BARRON'S

PRAXIS®

CORE • PLT

ELEMENTARY SCHOOL ASSESSMENTS

CORE ACADEMIC SKILLS FOR EDUCATORS

PRINCIPLES OF LEARNING AND TEACHING (PLT)

7TH EDITION

Dr. Robert D. Postman

Professor

Mercy College

Westchester County, New York

BARRON'S

To my wife Liz,
who showed me the way

And particularly to

my first grandchild, Quinn,
who is now in charge

All inquiries should be addressed to:
Barron's Educational Series, Inc.
250 Wireless Boulevard
Hauppauge, New York 11788
www.barronseduc.com

ISBN: 978-1-4380-0378-8

Library of Congress Control Number: 2014946043

PRINTED IN THE UNITED STATES OF AMERICA
9 8 7 6 5 4 3 2

10%
POST-CONSUMER
WASTE
Paper contains a minimum
of 10% post-consumer
waste (PCW). Paper used
in this book was derived
from certified, sustainable
forestlands.

CONTENTS

PART IV: PRACTICE CORE TESTS WITH EXPLAINED ANSWERS

PART V: PRINCIPLES OF LEARNING AND TEACHING

Preface

This completely updated and expanded seventh edition shows you how to do your absolute best on the Praxis Teacher Certification examinations including the new Core tests. The book helps you get started in a teaching career. Hundreds of prospective teachers field-tested preliminary versions of this book, and dozens of experienced teachers and subject matter specialists reviewed the book to ensure that it provides you with the subject matter preparation and practice tests you need.

The practice tests in this book have the same question types and the same question-and-answer formats as the real tests. The practice tests also have the look and feel of the real thing.

My wife Liz, a teacher, was a constant source of support, and she made significant contributions to this book. I hope she accepts my regrets for the lost months and believes my promises that it won't happen again. My children Chad, Blaire, and Ryan, and my grandson Quinn, have also been a source of support as I worked on this and other books.

I can attest that Barron's is simply the best publisher of test preparation books. The editorial department spared no effort to ensure that this book will be most helpful to you, the test taker.

Kristen Girardi, my editor at Barron's, did another fine job with a mammoth and complex manuscript. Kris and I have worked on other books and, as usual, many of the special touches are due to her caring attention.

Special thanks to the undergraduate and graduate students and those changing careers who field-tested sections of this book and to those at the Educational Testing Service. Special thanks also to Benjamin, Edith, and Pamela, who would have liked seeing their names in a book. I am also grateful to experts at state education departments for taking the time to talk with me about the teacher certification requirements in their states.

I wish you well as you pursue a rewarding and fulfilling teaching career.

Robert D. Postman

PART I
Tests and Strategies

PRAXIS Tests

1

TEST INFO BOX

Most chapters begin with a Test Info Box. Read it for information about the Praxis tests.
The Educational Testing Service (ETS) offers the Praxis tests. Contact ETS for registration forms, admission tickets, testing accommodations, or test scores. You can register online.

Educational Testing Service
Praxis Series
Box 6501
Princeton, NJ 08541-6051
800-772-9476   TTY 609-771-7714
www.ets.org/praxis/   *praxis@ets.org*

PRAXIS TESTS REVIEWED IN THIS BOOK*

PRAXIS I
Computer-Delivered Core Academic Skills Test for Educators (Core)
Reading (5712)
Writing (5722)
Mathematics (5732)

PRAXIS II—Computer Delivered
Principles of Learning and Teaching (PLT)
Early Childhood (5621), Grades K–6 (5622), Grades 5–9 (5623), Grades 7–12 (5624)
Elementary Subject Assessments
Curriculum, Instruction, and Assessment (5011)
Elementary Education Multiple Subjects (5032, 5033, 5034, 5035)
Content Knowledge (5014)

PARAPRO ASSESSMENT (Paper Delivered and Internet Based) (0755, 1755)

This section explains the steps you should take in beginning your test preparation. Read it before going on.

What's Going on with Praxis?

Some Praxis tests, such as the Core Academic Skills for Educators Tests are available only in computer-delivered format. Some Praxis tests are given in a paper-delivered format on scheduled dates at national test centers. In the paper-delivered format, you work from a test booklet and mark your multiple-choice answers on an answer sheet. In the computer-delivered format, you work on a computer and mark your multiple-choice answers by clicking an oval next to your answer choice. You type all essays.

THE PRACTICE TESTS

Our tests have the same format and structure as the real tests. However, ETS uses many versions of each test. That means the test you take may have a different subject emphasis than the test you find here.

Which Tests Should I Take?

Check the tests you have to take in the following Review Checklist. It shows which part(s) of this book to use.

TAKING THE PRAXIS TESTS

REVIEW CHECKLIST AND TEST SECTION IDENTIFIER

Use this page to plan your study and to find the marked test preparation sections.

☐ **Computer-Delivered Core Academic Skills Tests for Educators (Core)**
(5712–Reading, 5722–Writing, 5732–Mathematics)

☐ Subject Matter Review	Page 25
☐ Practice Core 1	Page 233
☐ Practice Core 2	Page 301

☐ **Principles of Learning and Teaching (PLT)**   **Page 363**

☐ **Elementary Education Subject Assessments**   **Page 465**

☐ Curriculum, Instruction, and Assessment (0011), (5011)	Page 467
☐ Elementary Education Multiple Subjects (5031) (5032–Reading and Language Arts, 5033–Mathematics, 5034–Social Studies, 5035–Science)	Page 521

☐ **ParaPro Assessment Overview**   **Page 619**

The Praxis Bulletin lists a code for each organization that can receive scores. List the code for each certification agency or college you want to receive your scores. The scores are usually sent directly to the agencies from ETS.

Although you may want to wait until you know you have gotten a passing score before sending it in, it is not necessary. You will just slow the process down and incur extra expense. Certification agencies do not use these scores for evaluative purposes. They just need to see a passing score, and ETS reports only your highest score.

You will receive your own report, and you are entitled to have four score reports sent to the certification agency or colleges you choose. Any extra reports will be sent to you.

Special Test Arrangements

Many test takers require special testing arrangements. Requests for an accommodation must be approved well in advance of the test. The first step is to contact ETS Disability Services directly. The current phone number and email address are given below.

> ETS Special Accommodations
> 866-287-8602
> *stassd@ets.org*

Reasons for a special arrangement include, but are not limited to, a learning disability, or a physical, visual, or hearing impairment.

You may qualify for extended testing time or for additional breaks during the test, a reader, a scribe, a Braille slate, or other Braille equipment.

For computer-delivered tests, you may qualify to use a different type of keyboard, a magnified computer screen, specialized screen colors, a trackball mouse, and so on.

A range of accommodations are available for those with health-related issues.

Test Preparation and Test-Taking Strategies

2

This chapter shows you how to set up a test preparation schedule and offers test-taking strategies that will help you improve your score. The most important strategies are discussed below.

MULTIPLE CHOICE

Eliminate and then guess. There is no penalty for wrong answers. Never leave any answer blank.

Suppose a test has 40 items with four answer choices. If you eliminate two incorrect answer choices on all the items and guess every answer, then on average, you would get 20 correct.

On the computer-delivered tests, be sure that you have answered all the questions. Check the review screen for questions you may not have answered.

ESSAY

Write an outline first, then write the essay.

TOPIC PARAGRAPH: Begin the written assignment with an introduction to orient the reader to the topic. The first paragraph should clearly state the main idea of your entire written assignment.

TOPIC SENTENCE: Begin each paragraph with a topic sentence that supports the main idea.

DETAILS: Provide details, examples, and arguments to support the topic sentence.

CONCLUSION: End the written assignment with a paragraph that summarizes your main points.

GRAMMAR, PUNCTUATION, SPELLING: Edit sentences to conform to standard usage.

AVOID PASSIVE CONSTRUCTION: Write actively and avoid the passive voice.

PLT CONSTRUCTED RESPONSE

Use the PLT constructed-response strategies in Chapter 11. Although you have only about seven minutes to write each response, still plan before you write.

PROVEN TEST-PREPARATION STRATEGIES

Here are several strategies and steps to follow as you prepare for the test. These strategies take you right up to test day.

Get Yourself Ready for the Test

Most people feel at least a little bit uncomfortable about tests. You are probably one of them. No book is going to make you feel comfortable, but here are some suggestions to help ease your concerns.

Most people are less tense when they exercise. Set up a *reasonable* exercise program for yourself. The program should involve exercising in a way that is appropriate for you. Aim for 30 to 45 minutes of exercise each day. This exercise may be just as important as other preparation.

Prepare with another person. You will feel less isolated if you have a friend or colleague to study with.

Accept this important truth: You are not going to get all the answers correct, and you do not have to. You can take this test again if necessary. There is no penalty for taking the test again. This is not a do-or-die, life-or-death situation. You will survive.

Follow This Study Plan

Begin preparing four to ten weeks before the test. Use the longer time if you are very busy or you don't feel comfortable about the test.

Look in turn at each chapter you have to use and review the description of each test you have to take. Then, take each appropriate review quiz when one is available. Use the answer key to mark the review quiz. Each incorrect answer will point you to a specific portion of the review.

Use the subject matter review indicated by the review quiz when one is available. Do not spend your time reviewing things you already know.

After the review of each chapter is complete, take the targeted test when one is available. It will let you know what further review may be necessary. Complete your review two weeks before the test. Then, complete the practice test. Have someone proctor the test. Take the test under exact test conditions. No television. No extra time. No breaks that are not normally included in the test. Nothing. We recommend that you take the practice test on the same day of the week and during the same time period that you will take the actual test.

Grade your own test or have someone grade it for you. Either way, review each incorrect answer and read all the explanations. Every answer is explained in detail.

TWO WEEKS TO GO

During this week look over those areas you answered incorrectly on the practice test. Go over the answer explanations and go back to the review sections.

ONE WEEK TO GO

The hard work is over. You are coasting in for a landing. You know the material on the test. You do not even have to get an A. You just have to pass.

Get up each day at the time you will have to get up on test day. Sit down at the time the test will start and spend about one hour answering questions on the targeted test or the practice tests. It is okay that you have answered these questions before.

FOUR DAYS TO GO

Make sure you:

- have your admission ticket.
- know where the test is given.
- know how you will get there.

THREE DAYS TO GO

- Write on 3 × 5 index cards any special terms or formulas you must remember for the test.
- Visit the test site or the test center, if you have not done so already. You do not want any surprises.

TWO DAYS TO GO

- Get some sharpened No. 2 pencils and an eraser and put them aside.

ONE DAY TO GO

- Review your index cards one last time.
- Complete any forms you have to take to the test.
- Prepare any snacks or food you want to bring with you.
- Talk to someone who makes you feel good or do something enjoyable and relaxing.
- Have a good night's sleep.

TEST DAY

- Plan to be at the test site or center for at least four hours.
- Dress comfortably. There are no points for appearance.
- Do not eat too much before the test. You want your blood racing through your brain, not your stomach.
- Get to the test room or the test center, not the parking lot, about 10 to 15 minutes before the test starts. Remember to leave time for parking and walking to the test site or test center.
- Hand in your forms. You are ready. This is the easy part.
- Follow the test-taking strategies in the next section.

PROVEN TEST-TAKING STRATEGIES

Testing companies like to pretend that test-taking strategies do not help that much. They act like that because they want everyone to think that their tests only measure your knowledge of the subject. Of course, they are just pretending; test-taking strategies can make a big difference.

However, there is nothing better than being prepared for the subject matter on the test. These strategies will do you little good if you lack this fundamental knowledge. If you are prepared, then these strategies can make a difference. Not using them may very well lower your score.

Be Comfortable

Be sure you get an appropriate seat in the paper-delivered test center. Be sure the computer is working properly at the computer testing center.

You Will Make Mistakes

You are going to make mistakes on this test. The people who wrote the test expect you to make them.

You Are Not Competing with Anyone

Do not worry about how anyone else is doing. Your score does not depend on others. When the score report comes out it does not say, "Nancy got a 661, but Blaire got a 670." You just want to get the score required for your state. If you can do better, that is great. Stay focused. Remember your goal. Passing scores for most tests are at or below the 25th percentile.

Some Multiple-Choice Questions Are Traps

Some questions include the words *not*, *least*, or *except*. You are being asked for the answer that does not fit with the rest. Be alert for these types of questions.

Save the Hard Questions for Last

You are not supposed to get all the questions correct, and some of them will be too difficult for you. Work through the questions and answer the easy ones. Pass by the other ones. If a question seems really hard, draw a circle around the question number in the test booklet. Save these questions until the very end.

They Show You the Answer

Every multiple-choice test shows you the correct answer for each question. The answer is staring right at you. You just have to figure out which one it is. There is a 20 or 25 percent chance you will get it right by just closing your eyes and pointing.

Some Answers Are Traps

When a test writer writes a test question, he or she often include distracters. Distracters are traps—incorrect answers that look like correct answers. It might be an answer to an addition problem when you should be multiplying. It might be a correct answer to a different question. It might just be an answer that catches your eye. Watch out for this type of incorrect answer.

Eliminate the Incorrect Answers

If you cannot figure out which answer is correct, then decide which answers can't be correct. Choose the answers you are sure are incorrect. Cross them off in the test booklet. Only one left? That is the correct answer.

Guess, Guess, Guess

If there are still two or more answers left, then guess. Guess the answer from those remaining. Never leave any item blank. There is no penalty for guessing.

It Is Not What You Know That Matters, It Is Just Which Circle You Fill In

No one you know or care about will see your test. An impersonal machine scores all multiple-choice questions. The machine just senses whether the correct circle on the computer screen is selected. That is the way the test makers want it. If that is good enough for them, it should be good enough for you. Concentrate on filling in the correct circle.

You Can Be Right but Be Marked Wrong

If you get the right answer but fill in the wrong circle, the machine will mark it wrong. We told you that filling in the right circle was what mattered. We strongly recommend that you use the following strategy.

You can write the letter for your answer big on the scrap paper next to the number for the problem. If you change your mind about an answer, cross off the "old" letter and write the "new" one. At the end of each section, transfer all the answers together from the scrap paper to the computer screen.

You Type Your Constructed Responses on the Computer Screen

You will type your constructed responses directly on the computer screen. You will not be able to use a grammar checker or a spell checker. Be sure to practice typing your constructed responses on a word processor with the grammar check and spell check turned off.

Leave time to review your essay and correct any typos. Follow the guidelines in this book for the minimum number of words for each type of constructed response.

Write an Outline for Each Constructed Response

Use the scrap paper to write a brief outline before you type your constructed response. Be sure your outline is based on the topic or question in the prompt. Focus on planning your response as you write your outline. Focus on writing well as you type your response.

Pay Attention During the Tutorial

The tutorial shows you how to use the computer, how to mark your answers, how to use a tool to mark items to which you want to return, and how to use the review page to see the items you marked. Pay close attention. There is no way to get additional help once the test is underway.

You Do Not Have to Answer Every Item When It First Appears

If you come across an item you are not ready to answer, mark it with the special marking tool you learned about during the tutorial. You can also mark an item you have not answered as a reminder to review the item later and/or perhaps change an answer.

All the items you mark are recorded on the review screen.

Use the Review Screen

Leave time at the end of the test to look at the review screen. The screen shows all the items you marked with the marking tool, as well as those items you revisited. Use the information on this screen to be sure you entered an answer for every item. There is no penalty for guessing.

It Is Easy to Change Your Answer

You can change the answer to any multiple-choice item. Just click on the oval for another answer.

Use the Scrap Paper

The test center staff should provide you with scrap paper. Use the scrap paper to do calculations, draw diagrams, or to make any notes you need to arrive at the correct answer.

Take the Optional 15-Minute Break

You have the right to a 15-minute break between tests. Take it. You do not want to waste time during the next test to excuse yourself.

Your Constructed Responses Are Graded Holistically

Holistic rating means the readers assign a score based on their informed sense about your writing. Readers read a lot of essays, and they do not do a detailed analysis.

ETS sends your essay to readers typically on a computer. Readers can review the essays anywhere there is Internet or cell phone access. Readers typically consist of teachers. At first, representatives of ETS show the readers the topics for the recent test and review the types of responses that should be rated. The readers are trained to evaluate the responses according to the ETS guidelines.

Each written assignment is evaluated twice, without the second reader knowing the evaluation given by the first reader. If the two evaluations differ significantly, other readers review the assignment.

Readers have a tedious, tiring assignment, and they work quickly. Think about them as you write. Write a response that makes it easy for the reader to give you a high score.

PART II
Core Tests and Strategies

Computer-Delivered
Core Tests

3

TEST INFO BOX

Most chapters begin with a Test Info Box. Read it for information about these tests.

The Educational Testing Service (ETS) offers the Core Tests. Contact ETS for registration forms, admission tickets, testing accommodations, and test scores.

You can register online. All Core tests are computer delivered.

Educational Testing Service
Box 6501
Princeton, NJ 08541-6051
Website: *www.ets.org/praxis*
609-771-7395
TTY 609-771-7714
FAX (609) 530-0581 (24 hours)
E-mail: *praxis@ets.org*

The Core Tests
Computer-delivered

Reading (5712)
Writing (5722)
Mathematics (5732)

READ ME FIRST!

This section explains the steps you should take in beginning your test preparation. Read it before continuing on.

What's Going on with the Core Academic Skills for Educators (Core)?

Teacher certification examinations have been around for years. Until recently, most states relied on the PPST. The PPST is no longer given. Recently, states have focused on the reading, writing, and mathematics skills tested by the computer-delivered Core tests.

The Good News

The good news is that the Core tests focus on a central core of reading, writing, and mathematics skills. In this book, you will learn how to prepare successfully for each test.

CORE TESTS—THE INSIDE STORY

The Computer-delivered Core tests were developed by the Educational Testing Service in conjunction with a number of states. The Core tests consist of three separate tests: (1) Reading, (2) Mathematics, and (3) Writing—multiple choice and essays.

Some questions on the test do not count toward the scoring, but you will not know which questions these are.

Core Tests Summary

Computer-delivered Only		
Reading	56 multiple-choice questions*	85 minutes
Writing Multiple choice	40 multiple-choice questions	40 minutes
Constructed Response	2 typed responses	30 minutes each
Mathematics	56 multiple-choice questions*	85 minutes

*Multiple-choice items with more than one correct answer will have a box (☐) to mark and not an oval.

What Are the Tests Like?

The computer-delivered Core tests assess reading, writing, and mathematics skills. The Core is a computer-based multiple-choice test with two typed essays.

You take the computer-delivered Core tests on the scheduled days set by ETS. You sit in a cubicle in front of a computer screen while a video camera mounted overhead records your actions. The computer selects all the items before you take the test. You use a mouse and a keyboard to enter your answers directly on the test screen. You type your essays.

A special "mark tool" lets you mark a question so that you may return later to answer the question or change your answer. A review screen shows the questions you have answered, those marked for return, and those not seen at all.

MULTIPLE-CHOICE ITEM TYPES

MOST MULTIPLE-CHOICE: These are standard multiple-choice items with five answer choices and one correct answer. The answer choices will appear within ovals.

MULTIPLE-CHOICE WITH MORE THAN ONE CORRECT ANSWER: These items will have more than one correct answer. The answer choices for these items will appear in a box rather than an oval.

NUMERIC ENTRY: For these questions, you will be asked to type your answer in a box. You can also use the calculator and transfer your answer directly from the onscreen calculator to the box by clicking on "Transfer Display."

READING (5712)

The 85-minute reading test has 56 multiple-choice items. Some items have several correct answer choices. You indicate your answer by clicking an oval. For questions with more than one correct answer, you will click on the appropriate boxes. According to ETS, test items are partitioned as follows: 35 percent Key Ideas and Details, 30 percent Craft Structure and Language Skills, and 30 percent Integration of Knowledge

WRITING (5722)

The writing test has a 40-minute multiple-choice section with about 18 error recognition and 22 sentence correction items and two 30-minute essays. For error correction, you indicate your answer by highlighting the part of a sentence that contains an error, or by highlighting "No error." For sentence correction, you click an oval or a box to indicate your choices. There is one Argumentative Essay and one Informative Explanation (source-based) essay. You type your essays in the space provided on the computer screen.

MATHEMATICS (5732)

The 85-minute mathematics test has 56 items. Some items have several correct answer choices. You indicate your answer by clicking on an oval. According to ETS, test items are partitioned as follows: Number and Quantity–30 percent, Algebra and Functions–30 percent, Geometry–20 percent, and Statistics and Probability–20 percent. A basic four-function on–screen calculator is available throughout the test.

CORE TEST REGISTRATION AND SCORING

Core Test Registration

Visit the Praxis website at *www.ets.org/praxis/* to register for your test. Enter your zip code to find centers near you.

The computer-delivered Core is offered at more than 300 centers and colleges. Early registration is strongly advised.

Test Scores

Computer-delivered Core scores are available later through the Praxis website.

Where to Send Your Scores

The Praxis Bulletin lists a code for each organization that can receive scores. You should list the code for each certification agency or college you want to receive your scores. The scores must usually be sent directly to the agencies from ETS.

You may feel that you should wait until you know you have gotten a passing score before sending it in, but that is not necessary. You will just slow down the process and incur extra expense. Certification agencies do not use these scores for evaluative purposes. They just need to see a passing score, and ETS reports only your highest score.

You will receive your own report, and you are entitled to have four score reports sent to the certification agency or colleges you choose.

PASSING THE CORE TESTS

This section reviews Core scoring and gives you some information about what it takes to get a passing score.

Raw Scores and Scale Scores

Your raw score is the number of items you answer correctly, or the number of points you actually earn. Your scale score converts your raw score to a score that can be compared to those of everyone else who has taken that test.

It works this way. Test items, test sections, and different forms of the test have different difficulty levels. For example, an item on one form might be harder than a comparable item on another form. To make up for this difference in difficulty, the harder item might earn a 0.9 scale point, while the easier item might earn a 0.8 scale point. A scale score can be compared to the scale score on all forms of a test.

This is the fair way to do it. To maintain this fairness, Core scores are reported to you as scale scores. All the scores discussed here are scale scores.

CORE SCALE SCORING

The scoring for each Core test is summarized on the following pages. The tables show the scale score range and score interval for each test, along with the scale scores at the first quartile, second quartile, and third quartile. An explanation of quartiles is given below.

	Percent of test takers who scored at or below this scale score	Percent of test takers who scored above this scale score
First quartile	25%	75%
Second quartile	50%	50%
Third quartile	75%	25%

Passing scores for most states are shown below. Check for most recent requirements.

Math (5732): 150
Reading (5712): 156
Writing (5722): 162

Scores may vary for individual college programs. ETS has not yet released the quartile scores for these tests.

CORE PASSING RAW SCORES

It is tricky to figure out the raw score you will need to get a passing scale score. That is because a passing raw score varies from one test version to another. Even ETS does not know the conversion of a raw score to a scale score until after the test has been given. The passing raw scores on tests released by ETS vary widely.

This means we have to be cautious. However, this is information readers often request, so we will help as best we can. Please remember that these are just estimates. ETS may adjust its scaling, or the Core versions it designs may be harder or easier. The test you take may be a harder or easier version. Any of these things will significantly reduce the meaning of these estimates.

Of course, the idea is to do your best. Remember that you can pick up raw score points by using the fundamental test strategies. Eliminate every answer you know is incorrect. Never leave an answer blank. You will also see that a good essay score can significantly reduce the writing multiple-choice raw score you will need.

So here it is—ESTIMATES. There is absolutely no assurance that they will apply to the test you take. The best approach is to assume you will have to do better than these guidelines indicate.

Generally speaking, a multiple-choice raw score of 70 percent correct is a good score for most test takers. An essay score of 8 points out of 12 points is also a good score for most test takers. Here are our recommended goals for most state passing score requirements:

> **MATHEMATICS**—65 percent correct
>
> **READING**—75 percent correct
>
> **WRITING**—8 of 12 essay points and 65 percent of the multiple-choice points

Core Test Preparation and Test-Taking Strategies

4

This chapter shows you how to set up a test preparation schedule and shows you some test-taking strategies that will help you improve your score. The important strategies are discussed below.

MULTIPLE CHOICE

Eliminate and then guess. There is no penalty for wrong answers. Never leave any answer blank.

Suppose a multiple-choice test has 40 items with four answer choices. Eliminate two incorrect answer choices on all the items, guess every answer, and, on average, you would get 20 correct, although your actual score may be higher or lower.

Multiple-choice questions that have more than one correct answer will have boxes rather than ovals for the answer choices.

CONSTRUCTED RESPONSE

General Guidelines

There are two 30-minute responses—Argumentative and Informative/Explanatory. The approaches to each response are somewhat different. The writing review section provides specific steps for each response and scored sample responses.

Write an outline first, then write the response. Handwrite your brief outline on scrap paper.

TOPIC PARAGRAPH: Begin the written assignment with an introduction to orient the reader to the topic. The first paragraph should clearly state the main idea of your entire written assignment.

TOPIC SENTENCE: Begin each paragraph with a topic sentence that supports the main idea.

DETAILS: Provide details, examples, and arguments to support the topic sentence.

CONCLUSION: End the written assignment with a paragraph that summarizes your main points.

GRAMMAR, PUNCTUATION, SPELLING: Edit sentences to conform to standard usage.

AVOID PASSIVE CONSTRUCTION: Write actively and avoid the passive voice.

PROVEN TEST-PREPARATION STRATEGIES

Here are several strategies and steps to follow as you prepare for the test. These strategies take you right up to test day.

Get Yourself Ready for the Test

Most people are less tense when they exercise. Set up a *reasonable* exercise program for yourself. The program should involve exercising in a way that is appropriate for you 30 to 45 minutes each day. This exercise may be just as important as other preparation.

Prepare with another person. You will feel less isolated if you have a friend or colleague to study with.

Follow This Study Plan

Begin working four to ten weeks before the test. Review the description of each test you have to take and then take each appropriate review quiz. Use the answer key to mark the review quiz. Each incorrect answer will point you to a specific portion of the review.

Use the subject matter review indicated by the review quiz. Don't spend your time reviewing things you already know.

Take the targeted test after the review of each chapter is complete. It will let you know what further review may be necessary. Complete your review two weeks before the test. Then, complete the practice test. Take the test under exact test conditions.

Grade your own test or have someone do it for you. Either way, review each incorrect answer and read all the explanations. Every answer is explained in detail.

TWO WEEKS TO GO

Be sure you are registered. Look over those areas you answered incorrectly on the practice test. Go over the answer explanations and go back to the review sections. Practice using a computer mouse, a keyboard, and a word processor.

ONE WEEK TO GO

Get up each day at the time you will have to get up the following Saturday. Sit down at the time the test will start and spend at least one hour answering questions on targeted tests or practice tests even if you've answered these questions before.

Follow this schedule for the week leading up to test day.

FIVE DAYS TO GO

Make sure you

- have your admission ticket.
- know where the test is given.
- know how you're getting there.

THREE DAYS TO GO

Visit the test site, if you haven't done so already.

TWO DAYS TO GO

Get some sharpened No. 2 pencils and an eraser.

ONE DAYS TO GO

- Complete any forms you have to bring to the test.
- Prepare any snacks or food you want to bring with you.
- Talk to someone who makes you feel good or do something enjoyable and relaxing.
- Have a good night's sleep.

TEST DAY

- Dress comfortably.
- Eat the same kind of breakfast you've been eating each morning.
- Get together things to bring to the test, including: registration ticket, identification forms, pencils, eraser, and snacks.
- Get to the site about 10 to 15 minutes before the start time. Remember to leave time for parking and walking to the test site.
- Hand in your forms.
- Let the test center director know if there are problems with your cubicle or computer.
- Follow the test-taking strategies in the next section.

TIP

Test Day Necessities

- **Admission Ticket**
- **Completed forms**
- **Identification**
- **Sharpened No. 2 pencils**
- **Eraser**
- **Snacks**

PROVEN TEST-TAKING STRATEGIES

These strategies are for all of the Core tests. This book also has strategies for each individual Core test.

Writing	page 57
Mathematics	page 161
Reading	page 197

It's Not What You Know That Matters, It's Just Which Answer You Mark

An impersonal machine scores every item except the essay. The machine just senses whether the correct answer oval is filled in. That is the way the test makers want it. If that's good enough for them, it should be good enough for you. Concentrate on marking the correct answer.

Use the Scrap Paper

Use the scrap paper provided at the test center. Use it to do calculations, to jot down possible answers, and to write reminder notes.

Some Questions Are Traps

Some questions include the words "not," "least," or "except." You are being asked for the answer that doesn't fit with the rest. Be alert for these types of questions.

Work Backward from the Answers

Back solving is particularly useful for answering mathematics questions. This strategy is discussed in detail in the mathematics section, page 162.

They Show You the Answer

Every multiple-choice test shows you the correct answer for each question. The answer is staring right at you. You just have to figure out which one it is.

Some Answers Are Traps

When a test writer writes a test question, he or she often includes distracters. Distracters are traps—incorrect answers that look like correct answers. It might be an answer to an addition problem when you should be multiplying. It might be a correct answer to a different question. It might just be an answer that catches your eye. Watch out for this type of incorrect answer.

Eliminate the Incorrect Answers

If you can't figure out which answer is correct, then decide which answers can't be correct. Choose the answers you're sure are incorrect. Keep track on the scrap paper. Only one left? That's the correct answer.

Guess, Guess, Guess

If there are still two or more answers left, then guess. Guess the answer from those remaining. Never leave any item blank. There is no penalty for guessing.

Use the Tutorial

There is an untimed tutorial before each test that shows you how to use the computer, how to indicate your answer, and how to use the "mark tool" and review page. Pay careful attention to the tutorial. It will speed things up when you take the test. Take as much time as you need.

Mark Every Item You Might Come Back To

Before you skip an item, mark it with the "mark tool." Mark each item you answer if you think you may want to come back to it.

Use the Review Screen

Before you finish the test, check the review page to be sure you have answered each item. You can use the review screen to check your progress during the test. Be sure to answer every item.

Your Responses Are Graded Holistically

Holistic scoring means the raters assign a score based on their informed sense about your writing. Raters have a lot of answers to look at and they do not do a detailed analysis. The ETS sends your essay to readers over the Internet. Representatives of ETS show the readers the topics for the test and review the types of responses that should be rated 1–6. The rating guidelines for the Argumentative and Informative/Explanatory essays are on pages 32–33. The readers are trained to evaluate the responses according to the ETS guidelines.

Each written assignment is evaluated twice, without the second reader knowing the evaluation given by the first reader. If the two evaluations differ by more than one point, other readers review the assignment.

Readers have a tedious, tiring assignment. Think about those readers as you write. Write a response that makes it easy for them to give you a high score.

You will find detailed steps for writing essays on pages 61–62.

PART III
Core Subject Matter Preparation

Writing

5

TEST INFO BOX		
Computer-delivered Core	40 Multiple-Choice Items	40 minutes
	Usage	about 18–19 Items
	Sentence Correction	about 13–14 Items
	Revision in Context	about 6 Items
	Research Skills	about 3 Items
	2 Typed Responses	30 minutes each

USING THIS CHAPTER

This chapter prepares you to take the multiple-choice writing section and the essay sections of the computer-delivered Core. You may want to find an English professor, teacher, or tutor to mark the essay portion of the review test. This person may also be able to help you prepare for the essay section of the test. Choose one of these approaches.

- **I WANT ALL THE WRITING HELP I CAN GET.** Skip the review quiz and read the writing review. Then take the English review quiz. Correct the test and reread the indicated parts of the writing review. Take the targeted test at the end of the chapter.
- **I WANT WRITING HELP.** Take the review quiz. Correct the quiz and review the indicated parts of the English review. Take the targeted test at the end of the chapter.
- **I WANT A QUICK WRITING REVIEW.** Take the review quiz. Correct the quiz. Then take the targeted test at the end of the chapter.
- **I WANT TO PRACTICE A WRITING TEST.** Take the targeted test at the end of the chapter.

The English Review Quiz assesses your knowledge of the English topics included in the Core writing test. The first part of the quiz consists of sentences to mark or correct. Make your marks or corrections right on the sentences.

This quiz is not like the real test. It will be more difficult than the questions on the actual certification test. The key is to find out what you know. It is not important to answer all these questions correctly, and do not be concerned if you miss many of them.

The answers are found immediately after the quiz. It is to your advantage not to look until you have completed the quiz. Once you have completed and marked this review quiz, use the checklist to decide which sections to study.

Sentence Correction

Directions: Correct the sentence. Some sentences may not contain errors.

1. Ron and James fathers each sent them to players camp to learn the mysterys of sport.

2. They go to the camp, ridden horses while they were there, and had write letters home.

3. James went to the water and goes skiing.

4. Ron and James called his coach. The operator never answered, and they wondered what happened to her.

5. Bob and Liz went to the store and got some groceries.

6. Dad want me to do my homework. My sisters try their best to help me.

Directions: Underline the subject in each sentence.

7. Chad's project that he showed the teacher improved his final grade.

8. The legs pumped hard, and the racer finished in first place.

9. Through the halls and down the stairs ran the harried student.

10. Where is the dog's leash?

11. Chad was sure correct, the food tastes bad and the singer sang bad but Ryan played really well. Ryan was more happy than Chad who sat closer to the stage than Ryan.

12. The larger table in the restaurant was full.

13. The waiter brought food to the table on a large tray. The waiter wanted a job in the suburbs that paid well.

14. Waiting for the food to come, the complaining began.

15. The food arrived, the eating began. The waiter stood by he was tired.

16. The coach realized that new selection rules to go into effect in May. She also knew what it would take for Ryan to be selected. Ryan winning every game. But the coach and Ryan had a common goal. To see Ryan on the team.

17. Ryan's parents wanted a success rather than see him fail. They knew he stayed in shape by eating right and exercising daily. Ryan was a person who works hard and has talent.

18. Chad was dog tired after soccer practice. He became a coach for the purpose of helping the college to the soccer finals. During the rein of the former coach, the team had miserable seasons. Chad would stay at the job until such time as he could except the first place trophy.

19. Chad was satisfied but the players were grumbling. The players wanted to practice less have more free time. The players didn't like their light blue uniforms! The finals began in May 2012. The first game was scheduled for Tuesday May 9 at 1:00 P.M. The time for the game was here the players were on the field. Chad had the essential materials with him player list score book soccer balls and a cup of hope.

Part I—Sentence Correction
The answers are organized by review sections. Check your answers. If you miss any item in a section, check the box and review that section.

☐ Nouns, page 34

1. Ron's and James's fathers each sent them to players' camp to learn the mysteries of sport.

☐ Verbs, page 35

2. They went to the camp, rode horses while they were there, and wrote letters home.

☐ Tense Shift, page 37

3. James went to the water and went skiing. James goes to the water and goes skiing.

☐ Pronouns, page 38

4. Ron and James called (Ron's, James's, their) coach. The operator never answered, and they wondered what happened to him or her.

☐ Subject-Verb Agreement, page 41
5. No error
6. Dad wants me to do my homework. My sisters try their best to help me.
7. Chad's project that he showed the teacher improved his final grade.
8. The legs pumped hard, and the racer finished in first place.
9. Through the halls and down the stairs ran the harried student.
10. Where is the dog's leash?

☐ Adjectives and Adverbs, page 42

11. Chad was surely correct, the food tastes bad and the singer sang badly but Ryan played really well. Ryan was happier than Chad who sat closer to the stage than Ryan did.

☐ Comparison, page 43

12. The largest table in the restaurant was full.

☐ Misplaced and Dangling Modifiers, page 45

13. The waiter brought food on a large tray to the table. The waiter wanted a well-paying job in the suburbs.
14. Waiting for the food to come, the (patrons, diners) complained. The (patrons, diners) complained about waiting for the food to come.

☐ Comma Splices and Run-on Sentences, page 46

15. The food arrived. The eating began.
The food arrived; the eating began.
The food arrived, and the eating began. The waiter stood by. He was tired.
The waiter stood by; he was tired.
The waiter stood by, and he was tired.

□ Sentence Fragments, page 47

16. The coach realized that new selection rules <u>would</u> go into effect in May. She also knew what it would take for Ryan to be selected. Ryan <u>would have to win</u> every game. But the coach and Ryan had a common goal. <u>They wanted</u> to see Ryan on the team.

□ Parallelism, page 48

17. Ryan's parents wanted a success rather than <u>a failure</u> (wanted success rather than failure). They knew he stayed in shape by eating right and <u>by</u> exercising daily. Ryan is a person who works hard and <u>who</u> has talent. (Ryan is hardworking and talented.)

□ Diction, page 49

18. Chad was [delete "dog"] tired after soccer practice. He became a coach <u>to help</u> the college <u>ascend</u> to the soccer finals. During the <u>reign</u> of the former coach, the team had miserable seasons. Chad would stay at the job until [delete "such time as"] he could <u>accept the first place trophy</u>.

□ Punctuation, page 52

19. Chad was satisfied<u>,</u> but the players were grumbling. The players wanted to practice less <u>and</u> have more free time. The players didn't like their light blue uniforms<u>.</u> The finals began in May 2012. The first game was scheduled for Tuesday<u>,</u> May 9<u>,</u> at 1:00 P.M. The time for the game was here; the players were on the field. Chad had the essential materials with him: player list<u>,</u> score book<u>,</u> soccer balls<u>,</u> (optional) and a cup of hope.

RATING ESSAYS

Each essay is graded holistically by two raters, using two different 6-point scales described on pages 32 and 33. Holistic rating means that the raters base the scores on their informed sense of your essay and the elements it contains, not on a detailed analysis of the essay.

In practice, a rater often assigns an essay to top third, middle third, or bottom third. Then the rater decides which of the two scores in each third to assign to that essay. If the scores assigned to an essay differ by 2 points or more, the essay is resubmitted for further review.

Rating is not an exact science, and it is not unusual for raters to differ by 1 point. That is a bigger difference than you might think because a rating of 3 with a 1-point difference could be a rating of a 2 or 4. That range represents 50 percent of the available scores. This just emphasizes how important it is to focus your efforts on making it easy for a rater to give you a high score.

The rating scales for each essay type are given on pages 32 and 33.

6 This is the highest score. Essays with some minor errors can still receive a score of 6.

    To score a 6 an essay will:

- perceptively present the main issues under discussion, citing both paraphrased and quoted parts of the both accompanying position papers
- demonstrate a clear logical development, a variety of sentence types, and effective use of language
- essentially be free of grammatical and usage errors

5 This is an excellent score, just a little short of a score of 6. Essays with some minor errors can still receive a score of 5. The absence of the word *perceptively* is the primary difference between a 6 and a 5, indicating that essays scored 6 provide more insight than essays scored 5.

    To score a 5 an essay will:

- present the main issues under discussion, citing both paraphrased and quoted parts of the accompanying position papers
- demonstrate a clear logical development, a variety of sentence types, and effective use of language
- essentially be free of grammatical and usage errors

4 This essay is best characterized as satisfactory.

    To score a 4 an essay will:

- satisfactorally present the main issues under discussion, citing both paraphrased and quoted parts of the accompanying position papers
- demonstrate adequate development, a variety of sentence types, and effective use of language
- may have grammatical and usage errors

3 This essay is best characterized as limited.

    To score a 3 an essay will:

- partially present the main issues under discussion, citing one, or partially citing two, paraphrased and quoted parts of the accompanying position papers
- have limited development, a limited variety of sentence types, and limited use of language
- have a number of grammatical and usage errors

2 This essay is best characterized as very limited.

    To score a 2 an essay will:

- not present the main issues under discussion, citing none, and inadequately mentioning one or not mentioning any of the accompanying position papers
- have poor development, a very limited variety of sentence types, and very limited use of language
- have a large number of grammatical and usage errors

1 This essay is best characterized as unacceptable.

    To score a 1, an essay will:

- completely lack development and contain repeated and serious errors or be incomprehensible

ARGUMENTATIVE ESSAY RATING SCALE

6 This essay is extremely well written. It is the equivalent of an A on an in-class assignment. The essay addresses the question and provides clear supporting arguments, illustrations, or examples. The paragraphs and sentences are well organized and show a variety of language and syntax. The essay may contain some minor errors.

5 This essay is well written. It is the equivalent of a B+ on an in-class assignment. The essay addresses the question and provides some supporting arguments, illustrations, or examples. The paragraphs and sentences are fairly well organized and show a variety of language and syntax. The essay may contain some minor mechanical or linguistic errors.

4 This essay is fairly well written. It is the equivalent of a B on an in-class assignment. The essay adequately addresses the question and provides some supporting arguments, illustrations, or examples for some points. The paragraphs and sentences are acceptably organized and show a variety of language and syntax. The essay may contain mechanical or linguistic errors but is free from an identifiable pattern of errors.

3 This essay may demonstrate some writing ability, but it contains obvious errors. It is the equivalent of a C or C+ on an in-class assignment. The essay may not clearly address the question and may not give supporting arguments or details. The essay may show problems in diction including inappropriate word choice. The paragraphs and sentences may not be acceptably developed. There will be an identifiable pattern or grouping of errors.

2 This essay shows only the most limited writing ability. It is the equivalent of a C on an in-class assignment. It contains serious errors and flaws. This essay may not address the question, be poorly organized, or provide no supporting arguments or detail. It usually shows serious errors in diction, usage, and mechanics.

1 This essay does not demonstrate minimal writing ability. It is the equivalent of a D or F on an in-class assignment. This essay may contain serious and continuing errors, or it may not be coherent.

This review section targets the skills and concepts you need to know in order to pass the Writing Section of the Core.

NOUNS AND VERBS

Every sentence has a subject and a predicate. Most sentences are statements. The sentence usually names something (subject). Then the sentence describes the subject or tells what that subject is doing (predicate). Sentences that ask questions also have a subject and a predicate. Here are some examples.

Subject	Predicate
The car	moved.
The tree	grew.
The street	was dark.
The forest	teemed with plants of every type and size.

Many subjects are nouns. Every predicate has a verb. A list of the nouns and verbs from the preceding sentences follows.

Noun	Verb
car	moved
tree	grew
street	was
forest, plants	teemed

Nouns

Nouns name a person, place, thing, characteristic, or concept. Nouns give a name to everything that is, has been, or will be. Here are some simple examples.

Person	Place	Thing	Characteristic	Concept(Idea)
Abe Lincoln	Lincoln Memorial	beard	mystery	freedom
judge	courthouse	gavel	fairness	justice
professor	college	chalkboard	intelligence	number

SINGULAR AND PLURAL NOUNS

Singular nouns refer to only one thing. Plural nouns refer to more than one thing. Plurals are usually formed by adding an *s* or dropping a *y* and adding *ies*. Here are some examples.

Singular	Plural
college	colleges
professor	professors
Lincoln Memorial	Lincoln Memorials
mystery	mysteries

POSSESSIVE NOUNS

Possessive nouns show that the noun possesses a thing or a characteristic. Make a singular noun possessive by adding *'s*. Here are some examples.

> The *child's* sled was in the garage ready for use.
> The *school's* mascot was loose again.
>
> The rain interfered with *Jane's* vacation.
>
> *Ron's* and *Doug's* fathers were born in the same year.
> Ron and *Doug's* teacher kept them after school.

Make a singular noun ending in *s* possessive by adding *'s* unless the pronunciation is too difficult.

> The teacher read *James's* paper several times.
> The angler grabbed the *bass'* fin.

Make a plural noun possessive by adding an apostrophe (') only.

> The *principals'* meeting was delayed.
> The report indicated that *students'* scores had declined.

Practice

Directions: Write the plural of each singular noun.

1. sheaf
2. deer
3. fry
4. lunch
5. knee

6. lady
7. octopus
8. echo
9. foot
10. half

Answers on page 73.

Verbs

Some verbs are action verbs. Other verbs are linking verbs that link the subject to words that describe it. Here are some examples.

Action Verbs
Blaire *runs* down the street.
Blaire *told* her story.
The crowd *roared*.
The old ship *rusted*.

Linking Verbs
Blaire *is* tired.
The class *was* bored.
The players *were* inspired.
It *had been* a proud ship.

TENSE

A verb has three principal tenses: present tense, past tense, and future tense. The present tense shows that the action is happening now. The past tense shows that the action happened in the past. The future tense shows that something will happen. Here are some examples.

Present:	I *enjoy* my time off.
Past:	I *enjoyed* my time off.
Future:	I *will enjoy* my time off.
Present:	I *hate* working late.
Past:	I *hated* working late.
Future:	I *will hate* working late.

REGULAR AND IRREGULAR VERBS

Regular verbs follow the consistent pattern noted previously. However, a number of verbs are irregular. Irregular verbs have their own unique forms for each tense. A partial list of irregular verbs follows. The past participle is usually preceded by *had, has,* or *have.*

Some Irregular Verbs

Present Tense	Past Tense	Past Participle
am, is, are	was, were	been
begin	began	begun
break	broke	broken
bring	brought	brought
catch	caught	caught
choose	chose	chosen
come	came	come
do	did	done
eat	ate	eaten
give	gave	given
go	went	gone
grow	grew	grown
know	knew	known
lie	lay	lain
lay	laid	laid
raise	raised	raised
ride	rode	ridden
see	saw	seen
set	set	set
sit	sat	sat
speak	spoke	spoken
take	took	taken
tear	tore	torn
throw	threw	thrown
write	wrote	written

TENSE SHIFT

Verbs in a sentence should reflect time sequence. If the actions represented by the verbs happened at the same time, the verbs should have the same tense.

Incorrect:	Beth sits in the boat while she wore a life jacket.
Correct:	Beth sits in the boat while she wears a life jacket. [Both verbs are present tense.]
Correct:	Beth sat in the boat while she wore a life jacket. [Both verbs are past tense.]
Correct:	Beth wears the life jacket she wore last week. [The verbs show time order.]

Practice

Directions: Correct the tense errors. Some sentences may be correct.

1. Ryan driven to Florida.

2. Refereeing soccer games is not work.

3. Chad ride to the game with his team last week.

4. Why did Mary ran her errands now?

5. I have speak to my teacher about the grade.

6. Carl paddled across the river every Saturday.

7. Blaire thrown out the ball for the players to use.

8. Joann will lost her bag if she leaves it in the store.

9. Bob is standing on a stool next to the green table.

10. Liz begun to grasp the depth of her happiness.

Answers on page 73.

Practice

Directions: Correct the tense shifts. Some sentences may be correct.

1. Lisa already went to the North Pole but she is not going there again.

2. Dennis will take his airline tickets with him because he is leaving for his flight.

3. The runner gasped as she crosses the finish line.

4. I like to hear music so I played the clarinet.

5. Chris wanted to be a producer so he puts in long hours every day.

6. Bertha sews five hours a day because she will need her dress by next month.

7. The car turns over and then bounced down the hill.

8. Lois handed over her money because she wants to buy the computer.

9. The captain wandered out on the deck as she calls to her friends on shore.

10. The sun sets in the west as the moon rose in the east.

Answers on page 74.

PRONOUNS

Pronouns take the place of nouns or noun phrases and help avoid constant repetition of the noun or phrase. Here is an example.

> *Blaire* is in law school. *She* studies in *her* room every day.
> [The pronouns *she* and *her* refer to the noun *Blaire*.]

Pronoun Cases

Pronouns take three case forms: subjective, objective, and possessive. The personal pronouns *I, he, she, it, we, they, you* refer to an individual or individuals. The relative pronoun *who* refers to these personal pronouns as well as to an individual or individuals. These pronouns change their case form depending on their use in the sentence.

SUBJECTIVE PRONOUNS: I, WE, HE, IT, SHE, THEY, WHO, YOU

Use the subjective form if the pronoun is, or refers to, the subject of a clause or sentence.

> *He* and *I* studied for the Core.
>
> The proctors for the test were *she* and *I*.
> [*She* and *I* refer to the subject *proctors*.]
>
> She is the woman *who* answered every question correctly.
>
> I do not expect to do as well as *she*.
> [*She* is the subject for the understood verb *does*.]

OBJECTIVE PRONOUNS: ME, US, HIM, IT, HER, THEM, WHOM, YOU

Use the objective form if the pronoun is the object of a verb or preposition.

> Cathy helps both *him* and *me*.
>
> She wanted *them* to pass.
>
> I do not know *whom* she helped most.

POSSESSIVE PRONOUNS: MY, OUR, HIS, ITS, HER, THEIR, WHOSE, YOUR

Use the objective form if the pronoun shows possession.

I recommended they reduce the time they study with *their* friends.

He was the person *whose* help they relied on.

Clear Reference

The pronoun must clearly refer to a particular noun or noun phrase. Here are some examples.

Unclear

Gary and Blaire took turns feeding *her* cat.
[We can't tell which person *her* refers to. Blaire is involved but we do not know it is her cat.]

Gary gave *it* to Blaire.
[The pronoun *it* refers to a noun that is not stated.]

Clear

Gary and Blaire took turns feeding Blaire's cat.
[A pronoun doesn't work here. Use a noun.]

Gary got the book and gave it to Blaire.
[The pronoun works once the noun is stated.]

Agreement

Each pronoun must agree in number (singular or plural) and gender (male or female) with the noun it refers to. Here are some examples.

Nonagreement in Number

The children played all day, and *she* came in exhausted.
[*Children* is plural, but *she* is singular.]

The child picked up the hat and brought *them* into the house.
[*Hat* is singular, but *them* is plural.]

Agreement

The children played all day, and *they* came in exhausted.
The child picked up the hat and brought *it* into the house.

Nonagreement in Gender

The lioness picked up *his* cub.
[*Lioness* is female, and *his* is male.]

A child must bring in a doctor's note before *she* comes to school.
[The child may be a male or female but *she* is female.]

Agreement

The lioness picked up *her* cub.
A child must bring in a doctor's note before *he* or *she* comes to school.

Practice

Directions: Correct the pronoun reference and case and number errors in these sentences. Some sentences may not have errors.

1. His was the best table tennis player.

2. Whom was the worst table tennis player?

3. Where are the table tennis balls?

4. Before the game everyone are going to choose teams.

5. The names of the winning teams are sent to we.

6. Them are the best table tennis team.

7. Ron and Jeff wanted to use his skates.

8. Jeff went to get them.

9. The couch looked different, depending on how they were arranged.

10. Bob won most of his table tennis games.

11. The student waited for their school bus to come.

12. Either of the buses can arrive on time if they do not break down.

13. The book was most interesting near her beginning.

14. She read the book to find her most interesting parts.

15. I am the winner; victory is ours.

16. His friends got out of the car, and he went over to talk to them.

17. The rain clouds moved toward the pool, and the swimmers tried to wish it away.

18. Was Les disappointed that him team did not win?

19. Whom has more experience than Nicky does?

20. You play better after you have experience.

Answers on page 74.

SUBJECT-VERB AGREEMENT

Singular and Plural

Singular nouns take singular verbs. Plural nouns take plural verbs. Singular verbs usually end in *s*, and plural verbs usually do not. Here are some examples.

Singular:	My father wants me home early.
Plural:	My parents want me home early.
Singular:	Ryan runs a mile each day.
Plural:	Ryan and Chad run a mile each day.
Singular:	She tries her best to do a good job.
Plural:	Liz and Ann try their best to do a good job.

Correctly Identify Subject and Verb

The subject may not be in front of the verb. In fact, the subject may not be anywhere near the verb. Say the subject and the verb to yourself. If it makes sense, you probably have it right.

Words may come between the subject and the verb.

Chad's final exam score, which he showed to his mother, improved his final grade.

The verb is *improved*. The word *mother* appears just before *improved*.

Is this the subject? Say it to yourself. [Mother improved the grade.]

That cannot be right. *Score* must be the subject. Say it to yourself. [Score improved the grade.] That is right. *Score* is the subject, and *improved* is the verb.

The racer running with a sore arm finished first.

Say it to yourself. [Racer finished first.] *Racer* is the noun, and *finished* is the verb.

It would not make any sense to say the arm finished first.

The verb may come before the subject.

Over the river and through the woods romps the merry leprechaun.

Leprechaun is the subject, and *romps* is the verb. [Think: Leprechaun romps.]

Where are the car keys?

Keys is the subject, and *are* is the verb. [Think: The car keys are where?]

Examples of Subject-Verb Agreement

Words such as *each, neither, everyone, nobody, someone,* and *anyone* are singular pronouns. They always take a singular verb.

Everyone needs a good laugh now and then.
Nobody knows more about computers than Bob.

Words that refer to number such as *one-half, any, most,* and *some* can be singular or plural.

One-fifth of the students were absent. [*Students* is plural.]
One-fifth of the cake was eaten. [There is only one cake.]

Practice

Directions: Correct any subject-verb agreement errors. Some sentences may be correct.

1. The chess set are still on the shelf.

2. The shortest route to the college are shown in the catalog.

3. The golf pro drive a golf cart every day.

4. Derek and Ann walks every morning.

5. The tropical birds in the tree adds a festive air to the occasion.

6. No one, not even Rick or Ronnie, walk to school today.

7. Do you know who they is?

8. Ron prepare a paper for submission to the committee.

9. The 15 employees of the coffee house shows up each day at 6:00 A.M.

10. Each person who takes the 12 steps improve his or her view.

Answers on page 76.

ADJECTIVES AND ADVERBS

Adjectives

Adjectives modify nouns and pronouns. Adjectives add detail and clarify nouns and pronouns. Frequently, adjectives come immediately before the nouns or pronouns they are modifying. At other times, the nouns or pronouns come first and are connected directly to the adjectives by linking verbs. Here are some examples.

Direct	**With a Linking Verb**
That is a *large* dog.	That dog is *large*.
He's an *angry* man.	The man seems *angry*.

Adverbs

Adverbs are often formed by adding *ly* to an adjective. However, many adverbs do not end in *ly* (e.g., *always*). Adverbs modify verbs, adjectives, and adverbs. Adverbs can also modify phrases, clauses, and sentences. Here are some examples.

Modify verb:	Ryan *quickly* sought a solution.
Modify adjective:	That is an *exceedingly* large dog.
Modify adverb:	Lisa told her story *quite* truthfully.
Modify sentence:	*Unfortunately*, all good things must end.
Modify phrase:	The instructor arrived *just* in time to start the class.

AVOIDING ADJECTIVE AND ADVERB ERRORS

■ Do not use adjectives in place of adverbs.

Correct	**Incorrect**
Lynne read the book quickly.	Lynne read the book quick.
Stan finished his work easily.	Stan finished his work easy.

■ Do not confuse the adjectives *good* and *bad* with the adverbs *well* and *badly*.

Correct	**Incorrect**
Adverbs	
She wanted to play the piano well.	She wanted to play the piano good.
Bob sang badly.	Bob sang bad.
Adjectives	
The food tastes good.	The food tastes well.
The food tastes bad.	The food tastes badly.

■ Do not confuse the adjectives *real* and *sure* with the adverbs *really* and *surely*.

Correct	**Incorrect**
Chuck played really well.	Chuck played real well.
He was surely correct.	He was sure correct.

Comparison

Adjectives and adverbs can show comparisons. Avoid clumsy modifiers.

Correct	**Incorrect**
Jim is more clingy than Ray.	Jim is clingier than Ray.
Ray is much taller than Jim.	Ray is more taller than Jim.
Jim is more interesting than Ray.	Jim is interesting than Ray.
Ray is happier than Jim.	Ray is more happy than Jim.

Use word comparisons carefully to be sure that the comparison is clear.

Unclear:	Chad lives closer to Ryan than Blaire.
Clear:	Chad lives closer to Ryan than Blaire does.
Clear:	Chad lives closer to Ryan than he does to Blaire.
Unclear:	The bus engines are bigger than cars.
Clear:	The bus engines are bigger than cars' engines.

Practice

> **Directions:** Correct the adjective and adverb errors. Some sentences may contain no errors.

1. The view of the Grand Canyon was real spectacular.

2. The trainer said the dog behaved very good today.

3. Unfortunate, the tickets for the concert were sold out.

4. Things went smooth.

5. The judge took extremely exception to the defendant's actions.

6. The accident was silly, particularly since driving more careful would have avoided the whole thing.

7. But the reviews said the performance was truly horrible.

8. The manager conveniently forgot that she promised the employee a raise.

9. The bonus was a welcome surprise; it was a real large check.

10. I didn't do good, but didn't do bad either.

Answers on page 77.

Practice

> **Directions:** Correct the comparison errors. Some sentences may be correct.

1. Leon was the happier chef in the restaurant.

2. But some of the people eating in the restaurant were happier than Leon.

3. The jet was the faster plane at the airport.

4. John was the fastest of the twins.

5. The taller of the apartment buildings is under repair.

6. The lightest of the two weights is missing.

7. Lonnie was among the most creative students in the school.

8. Ron is the least able of the two drivers.

9. His shoe size is the smallest in his class.

10. She was the more capable of the two referees.

Answers on page 77.

MISPLACED AND DANGLING MODIFIERS

Modifiers may be words or groups of words. Modifiers change or qualify the meaning of another word or group of words. Modifiers belong near the words they modify.

Misplaced modifiers appear to modify words in a way that does not make sense.

The modifier in the following sentence is *in a large box*. It does not make sense for *in a large box* to modify *house*. Move the modifier near *pizza* where it belongs.

> Misplaced: Les delivered pizza to the house in a large box.
>
> Revised: Les delivered pizza in a large box to the house.

The modifier in the next sentence is *paid well*. *Paid well* can't modify *city*. Move it next to *the job* where it belongs.

> Misplaced: Gail wanted the job in the city that paid well.
>
> Revised: Gail wanted the well-paying job in the city.

Dangling modifiers modify words not present in the sentence. The modifier in the following sentence is *waiting for the concert to begin*.

This modifier describes the audience, but audience is not mentioned in the sentence. The modifier is left dangling with nothing to describe.

> Dangling: Waiting for the concert to begin, the chanting started.
>
> Revised: Waiting for the concert to begin, the audience began chanting.
>
> Revised: The audience began chanting while waiting for the concert to begin.

The modifier in the next sentence is *after three weeks in the country*. The modifier describes the person, not the license. But the person is not mentioned in the sentence. The modifier is dangling.

> Dangling: After three weeks in the country, the license was revoked.
>
> Revised: After he was in the country for three weeks, his license was revoked.
>
> Revised: His license was revoked after he was in the country three weeks.

Practice

> **Directions:** Correct the misplaced modifiers. Some sentences may be correct.

1. Les was reading his book through glasses with dirty lenses.

2. Jim left work early to go to the doctor on the train.

3. The first train car was crowded; which had to go to the next car.

4. Ron's car ran out of gas when on the way to the store.

5. Zena was jogging, when caused her to fall.

6. Derek wrapped the flowers and put them in the delivery van with colorful paper.

7. Which bus stops at the corner where the stop sign is?

8. Fran is going on the plane, which is just pulling up to the gate.

9. Lisa bought a shirt in the store, which was expensive.

10. The car turned around and the headlights shone quickly into the garage.

Answers on page 78.

COMMA SPLICES AND RUN-ON SENTENCES

An *independent clause* is a clause that could be a sentence.

Independent clauses should be joined by a semicolon, or by a comma and a conjunction.

A *comma splice* consists of two independent clauses joined by just a comma.

A *run-on* sentence consists of two independent clauses incorrectly joined.

Correct: The whole family went on vacation; the parents took turns driving.
[Two independent clauses are joined by a semicolon.]

The whole family went on vacation, and the parents took turns driving.
[Two independent clauses are joined by a comma and a conjunction.]

Incorrect: The whole family went on vacation, the parents took turns driving.
[Comma splice. Two independent clauses are joined by just a comma.]

The whole family went on vacation the parents took turns driving.
[Run-on sentence. Two independent clauses are incorrectly joined.]

Practice

> **Directions:** Correct the run-on sentences and comma splices. Some sentences may be correct.

1. It will be tomorrow before the sea is calm enough to go out.

2. It started to rain unexpectedly the boaters were soaked.

3. But right now my sneakers are soaking wet the towel is too wet to help me.

4. The Marine Police sounded the siren the boat stopped immediately.

5. I put the sneakers next to the fire to dry, although they started to steam after a while.

6. The Coast Guard monitors boats as they enter the river they use the data to monitor water pollution.

7. I like to use my compass when I go out on the boat.

8. When the boat breaks down, Liz calls Sea Tow.

9. The fire went out the sun came up.

10. Splashing through the waves, the water skier was covered with salt spray.

Answers on page 79.

SENTENCE FRAGMENTS

English sentences require a subject and a predicate (see page 34). Fragments are parts of sentences written as though they were sentences. Fragments are writing mistakes that lack a subject, a predicate, or both subject and predicate. Here are some examples.

> Since when.
> To enjoy the summer months.
> Because he isn't working hard.
> If you can fix old cars.
> What the principal wanted to hear.

Include a subject and/or a verb to rewrite a fragment as a sentence.

Fragment	**Sentence**
Should be coming up the driveway now.	The *car* should be coming up the driveway now.
Both the lawyer and her client.	Both the lawyer and her client *waited* in court.
Which is my favorite subject.	*I took math*, which is my favorite subject.
If you can play.	If you can play, *you'll improve with* practice.

Verbs such as *to be, to go, winning, starring,* etc., need a main verb.

Fragment	**Sentence**
The new rules to go into effect in April.	The new rules *will* go into effect in April.
The team winning every game.	The team *was* winning every game.

Often, a fragment is related to a complete sentence. Combine the two to make a single sentence.

Fragment: Reni loved vegetables. *Particularly corn, celery, lettuce, squash, and eggplant.*

Revised: Reni loved vegetables, particularly corn, celery, lettuce, squash, and eggplant.

Fragment: *To see people standing on Mars.* This could happen in the twenty-first century.

Revised: To see people standing on Mars is one of the things that could happen in the twenty-first century.

Sometimes short fragments can be used for emphasis. However, you should not use fragments in your essay. Here are some examples.

> *Stop!* Do not take one more step toward that apple pie.
> I need some time to myself. *That's why.*

Practice

Directions: Correct the sentence fragments. Some items may be correct.

1. A golf bag, golf clubs, and golf balls. That's what she needed to play.

2. As the rocket prepared for blast-off. Mary saw birds flying in the distance.

3. Jim is mowing the lawn. Then, the mower stopped.

4. The lawn looked lush and green. Like a golf course.

5. The polar bears swept across the ice. Like white ghosts in fur jackets.

6. Jim looked across at the igloo. Like an ice fort, it stood a lonely vigil.

7. Astronauts and their equipment went by. These were the people who would go into space.

8. This was what Joe had been waiting for. To graduate from college.

9. To be finished with this test. That's what I'm waiting for.

10. The test finished and done. The papers graded and good.

Answers on page 79.

PARALLELISM

When two or more ideas are connected, use a parallel structure. Parallelism helps the reader follow the passage more clearly. Here are some examples.

Not Parallel:	Toni stayed in shape by eating right and exercising daily.
Parallel:	Toni stayed in shape by eating right and *by* exercising daily.
Not Parallel:	Lisa is a student who works hard and has genuine insight.
Parallel:	Lisa is a student who works hard and *who* has genuine insight.
Not Parallel:	Art had a choice either to clean his room or take out the garbage.
Parallel:	Art had a choice either to clean his room or *to* take out the garbage.
Not Parallel:	Derek wanted a success rather than failing.
Parallel:	Derek wanted a success rather than a failure.
Parallel:	Derek wanted success rather than failure.

Practice

Directions: Correct any parallel form errors. Some sentences may not have errors.

1. I have to get to work, but first I have to find my way to breakfast.

2. The road was dry; the day was hot and sultry.

3. Jane likes to eat and go shopping when she is at the mall.

4. April chose to be a cameraperson rather than to be a technician who works the sound board.

5. Since I have not heard from you, I decided to write this letter.

6. Although she had driven the road before, Sally proceeded slowly, keeping her eye on the yellow line.

7. The tree withstood the hurricane, but the branches on the tree snapped off.

8. His work on the Board of Education revealed his dedication to the community.

9. Cars, taxis, and buses were my transportation to the airport.

10. The subject matter and the preparation for class created an excellent lesson.

Answers on page 80.

DICTION

Diction is choosing and using appropriate words. Good diction conveys a thought clearly without unnecessary words. Good diction develops fully over a number of years; however, there are some rules and tips you can follow.

Do not use slang, colloquialisms, or other non-standard English.
One person's slang is another person's confusion. Slang is often regional, and slang meanings change rapidly. We do not give examples of slang here for that very reason. Do not use slang words in your formal writing.

Colloquialisms are words used frequently in spoken language. This informal use of terms such as *dog tired*, *kids*, and *hanging around* is not generally accepted in formal writing. Save these informal terms for daily speech and omit or remove them from your writing except as quotations.

Omit any other non-standard English. Always choose standard English terms that accurately reflect the thought to be conveyed.

> ## AVOID WORDY, REDUNDANT, OR PRETENTIOUS WRITING
>
> Good writing is clear and economical.
>
> Wordy: I chose my career as a teacher because of its high ideals, the truly self-sacrificing idealism of a career in teaching, and for the purpose of receiving the myriad and cascading recognition that one can receive from the community as a whole and from its constituents.
>
> Revised: I chose a career in teaching for its high ideals and for community recognition.

Given below is a partial list of wordy phrases and the replacement word.

Wordy Phrases and Replacements

at the present time	now	because of the fact that	because
for the purpose of	for	in the final analysis	finally
in the event that	if	until such time as	until

HOMONYMS

Homonyms are words that sound alike but do not have the same meaning. These words can be confusing and you may use the incorrect spelling of a word. If words are homonyms, be sure you choose the correct spelling for the meaning you intend.

Homonyms

accept (receive)	lessen (make less)
except (other than)	lesson (learning experience)
affect (to influence)	past (gone before)
effect (a result)	passed (moved by)
ascent (rise)	peace (no war)
assent (agreement)	piece (portion)
board (wood)	rain (precipitation)
bored (uninterested)	reign (rule)
fair (average)	rein (animal strap)
fare (a charge)	their (possessive pronoun)
its (shows possession)	there (location)
it's (it is)	they're (they are)
led (guided)	to (toward)
lead (metal)	too (also)
	two (a number)

IDIOMS

Idioms are expressions with special meanings and often break the rules of grammar. Idioms are acceptable in formal writing, but they must be used carefully. Here are some examples.

Idioms

in accordance with	inferior to
angry with	occupied by (someone)
differ from (someone)	occupied with (something)
differ about (an issue)	prior to
independent of	rewarded with (something)

Practice

Directions: Write the word or phrase that fits best in the blank.

1. Many _____ diseases, including pneumonia and swelling in cuts, are caused by bacteria.

   innocuous   unfortunate   infectious   ill-fated

2. Sigmund Freud's views of sexuality had become _____, and the country entered the sexual revolution.

   well known   all knowing   universal   inculcated

3. After crossing the land bridge near the Bering Strait, groups of Native Americans _____ spread throughout all of North, Central, and South America.

   inclusively   eventually   regardless   remotely

4. During the early 1500s Cortez and Pizarro opened up Central America to the Spanish who began _____ slaves from Africa.

   importing   exporting   imparting   immigrating

5. The Stamp Act requiring every legal paper to carry a tax stamp was vehemently _____ and eventually repealed by England.

   denied   deported   proclaimed   protested

Directions: Circle the underlined portion that is unnecessary in the passage.

6. No goal is more noble—no feat more revealing—than the strikingly brave exploration of space.

7. As many as a ton of bananas may have spoiled when the ship was stuck and delayed in the Panama Canal.

8. He was concerned about crossing the bridge, but the officer said that it was all right to cross and he need not worry.

9. A professional golfer told the novice beginning golfer that professional instruction or more practice improves most golfers' scores.

10. The soccer player's slight strain from the shot on goal that won the game led to a pulled muscle that would keep her from playing the next match.

11. He went to the bird's nest near the river, only too realize he missed its assent.

12. The rider pulled back on the horse's reign before the whether turned rainy.

13. The whether turned rainy as he led the hikers on there ascent.

14. The lessen was clear; it was fare, but not easy to accept.

15. They're board relatives were not fare too her father.

16. Her grades had everything to do of her efforts.

17. Joanie expected him to wait to the house until she arrived home.

18. She could spend months absorbed in her studies.

19. The two coaches differ significantly with each other's style.

20. That person is wearing the same coat from you.

Answers on page 81.

PUNCTUATION

The Comma (,)

The comma may be the most used punctuation mark. This section details a few of these uses.

A clause is part of a sentence that could be a sentence itself. If a clause begins with a conjunction, use a comma before the conjunction.

Incorrect:	I was satisfied with the food but John was grumbling.
Correct:	I was satisfied with the food, but John was grumbling.

Incorrect:	Larry was going fishing or he was going to paint his house.
Correct:	Larry was going fishing, or he was going to paint his house.

A clause or a phrase often introduces a sentence. Introductory phrases or clauses should be set off by a comma. If the introductory element is very short, the comma is optional. Here are some examples.

However, there are other options you may want to consider.

When the deicer hit the plane's wing, the ice began to melt.

To get a driver's license, go to the motor vehicle bureau.

It doesn't matter what you want, you have to take what you get.

Parenthetical expressions interrupt the flow of a sentence. Set off the parenthetical expression with commas. Do not set off expressions that are essential to understanding the sentence. Here are some examples.

Tom, an old friend, showed up at my house the other day.

I was traveling on a train, in car 8200, on my way to Florida.

John and Ron, who are seniors, went on break to Florida.
[Use a comma. The phrase "who are seniors" is extra information.]

All the students who are seniors take an additional course.
[Do not use a comma. The phrase "who are seniors" is essential information.]

Commas are used to set off items in a list or series. Here are some examples.

Jed is interested in computers, surfing, and fishing.
[Notice the comma before the conjunction *and*.]

Mario drives a fast, red car.
[The sentence would make sense with *and* in place of the comma.]

Andy hoped for a bright, sunny, balmy day.
[The sentence would make sense with *and* in place of the commas.]

Lucy had a pale green dress.
[The sentence would not make sense with *and*. The word *pale* modifies *green*. Do not use a comma.]

Randy will go to the movies, pick up some groceries, and then go home.

Practice

Directions: Correct the comma errors. Some sentences may have no comma errors.

1. I had a slow day yesterday, but I worked hard in my junior year.

2. Passing calculus seems a difficult, but achievable, result.

3. After making the sandwich, I looked for some pickles, but the jar was empty.

4. Write an outline first and be sure to leave enough time to write the essay.

5. In the attic I found some old clothes, an old trunk, and a shoe.

6. Chad, Blaire, and Ryan have advanced degrees but they are still children at heart.

7. Using a computer the Core tests reading, writing, and arithmetic.

8. Either walk the dog or wash the dishes.

9. Every pilot, who has flown over 20 missions, receives an award.

10. Each time I ate lunch at home, my mother made liverwurst sandwiches.

Answers on page 83.

Semicolon and Colon

THE SEMICOLON (;)

Use the semicolon to connect main clauses not connected by a conjunction. Include a semicolon with very long clauses connected by a conjunction. Here are some examples.

> The puck was dropped; the hockey game began.
>
> The puck was dropped, and the hockey game began.
>
> The general manager of the hockey team was not sure what should be done about the player who was injured during the game; but he did know that the player's contract stipulated that his pay would continue whether he was able to play or not.

THE COLON (:)

Use the colon after a main clause to introduce a list. Here are some examples.

> Liz kept these items in her car: spare tire, jack, flares, and a blanket.
>
> Liz kept a spare tire, jack, flares, and a blanket in her car.

Practice

Directions: Correct any semicolon or colon errors. Some sentences may be correct.

1. Pack these other things for camp; a bathing suit, some socks, and a shirt.

2. In your wallet put: your camp information card and your bus pass.

3. I have one thing left to do; say good-bye.

4. We went to the store; and the parking lot was filled with cars.

5. We fought our way through the crowds, the store was even more crowded than the parking lot.

Answers on page 83.

Period, Question Mark, Exclamation Point

THE PERIOD (.)

Use a period to end every sentence, unless the sentence is a direct question, a strong command, or an interjection.

> You will do well on the Core test.

THE QUESTION MARK (?)

Use a question mark to end every sentence that is a direct question.

> What is the passing score for the Core test?

THE EXCLAMATION POINT (!)

Use an exclamation point to end every sentence that is a strong command or interjection. Do not overuse exclamation points.

> Interjection: Pass that test!
> Command: Avalanche, head for cover!

Practice

Directions: Correct any punctuation errors.

1. I was so worn out after swimming!

2. Avalanche.

3. Who said that!

4. Warning. The danger signal blared in the background.

5. I can't believe this is the last day of camp?

Answers on page 84.

This section shows you how to pass the multiple-choice writing portion of the computer-delivered Core writing test.

Types of Questions

The multiple-choice writing test gives you a chance to show what you know about grammar, sentence structure, and word usage. You should be familiar with the subjects covered in the English Review section.

You may be able to get the correct answer from your sense or feel about the sentence. If you are someone who has an intuitive grasp of English usage, you should rely on your intuition as you complete this section of the tests.

There are four types of questions on the computer-delivered Core. Most are usage and sentence correction questions. Examples of these questions are found below.

USAGE

You are shown a sentence with four parts underlined and lettered (A), (B), (C), and (D). There is a fifth choice: (E) No error. You choose the letter of the flawed part or E if there is no error. You do not have to explain what the error is or what makes the other parts correct. No sentence contains more than one error. You just have to recognize the error or realize that there is no error.

EXAMPLE

Every week, Doug took a child from the class on a visit to the art room until he
    Ⓐ   Ⓑ   Ⓒ   Ⓓ

got tired. No error.
        Ⓔ

SENTENCE CORRECTION

You are shown a sentence or a passage with one part underlined. Choice (A) repeats the underlined selection exactly. Choices (B) through (E) give suggested changes for the underlined part. You choose the letter of the best choice that does not change the meaning of the original sentence. If the original is best, choose (A). Otherwise, select one of the suggested changes.

EXAMPLE

Many times a shopper will prefer value to price.

Ⓐ to price
Ⓑ instead of price
Ⓒ rather than price
Ⓓ more than price
Ⓔ than price

There are fewer Revision in Context and Research Skills questions.

REVISION IN CONTEXT

These questions ask you to choose the correct revision for a sentence in a passage.

RESEARCH SKILLS

These questions ask you about basic research skills.

You will find all four question types in the Targeted Writing Test on page 89.

STRATEGIES FOR PASSING THE MULTIPLE-CHOICE TEST

Read Carefully

In this section, it is often small details that count. Read each sentence carefully. Read the whole sentence and not just the underlined sections. Remember that an underlined section by itself can look fine but be incorrect in the context of the whole sentence or passage. Read each sentence a few times until you get a sense for its rhythm and flow.

This Is a Test of Written English

Evaluate each sentence as written English. Do not apply the more informal rules of spoken English.

Do Not Focus on Punctuation

Use the English rules discussed in the English Review section. However, do not be overly concerned about punctuation. Punctuation rules are seldom tested.

Eliminate and Guess

Eliminate the answers you know are incorrect. If you cannot pick out the correct answer, guess from among the remaining choices.

Usage

| **Directions:** Choose the letter that indicates an error or choose (E) for no error. |

1. Every week, Doug took a child from the class on a visit to the art room until he got tired.
      (A)   (B)   (C)   (D)

   No error.
   (E)

2. Doug walks two miles every day and he rubbed off the dirt on his shoes as he went.
     (A)   (B)   (C)   (D)

   No error.
   (E)

3. Jim and Tom, the salesman, was doing a good job directing the under twelve soccer
        (A)   (B)   (C)   (D)

   league. No error.
     (E)

4. The students were greatly effected by the retirement of a very popular teacher.
     (A)   (B) (C)   (D)

   No error.
   (E)

5. The Rathburn is a high rated and singularly successful Italian restaurant near
         (A)   (B)   (C)

   the beach in Avalon. No error.
   (D)   (E)

Sentence Correction

Directions: Choose the letter of the best choice for the underlined section, without changing the meaning of the sentence. If the original is best, choose (A). Otherwise, select one of the suggested changes.

6. Many times a shopper will prefer value <u>to price</u>.

   Ⓐ to price
   Ⓑ instead of price
   Ⓒ rather than price
   Ⓓ more than price
   Ⓔ than price

7. After it had snowed steadily for days, the snow plows and snow blowers <u>most important priorities.</u>

   Ⓐ most important priorities.
   Ⓑ were ready for action.
   Ⓒ concentrated on the most important priorities.
   Ⓓ most significant priorities.
   Ⓔ most frequent difficulties.

8. The tug boat strained against the ship, revved up its engines <u>and was able to maneuver the ship into the middle of the channel.</u>

   Ⓐ and was able to maneuver the ship into the middle of the channel.
   Ⓑ and moves the ship into the middle of the channel.
   Ⓒ moving the ship into the middle of the channel.
   Ⓓ and moved the ship into the middle of the channel.
   Ⓔ with the ship moved into the middle of the channel.

9. The zoo opened for <u>the day, the children ran</u> to the exhibits.

   Ⓐ the day, the children ran
   Ⓑ the day. the children ran
   Ⓒ the day; the children ran
   Ⓓ the day: the children ran
   Ⓔ the day the children ran

Answers Explained

USAGE

1. **(D)** Pronoun error—it is not clear which noun the pronoun *he* refers to.

2. **(A)** Verb tense error—the verb *walks* should be *walked* to agree with the verb *rubbed*.

3. **(B)** Number error—the subject, *Jim and Tom*, is plural. The verb *was* should be the plural verb *were*.

4. **(C)** Diction error—the word *effected* should be replaced by the word *affected*.

5. **(A)** Adjective-adverb error—the adjective *high* should be changed to the adverb *highly*.

SENTENCE CORRECTION

6. **(A)** No error—Always choose (A) if there is no error.

7. **(C)** Sentence fragment error—The original choice is a sentence fragment. There is no verb for the subject *snow plows and snow blowers*. Choice (B) is grammatically correct but changes the meaning of the sentence.

8. **(D)** Parallelism error—Choice (D) maintains the parallel development of the sentence.

9. **(C)** Run-on sentence error—Use a semicolon to separate two independent clauses.

Form of the Essays

You will be given two essay topics, one after the other. One essay is called the Argumentative Essay and the other is called the Informative/Explanatory Essay. You will have 30 minutes to plan and type each essay. Type the essay in the space provided on the computer screen, below the essay prompt. You may use the scrap paper to write a brief outline.

What follows is a review of each essay type, prompts from these essays, and some strategies to follow. You will write an essay based on these prompts in the Review Test at the end of the chapter and see examples of rated essays.

Argumentative Essay (30 MINUTES)

The first essay is called an Argumentative Essay. You will read an opinion and then discuss the extent to which you agree or disagree with the opinion (with supporting details). There is no right or wrong answer. It is the quality of your essay that counts.

Here is one example of an opinion you may see on the test.

ESSAY OPINION

"Machines hurt people. A machine is just a way of replacing a human in the workplace. Over 30,000 people are killed and hundreds of thousands injured or maimed in accidents involving the machine we call a car."

The main opinion is "machines hurt people." That is clear and unequivocal. The rest of the statement includes details provided to support the opinion. We are going to focus on the opinion "Machines hurt people." This kind of topic gives a lot of room for reasonable agreement or disagreement, which is what the authors of the test want to accomplish.

You can choose to agree with the opinion or to disagree. Once you make your decision you have got to stick with it and make the best argument and be as persuasive as you can, and support that point of view. You should choose the side of the opinion that is easiest for you to argue in your essay.

Remember, there is no right or wrong position, but you must stick to the position you choose. There is no "On the one hand this, but on the other hand that." You have got to write in favor or opposed to the opinion given. Do not write about an opinion not included in the prompt. Well-written but off-topic essays earn the lowest score.

> ### STRATEGIES FOR WRITING THE ARGUMENTATIVE ESSAY
>
> ■ Read and understand the topic.
> ■ Choose your position.
> ■ Outline your essay.
> ■ Type the essay.
> ■ Review and correct the essay.

TIP
Use the rules of grammar as you write your essay. Punctuate as carefully as you can but do not spend an inordinate amount of time on punctuation. Raters will often ignore minor grammatical or spelling errors if the essay is well developed.

Informative/Explanatory Essay (30 MINUTES)

The second essay is called an Informative/Explanatory Essay. You will read a topic and then read two sources about that topic. Your essay must be based on these sources. There is no right or wrong answer. It is the quality of your essay, how well it discusses the sources' main points, and how well you use and cite the sources that counts.

The Informative/Explanatory Essay is part reading and part writing. You will read information about a particular topic. Then you are presented with two relatively long position papers on that topic, usually totaling 500 words or more.

You scan these position papers to understand the points of view of each author, which usually present differing opinions about the topic. Use the following steps as you work:

STRATEGIES FOR WRITING AN INFORMATIVE/EXPLANATORY ESSAY

- Read and understand the topic and the positions in the two sources.
- Outline your essay incorporating points from the position papers.
- Write the essay and include sources and citations.
- Review and correct the essay.

Your focus for this essay is to identify the important issues raised in the sources and to discuss them using references from the two position papers. You can bring in your own experiences. Your essay will be necessarily shorter than the Argumentative Essay because you have to use part of your 30 minutes to review the position papers. Focus on the points in the position papers and build your essay around them.

Here is an example of a Informative/Explanatory Essay:

You have 30 minutes to read two position papers on a topic and then write an essay based on the topic. The essay will discuss the important points in the two sources.

Read the topic and sources below. Organize your thoughts and plan your essay before you start to write. You MUST write on the given topic and you MUST include references to the sources.

This essay gives you a chance to demonstrate how well you can write and include sources in your writing. That means you should focus on writing well and using examples and references, while being sure to cover the topic presented. While how much you write is not a specific scoring criterion, you will certainly want to write several meaningful paragraphs.

TOPIC

Tracking is a sweeping educational grouping system in which students are assigned to all subjects and classes by academic achievement. Tracking systems are most commonly found in secondary schools where students take each subject class with a different instructor. When the system is used, it is not unusual to find three general tracks—advanced academic, academic, and vocational. Typically, students in one track do not take classes with students from another track. Ability grouping is not the same as tracking. Ability groups are typically found in a single classroom. An assignment to an ability group can change as soon as a change in performance is noted.

Read the two source passages below. Then write an essay that highlights the most important aspects and then explain why they are important. Your essay should refer to EACH of the sources and must CITE the sources as you refer to them or you must provide direct quotes. You may also use your own experiences and readings.

Finding a Track to Success . . . Tracking in the Schools, from Robertson (web accessed 10/2/2014)

There is nothing worse than seeing students forced into academic classes that are inappropriate for them. Taking those inappropriate courses seldom prepares students for the real world and they frequently leave school with knowledge they can't use and without the skills and preparation that would enable them to pursue a fruitful career. While no system is perfect, tracking, properly used, helps students prepare for the real world they will live in.

A carefully implemented tracking system enables teachers to structure lessons to the specific needs of students in a class—lessons that challenge students, but challenge them at a level they are capable of achieving. For students in an upper track, it removes the lid placed on instruction for academically talented students that would be present if they were in class with students of lesser ability. At the same time, it ensures that students of lesser ability in a comparable class will also have a chance to achieve at their highest level of potential. Yes, the students most negatively impacted by a nontracked system will be denied the opportunity to achieve at the level expected of them. And look at the students who might be at the lowest educational track. They consist primarily of students who will pursue a career after high school, perhaps in some trade. Those students deserve the opportunities for a track aimed at career preparation. In a world of imperfect solutions, a well-managed tracking system is the best approach.

A Track to Nowhere—the Failure of Tracking,
from Pismenny (web accessed 10/15/2014)

Educators try to dress up student tracking as an approach that benefits all levels of the achievement spectrum. The truth is that tracking only helps more able students from affluent families. In fact, tracking is just a way to assign poor and minority students to the lowest tracks, where one finds the least-qualified teachers. These low-tracked students never have an opportunity to escape the low track and are essentially given a one-way ticket to the same low track of society. Put more simply, tracking is just another form of race and class discrimination. It is more insidious than overt discrimination because it hides behind a cloak of what appears to be a useful educational practice.

Beyond that, even when initial tracks are fairly homogeneous, things change over time. Students learn at different rates and learning impediments decrease in some students. The similarities among students in a track tend to widen or disappear. Accounting for this increasing heterogeneity would require regular reevaluation of students and placement in different tracks when indicated. In practice, the best systems make the reassignment once a year. In most tracking systems it takes an extraordinary event for a student to move from one track to another. If we are talking about a tracking system in a high school, students who stay in one track are more different at the end of high school than they are the same.

In addition to these serious problems, tracking systems often determine a student's peer group. Students in the low track suffer from social stigmatization. Since lower-class and minority students are overrepresented in low tracks with whites and Asians generally dominating high tracks, interaction among these groups can be discouraged by tracking. It is easy to see how for students a tracking system is a track to nowhere.

TARGETED WRITING TEST

This targeted test is designed to help you practice the strategies presented in this chapter. For that reason, questions may have a different emphasis than the actual test, and the actual test will certainly be more complete.

Mark your choice, then check your answers on pages 84–85.

Use the strategies on page 57.

Part A: Usage

> **Directions:** Choose the letter that indicates an error, or choose (E) for no error.

1. Kitty and Harry's anniversary will fall on Father's Day this year. No error.
   Ⓐ   Ⓑ   Ⓒ   Ⓓ   Ⓔ

2. The trees leaves provide a fall festival called "Fall Foliage" in most New England states.
   Ⓐ   Ⓑ   Ⓒ   Ⓓ
   No error.
   Ⓔ

3. Most colleges require a specific number of academic credits for admission.
   Ⓐ   Ⓑ   Ⓒ   Ⓓ
   No error.
   Ⓔ

4. My brother Robert loves to read novels but would enjoy good mystery's more.
   Ⓐ   Ⓑ   Ⓒ   Ⓓ
   No error.
   Ⓔ

5. Louise had lay her mitt on the bench when she got a glass of water. No error.
   Ⓐ   Ⓑ   Ⓒ   Ⓓ   Ⓔ

6. It seems to me that I had spoke to my landlord about the crack in the ceiling
   Ⓐ   Ⓑ   Ⓒ
   about two months ago. No error.
   Ⓓ   Ⓔ

7. The committee on fund-raising gathers in the hall, but Joe went to the room.
   Ⓐ   Ⓑ   Ⓒ   Ⓓ
   No error.
   Ⓔ

8. The administrator wanted all lesson plan books handed in by Friday. No error.
   Ⓐ   Ⓑ   Ⓒ   Ⓓ   Ⓔ

9. Behind the tree, she was reading a book, eating a banana, and she waited for the
    <u>A</u>   <u>B</u>   <u>C</u>   <u>D</u>

    sunset. No error.
    <u>E</u>

10. Is Washington, D. C. closer to Arlington Cemetery than Charleston? No error.
    <u>A</u>   <u>B</u>   <u>C</u>   <u>D</u>   <u>E</u>

11. The student would not do nothing to redeem himself in the eyes of the principal.
    <u>A</u>   <u>B</u>   <u>C</u>   <u>D</u>

    No error.
    <u>E</u>

12. Good teachers are distinguished by their enthusiasm and organization. No error.
    <u>A</u>   <u>B</u>   <u>C</u>   <u>D</u>   <u>E</u>

13. The principle of the middle school wanted to reorganize the lunch schedule. No error.
    <u>A</u>   <u>B</u>   <u>C</u>   <u>D</u>   <u>E</u>

14. Grandmother's shopping list consisted of mustard, green beans, buttermilk, and
    <u>A</u>   <u>B</u>   <u>C</u>

    included some eggs. No error.
    <u>D</u>   <u>E</u>

15. Unless you arm yourself with insect repellent, you will get a bight. No error.
    <u>A</u>   <u>B</u>   <u>C</u> <u>D</u>   <u>E</u>

16. Graduation exercises will be held on ___ Friday ___ June 19th, at 7:00 P.M. No error.
    <u>A</u>   <u>B</u>   <u>C</u>   <u>D</u>   <u>E</u>

17. With a quick glance the noisy room was silenced. No error.
    <u>A</u>   <u>B</u>   <u>C</u>   <u>D</u>   <u>E</u>

18. Without even trying, the sprinter passed the world record by five tenths of a second.
    <u>A</u>   <u>B</u>   <u>C</u>   <u>D</u>

    No error.
    <u>E</u>

19. Prior to the passage of PL 94-142, special education students
    <u>A</u>   <u>B</u>   <u>C</u>

    were not unrepresented legally. No error.
    <u>D</u>   <u>E</u>

20. Combine the sugar, waters, cornstarch, and eggs. No error.
    <u>A</u>   <u>B</u>   <u>C</u>   <u>D</u>   <u>E</u>

Part B: Sentence Correction

Directions: Choose the letter of the best choice for the underlined section, without changing the meaning of the sentence. If the original is best, choose (A). Otherwise, select one of the suggested changes.

21. Postman's talents were missed <u>not any more</u> as a student but also in his extracurricular activities on campus.

    (A) not any more
    (B) not
    (C) not only
    (D) never any
    (E) any

22. <u>Piled on the table, the students started sorting through their projects.</u>

    (A) Piled on the table, the students started sorting through their projects.
    (B) The students started sorting through their projects, which were piled on the table.
    (C) Piled on the table, the students sorted through their projects.
    (D) The students sorted through their projects as they piled on the table.
    (E) Students started sorting through the table piled with projects.

23. All the soccer players, <u>who are injured,</u> must not play the game.

    (A) , who are injured,
    (B) , who are injured
    (C) who are injured,
    (D) who are injured
    (E) (who are injured)

24. The plumber kept these tools in his <u>truck; plunger, snake, washers and faucets.</u>

    (A) truck; plunger, snake, washers and faucets
    (B) truck (plunger, snake, washers and faucets)
    (C) truck: plunger; snake; washers and faucets
    (D) truck; plunger, snake, washers, and faucets
    (E) truck: plunger, snake, washers, and faucets.

25. The two <u>attorneys meet</u> and agreed on an out-of-court settlement.

    (A) attorneys meet
    (B) attorney's meet
    (C) attorney's met
    (D) attorneys met
    (E) attorney meets

Part C: Revision in Context

Directions: Choose the correct revision for the underlined sentence.

Little Big Horn

(1) In 1875 the United States ordered all nomadic Lakota and Cheyenne to return to the Great Sioux Reservation, established by the Treaty of 1868, or be considered hostile. (2) The immediate issues leading to the conflict, which became known as the Great Sioux War, were the Black Hills Expedition of 1874 and the invasion of the Black Hills by gold miners. (3) The U.S. attempted to acquire the Black Hills by purchase but had been rebuffed by the Lakota. (4) The Grant administration then unilaterally declared the Black Hills outside of the control of the Great Sioux Reservation.

(5) In the early morning hours of June 25, 1876, the large village of the Lakota and Cheyenne was observed from a high promontory in the Wolf Mountains. (6) George Custer's regiment went into the "Battle of the Little Big Horn" piecemeal. (7) It became apparent that the assumptions of the early morning observations, that of a village escaping, were incorrect.

(8) The village was largely intact and from accounts had been surprised by the approaching cavalry contingents. (9) Fortunately, the warrior fighting force was able to concentrate overwhelming numbers against a now divided regiment and defeat it in detail. (10) Approximately 380 members of the 7th Cavalry survived the battle after Major Marcus Reno and Captain Frederick Benteen reunited and developed a strong defensive position on high ground. (11) Custer and the 209 men in his immediate command were killed to a person because they had advanced to a position beyond the ability of the surviving parts of the regiment to support them.

26. In context of this passage, which of the choices below is the best suggestion to place at the beginning of sentence 4, which is reproduced below?

    The Grant administration then unilaterally declared the Black Hills outside of the control of the Great Sioux Reservation.

    (A) Regrettably,
    (B) In retaliation,
    (C) Against his better intentions,
    (D) After 7 years,
    (E) At the Lakota's request,

27. In the context of this passage, which is the best way to reword the underlined portion of sentence 11, which is reproduced below?

    killed to a person because they had advanced to a position beyond the ability of the surviving parts

    (A) Leave as is
    (B) killed in advance of their ability to reach the surviving parts
    (C) all killed because they were too far from reinforcements
    (D) all killed because they were outnumbered
    (E) killed because they had advanced to a position that was within the reach of the surviving elements

Part D: Research Skills

28. Pismenny, Aaron R. "The First 'R' of Teaching." *Best Teaching Approaches* 215 (2014): pp. 286–387.

    The citation above is from which of the following types of sources?

    Ⓐ A periodical
    Ⓑ A textbook
    Ⓒ An article from a newspaper
    Ⓓ An Internet source
    Ⓔ A textbook chapter

29. You are writing a paper on the role of social media in advertising. Which of the following selections is NOT directly relevant to your paper?

    Ⓐ Social media actually account for a fairly high percentage of contacts that lead to lasting relationships.
    Ⓑ Twitter advertisements can be easily accessed on handheld devices, such as cell phones.
    Ⓒ Facebook can target specific subscribers to receive pictures and messages.
    Ⓓ Opinions vary about the relative merits of social media ads or ads generated by Internet searches.
    Ⓔ The use of social media is still a relatively recent form of communication, and many still think that social media is a fad that will fade with time.

Part E: Constructed Response

> The Core Writing test has two constructed responses.
>
> You have 30 minutes to complete each response.
>
> Rated response examples are found on pages 85–89.

Argumentative Constructed Response

Directions: Use a word processor, but not the spell check or the grammar check features, to type your response.

OPINION

"Machines hurt people. A machine is just a way of replacing a human in the workplace. Over 30,000 people are killed and hundreds of thousands injured or maimed in accidents involving the machine we call a car."

Use this space to write a brief outline before you type your constructed response:

Informative/Explanatory Constructed Response

> **Directions:** Use a word processor, but not the spell check or the grammar check features, to type your response.

TOPIC

Tracking is a sweeping educational grouping system in which students are assigned to all subjects and classes by academic achievement. Tracking systems are most commonly found in secondary schools where students take each subject class with a different instructor. When the system is used, it is not unusual to find three general tracks—advanced academic, academic, and vocational. Typically, students in one track do not take classes with students from another track. Ability grouping is not the same as tracking. Ability groups are typically found in a single classroom. An assignment to an ability group can change as soon as a change in performance is noted.

Read the two source passages below. Then write an essay that highlights the most important aspects of them and explain why they are important. Your essay should refer to EACH of the sources and must CITE the sources as you refer to them or you must provide direct quotes. You may also use your own experiences and readings.

Source Passages

Finding a Track to Success . . . Tracking in the Schools, from Robertson (web accessed 10/2/2014)

There is nothing worse than seeing students forced into academic classes that are inappropriate for them. Taking those inappropriate courses seldom prepares students for the real world and they frequently leave school with knowledge they can't use and without the skills and preparation that would enable them to pursue a fruitful career. While no system is perfect, tracking, properly used, helps students prepare for the real world they will live in.

A carefully implemented tracking system enables teachers to structure lessons to the specific needs of students in a class—lessons that challenge students, but challenge them at a level they are capable of achieving. For students in an upper track, it removes the lid placed on instruction for academically talented students that would be present if they were in class with students of lesser ability. At the same time, it ensures that students of lesser ability in a comparable class will also have a chance to achieve at their highest level of potential. Yes, the students most negatively impacted by a nontracked system will be denied the opportunity to achieve at the level expected of them. And look at the students who might be at the lowest educational track. They consist primarily of students who will pursue a career after high school, perhaps in some trade. Those students deserve the opportunities for a track aimed at career preparation. In a world of imperfect solutions, a well-managed tracking system is the best approach.

**A Track to Nowhere—the Failure of Tracking,
from Pismenny (web accessed 10/15/2016)**

Educators try to dress up student tracking as an approach that benefits all levels of the achievement spectrum. The truth is that tracking only helps more able students from affluent families. In fact, tracking is just a way to assign poor and minority students to the lowest tracks, where one finds the least-qualified teachers. These low-tracked students never have an opportunity to escape the low track and are essentially given a one-way ticket to the same low track of society. Put more simply, tracking is just another form of race and class discrimination. It is more insidious than overt discrimination because it hides behind a cloak of what appears to be a useful educational practice.

Beyond that, even when initial tracks are fairly homogeneous, things change over time. Students learn at different rates and learning impediments decrease in some students. The similarities among students in a track tend to widen or disappear. Accounting for this increasing heterogeneity would require regular reevaluation of students and placement in different tracks when indicated. In practice, the best systems make the reassignment once a year. In most tracking systems it takes an extraordinary event for a student to move from one track to another.

If we are talking about a tracking system in a high school, students who stay in one track are more different at the end of high school than they are the same.

In addition to these serious problems, tracking systems often determine a student's peer group. Students in the low track suffer from social stigmatization. Since lower-class and minority students are overrepresented in low tracks with whites and Asians generally dominating high tracks, interaction among these groups can be discouraged by tracking. It is easy to see how for students a tracking system is a track to nowhere.

Use this space to write a brief outline before you type your essay:

ANSWERS FOR ENGLISH PRACTICE

Nouns, page 35

1. sheaves
2. deer
3. fries
4. lunches
5. knees
6. ladies
7. octopi
8. echoes
9. feet
10. halves

Verbs, page 37

      drove
1. Ryan ~~driven~~ to Florida.

2. Refereeing soccer games is not work.
   [No tense errors.]

      rode
3. Chad ~~ride~~ to the game with his team last week.
   [The words *last week* indicate that the verb must be past tense.]

      run
4. Why did Mary ~~ran~~ her errands now?

      spoken
5. I have ~~speak~~ to my teacher about the grade.

      paddles
6. Carl ~~paddled~~ across the river every Saturday.
   [Use the present tense because it is a regular event.]

      had thrown
7. Blaire ~~thrown~~ out the ball for the players to use.

      lose
8. Joann will ~~lost~~ her bag if she leaves it in the store.

9. Bob is standing on a stool next to the green table.
   [No tense errors.]

      began
10. Liz ~~begun~~ to grasp the depth of her happiness.

Tense Shift, page 37

1. Lisa already went to the North Pole but she is not going there again.
   [No tense shift errors.]

   took
2. Dennis ~~will take~~ his airline tickets with him because he is leaving for his flight.

3. The runner gasped as she crosses the finish line.

   The runner gasped as she crossed the finish line.
   The runner gasps as she crosses the finish line.

   play
4. I like to hear music so I ~~played~~ the clarinet.
   liked
   I ~~like~~ to hear music, so I played the clarinet.

   wants
5. Chris ~~wanted~~ to be a producer so he puts in long hours every day.

6. Bertha sews five hours a day because she will need her dress by next month.
   [No tense shift errors.]

7. The car turns over and then bounced down the hill.

   The car turned over and then bounced down the hill.
   The car turns over and then bounces down the hill.

8. Lois handed over her money because she wants to buy the computer.

   Lois hands over her money because she wants to buy the computer.
   Lois handed over her money because she wanted to buy the computer.

9. The captain wandered out on the deck as she calls to her friends on shore.

   The captain wandered out on the deck as she called to her friends on shore.
   The captain wanders out on the deck as she calls to her friends on shore.

10. The sun sets in the west as the moon rose in the east.

    The sun set in the west as the moon rose in the east.
    The sun sets in the west as the moon rises in the east.

Pronouns, page 40

   He
1. ~~His~~ was the best table tennis player.

   Who
2. ~~Whom~~ was the worst table tennis player?

3. Where are the table tennis balls?
   [No errors.]

is

4. Before the game everyone ~~are~~ going to choose teams.

us

5. The names of the winning teams are sent to ~~we~~.

They

6. ~~Them~~ are the best table tennis team.

Ron's

7. Ron and Jeff wanted to use ~~his~~ skates.
   [Jeff's, or any other name, could be used in place of Ron's.]

the skates

8. Jeff went to get ~~them~~.
   [Other nouns that make sense in this context could be used in place of skates.]

the pillows

9. The couch looked different, depending on how ~~they~~ were arranged.

10. Bob won most of his table tennis games.
    [No errors.]

her or his

11. The student waited for ~~their~~ school bus to come.

it doesn't

12. Either of the buses can arrive on time if ~~they do not~~ break down.

its

13. The book was most interesting near ~~her~~ beginning.

the

14. She read the book to find ~~her~~ most interesting parts.
    [There are other possible substitutes for *her*.]

15. I am the winner; victory is ours.

    I am the winner; victory is mine.
    We are the winners; victory is ours.

16. His friends got out of the car, and he went over to talk to them.
    [No errors.]

17. The rain clouds moved toward the pool, and the swimmers tried to wish it away.

The rain cloud moved toward the pool, and the swimmers tried to wish it away.
The rain clouds moved toward the pool, and the swimmers tried to wish them away.

          his
18. Was Les disappointed that ~~him~~ team did not win?

    Who
19. ~~Whom~~ has more experience than Nicky does?

20. You play better after you have experience.
    [No errors.]

Subject-Verb Agreement, page 42

       is
1. The chess set ~~are~~ still on the shelf.

           is
2. The shortest route to the college ~~are~~ shown in the catalog.

     drives
3. The golf pro ~~drive~~ a golf cart every day.

     walk
4. Derek and Ann ~~walks~~ every morning.

        add
5. The tropical birds in the tree ~~adds~~ a festive air to the occasion.

       walks
6. No one, not even Rick or Ronnie, ~~walk~~ to school today.

      are
7. Do you know who they ~~is~~?

   prepares
8. Ron ~~prepare~~ a paper for submission to the committee.

        show
9. The 15 employees of the coffee house ~~shows~~ up each day at 6:00 A.M.

        improves
10. Each person who takes the 12 steps ~~improve~~ his or her view.

Adjectives and Adverbs, page 43

                        really
1. The view of the Grand Canyon was ~~real~~ spectacular.

                               well
2. The trainer said the dog behaved very ~~good~~ today.

    Unfortunately
3. ~~Unfortunate~~, the tickets for the concert were sold out.

                smoothly
4. Things went ~~smooth~~.

                 extreme
5. The judge took ~~extremely~~ exception to the defendant's actions.

                                      carefully
6. The accident was silly, particularly since driving more ~~careful~~ would have avoided the whole thing.

7. But the reviews said the performance was truly horrible.
    [No adjective or adverb errors.]

8. The manager conveniently forgot that she promised the employee a raise.
    [No adjective or adverb errors.]

                            really
9. The bonus was a welcome surprise; it was a ~~real~~ large check.

             well   **badly**
10. I didn't do ~~good~~, but didn't do ~~bad~~ either.

Comparison, page 44

               happiest
1. Leon was the ~~happieer~~ chef in the restaurant.

2. But some of the people eating in the restaurant were happier than Leon.
    [No error.]

               fastest
3. The jet was the ~~faster~~ plane at the airport.

               faster
4. John was the ~~fastest~~ of the twins.

tallest

5. The ~~taller~~ of the apartment buildings is under repair.

lighter

6. The ~~lightest~~ of the two weights is missing.

7. Lonnie was among the most creative students in the school.
   [No error.]

less

8. Ron is the ~~least~~ able of the two drivers.

9. His shoe size is the smallest in his class.
   [No error.]

10. She was the more capable of the two referees.
    [No error.]

Misplaced and Dangling Modifiers, page 45

1. Les was reading his book through glasses with dirty lenses.
   [No modifier errors.]

2. Jim left work early to go to the doctor on the train.

   Jim left work early to go on a train to the doctor.

3. The first train car was crowded; which had to go to the next car.

   The first train car was crowded; someone (he) (she) had to go to the next car.

4. Ron's car ran out of gas when on the way to the store.

   Ron's car ran out of gas when he was on the way to the store.
   [Many other substitutions are possible for *he was.*]

5. Zena was jogging, when caused her to fall.

   Zena was jogging, when a hole caused her to fall.
   [Many other substitutions are possible for *a hole.*]

6. Derek wrapped the flowers and put them in the delivery van with colorful paper.

   Derek wrapped the flowers with colorful paper and put them in the delivery van.

7. Which bus stops at the corner where the stop sign is?
   [No modifier errors.]

8. Fran is going on the plane, which is just pulling up to the gate.
   [No modifier errors.]

9. Lisa bought a shirt in the store, which was expensive.

   Lisa bought an expensive shirt in the store.
   Lisa bought a shirt in an expensive store.
   Lisa bought an expensive shirt in an expensive store.

10. The car turned around and the headlights shone quickly into the garage.

    The car turned around quickly and the headlights shone into the garage.

Comma Splices and Run-On Sentences, page 46

There are three ways to remedy run-on sentence errors and comma splice errors. You can create two sentences, put a comma and a conjunction between the clauses, or put a semicolon between the two clauses. Only one of these options is shown in the answers.

1. It will be tomorrow before the sea is calm enough to go out.
   [No errors.]

2. It started to rain unexpectedly; the boaters were soaked.

3. But right now my sneakers are soaking wet; the towel is too wet to help me.

4. The Marine Police sounded the siren; the boat stopped immediately.

5. I put the sneakers next to the fire to dry, although they started to steam after a while.
   [No errors.]

6. The Coast Guard monitors boats as they enter the river; they use the data to monitor water pollution.

7. I like to use my compass when I go out on the boat.
   [No errors.]

8. When the boat breaks down, Liz calls Sea Tow.
   [No errors.]

9. The fire went out; the sun came up.

10. Splashing through the waves, the water skier was covered with salt spray.
    [No errors.]

Sentence Fragments, page 48

1. A golf bag, golf clubs, and golf balls. That's what she needed to play.

   A golf bag, golf clubs, and golf balls were what she needed to play.

2. As the rocket prepared for blast-off. Mary saw birds flying in the distance.

   The rocket prepared for blast-off. Mary saw birds flying in the distance.
   As the rocket prepared for blast-off, Mary saw birds flying in the distance.

3. Jim is mowing the lawn. Then, the mower stopped.
   [No sentence fragment errors.]

4. The lawn looked lush and green. Like a golf course.

   The lawn looked lush and green, like a golf course.

5. The polar bears swept across the ice. Like white ghosts in fur jackets.

   The polar bears swept across the ice, like white ghosts in fur jackets.

6. Jim looked across at the igloo. Like an ice fort, it stood a lonely vigil.
   [No sentence fragment errors.]

7. Astronauts and their equipment went by. These were the people who would go into space.
   [No sentence fragment errors.]

8. This was what Joe had been waiting for. To graduate from college.

   This was what Joe had been waiting for, to graduate from college.

9. To be finished with this test. That's what I'm waiting for.

   To be finished with this test is what I'm waiting for.

10. The test finished and done. The papers graded and good.

    The tests were finished and done.
    The papers were graded and good.

Parallelism, page 49

1. I have to get to work, but first I have to ~~find my way~~ **get** to breakfast.

2. The road was dry; the day was hot and sultry.
   [No parallel form errors.]

3. Jane likes to eat and go shopping when she is at the mall.
   [No parallel form errors.]

4. April chose to be a cameraperson rather than to be a ~~technician who works the sound board.~~ **sound technician**

5. Since I have not heard from you, I decided to write this letter.
   [No parallel form errors. The conjunction *since* shows subordination.]

6. Although she had driven the road before, Sally proceeded slowly, keeping her eye on the yellow line.
   [No parallel form errors. The conjunction *although* shows subordination.]

tree branches

7. The tree withstood the hurricane, but ~~the branches on the tree~~ snapped off.

8. His work on the Board of Education revealed his dedication to the community.
   [No parallel form errors.]

9. Cars, taxis, and buses were my transportation to the airport.
   [No parallel form errors.]

class preparation

10. The subject matter and the ~~preparation for class~~ created an excellent lesson.

Diction, page 51

1. Many <u>infectious</u> diseases, including pneumonia and swelling in cuts, are caused by bacteria.
   Infectious means a disease caused by bacteria. While the disease may be unfortunate, the context of the sentence calls for a word that means *caused by bacteria*.

2. Sigmund Freud's views of sexuality had become <u>well known</u>, and the country entered the sexual revolution.
   Well known means known by many people. *Universal* means known everywhere, which does not fit the context of this sentence.

3. After crossing the land bridge near the Bering Strait, groups of Native Americans <u>eventually</u> spread throughout all of North, Central, and South America.
   Eventually means over a period of time. The other words do not make sense in this context.

4. During the early 1500s Cortez and Pizarro opened up Central America to the Spanish who began <u>importing</u> slaves from Africa.
   Importing means to bring in. Exporting means to send out, which does not fit the context of the sentence.

5. The Stamp Act requiring every legal paper to carry a tax stamp was vehemently <u>protested</u> and eventually repealed by England.
   The act could only be *protested* in this context. It was not *denied*, and it does not make sense to say it was *vehemently* denied.

The circled phrases make the sentence too wordy.

6. No goal <u>is more noble</u>—<u>no feat more revealing</u>—than the (strikingly) brave <u>exploration</u>
   <u>of space</u>.

7. As <u>many</u> as a <u>ton of</u> bananas <u>may have</u> spoiled when <u>the ship</u> was stuck (and delayed) in
   the Panama Canal.

8. He <u>was concerned</u> about <u>crossing</u> the bridge, <u>but the officer</u> said that it was all right to
   cross (and he need not worry.)

9. A <u>professional</u> golfer told the (novice) beginning golfer that <u>professional instruction</u> or
   more practice <u>improves most golfers' scores</u>.

10. The soccer player's <u>slight</u> strain from the shot on goal (that won the game) led to a <u>pulled</u>
    muscle that <u>would</u> keep her from <u>playing</u> the next match.

The circled words are homonym errors.

11. He went to the bird's nest near the river, only (too) realize he missed its (assent.)

12. The rider pulled back on the horse's (reign) before the (whether) turned rainy.

13. The (whether) turned rainy as he led the hikers on (there) ascent.

14. The (lessen) was clear; it was (fare), but not easy to accept.

15. (They're) (board) relatives were not (fare) (too) her father.

Refer to page 50 for a list of idioms.

with
16. Her grades had everything to do ~~of~~ her efforts.

at
17. Joanie expected him to wait ~~to~~ the house until she arrived home.

18. She could spend months absorbed in her studies.
    [No idiom error.]

from
19. The two coaches differ significantly ~~with~~ each other's style.

as
20. That person is wearing the same coat ~~from~~ you.

Commas, page 53

1. I had a slow day yesterday, but I worked hard in my junior year.
   [No comma errors.]

2. Passing calculus seems a difficult, but achievable, result.
   [No comma errors.]

3. After making the sandwich, I looked for some pickles, but the jar was empty.
   [No comma errors.]

4. Write an outline first, and be sure to leave enough time to write the essay.
   [Add a comma before the conjunction to separate the two clauses.]

5. In the attic I found some old clothes, an old trunk, and a shoe.
   [No comma errors.]

6. Chad, Blaire, and Ryan have advanced degrees, but they are still children at heart.
   [Add a comma to separate the clauses.]

7. Using a computer, the Core tests reading, writing, and arithmetic.
   [Add a comma to set off the introductory phrase.]

8. Either walk the dog or wash the dishes.
   [No comma errors.]

9. Every pilot who has flown over 20 missions receives an award.
   [Remove the commas.]

10. Each time I ate lunch at home my mother made liverwurst sandwiches.
    [Remove the comma.]

Semicolons and Colons, page 54

1. Pack these other things for camp: a bathing suit, some socks, and a shirt.
   [Replace the semicolon with a colon.]

2. In your wallet put your camp information card and your bus pass.
   [Remove the colon.]

3. I have one thing left to do: say good-bye.
   [Replace the semicolon with a colon.]

4. We went to the store, and the parking lot was filled with cars.
   [Replace the semicolon with a comma.]

5. We fought our way through the crowds; the store was even more crowded than the parking lot.
   [Replace the comma with a semicolon.]

Period, Question Mark, and Exclamation Point, page 55

1. I was so worn out after swimming.
    [Change the exclamation point to a period.]

2. Avalanche!
    [Change the period to an exclamation point.]

3. Who said that?
    [Change the exclamation point to a question mark.]

4. Warning! The danger signal blared in the background.
    [Change the period to an exclamation point.]

5. I can't believe this is the last day of camp.
    [Change the question mark to a period.]

TARGETED WRITING TEST ANSWERS, PAGE 65

Part A

1. **(E)** The underlined sections are all correct.

2. **(A)** Replace the word *trees* with the possessive *trees'*.

3. **(E)** The underlined sections are all correct.

4. **(D)** Replace the word *mystery's* with the plural *mysteries*.

5. **(A)** Replace the words *had lay* with *laid* to show the past tense.

6. **(B)** Replace the words *had spoke* with *spoke* or *had spoken* to show the past tense.

7. **(C)** Replace *gathers* with *gathered* to show past tense and agree with the plural *committee*.

8. **(E)** The underlined sections are all correct.

9. **(D)** Replace the phrase with *and waiting* to maintain the parallel form.

10. **(D)** Replace the phrase with *than to Charleston* to maintain the parallel form.

11. **(B)** Replace the phrase with *would do nothing,* or similar phrases to eliminate the double negative.

12. **(E)** The underlined sections are all correct.

13. **(A)** Replace the word *principle* with the correct spelling *principal*.

14. **(D)** Replace the phrase with *eggs* to maintain the parallel form.

15. **(D)** Replace the phrase with *bitten* to show the future tense.

16. **(C)** Replace the blank space with a comma.

17. **(E)** The underlined sections are all correct.

18. **(D)** Replace *five tenths* with the hyphenated *five-tenths.*

19. **(D)** Replace *unrepresented* with *represented* to eliminate the double negative.

20. **(C)** Replace the word *waters* with the singular *water.*

Part B

21. **(C)** The conjunction pair *not only . . . but also* is the correct coordination for this sentence.

22. **(B)** This wording conveys the meaning of students sorting through projects, which are piled on the table.

23. **(D)** The phrase *who are injured* is essential to the sentence, and it is not set off by commas.

24. **(E)** This choice shows the correct combination of punctuation, a colon, and three commas.

25. **(D)** This choice shows the correct combination of a plural noun and a past tense verb.

Part C

26. **(C)** The Grant administration was reacting against the Lakota's rebuff of Grant's attempts to purchase the land, and his decision to just take the land was in clear retaliation for the Lakota's acts.

27. **(C)** This choice clearly and accurately restates the sentence's meaning and is less wordy than the original sentence. Choice (D) is incorrect because, while the troops may have been outnumbered, this choice changes the meaning of the sentence.

Part D

28. **(A)** The volume number, 215, is the best clue that this citation refers to a periodical, a publication such as a magazine published on a regular schedule. The second clue is that we see a specific name for an article, "The First 'R' of Teaching," together with the name of the publication, *Best Teaching Approaches.* These clues, together with the absence of a name for a newspaper, establish the publication as a periodical.

29. **(E)** This choice gives no insight into the use of social media for advertising. You might have been drawn to Choice A, but personal contacts are a form of advertising and give some insight into the role social media plays in advertising.

Part E

Compare your responses to the sample responses that follow. You may want to show your responses to an English expert for further evaluation.

RATED CONSTRUCTED RESPONSES

Rated argumentative responses and Informative/Explanatory responses are given below. There are literally many thousands of different approaches and responses that would earn high scores. ETS gives a free example of another approach on pages 29–34 and pages 35–40 at *www.ets.org/s/praxis/pdf/5722.pdf.*

RATED ARGUMENTATIVE ESSAYS EXAMPLES

Essay Opinion

"Machines hurt people. A machine is just a way of replacing a human in the workplace. Over 30,000 people are killed and hundreds of thousands injured or maimed in accidents involving the machine we call a car."

This essay would likely receive a rating of 5 or 6.

It is hard to disagree with the point made in the prompt about automobile fatalities. It is a serious problem in this country. There are still impaired drivers behind the wheels of cars who are too disoriented to make good decisions. Lately, many drivers are distracted by cell phones and tablets, which has increasingly become a cause of accidents. In this day there are still some people who do not wear seatbelts. Most automobile accidents are caused by drivers themselves and through education and laws we need to address these problems and reduce the number of automobile accidents.

However I completely disagree with the notion that a problem with car safety means that, as a general rule, machines harm people. I have one particular example in mind that has to do with my mother. Several years ago she had to undergo serious heart surgery. I didn't know anything about it, but I quickly learned that she would not be breathing on her own nor would her heart be beating on its own during the surgery. It was a very scary proposition.

I learned that my mother would be connected to a heart lung machine during the surgery. For the purposes of this essay—the word "machine" is very important. As I read the opinion for this essay I thought that someone may not have thought of this lifesaving machine—a machine that made such a positive difference in my life. I learned that doctors would be operating inside the heart and that the flow of blood through the heart would actually have to be stopped. I learned that the heart lung machine was a wonderful machine that makes open heart surgery possible. By pumping and cleaning blood during surgery. Without the heart lung machine this type of surgery would not be as successful and my mother may have died. Fortunately, the surgeons were good and the machine was available and my mother is now fine.

Whenever I think of a machine I think of the heart lung machine that probably saved my mother's life. And I think of some of the other machines used in the hospital to keep her breathing and to keep her alive during recovery. There may be some machines that hurt people, but there are more that do not. When I think machine, I think good.

Discussion

While this essay begins by agreeing with one part of the prompt, it quickly turns to the main point and clearly establishes that the writer does not agree with the main proposition that "machines hurt people." The details to support her position come from a very personal experience with a machine that probably saved her mother's life. The essay is well developed with a minimum of grammatical errors. The force of the writer's experiences and the conclusions make this a particularly compelling essay.

This essay would likely receive a rating of 4 or 3.

I disagree with the opinion that machines hurt people. It is such a sweeping statement that you just need one counterexample to show that it is not true. Personally, I can think of lots of machines that help people. I could not live without my fax machine or my garbage disposal. People undergoing open heart surgery could not live without a heart-lung machine or a respirator. Those are machines.

I guess what bothers me is that the statement is so silly. How can you make a general statement that machines hurt people. It just does not make any sense. The list of machines that help people is practically endless. Even the automobile casualties cited in the opinion are most often caused by human error, and it is certainly clear that ambulances, a car of sorts, are extremely helpful and certainly save more lives than those lost in automobile accidents.

An opinion as sweeping and general as the one found on this test can be proven false through many examples including the one described here in detail, and the few others alluded to. It just takes one true counterexample to prove the statement untrue and to conclusively support position that the statement "machines hurt people" is simply not true.

Discussion

This essay clearly states the author's position about the opinion that "machines hurt people." It provides some logic-based arguments that a sweeping statement can be proven false with a single counterexample, and offers several counterexamples to bolster that point. The essay lacks the development and detail necessary to place it in the upper third of essays and consequently earns a 3 or 4.

This essay would likely receive a 2.

The general statement that machines hurt people is simply not true. I just think of the heart lung machine. It is a machine and it does not hurt people. Really, what more is there to say. That simple counterexample proves that the statement is false. You do not need more than that.

But there are other examples. You do not even have to talk about a hospital and saving lives. I have clothes that need to be washed. I'd rather not do that by hand so I use a washing machine—I use that "machine." I can absolutely tell you that a washing machine helps me. So there are two examples and there are plenty more of why I disagree with the opinion.

Discussion

There is nothing wrong with this very brief essay, and it makes the point. The intent of this essay is not to prove you can make a point, but that you can write a well-developed essay supported by details. This essay lacks the development, detail, and length to receive a score above 2.

Essays that would receive lower scores than a 2 would be shorter and less well developed, or would be completely off topic.

RATED INFORMATIVE/EXPLANATORY ESSAYS EXAMPLES

Here is an essay that would receive a score of 5 or 6.

The primary concerns about school tracking are its effectiveness as an instructional structure, its unfairness to minority students and the potential for locking students into a plan of study after they show growth. Both author's seem to agree that tracking helps more able students. But the reasons for that view are quite different. Robertson points to the beneficial impact of tracking, while writing that "tracking only helps more able students from more afflu-ent families" (Pismenny), that author finds tracking to be discriminatory.

The differences grow as we move to the next point. The first position paper (Robertson) finds little wrong with tracking, even finding vocational benefits for students in the lowest track when the author points out that "students deserve the opportunities for a track aimed at a career." (Robertson). Pismenny is having none of that and labels tracking programs as discriminatory and goes on to point out that tracking is "insidious" (Pismenny) because it presents itself as an effective educational practice.

Robertson is completely silent on the issue of locking students into a plan of study, while Pismenny highlights that point in a "Track to Nowhere," which condemns tracking because it can take an "extraordinary event" for a students to move up to the next track.

A fair summary seems to be that tracking is a system that seems to work well for more able students from more affluent families. Each position paper makes that point. The main differ-ence appears when Robertson, who supports tracking, finds the advantages of a lower track, while Pismenny opposes tracking and sees it as a discriminatory system that locks in students.

Discussion

This essay does what every high-scoring essay does. It identifies the three main issues. The essay addresses the three issues in turn, bringing information in from both sources into a discussion of each issue, and clearly associates the information presented with the source. It clearly shows the points of agreement and disagreement in the position. The essay is free of meaningful errors, uses an array of sentence types, and shows a notable language structure. The 269 words in this essay will make raters comfortable about placing the essay in the upper third. The difference between a 5 and a 6 will hinge on the raters' perception that the analysis was sophisticated enough to receive a 6.

This essay would likely receive a 3 or 4.

There seem to be a range of positive things and negative things about tracking. The first paper by Robertson focuses mainly on the positive with an emphasis on benefits to higher achieving learners. Pismenny's essay focuses on the faults, primarily noting that tracking is just one form of discrimination.

It is obvious that Pismenny does not support tracking. It's the discriminatory nature of tracking that seems to cause this author the most trouble. It just seems to Pismenny that there are more potential problems to make the tracking thing worthwhile. That point is really ham-mered home when we read "It (tracking) is more insidious than overt discrimination because it hides behind a cloak of what appears to be a useful educational practice." (Pismenny) That is powerful language. Another point Pismenny make is that students are forever stuck in the track they start with at the beginning of high school. They can never escape. It is obvious that tracking is one type of approach with many problems. After reading Pismenny's position I am left wonder just whether there is enough there alone to say that tracking is bad.

Robertson's essay supports tracking as much as we see Pismenny's paper saying that it is bad. Robertson really like how much tracking helps better students. That position is really hammered home by the quote, "For students in an upper track, it removes the lid placed on instruction for academically talented students that would be present if they were in class with students of lesser ability." (Robertson). Robertson also. The system for low track students by saying that it will help these students prepare for careers. In this age when jobs are not really available, I guess that can be a strong argument. Roberson really seems to be saying that tracking is great for all students, but really great for more affluent students. I guess if you are a better students you'll agree with Robertson's position. Some people would say that's the way it is supposed to be. Students who can do the work should be in the top classes.

Robertson says that tracking is the best choice of imperfect choices. If you look at it another way Pismenny says it's just a bad idea all around. I guess every school uses some kind of tracking. The high school I went to had Advanced Placement courses for better students. Since most schools have one I guess it can't be a terrible idea.

Discussion

This essay does a fairly good job discussing the main positions of each position paper, and brings in the writer's own experiences. However, it does not clearly identify the main issues. It discusses one writer's position and then the other's instead of synthesizing them. There is fairly effective use of grammar, mechanics, and usage but with some errors including grammar, sentence fragments (Robertson also. The system . . .), and repetition. The referenced explanation and language usage likely earn this essay a 3 or 4.

This essay would receive a 2.

These two writers seem to have two completely different opinions of tracking. One likes it and the other do not. "In a world of imperfect solutions, a well-managed tracking system is the best approach." It is an imperfect world and I guess that is why these two positions are very different.

Just the whole idea of tracking gets so complicated. You have all these students assigned to classes and if one of those students does better in the middle of this year how can it be so easy to make a change. Besides tracking means different things to different people. "It is easy to see how for students a tracking system is a track to nowhere." That seems hard to disagree with too.

To draw a conclusion you could say that if you like tracking then you do, but there could be very good reasons for not liking tracking. I guess it is up to each person.

Discussion

This essay suffers from two problems. It mentions material from the sources, if inadequately, but it does not reference those sources. The essay also suffers from poor and inadequate development. Either one of these shortcomings would lead to a score of 2 for this essay.

Mathematics

6

TEST INFO BOX

Core Academic Skills For Educators: Mathematics

Computer-Delivered Only
56 items   85 minutes

Most are multiple-choice items with one correct answer choice.
Some are multiple-choice items that have more than one correct answer choice.
A few items require you to directly enter a numeric answer.
See the next page for sample mathematics items.

A basic calculator described below is available onscreen during the test.

USING THIS CHAPTER

This chapter prepares you to take the mathematics part of the Core Academic Skills Test for Educators (Core). Choose one of the approaches.

I want all the mathematics review I can get.

- Skip the Review Quiz and complete the entire review section starting on page 98.
- Take the Mathematics Review Quiz on page 93.
- Correct the Review Quiz and reread the indicated parts of the review.
- Go over the Special Strategies for Answering the Mathematics items on pages 161–162.
- Complete the Targeted Test items on page 163.

I want a thorough Mathematics review.

- Take the Mathematics Review Quiz on page 93.
- Correct the Review Quiz and reread the indicated parts of the review.
- Go over the Special Strategies for Answering the Mathematics items on pages 161–162.
- Complete the Targeted Test items on page 163.

I want a quick Mathematics review.

- Take and correct the Mathematics Review Quiz on page 93.
- Go over the Special Strategies for Answering the Mathematics items on pages 161–162.
- Complete the Targeted Test items on page 163.

SAMPLE MATHEMATICS ITEMS

Most mathematics multiple-choice items look like this.

If $x = \dfrac{5}{6}$, which of the following inequalities is correct?

Ⓐ $\dfrac{5}{9} < x < \dfrac{7}{9}$

Ⓑ $\dfrac{5}{8} < x < \dfrac{3}{4}$

Ⓒ $\dfrac{3}{4} < x < \dfrac{7}{8}$

Ⓓ $\dfrac{7}{8} < x < \dfrac{5}{16}$

Ⓔ $\dfrac{5}{6} < x < \dfrac{6}{5}$

You know the equation of a line 1 is $y = \dfrac{-3x}{4} + 2$.

Which of the following is an equation of a line parallel to line 1?

Select all that apply.

A $y = \dfrac{3x}{4} + 2$

B $y = \dfrac{-3x}{4} - 2$

C $y = \dfrac{-3x}{4} + 4$

D $y = \dfrac{3x}{4} + 2$

E $y = \dfrac{3x}{4} - 2$

A numeric-entry item might look like this:

$(3x - 7) + 3 = 4(x - 2)$

What is the value of x?

MATHEMATICS REVIEW QUIZ

This quiz uses a short-answer format to help you find out what you know about the mathematics topics reviewed in this chapter. The quiz results direct you to the portions of the chapter you should review. You do not have to take the quiz in one sitting.

This quiz will also help focus your thinking about mathematics, and these questions and answers are a good review in themselves. It is not important to answer all these questions correctly, and do not be concerned if you miss many of them.

The answers are found immediately after the quiz. It is to your advantage NOT to look at them until you have completed the quiz. Once you have completed and corrected this review quiz, use the answer checklist to decide which sections of the review to study.

It is to your advantage to not use a calculator for this review quiz.

1. Which number is missing from this sequence?

   6 ____ 12

Questions 2–4: Use symbols for less than, greater than, and equal to, and compare these numbers:

2. 23 ____ 32

3. 18 ____ 4 + 14

4. 9 ____ 10 ____ 11

5. Write the place value of the digit 7 in the numeral 476,891,202,593.

6. Write this number in words: 600,000,000,000.

7. $2^2 \times 2^3 =$

8. $6^9 \div 6^7 =$ _____

9. $3^2 \times 2^3 =$ _____

10. Write 8,342 in scientific notation.

   _____

11. Write the place value of the digit 4 in the numeral 529.354.

   _____

Questions 12–13: Use symbols for less than, greater than, and equal to, and compare these numbers:

12. 9,879 _____ 12,021

13. 98.1589 _____ 98.162

Questions 14–15: Round 234,489.0754 to the:

14. thousands place _____

15. hundredths place _____

16. Is 0.333 . . . a rational or irrational number?

   _____

17. Write these fractions from least to greatest.

   $$\frac{7}{8}, \frac{11}{12}, \frac{17}{20}$$

   _____, _____, _____

18. Which integer is one smaller than –6?

   _____

19. $5 + 7 \times 3^2$ _____

20. $5 \times 8 - (15 - 7 \times 2)$ _____

21. Is 4 a factor of 1,528? Why?

   _____

22. Write the GCF and LCM of 6 and 14.

   _____

23. $426 \div 16 =$ _____

24. Write the property illustrated by:

   $$x(x + 2) = x^2 + 2x$$

   _____

25. $30.916 - 8.72$ _____

26. 3.4×0.0021 _____

27. $0.576 \div 0.32$ _____

28. $1\frac{2}{3} \times 3\frac{3}{4}$ _____

29. $1\frac{2}{3} \div \frac{3}{8}$ _____

30. $1\frac{4}{9} + \frac{5}{6}$ _____

31. $4\frac{5}{6} - 2\frac{3}{5}$ _____

32. Simplify this square root

   $\sqrt{98}$ = _____

33. Complete the following ratio so that it is equivalent to 4 : 5

28 : _____

34. Use a proportion and solve this problem. Bob uses jelly and peanut butter in a ratio of 5 : 2. He uses 10 teaspoons of jelly. How much peanut butter will he use?

_____

Questions 35–40: Change among decimals, percents, and fractions to complete the table.

Decimal	Percent	Fraction
0.56	35. _____	36. _____
37. _____	15.2%	38. _____
39. _____	40. _____	$\frac{3}{8}$

41. What is 35 percent of 50?

42. What percent of 120 is 40?

43. A $25 item is on sale for $23.50. What percent of decrease is that?

44. What is the probability of rolling one die and getting a 7? _____

45. You flip a fair coin five times in a row and it comes up heads each time. What is the probability that it will come up tails on the next flip?

_____

46. You pick one card from a deck. Then you pick another one without replacing the first. Are these dependent or independent events? Explain.

_____

47. Anna has four pictures. How many different pairs can she make?

Questions 48–49: Find the median and mode of this set of data.

10, 5, 2, 1, 8, 5, 3, 0

48. Median _____

49. Mode _____

50. What type of correlation does this scatter plot show?

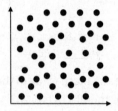

_____

51. A recreation center is going to be built. The builders randomly poll people in town of various ages, male and female, to find out what is wanted in the recreation center. Is this an appropriate or inappropriate form of sampling?

_____

52. The graph below represents the percentage of money that is given to each department at Ryan's college. If there is $3,000,000 in available funds, how much does the mathematics department get?

_____

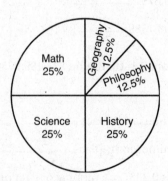

53. $+85 + -103 =$

54. $-12 - +7 =$ _____

55. $-72 - -28 =$ _____

56. $-12 \times -6 =$ _____

57. $-28 \div +7 =$ _____

58. $-72 \div -9 =$ _____

59. Add $(3x^2 + 4xy^2 - 2xy - 3) + (4x^2y - 2y)$

   _____

60. Find the area of a triangle with a base of 3 and a height of 2.

   _____

61. Find the area of a square with a side of 5.

   _____

62. Find the area of a circle with a radius of 6.

   _____

Write the value of the variable.

63. $x - 35 = 26$ _____

64. $x + 81 = 7$ _____

65. $y \div 8 < 3$ _____

66. $3z \geq 54$ _____

67. $4y - 9 = 19$ _____

Questions 68–71: Draw a model of:

68. an acute angle

69. complementary angles

70. an isosceles triangle

71. a rectangle

72. Triangle *PQR* and triangle *LMN* are similar. What is the length of side *LN*?

   _____

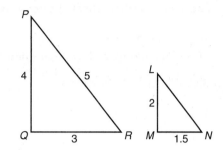

73. Use this coordinate grid and plot these points: $A\,(3, 2)$ $B\,(-4, -2)$, $C\,(2, 0)$. Connect the points to form a triangle.

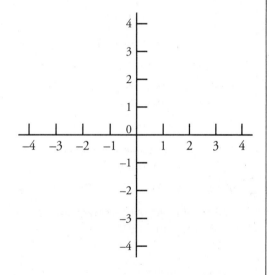

74. The figure in the preceding diagram is shifted up 3 units. What is the coordinate of point *B*?

75. The figure in the preceding diagram is shifted left 2 units. What is the coordinate of point *C*?

The answers are organized by review sections. Check your answers. If you miss any questions in a section, check the box and review that section.

☐ **Calculator page 98**
Everyone should review this section.

NUMBER AND QUANTITY

☐ **Understanding and Ordering Whole Numbers, page 101**

1. 9   3. =
2. <   4. <, <

☐ **Place Value, page 101**

5. 10 billion
6. six trillion

☐ **Positive Exponents, page 102**

7. 32   9. 72
8. 36

☐ **Scientific Notation, page 103**

10. 8.342×10^3

☐ **Understanding and Ordering Decimals, page 104**

11. thousandths

☐ **Comparing Whole Numbers and Decimals, page 104**

12. <   13. <

☐ **Rounding Whole Numbers and Decimals, page 105**

14. 234,000
15. 234,489.08
16. Rational $0.333 \ldots = \dfrac{1}{3}$

☐ **Rational, Irrational Numbers and Fractions, page 105**

17. $\dfrac{17}{20}, \dfrac{7}{8}, \dfrac{11}{12}$

☐ **Integers, page 109**

18. −7

☐ **How and When to Add, Subtract, Multiply, and Divide, page 109**

19. 68
20. 39

☐ **Common Factors and Multiples, page 111**

21. Yes, $1{,}528 \div 4 = 382$. There is no remainder.
22. GCF is 2. LCM is 42.

☐ **Whole Number Computation, page 112**

23. 26 R 10

☐ **Properties of Operations, page 114**

24. Distributive

☐ **Add, Subtract, Multiply, and Divide Decimals, page 115**

25. 22.196
26. 0.00714
27. 1.8

☐ **Multiplying, Dividing, Adding, and Subtracting Fractions and Mixed Numbers, page 117**

28. $6\dfrac{1}{4}$ 30. $2\dfrac{5}{18}$
29. $4\dfrac{4}{9}$ 31. $2\dfrac{7}{30}$

☐ **Square Roots, page 118**

32. $7\sqrt{2}$

☐ **Ratio and Proportion, page 119**

33. 35
34. 4

☐ **Percent, page 120**

Decimal	Percent	Fraction
0.56	35. 56%	36. $\dfrac{14}{25}$
37. 0.152	15.2%	38. $\dfrac{19}{25}$
39. 0.375	40. 37.5%	$\dfrac{3}{8}$

☐ **Three Types of Percent Problems, page 121**

41. 17.5   42. $33\dfrac{1}{3}$ %

☐ **Percent of Increase and Decrease, page 122**

43. 6%

PROBABILITY AND STATISTICS

☐ **Probability, page 124**

44. Zero

45. $\frac{1}{2}$

☐ **Independent and Dependent Events, page 125**

46. Dependent. The outcome of one event affects the probability of the other event.

☐ **Permutations, Combinations, and the Fundamental Counting Principle, page 125**

47. 6

☐ **Statistics and Scatter Plots, page 126**

48. 4

49. 5

50. There is no correlation.

51. Appropriate

52. $750,000

ALGEBRA AND FUNCTIONS

☐ **Adding and Subtracting Integers, page 130**

53. –18

54. –19

55. –44

☐ **Multiplying and Dividing Integers, page 131**

56. +72

57. –4

58. +8

☐ **Polynomials, page 131**

59. $3x^2 + 4xy^2 + 4x^2y - 2xy - 2y - 3^n$

☐ **Formulas, page 133**

60. 3

61. 25

62. about 113 (113.097...)

☐ **Equations and Inequalities, page 136**

63. 61

64. –74

65. $y < 24$

66. $z \geq 18$

67. 7

GEOMETRY AND MEASUREMENT

☐ **Two-Dimensional Geometry, page 139**

68. Acute angle

69. Complementary angles

70. Isosceles triangle

71. Rectangle

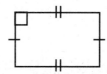

☐ **Similar Triangles, page 143**

72. 2.5

☐ **Coordinate Grid and Translations, page 145**

73.

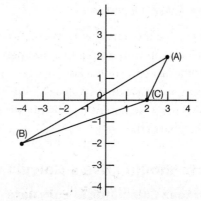

74. (–4, 1)

75. (0, 0)

☐ **Problem Solving, page 148**

Everyone should review this section.

This review section targets the skills and concepts you need to know to pass the mathematics part of the Core Academic Skills for Educators (Core).

USING THE ON-SCREEN CALCULATOR

This calculator will always be available on the screen to use during the mathematics test. You can use it, when appropriate. For numeric-entry items press TRANSFER to transfer an answer from the calculator directly to an answer box.

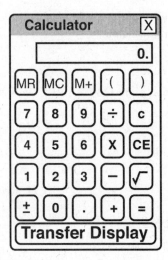

It is a good idea to get a very simple calculator like this one to prepare for the test. The TI-108 is an example of an inexpensive calculator. The TI-108 has the same keys as the on-screen calculator, except for the parentheses keys. Also the TI-108 keys are arranged a little differently. Although there are other basic calculators available, DO NOT use a calculator with more capabilities than the on-screen calculator.

Key Entry Errors

Many calculator mistakes come from key entry errors. Avoid that at all costs.

When you work with paper and pencil, you see all your work. On this calculator, you see only the last entry or the last answer. It is possible to make a key entry error and, in a flurry of entries, never catch your mistake. We all put an enormous amount of trust in the calculator answer, and we do not usually question the answer it produces. This makes us particularly vulnerable to the results of these key entry errors.

How Should I Use a Calculator?

Use Your Calculator to Calculate

Remember that the calculator is best at helping you find answers quickly. Use it to calculate the answers to numerical problems. Use it to try out answers quickly to find which is correct. Whenever you come across a problem involving calculation, you can use the calculator to do or check your work.

Estimate Before You Calculate

Earlier we mentioned that many calculator errors are caused by key entry mistakes. You think you put in one number, but you really put in another. One way to avoid this type of error is to estimate before you calculate. Then compare the estimate to your answer. If they are not close, then either your estimate or your calculation is off.

Recognize When Your Calculator Will Be Helpful

Think of problems in three categories. The calculator can be a big help, some help, or no help. The idea is to use your calculator on the first two types of problems and not to use it when it will not help.

BIG HELP

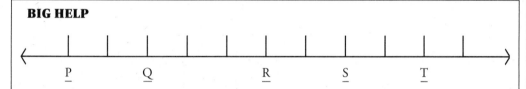

The segment $\overline{PT}$ has a length of 31.5. What is the length of segment $\overline{QS}$?

A calculator is a big help here. There are 9 units from P to T. So divide 31.5 by $9 = 3.5$ to find the length of each unit. Multiply 3.5 by $5 = 17.5$ to find the length of QS.

SOME HELP

A rectangle has a length 3 and width 5. What is the area?

You can do this computation in your head. A calculator could help you check the answer, but you do not absolutely need it.

NO HELP

Calculators are no help with problems involving equations or nonnumerical solutions. Using a calculator when it will not help will cause trouble and waste time.

Order of Operations

There is a difficulty with the TI-108 that you'll have to work around during the test. The TI-108 does not use order of operations, and it does not include keys with parentheses. The TI-108 just does the calculations in the order you press the keys.

You will have to be sure you follow this order of operations.

1. Parentheses (operations in parentheses are done first.)
2. Exponents
3. Multiplication
4. Division
5. Addition
6. Subtraction

Find the answer: $4 + 6 \times 5$

Using order of operation: $4 + 6 \times 5 = 4 + 30 = 34$

That is because you multiply first and then add.

But press $4 + 6 \times 5$ on a TI-108 and the answer is 50. That's wrong!
That is because the TI-108 just completes the calculation in the order you press the keys.

You have to press the TI-108 calculator keys as shown below to find the correct answer. $6 \times 5 + 4 =$

How Are Calculator Keys Used?

Press the numeral keys and the decimal point to represent numbers.

Press the $\boxed{+}$, $\boxed{-}$, $\boxed{\times}$, and $\boxed{\div}$ keys to add, subtract, multiply, and divide.

Press the equal $\boxed{=}$ key when you are through to get the final answer.

4 $\boxed{\times}$ 7 $\boxed{+}$ 9 $\boxed{=}$ 37   12 $\boxed{-}$ 18 $\boxed{=}$ -6

6 $\boxed{\times}$ 4 $\boxed{\times}$ 3 $\boxed{=}$ 72   10 $\boxed{\div}$ 3 $\boxed{=}$ 3.3333333

Square Root Key. $\boxed{\sqrt{}}$ To find the square root of 38.44 enter 38.44 $\boxed{\sqrt{}}$ =.
Note also that the square root key will not simplify a square root. So the square root shows up as 2.8284, not $2\sqrt{2}$.

Integer Key. $\boxed{+/-}$ The subtraction key on the calculator cannot be used to represent negative integers. Use the $\boxed{+/-}$ key on the calculator after a number to change the sign. For example, to subtract –62 – +25, enter 62 $\boxed{+/-}$ $\boxed{-}$ 25 $\boxed{=}$. To multiply –8 × –6, enter 8 $\boxed{+/-}$ $\boxed{\times}$ 6 $\boxed{+/-}$ $\boxed{=}$.

Percent Key $\boxed{\%}$

Use the percent key to find percent of increase or percent of decrease, such as the price after a sales tax is added or the price after a percent discount.

Find the cost of an item sold for $16 after a 7% sales tax.
Use these key strokes.

16 $\boxed{+}$ 7 $\boxed{\%}$ 17.12 [Do not press the equal sign.]

The cost with sales tax is $17.12.

Find the price of a $15.50 item sold at a 20% discount.
Use these key strokes.

15.50 $\boxed{-}$ 20 $\boxed{\%}$ 12.40 [Do not press the equal sign.]

The cost after the discount is $12.40.

Memory Keys $\boxed{M+}$ $\boxed{M-}$ $\boxed{MRC}$

The memory can be a handy place to store a number. The keys let you add and subtract values in memory, recall the value from memory, and erase that number.

13 M+ places the 13 in memory.

5 M– subtracts 5 from memory.

32.5 M+ adds 32 to the memory

Press MRC after this series of key strokes and the display shows 40.5, the value stored in memory.

Press the MRC a second time and the value in memory is erased.

ON/C

This key turns the calculator on. Press the key once after the calculator is on to erase the display. Press the key a second time to erase all the work you have done. Pressing this key does not erase the memory.

NUMBERS

Understanding and Ordering Whole Numbers

Whole numbers are the numbers you use to tell how many. They include 0, 1, 2, 3, 4, 5, 6 . . . . The dots tell us that these numbers keep going on forever. There are an infinite number of whole numbers, which means you will never reach the last one.

Cardinal numbers such as 1, 9, and 18 tell how many. There are 9 players on the field in a baseball game. Ordinal numbers such as 1st, 2nd, 9th, and 18th tell about order. For example, Lynne batted 1st this inning.

You can visualize whole numbers evenly spaced on a number line.

You can use the number line to compare numbers. Numbers get smaller as you go to the left and larger as you go to the right. The terms *equal to* (=), *less than* (<), *greater than* (>), and *between* are used to compare numbers.

12 equals 10 + 2	2 is less than 5	9 is greater than 4	6 is between 5 and 7
12 = 10 + 2	2 < 5	9 > 4	5 < 6 < 7

Place Value

We use ten digits, 0–9, to write out numerals. We also use a place value system of numeration. The value of a digit depends on the place it occupies. Look at the following place value chart.

millions	hundred thousands	ten thousands	thousands	hundreds	tens	ones
3	5	7	9	4	1	0

The value of the 9 is 9,000. The 9 is in the thousands place. The value of the 5 is 500,000. The 5 is in the hundred thousands place. Read the number three million, five hundred seventy-nine thousand, four hundred ten.

Some whole numbers are very large. The distance from Earth to the planet Pluto is about six trillion (6,000,000,000,000) yards. The distance from Earth to the nearest star is about 40 quadrillion (40,000,000,000,000,000) yards.

A. What is the value of 8 in the numeral 47,829?

The value of the 8 is 800; this is because the 8 is in the hundreds place.

B. Use <, >, or = to compare 2 and 7.

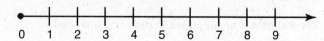

Use the number line to see that 2 < 7 (2 is less than 7).

Practice

Fill in the space with =, <, or > to make each statement true.

1. 2 _____ 3

2. 4 _____ 1

3. 8 _____ 9

4. 1 _____ 1

5. 7 _____ 6

6. Write a numeral in which the value of 7 is seven, the value of 9 is nine thousand, the value of 3 is thirty, and the 0 is in the hundreds place.

7. Write a numeral in which the value of 5 is fifty, the value of 2 is two thousand, the value of 1 is one, and the value of 8 is eight hundred.

8. What place values in the numeral 65,747 contain the same digit?

9. Write the whole numbers between 0 and 15.

10. How many whole numbers are there between 0 and 50?

Answers on page 179.

Positive Exponents

You can show repeated multiplication as an exponent. The exponent shows how many times the factor appears.

$$\text{Base—}3^5 = 3 \times 3 \times 3 \times 3 \times 3 = 243$$

[Exponent]

[Factors]

RULES FOR EXPONENTS

Use these rules to multiply and divide exponents with the *same base*.

$$7^8 \times 7^5 = 7^{13} \qquad\qquad a^n \times a^m = a^{m+n}$$
$$7^8 \div 7^5 = 7^3 \qquad\qquad a^n \div a^m = a^{n-m}$$

A. $4^3 + 6^2$ $= 4 \times 4 \times 4 + 6 \times 6$ $= 64 + 36$ $= 100$

B. $(2^3)(4^2)$ $= (2 \times 2 \times 2) \times (4 \times 4)$ $= 8 \times 16$ $= 128$

C. $(3^2)^2$ $= 3^4$ $= 3 \times 3 \times 3 \times 3$ $= 81$

D. $(10 - 9)^2$ $= 1^2$ $= 1$

Practice

1. $5^2 + 6^3 =$
2. $(3^2)^2 =$
3. $(8 - 6)^3 =$
4. $(5^2)(6^2) =$

5. $3^3 + 2^3 =$
6. $10^2 - 7^2 =$
7. $(4^3)^2 =$
8. $(2^4)^5 =$

9. $6^2 + 2^3 =$
10. $(25 - 15)^3 =$
11. $(4^2)^2 =$
12. $(2^3)(3^2) =$

Answers on page 179.

Scientific Notation

Scientific notation uses powers of 10. The power shows how many zeros to use.

$$10^0 = 1 \qquad 10^1 = 10 \qquad 10^2 = 100 \qquad 10^3 = 1,000 \qquad 10^4 = 10,000$$
$$10^{-1} = 0.1 \qquad 10^{-2} = 0.01 \qquad 10^{-3} = 0.001 \qquad 10^{-4} = 0.0001$$
$$10^5 = 100,000$$
$$10^{-5} = 0.00001$$

Write whole numbers and decimals in scientific notation. Use a decimal with one numeral to the left of the decimal point.

$2{,}345 \quad = \quad 2.345 \times 10^3$ The decimal point moved three places to the left. Use 10^3.

$176.8 \quad = \quad 1.768 \times 10^2$ The decimal point moved two places to the left. Use 10^2.

$0.0034 \quad = \quad 3.4 \times 10^{-3}$ The decimal point moved three places to the right. Use 10^{-3}.

$2.0735 \quad = \quad 2.0735 \times 10^0$ The decimal is in the correct form. Use 10^0 to stand for 1.

EXAMPLES

A. Write 7,952 in scientific notation.

Move the decimal point three places to the left and write $7{,}952 = 7.952 \times 10^3$.

B. Write 0.03254 in scientific notation.

Move the decimal point two places to the right and write 3.254×10^{-2}.

Practice

Rewrite using scientific notation.

1. 0.0564
2. 0.00897

3. 0.06501
4. 0.000354

5. 545
6. 7,790

7. 289,705
8. 1,801,319

Answers on page 179.

Understanding and Ordering Decimals

Decimals are used to represent numbers between 0 and 1. Decimals can also be written on a number line.

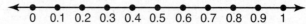

We also use ten digits 0–9 and a place value system of numeration to write decimals. The value of a digit depends on the place it occupies. Look at the following place value chart.

ones	tenths	hundredths	thousandths	ten thousandths	hundred thousandths	millionths	ten millionths	hundred millionths	billionths
0.	3	6	8	7					

The value of 3 is three tenths. The 3 is in the tenths place. The value of 8 is eight thousandths. The 8 is in the thousandths place.

Comparing Whole Numbers and Decimals

To compare two numbers line up the place values. Start at the left and keep going until the digits in the same place are different.

Compare	9,879 and 16,459	23,**8**01 and 23,798	58.1289 and 58.132
Line up the	9,879	23,**8**01	58.1289
place values	16,459	23,798	58.**1**32
	9,879 < 16,459	23,801 > 23,798	58.1289 < 58.132
	Less than	Greater than	Less than

EXAMPLES

A. What is the value of the digit 2 in the decimal 35.6829?

The 2 is in the thousandths place. $2 \times 0.001 = 0.002$.
The value of the 2 is 0.002 or 2 thousandths.

B. Use <, >, or = to compare 1248.9234 and 1248.9229.

1248.9234 ◯ 1248.9229. The digits in the numerals are the same until you reach the thousandths place where 3 > 2. Since 3 > 2, then 1248.9234 > 1248.9229.

Practice

Use <, >, or = to compare.

1. 0.02 _____ 0.003

2. 4.6 _____ 1.98

3. 0.0008 _____ 0.00009

4. 1.0 _____ 1

5. 7.6274 _____ 7.6269

Write the answer.

6. Write a numeral in which the value of 5 is five tenths, the value of 2 is two, the value of 6 is six thousandths, and the value of 8 is eight hundredths.

7. Write a numeral in which the value of 4 is in the ten thousandths place, the value of 3 is three hundred, the 7 is in the hundredths place, the 1 is in the tens place, the 9 is in the ten thousands place, and the rest of the digits are zeros.

8. In the numeral 6.238935, which place values contain the same digit?

9. Using only the tenths place, write all the decimals from 0 to 1.

10. If you used only the tenths and hundredths places, how many decimals are between 0 and 1?

Answers on page 179.

Rounding Whole Numbers and Decimals

Follow these steps to round a number to a place.

- Look at the digit to the right of the number.
- If the digit to the right is 5 or more, round up. If the digit is less than 5, leave the numeral to be rounded as written.

EXAMPLES

A. *Round 859,465 to the thousands place.*
Underline the thousands place.
Look to the right. The digit 4 is less than 5 so leave as written.
859,465 rounded to the thousands place is 859,000.
859,465 rounded to the ten-thousands place 860,000.

B. *Round 8.647 to the hundredths place.*
Underline the hundredths place.
Look to the right. The digit 7 is 5 or more so you round up.
8.647 rounded to the *hundredths* place is 8.65.
8.647 rounded to the *tenths* place is 8.6.

Practice

1. Round 23,465 to the hundreds place.

2. Round 74.1508 to the thousandths place.

3. Round 975,540 to the ten thousands place.

4. Round 302.787 to the tenths place.

5. Round 495,244 to the tens place.

6. Round 1508.75 to the hundreds place.

7. Round 13.097 to the hundredths place.

8. Round 198,704 to the hundred thousands place.

9. Round 51.8985 to the ones place.

10. Round 23,457 to the hundreds place.

Answers on page 179.

Rational and Irrational Numbers and Fractions

Most numbers can be written as a fraction or a ratio, with an integer in the numerator and in the denominator. These are called rational numbers.

Some numbers cannot be written as fractions with an integer in the numerator and denominator. These are called irrational numbers.

Never write 0 in the denominator. These numbers are undefined.

Look at these examples.

9 is rational because it can be written as the ratio 9/1 (or 18/2 and so on).

0.25 is rational because it can be written as the ratio ¼.

0.4 is rational because it can be written as the ratio 4/10 (2/5 in simplest form).

0.666 . . . (6 continues to repeat) is rational because it can be written as the ratio 2/3.

Rational numbers can be written as decimals that terminate or repeat.

0.25 and 0.4 are examples of decimals that terminate.

$\frac{1}{3}$ = 0.333 . . . and $\frac{1}{7}$ = 0.14285714285 . . . (the "142857" repeats) are examples of decimals that repeat.

Every fraction can be represented by a decimal that terminates or repeats.

IRRATIONAL NUMBERS

Irrational numbers cannot be written as a fraction.

The most famous irrational number is π.

You could try forever and never find a fraction or a terminating or repeating decimal that equals π.

$\pi = 3.141592653 . . .$

The calculator for this test does not have a π key, so you will have to use rational numbers to approximate π. Use 3.14, 3.1416 or 22/7 (= 3.14285). The test item will indicate which approximation to use or the answer will be so obvious that you will not need that specific information.

Square Root of 2

Another famous irrational number is the square root of $2(\sqrt{2})$. If you draw a diagonal in a square with sides equal to 1, the Pythagorean theorem tells you that the length of that diagonal is $\sqrt{2}$.

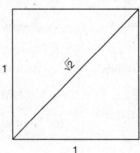

$$a^2 + b^2 = c^2 = 1^2 + 1^2 \qquad c^2 = 1 + 1 = 2: c = \sqrt{2}$$

$\sqrt{2} = 1.41421356 . . .$

You can use 99/70 ($\approx$ 1.41429) to approximate $\sqrt{2}$. You can see that this approximation is very close to the decimal value of the number.

The test calculator has a square root key so you could approximate the square root of 2. Most often just leave it as is and write the answer in radical form, such as $3\sqrt{2}$.

Practice

Write these fractions as terminating or repeating decimals. You can use a calculator.

1. $\dfrac{2}{3}$ 2. $\dfrac{8}{12}$ 3. $\dfrac{5}{9}$ 4. $\dfrac{7}{12}$

5. What is a reasonable approximation of 7π?

6. What is a reasonable approximation of $105\sqrt{2}$?

Answers on page 179.

Understanding and Ordering Fractions

A fraction names a part of a whole or of a group. A fraction has two parts, a numerator and a denominator. The denominator tells how many parts in all. The numerator tells how many parts are identified.

$$\frac{3}{4} \quad \begin{array}{l} \text{Numerator} \\ \text{Denominator} \end{array}$$

EQUIVALENT FRACTIONS

Two fractions that stand for the same number are called equivalent fractions. Multiply or divide the numerator and denominator by the same number to find an equivalent fraction.

$$\frac{2\times3}{5\times3}=\frac{6}{15} \qquad \frac{6\div3}{9\div3}=\frac{2}{3} \qquad \frac{6\times4}{8\times4}=\frac{24}{32} \qquad \frac{8\div2}{10\div2}=\frac{4}{5}$$

Fractions can also be written and ordered on a number line. You can use the number line to compare fractions. Fractions get smaller as you go to the left and larger as you go to the right. Use the terms equivalent to (=), less than (<), greater than (>), and between to compare fractions.

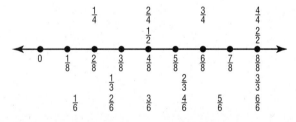

$\dfrac{1}{2}$ is equivalent to $\dfrac{2}{4}$ $\dfrac{2}{3}$ is less than $\dfrac{3}{4}$ $\dfrac{5}{8}$ is greater than $\dfrac{1}{2}$ $\dfrac{1}{3}$ is between $\dfrac{1}{4}$ and $\dfrac{3}{8}$

$\dfrac{1}{2} = \dfrac{2}{4}$ $\dfrac{2}{3} < \dfrac{3}{4}$ $\dfrac{5}{8} > \dfrac{1}{2}$ $\dfrac{1}{4} < \dfrac{1}{3} < \dfrac{3}{8}$

COMPARE TWO FRACTIONS

Use this method to compare two fractions. For example, compare $\frac{13}{18}$ and $\frac{5}{7}$. First write the two fractions and cross multiply as shown. The larger cross product appears next to the larger fraction. If cross products are equal, then the fractions are equivalent.

$$91 = \qquad = 90$$

$$91 > 90 \text{ so } \frac{13}{18} > \frac{5}{7}$$

MIXED NUMBERS AND IMPROPER FRACTIONS

Change an improper fraction to a mixed number:

$$\frac{23}{8} = 8\overline{)23}\,^{\displaystyle 2\frac{7}{8}}$$

Change a mixed number to an improper fraction:

$$3\frac{2}{5} = \frac{17}{5}$$

Multiply denominator and whole number. Then add the numerator.

$$\frac{(3\times5)+2}{5} = \frac{15+2}{5} = \frac{17}{5}$$

EXAMPLES

A. Compare $\frac{5}{7}$ and $\frac{18}{19}$,

Use cross multiplication.

$\frac{5}{7} \times \frac{18}{19}$, $5 \times 19 = 95$ and $7 \times 18 = 126$, therefore $\frac{5}{7} < \frac{18}{19}$.

B. Write $\frac{27}{7}$ as a mixed number.

$$7\overline{)27}\,^{\displaystyle 3\,\text{R}6}$$

$$\frac{21}{6}$$

$$\frac{27}{7} = 3\frac{6}{7}$$

C. Write $6\frac{5}{8}$ as a fraction.

$6 \times 8 = 48$. Multiply the denominator and the whole number.

$48 + 5 = 53$. Add the numerator to the product.

$$6\frac{5}{8} = \frac{53}{8}$$

Practice

Write the improper fraction as a mixed number.

1. $\dfrac{5}{3}$
2. $\dfrac{15}{7}$
3. $\dfrac{24}{9}$

Write the mixed number as an improper fraction.

4. $8\dfrac{1}{5}$
5. $6\dfrac{7}{8}$
6. $9\dfrac{5}{7}$

Use $>$, $<$, $=$ to compare the fractions.

7. $\dfrac{3}{7}, \dfrac{4}{9}$
8. $\dfrac{5}{6}, \dfrac{25}{30}$
9. $\dfrac{4}{5}, \dfrac{7}{8}$

Answers on page 179.

Integers

The number line can also show negative numbers. There is a negative whole number for every positive whole number. Zero is neither positive nor negative. The negative whole numbers, the positive whole numbers, and zero, together, are called integers. Integers are smaller as you go left on the number line and larger as you go to the right.

$$^-10 < {}^-1 \qquad {}^-8 < {}^-3 \qquad {}^+1 > {}^-9 \qquad {}^+6 > {}^+4$$

How and When to Add, Subtract, Multiply, and Divide

ORDER OF OPERATIONS

Use this phrase to remember the order to do operations:

Please Excuse My Dear Aunt Sally

(1) **P**arentheses (2) **E**xponents (3) **M**ultiplication or **D**ivision (4) **A**ddition or **S**ubtraction

For example,

$$4 + 3 \times 7^2 \quad = \quad 4 + 3 \times 49 \quad = \quad 4 + 147 \quad = \quad 151$$
$$(4 + 3) \times 7^2 \quad = \quad 7 \times 7^2 \quad = \quad 7 \times 49 \quad = \quad 343$$
$$(6 - 10 \div 5) + 6 \times 3 = (6 - 2) + 6 \times 3 = 4 + 6 \times 3 = 4 + 18 = 22$$

EXAMPLES

$$7 + 3 \times 6 + 4^2 - (8 + 4) \quad = \quad 7 + 3 \times 6 + 4^2 - \underline{12} \quad =$$
$$7 + 3 \times 6 + \underline{16} - 12 \quad = \quad 7 + \underline{18} + 16 - 12 \quad = 29$$

DECIDE WHETHER TO ADD, SUBTRACT, MULTIPLY, OR DIVIDE

Before you can solve a problem, you should know which operation to use. You can use key words to decide which operation to use or you can use a problem-solving strategy called choosing the operation.

Key Words

Addition	sum, and, more, increased by
Subtraction	less, difference, decreased by
Multiplication	of, product, times
Division	per, quotient, shared, ratio
Equals	is, equals

You cannot just use these key words without thinking. You must check to be sure that the operation makes sense when it replaces the key word. See the examples below.

EXAMPLES

19 and 23 is 42   16 is 4 more than 12   What percent of 19 is 5.7

$19 + 23 = 42$ $16 = 4 + 12$ _____$\% \times 19 = 5.7$

Practice

Find the answer.

1. $4 \times 5 + 4 \div 2 =$

2. $(5 + 7 - 9) \times 8^2 + 2 =$

3. $((7 + 4) - (1 + 4)) \times 6 =$

4. $6^2 + 3(9 - 5 + 7)^2 =$

5. $(12 + 5) \times 3 - 6^2 =$

6. $8 \times 5 + 4 - 8 \div 2 =$

7. $100 - 30 \times 5 + 7 =$

8. $((5 + 2)^2 + 16) \times 8 =$

Answers on page 180.

CHOOSING THE OPERATION

To use the choosing-the-operation strategy, you think of each situation in this way. What do I know? What am I trying to find? The answers to these questions lead you directly to the correct operation.

You Know	You Want to Find
Add	
1. How many in two or more groups	How many in all
2. How many in one group How many join it	The total amount
3. How many in one group How many more in the second group	How many in the second group
Subtract	
4. How many in one group Number taken away	How many are left
5. How many in each of two groups	How much larger one group is than the other
6. How many in one group How many in part of that group	How many in the rest of the group

You Know	You Want to Find
Multiply	
7. How many in each group	How many in all
There is the same number in each group	
How many groups	
Divide	
8. Same number in each group	How many groups
How many in all	
How many in each group	
9. Same number in each group	How many in each group
How many in all	
How many groups	

Common Factors and Multiples

FACTORS

The factors of a number evenly divide the number with no remainder. For example, 2 is a factor of 6, but 2 is not a factor of 5.

Here are the factors for the numbers 1–10.

The number 1 is a factor of every number. Each number is a factor of itself.

1	The only factor is 1	6	1, 2, 3, 6
2	1, 2	7	1, 7
3	1, 3	8	1, 2, 4, 8
4	1, 2, 4	9	1, 3, 9
5	1, 5	10	1, 2, 5, 10

LEAST COMMON MULTIPLE (LCM), GREATEST COMMON FACTOR (GCF)

Multiples

The multiples of a number are all the numbers you get when you count by that number. Here are some examples.

Multiples of 1: 1, 2, 3, 4, 5, . . .
Multiples of 2: 2, 4, 6, 8, 10, . . .
Multiples of 3: 3, 6, 9, 12, 15, . . .
Multiples of 4: 4, 8, 12, 16, 20, . . .
Multiples of 5: 5, 10, 15, 20, 25, . . .

Least Common Multiple

The least common multiple is the smallest multiple shared by two numbers.

The least common multiple of 6 and 8 is 24.

List the multiples of 6 and 8. Notice that 24 is the smallest multiple common to both numbers.

Multiples of 6: 6, 12, 18, **24**, 30, 36
Multiples of 8: 8, 16, **24**, 32, 40

Greatest Common Factor

The greatest common factor is the largest factor shared by two numbers.

The greatest common factor of 28 and 36 is 4.

List the factors of 28 and 36.

Factors of 28: 1, 2, **4**, 7, 28
Factors of 36: 1, 2, 3, **4**, 9, 12, 18, 36

EXAMPLES

A. Find the factors of 24.

The factors are 1, 2, 3, 4, 6, 8, 12, and 24.
These are the only numbers that divide 24 with no remainder.

B. Find the GCF of 14 and 22.

Write out the factors of each number.
14: 1, 2, 7, 14
22: 1, 2, 11, 22

The greatest common factor is 2.

C. Find the LCM of 6 and 9.

List some of the multiples of each number.
6: 6, 12, 18, 24, . . .
9: 9, 18, 27, . . .

The least common multiple is 18.

Practice

Write the factors of each number.

1. 13   2. 26   3. 40   4. 23

Find the LCM of the two numbers.

5. 6 and 8   6. 5 and 12   7. 7 and 35   8. 4 and 14

Find the GCF of the two numbers.

9. 24 and 30   10. 15 and 40   11. 32 and 64   12. 56 and 84

Answers on page 180.

Whole Number Computation

You have a calculator, but it may help to review these steps.

Follow these steps to add, subtract, multiply, and divide whole numbers.
Estimate first and then check to be sure your answer is reasonable.

Add

24,262 + 8,921.

Estimate first.

24,262 rounded to the nearest ten thousand is 24,000.

8,921 rounded to the nearest thousand is 9,000.

24,000 + 9,000 = 33,000. The answer should be close to 33,000.

Add.

```
                          1 1
    2 4 2 6 2          2 4 2 6 2
  +   8 9 2 1        +   8 9 2 1
                      3 3 1 8 3

   Align digits.          Add.
```

33,183 is close to 33,000, so the answer is reasonable.

Subtract

20,274 − 17,235.

Estimate first.

20,274 rounded to the nearest thousand is 20,000.

17,235 rounded to the nearest thousand is 17,000.

20,000 − 17,000 = 3,000.

The answer should be close to 3,000.

Subtract.

```
                       1 10   6 14
    2 0 2 7 4          2 0 2 7 4
  − 1 7 2 3 5        − 1 7 2 3 5
                          3 0 3 9

   Align digits.        Subtract.
```

3,039 is close to 3000, so the answer seems reasonable.

Multiply

32 × 181.

Estimate first.

Multiplication answers may look correct but may be wrong by a multiple of 10.

32 rounded to the nearest ten is 30.
181 rounded to the nearest hundred is 200.

30 × 200 = 6,000.

The answer should be near 6,000.

Multiply.

```
      181                 181
   ×   32              ×   32
      362                 362
      543                 543
                         5792

Find the partial products.   Add the partial products.
```

The answer is close to 6,000.

The answer seems reasonable.

Divide

$927 \div 43$.

Estimate first.

You may make a division error if you misalign digits.

927 rounded to the nearest hundred is 900.

43 is close to 45.

$900 \div 45 = 20$

The answer should be somewhere near 20.

Divide.

$$43\overline{)927}$$

$$\begin{array}{r} 21 \text{ R}24 \\ 43\overline{)927} \\ \underline{86} \\ 67 \\ \underline{43} \\ 24 \end{array}$$

        Divide.   Find the quotient and the remainder.

The answer is close to 20.

The answer seems reasonable.

Practice

Find the answer.

1. $97,218$ $\underline{+\ 1,187}$	2. $23,045$ $\underline{+\ 4,034}$	3. $67,914$ $\underline{+27,895}$	4. $48,549$ $\underline{+17,635}$
5. $20,591$ $\underline{-\ 4,578}$	6. $34,504$ $\underline{-\ \ \ 405}$	7. $57,895$ $\underline{-23,207}$	8. $84,403$ $\underline{-42,194}$
9. 240 $\underline{\times\ \ 57}$	10. 302 $\underline{\times\ \ 91}$	11. 725 $\underline{\times\ \ 41}$	12. 146 $\underline{\times\ \ 36}$

13. $328 \div 41 =$ 14. $240 \div 59 =$ 15. $754 \div 26 =$ 16. $2,370 \div 74 =$

Answers on page 180.

PROPERTIES OF OPERATIONS

Subtraction and division are not commutative or associative.

Commutative	$a + b = b + a$	$a \times b = b \times a$
	$3 + 5 = 5 + 3$	$3 \times 5 = 5 \times 3$
Associative	$(a + b) + c = a + (b + c)$	$(a \times b) \times c = a \times (b \times c)$
	$(3 + 4) + 5 = 3 + (4 + 5)$	$(3 \times 4) \times 5 = 3 \times (4 \times 5)$

Identity	$a + 0 = a$	$a \times 1 = a$
	$5 + 0 = 5$	$5 \times 1 = 5$

Inverse	$a + (-a) = 0$	$a \times \dfrac{1}{a} = 1$
	$5 + (-5) = 0$	$5 \times \dfrac{1}{5} = 1 \; (a \neq 0)$

Distributive property of $a(b + c) = (a \times b) + (a \times c)$
multiplication over addition $3(4 + 5) = (3 \times 4) + (3 \times 5)$

EXAMPLES

A. Use a property of operations to write an expression equivalent to $8y - 4x$. These items ask you to identify equivalent statements produced by the properties.
The distributive property creates the equivalent expressions $4(2y - x)$ or $2(4y - 2x)$.

B. What property is illustrated by $7^2 + 8^3 = 8^3 + 7^2$?
This statement demonstrates the commutative property.

Practice

1. Use a property to write an expression equivalent to $\dfrac{6}{8} \times \dfrac{7}{9}$.
2. What property is illustrated by $(2 + 3) + 4 = 2 + (3 + 4)$?
3. What property is illustrated by $3x(x + 2y) = 3x^2 + 6xy$?
4. Write an expression equivalent to $a(6) + a(3)$.
5. What property is illustrated by $3a + 3b = 3b + 3a$?
6. Choose a statement that is *not* true for all real numbers.

   Ⓐ A $(1/A) = 0$ for A $\neq 0$.
   Ⓑ $x^2 (y^2) = (xy)^2$
   Ⓒ $(3x + y)(x - y) = (x - y)(3x + y)$
   Ⓓ $10^2 + 12 = 12 + 10^2$

Answers on page 180.

Add, Subtract, Multiply, and Divide Decimals

ADD AND SUBTRACT DECIMALS

Line up the decimal points and add or subtract.

Add: $14.9 + 3.108 + 0.16$ Subtract $14.234 - 7.14$

$$
\begin{array}{r}
14.9 \\
3.108 \\
+\,0.16 \\
\hline
18.168
\end{array}
\qquad\qquad
\begin{array}{r}
14.234 \\
-\,7.14 \\
\hline
7.094
\end{array}
$$

MULTIPLY DECIMALS

Multiply as with whole numbers. Count the total number of decimal places in the factors. Put that many decimal places in the product. You may have to write leading zeros.

Multiply: 17.4×1.3

$$
\begin{array}{r}
17.4 \\
\times\ 1.3 \\
\hline
522 \\
174 \\
\hline
22\ 6\ 2
\end{array}
$$

Multiply: 0.016×1.7

$$
\begin{array}{r}
0.016 \\
\times\ 1.7 \\
\hline
112 \\
16 \\
\hline
02\ 7\ 2
\end{array}
$$

DIVIDE DECIMALS

Make the divisor a whole number. Match the movement in the dividend and then divide.

$$0.16\overline{)1.328}$$

$$0.16.\overline{)1.32.8}$$

$$
\begin{array}{r}
8.3 \\
16\overline{)132.8} \\
128 \\
\hline
48 \\
48 \\
\hline
0
\end{array}
$$

Practice

1. $\begin{array}{r} 12.79 \\ 8.1 \\ +\ 5.2 \\ \hline \end{array}$

2. $\begin{array}{r} 40.267 \\ 23.2 \\ +\ 9.15 \\ \hline \end{array}$

3. $\begin{array}{r} 940.17 \\ 36.15 \\ +\ 12.07 \\ \hline \end{array}$

4. $\begin{array}{r} 5290.3 \\ 167.81 \\ +\ 15.09 \\ \hline \end{array}$

5. $\begin{array}{r} 37.9 \\ -\ 29.7 \\ \hline \end{array}$

6. $\begin{array}{r} 136.804 \\ -\ 65.7944 \\ \hline \end{array}$

7. $\begin{array}{r} 513.72 \\ -\ 59.75 \\ \hline \end{array}$

8. $\begin{array}{r} 2451.06 \\ -\ 683.19 \\ \hline \end{array}$

9. $\begin{array}{r} 0.249 \\ \times\ 2.5 \\ \hline \end{array}$

10. $\begin{array}{r} 46.7 \\ \times\ 3.5 \\ \hline \end{array}$

11. $\begin{array}{r} 56.2 \\ \times\ 65.49 \\ \hline \end{array}$

12. $\begin{array}{r} 93.57 \\ \times\ 40.2 \\ \hline \end{array}$

13. $10.32 \div 2.1\,5$ 14. $16.8 \div 1.7\,5$ 15. $258.32 \div 7.4\,5$ 16. $659.5575 \div 5.2\,5$

Answers on page 180.

Multiply, Divide, Add, and Subtract Fractions and Mixed Numbers

MULTIPLY FRACTIONS AND MIXED NUMBERS

Write any mixed number as an improper fraction. Multiply numerator and denominator. Write the product in simplest form. For example, multiply $\frac{3}{4}$ and $\frac{1}{6}$.

$$\frac{3}{4} \times \frac{1}{6} = \frac{3}{24} = \frac{1}{8}$$

Now, multiply $3\frac{1}{3}$ times $\frac{3}{5}$.

$$3\frac{1}{3} \times \frac{3}{5} = \frac{10}{3} \times \frac{3}{5} = \frac{30}{15} = 2$$

DIVIDE FRACTIONS AND MIXED NUMBERS

To divide $1\frac{4}{5}$ by $\frac{3}{8}$:

$$1\frac{4}{5} \div \frac{3}{8} = \frac{9}{5} \div \frac{3}{8} = \frac{9}{5} \times \frac{8}{3} = \frac{72}{15} = 4\frac{12}{15} = 4\frac{4}{5}$$

Write any mixed numbers · · · · · · Invert the divisor · · · · · Write the · · · · · Write in
as improper fractions · · · · · · · and multiply · · · · · · · · product · · · · · simplest form

ADD FRACTIONS AND MIXED NUMBERS

Write fractions with common denominators. Add and then write in simplest form.

Add: $\frac{3}{8} + \frac{1}{4}$

$$\frac{3}{8} = \frac{3}{8}$$
$$+\frac{1}{4} = \frac{2}{8}$$
$$\frac{5}{8}$$

Add: $\frac{7}{8} + \frac{5}{12}$

$$\frac{7}{8} = \frac{21}{24}$$
$$+\frac{5}{12} = \frac{10}{24}$$
$$\frac{31}{24} = 1\frac{7}{24}$$

Add: $2\frac{1}{3} + \frac{5}{7}$

$$2\frac{1}{3} = 2\frac{7}{21}$$
$$+\frac{5}{7} = \frac{15}{21}$$
$$2\frac{22}{21} = 3\frac{1}{21}$$

SUBTRACT FRACTIONS AND MIXED NUMBERS

Write fractions with common denominators. Subtract and then write in simplest form.

Subtract: $\frac{5}{6} - \frac{1}{3}$

$$\frac{5}{6} = \frac{5}{6}$$
$$-\frac{1}{3} = \frac{2}{6}$$
$$\frac{3}{6} = \frac{1}{2}$$

Subtract: $\frac{3}{8} - \frac{1}{5}$

$$\frac{3}{8} = \frac{15}{40}$$
$$-\frac{1}{5} = \frac{8}{40}$$
$$\frac{7}{40}$$

Subtract: $3\frac{1}{6} - 1\frac{1}{3}$

$$3\frac{1}{6} = 3\frac{1}{6} = 2\frac{7}{6}$$
$$-1\frac{1}{3} = 1\frac{2}{6} = 1\frac{2}{6}$$
$$1\frac{5}{6}$$

Practice

1. $\dfrac{1}{3} \times \dfrac{5}{9} =$

2. $\dfrac{2}{3} \times \dfrac{1}{4} =$

3. $3\dfrac{3}{8} \times 4\dfrac{1}{8} =$

4. $3\dfrac{1}{5} \times 2\dfrac{4}{7} =$

5. $\dfrac{3}{4} \div \dfrac{7}{8} =$

6. $\dfrac{2}{5} \div \dfrac{7}{9} =$

7. $9\dfrac{5}{7} \div 4\dfrac{1}{3} =$

8. $2\dfrac{4}{5} \div 7\dfrac{3}{5} =$

9. $\dfrac{5}{9} + \dfrac{2}{3} =$

10. $\dfrac{7}{10} + \dfrac{2}{4} =$

11. $1\dfrac{6}{7} + 2\dfrac{3}{14} =$

12. $5\dfrac{2}{3} + 6\dfrac{5}{6} =$

13. $\dfrac{2}{7} - \dfrac{5}{21} =$

14. $\dfrac{2}{5} - \dfrac{3}{8} =$

15. $3\dfrac{4}{5} - 3\dfrac{2}{15} =$

16. $8\dfrac{1}{7} - 4\dfrac{2}{9} =$

Answers on page 180.

Square Roots

The square root of a given number, when multiplied by itself, equals the given number. This symbol means the square root of 25: $\sqrt{25}$. The square root of 25 is 5. $5 \times 5 = 25$.

SOME SQUARE ROOTS ARE WHOLE NUMBERS

The numbers with whole-number square roots are called perfect squares.

$$\sqrt{1} = 1 \qquad \sqrt{4} = 2 \qquad \sqrt{9} = 3 \qquad \sqrt{16} = 4 \qquad \sqrt{25} = 5 \qquad \sqrt{36} = 6$$

$$\sqrt{49} = 7 \qquad \sqrt{64} = 8 \qquad \sqrt{81} = 9 \qquad \sqrt{100} = 10 \qquad \sqrt{121} = 11 \qquad \sqrt{144} = 12$$

The fractional exponent $a^{\frac{1}{2}}$ is another way to write square root.

$$16^{\frac{1}{2}} = \sqrt{16} = 4 \qquad 324^{\frac{1}{2}} = \sqrt{324} = 18$$

USE THIS RULE TO WRITE A SQUARE ROOT IN ITS SIMPLEST FORM

$$\sqrt{a \times b} = \sqrt{a} \times \sqrt{b} \qquad \sqrt{5 \times 3} = \sqrt{5} \times \sqrt{3}$$

$$\sqrt{72} = \sqrt{36 \times 2} = \sqrt{36} \times \sqrt{2} = 6 \times \sqrt{2}$$

EXAMPLES

A. Write the square root of 162 in simplest form.

$$\sqrt{162} = \sqrt{81 \times 2} = \sqrt{81} \times \sqrt{2} = 9\sqrt{2}$$

B. Write the square root of 112 in simplest form.

$$\sqrt{112} = \sqrt{16 \times 7} = \sqrt{16} \times \sqrt{7} = 4\sqrt{7}$$

Practice

Simplify.

1. $\sqrt{256}$

2. $\sqrt{400}$

3. $\sqrt{576}$

4. $\sqrt{900}$

5. $\sqrt{1225}$

6. $\sqrt{48}$

7. $\sqrt{245}$

8. $\sqrt{396}$

9. $\sqrt{567}$

10. $\sqrt{832}$

Answers on page 180.

Ratio and Proportion

RATIO

A ratio is a way of comparing two numbers with division. It conveys the same meaning as a fraction. There are three ways to write a ratio.

Using words   3 to 4   As a fraction $\frac{3}{4}$ Using a colon   3 : 4

PROPORTION

A proportion shows two ratios that have the same value; that is, the fractions representing the ratios are equivalent. Use cross multiplication. If the cross products are equal, then the two ratios form a proportion.

$\frac{3}{8}$ and $\frac{27}{72}$ form a proportion. The cross products are equal. ($3 \times 72 = 8 \times 27$)

$\frac{3}{8}$ and $\frac{24}{56}$ do not form a proportion. The cross products are not equal.

SOLVING A PROPORTION

You may have to write a proportion to solve a problem. For example, the mason mixes cement and sand using a ratio of 2 : 5. Twelve bags of cement will be used. How much sand is needed?

To solve, use the numerator to stand for cement. The denominator will stand for sand.

$$\frac{2}{5} = \frac{12}{S} \qquad\qquad \frac{2}{5} = \frac{12}{S}$$

$$2 \times S = 5 \times 12$$
$$2S = 60$$
$$S = 30$$

Write the proportion   Cross multiply to solve

Thirty bags of sand are needed.

EXAMPLE

The problem compares loaves of whole wheat bread with loaves of rye bread. Let the numerators stand for loaves of whole wheat bread. The denominators stand for loaves of rye bread.

Ratio of whole wheat to rye. $\frac{3}{7}$ Ratio of whole wheat to rye for $\frac{51}{R}$
                                             51 loaves of whole wheat.

Write a proportion. $\frac{3}{7} = \frac{51}{R}$

Solution: $3R = 357$ $R = 119$

There are 119 loaves of bread.

Practice

1. A salesperson sells 7 vacuum cleaners for every 140 potential buyers. If there are 280 potential buyers, how many vacuums are sold?

2. There is one teacher for every 8 preschool students. How many teachers are needed if there are 32 preschool students?

3. There are 3 rest stops for every 20 miles of highway. How many rest stops would there be on 140 miles of highway?

4. Does $\frac{7}{9}$ and $\frac{28}{36}$ form a proportion? Explain.

Answers on page 181.

Percent

Percent comes from per centum, which means per hundred. Whenever you see a number followed by a percent sign it means that number out of 100.

DECIMALS AND PERCENTS

To write a decimal as a percent, move the decimal point two places to the right and write the percent sign.

$$0.34 = 34\% \qquad 0.297 = 29.7\% \qquad 0.6 = 60\% \qquad 0.001 = 0.1\%$$

To write a percent as a decimal, move the decimal point two places to the left and delete the percent sign.

$$51\% = 0.51 \qquad 34.18\% = 0.3418 \qquad 0.9\% = 0.009$$

FRACTIONS AND PERCENTS

Writing Fractions as Percents

- Divide the numerator by the denominator. Write the answer as a percent.

Write $\frac{3}{5}$ as a percent.   Write $\frac{5}{8}$ as a percent.

$$5\overline{)3.0}^{\,0.6} \qquad 0.6 = 60\% \qquad\qquad 8\overline{)5.000}^{\,0.625} \qquad 0.625 = 62.5\%$$

- Write an equivalent fraction with 100 in the denominator. Write the numerator followed by a percent sign.

Write $\frac{13}{25}$ as a percent.

$$\frac{13}{25} = \frac{52}{100} = 52\%$$

- Use these equivalencies.

$\frac{1}{4} = 25\%$	$\frac{1}{2} = 50\%$	$\frac{3}{4} = 75\%$	$\frac{4}{4} = 100\%$
$\frac{1}{5} = 20\%$	$\frac{2}{5} = 40\%$	$\frac{3}{5} = 60\%$	$\frac{4}{5} = 80\%$
$\frac{1}{6} = 16\frac{2}{3}\%$	$\frac{1}{3} = 33\frac{1}{3}\%$	$\frac{2}{3} = 66\frac{2}{3}\%$	$\frac{5}{6} = 83\frac{1}{3}\%$
$\frac{1}{8} = 12\frac{1}{2}\%$	$\frac{3}{8} = 12\frac{1}{2}\%$	$\frac{5}{8} = 62\frac{1}{2}\%$	$\frac{7}{8} = 87\frac{1}{2}\%$

Writing Percents as Fractions

Write a fraction with 100 in the denominator and the percent in the numerator. Simplify.

$$18\% = \frac{18}{100} = \frac{9}{50} \qquad\qquad 7.5\% = \frac{7.5}{100} = \frac{75}{1000} = \frac{3}{40}$$

EXAMPLES

A. Write 0.567 as a percent.

Move the decimal two places to the right and write a percent sign, therefore, $0.567 = 56.7\%$.

B. Write $\frac{1}{4}$ as a percent.

Write $\frac{1}{4}$ as a decimal $(1 \div 4) = 0.25$

Write 0.25 as a decimal $0.25 = 25\%$

C. Write 26% as a fraction.

Place the percent number in the numerator and 100 in the denominator.

$26\% = \frac{26}{100} = \frac{13}{50}$. Simplify: $\frac{26}{100} = \frac{13}{50}$

Practice

Write the decimal as a percent.

1. 0.359   2. 0.78   3. 0.215   4. 0.041

Write the fraction as a percent.

5. $\frac{1}{9}$ 6. $\frac{5}{8}$ 7. $\frac{3}{10}$ 8. $\frac{4}{9}$

Write the percents as fractions in simplest form.

9. 58%   10. 79%   11. 85.2%   12. 97.4%

Answers on page 181.

Three Types of Percent Problems

FINDING A PERCENT OF A NUMBER

To find a percent of a number, write a number sentence with a decimal for the percent and solve.

$$\text{Find } 40\% \text{ of } 90.$$
$$0.4 \times 90 = 36$$

It may be easier to write a fraction for the percent.

$$\text{Find } 62\frac{1}{2}\% \text{ of } 64.$$
$$\frac{5}{8} \times 64 = 5 \times 8 = 40$$

FINDING WHAT PERCENT ONE NUMBER IS OF ANOTHER

To find what percent one number is of another, write a number sentence and solve to find the percent.

What percent of 5 is 3?

$$n \times 5 = 3$$
$$n = \frac{3}{5} = 0.6 = 60\%$$

FINDING A NUMBER WHEN A PERCENT OF IT IS KNOWN

To find a number when a percent of it is known, write a number sentence with a decimal or a fraction for the percent and solve to find the number.

5% of what number is 2?

$$0.05 \times n = 2$$
$$n = 2 \div 0.05$$
$$n = 40$$

EXAMPLES

A. What percent of 70 is 28?

$\square \times 70 = 28$

$\square = \frac{28}{70} = \frac{4}{10}$

$\square = 40\%$

B. 30% of 60 is what number?

$30\% \times 60 = \square$

$0.3 \times 60 = \square$

$\square = 18$

C. 40% of what number is 16?

$0.40 \times \square = 16$

$\square = \frac{16}{0.4}$

$\square = 40$

Practice

1. 120 is what percent of 240?

2. 15% of 70 is what number?

3. 60% of 300 is what number?

4. What percent of 60 is 42?

5. What percent of 25 is 2.5?

6. 40% of what number is 22?

7. 70% of what number is 85?

8. 25% of 38 is what number?

9. 35% of what number is 24?

10. 24 is what percent of 80?

Answers on page 181.

Percent of Increase and Decrease

PERCENT OF INCREASE

A price increases from $50 to $65. What is the percent of increase?

Subtract to find the amount of increase. $65 - $50 = $15

$15 is the amount of increase

Write a fraction. The amount of increase is the numerator. The original amount is the denominator.

$15   Amount of increase
—————————————————
$50   Original amount

Write the fraction as a percent. The percent of increase is 30%.

$$50\overline{)15.00}^{0.3} \qquad 0.3 = 30\%$$

PERCENT OF DECREASE

A price decreases from $35 to $28. What is the percent of decrease?

Subtract to find the amount of decrease.

$35 − $28 = $7

$7 is the amount of decrease

Write a fraction. The amount of decrease is the numerator. The original amount is the denominator.

$7   Amount of decrease
—————————————————
$35   Original amount

Write the fraction as a percent. The percent of decrease is 20%.

$$\frac{7}{35} = \frac{1}{5} = 20\%$$

EXAMPLES

A. The price increased from $30 to $36. What is the percent of increase?

   $36 − $30 = $6

   $$\frac{6}{30} = \frac{1}{5} = 20\%$$

B. An $80 item goes on sale for 25% off. What is the sale price?

   $80 × 25% = $80 × 0.25 = $20

   $80 − $20 = $60. $60 is the sale price.

Practice

1. The price increased from $25 to $35. What is the percent of increase?

2. A sale marks down a $100 item 25%. What is the sale price?

3. The price decreases from $80 by 15%. What is the new price?

4. The price increased from $120 to $150. What is the percent of increase?

5. A sale marks down a $75 item 10%. What is the sale price?

6. The price decreases from $18 to $6. What is the percent of decrease?

7. A sale marks down a $225 item to $180. What is the percent of decrease?

8. A sale price of $150 was 25% off the original price. What was the original price?

Answers on page 181.

PROBABILITY AND STATISTICS
Probability

The probability of an occurrence is the likelihood that it will happen. Most often, you write probability as a fraction.

Flip a fair coin and the probability that it will come up heads is $\frac{1}{2}$. The same is true for tails. Write the probability this way.

$$P(\text{H}) = \frac{1}{2} \qquad P(\text{T}) = \frac{1}{2}$$

If something will never occur the probability is 0. If something will always occur, the probability is 1. Therefore, if you flip a fair coin,

$$P(7) = 0 \qquad P(\text{H or T}) = 1$$

Write the letters A, B, C, D, and E on pieces of paper. Pick them randomly without looking. The probability of picking any letter is $\frac{1}{5}$.

$$P(\text{vowel}) = \frac{2}{5} \qquad P(\text{consonant}) = \frac{3}{5}$$

RULES FOR COMPUTING PROBABILITY

$$P(A \text{ or } B) = P(A) + P(B) = \frac{1}{5} + \frac{1}{5} = \frac{2}{5}$$

when A and B have no common elements

$$P(A \text{ and } B) = P(A) \times P(B) = \frac{1}{5} \times \frac{1}{5} = \frac{1}{25}$$

$$P(\text{not } C) = 1 - P(C) = 1 - \frac{1}{5} = \frac{4}{5}$$

EXAMPLE

In one high school, 40% of the students go on to college. Two graduates of the high school are chosen at random. What is the probability that they both went to college?

Write the probabilities you know.

$$P(\text{college}) = \frac{40}{100} = \frac{2}{5}$$

Solve the problem.

$P(A \text{ and } B)$ probability the two students went to college.

$$P(A \text{ and } B) = P(A) \times P(B) = \frac{2}{5} \times \frac{2}{5} = \frac{4}{25}$$

The probability that they both went to college is $\frac{4}{25}$.

Practice

1. There are 3 black, 2 white, 2 gray, and 3 blue socks in a drawer. What is the probability of drawing a sock that is not black?

2. Six goldfish are in a tank; 4 are female and 2 are male. What is the probability of scooping out a male?

3. A standard deck of 52 playing cards is spread facedown on a table. What is the probability of choosing a card that is a king or a queen?

4. Six names are written on pieces of paper. The names are Aaron, Ben, Carl, Edith, Elizabeth, and Phyllis. One name is picked and replaced. Then another name is picked. What is the probability that the names were Carl and Phyllis?

5. A fair die having six sides is rolled. What is the probability that the side facing up is a prime number?

6. A fair coin is tossed in the air 5 times. What is the probability of getting five tails?

Answers on page 182.

Independent and Dependent Events

Events are *independent* when the outcome of one event does not affect the probability of the other event. Each coin flip is an independent event. No matter the outcome of one flip, the probability of the next flip remains the same.

Flip heads 10 times in a row with a fair coin. On the next flip, the $P(H)$ is still 1/2. Coin flips are independent events.

Events are *dependent* where the outcome of one event does affect the probability of the other event. For example, you have a full deck of cards. The probability of picking the Queen of Hearts is 1/52.

You pick one card and it is not the Queen of Hearts. You do not put the card back. The probability of picking the Queen of Hearts is now 1/51. Cards picked without replacement are dependent events.

Permutations, Combinations, and the Fundamental Counting Principle

PERMUTATIONS

A permutation is the way a set of things can be arranged in order. There are 6 permutations of the letters A, B, and C.

ABC   ACB   BAC   BCA   CAB   CBA

Permutation Formula

The formula for the number of permutations of n things is **n! (n factorial)**.

$$6! = 6 \times 5 \times 4 \times 3 \times 2 \times 1 \qquad 4! = 4 \times 3 \times 2 \times 1 \qquad 2! = 2 \times 1$$

There are 120 permutations of 5 things.

$$n! = 5! = 5 \times 4 \times 3 \times 2 \times 1 = 120$$

COMBINATIONS

A combination is the number of ways of choosing a given number of elements from a set. The order of the elements does not matter. There are 3 ways of choosing 2 letters from the letters A, B, and C.

AB AC BC

FUNDAMENTAL COUNTING PRINCIPLE

The fundamental counting principle is used to find the total number of possibilities. Multiply the number of possibilities from each category.

EXAMPLE

An ice cream stand has a sundae with choices of 28 flavors of ice cream, 8 types of syrups, and 5 types of toppings. How many different sundae combinations are available?

$$28 \quad \times \quad 8 \quad \times \quad 5 \quad = \quad 1{,}120$$

flavors   syrups   toppings   sundaes

There are 1,120 possible sundaes.

Practice

1. There are 2 chairs left in the auditorium, but 4 people are without seats. In how many ways could 2 people be chosen to sit in the chairs?

2. The books *Little Women*, *Crime & Punishment*, *Trinity*, *The Great Santini*, *Pygmalion*, *The Scarlet Letter*, and *War and Peace* are on a shelf. In how many different ways can they be arranged?

3. A license plate consists of 2 letters and 2 digits. How many different license plates can be formed?

4. There are four students on line for the bus, but there is only room for three students on this bus. How many different ways can 3 of the 4 students get on the bus?

Answers on page 182.

Statistics and Scatter Plots

Descriptive statistics are used to explain or describe a set of numbers. Most often you use the mean, median, or mode to describe these numbers.

MEAN (AVERAGE)

The mean is a position midway between two extremes. To find the mean:

1. Add the items or scores.
2. Divide by the number of items.

For example, find the mean of 24, 17, 42, 51, 36.

$$24 + 17 + 42 + 51 + 36 = 170 \qquad 170 \div 5 = 34$$

The mean or average is 34.

MEDIAN

The median is the middle number. To find the median:

1. Arrange the numbers from least to greatest.
2. If there are an odd number of scores, then find the middle score.
3. If there is an even number of scores, average the two middle scores.

For example, find the median of these numbers.

$$6, 9, 11, \underline{17}, \underline{21}, 33, 45, 71$$

There are an even number of scores.

$$17 + 21 = 38 \qquad 38 \div 2 = 19$$

The median is 19.

Do not forget to arrange the scores in order before finding the middle score!

MODE

The mode is the number that occurs most often.

For example, find the mode of these numbers.

$$6, 3, 7, 6, 9, 3, 6, 1, 2, 6, 7, 3$$

The number 6 occurs most often so 6 is the mode.

Not all sets of numbers have a mode. Some sets of numbers may have more than one mode.

EXAMPLE

What is the mean, median, and mode of 7, 13, 18, 4, 14, 22?

Mean Add the scores and divide by the number of scores.

$$7 + 13 + 18 + 4 + 14 + 22 = 78 \div 6 = 13 \qquad \text{The mean is 13.}$$

Median Arrange the scores in order. Find the middle score.

$$4, 7, 13, 14, 18, 22 \quad 13 + 14 = 27 \div 2 = 13.5 \qquad \text{The median is 13.5.}$$

Mode Find the score that occurs most often.

Each score occurs only once.   There is no mode.

Practice

1. A group of fourth graders received the following scores on a science test.

   $$80, 87, 94, 100, 75, 80, 98, 85, 80, 95, 92$$

   Which score represents the mode?

2. What is the mean of the following set of data?

   $$44, 13, 84, 42, 12, 18$$

3. What is the median of the following set of data?

   $$8, 9, 10, 10, 8, 10, 7, 6, 9$$

4. What measure of central tendency does the number 16 represent in the following data?

   $$14, 15, 17, 16, 19, 20, 16, 14, 16$$

5. What is the mean of the following set of scores?

100, 98, 95, 70, 85, 90, 94, 78, 80, 100

6. What is the mode of the following data?

25, 30, 25, 15, 40, 45, 30, 20, 30

Answers on page 182.

Scatter Plots

Scatter plots are an indication about the trend of a set of data. They indicate how the data are correlated. Correlation can be complicated, but test questions will not ask for a sophisticated understanding of scatter plots or correlation.

Look at these examples.

Example A shows a positive correlation. The dots in the plot move generally from lower left to upper right. Example B shows a negative correlation. The dots move generally from upper left to lower right. Example C shows little or no correlation. The dots do not show any organized pattern.

Negative and positive linear correlations are also called negative and positive linear relationships. You may come across this term on the test.

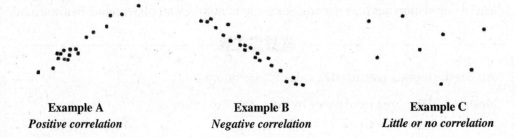

Example A	Example B	Example C
Positive correlation	*Negative correlation*	*Little or no correlation*

Scatter plots are usually based on sets of data.

Practice

Plot this data on the graph below. Then answer the other questions.

Students chose a number from 1 to 5 to indicate their preference for school subjects and activities. School subjects and activities students prefer.

Student	Computers	Art
1	5	4
2	3	2
3	1	2
4	5	5
5	2	3
6	1	1
7	5	3
8	3	3
9	4	5
10	2	4

1. Plot the responses to create a scatter plot. The first response of 5 for computers and 4 for art is plotted for you.

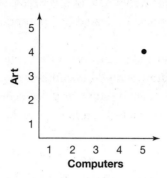

2. Does the scatter plot generally show a positive correlation, a negative correlation, or no correlation? How can you tell?

3. Would the correlation change if the values for art and computers were switched?

Answers on page 182.

Choose a Process That Involves Random Selection

Random selection means that the sample is picked by chance. Every person in the larger population has an equal chance of being picked.

Examples of random sampling:

Pick a sample of names by chance out of a container with all the names.

Have a computer use a random selection program to choose the sample.

Partition a group into a male group and a female group, and then choose names at random from each group.

Examples of nonrandom sampling:

Sample the first 100 people you meet.

Choose every sixth person from a list of names.

Rely on voluntary responses.

Choose Your Sample from the Correct Population

The random selection must be from the group you want to study.

Examples of sampling from the wrong population:

Sample college alumni to determine current reactions to the cafeteria.

Sample from one town to determine statewide views.

Sample from 18- to 22-year-old military recruits to determine the views of college students.

The college cafeteria manager wants to find out which new selections students want added to the menu. What procedure would be appropriate for selecting an unbiased sample?

The manager could gather the names of all the students who ate in the cafeteria during the week and then draw a random sample from those names. The manager should not draw a sample from all the students in the school. You should not interview every fifth student entering the cafeteria during the week.

Practice

1. A group is taking a poll to determine working parents' day-care needs. They interview parents at work. Give examples of good and poor sampling techniques.

2. The town architect wants to find out about senior community members' ideas for the new senior center. Give examples of good and poor sampling techniques.

Answers on page 183.

ALGEBRA AND FUNCTIONS

Add, Subtract, Multiply, and Divide Integers

ADDITION

When the signs are the same, keep the sign and add.

$$\begin{array}{r} +7 \\ +\ +8 \\ \hline +15 \end{array} \qquad \begin{array}{r} -3 \\ +\ -11 \\ \hline -14 \end{array}$$

When the signs are different, disregard the signs, subtract the numbers, and keep the sign of the larger number.

$$\begin{array}{r} +28 \\ +\ -49 \\ \hline -21 \end{array} \qquad \begin{array}{r} -86 \\ +\ +135 \\ \hline +49 \end{array}$$

SUBTRACTION

Change the sign of the number being subtracted. Then add using the preceding rules.

$$\begin{array}{r} +13 \\ -\ -18 \\ \downarrow \\ +13 \\ +\ +18 \\ \hline +31 \end{array} \qquad \begin{array}{r} -43 \\ -\ -17 \\ \downarrow \\ -43 \\ +\ +17 \\ \hline -26 \end{array} \qquad \begin{array}{r} +29 \\ -\ -49 \\ \downarrow \\ +29 \\ +\ +49 \\ \hline +78 \end{array} \qquad \begin{array}{r} -92 \\ -\ +135 \\ \downarrow \\ -92 \\ +\ -135 \\ \hline -227 \end{array}$$

MULTIPLY

Multiply as you would whole numbers. The product is *positive* if there are an even number of negative factors. The product is *negative* if there are an odd number of negative factors.

$$-2 \times +4 \times -6 \times +3 = +144 \qquad -2 \times -4 \times +6 \times -3 = -144$$

DIVIDE

Forget the signs and divide. The quotient is *positive* if both integers have the same sign. The quotient is *negative* if the integers have different signs.

$$+24 \div +4 = +6 \quad -24 \div -4 = +6 \quad +24 \div -4 = -6 \quad -24 \div +4 = -6$$

Practice

1. $6 + 9 =$
2. $18 + -17 =$
3. $-24 + -45 =$
4. $-38 + 29 =$

5. $7 - 6 =$
6. $15 - -39 =$
7. $-36 - -58 =$
8. $-27 - 53 =$

9. $9 \times 11 =$
10. $26 \times -25 =$
11. $-31 \times -59 =$
12. $-42 \times 35 =$

13. $120 \div 8 =$
14. $68 \div -4 =$
15. $-352 \div -8 =$
16. $-66 \div 3 =$

Answers on page 183.

POLYNOMIALS

Polynomials are made up of constants and variables.

Constant—A constant is a number such as 9, $\frac{1}{2}$, 0.56.

Variable—A variable is represented by a letter (such as x, a, c) to show that we do not know the value.

Polynomials do not have equal signs.

Polynomials are described by the number of terms. Terms are separated by addition or subtraction.

A term can be a constant, a variable, or the product of constants and variables.

In a term with a constant and a variable or variables, the constant is called the coefficient.

In the term $9x$, the coefficient is 9 and the variable is x.

MONOMIALS

A monomial has one term.

There are no addition or subtraction signs in a monomial.

Here are some monomials.

$$7, x, 3x, \frac{6}{27}, y^2, -16$$

BINOMIALS

A binomial has two terms.

Here are some binomials.

$$5x - 6, \qquad 3y^2 + 7, \qquad 13x^2 + 0.5y^2$$

TRINOMIALS

A trinomial has three terms.

Here are some trinomials.

$$6x^2 \;+\; 12y^2 \;+\; 12y, \quad 13x^6z^5 \;+\; 12y^2 \;+\; 12y$$

SIMPLIFY POLYNOMIALS

Combine similar terms to simplify a polynomial.

Similar terms have the same variable part. The order of the variables is not important. $3x$ is similar to $5x$ and $0.9x$. The variable in each term is x.

$2\,x^3y$ is similar to $12\,yx^3$.

$3\,x^3y$ is not similar to $3\,y^3x$.

Combine Similar Terms

Add or subtract the coefficient and keep the variable part.

Combine the terms in $\quad 5x + 9xy + 2y^3 - 8x + 2x^2 - 8y^3$

Rearrange the terms so that similar terms are next to one another.

The similar terms are $2y^3$ and $8y^3$.

$$5x + 9xy \underline{+ 2y^3 - 8y^3} - 8x + 2x^2$$

$$5x + 9xy \underline{- 6y^3} - 8x + 2x^2$$

ADD AND SUBTRACT POLYNOMIALS

Add Polynomials

Combine similar terms.

Add:	$(5x^6 + 7x^3y - y^2 + 9) + (7x^5 - 3x^3y + y^2z)$
Write as a polynomial:	$5x^6 + 7x^3y - y^2 + 9 + 7x^5 - 3x^3y + y^2z$

The common terms are $7x^3y$ and $3x^3y$.

Rearrange terms:	$5x^6 + \underline{7x^3y - 3x^3y} - y^2 + 9 + 7x^5 + y^2z$
Combine:	$5x^6 + 4x^3y - y^2 + 9 + 7x^5 + y^2z$

Subtract Polynomials

Change the signs in the polynomial being subtracted.
Then combine similar terms.

Subtract: $(2x^4 + 15x^2 - y^2 + x) - (x^4 - 8x^3y + y^2z - 3x + 4)$

Change the signs in the polynomial
being subtracted and add: $(2x^4 + 15x^2 - y^2 + x) + (-x^4 + 8x^3y - y^2z + 3x + 4)$

The common terms are $2x^4$ and $-x^4$, x and $3x$.

Rearrange terms: $\underline{2x^4 - x^4} + 15x^2 - y^2 + \underline{x + 3x} + 8x^3y - y^2z + 4$

Combine: $x^4 + 15x^2 - y^2 + 4\underline{x} + 8x^3y - y^2z + 4$

Practice

Combine terms.

1. $3x^2 + 4y + 3x^2y + 6y$

2. $7x + 3x^2y + 17x + 3yx^2 + 7x^2y^2$

Add.

3. $(3x^5 + 3x^2 - 5x^2y + 6xy^2) + (3x^5 - 2x^2 + 4x^3y - x^2y + 3xy^3 - y^2)$

4. $(x^4 - 4x^3 + 2x^2y^2 - 4xy^2) + (3x^5 - 7x^4 + 3x^3 - 2x^2y^3 + 7xy^2)$

Subtract.

5. $(6x^7 + 9x^4 - 3x^2y + 5xy^3) - (6x^8 - 15x^4 - 3x^3y + x^2y)$

6. $(7x^2 - 9x + 3xy^2 + 3y^3 - 12) - (x^3 - 9x^2 + 2xy^2 - 3y^5 - 18)$

Answers on page 183.

Formulas

EVALUATING AN EXPRESSION

Evaluate an expression by replacing the variables with values. Remember to use the correct order of operations. For example, evaluate

$$3x - \frac{y}{z} \text{ for } x = 3, y = 8, \text{ and } z = 4$$

$$3(3) - \frac{8}{4} = 9 - 2 = 7$$

Using Formulas

Using a formula is like evaluating an expression. Just replace the variables with values. Here are some important formulas to know. The area of a figure is the amount of space it occupies in two dimensions. The perimeter of a figure is the distance around the figure. Use 3.14 for π.

FIGURE	FORMULA	DESCRIPTION
Triangle	Area $= \frac{1}{2} bh$ Perimeter $= s_1 + s_2 + s_3$	
Square	Area $= s^2$ Perimeter $= 4s$	
Rectangle	Area $= lw$ Perimeter $= 2l + 2w$	
Parallelogram	Area $= bh$ Perimeter $= 2s + 2b$	
Trapezoid	Area $= \frac{1}{2} h(b_1 + b_2)$ Perimeter $= b_1 + b_2 + s_1 + s_2$	
Circle	Area $= \pi r^2$ Circumference $= 2\pi r$ or $= \pi d$	

Pythagorean Formula

The Pythagorean formula for right triangles states that the sum of the square of the legs equals the square of the hypotenuse:

$$a^2 + b^2 = c^2$$

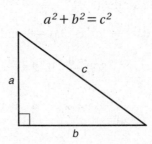

Other Polygons

Pentagon	5 sides	Octagon	8 sides
Hexagon	6 sides	Nonagon	9 sides
Heptagon	7 sides	Decagon	10 sides

Regular Polygon—All sides are the same length.

EXAMPLES

DISTANCE AND AREA

Solve the distance and area problems.

A. How many meters is it around a regular hexagon with a side of 87 centimeters?
A hexagon has 6 sides. It is a regular hexagon, so all the sides are the same length.
$6 \times 87 = 522$. The perimeter is 522 centimeters, which equals 5.22 meters.

B. What is the area of this figure?
The formula for the area of a circle is πr^2.
The diameter is 18, so the radius is 9. Use 3.14 for π.
$A = 3.14 \times (9)^2 = 3.14 \times 81 = 254.34$ or
about 254 square units.

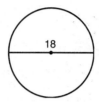

Volume

Volume—The amount of space occupied by a three-dimensional figure.
The test will give you the formulas.

FORMULAS FOR VOLUME

FIGURE	FORMULA	DESCRIPTION
Cube	Volume $= s^3$	
Rectangular Prism	Volume $= lwh$	
Sphere	Volume $= \dfrac{4}{3}\pi r^3$	
Cone	Volume $= \dfrac{1}{3}\pi r^2 h$	
Cylinder	Volume $= \pi r^2 h$ Surface Area $= 2\pi r(h+r)$	

VOLUME

A circular cone has a radius of 8 cm and a height of 10 cm. What is the volume?

Formula for the volume of a cone $= \frac{1}{3} \pi r^2 h$.

$$V = \left(\frac{1}{3}\right)(3.14)(8^2)(10) = \left(\frac{1}{3}\right)(3.14)(64)(10) = \left(\frac{1}{3}\right)(3.14)(640) = 669.87$$

The volume of the cone is 669.87 cubic centimeters or about 670 cubic centimeters.

Practice

1. A circle has a radius of 9 meters. What is the area?

2. The faces of a pyramid are equilateral triangles. What is the surface area of the pyramid if the sides of the triangles equal 3 inches and the height is 2.6 inches?

3. A regular hexagon has one side 5 feet long. What is the distance around its edge?

4. What is the surface area of the side of a cylinder (not top and bottom) with a height of 10 cm and a diameter of 2.5 cm?

5. A rectangle has a width x and a length $(x + 5)$. If the perimeter is 90 feet, what is the length?

6. The perimeter of one face of a cube is 20 cm. What is the surface area?

7. What is the length of the third side in the right triangle below?

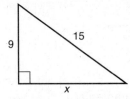

8. What is the area of a trapezoid whose height is 5 inches, the length of one base is 5 inches, and the length of the other base is 8 inches?

9. What is the volume of a sphere that has a diameter of length 20 cm?

10. What is the volume of a cube having a side length of 15 inches.

Answers on page 183.

Solve Linear Equations and Inequalities

EQUATIONS AND INEQUALITIES

The whole idea of solving equations and inequalities is to isolate the variable on one side. The value of the variable is what is on the other side. Substitute your answer in the original equation or inequality to check your solution.

Solving Equations and Inequalities by Adding or Subtracting

$$\text{Solve: } y + 19 = 23$$

Subtract 19 $\quad y + 19 - 19 = 23 - 19$

$$y = 4$$

Check: Does $4 + 19 = 23$? Yes. It checks.

$$\text{Solve: } x - 23 \leq 51$$

Add 23 $\quad x - 23 + 23 \leq 51 + 23$

$$x \leq 74$$

Check: Is $74 - 23 \leq 51$. Yes. It checks.

Solving Equations and Inequalities by Multiplying or Dividing

$$\text{Solve: } \frac{z}{7} \geq 6$$

Multiply by 7 $\quad \frac{x}{7} \times 7 \geq 6 \times 7$

$$z \geq 42$$

Check: Is $\frac{42}{7} \geq 6$? Yes. It checks.

$$\text{Solve: } 21 = -3x$$

Divide by –3 $\quad \dfrac{21}{-3} = \dfrac{-3x}{-3}$

$$-7 = x$$

Check: Does $21 = (-3)(-7)$? Yes. It checks.

EXAMPLES

A. Solve for x $\qquad x - 7 = 4$

Add 7 $\qquad \dfrac{+7 \ +7}{}$

$$x = \ 11$$

B. Solve for n $\qquad 5n > 2$

Divide by 5 $\qquad \dfrac{5n}{5} > \dfrac{2}{5}$

Simplify $\qquad n > \dfrac{2}{5}$

Practice

1. Solve for x: $x + \dfrac{2}{5} = 17$

2. Solve for y: $6y > -32$

3. Solve for x: $15 < 4x$

4. Solve for y: $22 = -2y$

Answers on page 184.

GEOMETRY AND MEASUREMENT
Symmetry

Symmetric objects, figures, and designs have a pleasing, balanced appearance.

There are three primary types of symmetry—line (reflection), rotational, and translational.

LINE OR REFLECTIVE SYMMETRY

A figure with line symmetry can be folded in half so that one half exactly matches the other half.

This letter M has line symmetry.

Fold the M in half at the line and one half exactly matches the other half.

Flip the M over the line and it looks the same.

Place a mirror on that line and half the M and the reflection will form the entire M.

The line is called the line of symmetry.

ROTATIONAL SYMMETRY

A figure has rotational symmetry if it can be turned less than a full turn and look exactly as it did before it was turned.

This letter N has rotational symmetry.

N ⭭ Z ⭭ N

Turn the Z half a turn and it looks exactly as it did before the turn.

TRANSLATIONAL SYMMETRY

A design has translational symmetry if it repeats a pattern.

Many wallpaper patterns have translational symmetry.

This simple pattern has translational symmetry because it shows a repeating pattern.

A   B   C   A   B   C

EXAMPLES

A. Which of these letters has line symmetry?

B. Which of these letters has rotational symmetry?

A   B   C   D   E   F   G   H   I

These letters have both line and rotational symmetry: H, I

These letters have only line symmetry: A, B, C, D, E

None of the letters has only rotational symmetry.

These letters have neither type of symmetry: F, G

Practice

1. Which of these numerals has rotational or line symmetry?

   1   2   3   4   5   6   7   8   9   0

2. Complete this pattern so that the final pattern has translational symmetry.

   2   3   4

Answers on page 184.

Two-Dimensional Geometry

Geometry has two or three dimensions. A two-dimensional model is this page. A three-dimensional model is the room where you will take the test.

DEFINITION	MODEL	SYMBOL
Point—a location	. A	A
Plane—a flat surface that extends infinitely in all directions	A· ·B ·C	plane ABC
Line—a set of points in a straight path that extends infinitely in two directions	A B	$\overleftrightarrow{AB}$
Line segment—part of a line with two endpoints	B A	$\overline{AB}$
Ray—part of a line with one endpoint	A B	$\overrightarrow{AB}$
Parallel lines—lines that stay the same distance apart and never touch	A B D F	$\overleftrightarrow{AB} \parallel \overleftrightarrow{DF}$
Perpendicular lines—lines that meet at right angles	C A B D	$AB \perp CD$

DEFINITION	MODEL	SYMBOL
Angle—two rays with a common endpoint, which is called the vertex		$\angle ABC$
Acute angle—angle that measures between 0° and 90°		
Right angle—angle that measures 90°		
Obtuse angle—angle that measures between 90° and 180°		
Complementary angles—angles that have a total measure of 90°		
Supplementary angles—angles that have a total measure of 180°		
Congruent angles have the same angle measure. $\angle p$ and $\angle q$ measure 90°. $\angle p$ and $\angle q$ are congruent. $m\angle p = m\angle q$		$\angle p \cong \angle q$

CIRCLES

A circle is a shape with all points the same distance from its center. A circle is named by its center. The distance around the circle is called the circumference.

The region inside a circle is not part of the circle. It is called the area of a circle.

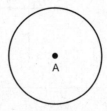

The diameter of a circle is a line segment across a circle through the center.

The radius of a circle is a line segment from the center of the circle to any point on the circle. Two radii lined up end-to-end form a diameter. The diameter and radius each has a length, and the length of the diameter is twice the length of the radius.

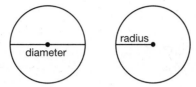

A chord is a line segment with endpoints on a circle. A diameter is the longest chord of a circle. Every diameter is a chord but not every chord is a diameter.

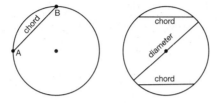

Practice

1. Can a circle have more than one diameter?

2. Can part of a chord not be on the circle?

3. Do two radii always form a diameter?

4. Can two separate chords form a diameter?

Answers on page 184.

Polygon

A closed figure made up of line segments; if all sides are the same length, the figure is a regular polygon.

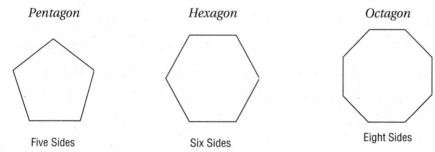

| *Pentagon* | *Hexagon* | *Octagon* |

| Five Sides | Six Sides | Eight Sides |

TRIANGLE

A polygon with three sides and three angles; the sum of the angles is always 180°.

Equilateral triangle—all the sides are the same length; all the angles are the same size, 60°.

Isosceles triangle—two sides the same length; two angles the same size.

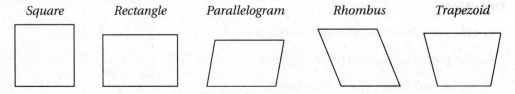

Scalene triangle—all sides different lengths; all angles different sizes.

Congruent triangle—Two triangles are congruent if the lengths of each corresponding pair of sides are equal and the measures of each corresponding pair of angles are equal. That means one triangle fits exactly on top of the other triangle.

QUADRILATERAL

A polygon with four sides

| Square | Rectangle | Parallelogram | Rhombus | Trapezoid |

EXAMPLE

Which types of quadrilaterals can be constructed using four congruent line segments *AB*, *BC*, *CD*, and *DA*?

You can create a square and a rhombus.

Practice

Be certain to use proper markings to indicate congruent segments and congruent angles.

1. What is the name of a quadrilateral that has exactly one pair of parallel sides?

2. Use the figure below. The m∠1 = 45°. What is m∠2?

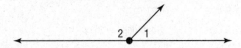

3. In the triangle below, *AB* = *AC* and m∠*BAC* = 80°.

    What are the measures of ∠*ABC* and ∠*ACB*?

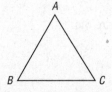

4. Draw a diagram of an equilateral triangle.

5. Which has more sides, an octagon or a hexagon?
   What is the difference in the number of sides for these figures?

6. What type of angle with a measure less than 180° is neither obtuse nor acute?

7. Draw a diagram in which ray (*AB*) intersects ray (*AC*) at point *A*, and name the new figure that is formed.

8. Draw a diagram of line *AB* intersecting line segment *CD* at point *E*.

9. Draw a diagram of two parallel lines perpendicular to a third line.

10. Given a triangle *ABC*, describe the relationship among the measures of the three angles.

Answers on page 184.

SIMILAR TRIANGLES

In similar triangles, corresponding angles are congruent. The ratio of the lengths of corresponding sides are equal.

These triangles are similar.

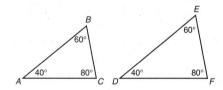

Corresponding angles of the two triangles are congruent.

$\angle A$ and $\angle D$ $\qquad$ $\angle B$ and $\angle E$ $\qquad$ $\angle C$ and $\angle F$

That means the measures of congruent angles are equal.

measure of $\angle A$ = measure of $\angle D$ = 40°
measure of $\angle B$ = measure of $\angle E$ = 60°
measure of $\angle C$ = measure of $\angle F$ = 80°

Corresponding sides (Corresponding sides are opposite corresponding angles)

$\overline{BC}$ and $\overline{EF}$ $\qquad$ $\overline{AC}$ and $\overline{DF}$ $\qquad$ $\overline{AB}$ and $\overline{DE}$

The ratios of the lengths of corresponding sides are equal.

$$\frac{BC}{EF} = \frac{AC}{DF} = \frac{AB}{DE}$$

Are these triangles similar?

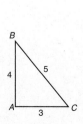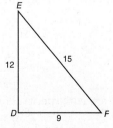

Corresponding sides: $\overline{AB}$ and $\overline{DE}$, $\overline{BC}$ and $\overline{EF}$, $\overline{AC}$ and $\overline{DF}$

Does $\dfrac{AB}{DE} = \dfrac{BC}{EF}$? $\dfrac{AB}{DE} = \dfrac{4}{12}$; $\dfrac{BC}{EF} = \dfrac{5}{15}$; $\dfrac{4}{12} = \dfrac{1}{3}$; $\dfrac{5}{15} = \dfrac{1}{3}$

These triangles are similar. Ratios of corresponding sides of the two triangles are equal.

EXAMPLE

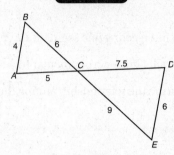

Are triangle *ABC* and triangle *CDE* similar triangles?

The ratios of the lengths of corresponding sides are equal.

$\overline{AB}$ and $\overline{DE}$ are corresponding sides.

Does $\dfrac{AC}{CD} = \dfrac{AB}{DE}$?   Yes. $\dfrac{5}{7.5} = \dfrac{4}{6}$ $\left(\dfrac{20}{30} = \dfrac{20}{30} \right)$

Practice

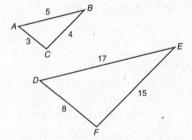

1. Are △*PQR* and △*SVT* similar?

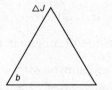

2. The triangles above are similar. What is the measure of ∠*b*?

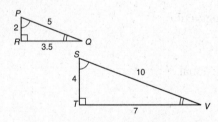

3. Which of these statements is true for the triangles above?

   Ⓐ ∠*C* is congruent to ∠*F*

   Ⓑ ∠*B* is congruent to ∠*E*

   Ⓒ $\dfrac{AB}{DE} = \dfrac{CB}{FE}$

   Ⓓ △*ABC* and △*DEF* are congruent

Answers on page 184.

Coordinate Grid and Translations

You can plot ordered pairs of numbers on a coordinate grid.

The *x* axis goes horizontally from left to right. The first number in the pair tells how far to move left or right from the origin. A minus sign means move left. A plus sign means move right.

The *y* axis goes vertically up and down. The second number in the pair tells how far to move up or down from the origin. A minus sign means move down. A plus sign means move up.

Pairs of numbers show the *x* coordinate first and the *y* coordinate second (*x*, *y*). The origin is point (0, 0) where the *x* axis and the *y* axis meet.

Plot these pairs of numbers on the grid.

$$\textbf{A}\,(+3, -7) \qquad \textbf{B}\,(+5, +3) \qquad \textbf{C}\,(-6, +2) \qquad \textbf{D}\,(-3, -6)$$

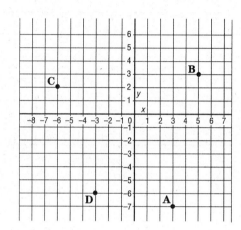

Practice

The following grid is for questions 1 and 2.

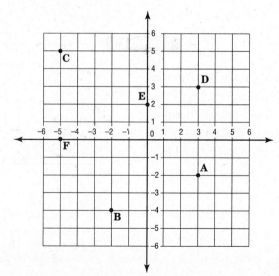

1. Write the coordinates of the points on the grid provided.

   A _____   *B* _____   *C* _____   *D* _____   *E* _____   *F* _____

2. Plot these points on the grid provided.

   G (3, −1)   *H* (2, −3)   *I* (5, 6)   *J* (−4, 0)   *K* (−5, −2)   *L* (−1, 6)   *M* (0, 3)   *N* (−5, 2)

3. Plot these points on the grid below and connect them in alphabetical order.

$Z\,(-5, 5)$ $Y\,(-2, 0)$ $X\,(2, -6)$ $W\,(3, 5)$ $V\,(-6, -2)$ $U\,(2, 0)$ $T\,(6, 1)$ $S\,(-5, 5)$

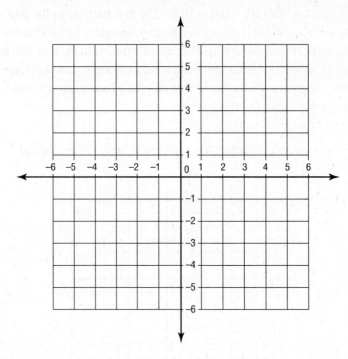

Answers on page 185.

TRANSLATIONS ON A COORDINATE GRID

You can slide or translate points and geometric shapes on the coordinate grid. You can describe the translations by what happens to the positions of the vertices. Look at these simple examples:

EXAMPLE 1

This triangle slid right 4 units horizontally on the coordinate plane. The y values remain the same. The x values increase by 4. The coordinates of point $A\,(-4, 3)$ on the triangle became $(0, 3)$ after the slide.

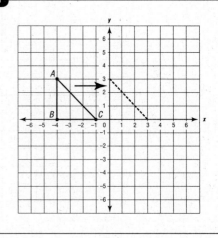

EXAMPLE 2

This triangle slid down five units vertically. The *x* values remain the same. The *y* values decrease by 3. The coordinate of point *Q* (4, 3) became (4, –2) after the slide.

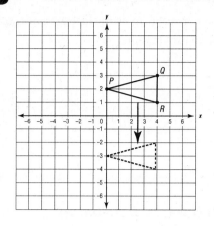

EXAMPLE 3

This triangle slid right 6 units and up 3 units. The *x* values increased by 6 and the *y* values increased by 5. The coordinate of point *M* (–2, –2) became (4, 1) after the slide.

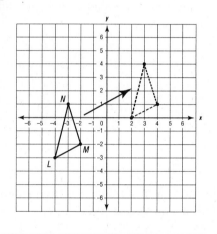

Practice

1. In Example 1, what is the coordinate of point *C* if the triangle moved down 4 units and left 3 units?

2. In Example 3, what are the coordinates of point *M* if point *L* slid up and over to the coordinate (0, 0)?

3. A triangle slid right 3 units and down 4 units. What is the new coordinate of a point that started at (–7, 2) before the slide?

4. Point *B* is at the right angle of a right triangle. Point *A* is at coordinates (–2, 3). The triangle is shifted up 2 units and right 3 units. What can you tell about the other vertices of the triangle?

Answers on page 185.

ALL, SOME, AND NONE

Diagrams can show the logical connectives *all*, *some*, and *none*. View the following diagrams for an explanation.

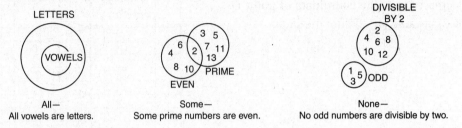

All—
All vowels are letters.

Some—
Some prime numbers are even.

None—
No odd numbers are divisible by two.

Deductive Reasoning

Deductive reasoning draws conclusions from statements or assumptions. Diagrams may help you draw a conclusion. Consider this simple example.

Assume that all even numbers are divisible by two and that all multiples of ten are even. Draw a diagram:

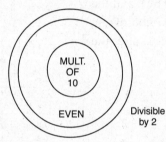

The multiple of ten circle is entirely within the divisible by two circle. Conclusion: All multiples of ten are divisible by two.

Practice

Write whether the statement is true or false. Explain your answer.

1. A ball is used in all sports.

2. Some numbers divisible by 5 are also divisible by 7.

3. There are no even numbers divisible by 3.

4. Some prime numbers are divisible by 2.

Answers on page 185.

PROBLEM SOLVING

The problem-solving strategies of choosing a reasonable answer, estimating, choosing the operation, writing a number sentence, and identifying extra or needed information were discussed earlier in the review. This section shows you how to use more problem-solving strategies.

Estimate to Be Sure Your Answer Is Reasonable

You can use estimation and common sense to be sure that the answer is reasonable. You may make a multiplication error or misalign decimal points. You may be so engrossed in a problem that you miss the big picture because of the details. These difficulties can be headed off by making sure your answer is reasonable.

A few examples follow.

A question involves dividing or multiplying. Multiply: 28×72.

Estimate first: $30 \times 70 = 2,100$. Your answer should be close to 2,100. If not, then your answer is not reasonable. A mistake was probably made in multiplication.

A question involves subtracting or adding. Add: $12.9 + 0.63 + 10.29 + 4.3$.

Estimate first: $13 + 1 + 10 + 4 = 28$. Your answer should be close to 28. If not, then your answer is not reasonable. The decimal points may not have been aligned.

A question asks you to compare fractions to $\frac{11}{10}$.

Think: $\frac{11}{10}$ is more than 1. Any number 1 or less will be less than $\frac{11}{10}$. Any number larger than $1\frac{1}{10}$ will be more than $\frac{11}{10}$. You have to look closely only at numbers from 1 to $1\frac{1}{10}$.

A question asks you to multiply two fractions or decimals.

The fractions or decimals are less than 1. The product of two fractions or decimals less than one is less than either of the two fractions or decimals. If not, you know that your answer is not reasonable.

Stand back for a second after you answer each question and ask, "Is this reasonable? Is this at least approximately correct? Does this make sense?"

Check answers to computation, particularly division and subtraction. When you have completed a division or subtraction example, do a quick, approximate check. Your check should confirm your answer. If not, your answer is probably not reasonable.

Circle Important Information and Key Words
Eliminate Extra Information

This approach will draw your attention to the information needed to answer the question. A common mistake is to use facts from the question that have nothing to do with the solution.

In the morning, a train travels at a constant speed over an 800 kilometer distance. In the afternoon the train travels back over this same route. There is less traffic and the train travels four times as fast as it did that morning. However, there are more people on the train during the afternoon. Which of the following do you know about the train's afternoon trip?

Ⓐ The time is divided by four
Ⓑ The time is multiplied by four
Ⓒ The rate and time are divided by four
Ⓓ The rate is divided by four
Ⓔ The distance is the same, so the rate is the same

To solve the problem you just need to know that the speed is constant, four times as fast, and the same route was covered. Circle this information you need to solve the problem.

The distance traveled or that there were more people in the afternoon is extra information. Cross off this extra information, which may interfere with your ability to solve the problem.

In the morning, a train travels at a constant speed over an 800 kilometer distance. In the afternoon the train travels back over this same route. There is less traffic and the train travels four times as fast as it did that morning. However, there are more people on the train during the afternoon. Which of the following do you know about the train's afternoon trip?

The correct answer is (A), the time is divided by four. The route is the same, but the train travels four times as fast. Therefore, the time to make the trip is divided by four. Rate means the same thing as speed, and we know that the speed has been multiplied by four.

Words to Symbols Problems

Before you solve a problem, you may have to decide which operation to use. You can use key words to help you decide which operation to use.

Key Words

Addition	sum, and, more, increased by
Subtraction	less, difference, decreased by
Multiplication	of, product, times
Division	per, quotient, shared, ratio
Equals	is, equals

You cannot just use these key words without thinking. You must be sure that the operation makes sense when it replaces the key word. For example,

19 and 23 is 42	16 is 4 more than 12	30% of 19 is 5.7?
$19 + 23 = 42$	$16 = 4 + 12$	$0.3 \times 19 = 5.7$

three more than y	$y + 3$	The product of 3 and y	$3y$
y increased by 3	$y + 3$	3 times y	$3y$
y more than 3	$3 + y$	3% of y	$0.03y$

3 less than y	$y-3$	3 divided by y	$\dfrac{3}{y}$
y decreased by 3	$y-3$	y divided by 3	$\dfrac{y}{3}$
3 decreased y	$3-y$	ratio of 3 to y	$\dfrac{3}{y}$
The opposite of y	$-y$	The reciprocal of y	$\dfrac{1}{y}$

EXAMPLES

A. 18 divided by what number is 3?

$18 \div y = 3$ $18 = 3y$ $y = 6$

B. 25 less 6 is what number?

$25 - 6 = y$ $y = 19$

C. A student correctly answered 80% of 120 mathematics problems. How many mathematics problems did he answer correctly?

$0.8 \times 120 = y$ $y = 96$

The student correctly answered 96 problems.

D. The product of a number and its opposite is –25. What is the number?

$(y) \times (-y) = -25$ $y = 5$

The number is 5.

Practice

Solve the problems.

1. What number decreased by 9 is 25?

2. What is 60% of 90?

3. Bob lives $\dfrac{2}{3}$ mile from Gina and $\dfrac{1}{2}$ mile from Sam. Bob's walk to the school is three times the sum of these distances. How far is Bob's walk to school?

4. The ratio of two gears is 20 to y. If the ratio equals 2.5, what is the value of y?

5. The sum of 5 and the reciprocal of another number is $5\dfrac{1}{8}$. What is the other number?

6. Car A travels at a constant speed of 60 mph for 2.5 hours. Car B travels at a constant speed of 70 mph for 2 hours. What is the total distance traveled by both cars?

Answers on page 185.

Finding and Interpreting Patterns

SEQUENCES

Arithmetic Sequence

A sequence of numbers formed by adding the same nonzero number.

| 3, 11, 19, 27, 35, 43, 51 | Add 8 to get each successive term. |
| 52, 48, 44, 40, 36, 32 | Add (-4) to get each successive term. |

Geometric Sequence

A sequence of numbers formed by multiplying the same nonzero number.

| 3, 15, 75, 375 | Multiply by 5 to get each successive term. |
| 160, 40, 10, $2\frac{1}{2}$ | Multiply by $\frac{1}{4}$ to get each successive term. |

Harmonic Sequence

A sequence of fractions with a numerator of 1 in which the denominators form an arithmetic sequence.

$$\frac{1}{2} \quad \frac{1}{9} \quad \frac{1}{16} \quad \frac{1}{23} \quad \frac{1}{30}$$

Each numerator is 1. The denominators form an arithmetic sequence.

Relationships

Linear Relationships

Linear relationships are pairs of numbers formed by adding or multiplying the same number to the first term in a pair. Here are some examples.

(3, 12), (5, 14), (11, 20), (15, 24)	Add 9 to the first term to get the second.
(1, 6), (2, 12), (3, 18), (4, 24), (5, 30)	Multiply the first term by 6 to get the second.
(96, 12), (72, 9), (56, 7), (24, 3), (16, 2)	Multiply the first term by $\frac{1}{4}$ to get the second.

EXAMPLES

A. What term is missing in this number pattern?

$$2 \quad\quad 5 \quad\quad 10 \quad\quad 17 \quad\quad \underline{}$$
$$+3 \quad +5 \quad +7 \quad +9$$

26 is the missing term.

B. These points are all on the same line.
Find the missing term.

$$(-7, -15) \left(\frac{2}{3}, \frac{1}{3}\right) (2, 3)\ (4, 7)\ (8, \underline{})$$

Multiply the first term by 2 and subtract 1.
The missing term is (8, 15).

Practice

Find the missing term in each pattern below.

1. 4, 2, 0, −2, −4, ___ −8, −10 ___

2. 4, 6.5, 9, 11.5, ___

3. 120, 60, 30, 15, ___

4. 1, 2, 6, 24, 120,

5. 5, 9, 13, 17 ___

The points in each sequence below are on the same line. Find the missing term.

6. (4, 12), (2, 10), (10, 18), (18, 26), (22, ___)

7. (100, 11), (70, 8), (90, 10), (40, 5), (30, ___)

8. (3, 9), (7, 49), (2, 4), (100, 10,000), (5, ___)

9. A meteorologist placed remote thermometers at sea level and up the side of the mountain at 1,000, 2,000, 5,000, and 6,000 feet. Readings were taken simultaneously and entered in the following table. What temperatures would you predict for the missing readings?

Temperature

0	1,000	2,000	3,000	4,000	5,000	6,000	7,000	8,000	9,000	10,000
52°	49°	46°			37°	34°				

10. Consider another example. A space capsule is moving in a straight line and is being tracked on a grid. The first four positions on the grid are recorded in the following table. Where will the capsule be on the grid when the x position is 13?

x-value	1	2	3	4
y-value	1	4	7	10

Answers on page 186.

Estimation Problems

Follow these steps.

1. Round the numbers.
2. Use the rounded numbers to estimate the answer.

EXAMPLE

It takes a person about $7\frac{1}{2}$ minutes to run a mile. The person runs 176 miles in a month. What is a reasonable estimate of the time it takes for the person to run that distance?

Round $7\frac{1}{2}$ to 8.

Round 174 to 180.

$180 \times 8 = 1,440$ minutes or 24 hours.

24 hours is a reasonable estimate of the answer.

Practice

1. A class took a spelling quiz and the grades were 93, 97, 87, 88, 98, 91. What is a reasonable estimate of the average of these grades?

2. To build a sandbox, you need lumber in the following lengths: 12 ft, 16 ft, 18 ft, and 23 ft. What is a reasonable estimate of the total length of the lumber?

3. Each batch of cookies yields 11 dozen. You need 165 dozen. What is a reasonable estimate for the number of batches you will need?

4. It takes 48 minutes for a commuter to travel back and forth from work each day. If the commuter drives back and forth 26 days a month, what is a reasonable estimate of the number of hours that are spent driving?

Answers on page 186.

Chart Problems

Follow these steps:

1. Identify the data in the chart.
2. Add when necessary to find the total probability.

EXAMPLE

	Air Express	Rail	Truck
5 pounds and over	0.07	0.34	0.18
Under 5 pounds	0.23	0.02	0.16

The table shows the percent of packages shipped by the method used and the weight classes.

What is the probability that a package picked at random was sent Air Express?

Add the two decimals for Air Express.

$$0.07 + 0.23 = 0.30$$

The probability that a randomly picked package was sent Air Express is 0.3.

What is the probability that a package picked at random weighed under five pounds?

Add the three decimals for under five pounds.

$$0.23 + 0.02 + 0.16 = 0.41.$$

The probability that a randomly chosen package weighed under five pounds is 0.42.

What is the probability that a package picked at random weighing under five pounds was sent by rail?

Look at the cell in the table where *under five pounds* and *rail* intersect.

That decimal is 0.02.

The probability that a randomly chosen package under five pounds was sent by rail is 0.02.

Practice

Use Table 1 above.

1. What is the probability that a package was sent by truck?

2. What is the probability of a package five pounds and over being randomly chosen?

3. What is the probability that a package five pounds and over picked at random was sent by Air Express?

4. What is the probability of randomly choosing a package under five pounds that was sent other than by rail?

Answers on page 186.

Frequency Table Problems

PERCENT

Percent tables show the percent or proportion of a particular score or characteristic. You can see from the table below that 13% of the students got a score from 90 through 100.

EXAMPLE

Scores	Percent of Students
0-59	2
60-69	8
70-79	39
80-89	38
90-100	13

Which score interval contains the mode?

The largest percentage is 39% for 70–79. The interval 70–79 contains the mode.

Which score interval contains the median?

The cumulative percentage of 0–79 is 49%.

The median is in the interval in which the cumulative percentage of 50% occurs. The score interval 80–89 contains the median.

What percent of the students scored above 79?

Add the percentiles of the intervals above 79. $38 + 13 = 51$

51% of the students scored above 79.

PERCENTILE RANK

The percentile rank shows the percent of scores below a given value. You can see from the table below that 68% of the scores fell below 60.

EXAMPLE

Standardized Score	Percentile Rank
80	99
70	93
60	68
50	39
40	22
30	13
20	2

What percent of the scores are below 50?

The percentile rank next to 50 is 39. That means 39% of the scores are below 50.

What percent of the scores are between 30 and 70?

Subtract the percentile rank for 30 from the percentile rank for 70.

93% − 13% = 80%. 80% of the scores are between 30 and 70.

What percent of the scores are at or above 60?

Subtract the percentile rank for 60 from 100%.

100% − 68% = 32%. 32% of the scores are at or above 60.

Practice

Use the table above and the table on page 155.

Table 1

1. What percent of the scores are below 70?

2. In which score interval is the median?

3. What percent of the scores are from 80 to 100?

Table 2

4. The lowest passing score is 50. What percent of the scores are passing?

5. What percent of the scores are from 20 to 50?

Answers on page 187.

Formula Problems

Concentrate on substituting values for variables. If you see a problem to be solved with a proportion, set up the proportion and solve.

EXAMPLES

A. A mechanic uses this formula to estimate the displacement (P) of an engine. $P = 0.8$ $(d^2)(s)(n)$ where d is the diameter, s is the stroke length of each cylinder, and n is the number of cylinders. Estimate the displacement of a 6-cylinder car whose cylinders have a diameter of 2 inches and a stroke length of 4 inches.

1. Write the formula. $P = 0.8(d^2)(s)(n)$
2. Write the values of the variables. $d = 2,\ s = 4,\ n = 6$
3. Substitute the values for the variables. $P = 0.8(2^2)(4)(6)$
4. Solve. $P = 0.8(4)(24) = (3.2)(24)$
                                         $P = 76.8$

The displacement of the engine is about 76.8 cubic inches.

B. The accountant calculates that it takes $3 in sales to generate $0.42 in profit. How much cost does it take to generate a profit of $5.46?

1. Write a proportion
Use s for sales. $\dfrac{3}{0.42} = \dfrac{s}{5.46}$

2. Cross multiply. $0.42s = 16.38$

3. Solve. $s = \dfrac{16.38}{0.42}$
                          $s = 39$

It will take $39 in sales to generate $5.46 in profits.

Practice

1. A retail store makes a profit of $3.75 for each $10 of goods sold. How much profit would the store make on a $45 purchase?

2. The formula for calculating average speed is $d/(T_2 - T_1)$. If T_1 (start time) is 5:00 P.M. and T_2 (end time) is midnight the same day, and 287 miles were traveled, what was the average speed?

3. A car purchased for $12,000 ($O$) depreciates 10% ($P$) a year ($Y$). If the car is sold in 3 years, what is its depreciated value if $V = O - POY$?

4. There is a square grid of dots. A figure is made of line segments that connect the dots. The formula for the area of a figure on the grid is $\dfrac{T-2}{2} + I$. T is the number of dots touching the figure, and I is the number of dots inside. What is the area of a figure with 14 dots touching and 5 dots inside?

Answers on page 187.

Pythagorean Theorem Problems

Follow these steps to solve this type of problem.

1. Sketch and label the right triangle.
2. Use the Pythagorean formula.
3. Solve the problem.

EXAMPLE

A radio tower sticks 40 feet straight up into the air. Engineers attached a wire with no slack from the top of the tower to the ground 30 feet away from the tower. If it costs $95 a foot to attach the wire, how much did the wire cost?

1. Sketch and label the right triangle.

2. Use the Pythagorean formula.

   $a^2 + b^2 = c^2$
   $(40)^2 + (30)^2 = c^2$
   $1{,}600 + 900 = c^2$
   $2{,}500 = c^2$
   $50 = c$
   The wire is 50 feet long.

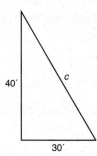

3. Solve the problem.

   50 feet at $95 a foot.
   $50 \times 95 = 4{,}750$. The wire costs $4,750 to install.

Practice

1. A 20-foot ladder is leaning against the side of a tall apartment building. The bottom of the ladder is 15 feet from the wall. At what height on the wall does the top of the ladder touch the building?

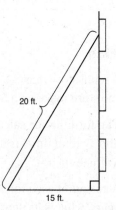

2. A truck ramp is shaped like a right triangle. The base of the ramp is 300 feet long. The ramp itself is 340 feet long. How high is the third side of the ramp?

3. A 25-meter telephone pole casts a shadow. The shadow ends 17 meters from the base of the pole. How long is it straight from the top of the pole to the end of the shadow?

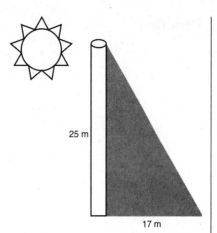

25 m

17 m

4. You are building a staircase. The wall is 14 feet wide and the stairs are 40 feet long. How high is the wall where it touches the top of the stairs?

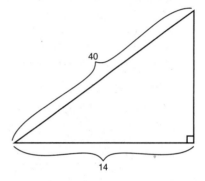

40

14

Answers on page 187.

Geometric Figure Problems

Follow these steps to solve this type of problem.

1. Identify the figure or figures involved.
2. Use the formulas for these figures.
3. Use the results of the formulas to solve the problem.

EXAMPLE

A circular pool with a radius of 10 feet is inscribed inside a square wall. What is the area of the region outside the pool but inside the fence?

10

1. There is a square with $s = 20$ and a circle with $r = 10$. The side of the square is twice the radius of the circle.

2. Find the areas.
   Square: $(A = s^2)$ $(20) \times (20) = 400$
   Circle: $(A = \pi r^2)$ $3.14 \times 10^2 = 3.14 \times 100 = 314$

3. Subtract to find the area inside the square but outside the circle.
   $400 - 314 = 86$

Practice

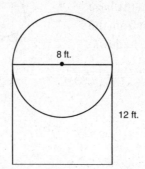

1. The dimensions of part of a basketball court are shown in the diagram above. One pint of paint covers 35 square feet. How much paint would it take to paint the inside region of this part of the court?

2. A roofer uses one bushel of shingles to cover 1,200 square feet. How many bushels of shingles are needed to cover these three rectangular roofs?

   Roof 1: 115 ft by 65 ft
   Roof 2: 112 ft by 65 ft
   Roof 3: 72 ft by 52 ft

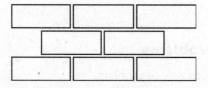

3. The bricks in the wall pictured here measure 2 inches by 4 inches by 8 inches. What is the volume of the bricks in this section of the wall?

4. A circular cone has a radius of 4 cm. If the volume is 134 cm^3, what is the height?

5. The official basketball has a radius of 6.5 inches. What is the volume?

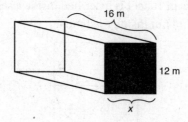

6. The rectangular solid shown here has a volume of 1,920 m^3. What is the area of the shaded side?

Answers on page 188.

Interpreting Remainder Problems

When you divide to solve a problem there may be both a quotient and a remainder. You may need to (1) use only the quotient, (2) round the quotient to the next greater whole number, or (3) use only the remainder.

EXAMPLE

Stereo speakers are packed 4 to a box. There are 315 stereo speakers to be packed.

Questions:
1. How many boxes can be filled?
2. How many boxes would be needed to hold all the stereo speakers?
3. How many stereo speakers will be in the box that is not completely full?

Divide 315 by 4.

$$\begin{array}{r} 78\ R3 \\ 4\overline{)315} \\ 28 \\ \hline 35 \\ 32 \\ \hline 3 \end{array}$$

Answers:
1. Use only the quotient—78 of the boxes can be filled.
2. Round the quotient to the next higher number. It would take 79 boxes to hold all the stereo speakers.
3. Use only the remainder. Three stereo speakers would be in the partially filled box.

Practice

At the quarry, workers are putting 830 pounds of sand into bags that hold 25 pounds.

1. How much sand is left over after the bags are filled?

2. How many bags are needed to hold all the sand?

3. How many bags can be filled with sand?

Answers on page 188.

STRATEGIES FOR TAKING THE MATHEMATICS TEST

The mathematics tested is the kind you probably had in high school and in college. It is the kind of mathematics you will use as you teach and go about your everyday life. Computational ability alone is expected but is held to a minimum. Remember to use the general test strategies discussed in the Introduction.

Write on the Scrap Paper Provided

It is particularly important to use the provided scrap paper while taking the mathematics portion of the test.

Draw Diagrams and Figures on the Scrap Paper

When you come across a geometry problem or related problem, draw a diagram on the scrap paper to help.

All sides of a rectangle are shrunk in half. What happens to the area?

Ⓐ Divided by 2
Ⓑ Divided by 4
Ⓒ Multiplied by 2
Ⓓ Multiplied by 6

Answer (B), divided by 4, is the correct answer. The original area is evenly divided into four parts.

Work from the Answers

If you do not know how to solve a formula or relation try out each answer choice until you get the correct answer. Look at this example.

What percent times $\frac{1}{4}$ is $\frac{1}{5}$?

Ⓐ 25%
Ⓑ 40%
Ⓒ 80%
Ⓓ 120%

Just take each answer in turn and try it out.

$$0.25 \times \frac{1}{4} = \frac{1}{4} \times \frac{1}{4} = \frac{1}{16} \qquad \text{That is not it.}$$

$$0.40 \times \frac{1}{4} = \frac{4}{10} \times \frac{1}{4} = \frac{4}{40} = \frac{1}{10} \qquad \text{That is not it either.}$$

$$0.8 \times \frac{1}{4} = \frac{4}{5} \times \frac{1}{4} = \frac{4}{20} = \frac{1}{5}$$

You know that 0.8 is the correct answer, so choice (C) is correct.

Try Out Numbers

Look at the preceding question.

Work with fractions at first. Ask: What number times $\frac{1}{4}$ equals $\frac{1}{5}$?

Through trial and error you find out that $\frac{4}{5} \times \frac{1}{4} = \frac{1}{5}$. The answer in fractions is $\frac{4}{5}$.

$$\frac{4}{5} = 0.8 = 80\%$$

The correct choice is (C).

In this example, you can find the answer without ever solving an equation by trying out numbers until you find the one that works.

Eliminate and Guess

Use this approach when all else has failed. Begin by eliminating the answers you know are wrong. Sometimes you know with certainty that an answer is incorrect. Other times, an answer looks so unreasonable that you can be fairly sure that it is not correct.

Once you have eliminated incorrect answers, a few will probably be left. Just guess among these choices. There is no method that will increase your chances of guessing correctly.

There is nothing better than mathematics practice. This targeted test is designed to help you practice the problem-solving and test-taking strategies presented in this chapter. For that reason, questions may have a different emphasis than the actual test, and the actual test will certainly be more complete. Answers are on pages 189–193.

Directions: Mark your choice, then check your answers. You may use a calculator, like the one used on the test.

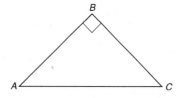

1. This is an isosceles triangle. What is the measure of angle *A*?

    Ⓐ 10°
    Ⓑ 40°
    Ⓒ 90°
    Ⓓ 45°
    Ⓔ 180°

2. After a discount of 25 percent, the savings on a pair of roller blades was $12.00. What was the sale price?

    Ⓐ $48.00
    Ⓑ $36.00
    Ⓒ $24.00
    Ⓓ $25.00
    Ⓔ $60.00

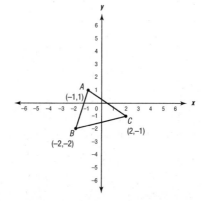

3. In the graph above, the triangle is shifted up 3 units and to the right 6 units. What would be the coordinates of point *B* after that shift?

    Ⓐ (1, –6)
    Ⓑ (1, 3)
    Ⓒ (3, 2)
    Ⓓ (4, 1)
    Ⓔ (1, 4)

4. Chad rolls a fair die. The sides of the die are numbered from 1 to 6. Ten times in a row he rolls a 5. What is the probability that he will roll a 5 on his next roll?

Ⓐ $\frac{1}{5}$

Ⓑ $\frac{5}{6}$

Ⓒ $\frac{1}{50}$

Ⓓ $\frac{1}{11}$

Ⓔ $\frac{1}{10}$

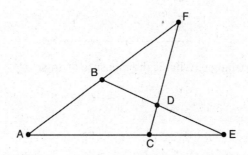

5. Which of the following set of points do not form an angle in the diagram?

Ⓐ ABF
Ⓑ ABE
Ⓒ AFC
Ⓓ ABC
Ⓔ CDE

6. An apple costs (C). You have (D) dollars. What equation would represent the amount of apples you could buy for the money you have?

Ⓐ C/D
Ⓑ CD
Ⓒ C + D
Ⓓ D/C
Ⓔ C + 2D

7. If a worker gets $144.00 for 18 hours' work, how much would that worker get for 32 hours' work?

Ⓐ $200.00
Ⓑ $288.00
Ⓒ $400.00
Ⓓ $432.00
Ⓔ $256.00

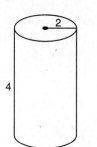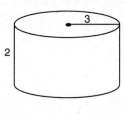

$V = \pi r^2 h$

8. Find the difference between the volumes of these two cylinders?

Ⓐ 2π
Ⓑ 4π
Ⓒ 9π
Ⓓ 16π
Ⓔ 18π

9. r = regular price
d = discount
s = sale price

What equation would represent the calculations for finding the discount?

Ⓐ $d = r - s$
Ⓑ $d = s - r$
Ⓒ $d = sr$
Ⓓ $d = s + r$
Ⓔ $d = \dfrac{1}{2} r$

10. A printing company makes pamphlets that cost $.75 per copy plus $5.00 as a setter's fee. If $80 were spent printing a pamphlet, how many pamphlets were ordered?

Ⓐ 50
Ⓑ 75
Ⓒ 100
Ⓓ 150
Ⓔ 225

11. Which is farthest from $\dfrac{1}{2}$ on a number line?

Ⓐ $\dfrac{1}{12}$

Ⓑ $\dfrac{7}{8}$

Ⓒ $\dfrac{3}{4}$

Ⓓ $\dfrac{2}{3}$

Ⓔ $\dfrac{5}{6}$

12. Which of the following could be about 25 centimeters long?

    Ⓐ a human thumb
    Ⓑ a doorway
    Ⓒ a car
    Ⓓ a house
    Ⓔ a notebook

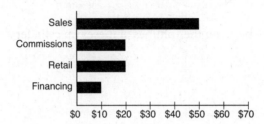

13. The sales department staff draws its salary from four areas of the company's income. Using the above graph, determine what percentage is drawn from the retail fund.

    Ⓐ 10%
    Ⓑ 20%
    Ⓒ 25%
    Ⓓ 30%
    Ⓔ 15%

14. If 250 is lowered by 40%, what percent of the new number is 30?

    Ⓐ 5%
    Ⓑ 10%
    Ⓒ 20%
    Ⓓ 25%
    Ⓔ 50%

15. For a fund-raiser the Science and Technology Club is selling raffles at the cost of six raffles for $5.00. It cost the club $250.00 for the prizes and tickets that will be given away. How many raffles will the club have to sell in order to make $1,000.00?

    Ⓐ 300
    Ⓑ 600
    Ⓒ 750
    Ⓓ 1,200
    Ⓔ 1,500

16. What value for n makes the number sentence true?

$5.3 \times 10^4 = 0.0053 \times 10^n$

    Ⓐ 4
    Ⓑ 5
    Ⓒ 6
    Ⓓ 7
    Ⓔ 8

17. Which of the following represents complementary angles?

Ⓐ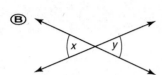

Ⓑ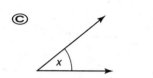

Ⓒ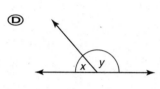

Ⓓ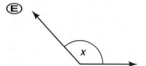

Ⓔ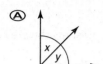

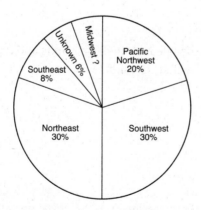

18. The above graph shows the percentage of students who attend college by the location of their home towns. How many more college students come from the Northeast than come from the Midwest?

Ⓐ twice as many
Ⓑ three times as many
Ⓒ half as many
Ⓓ five times as many
Ⓔ ten times as many

19. Each rectangle has a total area of 1 square unit. What number represents the area of the shaded regions?

Ⓐ $\frac{5}{6}$ square units

Ⓑ $\frac{7}{8}$ square units

Ⓒ $1\frac{3}{4}$ square units

Ⓓ $1\frac{1}{3}$ square units

Ⓔ $1\frac{5}{24}$ square units

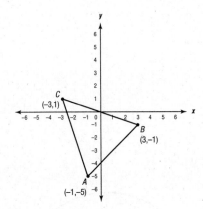

20. In the graph above, the triangle is shifted left 2 units and down 4 units. What would be the coordinates of point A after that shift?

Ⓐ (1, 1)
Ⓑ (2, 4)
Ⓒ (−2, −4)
Ⓓ (−8, −3)
Ⓔ (−3, −8)

21. The sum of the measures of two angles is 90°. What do we know about these two angles?

Ⓐ They are right angles.
Ⓑ The are supplementary angles.
Ⓒ They are acute angles.
Ⓓ The are obtuse angles.
Ⓔ They are supplementary angles.

22. Three very bright light beams go out into space from the same spot on Earth. None of the beams are parallel and none point in the same direction. What conclusion can we reach?

    Ⓐ All three beams will cross at the same point.
    Ⓑ Exactly two of the beams will cross.
    Ⓒ At least two of the beams will cross.
    Ⓓ Two of the beams are perpendicular.
    Ⓔ At least two of the beams may be skewed.

23. Bob walked about 2,750 meters to school every day. About how many kilometers is that?

    Ⓐ 2.750
    Ⓑ 27.50
    Ⓒ 275
    Ⓓ 275,000
    Ⓔ 27.5 × 1,000

24. You buy 20 shares of stock on March 10 for $17 \frac{7}{8}$ a share. You sell the 20 shares of the same stock on May 5 for $19 \frac{5}{8}$ a share. How much in dollars and cents did you make on the stock sale?

    Ⓐ $75.00
    Ⓑ $4.50
    Ⓒ $37.50
    Ⓓ $35.00
    Ⓔ $3.50

25. Alpha Centauri is about 4 light years from Earth. Light travels about 186,000 miles in a second. About how far is it from Alpha Centauri to Earth?

    Ⓐ 23 quintillion miles
    Ⓑ 23 quadrillion miles
    Ⓒ 23 trillion miles
    Ⓓ 23 billion miles
    Ⓔ 28 million miles

26. An unusual plant is 10 feet tall when planted and then, starting the next day, grows 20 percent of each of the previous day's final height. About how tall is the tree at the end of the fourth day after planting?

    Ⓐ 8 feet
    Ⓑ 19.4 feet
    Ⓒ 18 feet
    Ⓓ 16 feet
    Ⓔ 20.47 feet

27. A block of stone is 9 feet wide by 12 feet long by 8 feet high. A stone mason cuts the stone to form the biggest cube possible. What is the volume of the cube?

   Ⓐ 864 cubic feet
   Ⓑ 144 cubic feet
   Ⓒ 81 cubic feet
   Ⓓ 526 cubic feet
   Ⓔ 512 cubic feet

USE THE BELOW INFORMATION FOR QUESTIONS 28 AND 29.

An archaeologist was investigating the books of an old civilization. She found the following table, which showed the number of hunters on top and the number of people they could feed on the bottom. For example, 3 hunters could feed 12 people. The archaeologist found a pattern in the table.

Hunters	1	2	3	4	5	6	7
Eaters	2	6	12	20	30		

28. Look for the pattern. How many eaters can 6 hunters feed?

   Ⓐ 42
   Ⓑ 40
   Ⓒ 30
   Ⓓ 36
   Ⓔ 34

29. What is the formula for the pattern:

   H stands for hunters and
   E stands for eaters?

   Ⓐ $E = 3 \times H$
   Ⓑ $E = 4 \times H$
   Ⓒ $E = H^2 + H$
   Ⓓ $E = 3 \times (H + 1)$
   Ⓔ $E = (H + 1)(H + 1)$

   _____

30. The school is planning a class trip. They will go by bus. There will be 328 people going on the trip, and each bus holds 31 people. How many buses will be needed for the trip?

   Ⓐ 7
   Ⓑ 8
   Ⓒ 9
   Ⓓ 10
   Ⓔ 11

1	2	3	4	5	6	7	8	9	10
11	12	13	14	15	16	17	18	19	20
21	22	23	24	25	26	27	28	29	30
31	32	33	34	35	36	37	38	39	40
41	42	43	44	45	46	47	48	49	50
51	52	53	54	55	56	57	58	59	60
61	62	63	64	65	66	67	68	69	70
71	72	73	74	75	76	77	78	79	80
81	82	83	84	85	86	87	88	89	90
91	92	93	94	95	96	97	98	99	100

31. Cross off the multiples of 2, 3, 4, 5, 6, 7, and 8 in the above hundreds square. Which numbers in the 80s are not crossed off?

Ⓐ 83, 87

Ⓑ 81, 89

Ⓒ 83, 89

Ⓓ 81, 83, 89

Ⓔ 82, 85, 88

USE THE BELOW GRAPH TO ANSWER QUESTIONS 32 AND 33.

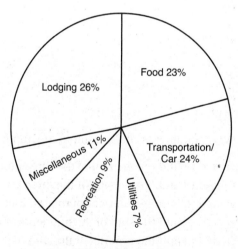

Jane's Monthly Budget

32. Jane spends $2,600 in the month of March. How much did she spend on food?

Ⓐ $624

Ⓑ $598

Ⓒ $312

Ⓓ $400

Ⓔ $600

33. Jane spends $2,600 in May. She needs $858 that month for transportation/car expenses, which is more than the budget allows. Any needed money will come from miscellaneous. When she recalculates her budget chart, what percent is left for miscellaneous?

Ⓐ 13 percent

Ⓑ 11 percent

Ⓒ 9 percent

Ⓓ 6 percent

Ⓔ 2 percent

---

34. The bakers make brownies and cookies in a ratio of 2 : 9. Today the bakers made 1,350 cookies. How many brownies did the bakers make?

Ⓐ 150

Ⓑ 300

Ⓒ 675

Ⓓ 2,750

Ⓔ 3,000

35. A tent standing on level ground is 40 feet high. A taut rope extends from the top of the tent to the ground 30 feet from the bottom of the tent. About how long is the rope?

Ⓐ 26.455 feet

Ⓑ 50 feet

Ⓒ 63.255 feet

Ⓓ 70 feet

Ⓔ 2,500 feet

36. $(123 + 186 + 177) \div (3) =$

Which of the following statements could result in the number sentence given above?

Ⓐ The athlete wanted to find the median of the three jumps.

Ⓑ The athlete wanted to find the average of the three jumps.

Ⓒ The athlete wanted to find the quotient of the product of three jumps.

Ⓓ The athlete wanted to find the sum of the quotients of the three jumps.

Ⓔ The athlete wanted to find the product of the sum of the quotients.

37. Renee, Lisa, and Jan are all on the basketball team. Renee is the tallest player on the team. Lisa is not the shortest player on the team. Jan is not shorter than Lisa.

Which of the following conclusions can be drawn from this statement?

Ⓐ Jan is taller than Lisa.

Ⓑ Jan is the second-tallest player on the team.

Ⓒ Jan is not the shortest player on the team.

Ⓓ Either Jan or Lisa is the second tallest player on the team.

Ⓔ Lisa is the tallest player.

38. If $x = \dfrac{5}{6}$, which of the following inequalities is correct?

Ⓐ $\dfrac{5}{9} < x < \dfrac{7}{9}$

Ⓑ $\dfrac{5}{8} < x < \dfrac{3}{4}$

Ⓒ $\dfrac{3}{4} < x < \dfrac{7}{8}$

Ⓓ $\dfrac{7}{8} < x < \dfrac{15}{16}$

Ⓔ $\dfrac{5}{6} < x < \dfrac{9}{10}$

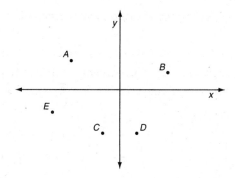

39. Which letter on the coordinate grid above could represent the point (–2, –5)?

Ⓐ A
Ⓑ B
Ⓒ C
Ⓓ D
Ⓔ E

40. The disaster relief specialist found that 289, or 85%, of the houses on the beach had been damaged by the storm. How many houses were on the beach?

Ⓐ 294
Ⓑ 332
Ⓒ 340
Ⓓ 400
Ⓔ 420

41. Light travels about 186,000 miles in a second. How would you find out how far light travels in an hour?

Ⓐ Multiply 186,000 by 24.
Ⓑ Multiply 186,000 by 60.
Ⓒ Multiply 186,000 by 360.
Ⓓ Multiply 186,000 by 3600.
Ⓔ Multiply 186,000 by 2,400.

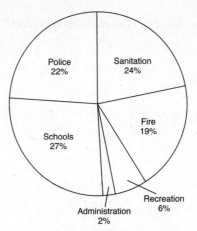

Tax money spent on town services.

42. A town collects $2,600,000 in taxes. The town needs $624,000 for police. Any needed money will come from sanitation. The percents in the circle graph are recalculated. What percent is left for sanitation?

    (A) 22%
    (B) 20%
    (C) 19%
    (D) 18%
    (E) 16%

43. A person flips a fair penny twice and it lands heads up each time. What is the probability that the penny will land heads up on the next flip?

    (A) 1
    (B) $\dfrac{1}{2}$
    (C) $\dfrac{1}{4}$
    (D) $\dfrac{1}{8}$
    (E) $\dfrac{1}{16}$

x	0	3	6	7	9
y	1	7	13	15	19

44. Which of the following expressions shows the relationship between x and y in the table above?

    (A) $y = 3x - 2$
    (B) $y = 2x + 1$
    (C) $y = x + 3$
    (D) $y = 2x - 2$
    (E) $y = 4x + 1$

45. What is the area of the shaded portion?

Ⓐ 45 square feet

Ⓑ 270 square feet

Ⓒ 170 square feet

Ⓓ 180 square feet

Ⓔ 150 square feet

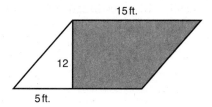

15 ft.

12

5 ft.

46. $2n + 3n^2 - 5n \times 3 - 6n^2 =$

Ⓐ $-12n$

Ⓑ $-13n - 3n^2$

Ⓒ $13n + 3n^2$

Ⓓ $-6n^2$

Ⓔ $-15n - n^2$

47. The formula for converting a kilogram weight (K) to a pound weight (P) is P = 2.2 K. If a dog weighs 15.6 pounds, how many kilograms does the dog weigh?

Ⓐ 3.43 kg

Ⓑ 34.32 kg

Ⓒ 7.09 kg

Ⓓ 70.9 kg

Ⓔ .709 kg

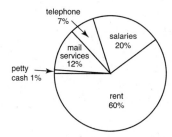

telephone
7%

salaries
20%

mail
services
12%

petty
cash 1%

rent
60%

48. The pie chart preceding this question represents the monthly expenses of a small business for August. In what area is the most money spent?

Ⓐ mail services, telephone, and salaries

Ⓑ salaries, telephone, and petty cash

Ⓒ petty cash and salaries

Ⓓ rent

Ⓔ petty cash, salaries, and mail services

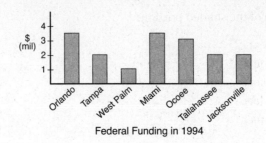

Federal Funding in 1994

49. In the bar graph that precedes this question, which city or cities likely represent the mode?

(A) Orlando
(B) Ocoee
(C) West Palm
(D) Tallahassee
(E) Miami

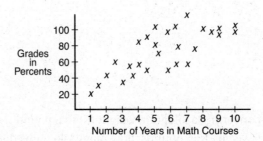

50. The graph shows the grade distribution on a standardized mathematics test. Which of the following best describes the relationships between test score and number of years in mathematics courses?

(A) People who took fewer years of math scored highest.
(B) People who took more math courses scored lower.
(C) There is a negative relationship.
(D) There is no relationship.
(E) There is a positive relationship.

You may also see items like these.

51. Which of the following expressions represents the area of the figure below?

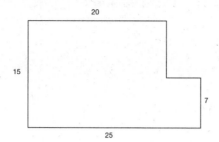

Choose all that apply.

- A. $(15 \times 20) + (7 \times 5)$
- B. $(20 \times 15) + (7 \times 25)$
- C. $(25 \times 15) - (8 \times 5)$
- D. $(20 \times 15) - (25 \times 7)$
- E. $(25 \times 15) + (7 \times 5)$

52. A rectangle is 48 inches wide with an area greater than 57 square feet. Which of the lengths listed below could be the length of the rectangle.

Choose all that apply.

- A. 12 feet
- B. 14 feet, 9 inches
- C. 14 feet, 3 inches
- D. 60 inches
- E. 175 inches

Final Exam Grades

Percent Correct	Class A	Class B	Class C	Class D	Class E
90–100	9	4	1	2	4
80–89	2	8	4	5	3
70–79	8	2	5	4	4
60–69	2	3	8	0	5
Below 60	5	11	2	6	7

53. The passing grade for a college course requires a score of at least 70% on the final exam. Which of the following classes has more than 60% of the students passing the course?

Choose all that apply.

- A. Class A
- B. Class B
- C. Class C
- D. Class D
- E. Class E

54. If $a > 0$ and $b > 0$, evaluate the expression below when $a = 2$ and $b = 3$.

$$\frac{(b^2 - a^2)^3 + 3}{(a + 2b)^2}$$

55. Write the fraction in simple form.

$$\frac{\frac{1}{4}}{\frac{2}{3} - \frac{1}{2}}$$

56. Write the expression below as a fraction in lowest terms.

$$\left(\frac{2}{3}\right)^3 \cdot \left(\frac{3}{5}\right)^2$$

MATHEMATICS PRACTICE ANSWERS

Understanding and Ordering Whole Numbers, page 102

1. $2 < 3$
2. $4 > 1$
3. $8 < 9$
4. $1 = 1$
5. $7 > 6$
6. 9,037
7. 2,851
8. The hundreds place and the ones place each contain a 7.
9. 1, 2, 3, 4, 5, 6, 7, 8, 9, 10, 11, 12, 13, 14 The problem asks for the numbers between 0 and 15, so 0 and 15 are not included.
10. There are 49. (1, 2, 3, . . . , 47, 48, 49)

Positive Exponents, page 103

1. 241
2. 81
3. 8
4. 900
5. 35
6. 51
7. $4^6 = 4,096$
8. $2^5 = 32$
9. 44
10. 1,000
11. $4^4 = 256$
12. 72

Scientific Notation, page 103

1. $0.0564 = 5.64 \times 10^{-2}$
2. $0.00897 = 8.97 \times 10^{-3}$
3. $0.06501 = 6.501 \times 10^{-2}$
4. $0.000354 = 3.54 \times 10^{-4}$
5. $545 = 5.45 \times 10^2$
6. $7,790 = 7.79 \times 10^3$
7. $289,705 = 2.89705 \times 10^5$
8. $1,801,319 = 1.801319 \times 10^6$

Understanding and Ordering Decimals, page 104

1. $0.02 > 0.003$
2. $4.6 > 1.98$
3. $0.0008 > 0.00009$
4. $1.0 = 1$
5. $7.6274 > 7.6269$
6. 2.586

7. 90310.0704
8. The hundredths place and the hundred thousandths place each contain a 3.
9. 0, 0.1, 0.2, 0.3, 0.4, 0.5, 0.6, 0.7, 0.8, 0.9, 1.0
10. There are 99—0.01, 0.02, 0.03, . . . , 0.50, 0.51, 0.52, . . . , 0.97, 0.98, 0.99

Rounding Whole Numbers and Decimals, page 105

1. 23,500
2. 74.151
3. 980,000
4. 302.8
5. 495,240
6. 1500
7. 13.1
8. 200,000
9. 52
10. 23,500

Rational and Irrational Numbers, page 107

1. $\dfrac{2}{3} = 0.666\ldots$
2. $\dfrac{8}{12} = \dfrac{3}{4} = .75$
3. $\dfrac{5}{9} = 0.555\ldots$
4. $\dfrac{7}{12} = 0.58333\ldots$
5. 7π is close to $7 \times \dfrac{22}{7}$, which is approximately equal to 22.
6. $105\sqrt{2}$ is close to $105 \times \dfrac{99}{70}$, or approximately 1.5×99, and approximately 1.485.

Understanding and Ordering Fractions, page 109

1. $1\dfrac{2}{3}$
2. $2\dfrac{1}{7}$
3. $2\dfrac{2}{3}$
4. $\dfrac{41}{5}$
5. $\dfrac{55}{8}$
6. $\dfrac{68}{7}$
7. $\dfrac{3}{7} < \dfrac{4}{9}$
8. $\dfrac{5}{6} = \dfrac{25}{30}$
9. $\dfrac{4}{5} < \dfrac{7}{8}$

Order of Operations, page 110

1. $4 \times 5 + 4 \div 2 = 20 + 2 = 22$
2. $(5 + 7 - 9) \times 8^2 + 2 = 3 \times 8^2 + 2 = 194$
3. $((7 + 4) - (1 + 4)) \times 6 = (11 - 5) \times 6 = 36$
4. $6^2 + 3(9 - 5 + 7)^2 = 36 + 3 \times 11^2 = 399$
5. $51 - 36 = 15$
6. $40 + 4 - 4 = 40$
7. $-50 + 7 = -43$
8. $(49 + 16) \times 8 = 520$

Number Theory, page 112

1. 13: 1 and 13
2. 26: 1, 2, 13, and 26
3. 40: 1, 2, 4, 5, 8, 10, 20, 40
4. 23: 1 and 23
5. 24
6. 60
7. 35
8. 28
9. 6
10. 5
11. 32
12. 28

Whole Number Computation, page 114

1. 98,405
2. 27,079
3. 95,809
4. 66,184
5. 16,013
6. 34,099
7. 34,688
8. 42,209
9. 13,680
10. 27,482
11. 29,725
12. 5,256
13. 8
14. 4 R4
15. 29
16. 32 R2

Properties of Operations, page 115

1. Commutative Property
   $\frac{6}{8} \times \frac{7}{9} = \frac{7}{9} \times \frac{6}{8}$
2. Associative Property
   $(2 + 3) + 4 = 2 + (3 + 4)$
3. The equation represents the distributive property.
4. Distributive property creates the expression $a(6 + 3)$.
5. The commutative property creates the expression.
6. (A) is not true for all real numbers. In fact the answer to A $\times$ (1/A) is always 1

Add, Subtract, Multiply, and Divide Decimals, pages 116

1. 26.09
2. 72.617
3. 988.39
4. 5473.2
5. 8.2
6. 71.0096
7. 453.97
8. 1767.87
9. .6225
10. 163.45
11. 3680.538
12. 3761.514
13. 4.8
14. 9.6
15. 33.6
16. 125.63

Multiply, Divide, Add, and Subtract Fractions and Mixed Numbers, page 118

1. $\frac{5}{27}$
2. $\frac{1}{6}$
3. $13\frac{59}{64}$
4. $8\frac{8}{35}$
5. $\frac{6}{7}$
6. $\frac{18}{35}$
7. $2\frac{22}{91}$
8. $\frac{7}{19}$
9. $1\frac{2}{9}$
10. $1\frac{1}{5}$
11. $4\frac{1}{14}$
12. $12\frac{1}{2}$
13. $\frac{1}{21}$
14. $\frac{1}{40}$
15. $\frac{2}{3}$
16. $3\frac{58}{63}$

Square Roots, page 118

1. $\sqrt{256} = 16$
2. $\sqrt{400} = 20$
3. $\sqrt{576} = 24$
4. $\sqrt{900} = 30$
5. $\sqrt{1225} = 35$
6. $\sqrt{48} = \sqrt{16 \times 3} = 4\sqrt{3}$
7. $\sqrt{245} = \sqrt{49 \times 5} = 7\sqrt{5}$
8. $\sqrt{396} = \sqrt{36 \times 11} = 6\sqrt{11}$
9. $\sqrt{567} = \sqrt{81 \times 7} = 9\sqrt{7}$
10. $\sqrt{832} = \sqrt{64 \times 13} = 8\sqrt{13}$

Ratio and Proportion, page 120

1. 14 vacuum cleaners for 280 houses
2. 4 teachers for 32 children
3. 21 rest stops for 140 miles
4. Yes. $\frac{7}{9} = \frac{28}{36}$ because $7 \times 36 = 252 = 9 \times 28$

Percent, page 121

1. 35.9%
2. 78%
3. 21.5%
4. 4.1%
5. $11\frac{1}{9}$%
6. 62.5%
7. 30%
8. $44\frac{4}{9}$%
9. $\frac{29}{50}$
10. $\frac{79}{100}$
11. $\frac{213}{250}$
12. $\frac{487}{500}$

Three Types of Percent Problems, page 122

1. $\square \times 240 = 120$
   $\square = \frac{120}{240}$
   $\square = .5 = 50\%$
2. $.15 \times 70 = \square$
   $.15 \times 70 = 10.5$
   $\square = 10.5$
3. $.6 \times 300 = \square$
   $.6 \times 300 = 180$
   $\square = 180$
4. $\square \times 60 = 42$
   $\square = \frac{42}{60}$
   $\square = 70\%$
5. $\square\% \times 25 = 2.5$
   $\square\% = \frac{25}{25}$
   $\square = 10\%$

6. $40\% \times \square = 22$
   $\square = \frac{22}{.4}$
   $\square = 55$
7. $.7 \times \square = 85$
   $\square = \frac{85}{.7}$
   $\square = 121\frac{3}{7}$
8. $25\% \times 38 = \square$
   $.25 \times 38 = 9.5$
   $\square = 9.5$
9. $.35 \times \square = 24$
   $\square = \frac{24}{.35}$
   $\square = 68\frac{4}{7}$
10. $24 = \square \times 80$
    $\frac{24}{80} = \square$
    $\square = 30\%$

Percent of Increase and Decrease, page 123

1. Amount of increase $35 − $25 = $10
   $\frac{10}{25} = 0.4 = 40\%$
   Percent of increase = 40%
2. Discount: $100 × .25 = $25
   $100 − $25 = $75
   Sale price = $75
3. Discount $80 × 15% = $12
   $80 − $12 = $68
   New price = $68
4. Amount of increase $150 − $120 = $30
   $\frac{30}{120} = \frac{1}{4} = 25\%$
   Percent of increase = 25%
5. Discount $75 × 10% = $7.50
   $75 − $7.50 = $67.50
   Sale price = $67.50

6. Amount of decrease $18 − $6 = $12

$$\frac{12}{18} = \frac{2}{3} = 66\frac{2}{3}\%$$

Percent of decrease $= 66\frac{2}{3}\%$

7. Amount of decrease $225 − $180 = $45

$$\frac{45}{225} = 0.2 = 20\%$$

Percent of decrease = 20%

8. Discount $150 = x − 0.25x
$150 = 0.75x$
$x = 200
Original price: $200

Probability, page 125

1. There are 10 socks in the drawer. 7 of the 10 are not black.

$$P\text{ (not black)} = \frac{7}{10}$$

2. There are 6 goldfish; 2 of the 6 are male.

$$P\text{ (male)} = \frac{2}{6} = \frac{1}{3}$$

3. There are 52 cards in a deck. There are 4 kings and 4 queens.
P (king or queen) =
P (king) + P (queen)

$$= \frac{4}{52} + \frac{4}{52} = \frac{8}{52} = \frac{2}{13}$$

4. There are 6 different names.
P (Carl and Phyllis) =
P (Carl) $\times$ P (Phyllis) =

$$\frac{1}{6} \times \frac{1}{6} = \frac{1}{36}$$

5. $\dfrac{1}{2}$

6. This is an "and" problem. Multiply the probability.

$$\left(\frac{1}{2}\right)\left(\frac{1}{2}\right)\left(\frac{1}{2}\right)\left(\frac{1}{2}\right)\left(\frac{1}{2}\right) = \frac{1}{32}$$

Permutations and Combinations, page 126

1. There are 6 combinations of 2 people to sit in the chairs.

2. There are 5,040 possible arrangements of the 7 books on the shelf.

3. 67,600 license plates
($26 \times 26 \times 10 \times 10$)

4. The positions on the bus are not specified. Order does not matter. This is a combination problem.

Four students   A   B   C   D
ABC   ABD   ACD   BCD

There are four ways for three of four students to board the bus.

Statistics, page 127

1. mode 80

2. mean (average) 35.5

3. median 9 (Remember to arrange the numbers in order.)

4. 16 is the median, the mode, and very close to the mean.

5. mean 89

6. mode 30

Scatter Plots, page 128

1.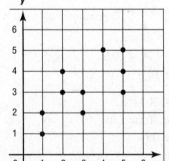

2. The scatter plot shows a trend from lower left to upper right, and it is generally a positive correlation.

3. The correlation will always be positive although the plot might look a little different.

Selecting Unbiased Samples, page 130

1. Good Sampling Techniques

   Randomly ask people at work about their child care needs.

   Randomly sample parents who have their children in day care.

   Poor Sampling Techniques

   Randomly sample women with children.

   Randomly sample people who have no children.

2. Good Sampling Technique

   Randomly sample residents identified as senior citizens.

   Poor Sampling Technique

   Randomly sample residents of senior housing.

Add, Subtract, Multiply, and Divide Integers, page 131

1. 15
2. 1
3. −69
4. −9
5. 1
6. 54
7. 22
8. −80
9. 99
10. −650
11. 1829
12. −1470
13. 15
14. −17
15. 44
16. −22

Polynomials, page 133

1. $3x^2 + 3x^2y + 10y$

2. $3x^2y + 24x + 3yx^2 + 7x^2y^2 = 7x^2y^2 + 6x^2y + 24x$

3. $(3x^5 + 3x^2 - 5x^2y + 6xy^2) + (3x^5 - 2x^2 + 4x^3y - x^2y + 3xy^3 - y^2) = \underline{3x^5 + 3x^5} + \underline{3x^2 - 2x^2} - \underline{5x^2y - x^2y} + 6xy^2 + 4x^3y + 3xy^3 - y^2 = 6x^5 + x^2 - 6x^2y + 6xy^2 + 4x^3y + 3xy^3 - y^2$

4. $(x^4 - 4x^3 + 2x^2y^2 - 4xy^2) + (3x^5 - 7x^4 + 3x^3 - 2x^2y^3 + 7xy^2) = x^4 \underline{- 4x^3 + 3x^3} + 2x^2y^2 \underline{- 4xy^2 + 7xy^2} + 3x^5 - 7x^4 - 2x^2y^3 = 3x^5 - 6x^4 - x^3 + 2x^2y^2 + 3xy^2 - 2x^2y^3$

5. $(6x^7 + 9x^4 - 3x^2y + 5xy^3) - (6x^8 - 15x^4 - 3x^3y + x^2y) = (6x^7 + 9x^4 - 3x^2y + 5xy^3) + (-6x^8 + 15x^4 + 3x^3y - x^2y) = 6x^7 + \underline{9x^4 + 15x^4} - \underline{3x^2y - x^2y} + 5xy^3 - 6x^8 + 3x^3y = -6x^8 + 6x^7 + 24x^4 + 3x^3y - 4x^2y + 5xy^3$

6. $(7x^2 - 9x + 3xy^2 + 3y^3 - 12) - (x^3 - 9x^2 + 2xy^2 - 3y^5 - 18) = (7x^2 - 9x + 3xy^2 + 3y^3 - 12) + (-x^3 + 9x^2 - 2xy^2 + 3y^5 + 18) = 7x^2 + 9x^2 - 9x + 3xy^2 - 2xy^2 + 3y^3 - 12 + 18 - x^3 + 3y^5 = 16x^2 - 9x + xy^2 + 3y^3 + 6 - x^3 + 3y^5 = [-x^3 + 16x^2 - 9x + xy^2 + 3y^3 + 3y^5 + 6]$

Formulas, page 136

1. πr^2

   $3.14 \times (9)^2 =$

   $3.14 \times 81 = 254.34 \text{ m}^2$

2. $b = 3, h = 2.6$

   $\left(\dfrac{1}{2}\right)(3)(2.6) = 3.9$

   $4 \times 3.9 = 15.6 \text{ in}^2$

3. Hexagon is 6-sided

   $6 \times 5 \text{ ft} = 30 \text{ ft perimeter}$

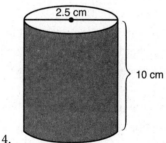

2.5 cm

10 cm

4.

   | 2 | π | r | h |

   $2\,(3.14)(1.25)(10)$

   $= 78.5 \text{ cm}^2$

5. $(x + 5) + (x + 5) + x + x = 90$

   $4x + 10 = 90$

   $4x = 80 \quad x = 20$

   length $= x + 5$

   length $= 25$ ft

6. Area of each side $= 25 \text{ cm}^2$

   Cube is 6-sided

   $6 \times 25 = 150 \text{ cm}^2$

7. $x = 12$

8. $A = 32.5$ in.^{2}

9. $V = 4186.\overline{6}\left(4186\frac{2}{3}\right)$ cm^3

10. $V = 3375$ in^3

Solving Linear Equations and Inequalities, page 137

1. $x = 16\frac{2}{5}$

2. $y > -56\frac{1}{3}$

3. $x > \frac{15}{4}$

4. $y = -11$

Symmetry, page 139

1. The numerals 8 and 0 have line and rotational symmetry.
   The numeral 3 has only line symmetry. The other numerals have neither type of symmetry.

2. The most obvious pattern is shown below.

   2   3   4   2   3   4

Circles, page 141

1. A circle has an infinite number of line segments that form a diameter. Each of these line segments is the same length.

2. Yes. The only parts of a chord on the circle are the two endpoints.

3. No. Two radii must form a single line segment across the circle to form a diameter. However, the lengths of two radii are always equal to the length of a diameter.

4. No. A diameter consists of a single chord.

Polygons, page 142

1. trapezoid

2. m∠2 = 135°

3. m∠ABC = 50° = m∠ACB

4.

5. An octagon (8 sides) has two more sides than a hexagon (6 sides).

6. A right angle, which has a measure of 90°.

7. (Picture may vary)

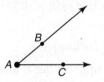

The new figure is ∠BAC.

8. (Picture may vary)

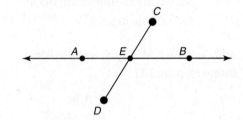

9. (Picture may vary)

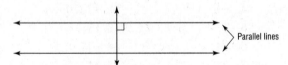

Parallel lines

10. The sum of the measures is 180° (m∠A + m∠B + m∠C = 180°).

Similar Triangles, page 144

1. Yes, the ratios of the lengths of corresponding sides are equal.

   $\frac{PR}{ST} = \frac{2}{4}$; $\frac{PQ}{SV} = \frac{5}{10}$; $\frac{2}{4} = \frac{5}{10}$

2. The measures of corresponding angles are equal.
   Find the measure of the angle in K.
   Angle b in triangle J is the same size.
   $180 - (50 + 55) = 75$.
   The measure of angle b is 75°.

3. A. True. Both are right angles because the triangles are right triangles.
(B), (C), and (D) are false because the triangles are not similar.

Coordinate Grid, page 145

1. A (3, −2)
   B (−2, −4)
   C (−5, 5)
   D (3, 3)
   E (0, 2)
   F (−5, 0)
2.

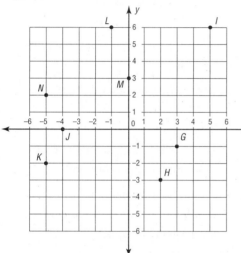

3.

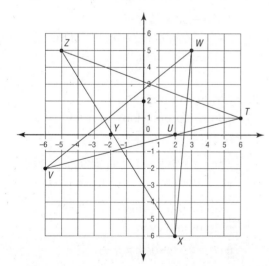

Translations on a Coordinate Grid, page 147

1. (−4, −4)
2. (2, 1)
3. (−4, −2)
4. You know that at least one of the vertices will have the same x value as point B and that at least one will have the same y value as point B. You cannot be sure about anything else.

Deductive Reasoning, page 148

1. False—Some sports, such as hockey, do not use a ball.
2. True—For example, 35 is divisible by both 5 and 7.
3. False—For example, 12 is divisible by 3.
4. True—For example, 2 is both prime and divisible by 2.

Words to Symbols Problems, page 151

1. 34; $34 - 9 = 25$
2. $0.6 \times 90 = 54$
3. Add: $\frac{2}{3} + \frac{1}{2} = \frac{7}{6}$

   Multiply: $\frac{7}{6} \times 3 = \frac{21}{6}$

   Divide: $21 \div 6 = 3 \frac{3}{6} = 3 \frac{1}{2}$.

   Bob's walk to school is $3 \frac{1}{2}$ miles.

4. $\frac{20}{y} = 2.5$ $20 = 2.5y$ $y = 8$

5. $5 \frac{1}{x} = 5 \frac{1}{8}$ $x = 8$

   The number is 8.

6. Multiply: $60 \times 2.5 = 150$
   $70 \times 2 = 140$
   Add: $150 + 140 = 290$
   The cars traveled a total distance of 290 miles.

Finding and Interpreting Patterns, page 153

1. **−6** is the missing term. Subtract 2 from each term.
2. **14** is the missing term. Add 2.5 to each term.
3. **7.5** is the missing term. Divide each term by 2 to get the next term.
4. **720** is the missing term. The sequence follows the pattern
$(1 \times 1)(1 \times 2)(1 \times 2 \times 3)(1 \times 2 \times 3 \times 4)\ldots$
5. **21** is the missing term. Add 4 to find the next term.
6. (22, **30**) is the missing term. Add 8 to the first term to find the second term.
7. (30, **4**) is the missing term. Divide the first term by 10 and add 1 to find the second term.
8. (5, **25**) is the missing term. Square the first term to get the second term.
9. The temperatures drops 3° from 52° to 49° and from 49° to 46°. If it drops at the same rate, the temperature drop at 3,000 feet would be 43° and at 4,000 feet would be 40° (followed by 37° and 34°). Continue to fill in the table accordingly, as follows.

Temperature

0	1,000	2,000	3,000	4,000	5,000
52°	49°	46°	43°	40°	37°
6,000	7,000	8,000	9,000	10,000	
34°	31°	28°	25°	22°	

10. Multiply three times the x value, subtract 2, and that gives the y value. The rule is y equals three times $x - 2$, so that the equation is $y = 3x - 2$. Substitute 13 for x:
$$y = 3(13) - 2 = 39 - 2 = 37$$
The capsule will be at position (13, 37).

Estimation Problems, page 154

1. Round all the scores and add the rounded scores.
$90 + 100 + 90 + 90 + 100 + 90 = 560$
Divide by the number of scores.
$560 \div 6 = 93.3$
93 is a reasonable estimate of the average.

2. Round the lengths and add the rounded lengths.
$10 + 20 + 20 + 20 = 70$
70 feet is a reasonable estimate of the amount of wood needed.

3. Round the number of dozens to the nearest 10.
Divide the rounded numbers.
$$\frac{170}{10} = 17$$
17 is a reasonable estimate of the number of batches needed.

4. Round the number of minutes and number of days to the nearest 10.
Multiply the rounded numbers.
$50 \times 30 = 1,500$
Divide to find hours.
$1,500 \div 60 = 25$
25 is a reasonable estimate of the number of hours.

Chart Problems, page 155

1. Add two proportions for truck.
$0.18 + 0.16 = 0.34$
The probability that a package picked at random was sent by truck is 34%.

2. Add the three proportions for 5 pounds and over.
$0.07 + 0.34 + 0.18 = 0.59$

3. The proportion for Air Express over 5 pounds is 0.07.

4. Add proportions for under 5 pounds by Air Express and under 5 pounds by truck.

$0.23 + 0.16 = 0.39$

Frequency Table Problems, page 156

1. Add the percentiles of the intervals below 70.

$2 + 8 = 10$

10% of the students scored below 70.

2. The median score is in the interval 80–89.

3. The percent of scores from 80 to 100 is
$38 + 13 = 51$

51% of the students scored from 80 to 100.

4. The question is asking for the number of scores that are above 50. The percentile rank next to 50 is 39. So 39% of the scores are below 50; 39% failed. $100 - 39 = 61$. 61% passed.

5. The percent of the scores from 20 to 50 is the percentile rank for 50, less the percentile rank for 20.

$39 - 2 = 37$

37% of the scores are from 20 to 50.

Formula Problems, page 157

1. $P =$ about \$16.88
2. $s = 41$ mph
3. $V = \$8,400$
4. $A = 11$

Pythagorean Theorem Problems, page 158

1.

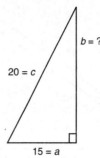

$a^2 + b^2 = c^2$
$(15)^2 + b^2 = (20)^2$
$225 + b^2 = 400$
$b^2 = 400 - 225 = 175$
$b =$ approximately 13.2 ft.

2.

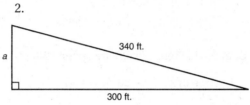

$a^2 + b^2 = c^2$
$a^2 + (300)^2 = (340)^2$
$a^2 = 115,600 - 90,000 = 25,600$
$a = 160$ ft
The ramp is 160 feet high.

3.

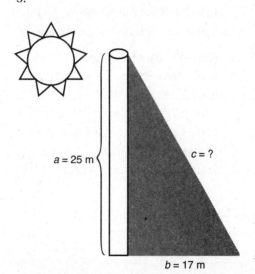

$a^2 + b^2 = c^2$
$(25)^2 + (17)^2 = c^2$
$625 + 289 = c^2$
$c^2 = 914$, $c =$ approximately 30.2 m.

4.

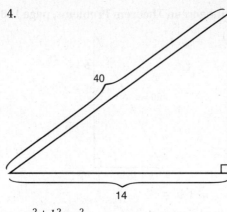

40

14

$a^2 + b^2 = c^2$
$(14)^2 + b^2 = (40)^2$
$196 + b^2 = 1,600$
$b^2 = 1,404$
$b =$ approximately 37.5
The height is about 37.5 feet.

Geometric Figure Problems, page 160

1. Area of half the circle ($r = 4$)

   $\frac{1}{2}(3.14)(16) = (3.14)(8)$ is

   approximately 25.12 sq ft
   Area of the rectangle
   $12 \times 8 = 96$ sq ft
   Area of the entire figure
   $25.12 + 96 = 121.12$ sq ft
   $121.12 \div 35$ is approximately 3.5 pints
   Round up. You need 4 pints of paint.

2. Find the area of the roofs.
   Roof 1: $115 \times 65 = 7,475$ sq ft
   Roof 2: $112 \times 65 = 7,280$ sq ft
   Roof 3: $72 \times 52 = \underline{3,744}$ sq ft
   TOTAL $ 18,499$ sq ft
   $18,499 \div 1,200 = 15.4$
   Round up. You need 16 bushels.

3. Volume of a brick $= lwh$
   $V = 2 \times 4 \times 8 = 64$ in^3
   8×64 in$^3 = 512$ in^3

4. Volume of a cone $= \frac{1}{3}\pi r^2 h$

   $134 \approx \frac{1}{3}(3.14)(4)^2 h$

   $134 \approx 16.7 h$
   $h \approx 8$ cm

5. Volume of a sphere $= \frac{4}{3}\pi r^3$

   $V = \frac{4}{3}(3.14)(274.6)$

   $V = 1149.76$ in^3

6. Volume of a rectangular solid $= lwh$
   $1920 = (16)(12) w$
   $1920 = 192 w$
   $w = 10$
   Shaded area $= 12 \times 10 = 120$ m^2

Interpreting Remainder Problems, page 161

1. 5 pounds
2. 34 bags
3. 33 bags

1. **(D)** $(180 - 90) \div 2 = 45°$. There is a total of 180° in a triangle. If it is an isosceles right triangle, that means one angle is 90° and the other two angles are equivalent.

2. **(B)** 25% of $48 = $12
   $48 − $12 = $36.

3. **(E)** Focus on point B. Recall that a shift up moves the y-coordinate and a shift right moves the x-coordinate. Shifting up 3 units from $y = -2$ takes you to $y = 1$. Shifting right 3 units from $x = -2$ takes you to $x = 4$. Write the result as an (x, y) ordered pair (4, 1).

4. **(B)** The probability of rolling a "5" is $\frac{1}{6}$, regardless of what happened on previous rolls.

5. **(D)** An angle is not formed because point B and point C are not connected in this diagram.

6. **(D)** Divide the money by the cost of an item to find the number of items you can afford.

7. **(E)** Estimate. 32 hours is not twice 18 hours, so eliminate (B), (C), and (D). 32 hours is about 75% more than 18 hours. 75% more than $144 is about $250. Answer E must be correct.

8. **(A)** $\pi(3^2 \times 2) - \pi(2^2 \times 4) = (9 \times 2 - 4 \times 4)\pi = 2\pi$.

9. **(A)** The discount is the regular price less the sale price.

10. **(C)** $80 − $5 = $75
    $75 \div $0.75 = 100$.

11. **(A)** The fraction farthest from $\frac{1}{2}$ will be closest to 0 or closest to 1. The answer is $\frac{1}{12}$ from 0. The other answers are greater than $\frac{1}{2}$ but farther than $\frac{1}{12}$ from 1.

12. **(E)** 25 centimeters is about 10 inches, a reasonable length for a notebook.

13. **(B)** The total spent was $100. Retail was $20. $20 \div 100 = .2 = 20\%$.

14. **(C)** $250 − .4 \times 250 = 150$. 30 out of $150 = 30 \div 150 = .2 = 20\%$.

15. **(E)** $1,000 + $250 = $1,250$, needed to make $1,000.
    $1,250 \div $5 = 250$
    $250 \times 6 = 1,500$ tickets

16. **(D)** $5.3 \times 10^4 = 53,000$. 0.0053 needs to have the decimal moved right 7 places.

17. **(A)** Complementary angles total 90°, the number of degrees in this right angle.

18. **(D)** $100\% − 94\% = 6\%$ (Midwest). Northeast = 30%. $6\% \times 5 = 30\%$.

19. **(E)** $\frac{1}{2} + \frac{1}{3} + \frac{3}{8} = \frac{12}{24} + \frac{8}{24} + \frac{3}{8} = \frac{27}{24} = 1\frac{5}{24}$.

20. **(E)** Focus on point A. Recall that a shift left moves the x-coordinate and a shift down moves the y-coordinate. Shifting left 2 units from $x = -1$ takes you to $x = -3$. Shifting down 4 units from $y = -2$ takes you to $y = -8$. Write the result as an (x, y) ordered pair (−3, −8).

21. **(C)** Each angle must measure less than 90° to total 90°. Acute angles have measures less than 90°.

22. **(E)** We just know that since the beams are not parallel and do not point in the same direction, at least two of them may be skewed (not touch).

23. **(A)** There are 1,000 meters in a kilometer. So, divide 2,750 by 1,000 to find the answer.

24. **(D)** The difference in the two stock prices ($19\frac{5}{8} - 17\frac{7}{8}$) is $1\frac{3}{4}$ dollars or $1.75. Multiply $1.75 by 20 to find the answer.

25. **(C)** There are about (60) × (60) × (24) or 86,400 seconds in a day. There are about (365) × (86,400) or 31,536,000 seconds in a year. There are about (4) × (31,536,000) or 126,144,000 seconds in 4 years. Light travels about (186,000) × (126,144,000) or about 23,000,000,000,000 (23 trillion) miles in 4 years.

26. **(E)** 10 feet + 20% = 12 feet + 20% = 14.4 feet +
   first   second
   20% = 17.28 feet + 20% = 20.736 or
   third   fourth
   about 20.7 feet.

27. **(E)** The maximum length of the side of the cube is the shortest of the three dimensions. The volume of the cube is 8^3 or 512.

28. **(A)** The correct answer is 42. The pattern increases by 4, 6, 8, 10, and then 12.

29. **(C)** This formula gives the correct answer. The formula $H \times (H + 1)$ is equivalent to this formula.

30. **(E)** Round the quotient (10) to 11 to have room for all the people to go on the class trip.

31. **(C)** This process crosses off all numbers but the prime numbers. The numbers in answer C are all the prime numbers in the 80s.

32. **(B)** Multiply 0.23 and $2,600 to find $598.

33. **(E)** Divide $858 by $2,600 to find the percent (33 percent) needed for transportation. Subtract the current transportation percentage from 33 percent to find the percent to be taken from miscellaneous (33% − 24% = 9%). Subtract 11% − 9% = 2% to find the percent left for miscellaneous.

34. **(B)** Solve a proportion. $\frac{2}{9} = \frac{x}{1,350}$

   $9x = 2,700 \; x = 300$

35. **(B)** This question asks you to apply the Pythagorean theorem $a^2 + b^2 = c^2$.
   $$30^2 + 40^2 = 50^2$$
   The rope is 50 feet long.

36. **(B)** The number sentence corresponds to finding an average. To find an average, you add the terms and divide by the number of terms.

37. **(C)** Jan is either the same height as Lisa or she is taller than Lisa. Because Lisa is not the shortest player, Jan cannot be the shortest player.

38. **(C)** You can cross multiply to find that $\frac{5}{6} > \frac{3}{4}$, but that $\frac{5}{6} < \frac{7}{8}$. You can also use a calculator to find that $\frac{5}{6} = 0.833$, and see that this decimal comes between $\frac{3}{4} = 0.75$ and $\frac{7}{8} = 0.875$.

39. **(C)** Only points in this quadrant of the coordinate grid have a negative x-value and a negative y-value. Point C is closer to $(-2, -5)$ than point E, which might be closer to $(-5, -2)$.

40. **(C)** This is another calculator problem.
    Think of the percent equation.
    $85\% \times \square = 289$
    So, $\square = 289 \div 0.85$
    Divide 289 by 0.85 to find how many houses there were altogether.
    $289 \div 0.85 = 340$

41. **(D)** There are 60 seconds in a minute and 60 minutes in an hour. So there are $60 \times 60 = 3600$ seconds in an hour. $186,000 \times 3600$ is about how far light travels in an hour.

42. **(A)** Use your calculator to find this answer. Divide to find what percent \$624,000 is of \$2,600,000. $624,000 \div 2,600,000 = 0.24 = 24\%$. The town needs 24% for police, 2% more than in the pie chart. Take the 2% from sanitation, leaving 22% for sanitation.

43. **(B)** The probability that a "fair" penny will land heads up is always $\frac{1}{2}$ regardless of what has occurred on previous flips.

44. **(B)** Multiply x by 2 and then add 1. Some of the other choices work for individual values of x, but only this choice works for all the values of x.

45. **(E)** To find the area of a triangle, use the formula $A = \frac{1}{2}bh = 30$.

    To find the area of a parallelogram, use the formula $A = (bh) = 180$.
    Subtract: Area (parallelogram) $-$ Area (triangle) $=$ Area (shaded portion)
    $180 - 30 = 150$

46. **(B)** Use the order of operations to combine to simplest terms.
    $$2n + 3n^2 - 5n \times 3 - 6n^2 = 2n + 3n^2 - 15n - 6n^2 = -13n - 3n^2$$

47. **(C)** Use formula $P = 2.2K$
    $K = P \div 2.2$
    $K = 15.6/2.2$
    $K = 7.09$

48. **(D)** Rent represents 60% of the monthly expenses, greater than all the other expenses combined.

49. **(D)** The mode is the amount that occurs most often. Tampa, Tallahassee, and Jacksonville have graphs of almost identical heights and most likely represent the mode. None of the other answer choices lists cities with nearly matching graphs.

50. **(E)** There is a positive relationship between the test score and the number of years in math courses.

51. **(A, C)** Choice A. Complete the missing measurements on the figure as shown below. Then use the area formula $A = l \times w$ to find the larger area (15×20) and the smaller area (7×5). Add the two areas as shown in the answer.

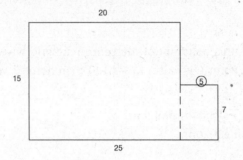

Choice C. Find that the area of the larger rectangle shown below is (25×15) and find the area of the "missing piece" is (5×8). Then subtract the area of the missing piece from the area of the larger rectangle as shown in the answer.

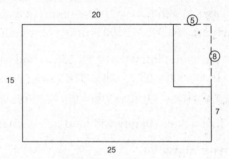

52. **(B, E)** Notice that 48 inches is 4 feet. Divide the area (57 square feet) by the width (4 feet). The result is 14.25 feet (14 feet, 3 inches). That means the length must be more than 14 feet, 3 inches (171 inches). Choice B is correct because 14 feet, 9 inches is greater than 14 feet, 3 inches. Choice E is correct because 175 inches is greater than 171 inches. Choice A is incorrect because 12 feet is less than 14 feet, 3 inches. Choice C is incorrect because 14 feet, 3 inches is not greater than 14 feet, 3 inches. Choice D is incorrect because 60 inches is less than 171 inches.

53. **(A, D)** Find the total number of students in each class. (A = 26, B = 28, C = 20, D = 17, E = 23). Calculate 60% of each class: A = 15.6, B = 16.8, C = 12, D = 10.2, E = 13.8. Next, find the sum of students from each class that scored 70% or higher. Compare this number to the 60% number for each class. If it is greater, it is the correct solution. Choice A is correct because 19 > 15.6. Choice B is incorrect because 14 < 16.8. Choice C is incorrect because 10 < 12. Choice D is correct because 11 > 10.2. Choice E is incorrect because 11 < 13.8.

54. **(2)** Follow these steps:

Substitute the given values for a and b.

$$\frac{\left(3^2 - 2^2\right)^3 + 3}{\left(2 + 2 \cdot 3\right)^2}$$

Compute inside the ( ).

$$\frac{(9-4)^3 + 3}{8^2} = \frac{5^3 + 3}{64}$$

Raise to the given powers and simplify.

$$\frac{125 + 3}{64} = \frac{128}{64} = 2$$

55. $\left(\dfrac{3}{2}\right)$ Do the computation in the denominator first.

$$\frac{\dfrac{1}{4}}{\dfrac{2}{3}-\dfrac{1}{2}}=\frac{\dfrac{1}{4}}{\dfrac{4}{6}-\dfrac{3}{6}}=\frac{\dfrac{1}{4}}{\dfrac{1}{6}}$$

Do the indicated division.

$$\frac{1}{4}\div\frac{1}{6}=\frac{1}{4}\times\frac{6}{1}$$

Simplify and multiply as indicated.

$$\frac{1}{\underset{2}{\cancel{4}}}\times\frac{\overset{3}{\cancel{6}}}{1}=\frac{3}{2}$$

56. $\left(\dfrac{8}{75}\right)$ Remove the ( ) applying the exponent to both the numerators and denominators of each factor.

$$\frac{8}{27}\cdot\frac{9}{25}$$

Simplify the fractions and multiply.

$$\frac{8}{\underset{3}{27}}\cdot\frac{\overset{1}{\cancel{9}}}{25}=\frac{8}{75}$$

Reading

7

---

56 Multiple-Choice Questions
85 Minutes

This computer-delivered test draws on a vast bank of items, which are all selected before you start the test. Tests vary in question type and difficulty.

There are 56 multiple-choice questions and 85 minutes to complete the test. That is about a minute and a half per question. Some of these questions may not count toward your final score. Do not try to figure out which ones they are. Treat every question as though it counts.

The primary item type is a passage followed by a question or questions that ask you to find the main idea or details, and to analyze the passage and draw inferences. A second item type is two passages on a single topic, followed by questions that ask you to compare and contrast the passages. Finally, you will see some items that involve tables or charts.

The sample items on pages 206–212 show you the types of questions you will encounter and give you a chance for further review before you take the practice tests.

USING THIS CHAPTER

This chapter prepares you to take the computer-delivered Core reading comprehension tests. Choose one of these approaches.

- **I WANT VOCABULARY AND READING HELP.** Review the entire chapter and take the targeted test at the end.
- **I JUST WANT READING HELP.** Read Strategies for Passing the Reading Test beginning on page 197. Take the targeted test at the end of the chapter.
- **I WANT TO PRACTICE READING ITEMS.** Take the targeted test at the end of the chapter.

You cannot read if you do not know the vocabulary. You do not have to know every word in the dictionary. Follow this reasonable approach to developing a good vocabulary for these tests.

CONTEXT CLUES

Many times you can figure out a word from its context. Look at these examples. Synonyms, antonyms, examples, or descriptions may help you figure out the word.

1. The woman's mind wandered as her two friends **prated** on. It really did not bother her though. In all the years she had known them, they had always <u>babbled</u> about their lives. It was almost comforting.
2. The wind **abated** in the late afternoon. Things were different yesterday when the wind had <u>picked up</u> toward the end of the day.
3. The argument with her boss had been her **Waterloo**. She wondered if the defeat suffered by Napoleon <u>at this famous place</u> had felt the same.
4. The events swept the politician into a **vortex** of controversy. The politician knew what it meant to be spun around like a toy boat in the <u>swirl of water</u> that swept down the bathtub drain.

Passage 1 gives a synonym for the unknown word. We can tell that *prated* means babbled. *Babbled* is used as a synonym of *prated* in the passage.

Passage 2 gives an antonym for the unknown word. We can tell that *abated* means slowed down or diminished because *picked up* is used as an antonym of *abated*.

Passage 3 gives a description of the unknown word. The description of Waterloo tells us that the word means defeat.

Passage 4 gives an example of the unknown word. The example of a *swirl of water* going down the bathtub drain gives us a good idea of what a *vortex* is.

ROOTS

A root is the basic element of a word. The root is usually related to the word's origin. Roots can often help you figure out the word's meaning. Here are some roots that may help you.

Root	Meaning	Examples
bio	life	biography, biology
circu	around	circumference, circulate
frac	break	fraction, refract
geo	earth	geology, geography
mal	bad	malicious, malcontent
matr, mater	mother	maternal, matron
neo	new	neonate, neoclassic
patr, pater	father	paternal, patron
spec	look	spectacles, specimen
tele	distant	telephone, television

PREFIXES

Prefixes are syllables that come at the beginning of a word. Prefixes usually have a standard meaning. They can often help you figure out the word's meaning. Here is a list of prefixes that may help you figure out a word.

Prefix	Meaning	Examples
a-	not	amoral, apolitical
il-, im-, ir-	not	illegitimate, immoral, irreversible
un-	not	unbearable, unknown
non-	not	nonbeliever, nonsense
ant-, anti-	against	antiwar, antidote
de-	opposite	defoliate, declaw
mis-	wrong	misstep, misdeed
ante-	before	antedate, antecedent
fore-	before	foretell, forecast
post-	after	postfight, postoperative
re-	again	refurbish, redo
super-	above	superior, superstar
sub-	below	subsonic, subpar

STRATEGIES FOR PASSING THE READING TEST

This section gives an integrated approach to answering the literal and figurative reading items on the computer-delivered Core.

You do not have to understand the entire passage. In fact, the most common error is to read the entire passage before reading the questions. Do not do that. It just wastes time. You only have to know enough to get the correct answer. Less than half, often less than 25 percent, of the details in a passage are needed to answer a question.

> A great way to develop a vocabulary is to read a paper every day and a news magazine every week, in addition to the other reading you are doing. There are also several inexpensive books, including *1,100 Words You Need to Know* and *Pocket Guide to Vocabulary* from Barron's, which may help you develop your vocabulary further.

THE READING COMPREHENSION STUDY PLAN

All reading questions call for either literal or figurative responses. There are examples and tips for answering each type. Then you will learn about the five steps for taking the Core reading test.

Next come passages and questions to try out. All the questions have explained answers. Do not skip anything. Do not look at the answers until you have answered all of the questions.

CORE READING QUESTION TYPES

This is how ETS classifies the three categories of reading items:

Key Ideas and Details

These questions usually ask for the stated main idea of a passage or about details in the passage.

Craft, Structure, and Language Skills

These questions are usually related to word or phrase meaning, the unstated purpose of a passage, the author's reason or purpose for writing the passage, or the general organization of the passage.

Integration of Knowledge and Ideas

These questions may ask you to draw an inference or implication or to identify the author's point of view, attitude, or reason for mentioning something. In addition, you will be asked about the meaning of a word in quotation, and to compare or contrast two paragraphs. The more difficult questions will ask about which listed statement would support or diminish the author's argument or would provide an alternate explanation.

It is not always easy to categorize questions. That is OK because there are really two categories of reading questions—literal comprehension and figurative comprehension. Literal questions typically ask directly about the passage. Figurative questions typically ask you to interpret, extend, and apply ideas in the passage. The test does not identify these categories.

> Let me repeat, do not begin by reading the passage in detail. In fact, that kind of careful reading will almost certainly get you into trouble. Only read in detail after you have read a question and you are looking for the answer. This section shows you how to do that.

Correct Answers

It all comes down to finding the correct answer. The correct answer will be the best choice available among the choices listed, even if there is a better answer. The correct answer will be based on the passage, not on something not in the passage that you may know is true or think is true.

Literal Comprehension

MAIN IDEA (MAIN PURPOSE)

These questions are the main focus of reading comprehension. Main idea and main purpose questions ask you to identify the topic of the passage or part of the passage, or the main reason the author wrote the passage or part of that passage.

Main idea questions often include the words "main idea":

Which of the following describes the main idea of the passage?

Main purpose questions also often include the words "primary purpose":

The primary purpose of this passage is . . .

Find the central idea of the passage to answer these questions. What was the author really trying to get at? Why did the author write the passage?

Some main ideas may not be directly stated in the passage. However, the main idea or purpose must be from the passage. It cannot be what you think the author might have in mind.

SUPPORTING DETAILS

Authors give details to support the main idea. These details may be facts, opinions, experiences, or discussions.

Here are some examples of supporting details questions:

Which of the following does the author use to support the main idea in the passage?

Which of the following details is not found in this passage?

To explain [a statement] in the passage the author writes. . .

When the passage describes the outcomes of [an event] it mentions. . .

The answer choices will usually include statements or summaries of statements found in the passage. Read the question carefully to be sure what details are asked for.

Answer choices frequently include details you know to be true but that are not found in the passage. Eliminate those. The correct answer will be found in the passage.

VOCABULARY QUESTIONS

A passage has lots of words and phrases. Vocabulary questions typically ask you to show that you know the meaning of one of those words or phrases.

Here are some examples of vocabulary questions:

Which of the following words is a synonym for (the word) in line 99 of the passage?

Which of the following gives the best definition of (word) in line 99 of the passage?

All of the following gives the best meaning for the (phrase/word) in line 99 EXCEPT. . .

The vocabulary section of this book (beginning on page 196) gives a vocabulary review. It also includes ways to identify words from their context. A word in context is not always a strict dictionary definition. Word meaning can be literal or figurative.

Here is an easy example. The author writes, "Stand up for what you believe in." The question asks about the meaning of "stand up." One of the answer choices is (A) "stand up straight." Another choice is (B) "take a position." The main dictionary definition is "stand up straight." However, that is not what these words mean in context. The words mean "take a position." That is the correct answer.

That is not to say that a literal definition will always be wrong, or often wrong. It does mean that you should think about the word's meaning in context.

ORGANIZATION

These questions ask you about the way a passage or part of a passage is organized. It sounds hard, but the answer choices are just plain language descriptions. It is usually more a matter of common sense than any specialized knowledge.

Organization questions are just what you would think they would be:

Which of the following choices best describes the way the passage is organized?

There may be some moderately difficult words in the choices for these types of questions. Use the vocabulary skills you will learn in this chapter to tackle those words if they occur.

Figurative Comprehension

INFERENCE

An inference question asks you to identify something that can be reasonably implied or inferred from a passage. The answers to inference questions will not be directly stated in the passage.

Inference questions look like this:

Which choice below can be inferred from this passage?

What can be inferred about [name or event] from lines ___-___ in the passage?

Test writers try to write five choices for which only one is clearly the "most correct" inference. They usually do a good job. However, sometimes other apparently reasonable inferences appear.

> Choose an inference based on the passage. Do not make a choice just because it is true—you will find choices like that. Do not make a choice because it has some other emotional appeal. The inference has to be based on information in the passage.

EVALUATE SUPPORTING DETAILS

Some of these questions may ask you to decide whether details support the main idea. Other times, the questions introduce other details and ask you to determine if they would strengthen or weaken the author's argument.

Evaluating supporting details questions look like this:

Which of the following statements, if added to the passage, would best support (weaken) the author's argument?

Which of the following information would be needed to fully support the author's claim?

A main idea, a position, or a claim needs appropriate support from details. Think about the author's claim or argument. Think about what in the argument convinces you, and about what information is questionable or missing.

Strengthening or weakening an argument does not mean to prove or disprove that argument. Here is an example:

An author writes, "All my shoes are black." Then someone says, "Did I see you wearing brown shoes the other day?" The second statement weakens the first. It does not disprove it. The second statement may be wrong, or it may be meant as a joke, or lots of other things. However, the second statement is enough to make us think and enough to weaken the author's statement.

ATTITUDE QUESTIONS

By attitude, these questions mean a position or point of view the author holds that is revealed in a passage. Author's tone may also be used to describe these questions. These questions typically have one-word answers. The idea is to figure out how someone feels about something and then find the vocabulary word that matches the feeling.

Attitude questions are what you would expect.

What is the author's attitude about [some idea or fact]?

Look for a statement in the passage that includes judgment terms such as "bad," "good," "well-thought-out," "I guess," or "questionable," and the like.

MAKING PREDICTIONS

These questions ask you to identify predictions that can be made from the information in the passage. A prediction is a statement about something that will happen. The questions may also ask you to identify something that a person may say or do based on information in the passage.

Here is an example that could lead to a prediction:

Derek loves to go out on his boat, but he did not go out yesterday because the waves were over three feet. It is reasonable to predict that Derek would not go out on his boat in the future if the waves were over three feet.

Making predictions questions look like this:

Which of the statements below is the author most likely to agree with?

Do not choose an answer because it seems correct (it may be the correct answer to a different question) or because you agree with it. The answer must be predictable from information in the passage.

> Making a prediction is not the same as saying you are absolutely sure. In the example, Derek might go out on the boat in special circumstances. The waves might be over three feet, but a friend might be out on a boat and need help. It is possible that Derek would go out on his boat under those circumstances. However, we would not predict that based on the information in the passage.

DRAWING CONCLUSIONS

These questions ask you to assume that everything in the passage is correct and then to draw a conclusion from that information. Drawing a conclusion usually means drawing a logical conclusion based on two pieces of information. These two pieces of information may not appear near one another in the passage.

Here is a simple example that could lead to a conclusion:

Whenever Liz meets someone she knows she always talks to him or her. (The first bit of information means talking.) Later we could read that when Liz talks to someone she knows she always shakes his or her hand.

We can conclude that if Liz met someone she knows she would shake his or her hand. We can't conclude that if she shakes hands with someone, then she knows him or her. That conclusion is not supported by the passage.

Drawing conclusions questions look like this:

> **Based on the information in the passage, which of the following is the most reasonable conclusion?**

Do not choose an answer just because it is correct or because you agree with it. The answer must flow logically from the information in the passage.

STEPS FOR ANSWERING READING QUESTIONS

This section describes five steps for answering any Core reading question. You will learn how to apply the steps, and then you will see the steps applied to sample passages.

Reading About Reading

Reading seems to be a natural process. Reading about reading and about steps to taking reading tests can seem contrived and confusing. However, we know that these steps and techniques work. Once you apply the steps to the practice exercises, your reading ability and scores will improve.

FIVE STEPS TO TAKING A READING TEST

During a reading test follow these steps:

STEP 1 Skim to find the topic of each paragraph.

STEP 2 Read the questions and the answers.

STEP 3 Identify the question type.

STEP 4 Eliminate incorrect answers.

STEP 5 Scan the details to find the answer.

STEP 1 **Skim to Find the Topic of Each Paragraph**

Your first job is to find the topic of each paragraph. The topic is what a paragraph or passage is about.

The topic of a paragraph is usually found in the first and last sentences. Read the first and last sentences just enough to find the topic. Use scrap paper for the Computer-Delivered Core.

READING SENTENCES

Every sentence has a subject that tells what the sentence is about. The sentence also has a verb that tells what the subject is doing or links the subject to the complement. The sentence may also contain a complement that receives the action or describes what is being said about the subject. The words underlined in the following examples are the ones you would focus on as you preview.

1. The famous educator John Dewey founded an educational movement called progressive education.

2. Sad to say, we have learned American school children of all ages are poorly nourished.

You may occasionally encounter a paragraph or passage in which the topic can't be summarized from the first and last sentences. This type of paragraph usually contains factual information. If this happens, you will have to skim the entire paragraph.

STEP 2 **Read the Questions and the Answers**

Now read the questions—one at a time. Read the answers for the question you are working on. Be sure that you understand what each question and its answers mean.

Before you answer a question, be sure you know whether it is asking for a fact or an inference. If the question asks for a fact, the correct answer will identify a main idea or supporting detail. The correct answer may also identify a cause and effect relationship among ideas or be a paraphrase or summary of parts of the passage. Look for these.

If the question asks for an inference, the correct answer will identify the author's purpose, assumptions, or attitude, and the difference between fact and the author's opinion. Look for these elements.

STEP 3 **Identify the Question Type**

Do your best to identify the question type. It will really help on the test.

STEP 4 **Eliminate Incorrect Answers**

Read the answers and eliminate the ones that you absolutely know are incorrect. Read the answers literally. Look for words such as *always, never, must, all.* If you can find a single exception to this type of sweeping statement, then the answer cannot be correct. Eliminate it.

STEP 5 **Scan the Details to Find the Answer**

Once you have eliminated answers, compare the other answers to the passage. When you find the answer that is confirmed by the passage—stop. That is your answer choice. Follow these other suggestions for finding the correct answer.

Who Wrote This Answer?

People who write tests go to great lengths to choose a correct answer that cannot be questioned. That is what they get paid for. They are not paid to write answers that have a higher meaning or include great truths.

Test writers want to be asked to write questions and answers again. They want to avoid valid complaints from test takers like you who raise legitimate concerns about their answers.

Try to think like the person who wrote the test.

A Vague Answer Can Be Correct

How can a person write a vague answer that is correct? Think of it this way. If I wrote that a person is 6 feet 5 inches tall, you could get out a tape measure to check my facts. Since I was very specific, you are more likely to be able to prove me wrong.

On the other hand, if I write that the same person is over 6 feet tall you would be hard pressed to find fault with my statement. So my vague statement was hard to argue with. If the person in question is near 6 feet 5 inches tall, then my vague answer is most likely to be the correct one.

Do not choose an answer just because it seems more detailed or specific. A vague answer may just as likely be correct.

APPLYING THE STEPS

Let's apply the five steps to this passage and items 1 and 2.

> Many vocational high schools in the United States give off-site work experience to their students. Students usually work in local businesses part of the school day and attend high school the other part. These programs have made American
>
> *Line* vocational schools world leaders in making job experience available to teenage
> *(5)* students.

1. According to this paragraph, American vocational high schools are world leaders in making job experience available to teenage students because they

   (A) have students attend school only part of the day.
   (B) were quick to move their students to schools off-site.
   (C) require students to work before they can attend the school.
   (D) involve their students in cooperative education programs.
   (E) involve their students in after-school part time work.

STEP 1 Skim to find the topic of each paragraph. Both the first and last sentences tell us that the topic is vocational schools and work experience.

STEP 2 Read the questions and the answers. Why are American vocational education high schools the world leaders in offering job experience?

STEP 3 Identify the question type. This is a details question.

STEP 4 Eliminate incorrect answers. Answer (C) is obviously wrong. It has to do with work before high school. Answer (B) is also incorrect. This has to do with attending school off-site. This leaves answers (A), (D), and (E).

STEP 5 Scan the details to find the answer. Scan the details and find that parts of answer (A) are found in the passage. In answer (D) you have to know that cooperative education is another name for off-site work during school. There is no reference to the after-school work found in answer (E).

It is down to answer (A) or answer (D). But answer (A) contains only part of the reason that vocational education high schools have gained such acclaim. Answer (D) is the correct answer.

Here's how to apply the steps to the following passage.

Problem Solving

Problem solving has become the main focus of mathematics learning. Students learn problem-solving strategies and then apply them to problems. Many tests now focus on problem solving and limit the number of computational problems. The problem-solving movement is traced to George Polya who wrote several problem-solving books for high school teachers.

Problem Solving Strategies

Problem-solving strategies include guess and check, draw a diagram, and make a list. Many of the strategies are taught as skills, which inhibits flexible and creative thinking. Problems in textbooks can also limit the power of the strategies. However, the problem-solving movement will be with us for some time, and a number of the strategies are useful.

2. According to this passage, a difficulty with teaching problem-solving strategies is:

   Ⓐ The strategies are too difficult for children.
   Ⓑ The strategies are taught as skills.
   Ⓒ The strategies are in textbooks.
   Ⓓ The strategies are part of a movement.
   Ⓔ Problem solving is for high school teachers.

STEP 1   Skim to find the topic of each paragraph. The topic of the first paragraph is problem solving. You find the topic in both the first and last sentences. Write the topic next to the paragraph. The topic for the second paragraph is problem-solving strategies. Write the topic next to the paragraph if you are taking the paper-delivered test.

Now look at the questions. If the question is about problem solving "in general" start looking in the first paragraph for the answer. If the question is about strategies, start looking in the second paragraph for the answer.

STEP 2   Read the questions and the answers. The answer will be a difficulty with teaching problem solving.

STEP 3   Identifying the question type. This is a details question.

STEP 4   Eliminate incorrect answers. Answer (A) cannot be right because difficulty is not mentioned in the passage. Choice (E) cannot be correct because it does not mention strategies at all. That leaves (B), (C), and (D) to consider.

STEP 5   Scan the details to find the answer. The question asks about strategies so look immediately to the second paragraph for the answer. The correct answer is (B). Choice (C) is not correct because the passage does not mention strategies in textbooks. There is no indication that (D) is correct.

The correct choice is (B).

Try Them Out

Here are passages with at least one of each question type. There are many examples of each question type, and you may see completely different examples on the Core you take.

Remember that you are looking for the best answer from among the ones listed, even if you can think of a better answer. Remember that the answer must be supported by the passage and that you should not pick an answer choice just because it is true or because you agree with it.

Apply the five steps. You can look back to remind yourself what question type it is. You cannot look ahead at the answers. Looking ahead at the answers will deny you important experiences, and it may well hurt your performance on the Core.

Cross off the answers you know are incorrect. Circle your choice of the correct answer.

Apply the five steps to these practice passages. Mark the letter of the correct answer. Follow the directions given below. The answers to these questions are found on pages 213–219. Do not look at the answers until you complete your work.

Read the following passage. After reading the passage, choose the best answer to each question from among the five choices. Answer all the questions following the passage on the basis of what is stated or implied in the passage.

Today's students have hand-held calculators that can graph one or even many equations. Students can even type in several equations and the calculator will "solve" them. This is the best way just to see a plotted graph quickly.

Line
(5)   This is the worst way to learn about graphing and equations. The calculator can't tell the students anything about the process of graphing and does not teach them how to plot a graph.

Left to this electronic graphing process, students will not have the hands-on experience needed to see the patterns and symmetry that characterize graphing and equations. They may become too dependent on the calculator and be unable to reason
(10)   effectively about equations and the process of graphing.

It may be true that graphing and solving equations is taught mechanically in some classrooms. There is also something to be said for these electronic devices, which give students the opportunity to try out several graphs and solutions quickly before deciding on a final solution.

(15)   For all their electronic accuracy and patience, these graphing calculators cannot replace the process of graphing and solving equations on your own. For mastery of equations and graphing comes not just from seeing the graph automatically displayed on a screen, but also comes from a hands-on involvement with graphing.

3.   The main idea of the passage is that:

   Ⓐ a child can be good at graphing equations only through hands-on experience.
   Ⓑ teaching approaches for graphing equations should be improved.
   Ⓒ accuracy and patience are the keys to effective graphing instruction.
   Ⓓ the new graphing calculators have limited ability to teach students about graphing.
   Ⓔ graphing calculators provide one of the best possible ways to practice graphing equations.

4. According to this passage, what negative impact will graphing calculators have on students who use them?

Ⓐ They will not have experience with four-function calculators.
Ⓑ They will become too dependent on the calculator.
Ⓒ They can quickly try out several graphs before coming up with a final answer.
Ⓓ They will get too much hands-on experience with calculators.
Ⓔ The teachers will not know how to use the electronic calculator because they use mechanical aids.

5. According to the passage, which of the following is a major drawback of the graphing calculator?

Ⓐ It graphs many equations with their solutions.
Ⓑ It does not give students hands-on experience with graphing.
Ⓒ It does not give students hands-on experience with calculators.
Ⓓ This electronic method interferes with the mechanical method.
Ⓔ It does not replace the patient teacher.

6. The passage includes information that would answer which of the following questions?

Ⓐ What are the shortcomings of graphing and solving equations as it sometimes takes place?
Ⓑ How many equations can you type into a graphing calculator?
Ⓒ What hands-on experience should students have as they learn about graphing equations?
Ⓓ What is the degree of accuracy and speed that can be attained by a graphing calculator?
Ⓔ What level of ability is needed to show mastery of equations and graphing?

7. The description of a graphing calculator found in this passage tells about which of the following?
Select all that apply.

Ⓐ The equations that can be graphed
Ⓑ The approximate size of the calculator
Ⓒ The advantages of the graphing calculator

On July 2, 1937, during her famed journey across
the Pacific Ocean to complete flying around the
world, noted aviator Amelia Earhart disappeared.

Line Speculation remains about the cause and validity of
(5) her elusive disappearance, and Earhart's whereabouts
remain a mystery. As one of the first female aviators
to attempt an around-the-world flight, Earhart
solidified her reputation as one of the most daring
women of her day. Having achieved a series of
(10) record-breaking flights—such as surpassing the
women's altitude record of 14,000 feet in 1922
and venturing solo across the Atlantic Ocean
in 1932—this trailblazer not only paved the way
for women aviators but advocated independence,
(15) self-reliance, and equal rights for all women.

Billed as the "First Lady of the Air" or "Lady Lindy"
(Charles A. Lindbergh's female counterpart),
Earhart challenged gender barriers and influenced
women's position in the nascent aviation industry.
(20) She was a founding member and president of the
Ninety-Nines, an international organization of
women pilots. In 1932, after completing her solo
flight across the Atlantic Ocean, President Herbert
Hoover presented Earhart with the National
(25) Geographic Society's gold medal, an honor never
before bestowed to a woman. She was also the
first woman to receive the National Aeronautical
Association's honorary membership.

8. Which of the following is most likely an assumption made by the author of this passage?

   (A) Amelia Earhart was an American spy captured by Japanese forces.
   (B) Charles Lindbergh would not have disappeared had he been the pilot on this mission.
   (C) Amelia Earhart's daring nature caused her to crash on her flight.
   (D) Amelia Earhart may not have died when she disappeared.
   (E) Amelia Earhart may have flown too high and passed out, leading to her disappearance.

9. Which of the following statements, if added to the passage, would weaken the author's statement that Amelia Earhart's whereabouts are unknown?

Ⓒ A strong storm was reported by a ship along the flight route that Amelia Earhart was following.

Ⓓ The last person to see Amelia Earhart's plane, a Lockheed Vega, reported that the plane seemed very heavy as it lifted off.

Ⓔ A search pilot reported signs of recent human habitation on a deserted island along the flight route that Amelia Earhart took.

Ⓕ Further research on the radio in Amelia Earhart's plane revealed that all the radios in that version of the Lockheed Vega often failed.

Ⓖ Fred Noonan, a noted aviator and navigator, was with Amelia Earhart as she made this flight in the Pacific Ocean.

10. The author's attitude toward Amelia Earhart can best be described as

Ⓒ condescending.

Ⓓ reverential.

Ⓔ unsettled.

Ⓕ abhorrent.

Ⓖ impartial.

11. This passage indicates that Earhart would most likely agree with which of the following?

Ⓒ Good planning is the secret to any successful endeavor.

Ⓓ Experience is the quality that is most likely to serve you well in times of trouble.

Ⓔ Life is full of unexpected events and outcomes.

Ⓕ The recognition of America's leaders is the best reward for effort.

Ⓖ In this life, a woman is as capable of success and achievement as any man.

———————————

USE THIS PASSAGE TO ANSWER ITEMS 12–18.

Thousands of different types of rocks and minerals have been found on Earth. Most rocks at the Earth's surface are formed from only eight elements (oxygen,
Line silicon, aluminum, iron, magnesium, calcium, potassium,
(5) and sodium), but these elements are combined in a number of ways to make rocks that are very different.

Rocks are continually changing. Wind and water wear them down and carry bits of rock away; the tiny particles accumulate in a lake or ocean and harden into rock again.
(10) Scientists say the oldest rock ever found is more than 3.9 billion years old. The Earth itself is at least 4.5 billion years old, but rocks from the beginning of Earth's history have changed so much from their original form that they have become new kinds of rock.

(15)   Rock-forming and rock-destroying processes have been
           active for billions of years. Today, in the Guadalupe
           Mountains of western Texas, you find limestone, a
           sedimentary rock, that was a coral reef in a tropical sea
           about 250 million years ago. Half Dome in Yosemite
(20)   Valley, California, about 8,800 feet above sea level, is
           composed of quartz monzonite, an igneous rock that
           solidified several thousand feet within the Earth. A
           simple rock collection captures the enormous sweep
           of the history of our planet.

12.   What is the main purpose of this passage?

      Ⓐ To provide information that rocks are continually changing
      Ⓑ To emphasize that the Earth is made of rock from the tallest mountains to the
          floor of the deepest ocean
      Ⓒ To examine that there are thousands of different types of rocks and minerals
          that have been found on Earth
      Ⓓ To prove that in a simple rock collection of a few dozen samples, one can
          capture an enormous sweep of the history of our planet and the process that
          formed it
      Ⓔ To provide information on the oldest rock that has ever been found more than
          3.9 billion years ago

13.   Which of the following words or phrases is the best substitute for the word *accumulate*
      in line 9?

      Ⓐ Disperse
      Ⓑ Renew
      Ⓒ Break down
      Ⓓ Gather
      Ⓔ Float

14.   According to the passage, most rocks at the Earth's surface are formed from

      Ⓐ oxygen, silicon, calcium, and potassium.
      Ⓑ aluminum, iron, and magnesium.
      Ⓒ one of eight elements.
      Ⓓ elements combined in a number of ways.
      Ⓔ what were once coral reefs.

15. What is the author's reason for mentioning that rocks are continually changing?

    Ⓐ To make the reading more technical
    Ⓑ To provide a visual description
    Ⓒ To provide the reader with a physical description of rocks
    Ⓓ To allow the reader to have a clearer understanding about the formation of rocks
    Ⓔ To provide information to the reader as to why all rocks look different

16. Which of the following is the best description of the organization of this passage?

    Ⓐ An overall description is followed by some specific examples.
    Ⓑ A discussion of one topic ends up with a discussion of an entirely different topic.
    Ⓒ Specific examples are given followed by an explanation of those examples.
    Ⓓ A significant question is raised followed by possible answers to that question.
    Ⓔ A theory is expressed and then examples and counterexamples of that theory are presented.

17. It can be reasonably inferred from the passage that the author

    Ⓐ believes only what the author can personally observe.
    Ⓑ is open to accepting theories presented by others.
    Ⓒ believes science is a mixture of fact and fiction.
    Ⓓ knows how the Earth itself was created.
    Ⓔ has an advanced degree in geology.

18. Which of the following statements from the paragraph is most convincingly an opinion as opposed to a fact?

    Ⓐ Thousands of different types of rocks and minerals have been found on Earth.
    Ⓑ Today, in the Guadalupe Mountains of western Texas you find limestone, a sedimentary rock, that was a coral reef in a tropical sea about 250 million years ago.
    Ⓒ Wind and water wear them down and carry bits of rock away; the tiny particles accumulate in a lake or ocean and again harden into rock.
    Ⓓ The Earth itself is at least 4.5 billion years old.
    Ⓔ A simple rock collection captures the enormous sweep of the history of our planet.

The potential for instruction provided by cable television
in the classroom is eclipsed by the number of
educational practitioners who remain uninformed
Line about the concept or who lack proficiency in the
(5) use of protocols and strategies necessary to
optimize its benefits. Teachers, trainers, and
educational administrators nationwide would
benefit from structured opportunities, rather
than trial and error, to learn how to maximize
(10) the potential of the medium. Cable television in the
classroom can introduce real events into
instruction by reporting the news from a
perspective with which young people are
familiar. Broadcasts received by television
(15) satellite can present issues as opportunities in
which young people can play an active role,
rather than as overwhelming problems no one
can solve. By incorporating current events and
televised symposia learners are exposed to
(20) perspectives beyond their teacher's own view
and can explore truth without sensationalism
or condescension. Thus cable television access
in the classroom allows learners to make informed
judgments about the content under study.

19. Which of the following conclusions can reasonably be drawn from this passage?

Ⓐ The potential for television in the classroom is more important than the
opposition against it.
Ⓑ A lack of understanding of appropriate strategies is the reason cable television in
the classroom has not been fully implemented.
Ⓒ The reason cable television in the classroom has not been accepted goes beyond
being informed about this instructional tool.
Ⓓ Cable television in the classroom ensures that the teacher's views will receive his
or her appropriate attention.
Ⓔ Learners have the ability and the capability, themselves, to make informed
decisions about any content area that might be under study.

20. If the analysis of this passage were applied to introducing a completely different type
of vacuum cleaner, one might say that success would most likely be a function of

Ⓐ effectiveness.
Ⓑ cost.
Ⓒ name.
Ⓓ size.
Ⓔ advertising.

Answers to Reading Questions Explained

Do not read this section until you have completed the practice passage. Here's how to apply the steps. Use this Step 1 for items 3–7. Complete your own Step 1 for the remaining passages.

STEP 1 Skim to find the topic of each paragraph. You may have written a topic next to each paragraph. Suggested topics are shown next to the following selection. Your topics do not have to be identical, but they should accurately reflect the paragraph's content.

Graphing Calculators

Today's students have hand-held calculators that can graph one or even many equations. Students can even type in several equations and the calculator will "solve" them. This is the best way to just see a plotted graph quickly.

Problem with Graphing Calculators

This is the worst way to learn about graphing and equations. The calculator can't tell the students anything about the process of graphing and does not teach them how to plot a graph.

Why it's a Problem

Left to this electronic graphing process, students will not have the hands-on experience needed to see the patterns and symmetry that characterize graphing and equations. They may become too dependent on the calculator and be unable to reason effectively about equations and the process of graphing.

Good Points

It may be true that graphing and solving equations is taught mechanically in some classrooms. There is also something to be said for these electronic devices, which give students the opportunity to try out several graphs and solutions quickly before deciding on a final solution.

For all their electronic accuracy and patience, these graphing calculators cannot replace the process of graphing and solving equations on your own. Mastery of equations and graphing comes not just from seeing the graph automatically displayed on a screen, but also from a hands-on involvement with graphing.

Apply Steps 2 through 5 to each of the questions.

3. **STEP 2** Read the question and the answers. You have to identify the main idea of the passage. This is a very common question on reading tests. Remember that the main idea is what the writer is trying to say or communicate in the passage.

   STEP 3 Identify the question type. This is a main idea question.

   STEP 4 Eliminate incorrect answers. Answers (B) and (C) are not correct. Answer (C) is not at all correct based on the passage. Even though (B) may be true, it does not reflect what the writer is trying to say in this passage. Answer (E) is also not the correct answer. You might be able to imply this answer from the paragraph, but it is not the main idea.

STEP 5 Scan the details to find the answer. As we review the details we see that both answer (A) and answer (D) are stated or implied in the passage. A scan of the details alone does not reveal which is the main idea. You must determine that on your own.

The correct answer is (D). The author certainly believes that (A) is true, but uses this point to support the main idea.

4. **STEP 2** Read the question and the answers. This is a straightforward comprehension question. What negative impact will calculators have on students who use them? The second and third paragraphs have topics related to problems with calculators. You will probably find the answer there.

STEP 3 Identify the question type. This is a main idea question.

STEP 4 Eliminate incorrect answers. Answer (E) is obviously incorrect. The question asks about students. This answer is about teachers. Answer (C) is not a negative impact of graphing calculators. Scan the details to find the correct answer from (A), (B), and (D).

STEP 5 Scan the details to find the answer. The only detail that matches the question is in paragraph 3. The author says that students may become too dependent on the calculators. That is the answer.

Answer (B) is the only correct choice.

5. **STEP 2** Read the question and the answers. This is another straightforward comprehension question. This question is somewhat different from Question 2. Notice that the question asks for a drawback of the calculator. It does not ask for something that is wrong with the calculator itself. The topics indicate that we will probably find the answer in paragraph 1 or paragraph 2.

STEP 3 Identify the question type. This is a details question.

STEP 4 Eliminate incorrect answers. Answer (C) is obviously wrong. Graphing calculators do give students hands-on experience with calculators. Be careful! It is easy to mix up (C) with (B). Answer (A) is a strength of the calculator and is also incorrect. Now move on to the details.

STEP 5 Scan the details to find the answer. Choices (B), (D), and (E) remain. The details in paragraph 2 reveal that the correct answer is (B).

Answer (B) is the only absolutely correct answer.

6. **STEP 2** Read the question and the answers. This is yet another type of reading comprehension question. You are asked to identify the questions that could be answered from the passage.

STEP 3 Identify the question type. This is a details question.

STEP 4 Eliminate incorrect answers. Choices (B), (D), and (E) are not correct. None of this information is included in the passage. This is not to say that these questions, particularly (E), are not important. Rather it means that the answers to these questions are not found in this passage.

STEP 5 Scan the details to find the answer. Both (A) and (C) are discussed in the passage. However, a scan of the details reveals that the answer to (C) is not found in the passage. The passage mentions hands-on experience, but it does not mention what types of hands-on experience students should have. There is an answer for (A). Graphing is taught mechanically in some classrooms.

Answer (A) is the correct answer. This is the only question that can be answered from the passage. The answer is not related to the writer's main idea, and this may make it more difficult to answer.

7. **STEP 2** Read the question and the answers. This is another classic type of reading comprehension question. You are given several choices. You must decide which combination of these choices is the absolutely correct answer.

STEP 3 Identify the question type. This is a details question.

STEP 4 Eliminate incorrect answers. If you can determine that A, for example, is not addressed in the passage, you can eliminate it.

STEP 5 Scan the details to find which of the original three statements is (are) true.

> [A] No, there is no description of which equations can be graphed.
> [B] Yes, paragraph 1 mentions that the calculators are hand-held.
> [C] Yes, paragraph 4 mentions the advantages.

Both B and C are correct.

8. **STEP 2** Read the question and the answers. You have to identify an assumption.

STEP 3 Identify the question type. This is an assumption question.

STEP 4 Eliminate incorrect answers. Always try to eliminate at least one answer. Eliminate (A). There is nothing here at all about this assumption.

STEP 5 Scan the details to find the answer. (D) is the correct answer. The author assumes that Amelia Earhart may not have died when she disappeared. The author never states it, but the author questions the validity of her disappearance and calls her whereabouts a mystery. (A) This choice was eliminated even though this is a popular theory among some people. But there is no mention of this assumption in this passage. (B) There is nothing to indicate anything about Lindbergh, except for a nickname for Earhart. (C) and (E) are incorrect because there is nothing in the passage to indicate any reason for her disappearance.

9. **STEP 2** Read the question and the answers. You have to find the statement that would weaken the author's argument that Earhart's whereabouts are unknown. Remember weaken does not mean disprove.

STEP 3 Identify the question type. This is a question about evaluating supporting details.

STEP 4 Eliminate incorrect answers. Eliminate (B) and (D) because each contains information about why Earhart's plane may have encountered trouble but not about her whereabouts.

STEP 5 Scan the details to find the answer. (C) The reports of human habitation on a deserted island is the only statement that would weaken that argument, although it would not by itself disprove the statement. The other statements are incorrect: (A) A strong storm, (B) a heavy plane, (D) a malfunctioning radio, and (E) a second member of her crew do not provide any information about her whereabouts. Do not be tempted by the specific information about Earhart's plane found in choices (B) and (D).

10. **STEP 2** Read the question and the answers. You have to understand how the author feels about Earhart.

STEP 3 Identify the question type. This is an attitude question—it says it is.

STEP 4 Eliminate incorrect answers. Eliminate (D) abhorrent. It is a negative word and the author thinks the world of Earhart.

STEP 5 Scan the details to find the answer. Choice (B) is correct. Reverential means to honor and respect. That is obviously how the author feels toward her. Choice (A) is incorrect because condescending means to look down on, someone or something. Choice (C) is incorrect because the author was settled in his opinion of Earhart. Choice (D) was eliminated. Abhorrent means to have strong negative feelings. (E) is incorrect because impartial means to have no strong views about someone. This author had very positive feelings about Earhart.

11. **STEP 2** Read the question and the answers. You have to identify what Earhart would say about something.

STEP 3 Identify the question type. This is a prediction question.

STEP 4 Eliminate incorrect answers. Eliminate (D). This passage is mainly about Earhart's disappearance, not about recognition or rewards.

STEP 5 Scan the details to find the answer. Choice (C) is correct. This passage is about Earhart's disappearance, and if she were able to draw anything from that, it would be the uncertainty of life. The other choices are incorrect because none of them meant anything on that fateful day that she likely crashed into the Pacific Ocean. Be careful of the emotional appeal of choice (E). This is true, but it is not what we would predict from this passage.

12. **STEP 2** Read the question and the answers. You have to identify which answer best summarizes the main purpose of the passage. Why was it written? Save lots of time by reading the question and answers before looking at the details in the passage.

STEP 3 Identify the question type. This is a main purpose question.

STEP 4 Eliminate incorrect answers. Answer (D) is clearly wrong. The main purpose is not about rock collections. You might be able to eliminate more, but you can be sure of this one. If you had to guess, eliminating just this one answer would increase the odds that you will guess correctly.

STEP 5 Scan the details to find the answer. The answer to this question is (C) because most of the passage examines that there are thousands of different types of rocks and minerals that have been found on Earth. (A) is incorrect because the passage was not written primarily to discuss that rocks continually change. (B) and (E) are incorrect because each states facts found in the passage that are too detailed to be the main purpose.

13. (STEP 2) Read the question and the answers. You have to determine the meaning of a word, perhaps from the context.

(STEP 3) Identify the question type. This is a vocabulary question.

(STEP 4) Eliminate incorrect answers. Eliminate (C) because "accumulate" does not mean "break down."

(STEP 5) Scan the details to find the answer. (D) is the correct answer. If you accumulate something, you gather it. You can actually tell from the context that (A) is incorrect because disperse means the opposite of accumulate. It is an antonym. (B) is incorrect because bits of rock do not renew themselves; rather they combine with other bits of rock. (C) was eliminated because break down also means the opposite of accumulate. The rocks broke down before they accumulated. (E) is incorrect because floating is not related to accumulating. Some of the bits of rock may have floated on the surface of a lake when they first landed there, but that had nothing to do with the accumulation.

14. (STEP 2) Read the question and the answers. You have to find information in the passage.

(STEP 3) Identify the question type. This is a question about details.

(STEP 4) Eliminate incorrect answers. Eliminate (A) and (B) because each of them is just a partial list of the elements from which most rocks are formed. Correctly eliminating two choices means you would have a one-third chance of guessing correctly instead of a one-fifth chance. That is a big difference if you had to guess.

(STEP 5) Scan the details to find the answer. The correct answer is (D), because the passage states that elements are combined in a number of ways to form rocks. (A) and (B) were eliminated because they do not list all of the eight elements from the passage. (C) is incorrect because the passage says that rocks are a combination of elements. (E) is incorrect because a rock may have been formed from a coral reef, but that is not the way most rocks near the Earth's surface were formed.

15. (STEP 2) Read the question and the answers. You have to find the author's purpose for writing something in the passage.

(STEP 3) Identify the question type. This is a purpose question.

(STEP 4) Eliminate incorrect answers. Eliminate all the choices except for (E). If you know that all the other choices are incorrect, then you can be sure (E) is correct. Eliminate (A) because the author does not mention that all rocks are continually changing, primarily to make the reading more technical. Eliminate (B) and (C) because telling the reader that rocks are continually changing does not give him/her a visual or a physical description of rocks. Eliminate (D) because the statement that rocks are continually changing does not give the reader a clearer understanding about the formation of rocks.

(STEP 5) Scan the details to find the answer. (E) is the correct answer. All the other answer choices were eliminated, and the author mentions that rocks are continually changing to explain why rocks look different.

16. **STEP 2** Read the question and the answers. You have to look at the overall structure of the passage to see how it is organized.

STEP 3 Identify the question type. This is an organization question.

STEP 4 Eliminate incorrect answers. Eliminate choice (D) because no significant question is raised in the passage.

STEP 5 Scan the details to find the answer. Choice (A) is correct. The author writes about how rocks are formed and then discusses rocks formed deep in the Earth or from a coral reef. (B) is incorrect because the last sentence mentions Earth's history, but there is no discussion of Earth's history. (C) is incorrect because this is more or less the opposite of the actual structure of the passage. (D) was eliminated because the author never raises a significant question, although some scientists may have questions about the exact dates in the second paragraph. (E) is incorrect because the author never presents a theory and gives no counterexamples.

17. **STEP 2** Read the question and the answers. You have to draw an inference from the passage.

STEP 3 Identify the question type. This is an inference question.

STEP 4 Eliminate incorrect answers. Eliminate (C) because there is nothing here to suggest that science is a mixture of fact and fiction.

STEP 5 Scan the details to find the answer. (B) is correct. In the second paragraph the author presents a theory from other scientists about the age of rocks found on Earth. (A) is incorrect because most of what the author presents can't be personally observed. (C) was eliminated because there is nothing to indicate that the author has presented or believes that science includes both fact and fiction. (D) is incorrect because the author presents information about the age of rocks and the age of the Earth but nothing about how the Earth was formed. (E) is incorrect because there is no evidence that the author has any advanced degree.

18. **STEP 2** Read the question and the answers. You have to identify the statement that is most likely an opinion.

STEP 3 Identify the question type. This is a fact or opinion question.

STEP 4 Eliminate incorrect answers. Eliminate the choices that are facts. There are many facts in this passage so you should be able to eliminate many of the choices. The first three choices, (A), (B), and (C), are facts. That leaves choices (D) and (E).

STEP 5 Scan the details to find the answer. (E) is the correct answer. It is clearly the author's opinion about a simple rock collection. It could never be proven true or false. (D) is tempting, but scientists have ways of proving this true or false. Besides, choice (E) is a much clearer example of an opinion, and the question asks for the most convincing example.

19. **STEP 2** Read the question and the answers. You have to look for several elements in the passage that will lead to a conclusion.

STEP 4 Identify the question type. This is a conclusion question.

STEP 4 Eliminate incorrect answers. Eliminate (D) because the passage says learners will be exposed to "perspectives beyond their teacher's own view."

(STEP 5) Scan the details to find the answer. (C) is the correct answer. The first five lines of the passage mention both technical ability and familiarity as the reasons cable television in the classroom has not been accepted. We use those two bits of information to draw the conclusion. (A) is incorrect because the beginning of the passage says the opposite—that acceptance of cable television in the classroom is eclipsed by the number of educational practitioners who do not use it. (B) is incorrect because the passage mentions other reasons beyond strategies as why cable television in the classroom has not been accepted. (D) was eliminated because the passage mentions that cable television in the classroom will be exposed to views other than the teacher's view. (E) is incorrect because the passage says the opposite of this. "Cable television access in the classroom allows learners to make informed judgments about the content under study."

20. (STEP 2) Read the question and the answers. You have to decide how to use the information from the passage in a different setting.

(STEP 3) Identify the question type. This is an application question.

(STEP 4) Eliminate incorrect answers. Eliminate everything but choice (E). The main point of the passage is that teachers do not use cable television in the classroom because they do not know about it and do not know how to use it. One part of that message, applied to introducing a new vacuum cleaner, is that you have to get the word out. One way to do that is through advertising. You can eliminate all the other choices, which will probably be important when the new vacuum cleaner is introduced. Some of them may turn out to be more important than advertising. But none of those other choices are related to knowing about the vacuum or knowing how to use the new vacuum.

(STEP 5) Scan the details to find the answer. (E) is the best answer. Advertising is the only choice from among those given that is supported by this passage.

This targeted test is designed to help you further practice the strategies presented in this chapter. The answers immediately follow the test. For that reason questions may have a different emphasis than the real test.

READING COMPREHENSION

> **Directions:** Mark your choice, then check your answers. Use the strategies beginning on page 202.

USE THIS PASSAGE TO ANSWER ITEMS 1 AND 2.

While becoming a teacher, I spent most of my time with books. I read books about the subjects I would teach in school and books that explained how to teach the subjects. As a new teacher, I relied on books to help my students learn. But I learned, and now the basis for my teaching is to help students apply what they have learned to the real world.

1. We can predict that which of the following would most likely be the next line of this passage?

   Ⓐ The world is a dangerous and intimidating place; be wary of it.
   Ⓑ Children should be taught to seek whatever the world has to offer.
   Ⓒ A teacher has to be in the world, not just study about the world.
   Ⓓ But you can't forget about books.
   Ⓔ Teaching is like learning.

2. Which of the following is best inferred from this passage?

   Ⓐ Teaching art is very rewarding.
   Ⓑ Children learn a lot from field trips.
   Ⓒ There is much to be said for teachers who think of their students' experiences first.
   Ⓓ Firsthand experiences are important for a teacher's development.
   Ⓔ You never know what you will end up teaching.

USE THIS PASSAGE TO ANSWER ITEMS 3 THROUGH 5.

The American alligator is found in Florida and Georgia, and has also been reported in other states, including North and South Carolina. Weighing in at more than 400 pounds, the length of an adult alligator is twice that of its tail. Adult alligators eat fish and small mammals while young alligators prefer insects, shrimp, and frogs.

An untrained person may mistake a crocodile for an alligator. Crocodiles are found in the same areas as alligators and both have prominent snouts with many teeth. The crocodile has a long thin snout with teeth in both jaws. The alligator's snout is wider with teeth only in the upper jaw.

3.   Which of the following would be a good title for this passage?

(A) Large Reptiles
(B) Eating Habits of Alligators
(C) The American Alligator
(D) How Alligators and Crocodiles Differ
(E) American Alligator: Endangered Species

4.   Which of the following would be a way to distinguish an alligator from a crocodile?

(A) Number of teeth
(B) Shape of snout
(C) Habitat
(D) Diet
(E) Mating rituals

5.   Which of the following best describes the purpose of the passage?

(A) All animals are noteworthy.
(B) Reptiles are interesting animals.
(C) To educate readers about differences in similar animals
(D) To describe the life cycle of wetland creatures
(E) To provide information about the American alligator

Remove the jack from the trunk. Set the jack under the car. Use the jack to raise the car. Remove the lug nuts. Remove the tire and replace it with the doughnut. Reset the lug nuts loosely and use the jack to lower the chassis to the ground. Tighten the lug nuts once the tire is touching the ground.

6.   Which of the following is the main idea of this passage?

(A) Using a jack
(B) Changing a tire on a car
(C) Maintaining a car
(D) Following directions
(E) Caring for a car

USE THIS PASSAGE TO ANSWER ITEMS 7 AND 8.

Farmers and animals are fighting over rain forests. The farmers are clearing the forests and driving out the animals to make room for crops. If this battle continues, the rain forest will disappear. Both the farmers and the animals will lose, and the soil in the cleared forest will form a hard crust.

Of course, there are global implications as well. Clearing the forests increases the amount of carbon dioxide in the atmosphere. The most promising solution to the problems caused by clearing the rain forests is the education of the local farmers.

7. Which information below is not provided in the passage?

   Ⓐ Reasons the animals are being run out
   Ⓑ Reasons the farmers need more land
   Ⓒ Effects of lost rain forests
   Ⓓ Ways that people can help globally
   Ⓔ Ways that people can help locally

8. What most likely would the attitude of the author be about wildlife conservation?

   Ⓐ All animals must fend for themselves.
   Ⓑ Damage to the earth affects both people and animals.
   Ⓒ Our greatest resource is education.
   Ⓓ Testing products on animals is a practice that should be outlawed.
   Ⓔ Animals and people should have equal rights.

I love gingerbread cookies, which are flavored with ginger and molasses. I can remember cold winter days when my brother and I huddled around the fire eating gingerbread cookies and sipping warm apple cider. In those days, gingerbread cookies came in many shapes and sizes. When you eat a gingerbread cookie today, you have to bite a "person's" head off.

9. Why did the author of the passage above put quotes around the word *person*?

   Ⓐ To emphasize the difference between gingerbread cookies that appear as people rather than windmills
   Ⓑ Because gingerbread cookies often don't look like people
   Ⓒ To emphasize the most popular current shape of gingerbread cookies
   Ⓓ To emphasize this word has a figurative meaning
   Ⓔ To emphasize how our culture now puts more importance on people than on things

The Frogs Who Wanted a King

The frogs lived a happy life in the pond. They jumped from lily pad to lily pad and sunned themselves without a care. But a few of the frogs were not satisfied with this relaxed and enjoyable life. These frogs thought that they needed a king to rule them. So they sent a note to the god Jupiter requesting that he appoint a king.

Jupiter was amused by this request. In a good-natured response, Jupiter threw a log into the pond, which landed with a big splash. All the frogs jumped to safety. Some time passed and one frog started to approach the log, which lay still in the pond. When nothing happened, the other frogs jumped on the floating giant, treating it with disdain.

The frogs were not satisfied with such a docile king. They sent another note to Jupiter asking for a strong king to rule over them. Jupiter was not amused by this second request and he was tired of the frogs' complaints.

So Jupiter sent a stork. The stork immediately devoured every frog in sight. The few surviving frogs gave Mercury a message to carry to Jupiter pleading for Jupiter to show them mercy.

Jupiter was very cold. He told Mercury to tell the frogs that they were responsible for their own problems. They had asked for a king to rule them and they would have to make the best of it.

10. Which of the following morals fits the passage?

   Ⓐ Let well enough alone.
   Ⓑ Familiarity breeds contempt.
   Ⓒ Slow and steady wins the race.
   Ⓓ Liberty is too high a price to pay for revenge.
   Ⓔ Misery loves company.

11. Why did the frogs treat the log with contempt?

   Ⓐ The log was sent by Jupiter.
   Ⓑ The log floated in the pond.
   Ⓒ The log was not alive.
   Ⓓ The log could not speak.
   Ⓔ The log was not assertive.

USE THIS PASSAGE TO ANSWER ITEMS 12 THROUGH 14.

You may want to go to a park on a virgin prairie in Minnesota. The park borders Canada and is just west of the Mississippi River. The thousands of acres of park land are home to hundreds of species of birds and mammals. In the evening, a sotto wind sweeps across the prairie, creating wave-like ripples in the tall grasses. This prairie park is just one of the wonders you can see when you visit marvelous Minnesota.

12. We can infer that this passage is most likely from a

    Ⓐ cookbook.
    Ⓑ travel brochure.
    Ⓒ hunting magazine.
    Ⓓ national parks guide.
    Ⓔ conservation organization mailing.

13. We can conclude that this part of the United States is in the

    Ⓐ Midwest
    Ⓑ Northeast
    Ⓒ Southeast
    Ⓓ Northwest
    Ⓔ Southwest

14. What does the author mean by "virgin prairie"?

    Ⓐ Desolate taiga
    Ⓑ Untouched grasslands
    Ⓒ Wooded plains
    Ⓓ Indian reservation
    Ⓔ Untainted meadows

USE THIS PASSAGE TO ANSWER ITEMS 15 THROUGH 18.

There was a time in the United States when a married woman was expected to take her husband's last name. Most women still follow this practice, but things are changing. In fact, Hawaii is the only state with a law requiring a woman to take her husband's last name when she marries.

Many women look forward to taking their husband's surname. They may enjoy the bond it establishes with their husband, or want to be identified with their husband's professional status. Other women want to keep their own last name. They may prefer their original last name, or want to maintain their professional identity.

Some women resolve this problem by choosing a last name that hyphenates their surname and their husband's surname. This practice of adopting elements of both surnames is common in other cultures.

15. What would be the best title for this passage?

   Ⓐ Women Have Rights
   Ⓑ Determining a Woman's Name After Marriage
   Ⓒ Determining a Woman's Name After Divorce
   Ⓓ Legal Aspects of Surname Changing
   Ⓔ Hawaii's Domestic Laws

16. What can we infer about the author's position on women's rights?

   Ⓐ For women but against men
   Ⓑ For women and against equality
   Ⓒ For women and for men
   Ⓓ Against women but for men
   Ⓔ Against women and against men

17. This passage would LEAST likely be found in a

   Ⓐ fashion magazine.
   Ⓑ woman's corporate magazine.
   Ⓒ teen magazine aimed at girls.
   Ⓓ fitness magazine.
   Ⓔ bridal magazine.

18. What is the main idea of this passage?

   Ⓐ Women are at the mercy of the law.
   Ⓑ Women in Hawaii have no options.
   Ⓒ Women today have many options related to surnames.
   Ⓓ Children should have the same name as their mother.
   Ⓔ Men have stopped demanding that women change their names.

USE THIS PASSAGE TO ANSWER ITEMS 19 AND 20.

In recent years, cooperative learning, which involves students in small group activities, has gained popularity as an instructional approach. Cooperative learning provides students with an opportunity to work on projects presented by the teacher. This type of learning emphasizes group goals, cooperative learning, and shared responsibility. All students must contribute in order for the group to be successful.

19. What is the main idea of this passage?

   Ⓐ To show different learning styles
   Ⓑ To examine the best way to teach
   Ⓒ To explain why cooperative learning is the best method for eliminating classrooms
   Ⓓ To illustrate the method of cooperative learning
   Ⓔ To show the role of the teacher in a cooperative learning environment

20. According to this passage what would be a good definition of cooperative learning?

Ⓐ An instructional arrangement in which children work in small groups in a manner that promotes student responsibility

Ⓑ An instructional arrangement in which the teacher pairs two students in a tutor–tutee relationship to promote learning of academic skills or subject content

Ⓒ An instructional arrangement consisting of three to seven students that represents a major format for teaching academic skills

Ⓓ An instructional arrangement that is appropriate for numerous classroom activities such as show and tell, discussing interesting events, taking a field trip, or watching a movie

Ⓔ An instructional arrangement in which the teaching responsibilities are shared

---

USE THESE PASSAGES TO ANSWER ITEMS 21 AND 22.

I

Extraterrestrial life means life on or from a planet other than Earth. Life can be as simple as bacteria. Scientists believe that bacteria are the ancestors of the first forms of life on Earth beginning about 3.5 billion years ago. Bacteria are microscopic, and for the first 3 billion years or so the first life on Earth were microscopic.

Most scientists agree that the universe has been around three or four times longer than Earth. Humans as we know them have been around for 100,000 years or so. That means similar life could have developed in the universe billions of years ago. When you consider this very low threshold for the presence of life, and scientists' estimate that there may be billions of earth-like planets, it's just hard to believe that life does not exist elsewhere.

II

I've been reading a lot about how likely it is that life exists on other planets. Scientists use probability to arrive at the small percentage chance that life exists elsewhere. The problem is that the same probability calculations could be used to prove life elsewhere is unlikely. So, as nice as it would be, I am unconvinced.

Think of it this way. You arrive at the probability of something by multiplying. I begin with the probability that extraterrestrial life has actually been discovered. That's zero. And no matter what you multiply the result will always be zero.

I know that Earth is a young planet by galactic standards. But to argue Earth's life processes are replicated elsewhere has to be assumed as false until it is proven true. So I'll know there is life beyond Earth when I see it. I'm not holding my breath.

21. Which of the following best describes the relationship of the passages?

Ⓐ Both support the possibility of the existence of extraterrestrial life.

Ⓑ Passage 2 indicates there is no extraterrestrial life, while Passage 1 says there is such life.

Ⓒ Passage 1 is less positive about extraterrestrial life than Passage 2.

Ⓓ Passage 2 is more equivocal about extraterrestrial life than Passage 1.

Ⓔ Both use probability to demonstrate the likely existence of extraterrestrial life.

22. Which of the following when added at the end of the first passage would most strengthen the author's position?

Ⓐ I firmly believe we will discover life on other planets.

Ⓑ That there is no specific evidence of extraterrestrial life does not mean that it does not exist.

Ⓒ It may be that life has been discovered but not revealed to us.

Ⓓ In addition, a recent study discovered a sugar molecule necessary for life on a distant planet.

Ⓔ I wish that the life I know would be proven to exist elsewhere.

USE THE BELOW INFORMATION TO ANSWER ITEMS 23 AND 24.

Mon	Tue	Wed	Thu	Fri	Sat
8:00 A.M. Priority Mail	8:00 A.M. Priority Mail	8:00 A.M. Priority Mail	8:00 A.M. Priority Mail	8:00 A.M. Priority Mail	8:00 A.M. Priority Mail
11:00 A.M. First Class	11:00 A.M. First Class	11:00 A.M. First Class	11:00 A.M. First Class	11:00 A.M. First Class	11:00 A.M. First Class
2:00 P.M. Parcel Post	2:00 P.M. Parcel Post	2:00 P.M. Parcel Post	2:00 P.M. Parcel Post	2:00 A.M. Parcel Post	2:00 A.M. Parcel Post
3:00 P.M. First Class	3:00 P.M. First Class	3:00 P.M. First Class	3:00 P.M. First Class	3:00 P.M. First Class	
4:00 P.M. Overnight Mail	4:00 P.M. Overnight Mail	4:00 P.M. Overnight Mail	4:00 P.M. Overnight Mail	4:00 P.M. Overnight Mail	

This chart shows the times during the week when letters and packages are sent out from the post office to the central sorting facility. The post office opens at 9:00 A.M.

Priority Mail is guaranteed to be delivered in three business days, Monday through Friday, after dropoff to reach its destination. Overnight Mail is guaranteed to be delivered the next day.

23. Which of the following best explains why Quinn would mail a Priority package on Monday when he wanted it to arrive four days later on Friday?

Ⓐ Quinn wants to be extra careful that the package arrives on time.

Ⓑ The package will not go out until Tuesday.

Ⓒ The package will go out too late on Monday.

Ⓓ Overnight Mail is too expensive.

Ⓔ There is no delivery guarantee for Parcel Post.

24. Which types of mail below, if dropped off on Monday, are sure to arrive by Friday of that week?
Choose all that apply.

Ⓐ First Class Mail

Ⓑ Priority Mail

Ⓒ Overnight Mail

TARGETED READING TEST ANSWERS

1. **(C)** The passage emphasizes the necessary balance of learning from books and learning from experience.

2. **(D)** The passage notes that firsthand experiences are an important part of a teacher's development.

3. **(D)** The passage gives some insight into how these two reptiles are different.

4. **(B)** The passage indicates that the alligator has a wider snout than the crocodile.

5. **(C)** The passage educates readers about differences between these similar animals.

6. **(B)** The passage gives directions for changing a tire on a car.

7. **(D)** The passage mentions global problems, but gives no advice for how people can help on a global scale.

8. **(C)** The author concludes that education of local farmers offers the most promising solution. (B) is incorrect because it is not an opinion about wildlife conservation.

9. **(D)** The quotes indicate the word *person* is not to be taken literally.

10. **(A)** Things would clearly have been better for the frogs if they had left well enough alone.

11. **(E)** The passage indicates the frogs were not satisfied with such a docile king.

12. **(B)** This passage has all the flowery and positive wording you would find in a travel guide.

13. **(A)** The passage indicates that the park is near the center of the country around the Mississippi River, so Midwest is best among the choices given to describe this area.

14. **(B)** In this context, virgin means pristine or untouched. The *prairie* is grassland.

15. **(B)** The entire passage discusses ways in which a woman can determine her name after marriage.

16. **(C)** The author is objective and takes a balanced view of women and men.

17. **(D)** The passage would be completely out of place in a fitness magazine.

18. **(C)** The passage describes a range of options for choosing a surname (last name).

19. **(D)** The passage describes cooperative learning without evaluating its effectiveness.

20. **(A)** This choice best paraphrases the passage's description of cooperative learning. The other choices include information about cooperative learning not found in the passsage.

21. **(D)** In this context, the term *more equivocal* means "more doubtful." The second paragraph is definitely more doubtful about extraterrestrial life than the first. The other choices are obviously incorrect, and you were likely drawn to this choice even if you did not know that *equivocal* meant "doubtful."

22. **(D)** This sentence most strengthens the author's view that "it's hard to believe that life exists elsewhere" because it presents specific information that supports the possible existence of extraterrestrial life.

23. **(A)** Choice A is the best answer. Quinn cannot drop the package off on Tuesday because the Priority Mail goes out after the post office opens. His best option is to drop it off on Monday to go out at 8:00 A.M. on Tuesday.

24. **(A)** and **(C)** are the only types of mail with guaranteed delivery times, and each would be guaranteed for delivery by Friday. First Class Mail carries no guarantee, so while it seems certain that it would arrive by Friday of that week, we cannot be sure.

PART IV
Practice Core Tests
with Explained Answers (5712, 5722, 5732)

Practice Core 1

8

TEST INFO BOX

Reading	56 items	85 minutes
Writing Multiple Choice	40 items	40 minutes
Writing Essays	2 responses	30 minutes each
Mathematics	56 items	85 minutes

Take this test in a realistic, timed setting. You should not take this practice test until you have completed your review.

The setting will be most realistic if another person times the test and ensures that the test rules are followed exactly. If another person is acting as test supervisor, he or she should review these instructions with you and say "Start" when you should begin a section and "Stop" when time has expired.

Use a pencil to mark the test or the answer sheet. Once the test is complete, review the answers and explanations for each item.

ANSWER SHEET
Practice Core 1

Reading Test—85 minutes

1. Ⓐ Ⓑ Ⓒ Ⓓ Ⓔ   16. Ⓐ Ⓑ Ⓒ Ⓓ Ⓔ   31. Ⓐ Ⓑ Ⓒ Ⓓ Ⓔ   46. Ⓐ Ⓑ Ⓒ Ⓓ Ⓔ
2. Ⓐ Ⓑ Ⓒ Ⓓ Ⓔ   17. Ⓐ Ⓑ Ⓒ Ⓓ Ⓔ   32. Ⓐ Ⓑ Ⓒ Ⓓ Ⓔ   47. Ⓐ Ⓑ Ⓒ Ⓓ Ⓔ
3. Ⓐ Ⓑ Ⓒ Ⓓ Ⓔ   18. Ⓐ Ⓑ Ⓒ Ⓓ Ⓔ   33. Ⓐ Ⓑ Ⓒ Ⓓ Ⓔ   48. Ⓐ Ⓑ Ⓒ Ⓓ Ⓔ
4. Ⓐ Ⓑ Ⓒ Ⓓ Ⓔ   19. Ⓐ Ⓑ Ⓒ Ⓓ Ⓔ   34. Ⓐ Ⓑ Ⓒ Ⓓ Ⓔ   49. Ⓐ Ⓑ Ⓒ Ⓓ Ⓔ
5. Ⓐ Ⓑ Ⓒ Ⓓ Ⓔ   20. Ⓐ Ⓑ Ⓒ Ⓓ Ⓔ   35. Ⓐ Ⓑ Ⓒ Ⓓ Ⓔ   50. Ⓐ Ⓑ Ⓒ Ⓓ Ⓔ
6. Ⓐ Ⓑ Ⓒ Ⓓ Ⓔ   21. Ⓐ Ⓑ Ⓒ Ⓓ Ⓔ   36. Ⓐ Ⓑ Ⓒ Ⓓ Ⓔ   51. Ⓐ Ⓑ Ⓒ Ⓓ Ⓔ
7. Ⓐ Ⓑ Ⓒ Ⓓ Ⓔ   22. Ⓐ Ⓑ Ⓒ Ⓓ Ⓔ   37. Ⓐ Ⓑ Ⓒ Ⓓ Ⓔ   52. Ⓐ Ⓑ Ⓒ Ⓓ Ⓔ
8. Ⓐ Ⓑ Ⓒ Ⓓ Ⓔ   23. Ⓐ Ⓑ Ⓒ Ⓓ Ⓔ   38. Ⓐ Ⓑ Ⓒ Ⓓ Ⓔ   53. Ⓐ Ⓑ Ⓒ Ⓓ Ⓔ
9. Ⓐ Ⓑ Ⓒ Ⓓ Ⓔ   24. Ⓐ Ⓑ Ⓒ Ⓓ Ⓔ   39. Ⓐ Ⓑ Ⓒ Ⓓ Ⓔ   54. Ⓐ Ⓑ Ⓒ Ⓓ Ⓔ
10. Ⓐ Ⓑ Ⓒ Ⓓ Ⓔ   25. Ⓐ Ⓑ Ⓒ Ⓓ Ⓔ   40. Ⓐ Ⓑ Ⓒ Ⓓ Ⓔ   55. Ａ Ｂ Ｃ
11. Ⓐ Ⓑ Ⓒ Ⓓ Ⓔ   26. Ⓐ Ⓑ Ⓒ Ⓓ Ⓔ   41. Ⓐ Ⓑ Ⓒ Ⓓ Ⓔ   56. Ⓐ Ⓑ Ⓒ Ⓓ Ⓔ
12. Ⓐ Ⓑ Ⓒ Ⓓ Ⓔ   27. Ⓐ Ⓑ Ⓒ Ⓓ Ⓔ   42. Ⓐ Ⓑ Ⓒ Ⓓ Ⓔ
13. Ａ Ｂ Ｃ Ｄ   28. Ⓐ Ⓑ Ⓒ Ⓓ Ⓔ   43. Ⓐ Ⓑ Ⓒ Ⓓ Ⓔ
14. Ａ Ｂ Ｃ   29. Ⓐ Ⓑ Ⓒ Ⓓ Ⓔ   44. Ⓐ Ⓑ Ⓒ Ⓓ Ⓔ
15. Ⓐ Ⓑ Ⓒ Ⓓ Ⓔ   30. Ａ Ｂ Ｃ   45. Ⓐ Ⓑ Ⓒ Ⓓ Ⓔ

Writing Test—40 minutes

1. Ⓐ Ⓑ Ⓒ Ⓓ Ⓔ   11. Ⓐ Ⓑ Ⓒ Ⓓ Ⓔ   21. Ⓐ Ⓑ Ⓒ Ⓓ Ⓔ   31. Ⓐ Ⓑ Ⓒ Ⓓ Ⓔ
2. Ⓐ Ⓑ Ⓒ Ⓓ Ⓔ   12. Ⓐ Ⓑ Ⓒ Ⓓ Ⓔ   22. Ⓐ Ⓑ Ⓒ Ⓓ Ⓔ   32. Ⓐ Ⓑ Ⓒ Ⓓ Ⓔ
3. Ⓐ Ⓑ Ⓒ Ⓓ Ⓔ   13. Ⓐ Ⓑ Ⓒ Ⓓ Ⓔ   23. Ⓐ Ⓑ Ⓒ Ⓓ Ⓔ   33. Ⓐ Ⓑ Ⓒ Ⓓ Ⓔ
4. Ⓐ Ⓑ Ⓒ Ⓓ Ⓔ   14. Ⓐ Ⓑ Ⓒ Ⓓ Ⓔ   24. Ⓐ Ⓑ Ⓒ Ⓓ Ⓔ   34. Ⓐ Ⓑ Ⓒ Ⓓ Ⓔ
5. Ⓐ Ⓑ Ⓒ Ⓓ Ⓔ   15. Ⓐ Ⓑ Ⓒ Ⓓ Ⓔ   25. Ⓐ Ⓑ Ⓒ Ⓓ Ⓔ   35. Ⓐ Ⓑ Ⓒ Ⓓ Ⓔ
6. Ⓐ Ⓑ Ⓒ Ⓓ Ⓔ   16. Ⓐ Ⓑ Ⓒ Ⓓ Ⓔ   26. Ⓐ Ⓑ Ⓒ Ⓓ Ⓔ   36. Ⓐ Ⓑ Ⓒ Ⓓ Ⓔ
7. Ⓐ Ⓑ Ⓒ Ⓓ Ⓔ   17. Ⓐ Ⓑ Ⓒ Ⓓ Ⓔ   27. Ⓐ Ⓑ Ⓒ Ⓓ Ⓔ   37. Ⓐ Ⓑ Ⓒ Ⓓ Ⓔ
8. Ⓐ Ⓑ Ⓒ Ⓓ Ⓔ   18. Ⓐ Ⓑ Ⓒ Ⓓ Ⓔ   28. Ⓐ Ⓑ Ⓒ Ⓓ Ⓔ   38. Ⓐ Ⓑ Ⓒ Ⓓ Ⓔ
9. Ⓐ Ⓑ Ⓒ Ⓓ Ⓔ   19. Ⓐ Ⓑ Ⓒ Ⓓ Ⓔ   29. Ⓐ Ⓑ Ⓒ Ⓓ Ⓔ   39. Ⓐ Ⓑ Ⓒ Ⓓ Ⓔ
10. Ⓐ Ⓑ Ⓒ Ⓓ Ⓔ   20. Ⓐ Ⓑ Ⓒ Ⓓ Ⓔ   30. Ⓐ Ⓑ Ⓒ Ⓓ Ⓔ   40. Ⓐ Ⓑ Ⓒ Ⓓ Ⓔ

ANSWER SHEET
Practice Core 1

Mathematics Test—85 minutes

1. Ⓐ Ⓑ Ⓒ Ⓓ Ⓔ
2. Ⓐ Ⓑ Ⓒ Ⓓ Ⓔ
3. ▭ / ▭
4. Ⓐ Ⓑ Ⓒ Ⓓ Ⓔ
5. Ⓐ Ⓑ Ⓒ Ⓓ Ⓔ
6. Ⓐ Ⓑ Ⓒ Ⓓ Ⓔ
7. Ⓐ Ⓑ Ⓒ Ⓓ Ⓔ
8. Ⓐ Ⓑ Ⓒ Ⓓ Ⓔ
9. Ⓐ Ⓑ Ⓒ Ⓓ Ⓔ
10. Ⓐ Ⓑ Ⓒ Ⓓ Ⓔ
11. Ⓐ Ⓑ Ⓒ Ⓓ Ⓔ
12. Ⓐ Ⓑ Ⓒ Ⓓ Ⓔ
13. Ⓐ Ⓑ Ⓒ Ⓓ Ⓔ

14. Ⓐ Ⓑ Ⓒ Ⓓ Ⓔ
15. Ⓐ Ⓑ Ⓒ Ⓓ Ⓔ
16. ▭
17. Ⓐ Ⓑ Ⓒ Ⓓ Ⓔ
18. Ⓐ Ⓑ Ⓒ Ⓓ Ⓔ
19. Ⓐ Ⓑ Ⓒ Ⓓ Ⓔ
20. Ⓐ Ⓑ Ⓒ Ⓓ Ⓔ
21. Ⓐ Ⓑ Ⓒ Ⓓ Ⓔ
22. Ⓐ Ⓑ Ⓒ Ⓓ Ⓔ
23. Ⓐ Ⓑ Ⓒ Ⓓ Ⓔ
24. Ⓐ Ⓑ Ⓒ Ⓓ Ⓔ
25. Ⓐ Ⓑ Ⓒ Ⓓ Ⓔ
26. Ⓐ Ⓑ Ⓒ Ⓓ Ⓔ
27. Ⓐ Ⓑ Ⓒ Ⓓ Ⓔ
28. Ⓐ Ⓑ Ⓒ Ⓓ Ⓔ

29. Ⓐ Ⓑ Ⓒ Ⓓ Ⓔ
30. Ⓐ Ⓑ Ⓒ Ⓓ Ⓔ
31. Ⓐ Ⓑ Ⓒ Ⓓ Ⓔ
32. Ⓐ Ⓑ Ⓒ Ⓓ Ⓔ
33. Ⓐ Ⓑ Ⓒ Ⓓ Ⓔ
34. Ⓐ Ⓑ Ⓒ Ⓓ Ⓔ
35. Ⓐ Ⓑ Ⓒ Ⓓ Ⓔ
36. Ⓐ Ⓑ Ⓒ Ⓓ Ⓔ
37. Ⓐ Ⓑ Ⓒ Ⓓ Ⓔ
38. Ⓐ Ⓑ Ⓒ Ⓓ Ⓔ
39. Ⓐ Ⓑ Ⓒ Ⓓ Ⓔ
40. Ⓐ Ⓑ Ⓒ Ⓓ Ⓔ
41. Ⓐ Ⓑ Ⓒ Ⓓ Ⓔ
42. Ⓐ Ⓑ Ⓒ Ⓓ Ⓔ
43. Ⓐ Ⓑ Ⓒ Ⓓ Ⓔ

44. Ⓐ Ⓑ Ⓒ Ⓓ Ⓔ
45. Ⓐ Ⓑ Ⓒ Ⓓ Ⓔ
46. Ⓐ Ⓑ Ⓒ Ⓓ Ⓔ
47. Ⓐ Ⓑ Ⓒ Ⓓ Ⓔ
48. Ⓐ Ⓑ Ⓒ Ⓓ Ⓔ
49. Ⓐ Ⓑ Ⓒ Ⓓ Ⓔ
50. Ⓐ Ⓑ Ⓒ Ⓓ Ⓔ
51. Ⓐ Ⓑ Ⓒ Ⓓ Ⓔ
52. Ⓐ Ⓑ Ⓒ Ⓓ Ⓔ
53. Ⓐ Ⓑ Ⓒ Ⓓ Ⓔ
54. Ⓐ Ⓑ Ⓒ Ⓓ Ⓔ
55. A B C D E
56. Ⓐ Ⓑ Ⓒ Ⓓ Ⓔ

READING TEST

56 ITEMS   85 MINUTES

Directions: You will read selections followed by one or more questions. Most items have five answer choices with one correct answer. A few items may have one or more correct answers. The answer choices for these questions will be within boxes. Select the best answer choices based on what the selection states or implies and mark that letter on the test or the answer sheet.

1. The computers in the college dormitories are actually more sophisticated than the computers in the college computer labs, and they cost less. It seems that the person who bought the dormitory computers looked around until she found powerful computers at a low price. The person who runs the labs just got the computers offered by the regular supplier.

   The best statement of the main idea of this paragraph is

   Ⓐ it is better to use the computers in the dorms.
   Ⓑ it is better to avoid the computers in the labs.
   Ⓒ the computers in the dorms are always in use so, for most purposes, it is better to use the computers in the labs.
   Ⓓ it is better to shop around before you buy.
   Ⓔ wholesale prices are usually better than retail prices.

QUESTIONS 2–4 ARE BASED ON THIS PASSAGE.

Researchers were not sure at first what caused AIDS or how it was transmitted. They did know early on that everyone who developed AIDS died. Then researchers began to understand that the disease is caused by the HIV virus, which could be transmitted through blood and blood products. Even after knowing this, some blood companies resisted testing blood for the HIV virus. Today we know that the HIV virus is transmitted through blood and other bodily fluids. Women may be more susceptible than men, and the prognosis hasn't changed.

2. The main purpose of this passage is to

   Ⓐ show that blood companies can't be trusted.
   Ⓑ detail the history of AIDS research.
   Ⓒ detail the causes and consequences of AIDS.
   Ⓓ warn women that they are susceptible to AIDS.
   Ⓔ raise awareness about AIDS.

3. Which of the following questions could be answered from this passage?

   Ⓐ How do intravenous drug users acquire AIDS?
   Ⓑ How many AIDS diagnoses were recorded last year?
   Ⓒ Through what mediums is AIDS transmitted?
   Ⓓ How do blood companies test for AIDS?
   Ⓔ What does AIDS mean?

4. Which of the following would be the best conclusion for this passage?

Ⓐ AIDS research continues to be underfunded in the United States.

Ⓑ Sexual activity and intravenous drug use continue to be the two primary ways that AIDS is transmitted.

Ⓒ People develop AIDS after being HIV positive.

Ⓓ Our understanding of AIDS has increased significantly over the past several years, but we are no closer to a cure.

Ⓔ It is better to be transfused with your own blood, if possible.

_____

5. The retired basketball player said that, while modern players were better athletes because there was so much emphasis on youth basketball and increased focus on training, he still believed that the players of his day were better because they were more committed to the game, better understood its nuances, and were more dedicated to team play.

In this passage, the retired basketball player believed that which of the following factors led to today's basketball players being better athletes?

Ⓐ More dedication

Ⓑ Increased salaries

Ⓒ Better nutrition

Ⓓ Youth basketball

Ⓔ More commitment

6. The way I look at it, Robert E. Lee was the worst general in the Civil War—he was the South's commanding general, and the South lost the war.

What assumption does the writer of this statement make?

Ⓐ War is horrible and should not be glorified.

Ⓑ Pickett's charge at Gettysburg was a terrible mistake.

Ⓒ A general should be judged by whether he wins or loses.

Ⓓ The South should have won the Civil War.

Ⓔ Slavery is wrong.

7. Advances in astronomy and space exploration during the past twenty-five years have been significant, and we now know more answers to questions about the universe than ever before, but we still cannot answer the ultimate question, "How did our universe originate?"

Which of the following best characterizes the author's view of how the advances in astronomy and space exploration affect our eventual ability to answer the ultimate question?

Ⓐ We now know more answers than ever before.

Ⓑ All the questions have not been answered.

Ⓒ Eventually we will probably find out.

Ⓓ The question can't be answered.

Ⓔ We will have the answer very soon.

The Board of Adjustment can exempt a person from the requirements of a particular land use ordinance. Several cases have come before the Board concerning three ordinances. One ordinance states that religious and other organizations cannot build places of worship or meeting halls in residential zones. A second ordinance states that any garage must be less than 25 percent of the size of a house on the same lot, while a third ordinance restricts a person's right to convert a one-family house to a two-family house.

It is interesting to note how a person can be in favor of an exemption in one case but opposed to exemption in another. For example, one homeowner applied to build a garage 45 percent of the size of her house but was opposed to a neighbor converting his house from a one-family to a two-family house. This second homeowner was opposed to a church being built in his neighborhood. The woman opposed to his proposal was all for the church construction project.

The pressure on Board of Adjustment members who also live in the community is tremendous. It must sometimes seem to them that any decision is the wrong one. But that is what Boards of Adjustment are for, and we can only hope that this example of America in action will best serve the community and those who live there.

8. Which of the following sentences is the author of the passage most likely to DISAGREE with?

    Ⓐ These Boards serve a useful purpose.
    Ⓑ No exemptions should be granted to any zoning ordinance.
    Ⓒ People can be very fickle when it comes to the exemptions they favor.
    Ⓓ Some people may try to influence Board of Adjustment members.
    Ⓔ The garage the woman wanted to build was about twice the allowable size.

9. The author finds people's reactions to exemption requests interesting because

    Ⓐ so many different types of exemptions are applied for.
    Ⓑ a person's reaction is often based on religious principles and beliefs.
    Ⓒ a person can both support and not support requested exemptions.
    Ⓓ people put so much pressure on Board members.
    Ⓔ men usually oppose exemptions sought by women.

10. In which of the following publications would you expect this passage to appear?

    Ⓐ A government textbook
    Ⓑ A local newspaper
    Ⓒ A national newspaper
    Ⓓ A civics textbook
    Ⓔ A news magazine

11. We can infer from this passage that the actions of a Board of Adjustment

Ⓐ oppress religious and community groups.

Ⓑ favor men over women.

Ⓒ enforce town ordinances.

Ⓓ are examples of America in action.

Ⓔ exempt people from property taxes.

12. Which of the following does the passage convey?

Ⓐ A person should be consistently for or against Board exemptions.

Ⓑ The Board of Adjustment should act only when all agree.

Ⓒ People are interested in their own needs when it comes to zoning.

Ⓓ Board of Adjustment members should not be from town.

Ⓔ The Board of Adjustment should not approve any of the requests.

---

13. The college sororities are "interviewed" by students during rush week. Rush week is a time when students get to know about the different sororities and decide which ones they want to join. Each student can pledge only one sorority. Once students have chosen the three they are most interested in, the intrigue begins. The sororities then choose from among the students who have chosen them.

Which of the following strategies will help assure a student that she will be chosen for at least one sorority and preferably get into a sorority she likes?

Select all that apply.

A Choose at least one sorority she is sure will choose her

B Choose one sorority she wants to get into

C Choose her three favorite sororities

D Choose three sororities she knows will choose her

14. During a Stage 4 alert, workers in an energy plant must wear protective pants, a protective shirt, and a helmet, except that protective coveralls can be worn in place of protective pants and shirt. When there is a Stage 5 alert, workers must also wear filter masks in addition to the requirements for the Stage 4 alert.

During a Stage 5 alert, which of the following could be worn?

Select all that apply.

A masks, pants, helmet

B coveralls, helmet, mask

C coveralls, mask

Using percentages to report growth patterns can be deceptive. If there are 100 new users for a cereal currently used by 100 other people, the growth rate is 100 percent. However, if there are 50,000 new users for a cereal currently used by 5,000,000 people, the growth rate is 1 percent. It seems obvious that the growth rate of 1 percent is preferable to the growth rate of 100 percent. So while percentages do provide a useful way to report growth patterns, we must know the initial number the growth percentage is based on before we make any conclusions.

15. Which of the following statements about growth rates is the author most likely to agree with?

   Ⓐ Lower growth rates mean higher actual growth.
   Ⓑ Higher growth rates mean higher actual growth.
   Ⓒ The growth rate depends on the starting point.
   Ⓓ The growth rate does not depend on the starting point.
   Ⓔ A lower starting point means a higher growth rate.

16. Which of the following can be inferred from this passage?

   Ⓐ Don't believe any advertisements.
   Ⓑ Question any percentage growth rate.
   Ⓒ Percentages should never be used.
   Ⓓ Any growth rate over 50 percent is invalid.
   Ⓔ Percentages are deceptive advertising.

---

17. (1) The science fiction story started with a description of the characters.
    (2) Some of the descriptions were hard for me to understand.
    (3) The book was about time travel in the 22nd century, an interesting subject.
    (4) The authors believed time travel would be possible by then.

In these four sentences, a person describes a science fiction book. Which of the following choices most accurately characterizes these statements made by the person describing the book?

   Ⓐ (2) alone states an opinion
   Ⓑ (1) and (4) alone state facts
   Ⓒ (3) states both facts and opinion
   Ⓓ (1), (3), and (4) state facts only
   Ⓔ (4) states an opinion

18. The public schools in Hinman have devoted extra resources to mathematics instruction for years. Their programs always reflect the most current thinking about the way mathematics should be taught, and the schools are always equipped with the most recent teaching aids. These extra resources have created a mathematics program that is now copied by other schools throughout America.

The mathematics program at the Hinman schools is copied by other schools because

(A) their programs always reflect the most current thinking about the way mathematics should be taught.
(B) the schools are always equipped with the most recent teaching aids.
(C) the schools use the NCTM standards.
(D) extra resources were devoted to mathematics instruction.
(E) their successful programs were publicized to other schools.

QUESTIONS 19–24 APPLY TO THIS PASSAGE.

Computer graphing programs are capable of graphing almost any equations, including advanced equations from calculus. The student just types in the equation and the graph appears on the computer screen. The graphing program can also show the numerical solution for any entered equation. I like having a computer program that performs the mechanical aspects of these difficult calculations. However, these programs do not teach about graphing or mathematics because the computer does not "explain" what is going on. A person could type in an equation, get an answer, and have not the slightest idea what either meant.

Relying on this mindless kind of graphing and calculation, students will be completely unfamiliar with the meaning of the equations they write or the results they get. They will not be able to understand how to create a graph from an equation or to understand the basis for the more complicated calculations.

It may be true that a strictly mechanical approach is used by some teachers. There certainly is a place for students who already understand equations and graphing to have a computer program that relieves the drudgery. But these computer programs should never and can never replace the teacher. Mathematical competence assumes that understanding precedes rote calculation.

19. What is the main idea of this passage?

(A) Mechanical calculation is one part of learning about mathematics.
(B) Teachers should use graphing programs as one part of instruction.
(C) Graphing programs are not effective for initially teaching mathematics.
(D) Students who use these programs won't learn mathematics.
(E) The programs rely too heavily on a student's typing ability.

20. Which of the following questions could be answered from the information in the passage?

    Ⓐ How does the program do integration and differentiation?
    Ⓑ What type of mathematics learning experiences should students have?
    Ⓒ When is it appropriate to use graphing programs?
    Ⓓ Why do schools buy these graphing programs?
    Ⓔ Which graphing program does the author recommend?

21. If the reasoning about learning to use a graphing calculator was applied to all learning, then all learning should emphasize

    Ⓐ competence.
    Ⓑ thoroughness.
    Ⓒ teaching.
    Ⓓ mathematics.
    Ⓔ understanding.

22. What can we infer about the aspect of graphing programs that the author of the passage likes?

    Ⓐ That you just have to type in the equation
    Ⓑ That the difficult mechanical operations are performed
    Ⓒ That the calculations and graphing are done very quickly
    Ⓓ That you don't have to know math to use them
    Ⓔ That they can't replace teachers

23. Which of the following could be used in place of the first sentence of the last paragraph?

    Ⓐ It may be true that some strict teachers use a mechanical approach.
    Ⓑ It may be true that some teachers use only a mechanical approach.
    Ⓒ It may be true that a stringently mechanical approach is used by some teachers.
    Ⓓ It may be true that inflexible mechanical approaches are used by some teachers.
    Ⓔ It may be true that the mechanical approach used by some teachers is too rigorous.

24. Which of the following conclusions is supported by the passage?

    Ⓐ Programs that display the graph of an equation are useful in the schools.
    Ⓑ Relying on mindless graphing and calculation can still help students learn mathematics.
    Ⓒ Strictly mechanical approaches are used by most teachers.
    Ⓓ Using programs to graph equations can replace understanding.
    Ⓔ Being able to type in equations can help students understand the solution.

25. An analysis of models of potential space vehicles prepared by engineers revealed that the parts of the hull of the vehicles that were strongest were the ones that had the most potential for being weak.

Which of the following statements about hull design is the author most likely to agree with?

Ⓐ The parts of the hull that are potentially strongest should not receive as much attention from engineers as those that are potentially weakest.

Ⓑ The potentially weaker parts of the hull are stronger in models than the potentially stronger parts of the hull.

Ⓒ Being potentially weaker, these parts of the hull appear relatively stronger in a model.

Ⓓ Potentially weaker parts of the hull have the most potential for being stronger.

Ⓔ The parts of the hull that are potentially weakest receive less attention from engineers than those parts that are potentially stronger.

QUESTIONS 26 AND 27 ARE BASED ON THIS PASSAGE.

The growth of the town led to a huge increase in the number of students applying for kindergarten admission. Before this time, students had been admitted to kindergarten even if they were "technically" too young. At first the school administrators considered a testing plan for those applicants too young for regular admission, admitting only those who passed the test. Luckily the administrators submitted a plan that just enforced the official, but previously ignored, birth cut-off date for kindergarten admission. This decision set the stage for fairness throughout the town.

26. What main idea is the author trying to convey?

Ⓐ Testing of young children doesn't work.

Ⓑ All children should be treated equally.

Ⓒ Tests are biased against minority children.

Ⓓ The testing program would be too expensive.

Ⓔ Age predicts a child's performance level.

27. Which of the following is the primary problem with this plan for the schools?

Ⓐ Parents will sue.

Ⓑ Parents will falsify birth certificates to get their children in school.

Ⓒ Next year the schools will have to admit a much larger kindergarten group.

Ⓓ Missing kindergarten because a child is born one day too late doesn't seem fair.

Ⓔ Parents would not be able to dispute the results of an objective testing plan.

28. A person who is not treated with respect cannot be expected to be a good worker.

Which of the following can be concluded from this statement?

Ⓐ A person treated with respect can be expected to be a good worker.
Ⓑ A person who is expected to be a good worker should be treated with respect.
Ⓒ A person who cannot be expected to be a good worker is not treated with respect.
Ⓓ A person not treated with respect can still be expected to be a good worker.
Ⓔ A person who is not a good worker can't expect to be treated with respect.

QUESTIONS 29 AND 30 ARE BASED ON THESE CIRCUMSTANCES.

The state highway department has sets of regulations for the number of lanes a highway can have and how these lanes are to be used. A summary of these regulations follows.

- All highways must be five lanes wide and either three or four of these lanes must be set aside for passenger cars only.
- If four lanes are set aside for passenger cars, then one of these lanes must be set aside for cars with three or more passengers, with a second lane of the four passenger lanes also usable by school vehicles such as buses, vans, and cars.
- If three lanes are set aside for passenger cars, then one of these lanes must be set aside for cars with two or more passengers, except that school buses, vans, and cars may also use this lane.

29. Officials in one county submit a plan for a five-lane highway, with three lanes set aside for passenger cars, and school buses able to use the lane set aside for cars with two or more passengers. Based on their regulations, which of the following is most likely to be the state highway department's response to this plan?

Ⓐ Your plan is approved because you have five lanes with three set aside for passenger cars and one set aside for passenger cars with two or more passengers.
Ⓑ Your plan is approved because you permitted school buses to use the passenger lanes.
Ⓒ Your plan is disapproved because you don't include school vans and school cars among the vehicles that can use the lane for cars with two or more passengers.
Ⓓ Your plan is disapproved because you include school buses in the lane for passenger cars with two or more passengers.
Ⓔ Your plan is disapproved because you set aside only three lanes for passenger cars when it should have been four.

30. County officials send a list of three possible highway plans to the state highway department. Using their regulations, which of the following plans would the state highway department approve?

Select all that apply.

- [A] 4 lanes—3 for passenger cars, 1 passenger lane for cars with 3 or more passengers, school buses and vans can also use the passenger lane for 3 or more people
- [B] 5 lanes—4 for passenger cars, 1 passenger lane for cars with 3 or more passengers, 1 of the 4 passenger lanes can be used by school buses, vans, and cars
- [C] 4 lanes—3 for passenger cars, 1 passenger lane for cars with 2 or more passengers, school vehicles can also use the passenger lane for 2 or more passengers

---

QUESTIONS 31–34 ARE BASED ON THIS PASSAGE.

The choice of educational practices sometimes seems like choosing fashions. Fashion is driven by the whims, tastes, and zeitgeist of the current day. The education system should not be driven by these same forces. But consider, for example, the way mathematics is taught. Three decades ago, teachers were told to use manipulative materials to teach mathematics. In the intervening years, the emphasis was on drill and practice. Now teachers are being told again to use manipulative materials. This cycle is more akin to random acts than to sound professional practice.

31. What does the author most likely mean by the word *zeitgeist* in the second sentence?

- Ⓐ Tenor
- Ⓑ Emotional feeling
- Ⓒ Fabric availability
- Ⓓ Teaching methods
- Ⓔ Intelligence

32. Which of the following sentences contains an opinion?

- Ⓐ "But consider for example . . . ."
- Ⓑ "Three decades ago . . . ."
- Ⓒ "In the intervening years . . . ."
- Ⓓ "Now teachers are being told . . . ."
- Ⓔ "This cycle is more akin . . . ."

33. Which of the following best describes how this passage is organized?

- Ⓐ The author presents the main idea followed by examples.
- Ⓑ A comparison is made between two dissimilar things followed by the author's main idea.
- Ⓒ The author describes chronological events followed by an explanation of those events.
- Ⓓ The author presents a trend and explains why that trend will not continue.
- Ⓔ The author describes effective techniques and then gives examples of those techniques.

34. Which of the following could be substituted for the phrase "random acts" in the last sentence?

Ⓐ Unsound practice
Ⓑ A fashion designer's dream
Ⓒ The movement of hemlines
Ⓓ A fashion show
Ⓔ Pressure from mathematics manipulative manufacturers

———————————————————

35. Empty halls and silent walls greeted me. A summer day seemed like a good day for me to take a look at the school in which I would student teach. I tiptoed from door to door looking. Suddenly the custodian appeared behind me and said, "Help you?" "No sir," I said. At that moment, he could have been Aristotle or Plato for all I knew. Things worked out.

Which of the following best describes the main character in the passage?

Ⓐ Timid and afraid
Ⓑ Confident and optimistic
Ⓒ Pessimistic and unsure
Ⓓ Curious and respectful
Ⓔ Careful and quiet

QUESTIONS 36–38 ARE BASED ON THE FOLLOWING READING.

I remember my childhood vacations at a bungalow colony near a lake. Always bare-foot, my friend and I spent endless hours playing and enjoying our fantasies. We were pirates, rocket pilots, and detectives. Everyday objects were transformed into swords,
Line ray guns, and two-way wrist radios. With a lake at hand, we swam, floated on our crude
(5) rafts made of old lumber, fished, and fell in. The adult world seemed so meaningless while our world seemed so full. Returning years later I saw the colony for what it was—tattered and torn. The lake was shallow and muddy. But the tree that had been our lookout was still there. And there was the house where the feared master spy hid from the FBI. There was the site of the launching pad for our imaginary rocket trips. The
(10) posts of the dock we had sailed from many times were still visible. But my fantasy play did not depend on this place. My child-mind would have been a buccaneer wherever it was.

36. Which of the following choices best characterizes this passage?

Ⓐ An adult describes disappointment at growing up.
Ⓑ A child describes the adult world through the child's eyes.
Ⓒ An adult discusses childhood viewed as a child and as an adult.
Ⓓ An adult discusses the meaning of fantasy play.
Ⓔ An adult describes a wish to return to childhood.

37. The sentence "The adult world seemed so meaningless while our world seemed so full," on lines 5 and 6 is used primarily to

Ⓐ emphasize the emptiness of most adult lives.
Ⓑ provide a transition from describing childhood to describing adulthood.
Ⓒ show how narcissistic children are.
Ⓓ describe the difficulty this child had relating to adults.
Ⓔ emphasize the limited world of the child compared to the more comprehensive world of the adult.

38. Which of the following best characterizes the last sentence in the passage?

Ⓐ The child would have been rebellious, no matter what.
Ⓑ Childhood is not a place but a state of mind.
Ⓒ We conform more as we grow older.
Ⓓ The writer will always feel rebellious.
Ⓔ A part of us all stays in childhood.

QUESTIONS 39–40 APPLY TO THIS PASSAGE.

Sometimes parents are more involved in little league games than their children. I remember seeing a game in which a player's parent came on the field to argue with the umpire. The umpire was not that much older than the player.

Before long, the umpire's mother was on the field. There the two parents stood, toe to toe. The players and the other umpires formed a ring around them and looked on in awe.

Of course, I have never gotten too involved in my children's sports. I have never yelled at an umpire at any of my kid's games. I have never even—well, I didn't mean it.

39. What other "sporting" event is the author trying to re-create in the second paragraph?

Ⓐ Bullfight
Ⓑ Wrestling match
Ⓒ Boxing match
Ⓓ Football game
Ⓔ Baseball game

40. The author portrays herself as "innocent" of being too involved in her children's sports. How would you characterize this portrayal?

Ⓐ False
Ⓑ A lie
Ⓒ Tongue in cheek
Ⓓ Noble
Ⓔ Self-effacing

In the 1796 presidential election, John Adams eked out a victory over Thomas Jefferson. In the controversial XYZ affair, France sought bribes from America. Concern about France led to the Alien and Sedition acts. These acts put pressure on noncitizens and forbade writing that criticized the government. Some Western states opposed those acts and wanted to nullify those acts for their state. This Nullification Theory, and the states' rights mentioned in the Tenth Amendment to the Constitution, raised issues still important today.

41. Which of the following best summarizes the Nullification Theory?

Ⓐ Individual states' rights are superior to federal government rights.
Ⓑ Individual states could nullify their statehood and leave the Union.
Ⓒ Individual states' rights did not apply to noncitizens.
Ⓓ Individual states could decide which laws applied in their states.
Ⓔ Individual states could nullify treaties made with foreign governments.

My love falls on silence nigh
I am alone in knowing the goodbye
For while a lost love has its day
A love unknown is a sadder way

42. The word *nigh* in the first line most nearly means

Ⓐ clear
Ⓑ complete
Ⓒ near
Ⓓ not
Ⓔ missing

43. I grew up in Kearny New Jersey, now known as Soccer Town USA. I played football in high school and barely knew that the soccer team existed. However, a look back at my high school yearbook revealed that the soccer team won the state championship, while the football team had a .500 record. So much for awareness.

The author wrote the passage to

Ⓐ describe a situation.
Ⓑ reflect on past events.
Ⓒ present a point of view.
Ⓓ express irony.
Ⓔ narrate a story.

44. Lyndon Johnson was born in a farmhouse in central Texas in 1908. He grew up in poverty and had to work his way through college. He was elected to the U.S. House of Representatives in 1937, and served in the U. S. Navy during World War II. Following twelve years in the House of Representatives, he was elected to the U.S. Senate, where he was the youngest person chosen by any party to be its Senate leader.

According to this passage, Lyndon Johnson

Ⓐ lived in a farmhouse when he went to college.
Ⓑ was the youngest person elected to the U.S. Senate.
Ⓒ joined the Navy while a U.S. Representative.
Ⓓ served in the Senate for twelve years.
Ⓔ was born in the 1930s.

45. Population experts estimate that there may be 300 million inhabitants in South America. About 7 percent of the inhabitants speak native languages, and pockets of native civilization can still be found in the countryside. Most of the inhabitants with European origins trace their roots to Portugal, Spain, and Italy.

When the passage refers to native languages, it most likely means

Ⓐ spoken by those born in South America.
Ⓑ of those residents of South America who are native to Portugal, Spain, and Italy.
Ⓒ of those living in the pockets of civilization in the countryside.
Ⓓ of those born in South America with European origins who are not from Portugal, Spain, or Italy.
Ⓔ of those natives of Europe who came to South America.

46. The space vehicle identification program is designed to show that the vehicle meets all design and performance specifications. The <u>verification</u> program also seeks to ensure that all hazards and sources of failure have been eliminated or reduced to acceptable levels. The specific spaceship verification is based on a series of carefully monitored testing protocols. The verification tests are conducted under the strictest controls, including temperature and stress levels.

Which of the following words could be used in place of the word *verification*, underlined in the second sentence?

Ⓐ Elimination
Ⓑ Corroboration
Ⓒ Allocation
Ⓓ Renovation
Ⓔ Containment

I.

The United States has the world's largest reserves of coal. Coal is the most common fuel for generating electricity in the United States. Recently, 42 percent of the country's nearly 4 trillion kilowatt hours of electricity used coal as its source of energy. That *Line* such an important resource is abundantly available in this country provides one road (5) to energy independence, with the promise of economic growth and jobs.

Coal has gotten a bad name. However, coal-fired plants have become more efficient; recent advances have developed coal furnaces that operate at 91 percent efficiency. Coal is primarily carbon, and in particular, older plants have had significant carbon dioxide emissions. But the argument that our abundant supply of coal (10) should be abandoned is nonsense, just as it would be nonsense to suggest that cars be abandoned because they kill about thirty thousand Americans each year at an estimated cost approaching $300 billion.

II.

Burning coal to produce energy is widespread and dangerous. During combustion, the reaction between coal and air emits CO_2 (a greenhouse gas), oxides of sulfur (mainly (15) sulfur dioxide; SO_2), and various oxides of nitrogen (NO_x). Hybrids and nitrides of carbon and sulfur are also produced during the combustion of coal in air. These include hydrogen cyanide (HCN), sulfur nitrate (SNO_3), and other toxic substances.

The World Health Organization reports pollution caused by coal likely shortens over twenty thousand lives a year in the United States. Coal mining itself has signifi- (20) cant adverse environmental health impacts, including underground coal fires, some of which are still burning in Pennsylvania.

The argument that this country should use coal just because it has a lot of it does not hold up.

47. Which of the following best describes the relationship of these passages?

Ⓐ Both passages emphasize that coal is an important source of energy.
Ⓑ The first passage emphasizes more the harmful environmental impact of coal more than the second passage.
Ⓒ The first passage emphasizes the potential uses of coal in transportation while the second passage does not.
Ⓓ The second passage opposes the use of coal to produce energy compared to the first passage.
Ⓔ The passages provide equal evidence about the dangers of coal.

48. The meaning of the word *combustion* in context on line 13 is

Ⓐ mixing.
Ⓑ burning.
Ⓒ crushing.
Ⓓ igniting.
Ⓔ washing.

49. Both passages mention carbon dioxide, which is referred to in the second passage as

    Ⓐ NO_x.
    Ⓑ HCN.
    Ⓒ SNO_3.
    Ⓓ CO_2.
    Ⓔ SO_3.

50. Choose the word below that the authors each associate with coal-fired furnaces.

    Ⓐ Dangerous
    Ⓑ Helpful
    Ⓒ Emissions
    Ⓓ Heat
    Ⓔ Light

51. Which of the following sentences, if added to the end of the second passage, would most strengthen the author's position?

    Ⓐ Besides, clean-burning natural gas is replacing coal-fired plants.
    Ⓑ It is true that using coal supports the mining sector of the economy.
    Ⓒ Things get worse when you take the plight of the miners into account.
    Ⓓ There might be some ways to use coal efficiently.
    Ⓔ It is striking that the United States has so much coal.

52. The essence of each passage addresses

    Ⓐ the disadvantages of using coal.
    Ⓑ the advantages of using coal.
    Ⓒ emissions created by coal-burning plants.
    Ⓓ U.S. coal reserves.
    Ⓔ using coal to create energy.

Sun	Mon	Tue	Wed	Thu	Fri	Sat
	1 8:00 A.M. History 10:00 A.M. Algebra 2:00 P.M. Physics	2 9:00 A.M. English 1:00 P.M. Theater	3 8:00 A.M. History 10:00 A.M. Algebra 3:00 P.M. Physics	4 11:00 A.M. English 1:00 P.M. Theater	5 11:00 A.M. Physics Lab A	6
7	8 8:00 A.M. History 10:00 A.M. Algebra 2:00 P.M. Physics	9 9:00 A.M. English 1:00 P.M. Theater	10 8:00 A.M. History 10:00 A.M. Algebra 3:00 P.M. Physics	11 10:00 A.M. English 1:00 P.M. Theater	12 11:00 A.M. Physics Lab B	13 8:00 P.M. PLAY
14	15 8:00 A.M. History 10:00 A.M. Algebra 2:00 P.M. Physics	16 9:00 A.M. English 1:00 P.M. Theater	17 8:00 A.M. History 10:00 A.M. Algebra 3:00 P.M. Physics	18 10:00 A.M. English 1:00 P.M. Theater	19 11:00 A.M. Physics Lab A	20
21	22 8:00 A.M. History 10:00 A.M. Algebra 2:00 P.M. Physics	23 9:00 A.M. English 1:00 P.M. Theater	24 8:00 A.M. History 10:00 A.M. Algebra 3:00 P.M. Physics	25 10:00 A.M. English 1:00 P.M. Theater	26 11:00 A.M. Physics Lab B	27 8:00 P.M. PLAY

The calendar shows when courses and labs are scheduled during the month. Each class meets twice a week.

53. Quinn has to participate in a play following three theater classes, and he wants to participate in the play on the 13th. Which of the following is the best reason for skipping a class on the fourth day of the month?

    Ⓐ That choice would permit Quinn to participate in the play on the 27th.

    Ⓑ That choice would let Quinn be there for the beginning of class and practice just before the play.

    Ⓒ That choice would let Quinn skip English on the 4th and give him the day off to prepare for the physics lab on the 5th.

    Ⓓ Thursday is the day Quinn plans to take a trip to visit his family.

    Ⓔ Most students will be absent on the first day of class.

54. Quinn has to attend two meetings of lab A OR two meetings of lab B. Which of the following is the best explanation of why Quinn would choose lab A?

 Ⓐ Lab A meets during the first week of class.
 Ⓑ Lab B meets on the next-to-last-day of the term.
 Ⓒ There is a play on the 13th.
 Ⓓ There is no play on the 20th.
 Ⓔ Lab B is more difficult than lab A.

55. Based on the calendar, which of the following activities could Quinn have partici-pated in *just one* single time?

Select all that apply.

 A An English class at 11:00 A.M.
 B Algebra on the 22nd
 C A play on the 27th

Music consists of pitch, the actual frequency or sound of a note, and duration. A tone has a specific pitch and duration. Different tones occurring simultaneously are called chords. A melody is the tones that produce the distinctive "sound" of the music. Harmony is chords with a duration. Pitches separated by specific intervals are called a scale. Most music is based on the diatonic scale found on a piano's white keys (C, D, E, F, G, A, B). The chromatic scale includes the seven notes on the diatonic scale with the five sharps and flats corresponding to the white and black keys on a piano.

56. According to the passage, the chromatic scale

 Ⓐ corresponds to the white keys on a piano.
 Ⓑ consists of the flats and sharps not contained in the diatonic scale.
 Ⓒ is contained in the diatonic scale.
 Ⓓ can be played only on a piano.
 Ⓔ includes notes corresponding to seven letters of the alphabet.

WRITING TEST

40 ITEMS 40 MINUTES

2 CONSTRUCTED RESPONSES   60 MINUTES

Usage

> **Directions:** You will read sentences with four parts underlined and lettered. Determine whether one of the underlined parts contains grammatical, word use, or punctuation errors. If so, mark that letter. If there are no errors, mark E.

1. Disgusted by the trash left behind by picnickers, the town council passed a
   A   B   C
   law requiring convicted litterers to spend five hours cleaning up the town
            D
   park. No error.
            E

2. The teacher was sure that the child's difficult home life effected her school work.
                  A   B   C   D
   No error.
      E

3. It took Ron a long time to realize that the townspeople were completely opposed
      A   B   C   D
   to his proposal. No error.
                     E

4. A newspaper columnist promised to print the people who were involved in
                A   B   C
   the secret negotiations concerning the sports stadium in the next column.
                                          D
   No error.
      E

5. The silent halo of a solar eclipse could be seen by astronomers across asia.
              A   B   C   D
   No error.
      E

6. Also found during the archaeological dig was a series of animal bone fragments,
      A   B   C
   fire signs, and arrow points. No error.
                   D   E

7. The <u>teacher</u> asked all of <u>her</u> students to bring in <u>they're</u> permission slips <u>to go on</u>
        Ⓐ   Ⓑ   Ⓒ   Ⓓ

   the Washington trip. <u>No error.</u>
                Ⓔ

8. The <u>plumber</u> <u>did not go</u> to the dripping water <u>than to</u> the place the water
        Ⓐ   Ⓑ   Ⓒ

   <u>seemed to be</u> coming from. <u>No error.</u>
       Ⓓ   Ⓔ

9. The driver realized that she <u>would either</u> have to <u>go completely out of</u>
                      Ⓐ   Ⓑ

   the <u>way</u> or have to wait for the <u>swollen creek</u> to subside. <u>No error.</u>
       Ⓒ   Ⓓ   Ⓔ

10. The <u>tracker</u> was so <u>good that</u> he could tell the <u>difference between</u> a hoofprint
        Ⓐ   Ⓑ   Ⓒ

   made by a horse with a saddle <u>or</u> a hoofprint made by a horse without a
                         Ⓓ

   saddle. <u>No error.</u>
          Ⓔ

11. The mayor <u>estimated</u> that it <u>would cost</u> $1,200 for each <u>citizen individually</u> to
           Ⓐ   Ⓑ   Ⓒ

   repair the storm damage <u>to the town.</u> <u>No error.</u>
                 Ⓓ   Ⓔ

12. <u>Sustaining</u> a <u>month-long</u> winning streak in the town baseball A B league, the
   Ⓐ   Ⓑ

   young team <u>pressed on</u> with <u>unwavering determination.</u> <u>No error.</u>
         Ⓒ   Ⓓ   Ⓔ

13. The fire chief, <u>like the police chief,</u> <u>has so much</u> responsibility, that <u>they often have</u>
           Ⓐ   Ⓑ   Ⓒ

   a personal <u>driver.</u> <u>No error.</u>
          Ⓓ   Ⓔ

14. A talented chef <u>making customers</u> smack their lips at her <u>great gustatorial delights,</u>
            Ⓐ   Ⓑ

   the likes of which <u>are not available</u> in any <u>ordinary restaurant.</u> <u>No error.</u>
              Ⓒ   Ⓓ   Ⓔ

15. The fate of small towns in America, which were <u>popularized</u> in movies when it
(A)

seemed that everyone came from a small town <u>and now</u> face <u>anonymity</u> as
(B)   (C)

cars on highways speed by, <u>is perilous.</u> <u>No error.</u>
(D)   (E)

16. The coach <u>not only</u> <u>works with</u> each pitcher and each catcher, but he <u>also has to</u>
(A)   (B)   (C)

change <u>him.</u> <u>No error.</u>
(D)   (E)

17. When I <u>was a child</u>, a wet washcloth was the <u>main method</u> of first <u>aid</u>; it reduced
(A)   (B)   (C)

swelling, eliminated pain, <u>and inflammation was</u> reduced. <u>No error.</u>
(D)   (E)

18. I am going to a <u>World Cup game</u> next week, and I <u>would be surprised</u> if <u>there is even</u>
(A)   (B)   (C)

one empty seat <u>in the stadium.</u> <u>No error.</u>
(D)   (E)

Sentence Correction

Directions: You will read sentences with some or all of the sentence underlined, followed by five answer choices. The first answer choice repeats the underlined portion and the other four present possible replacements. Select the answer choice that best represents standard English without altering the meaning of the original sentence. Mark that letter on the test or the answer sheet.

19. The quality of the parts received in the most recent shipment <u>was inferior to parts in the previous shipments, but still in accordance with</u> manufacturers' specifications.

(A) was inferior to parts in the previous shipments, but still in accordance with
(B) were inferior to the previous shipments' parts but still in accordance with
(C) was the inferior of the previous shipments' parts but still in accordance with
(D) was inferior to the previous parts' shipments but still not on par with
(E) was inferior to the previous parts' shipments and the manufacturers' specifications

20. <u>The painful rabies treatment first developed by Pasteur</u> saved the boy's life.

(A) The painful rabies treatment first developed by Pasteur
(B) The painful rabies treatment which was first discovered by Pasteur
(C) Pasteur developed the painful rabies treatment
(D) First developed by Pasteur the treatment for painful rabies
(E) The fact that Pasteur developed a rabies treatment

21. By 10:00 A.M. every morning, <u>the delivery service brought important papers to the house in sealed envelopes</u>.

    Ⓐ the delivery service brought important papers to the house in sealed envelopes
    Ⓑ important papers were brought to the house by the delivery service in sealed envelopes
    Ⓒ sealed envelopes were brought to the house by the delivery service with important papers
    Ⓓ the delivery service brought important papers in sealed envelopes to the house
    Ⓔ the deliver service brought sealed envelopes to the house containing important papers

22. The shadows shortened as the sun <u>begun the</u> ascent into the morning sky.

    Ⓐ begun the
    Ⓑ begin the
    Ⓒ began the
    Ⓓ begun that
    Ⓔ begun an

23. Liz and Ann spent all day climbing the mountain, and <u>she was almost</u> too exhausted for the descent.

    Ⓐ she was almost
    Ⓑ they were almost
    Ⓒ they were
    Ⓓ she almost was
    Ⓔ was

24. The embassy announced that at the present time, they could neither confirm <u>nor deny that the ambassador would return home in the event that</u> hostilities broke out.

    Ⓐ nor deny that the ambassador would return home in the event that
    Ⓑ or deny that the ambassador would return home in the event that
    Ⓒ nor deny that the ambassador would return home if
    Ⓓ nor deny that the ambassador would leave
    Ⓔ nor deny that ambassador will return home in the event that

25. Every person <u>has the ultimate capacity to</u> control his or her own destiny.

    Ⓐ has the ultimate capacity to
    Ⓑ ultimately has the capacity to
    Ⓒ has the capacity ultimately to
    Ⓓ can
    Ⓔ could

26. In all likelihood, her mother's absence would be devastating, <u>were it not</u> for the presence of her sister.

    (A) were it not

    (B) it was not

    (C) it were not

    (D) were they not

    (E) was it not

27. She had listened very carefully to all the candidates, and the Independent candidate was the only <u>one who had not said something that did not make sense.</u>

    (A) one who had not said something that did not make sense

    (B) one who did not make sense when he said something

    (C) one who had only said things that made sense

    (D) one to not say something that made sense

    (E) one who never said anything that made no sense

28. The author knew that the book would be finished <u>only by working every day and getting</u> lots of sleep at night.

    (A) only by working every day and getting

    (B) only working every day and getting

    (C) only by working every day and by getting

    (D) only through work and sleep

    (E) only by daily work and by sleepless nights

29. The teacher was sure that Tom's difficult home life affected <u>his school work.</u>

    (A) his school work

    (B) his school's work

    (C) him school work

    (D) his school works

    (E) him school works

30. Small town sheriffs in America, <u>whom were popularized in movies when it seemed that everyone came from a small town,</u> now face anonymity.

    (A) whom were popularized in movies when it seemed that everyone came from a small town

    (B) who were popularized in movies when it seemed that everyone came from a small town

    (C) whom were popularized in movies when it seemed that anyone came from a small town

    (D) whom were popularized in movies when they seemed that everyone came from a small town

    (E) whom were popularized in movies when it seemed that everyone comes from a small town

31. The professor asked the class to consider the development of the human race. She pointed out that, throughout the ages, <u>human beings has learned to communicate by nonverbal means</u>.

    Ⓐ human beings has learned to communicate by nonverbal means
    Ⓑ human beings had learned to communicate by nonverbal means
    Ⓒ human beings has learn to communicate by nonverbal means
    Ⓓ human beings have learn to communicate by nonverbal means
    Ⓔ human beings have learned to communicate by nonverbal means

QUESTIONS 32–36 ARE BASED ON THE FOLLOWING PASSAGE.

Constitution

(1) The Federal Convention convened in the State House (Independence Hall) in Philadelphia on May 14, 1787, to revise the Articles of Confederation. (2) Through discussion and debate it became clear by mid-June that, rather than amend the existing articles, the Convention would draft an entirely new frame of government. (3) All through the summer, in closed sessions, the delegates debated and redrafted the articles of the new Constitution. (4) Among the chief points at issue were how much power to allow the central government, how many representatives in Congress to allow each state, and how these representatives should be elected—directly by the people or by the state legislators. (5) The Constitution stands as a model of cooperative statesmanship and the art of compromise.

(6) For the Constitution to be amended, the amendment must be approved by Congress and sent to the various states to be ratified. (7) A proposed amendment becomes part of the Constitution as soon as it is ratified by three-fourths of the states (38 of 50 states at this time). (8) The first ten amendments were adopted and ratified simultaneously and are known collectively as the <u>Bill of Rights</u>.

(9) The ratification process is not described in detail. (10) Rather, appropriate officials follow procedures and customs established by the Secretary of State. (11) The Constitution provides that an amendment may be proposed either <u>by the Congress with a two-thirds majority vote in both the House of Representatives and the Senate</u> or by a constitutional convention called for by two-thirds of the state legislatures. (12) None of the twenty-seven amendments to the Constitution have been proposed by constitutional convention. (13) Six amendments adopted by Congress and sent to the states have not been ratified by the required number of states.

32. Which of the following sentences, added just after sentence 13, would provide the best conclusion to this paragraph?

    Ⓐ It makes you wonder whatever happened to those six amendments floating around somewhere, and whether it is just a few states or a lot of states that still have to ratify them.
    Ⓑ Six amendments out of thirty-three is not that bad.
    Ⓒ A constitutional convention might be a good idea if none of the amendments has ever been approved by Constitutional Convention.
    Ⓓ Four of these amendments are still technically open and pending.
    Ⓔ It makes you wonder about how unimportant state legislatures have become that they have never proposed a constitutional amendment on their own.

33. In the context of this passage, what is the best replacement for the underlined portion of the sentence shown below?

by the Congress with a two-thirds majority vote in both the House of Representatives and the Senate

   Ⓐ Leave as is
   Ⓑ by a two-thirds majority vote in Congress
   Ⓒ by two-thirds of the House of Representatives or Congress
   Ⓓ with a majority two-thirds vote of the House of Representatives or Congress
   Ⓔ by a two-thirds majority vote

34. In the context of this paragraph, which of the following is the best introduction to sentence 5?

   Ⓐ It goes without saying,
   Ⓑ Because of the secretiveness, the
   Ⓒ State's rights were respected, and
   Ⓓ Thankfully,
   Ⓔ The work of many minds,

35. Among the following choices, which is the best thing to do with sentence 9?

   Ⓐ Delete it.
   Ⓑ Change "ratification" to "clarification.
   Ⓒ Add "Essentially," at the beginning of the passage.
   Ⓓ Add the word *process* as the second word in the sentence.
   Ⓔ Change "majority" to plurality.

36. In context, what is the most effective way to revise and combine sentences 6 and 7, reproduced below?

(6) For the Constitution to be amended, the amendment must be approved by Congress and sent to the various states to be ratified. (7) A proposed amendment becomes part of the Constitution as soon as it is ratified by three-fourths of the states (38 of 50 states at this time).

   Ⓐ Constitutional amendments require approval by Congress and the states.
   Ⓑ Delete sentence (7).
   Ⓒ The Constitution can be amended when the proposed amendment is approved by Congress and ratified by three-fourths of the states.
   Ⓓ Congress approves proposed amendments and states ratify them.
   Ⓔ Constitutional amendments must be ratified by three-fourths of the states. We have 50 so 38 states must ratify, which is really 76 percent of the states.

37. Woodman, Bryna L., and Rae Craven, *Growing Up Nashville, 1953–1963* (Nashville, TN: Forest Street Publishing, 2003), p. 52.

    The citation above is from which of the following types of sources?

    Ⓐ An online article
    Ⓑ A newspaper article
    Ⓒ A blog
    Ⓓ A book
    Ⓔ An interview

38. Which of the following would be correctly cited as a secondary source about dinosaurs?

    Ⓐ Dinosaur bones in a museum
    Ⓑ Field notes from a scientist written as dinosaur bones were unearthed
    Ⓒ A book about reptiles by a scientist who is an expert on dinosaurs
    Ⓓ Dinosaur skeletal remains embedded in a rock outcropping
    Ⓔ An ancient drawing on a cave wall depicting dinosaurs

39. You are writing a paper about Benedict Arnold. Which of the following pieces of information is NOT directly relevant to the paper?

    Ⓐ Benedict Arnold was the commander of the American fortifications at West Point.
    Ⓑ Benedict Arnold secretly planned to surrender West Point to British forces.
    Ⓒ A British major was hanged in connection with the proposed West Point plan.
    Ⓓ The British army paid Arnold to desert the American army and join the British army.
    Ⓔ British raids against American forces in Virginia were led by Arnold.

40. A friend is writing a paper about beekeeping. Which of the following could NOT be a primary source for this paper?

    Ⓐ A book about beekeeping from an experienced beekeeper
    Ⓑ A recorded interview with a beekeeper
    Ⓒ A summary of a report about beekeeping
    Ⓓ Images of steps to follow when extracting honey from a bee hive
    Ⓔ A video showing the steps to control bee stings

ARGUMENTATIVE CONSTRUCTED RESPONSE

30 MINUTES

Directions: You have 30 minutes to complete this constructed-response question. Use a word processor, but not the spell or grammar check, to type a brief response based on this topic.

> To encourage talented people to enter teaching, teachers who score higher on standardized tests should make significantly more money than those teachers who receive lower test scores.

Describe the extent to which you agree or disagree with this statement. Support your response with specific details, examples, and experiences.

Write a brief outline here.

INFORMATIVE/EXPLANATORY CONSTRUCTED RESPONSE

30 MINUTES

> **Directions:** You have 30 minutes to read two position papers on a topic and then type a constructed response based on the topic. Use a word processor, but not the spell or grammar check. The response should discuss the important points in the topic.
>
> Read the topic and sources below. It is good to spend time organizing your thoughts and planning your essay before you start to write. You MUST write on the given topic, and you MUST include references to the sources.
>
> This response gives you a chance to demonstrate how well you can write and include sources in your writing. That means you should focus on writing well, and using examples and references, all while being sure to cover the topic presented. While how much you write is not a specific scoring criteria, you will certainly want to write several meaningful paragraphs.

Topic

Nuclear power uses nuclear processes to generate heat and electricity. The nuclear fission of elements produces the vast majority of nuclear energy. Nuclear fission power stations produce about 6 percent of the world's energy and 15 percent of the world's electricity. Nuclear fission is efficient, but fission and nuclear waste are radioactive, and there is danger, with short- and long-term health risks. The recent Fukushima nuclear accident at a fifty-year-old reactor has slowed but not stopped the construction of newer and safer reactors worldwide. Attempts, unlikely to yield results before the middle of this century, are ongoing to develop nuclear fusion sources, the type of nuclear energy produced by the sun.

Read the two source passages below. Then type an essay that highlights the most important aspects of each and then explain why they are important. Your essay should refer to EACH of the sources and must CITE the sources as you refer to them or provide direct quotations. You may also use your own experiences and readings.

Nuclear Energy . . . the Best Road to Energy Independence
(Quinson, web access 10/12/2014)

You have heard about problems with nuclear energy from older reactors. What you may not have heard is that it is the most efficient way of using renewable energy to create electricity. It is better than coal, which is still the main way electricity is produced, and it is better than oil or gas or any other non-renewable energy source. You have heard a lot about solar power, but the truth is solar power will not be a commercially viable energy source in this century.

Nuclear power has caused fewer fatalities per unit of energy generated. Nuclear energy produces no greenhouse gases and does not pollute the environment. The new reactors put into service are much safer than the reactors built 50 years ago, and many of those older reactors have already been retired. I am very comfortable living just miles from a reactor that has been safely providing energy to this community for decades with no problems. There are no smokestacks, no trains hauling in coal, and no huge pipeline delivering gas or oil. In truth, the air here is cleaner than in most other parts of the United States because coal used to create electricity in most places is simply not used. Beyond that there are over 150 naval vessels propelled by nuclear power, vessels which never have to be refueled at sea and never have to come into port for fuel. That is the benefit of an energy source that does not have to constantly be renewed.

I want to close this brief paper by mentioning the Fukushima Daiichi nuclear reactor accident in 2011. The universal assessment of this tragedy is that it was essentially man made. That is, all investigations agree that the reactor should never have been built where it was, and that a reactor like that one over 50 years old should have already been retired. About 20,000 people were killed by the tsunami and its aftermath. There will undoubtedly be some aftereffects, but not at the level of the number of people killed in the tsunami. Using this accident to argue against nuclear power production is a failed argument.

Nuclear Energy—a Ticking Atom Bomb
(Patrick, web access 9/28/2014)

Nuclear energy is not all bad, and I can think of some specific situations when it might be appropriate. A ship at sea might be one of them, or perhaps a tiny reactor at some remote location away from a populated area, and where the earthquake and tornado risks are close to zero. But that is about it.

A large reactor built anywhere else is nothing more than a ticking bomb—a nuclear bomb. There have been three major accidents in the last 25 years, and the number of nuclear reactors is steadily increasing. No one really knows the death toll from these accidents or the long-term impact of radiation exposure, but the toll will be in the many tens of thousands, with many more impairments and diseases. And that is the problem with radiation—you often do not see most of the impact for decades. Just to understand the real safety issue, consider if someone blew up a coal generating power plant or a nuclear generating plant. Neither is good, but the impact of a destroyed nuclear plant would be devastation. Millions might be killed and thousands of square miles of land made barren for a century. And all that danger for a power system that serves a tiny portion of electric users.

We do not even have to look at the serious safety issues to question nuclear power. Recently former members of the agency that regulates the nuclear industry have said that nuclear energy is simply not economically viable. They point out that solar energy could fill the void that would be left by the absence of nuclear power. It is just a fact that solar energy could never fill a void left if coal and gas were not available to produce energy. So I guess there is a choice, but I will take the choice that will not lead to the death of millions.

Write a brief outline here.

MATHEMATICS TEST

56 ITEMS   85 MINUTES

Directions: Choose the correct answer(s).

---

1. A fair two-sided coin has a heads side and a tails side. The odds that either side will face up when flipped is exactly $\frac{1}{2}$. Jeanette flips the coin three times and gets three heads. What is the probability that the coin will land heads up on the next flip?

   Ⓐ $\frac{1}{16}$

   Ⓑ $\frac{1}{8}$

   Ⓒ $\frac{1}{4}$

   Ⓓ $\frac{1}{2}$

   Ⓔ 1

2. Which of the expressions below is equivalent to $51 - 3y$ for every value of y?

   Ⓐ $(6 - 2)(y - 17)$

   Ⓑ $(10 + 7)(y - 1)$

   Ⓒ $(-12 - 5)(-3 + 3y/17)$

   Ⓓ $(51 - 14)(y - 13)$

   Ⓔ $(14 - 51)3y - 38)$

3. If $3x(5 + 2) = 4(2x + 3)$, what is the value of x? Write your answer below as a fraction.

4. The triangle *ABC* below is shifted 7 units down and 3 units right. What are the coordinates of point *A* after the shifts?

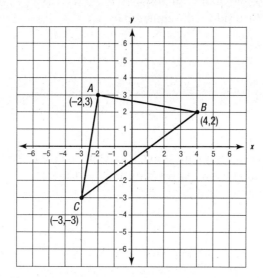

Ⓐ (–7, 0)
Ⓑ (5, –1)
Ⓒ (–6, 1)
Ⓓ (1, –4)
Ⓔ (–1, 6)

5. If $\frac{3}{4}x - 7 = 12$, then $x =$

Ⓐ $6\frac{2}{3}$

Ⓑ $19\frac{2}{3}$

Ⓒ $25\frac{1}{3}$

Ⓓ $36\frac{1}{3}$

Ⓔ $76\frac{1}{3}$

6. The numbers below are listed in order from least to greatest. Choose ALL the following numbers that could be the value of *x*.

$$0.5 \qquad \sqrt{2} \qquad x \qquad \frac{5}{2} \qquad \frac{8}{2}$$

Ⓐ 1.26
Ⓑ 2 333 . . .
Ⓒ $2\frac{3}{8}$
Ⓓ $2\frac{1}{2}$
Ⓔ 4

7. Which of the following equations can be solved using this set of steps?

   1. Add 8 to both sides of the equation.
   2. Then divide each side of the equation by 3.

   (A) $8 - 3x = 3$
   (B) $-8 + 3x = -4$
   (C) $8x - 3 = 3$
   (D) $3x + 8 = 4$
   (E) $-3x - 8 = 3$

8. The class kept track of rainy and sunny days. During 54 days the ratio of rainy days to sunny days was 7 to 14. How many sunny days were there?

   (A) 4
   (B) 8
   (C) 18
   (D) 24
   (E) 36

9. A car traveled along an interstate highway at a constant rate from 11:00 A.M. to 4:00 P.M. During that time the car traveled from mile marker 78 to mile marker 393. How far had the car traveled by 2:00 P.M.?

   (A) 126
   (B) 127
   (C) 128
   (D) 189
   (E) 282

10. The expression below represents the total number of two- and three-point baskets a basketball player scored in a season. The team scored a total of 233 points. What fraction of the total number of the team's points were from that player's three-point baskets?

$$3 \text{ (two)} + 12 \text{ (three)}$$

   (A) $\dfrac{12(\text{three})}{233}$

   (B) $\dfrac{(\text{three})}{233}$

   (C) $\dfrac{12(\text{three}) - 3(\text{two})}{233}$

   (D) $\dfrac{12(\text{three})}{233 - 3(\text{two})}$

   (E) $\dfrac{233}{3(\text{two}) + 12(\text{three})}$

11. All the letters of the alphabet were written on plastic discs and placed in a bag. The vowels in the bag were A, E, I, O, U. Two letters are randomly chosen and not replaced. Both letters are consonants. What is the probability that the next letter chosen will be a vowel?

(A) $\dfrac{1}{5}$

(B) $\dfrac{1}{3}$

(C) $\dfrac{5}{26}$

(D) $\dfrac{5}{24}$

(E) $\dfrac{24}{26}$

12. Accurate readings are taken of the amount of precipitation each day for 10 days. On 2 of the days there was no rainfall. The rainfall amounts in inches on the remaining 8 days are listed below.

0.132, 0.622, 0.093, 0.089, 0.0342, 0.601, 0.009, 0.499

What is the range of the rainfall on these days?

(A) 0.368
(B) 0.499
(C) 0.613
(D) 0.622
(E) 0.754

13. The coordinate plane below shows a graph of a linear equation. Which of the tables of values below could create this graph?

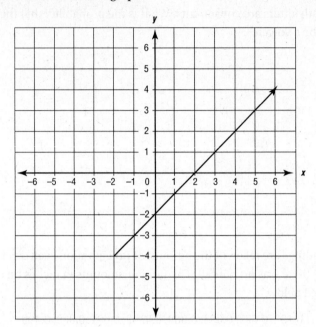

Ⓐ

x	y
2	4
4	6
−2	0
−4	−2

Ⓑ

x	y
0	−2
2	0
1	−1
−3	1

Ⓒ

x	y
1	−1
−1	−3
3	1
6	4

Ⓓ

x	y
4	6
6	4
3	1
1	3

Ⓔ

x	y
3	5
6	4
3	1
0	−3

14. There are four cylinders at the oil tank farm. You can see the first cylinder above. It has a height of 10 feet and a radius of 2 feet. The other three cylinders are hidden behind it. The second cylinder is half the height of this cylinder. The third is $\frac{1}{4}$ the height of this one, and the fourth cylinder is $\frac{1}{8}$ the height of this one. What is the combined volume of all four cylinders?

Use the formula for the volume of a cylinder: volume = $\pi \cdot r^2 \cdot$ height. Use 3.14 for π.

Ⓐ 235.5 cubic feet
Ⓑ 235.555 . . . cubic feet
Ⓒ 284.6 cubic feet
Ⓓ 286.7 cubic feet
Ⓔ 302.4 cubic feet

15. Serena is an account executive. She receives a base pay of $18 an hour plus a 15% bonus for all the sales she generates. Last week she generated $1,200 worth of business. What is the minimum number of hours she could have worked to make $500?

Ⓐ 17
Ⓑ 18
Ⓒ 25
Ⓓ 26
Ⓔ 35

16. If $5a + 3b = 19$ and $4c + 2d = 14$ where $a, b, c,$ and d are whole numbers greater than 0, where neither $a, b, c,$ or d have the same value, and where $a < b$ and $c < d$, then what is the value of the expression $(5a + 3c)(4b + 2d)$? Type your answer in the box below.

17. Which of the following scatter plots best represents a positive correlation?

Ⓐ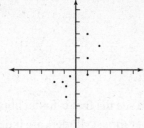

Ⓓ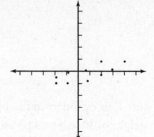

Ⓑ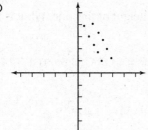

Ⓔ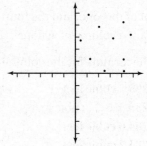

Ⓒ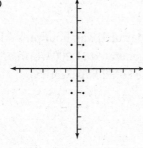

Police
22%

Sanitation
24%

Schools
27%

Fire
19%

Administration
2%

Recreation
6%

18. A town collects $2,600,000 in taxes. The town needs $624,000 for police. Any needed money will come from sanitation. The percents in the circle graph are recalculated. What percent is left for sanitation?

Ⓐ 22%

Ⓑ 20%

Ⓒ 19%

Ⓓ 18%

Ⓔ 16%

19. Steve pays $520 a month for rent, and his monthly paycheck after taxes is $1,300. Which computation shows the percent of Steve's paycheck that is used to pay rent?

Ⓐ $(1300 \div 520) \cdot 100$
Ⓑ $(520 \div 1300) \cdot 100$
Ⓒ $(5.2 \cdot 1300) \cdot 100$
Ⓓ $(13 \cdot 520) \cdot 100$
Ⓔ $(5.2 \cdot 13) \cdot 100$

20. All of the windows in the house are rectangles. None of the windows in the house are squares.

Based on this statement, which of the following conclusions are true?

Ⓐ Some of the windows have four sides of equal length.
Ⓑ None of the windows contain right angles.
Ⓒ None of the windows are parallelograms.
Ⓓ None of the windows have four sides of equal length.
Ⓔ All of the windows contain an acute angle.

21. The area of a square is 4 in². There is a larger square made up of 49 of these squares. What is the length of one side of the larger square?

Ⓐ 7 in
Ⓑ 14 in
Ⓒ 28 in
Ⓓ 56 in
Ⓔ 112 in

22. What is the value of the number in the table below that is expressed in scientific notation?

	A	B	C
1.	53794×10^1	537.94×10^4	5.3794×10^1
2.	5379.4×10^1	53.794×10^2	53794×10^2

Ⓐ 5.37940
Ⓑ 53794
Ⓒ 5379.4
Ⓓ 537.94
Ⓔ 53.794

NUMBER OF AWARDS

Person 1 🏆🏆🏆🏆

Person 2 🏆🏆

Person 3 🏆🏆🏆

Person 4 🏆🏆🏆🏆

Person 5 🏆🏆🏆🏆🏆🏆

Each 🏆 represents 20 awards

23. How many more awards did person 5 have than person 3?

    Ⓐ 20
    Ⓑ 40
    Ⓒ 60
    Ⓓ 80
    Ⓔ 100

24. If the function B 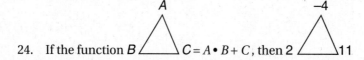 $C = A \cdot B + C$, then 2 △ 11

    Ⓐ −88
    Ⓑ −19
    Ⓒ −3
    Ⓓ 3
    Ⓔ 19

25. The following is a list of the ages of ten different people: 53, 27, 65, 21, 7, 16, 70, 41, 57, and 37.

    What is the difference between the mean age and the median age of the group?

    Ⓐ 0.4
    Ⓑ 4
    Ⓒ 39
    Ⓓ 39.4
    Ⓔ 13

26. A pizza has crust all around the edge. Which of the following figures shows a way to cut the pizza into four equal pieces where only two have crust?

(A)

(D)

(B)

(E)

(C)

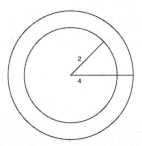

27. What is the difference between the area of the inner circle and the area of the outer circle?

(A) 2π
(B) 4π
(C) 6π
(D) 12π
(E) 14π

28. Frank has 2 dogs, some cats, and 1 bunny. If 62.5 percent of these animals are cats, how many cats are there?

(A) 2
(B) 3
(C) 5
(D) 7
(E) 10

Number of Students on Sports Teams

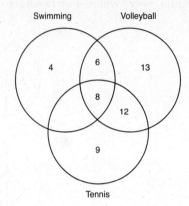

29. How many students participate in all of the sports except swimming?

Ⓐ 4
Ⓑ 8
Ⓒ 14
Ⓓ 30
Ⓔ 34

30. An old laser regenerates in 45,000 microseconds. By which factor does a new laser regenerate if the new laser regenerates every 0.45 microseconds?

Ⓐ 0.1
Ⓑ 0.01
Ⓒ 0.001
Ⓓ 0.0001
Ⓔ 0.00001

31. All of the following numbers are equal except for:

Ⓐ 4/9
Ⓑ 44/90
Ⓒ 404/909
Ⓓ 444/999
Ⓔ 4044/9099

32. Alice arrived at work at 7:45 A.M. and left work at 7 P.M. If she receives $20 an hour salary and no salary for her 1-hour lunch, how much did Alice earn as salary for the day?

Ⓐ $175
Ⓑ $195
Ⓒ $205
Ⓓ $215
Ⓔ $225

33. Which of the following shows a line with x- and y-intercepts equal to 1?

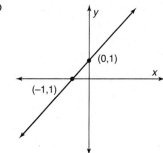

Ⓐ (0,1) (−1,1)

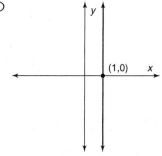

Ⓓ (0,1) (1,0)

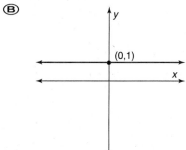

Ⓑ (0,1)

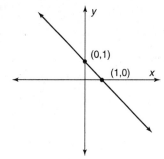

Ⓔ (1,0)

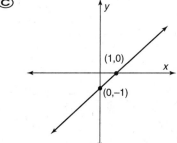

Ⓒ (1,0) (0,−1)

34.

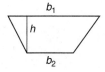

If the lengths of the bases in the trapezoid $(A = \dfrac{h}{2}(b_1 + b_2))$ above are doubled, the area of the new trapezoid is given by the formula:

Ⓐ $A = \dfrac{h}{2}(b_1 + b_2)$

Ⓑ $A = 2h(b_1 + b_2)$

Ⓒ $A = \dfrac{h}{4}(b_1 + b_2)$

Ⓓ $A = h(b_1 + b_2)$

Ⓔ $A = 4h(b_1 + b_2)$

where b_1 and b_2 are the lengths of the original bases.

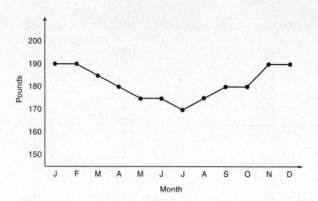

35. The above line graph displays Jack's weight over a 12-month period. Approximately what percentage of Jack's highest weight is Jack's lowest weight?

Ⓐ 97%

Ⓑ 94%

Ⓒ 91%

Ⓓ 89%

Ⓔ 85%

36. Which of the following figures could be used to disprove the following statement: "If a quadrilateral has one pair of congruent sides, then it has two pairs of congruent sides."

Ⓐ
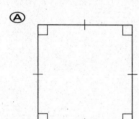

Ⓓ
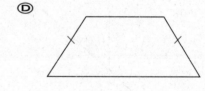

Ⓑ
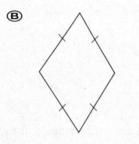

Ⓔ
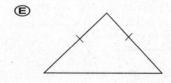

Ⓒ
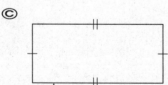

37. The five shapes seen below are made up of identical semi-circles and identical quarter-circles. Which of the five shapes has the greatest perimeter?

Ⓐ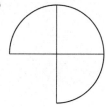

Ⓓ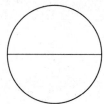

Ⓑ

Ⓔ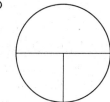

Ⓒ

38. Which of the following choices is not equivalent to the others?

Ⓐ $3^4 \times 9 \times 12$
Ⓑ $3^3 \times 27 \times 12$
Ⓒ $3^5 \times 36$
Ⓓ $3^3 \times 9^3 \times 4$
Ⓔ $3^5 \times 4 \times 9$

39. Company employees just received their earning report. The earnings of 4 individuals in a company are:

Person 1: $45,250
Person 2: $78,375
Person 3: $52,540
Person 4: $62,325

The total earnings of these individuals, in thousands of dollars, is closest to:

Ⓐ $237 thousand
Ⓑ $238 thousand
Ⓒ $239 thousand
Ⓓ $240 thousand
Ⓔ $241 thousand

40. Which of the following is true about the graph seen below?

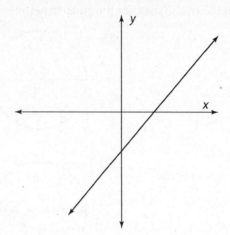

Ⓐ As *x* increases, *y* decreases
Ⓑ As *x* decreases, *y* does not change
Ⓒ As *x* decreases, *y* increases
Ⓓ As *x* increases, *y* increases
Ⓔ As *x* increases, *y* does not change

41. A computer costs 65 percent of its retail price of $400. What does the computer cost?

Ⓐ $660
Ⓑ $540
Ⓒ $260
Ⓓ $200
Ⓔ $140

42. What is the average of $\frac{1}{2}$, $\frac{2}{3}$, and $\frac{5}{12}$?

Ⓐ $\frac{19}{12}$

Ⓑ $\frac{19}{24}$

Ⓒ $\frac{19}{36}$

Ⓓ $\frac{19}{44}$

Ⓔ $\frac{19}{52}$

43. In a standard deck of 52 cards, what is the probability of being dealt a king, a queen, or a jack?

   Ⓐ $\frac{1}{3}$

   Ⓑ $\frac{2}{13}$

   Ⓒ $\frac{3}{13}$

   Ⓓ $\frac{4}{13}$

   Ⓔ $\frac{5}{13}$

44. To estimate 2.3×10^5 you could multiply 20 by

   Ⓐ 10
   Ⓑ 100
   Ⓒ 1,000
   Ⓓ 10,000
   Ⓔ 100,000

45. A circle can be a part of any of the following except a

   Ⓐ circle.
   Ⓑ sphere.
   Ⓒ cylinder.
   Ⓓ cone.
   Ⓔ cube.

46. The 2.00 P.M. temperature is shown on the thermometer. At 10:00 A.M. the temperature was 8° warmer. If the temperature changed at a constant rate, what was the temperature at noon?

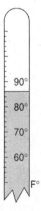

   Ⓐ 82°F
   Ⓑ 86°F
   Ⓒ 90°F
   Ⓓ 94°F
   Ⓔ 96°F

47. If $6x + 2y = 10$, which of the following choices are possible values for x and y?

   (A) $x = 2, y = -1$
   (B) $x = 2, y = 11$
   (C) $x = 3, y = 4$
   (D) $x = 3, y = 14$
   (E) $x = 4, y = -8$

48. Tickets for a baseball game are $8 each, or 4 tickets for $30. What is the lowest cost for 18 tickets?

   (A) $144
   (B) $136
   (C) $132
   (D) $130
   (E) $126

49. If $4A + 6 = 2(B - 1)$, then $B = ?$

   (A) $2A + 4$
   (B) $8A + 13$
   (C) $2A + 2$
   (D) $4A + 7$
   (E) $4A + 5$

50. Which of the following measurements is not equal to the others?

   (A)   230,000 millimeters
   (B)   0.23 kilometers
   (C)   23 meters
   (D)   23,000 centimeters
   (E)   2.3 hectometers

51. Which of the following choices is a multiple of 7 when 4 is added to it?

   (A)   58
   (B)   114
   (C)   168
   (D)   78
   (E)   101

52. Ryan has gone $3\frac{1}{5}$ miles of his 5-mile run.

How many more miles has he left to run?

Ⓐ A little less than 2 miles
Ⓑ A little more than 2 miles
Ⓒ A little less than 3 miles
Ⓓ A little more than 3 miles
Ⓔ A little less than 4 miles

53. For every 2 hours that Barbara works she earns $17. How much money will she earn if she works 45 hours?

Ⓐ $391
Ⓑ $382.50
Ⓒ $374
Ⓓ $365.50
Ⓔ $357

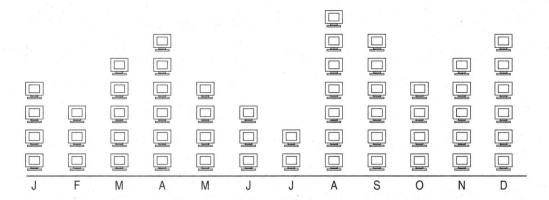

54. The pictograph shows TV sales for each month for all the stores in a chain. About how many times greater is the number of televisions sold in December than the number of televisions sold in January?

Ⓐ 1.5
Ⓑ 2
Ⓒ 2.5
Ⓓ 3
Ⓔ 3.5

55. Which of the below circles include measurements that would be possible?
Choose all that apply.

(Point B is the center of each circle.)

A

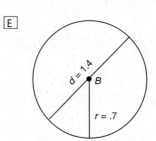

D

B

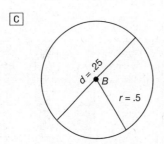

E

C

Ice Cream Cone Sales

Single Scoop	$2.50
Double Scoop	$4.00

56. The sign shows the cost of ice cream cones. A total of 100 cones were sold over a weekend. What additional information would be needed to determine how many double-scoop cones were sold?

Ⓐ The total number of the single-scoop cones sold.

Ⓑ The number of patrons who bought both single- and double-scoop cones.

Ⓒ The total dollar value of all the cones sold.

Ⓓ The total number of cones sold each day.

Ⓔ Amount of ice cream in each scoop.

ANSWER KEY
Practice Core 1

READING TEST

1. D	11. D	21. E	31. A	41. D	51. A
2. E	12. C	22. B	32. E	42. C	52. E
3. C	13. A, B	23. B	33. B	43. D	53. B
4. D	14. B	24. A	34. C	44. C	54. B
5. D	15. C	25. A	35. D	45. C	55. A, B, C
6. C	16. B	26. B	36. C	46. B	56. E
7. C	17. C	27. C	37. B	47. C	
8. B	18. D	28. B	38. B	48. B	
9. C	19. C	29. C	39. C	49. D	
10. B	20. C	30. B	40. C	50. C	

WRITING TEST

Usage

1. E	4. B	7. C	10. D	13. C	16. E
2. C	5. D	8. C	11. C	14. A	17. D
3. E	6. B	9. E	12. E	15. B	18. B

Sentence Correction

19. A	23. B	27. C	31. E	35. D	39. C
20. A	24. C	28. C	32. D	36. C	40. B
21. D	25. D	29. A	33. A	37. D	
22. C	26. A	30. B	34. E	38. B	

MATHEMATICS TEST

1. D	10. A	20. D	30. E	40. D	50. C
2. C	11. D	21. B	31. B	41. C	51. E
3. $\frac{12}{13}$	12. D	22. E	32. C	42. C	52. A
	13. C	23. C	33. D	43. C	53. B
4. D	14. A	24. D	34. D	44. D	54. A
5. C	15. B	25. A	35. D	45. E	55. B, E
6. B, C	16. 286	26. C	36. D	46. C	56. A
7. B	17. A	27. D	37. B	47. A	
8. E	18. A	28. C	38. D	48. B	
9. D	19. B	29. E	39. B	49. A	

EXPLAINED ANSWERS

Reading

1. **(D)** The paragraph describes how careful shopping can result in lower prices.

2. **(E)** The author is trying to raise AIDS awareness and not to present any particular fact.

3. **(C)** The passage explains that AIDS is transmitted through blood and other bodily fluids.

4. **(D)** The sentence for this choice is the best conclusion for this passage.

5. **(D)** The retired basketball player mentions youth basketball as one of the reasons why today's players were better athletes. The passage also mentions an increased focus on training. However, the question does not ask for all the factors the retired player mentioned.

6. **(C)** This writer believes that generals should be judged by results. Even if you do not agree, that is the view of this writer.

7. **(C)** The author writes that the question still cannot be answered. The author does not say that the question can never be answered.

8. **(B)** The author never discusses exemptions but indicates that Boards of Adjustment should do away with exemptions.

9. **(C)** The passage gives an example of a person who both supported and did not support requested exemptions.

10. **(B)** The author is writing about a local issue.

11. **(D)** In the last paragraph the author uses these words to describe Boards of Adjustment.

12. **(C)** The author gives several examples in which people support or don't support exemptions based on their own needs.

13. **(A, B)** A and B, together, assure the student that she will be chosen and give her a chance to get into a sorority she wants.

14. **(B)** B is the only list that meets all the requirements.

15. **(C)** The rate, alone, does not provide enough information. You must also know the starting point.

16. **(B)** You should question any growth rate when only the percentage is given.

17. **(C)** Choice C is correct. A sentence can state both a fact and an opinion. "(2) alone states an opinion" means that it is the only sentence that states an opinion.

18. **(D)** This choice gives the fundamental reason why the schools' programs are copied. The other reasons grow out of the decision to provide extra resources.

19. **(C)** The author objects to using these programs with students who don't know mathematics.

20. **(C)** This is the only question that can be answered from information in the passage. The answer is that it can be used when students already understand equations and graphing.

21. **(E)** The author emphasizes understanding in the second paragraph with a discussion of the "mindless kind of graphing . . ." that can occur with graphing calculators.

22. **(B)** The author mentions liking this aspect in the middle of the first paragraph.

23. **(B)** Choice B replicates the intent of the original sentence.

24. **(A)** The author provides support for this conclusion in the fourth sentence. The conclusions in the other choices are refuted in the passage.

25. **(A)** This is the only choice that reflects the author's observation that potentially weaker spots were actually stronger.

26. **(B)** The author's view is that all children should be treated the same.

27. **(C)** Choice C describes the problem. All the students who might have been admitted early this year will be admitted next year along with the other kindergarten students.

28. **(B)** Only this choice is a logical conclusion.

29. **(C)** When there are three lanes for passenger cars, school buses, school vans, and school cars can all use the lane for cars with two or more passengers.

30. **(B)** Only this choice meets all the rules.

31. **(A)** The context tells us that the answer, the tenor (direction, tendency) of the times, is the best choice to replace "zeitgeist."

32. **(E)** Of the listed sentences, only "This cycle is more akin . . ." contains an opinion.

33. **(B)** The author compares fashion to education, and then finally gets to the main point of the passage. That is, education practices seem random, like fashion, rather than based on sound educational practices.

34. **(C)** Hemlines move without apparent reason, which is this author's point about educational practices.

35. **(D)** The character visited the school and so is certainly curious. The character's reaction to the custodian shows respectfulness.

36. **(C)** The author discusses childhood from each of the perspectives described in C. Choice D is incorrect because the meaning of fantasy play is never discussed.

37. **(B)** This sentence juxtaposes adulthood and childhood and provides a transition to discussing adulthood.

38. **(B)** The author says that these childhood experiences would have occurred regardless of the location.

39. **(C)** The description of going toe to toe inside a ring reminds us of a boxing match.

40. **(C)** The author is not lying, but the story is obviously not meant to be taken seriously.

41. **(D)** You will find the answer in the third sentence. Some states wanted to nullify acts (laws) so these laws would not apply to their states. A and B are incorrect because the Nullification theory applied to laws on a case-by-case basis and were not as sweeping as the answers given in these choices.

42. **(C)** The word *nigh* most nearly means *near*, in time, place, or relationship. The writer's love has fallen on the deaf ears of someone near to the writer.

43. **(D)** Irony means an incongruity between the actual result and the expected result. It is ironic that the writer did not even know about the soccer team in Soccer Town USA.

44. **(C)** The third sentence indicates that he entered the Navy while he was in the House of Representatives.

45. **(C)** The passage indicates that the pockets of native civilizations, where native language would most likely be spoken, are in the countryside. Note that choice A is incorrect because births in South America can occur among nonnatives.

46. **(B)** Corroboration means "evidence of support for a finding," which has the same meaning as verification.

47. **(C)** The second passage clearly states opposition to the use of coal, which is supported in the first paragraph.

48. **(B)** Combustion means burning, which is what happens to coal as it is converted into energy.

49. **(D)** The main clues are the "di" in carbon dioxide, which means 2, the subscript in this answer choice, and that CO is the most likely abbreviation for carbon. You may know from your own experience that CO_2 is the abbreviation for carbon dioxide.

50. **(C)** The first passage includes the word *emit*, while the second passage includes the word *emissions*. Each word means the same thing, discharge(s), when applied to coal furnaces.

51. **(A)** The author's main point is that coal is a bad choice to create energy. Adding information about clean-burning natural gas supports that point of view. The other choices tend to weaken the author's anti-coal point of view.

52. **(E)** The common thread that runs through both passages is using coal to create energy.

53. **(B)** This choice is best because it gives Quinn two successive theater classes before the play, and allows him to be there for the first class when he is most likely to choose a part he wants. Choice D is incorrect because you do not know to which Thursday this choice refers.

54. **(B)** Quinn chooses lab A to avoid lab B, which comes at the end of the term. Lab A gives him more time off. The plays are not a factor, and you do not know anything about the difficulty of the labs.

55. **(A, B, C)** Quinn could only participate in each of these activities just once. None of the activities conflicts with the other. The other Algebra classes, plays on other days, and the English classes at other times are separate activities.

56. **(E)** The chromatic scale includes the diatonic scale, which includes the notes corresponding to the first seven letters of the alphabet. Remember, the black keys add sharps and flats but not more letters.

Writing

USAGE

1. **(E)** This sentence does not contain an error.

2. **(C)** The word *effected* is incorrect. It should be replaced by the word *affected*.

3. **(E)** This passage also contains no errors. *Townspeople* is an appropriate word.

4. **(B)** You can't print people. The underlined section should be *names of the people*.

5. **(D)** The word *Asia* is capitalized.

6. **(B)** The correct verb is *were*.

7. **(C)** The contraction *they're* (they are) is used incorrectly. *Their* is the correct word.

8. **(C)** The phrase *than to* is incorrectly used here. *But to* is the correct phrase.

9. **(E)** There are no underlined errors in this sentence.

10. **(D)** The conjunction *or* is incorrectly used here. The correct conjunction is *and*.

11. **(C)** There is no reason to use the word *individually*. Each citizen is an individual. The word *individually* should be removed.

12. **(E)** The passage contains no errors in underlined parts.

13. **(C)** The word *they* creates confusion because it could mean that there is one driver for both of them. A better usage is *each often has*.

14. **(A)** *Making* is the wrong verb. *Made* is the correct choice.

15. **(B)** The words *and now* should read *and which now*, in order to clarify just what faces anonymity.

16. **(E)** This sentence contains no underlined errors.

17. **(D)** This part of the sentence does not follow a parallel development. The correct usage is *reduced inflammation*.

18. **(B)** The correct replacement for *would be surprised* is *will be surprised*.

SENTENCE CORRECTION

19. **(A)** The underlined portion is appropriate.

20. **(A)** The underlined portion is appropriate.

21. **(D)** The rewording in D clarifies that the papers are in sealed envelopes—not in the house.

22. **(C)** This choice is the best wording from among the five choices available.

23. **(B)** This choice creates an agreement in number between nouns and pronoun.

24. **(C)** This choice replaces the wordy *in the event that* with *if*.

25. **(D)** This wordy expression is replaced by *can*.

26. **(A)** The underlined portion is appropriately worded.

27. **(C)** This choice appropriately replaces the double negative underlined in the original sentence.

28. **(C)** Adding the word *by* creates the desired parallel development in the sentence.

29. **(A)** The sentence is correct. The pronoun *his* agrees with the antecedent *Tom.*

30. **(B)** *Who* correctly shows the subjective case.

31. **(E)** *Have learned* indicates this has occurred and may continue.

32. **(D)** This sentence clarifies the status of the six unratified amendments and brings this paragraph to a conclusion.

33. **(A)** The existing sentence part is a better choice than any of the suggested replacements. These replacements are all incomplete in some way and do not accurately describe the amendment process.

34. **(E)** This choice captures the cooperation and compromise that led to the Constitution, which was not the work of a single person.

35. **(D)** The word *ratification* refers to the outcome. Adding the word *process* clarifies the sentence and indicates that the sentence describes the steps to ratification.

36. **(C)** The best answer is C. This sentence eliminates some of the wordiness of sentence 6 and sentence 7 and still conveys the essential meaning of these sentences.

37. **(D)** There is only one title and a publisher, indicating that this citation is for a book.

38. **(B)** The field notes are a secondary source. The scientist was not around when the dinosaurs were alive. Choices A and D are primary sources. Choice C is a general reference and not directly a source about dinosaurs. As for E, there were no drawings of any type made showing living dinosaurs.

39. **(C)** This statement about Major Andre is true, but it is not <u>directly</u> related to the topic of Benedict Arnold.

40. **(B)** In general, a summary cannot be a primary source. It is likely that the original report would have been a primary source.

Argumentative Essay

Compare your essay to the sample essay that follows. You may want to show your essay to an English expert for further evaluation.

This essay would likely receive a score of 5 or 6 out of 6 (515 words).

Paying Teachers Because They Score High Is a Bad Idea

A higher standardized test score does not tell anything about what a person will be like as a teacher. How many of us have known someone who could do very well on tests, but could not interact effectively with others? The same thing is true of people who do well on tests and can't explain what they know to another person. This does not mean that doing well on tests is a bad thing. It does seem to me that doing well on tests does not by itself mean that someone will be a good teacher. Besides that it is very hard to pay teachers on an incentive basis because there are so many differences among the pupils that teachers work with that you could never tell whether students did well because of a teacher or because of some other reason.

I don't agree that teacher's should be paid more to do something that lasts for a year because they scored higher on a test that lasts for hours, and I don't think it is possible to pay teachers by merit in most situations. I am going to write some things about each of these.

Just try to imagine this situation. There are two first grade teachers. One teacher scored much higher on a standardized test. Both teachers have to help their students learn about reading. But the teacher with the higher score for some reason or another can't deal with these young children. They do not have the patience to work with them all day long. It could be that the teacher with the higher score does not know how to teach reading. The teacher with the lower score is just the opposite. That other teacher works well with the children they have the patience to deal with them and they know how to teach reading. I do not think we could find a person anywhere who would not think that this low scoring teacher is the one we would want in the classroom.

The idea of paying teachers by merit is a part of this question. I think paying teachers in that way would be great if there was any way to tell that a teacher was the reason students were doing better or poorer as they learned. But I do not think there is. I can think of classes I was in where we did better because of the students who were in my class. To be honest the teacher did not help that much. But if you pay by merit then the teacher would have been paid more, not because of the teacher, but because of the students. That is not right.

In conclusion, I disagree with the statement because there is not evidence that indicates that teachers with higher standardized scores are better teachers. If some teachers have higher standardized scores, it is probably something about them and not the scores they received. This idea of paying teachers this way is an idea that should not be used in schools.

Informative/Explanatory Essay

Compare your essay to the sample essay that follows. You may want to show your essay to an English expert for further evaluation.

Here is an essay that would receive a 5 or a 6.

The issues raised in these essays have mainly to do with safety, but also with the continued use of nuclear reactors for power generation. Both authors agree that a strength of nuclear energy is that it is a renewable energy source with low greenhouse emissions.

Each author agrees there can be health risks associated with nuclear power generation. However, the Quinson seeks to minimize the risks, noting that, "Nuclear power has caused fewer fatalities per unit of energy generated." Personally, I don't find that particularly reassuring because the introduction notes that nuclear energy generates just 5% of the world's energy. Patrick takes a more ominous tone pointing out the three major nuclear accidents that occurred in the last 25 years writing ". . . nuclear reactor . . . is a ticking time bomb—a nuclear bomb." (Patrick)

The authors quite unusually each downplay the role of nuclear power in energy production. Quinson points out that coal is far and away the fuel used most often to produce power. Patrick seconds this idea, noting that solar power could fill the void left by the absence of nuclear energy but never the void left by the absence of coal.

Quinson brings in an additional point that there are "over 150 naval vessels powered by nuclear energy." (Quinson) Quite unusually, it seems to me, Patrick also believes a "ship at sea" (Patrick) might be an appropriate use of nuclear power.

Frankly, a somewhat confusing picture appears from these position papers. Quinson indicates that nuclear power is generally good, with some reservations. On the other hand Patrick says nuclear reactors are like nuclear bombs, most of the time. Each author likes nuclear power's reliability and absence of greenhouse emissions. I am drawn to Patrick's point that if some cataclysmic event occurs the results could be catastrophic. It's this final point that convinces me that Patrick's position is most appropriate.

Discussion

This essay identifies the main issues and notes that the issue of nuclear safety is the most prominent issue. The essay uses information from the two position papers, both by paraphrasing and by quoting, and in each case cites the appropriate position paper. This paper helps the reader see where the authors of the position papers actually agree and brings the essay writer's own perspectives to the issue. The essay is long enough for a rater to place it in the upper third, uses language well, and is free of any meaningful English errors.

This essay would receive a 3 or 4.

The best way to look at and see the main points about nuclear energy is to take each author's position one at a time. It seems that you either think it's good or you think it is bad. We can see that Quinson supports nuclear energy, while it looks like Patrick mainly opposes it.

As I see it Quinson mainly shows his support for nuclear energy by going to great lengths to explain off the nuclear accident with that tusomi in Japan. In this position paper. "Universal assessment of this tragedy is that it was essentially man made." I mean that may be true but it does not seem that should make much difference. The problem would not have happened if the reactor was not there. So what difference does it make. But this position paper sticks to its guns and add to "all investigations agree that the reactor should never have been built where it was." Quinson also brings all the ships that use reactors to make them work, but even Patrick seems to think that is OK too.

Patrick uses a title that shows opposition right away with the words "Nuclear Energy—A Ticking Atom Bomb." But when you start to read the paper it is hard to tell for sure that Patrick really is opposed. That's because of the fact that the first paragraph lists some ways that nuclear energy could be useful.

That all changes in the second paragraph. That is when we read that there "been three major accidents in the last 25 years." (Patrick) I remember reading about the one in Japan and it seemed pretty bad to me. Then Patrick goes further, "No one really knows the death toll from these accidents, and the long term impact of radiation exposure." I agree with that. I think that people were effected by the radiation from first atom bomb for decades and decades after the bomb was dropped. That would have to be true for other nuclear accidents.

Quinson is really on the defensive from the very beginning, and Patrick starts out too with a few positive things to say about nuclear power. But when you read on it seems that Quinson's paper is based on what Quinson believes, and that Patrick's paper provides more factual information.

Discussion

This essay lays out each position paper's point of view and frequently brings in the writer's own experiences. The essay mentions information from both sources and usually cites the source of the information. The essay summarizes the writer's opinion of the strength of the argument in each position paper. The essay does not fully integrate a discussion of the issues. While grammar and usage are generally fine, there are errors including sentence fragments, wordiness, and grammar. The appropriate references, completeness of the essay, and usage earn this essay a 4.

This essay would earn a 2.

The way I read these essays, the authors of the paper each agree that nuclear energy is a problem. One says nuclear energy is a ticking time bomb. The other says that nuclear energy is not all bad but doesn't that mean that it's at least somewhat bad. They writing about different stuff.

It's pretty hard to argue that radiation from a generator is not like radiation from a bomb. Once you see that the rest of it is just talk. These authors know how to make their own points, but is that the reason for writing a paper to show that you know how to make a point.

They each agree that nuclear energy is dangerous, it's just that one tries to convince you that it is not as dangerous as you might think it is. OK, I get it nuclear energy is dangerous.

Discussion

Even a well-written essay that cited sources, but was this short, could never earn a score above 3. The absence of any citations and the poor development mean that the highest score possible is a 2. The score could not be higher unless both the development and the citations were significantly improved.

Mathematics

1. **(D)** $\frac{1}{2}$

   The coin is a fair coin so no matter how many times you flip it the probability that the coin will land heads up is always $\frac{1}{2}$.

2. **(C)** Here is the best way to solve this problem. Find a product that equals 51.

   To see this only occurs in choice C, multiply $(-12 - 5) \times -3$ (the first term in the second expression). $(-12 - 5) \times -3 = -17 \times -3 = 51$

   To find out if C is correct, work out the entire problem. Remember to do the work in parentheses first.

   $(-12 - 5) (-3 + \frac{3y}{17}) =$

   $-17 (-3 + \frac{3y}{17}) =$

   $(-17) (-3) + (-17) (\frac{3y}{17})$ (That is the distributive property.)

   $= 51 - \frac{(17)(3y)}{17} = 51 - 3y$

3. $\left(\frac{12}{13}\right)$ Solve the equation.

   $3x (5 + 2) = 4 (2x + 3) = 15x + 6x = 8x + 12 \quad 21x = 8x + 12$

   Subtract $8x$ from each side of the equation.

   $21x \quad = \quad 8x + 12$
   $-8x \quad \quad -8x$
   $13x = 12$

   Solve for x

   $x = \frac{12}{13}$

4. **(D)** Remember that "up" (add) and "down" (subtract) describe the movement of the y coordinate, while "left" (subtract) and "right" (add) describe the movement of the x coordinate.

The original coordinates of point A are $(-2, 3)$

Add 3 to find the x coordinate $-2 + 3 = 1$. Subtract 7 to find the y coordinate: $3 - 7 = -4$

The coordinates of point A after the translation are $(1, -4)$.

You can trace the movement on the graph to confirm your answer.

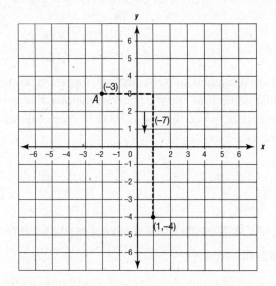

5. **(C)** Solve the equation.

$$\frac{3}{4}x - 7 = 12$$

$$\frac{3}{4}x (-7)(+7) = 12 + 7 \text{ (First add 7 to each side.)}$$

$$\frac{3}{4}x = 19$$

$$\left(\frac{3}{4}\right)\left(\frac{4}{3}\right)x = 19 \times \frac{4}{3} \text{ (Next multiply by } \frac{4}{3}.)$$

$$x = 19 \times \frac{4}{3}$$

$$x = \frac{76}{3}$$

$$x = 25\frac{1}{3}$$

6. **(B, C)** $\sqrt{2}$ is just to the left of x.

First use the calculator square root key to estimate that $\sqrt{2}$ is about 1.41.

x will be greater than 1.41.

$\frac{5}{2}$ is just to the right of x. x will be less than $2\frac{1}{2}$.

Look at each number in turn.

(A) 1.26; No, 1.26 is less than 1.41

(B) 2,333 . . . $\left(\frac{1}{333} \ldots = 2\frac{1}{3}\right)$; Yes, $2\frac{1}{3}$ is more than 1.42 and less than $2\frac{1}{2}$.

(C) $2\frac{3}{8}$; Yes, $2\frac{3}{8}$ is more than 1.41 and less than $2\frac{1}{2}$ $(2\frac{4}{8})$.

(D) $2\frac{1}{2}$; No, $2\frac{1}{2} = \frac{5}{2}$.

(E) 4 No, 4 is greater than $\frac{5}{2}$.

7. **(B)** These steps solve this equation.

   Here are the steps for the other equations.

   (A) Subtract 8 from each side and then divide each side by –3.
   (C) Add 3 to each side and divide each side by 8.
   (D) Subtract 8 from each side and then divide each side by 3.
   (E) Add 8 to each side and then divide each side by –3.

8. **(E)** The ratio 7 to 14 (7:14) can be expressed as 1:2. Use the equation $x + 2x = 54$, where x represents the number of rainy days and $2x$ the number of sunny days. The total number of days equals 54, so $x + 2x = 54$ and $3x = 54$, $x = 18$.

   $x = 18$, the number of rainy days

   $2x = 36$, the number of sunny days

   $18 + 36 = 54$. That checks.

9. **(D)** The car traveled for a total of 5 hours. Subtract to find how far the car traveled: $393 – 78 = 315$ miles. Divide by 5 to find the rate per hour: $315 \div 5 = 63$. The rate is 63 miles an hour. At 2:00 P.M. the car traveled for 3 hours. Multiply $63 \times 3 = 189$ to find how far the car had traveled at 2:00 P.M.

10. **(A)** The answer is a fraction with the total number of the team's points in the denominator and the total number of the player's three-point baskets in the numerator. There is no equation to solve.

11. **(D)** There are 26 letters in the alphabet. When 2 consonants were removed that left 24 letters, 5 of which were vowels. The probability of randomly picking a vowel is $\frac{5}{24}$.

12. **(D)** First find the lowest and highest rainfall amounts. The lowest amount is 0; there were two days with no rainfall.

    To find the highest amount look first in the tenths place. The largest digit in the tenths place is 6. There are two rainfall amounts with 6 in the tenths place: 0.622 and 0.601.

    0.622 is the largest of these two numbers.

    Subtract the smallest amount of rainfall from the largest amount to find the range. $0.622 – 0 = 0.622$

13. **(C)** First look at the graph to find two points where the graph crosses the intersection of two coordinate lines. The most obvious ones in this graph are (3, 1) and (–1, –3). Find a table with these two sets of values.

    There is just one table with these two points, table C. Check out the other two points to be sure they fit the pattern. They do. This is the correct choice.

14. **(A)** First find the volume of the main tank shown in the diagram.

    Use the calculator. Remember the answer is in cubic feet.

    $V = \pi \cdot r^2 \cdot h$

    $V = 3.14 \times 2^2 \times 10 = 3.14 \times 40 = 125.6$ cubic feet

    Now add to find the total size of all four cylinders

    $1 + \dfrac{1}{2} + \dfrac{1}{4} + \dfrac{1}{8} = 1 + \dfrac{4}{8} + \dfrac{2}{8} + \dfrac{1}{8} = 1\dfrac{7}{8}$

    It turns out $\dfrac{7}{8}$ has a decimal representation of 0.875. You would get the same answer

    if you used the fraction $\dfrac{7}{8}$.

    The total size of all four tanks is 1.875.

    Multiply $1.875 \times 125.6 = 235.5$. (Remember you have a calculator.)

    The total volume of all four tanks is 235.5 cubic feet.

15. **(B)** Multiply to find her bonus: $1,200 \times 15\% = \$180$

    She needs to work enough hours to make $500 – \$180 = \$320.

    Divide to find the number of hours: $\dfrac{\$320}{18} = 17$ R 14

    17 hours would be too few so she would have to work a minimum of 18 hours.

    Notice that choices C, D, and E are incorrect because they are *more* than the minimum number of hours she needed to work.

16. **(286)** You could probably see that you cannot find the values of *a*, *b*, *c*, and *d* directly. You need to use trial and error. We know that the numbers will be from the set 1, 2, 3, 4, 5, 6, 7, 8, 9, 10, 11, 12, 13, 14, 15 . . . That's going to make it a lot easier.

    $5a + 3b = 19$. Just a few guesses will show us that $a = 2$ and $b = 3$.

    $4c + 2d = 14$ Just a few more guesses shows us that $c = 1$ and $d = 5$.

    Substitute these values in the expression.

    $(5a + 3c)\ (4b + 2d)$
    $(5 \cdot 2 + 3 \cdot 1)\ (4 \cdot 3 + 2 \cdot 5) =$
    $(10 + 3)\ (12 + 10) =$ (Use the order of operations.)
    $13 \cdot 22 = 286$

17. **(A)** The "tight" diagonal pattern from lower left to upper right best shows a positive correlation. Choice B shows a negative correlation. Choices C and E show no correlation. Choice D suggests a slight positive correlation but not the strong positive correlation found in choice A.

18. **(A)** Divide to find what percent $624,000 is of $2,600,000. $624,000 \div 2,600,000 = 0.24 = 24$ percent. The town needs 24 percent for police, 2 percent more than in the pie chart. Take 2 percent from sanitation, leaving 22 percent for sanitation.

19. **(B)** To find what percent 520 is of 1300, divide 520 by 1300 to get the decimal representation of percent. Then multiply by 100 to get the answer into percent form.

20. **(D)** A is not true because none of the windows are squares. All of the windows are rectangles, so B, C, and E are not true. Choice D alone meets both of the requirements.

21. **(B)** The larger square has seven of the smaller squares along each side. The area of the smaller square is 4 in.^{2}, so each side of the smaller square is 2 in. The length of one side of the larger square is 2 in. $\times$ 7 = 14 in.

22. **(E)** The only number in the table written in scientific notation is (1C) 5.3794 $\times$ 10^1. Scientific notation is written as a number between 1 and 10 times a power of 10. (E) is the value of 5.3794 $\times$ 10^1.

23. **(C)** Person 5 had 3 more awards than person 3. Therefore person 5 had 3 • 20 = 60 more awards than person 3.

24. **(D)** $A \cdot B + C = -4 \cdot 2 + 11 = -8 + 11 = 3$

25. **(A)** The mean is 39.4 while the median is 39. The difference is 0.4 of a year.

26. **(C)** Only choices C and E have four pieces where two have crusts but in choice E the pieces clearly are not the same size.

27. **(D)** The formula for the area of a circle is πr^2.

    Area of the inner circle $= \pi(2)^2 = 4\pi$
    Area of the outer circle $= \pi(4)^2 = 16\pi$
    $16\pi - 4\pi = 12\pi$

    That is the area for the portion of the outer circle outside the inner circle. A, B, and C are all incorrect because these choices do not show the correct area.

28. **(C)** If 62.5 percent are cats, then 37.5 percent are not cats. Divide 37.5 by 3 to find that each animal is 12.5 percent of the total. Then divide 62.5 percent by 12.5 percent (62.5 ÷ 12.5 = 5) to find there are 5 cats.

29. **(E)** Add the numbers that are outside the "swimming circle." 13 + 12 + 9 = 34, the number of students who participate in sports except swimming.

30. **(E)** You are looking for the number multiplied by 45,000 that equals 0.45. Divide: 0.45 ÷ 45,000 = 0.00001.

31. **(B)** The decimal equivalents of each answer choice are:

    A. $0.\overline{4}$
    B. $0.4\overline{8}$
    C. $0.\overline{4}$
    D. $0.\overline{4}$
    E. $0.\overline{4}$

    Answer choices A, C, D, and E are equal.

32. **(C)** It is $11\frac{1}{4}$ hours from 7:45 A.M. to 7:00 P.M. Subtract 1 hour for lunch. That

    leaves $10\frac{1}{4}$ work hours.

    $10\frac{1}{4} \times \$20 = \$205.$

33. **(D)** (0, 1) shows a *y*-intercept of 1.

    (1, 0) shows an *x*-intercept of 1.

34. **(D)** The formula for the area of a trapezoid is $A = \frac{h}{2}(b_1 + b_2)$.

    However, in the new trapezoid the length of each base is doubled; therefore, the formula is

    $$A = \frac{h}{2}(2b_1 + 2b_2) = \frac{h}{2} \cdot 2(b_1 + b_2) = h(b_1 + b_2)$$

35. **(D)** Jack's lowest weight is 170 pounds and Jack's highest weight is 190 pounds.

    $170 \div 190 \approx 0.89 \approx 89\%$

36. **(D)** The trapezoid, choice D, has only one pair of congruent sides.

37. **(B)** Each diameter in choice B is part of the perimeter. When answering this question, consider only the perimeter and not any segments within a figure.

38. **(D)**

    A. $3^4 \times 9 \times 12 = 3^4 \times 9 \times 4 \times 3 = 3^5 \times 4 \times 9$

    B. $3^3 \times 27 \times 12 = 3^3 \times 9 \times 3 \times 4 \times 3 = 3^5 \times 4 \times 9$
    This is also choice A.

    C. $3^5 \times 36 = 3^5 \times 4 \times 9$
    This is also choice A.

    D. $3^3 \times 9^3 \times 4 = 3^3 \times 3^2 \times 9^2 \times 4 = 3^5 \times 4 \times 9^2 \neq 3^5 \times 4 \times 9$
    This is **not** choice E.

    E. $3^5 \times 4 \times 9$
    This is also choice A. We do not need to calculate.

    D is the only choice not equivalent to the others.

39. **(B)** $45{,}250 + 78{,}375 + 52{,}540 + 62{,}325 = 238{,}490 \approx 238{,}000$

40. **(D)** The *y*-value (vertical axis) moves up as the *x*-value (horizontal axis) moves right.

41. **(C)** $65\% = 0.65 \qquad (0.65) \cdot \$400 = \$260$

42. **(C)** $\frac{1}{2} = \frac{6}{12}, \frac{2}{3} = \frac{8}{12}, \frac{5}{12}$

    $\left(\frac{6}{12} + \frac{8}{12} + \frac{5}{12}\right) \div 3 = \frac{19}{12} \div 3 = \frac{19}{12} \cdot \frac{1}{3} = \frac{19}{36}$

43. **(C)** In a standard deck of cards there are 12 "face cards"—4 kings, 4 queens, and 4 jacks out of 52 possible cards.

    P(face card) $= \frac{12}{52} = \frac{3}{13}$

44. **(D)** Change 2.3 to 23 and then round to 20. (This involves multiplying by 10.) 10^5 means multiply by 100,000. So you need to move the decimal four more places to the right.

45. **(E)** Figures A, B, C, and D show a circle within a circle, a sphere, a cylinder, and a cone. A cube represented in Figure E does not contain a circle.

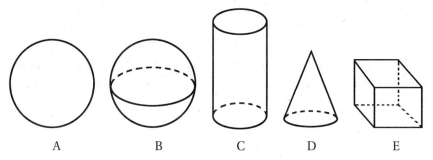

A   B   C   D   E

46. **(C)** The temperature on the thermometer is 86°F. It moved down 8° from 10:00 A.M. when it was 94°F. The temperature moved at a constant rate of 2° an hour, which means it moved down 4° from 10:00 A.M. to a noon temperature of 90°F. Be careful. The problem says the temperature is getting lower as the day goes on.

47. **(A)** $6(2) + 2(-1) = 12 - 2 = 10$

48. **(B)** There are 18 tickets and you can buy 16 of the tickets for $120 (4 • $30) and the remaining two tickets at $16.
$120 + $16 = $136

49. **(A)** $4A + 6 = 2(B - 1)$
Divide by 2 on both sides: $2A + 3 = B - 1$
Add 1 to both sides: $2A + 4 = B$

$B = 2A + 4$

50. **(C)** Use this chart

Kilo	Hecto	Deka	Unit	Deci	Centi	Milli
1,000	100	10	1	0.1	0.01	0.001

Given below is each answer choice in meters.

A. 230 meters
B. 230 meters
C. 23 meters
D. 230 meters
E. 230 meters

Choice C is not equal to the others.

51. **(E)** $101 + 4 = 105 = 7 • 15$

52. **(A)** $5 - 3\frac{1}{5} = 1\frac{4}{5}$, which is a little less than 2 miles.

53. **(B)** If Barbara earns $17 every 2 hours, she earns $\frac{\$17}{2} = \$8.50$ per hour. In 45 hours she earns $8.50 • 45 = $382.50.

54. **(A)** There are 4 pictures of televisions in January and 6 pictures of televisions in December; $\frac{6}{4} = 1.5$. It does not matter how many televisions each picture represents, the answer will still be the same.

55. **(B, E)** The diameter of a circle is twice the radius. This relationship is correctly shown in both choice B and choice E. Choices A, C, and D are incorrect because this relationship is not present.

56. **(A)** If we know the total value of the single-scoop cones sold, we can divide by $2.50 to find the number of single-scoop cones sold and then subtract that number from 100 to find the number of double-scoop cones sold. None of the other choices produces enough information.

Practice Core 2

9

TEST INFO BOX

Reading	56 items	85 minutes
Writing Multiple Choice	40 items	40 minutes
Writing Essays	2 responses	30 minutes each
Mathematics	56 items	85 minutes

Take this test in a realistic, timed setting. You should not take this practice test until you have completed your review.

The setting will be most realistic if another person times the test and ensures that the test rules are followed exactly. If another person is acting as test supervisor, he or she should review these instructions with you and say "Start" when you should begin a section and "Stop" when time has expired.

Use a pencil to mark the test or the answer sheet. Once the test is complete, review the answers and explanations for each item.

ANSWER SHEET
Practice Core 2

Reading Test—85 minutes

1. Ⓐ Ⓑ Ⓒ Ⓓ Ⓔ   16. Ⓐ Ⓑ Ⓒ Ⓓ Ⓔ   31. Ⓐ Ⓑ Ⓒ Ⓓ Ⓔ   46. Ⓐ Ⓑ Ⓒ Ⓓ Ⓔ
2. Ⓐ Ⓑ Ⓒ Ⓓ Ⓔ   17. Ⓐ Ⓑ Ⓒ Ⓓ Ⓔ   32. Ⓐ Ⓑ Ⓒ Ⓓ Ⓔ   47. Ⓐ Ⓑ Ⓒ Ⓓ Ⓔ
3. Ⓐ Ⓑ Ⓒ Ⓓ Ⓔ   18. Ⓐ Ⓑ Ⓒ Ⓓ Ⓔ   33. Ⓐ Ⓑ Ⓒ Ⓓ Ⓔ   48. Ⓐ Ⓑ Ⓒ Ⓓ Ⓔ
4. Ⓐ Ⓑ Ⓒ Ⓓ Ⓔ   19. Ⓐ Ⓑ Ⓒ Ⓓ Ⓔ   34. Ⓐ Ⓑ Ⓒ Ⓓ Ⓔ   49. Ⓐ Ⓑ Ⓒ Ⓓ Ⓔ
5. Ⓐ Ⓑ Ⓒ Ⓓ Ⓔ   20. Ａ Ｂ Ｃ   35. Ⓐ Ⓑ Ⓒ Ⓓ Ⓔ   50. Ⓐ Ⓑ Ⓒ Ⓓ Ⓔ
6. Ⓐ Ⓑ Ⓒ Ⓓ Ⓔ   21. Ⓐ Ⓑ Ⓒ Ⓓ Ⓔ   36. Ⓐ Ⓑ Ⓒ Ⓓ Ⓔ   51. Ⓐ Ⓑ Ⓒ Ⓓ Ⓔ
7. Ⓐ Ⓑ Ⓒ Ⓓ Ⓔ   22. Ⓐ Ⓑ Ⓒ Ⓓ Ⓔ   37. Ⓐ Ⓑ Ⓒ Ⓓ Ⓔ   52. Ⓐ Ⓑ Ⓒ Ⓓ Ⓔ
8. Ⓐ Ⓑ Ⓒ Ⓓ Ⓔ   23. Ⓐ Ⓑ Ⓒ Ⓓ Ⓔ   38. Ⓐ Ⓑ Ⓒ Ⓓ Ⓔ   53. Ⓐ Ⓑ Ⓒ Ⓓ Ⓔ
9. Ⓐ Ⓑ Ⓒ Ⓓ Ⓔ   24. Ⓐ Ⓑ Ⓒ Ⓓ Ⓔ   39. Ⓐ Ⓑ Ⓒ Ⓓ Ⓔ   54. Ⓐ Ⓑ Ⓒ Ⓓ Ⓔ
10. Ⓐ Ⓑ Ⓒ Ⓓ Ⓔ   25. Ⓐ Ⓑ Ⓒ Ⓓ Ⓔ   40. Ⓐ Ⓑ Ⓒ Ⓓ Ⓔ   55. Ａ Ｂ Ｃ
11. Ⓐ Ⓑ Ⓒ Ⓓ Ⓔ   26. Ⓐ Ⓑ Ⓒ Ⓓ Ⓔ   41. Ⓐ Ⓑ Ⓒ Ⓓ Ⓔ   56. Ⓐ Ⓑ Ⓒ Ⓓ Ⓔ
12. Ⓐ Ⓑ Ⓒ Ⓓ Ⓔ   27. Ⓐ Ⓑ Ⓒ Ⓓ Ⓔ   42. Ⓐ Ⓑ Ⓒ Ⓓ Ⓔ
13. Ⓐ Ⓑ Ⓒ Ⓓ Ⓔ   28. Ⓐ Ⓑ Ⓒ Ⓓ Ⓔ   43. Ⓐ Ⓑ Ⓒ Ⓓ Ⓔ
14. Ⓐ Ⓑ Ⓒ Ⓓ Ⓔ   29. Ⓐ Ⓑ Ⓒ Ⓓ Ⓔ   44. Ⓐ Ⓑ Ⓒ Ⓓ Ⓔ
15. Ⓐ Ⓑ Ⓒ Ⓓ Ⓔ   30. Ⓐ Ⓑ Ⓒ Ⓓ Ⓔ   45. Ⓐ Ⓑ Ⓒ Ⓓ Ⓔ

Writing Test—40 minutes

1. Ⓐ Ⓑ Ⓒ Ⓓ Ⓔ   11. Ⓐ Ⓑ Ⓒ Ⓓ Ⓔ   21. Ⓐ Ⓑ Ⓒ Ⓓ Ⓔ   31. Ⓐ Ⓑ Ⓒ Ⓓ Ⓔ
2. Ⓐ Ⓑ Ⓒ Ⓓ Ⓔ   12. Ⓐ Ⓑ Ⓒ Ⓓ Ⓔ   22. Ⓐ Ⓑ Ⓒ Ⓓ Ⓔ   32. Ⓐ Ⓑ Ⓒ Ⓓ Ⓔ
3. Ⓐ Ⓑ Ⓒ Ⓓ Ⓔ   13. Ⓐ Ⓑ Ⓒ Ⓓ Ⓔ   23. Ⓐ Ⓑ Ⓒ Ⓓ Ⓔ   33. Ⓐ Ⓑ Ⓒ Ⓓ Ⓔ
4. Ⓐ Ⓑ Ⓒ Ⓓ Ⓔ   14. Ⓐ Ⓑ Ⓒ Ⓓ Ⓔ   24. Ⓐ Ⓑ Ⓒ Ⓓ Ⓔ   34. Ⓐ Ⓑ Ⓒ Ⓓ Ⓔ
5. Ⓐ Ⓑ Ⓒ Ⓓ Ⓔ   15. Ⓐ Ⓑ Ⓒ Ⓓ Ⓔ   25. Ⓐ Ⓑ Ⓒ Ⓓ Ⓔ   35. Ⓐ Ⓑ Ⓒ Ⓓ Ⓔ
6. Ⓐ Ⓑ Ⓒ Ⓓ Ⓔ   16. Ⓐ Ⓑ Ⓒ Ⓓ Ⓔ   26. Ⓐ Ⓑ Ⓒ Ⓓ Ⓔ   36. Ⓐ Ⓑ Ⓒ Ⓓ Ⓔ
7. Ⓐ Ⓑ Ⓒ Ⓓ Ⓔ   17. Ⓐ Ⓑ Ⓒ Ⓓ Ⓔ   27. Ⓐ Ⓑ Ⓒ Ⓓ Ⓔ   37. Ⓐ Ⓑ Ⓒ Ⓓ Ⓔ
8. Ⓐ Ⓑ Ⓒ Ⓓ Ⓔ   18. Ⓐ Ⓑ Ⓒ Ⓓ Ⓔ   28. Ⓐ Ⓑ Ⓒ Ⓓ Ⓔ   38. Ⓐ Ⓑ Ⓒ Ⓓ Ⓔ
9. Ⓐ Ⓑ Ⓒ Ⓓ Ⓔ   19. Ⓐ Ⓑ Ⓒ Ⓓ Ⓔ   29. Ⓐ Ⓑ Ⓒ Ⓓ Ⓔ   39. Ⓐ Ⓑ Ⓒ Ⓓ Ⓔ
10. Ⓐ Ⓑ Ⓒ Ⓓ Ⓔ   20. Ⓐ Ⓑ Ⓒ Ⓓ Ⓔ   30. Ⓐ Ⓑ Ⓒ Ⓓ Ⓔ   40. Ⓐ Ⓑ Ⓒ Ⓓ Ⓔ

Mathematics Test—85 minutes

1. Ⓐ Ⓑ Ⓒ Ⓓ Ⓔ   16. Ⓐ Ⓑ Ⓒ Ⓓ Ⓔ   31. Ⓐ Ⓑ Ⓒ Ⓓ Ⓔ   46. Ⓐ Ⓑ Ⓒ Ⓓ Ⓔ

2. Ⓐ Ⓑ Ⓒ Ⓓ Ⓔ   17. Ⓐ Ⓑ Ⓒ Ⓓ Ⓔ   32. Ⓐ Ⓑ Ⓒ Ⓓ Ⓔ   47. Ⓐ Ⓑ Ⓒ Ⓓ Ⓔ

3. Ⓐ Ⓑ Ⓒ Ⓓ Ⓔ   18. Ⓐ Ⓑ Ⓒ Ⓓ Ⓔ   33. Ⓐ Ⓑ Ⓒ Ⓓ Ⓔ   48. Ⓐ Ⓑ Ⓒ Ⓓ Ⓔ

4. ☐   19. Ⓐ Ⓑ Ⓒ Ⓓ Ⓔ   34. Ⓐ Ⓑ Ⓒ Ⓓ Ⓔ   49. Ⓐ Ⓑ Ⓒ Ⓓ Ⓔ

5. Ⓐ Ⓑ Ⓒ Ⓓ Ⓔ   20. Ⓐ Ⓑ Ⓒ Ⓓ Ⓔ   35. Ⓐ Ⓑ Ⓒ Ⓓ Ⓔ   50. Ⓐ Ⓑ Ⓒ Ⓓ Ⓔ

6. Ⓐ Ⓑ Ⓒ Ⓓ Ⓔ   21. Ⓐ Ⓑ Ⓒ Ⓓ Ⓔ   36. Ⓐ Ⓑ Ⓒ Ⓓ Ⓔ   51. Ⓐ Ⓑ Ⓒ Ⓓ Ⓔ

7. Ⓐ Ⓑ Ⓒ Ⓓ Ⓔ   22. Ⓐ Ⓑ Ⓒ Ⓓ Ⓔ   37. Ⓐ Ⓑ Ⓒ Ⓓ Ⓔ   52. Ⓐ Ⓑ Ⓒ Ⓓ Ⓔ

8. Ⓐ Ⓑ Ⓒ Ⓓ Ⓔ   23. Ⓐ Ⓑ Ⓒ Ⓓ Ⓔ   38. Ⓐ Ⓑ Ⓒ Ⓓ Ⓔ   53. Ⓐ Ⓑ Ⓒ Ⓓ Ⓔ

9. Ⓐ Ⓑ Ⓒ Ⓓ Ⓔ   24. Ⓐ Ⓑ Ⓒ Ⓓ Ⓔ   39. Ⓐ Ⓑ Ⓒ Ⓓ Ⓔ   54. Ⓐ Ⓑ Ⓒ Ⓓ Ⓔ

10. Ⓐ Ⓑ Ⓒ Ⓓ Ⓔ   25. Ⓐ Ⓑ Ⓒ Ⓓ Ⓔ   40. Ⓐ Ⓑ Ⓒ Ⓓ Ⓔ   55. Ⓐ Ⓑ Ⓒ Ⓓ Ⓔ

11. Ⓐ Ⓑ Ⓒ Ⓓ Ⓔ   26. Ⓐ Ⓑ Ⓒ Ⓓ Ⓔ   41. Ⓐ Ⓑ Ⓒ Ⓓ Ⓔ   56. A B C D E

12. Ⓐ Ⓑ Ⓒ Ⓓ Ⓔ   27. Ⓐ Ⓑ Ⓒ Ⓓ Ⓔ   42. Ⓐ Ⓑ Ⓒ Ⓓ Ⓔ

13. Ⓐ Ⓑ Ⓒ Ⓓ Ⓔ   28. Ⓐ Ⓑ Ⓒ Ⓓ Ⓔ   43. Ⓐ Ⓑ Ⓒ Ⓓ Ⓔ

14. Ⓐ Ⓑ Ⓒ Ⓓ Ⓔ   29. Ⓐ Ⓑ Ⓒ Ⓓ Ⓔ   44. Ⓐ Ⓑ Ⓒ Ⓓ Ⓔ

15. Ⓐ Ⓑ Ⓒ Ⓓ Ⓔ   30. Ⓐ Ⓑ Ⓒ Ⓓ Ⓔ   45. Ⓐ Ⓑ Ⓒ Ⓓ Ⓔ

READING TEST

56 ITEMS   85 MINUTES

> **Directions:** You will read selections followed by one or more questions. Most items have five answer choices with one correct answer. A few items may have one or more correct answers. The answer choices for these questions will be within boxes. Select the best answer choices based on what the selection states or implies and mark that letter on the answer sheet.

1. Cellular phones, once used by the very rich, are now available to almost everyone. With one of these phones, you can call just about anywhere from just about anywhere. Since the use of these phones will increase, we need to find legal and effective ways for law enforcement agencies to monitor calls.

   Which of the following choices is the best summary of this passage?

   Ⓐ Criminals are taking advantage of cellular phones to avoid legal wiretaps.
   Ⓑ The ability to use a cellular phone to call from just about anywhere makes it harder to find people who are using the phones.
   Ⓒ The increase in cellular phone use means that we will have to find legal ways to monitor cellular calls.
   Ⓓ Cellular phones are like regular phones with a very long extension cord.
   Ⓔ Since cellular phones are more available to everyone, they are certainly more available to criminals.

2. The moon takes about 28 days to complete a cycle around the earth. Months, 28 days long, grew out of this cycle. Twelve of these months made up a year. But ancient astronomers realized that it took the earth about 365 days to make one revolution of the sun. Extra days were added to some months and the current calendar was born.

   What details does the author use to support the main purpose of the passage?

   Ⓐ Describes the moon's movement around the earth
   Ⓑ Is based on the sun's position
   Ⓒ Is based on the earth's rotation and position of the moon
   Ⓓ Combines features of the moon's cycle and the earth's revolution
   Ⓔ Was based on the number 12

3. Occasionally, college students will confuse correlation with cause and effect. Correlation just describes the degree of relationship between two factors. For example, there is a positive correlation between poor handwriting and intelligence. However, writing more poorly will not make you more intelligent.

   The author's main reason for writing this passage is to

   Ⓐ explain the difference between correlation and cause and effect.
   Ⓑ encourage improved penmanship.
   Ⓒ explain how college students can improve their intelligence.
   Ⓓ make those with poor penmanship feel more comfortable.
   Ⓔ describe a cause-and-effect relationship.

QUESTIONS 4–6 ARE BASED ON THIS PASSAGE.

It is striking how uninformed today's youth are about Acquired Immune Deficiency Syndrome. Because of their youth and ignorance, many young adults engage in high-risk behavior. Many of these young people do not realize that the disease can be contracted through almost any contact with an infected person's blood and bodily fluids. Some do not realize that symptoms of the disease may not appear for ten years or more. Others do not realize that the danger in sharing needles to inject intravenous drugs comes from the small amounts of another's blood injected during this process. A massive education campaign is needed to fully inform today's youth about AIDS.

4.   The main idea of this passage is

   Ⓐ   previous education campaigns have failed.
   Ⓑ   AIDS develops from the HIV virus.
   Ⓒ   the general public is not fully informed about AIDS.
   Ⓓ   people should not share intravenous needles.
   Ⓔ   young people are not adequately informed about AIDS.

5.   Which of the following is the best summary of the statement about what young people don't realize about how AIDS can be contracted?

   Ⓐ   The symptoms may not appear for ten years or more.
   Ⓑ   AIDS is contracted because of ignorance.
   Ⓒ   AIDS is contracted from intravenous needles.
   Ⓓ   AIDS is contracted through contact with infected blood or bodily fluids.
   Ⓔ   You will not contract AIDS if you know what to avoid.

6.   Which of the following words best describes how the author views young people and their knowledge of AIDS?

   Ⓐ   Stupid
   Ⓑ   Unaware
   Ⓒ   Dumb
   Ⓓ   Unintelligible
   Ⓔ   Reluctant

   _____

7.   When Lyndon Johnson succeeded John F. Kennedy, he was able to gain congressional approval for programs suggested by Kennedy but never implemented. These programs, called Great Society programs, included low-income housing and project Head Start. To some, this made Johnson a better president.

   Based on this statement, we can conclude that Johnson

   Ⓐ   was a better president than Kennedy.
   Ⓑ   gained approval for programs proposed by Kennedy.
   Ⓒ   was a member of a Great Society.
   Ⓓ   was president before Kennedy.
   Ⓔ   originally lived in low-income housing.

QUESTIONS 8–9 ARE BASED ON THIS PASSAGE.

I think women are discriminated against; however, I think men are discriminated against just as much as women. It's just a different type of discrimination. Consider these two facts: Men die about 6 years earlier than women, and men are the only people who can be drafted into the armed forces. That's discrimination!

8. What is the author's main point in writing this passage?

   Ⓐ Men are discriminated against more than women are.
   Ⓑ Both sexes are discriminated against.
   Ⓒ Women are not discriminated against.
   Ⓓ On average, men die earlier than women.
   Ⓔ Men are not discriminated against.

9. Which of the following could be substituted for the word *drafted* in the next to last sentence?

   Ⓐ Inducted against their will
   Ⓑ Signed up
   Ⓒ Pushed in by society
   Ⓓ Drawn in by peer pressure
   Ⓔ Serve in a foreign country

_____

QUESTIONS 10–11 ARE BASED ON THIS PASSAGE.

Alice in Wonderland, written by Charles Dodgson under the pen name Lewis Carroll, is full of symbolism, so much so that a book titled *Understanding Alice* was written containing the original text with marginal notes explaining the symbolic meanings.

10. By symbolism, the author of the passage above meant that much of *Alice in Wonderland*

    Ⓐ was written in a foreign language.
    Ⓑ contained many mathematical symbols.
    Ⓒ contained no pictures.
    Ⓓ had a figurative meaning.
    Ⓔ was set in a special type.

11. Which of the following details does the author use to support the description of *Understanding Alice*?

    Ⓐ Explanations of the musical meaning of the text
    Ⓑ Notes that may not have been completely correct
    Ⓒ Notes written next to the main text
    Ⓓ Marginal notes written by Carroll but not included in the original book
    Ⓔ An explanation of the text by Alice Liddell, the real Alice

12. Following a concert, a fan asked a popular singer why the songs sounded so different in person than on the recording. The singer responded, "I didn't record my emotions!"

Which of the following conclusions is suggested by this passage?

Ⓐ The singer was probably not in a good mood during that performance.
Ⓑ The fan was being intrusive, and the performer was "brushing her off."
Ⓒ The performance was outdoors where sound quality is different.
Ⓓ The fan didn't realize the controls available for studio recordings.
Ⓔ The performance may vary depending on the mood of the performer.

QUESTIONS 13–18 ARE BASED ON THIS PASSAGE.

The War of 1812 is one of the least understood conflicts in American history. However, many events associated with the war are among the best remembered from American History. The war began when the United States invaded British colonies
Line in Canada. The invasion failed, and the United States was quickly put on the defen-
(5) sive. Most Americans are not aware of how the conflict began. During the war, the *USS Constitution* (Old Ironsides) was active against British ships in the Atlantic. Captain William Perry, sailing on Lake Erie, was famous for yelling to his shipmates, "Don't give up the ship." Most Americans remember Perry and his famous plea, but not where or in which war he was engaged.
(10) Most notably, British troops sacked and burned Washington, D.C. during this conflict. Subsequent British attacks on Fort McHenry near Baltimore were repulsed by American forces. It was during one of these battles that Francis Scott Key wrote the "Star Spangled Banner" while a prisoner on a British ship. The "rockets red glare, bombs bursting in air" referred to ordnance used by the British to attack the fort.
(15) Many Americans mistakenly believe that the "Star Spangled Banner" was written dur-
— ing or shortly after the Revolutionary War.

13. All the following statements can be implied from the passage EXCEPT:

Ⓐ The British did not start the war.
Ⓑ Francis Scott Key was not at Fort McHenry when he wrote the "Star Spangled Banner."
Ⓒ The rockets referred to in the "Star Spangled Banner" were part of a celebration.
Ⓓ The British army entered Washington, D.C., during the war.
Ⓔ The nickname for the *USS Constitution* was Old Ironsides.

14. Which of the following words is the most appropriate replacement for "sacked" in line 10?

Ⓐ Entered
Ⓑ Ravished
Ⓒ Invaded
Ⓓ Enclosed
Ⓔ Encapsulated

15. With which of the following statements would the author agree about the difference referred to in the passage between Perry's involvement in the War of 1812 and the way many Americans remember his involvement?

   Ⓐ Perry was a drafter of the Constitution and later served on the *Constitution* in the Atlantic, although many Americans don't remember that.
   Ⓑ Perry served in the Great Lakes, but many Americans don't remember that.
   Ⓒ Perry served in Washington, D.C., although many Americans don't remember that.
   Ⓓ Perry served on the *Constitution* at Fort McHenry during the writing of the "Star Spangled Banner," although many Americans do not remember that.
   Ⓔ Perry served on the *Constitution* in the Atlantic, but many Americans don't remember that.

16. What can be inferred about Francis Scott Key from lines 12–13 of the passage?

   Ⓐ He was killed in the battle.
   Ⓑ All his papers were confiscated by the British after the battle.
   Ⓒ He was released by or escaped from the British after the battle.
   Ⓓ He returned to Britain where he settled down.
   Ⓔ He was a British spy.

17. Based on the passage, which of the following words best describes the United States' role in the War of 1812?

   Ⓐ Colonizer
   Ⓑ Neutral
   Ⓒ Winner
   Ⓓ Loser
   Ⓔ Aggressor

18. Which of the following questions is best answered from this passage?

   Ⓐ Why did the Americans fight the British in the War of 1812?
   Ⓑ Why did the Revolutionary War continue into the 1800s?
   Ⓒ Why did the British renew the Revolutionary War during the 1800s?
   Ⓓ Why were many Americans unaware of events associated with the War of 1812?
   Ⓔ Why should Americans remember the treachery of the army that invaded Washington during this war?

QUESTIONS 19–24 ARE BASED ON THIS PASSAGE.

Computer-based word processing programs have spelling checkers and even a thesaurus to find synonyms and antonyms for highlighted words. To use the thesaurus, the student just types in the word, and a series of synonyms and antonyms appears on the computer screen. The program can also show recommended spellings for misspelled words. I like having a computer program that performs these mechanical aspects of writing. However, these programs do not teach about spelling or word meanings. A person could type in a word, get a synonym and have not the slightest idea what either meant.

Relying on this mindless way of checking spelling and finding synonyms, students will be completely unfamiliar with the meanings of the words they use. In fact, one of the most common misuses is to include a word that is spelled correctly but used incorrectly in the sentence.

It may be true that a strictly mechanical approach to spelling is used by some teachers. There certainly is a place for students who already understand word meanings to use a computer program that relieves the drudgery of checking spelling and finding synonyms. But these computer programs should never and can never replace the teacher. Understanding words—their uses and meanings—should precede this more mechanistic approach.

19. What is the main idea of this passage?

   Ⓐ Mechanical spell checking is one part of learning about spelling.
   Ⓑ Programs are not effective for initially teaching about spelling and synonyms.
   Ⓒ Teachers should use word processing programs as one part of instruction.
   Ⓓ Students who use these programs won't learn about spelling.
   Ⓔ The programs rely too heavily on a student's typing ability.

20. Which of the following information is found in the passage?

   Select all that apply.

   [A] The type of computer that runs the word processor
   [B] The two main outputs of spell checking and thesaurus programs
   [C] An explanation of how to use the word-processing program to teach about spelling and synonyms

21. What is the author's attitude toward spell checking and thesaurus programs?

   Ⓐ That you just have to type in the word
   Ⓑ That the synonyms and alternative spellings are done very quickly
   Ⓒ That the difficult mechanical aspects are performed
   Ⓓ That you don't have to know how to spell to use them
   Ⓔ That they can't replace teachers

22. Which of the following questions could be answered from the information in the passage?

   Ⓐ When is it appropriate to use spell checking and thesaurus programs?
   Ⓑ How does the program come up with recommended spellings?
   Ⓒ What type of spelling learning experiences should students have?
   Ⓓ Why do schools buy these word processing programs?
   Ⓔ Which word program does the author recommend?

23. Which of the following statements could be used in place of the first sentence of the last paragraph?

   Ⓐ It may be true that some strict teachers use a mechanical approach.
   Ⓑ It may be true that a stringently mechanical approach is used by some teachers.
   Ⓒ It may be true that inflexible mechanical approaches are used by some teachers.
   Ⓓ It may be true that the mechanical approach used by some teachers is too rigorous.
   Ⓔ It may be true that some teachers use only a mechanical approach.

24. According to this passage, what could be the result of a student's unfamiliarity with the meanings of words or synonyms?

  (A) Using a program to display the alternative spellings
  (B) Relying on mindless ways of checking spelling and finding synonyms
  (C) Strictly mechanical approaches
  (D) Using microcomputers to find synonyms for highlighted words
  (E) Being able to just type in a word

QUESTIONS 25–28 ARE BASED ON THIS PASSAGE.

As a child he read the *Hardy Boys* series of books and was in awe of the author, Franklin Dixon. As an adult, he read a book entitled the *Ghost of the Hardy Boys,* which revealed that there was no Franklin Dixon and that ghost writers had authored the books. The authors were apparently working for a large publishing syndicate.

25. Which of the following is the likely intent of the author of this passage?

  (A) To describe a book-publishing practice
  (B) To contrast fiction and fact
  (C) To contrast childhood and adulthood
  (D) To correct the record
  (E) To dissuade children from reading the *Hardy Boys* books

26. Which of the following best describes the author's attitude toward Franklin Dixon?

  (A) Awe
  (B) Childlike
  (C) Syndicated
  (D) Disappointment
  (E) Satisfaction

27. What does the word *Ghost* in the title of the second mentioned book refer to?

  (A) A person who has died or was dead at the time the book was published
  (B) A person who writes books without credit
  (C) A person who influences the way a book is written
  (D) The mystical images of the mind that affect the way any author writes
  (E) A person who edits a book after the author has submitted it for publication

28. Which of the following would NOT be an acceptable replacement for the word *awe* in the first sentence?

  (A) Wonder
  (B) Admiration
  (C) Esteem
  (D) Aplomb
  (E) Respect

The Iroquois nation consisted of five main tribes—Cayuga, Mohawk, Oneida, Onondaga, and Seneca. Called the Five Nations or the League of Five Nations, these tribes occupied much of New York State. Since the tribes were arranged from east to west, the region they occupied was called the long house of the Iroquois.

The Iroquois economy was based mainly on agriculture. The main crop was corn, but they also grew pumpkins, beans, and fruit. The Iroquois used wampum (hollow beads) for money, and records were woven into wampum belts.

The Iroquoian Nation had a remarkable democratic structure, spoke a common Algonquin language, and were adept at fighting. These factors had made the Iroquois a dominant power by the early American colonial period. In the period just before the Revolutionary War, Iroquoian conquest had overcome most other Indian tribes in the northeastern United States as far west as the Mississippi River.

During the Revolutionary War, most Iroquoian tribes sided with the British. At the end of the Revolutionary War the tribes scattered, with some migrating to Canada. Only remnants of the Seneca and Onondaga tribes remained on their tribal lands.

29. Which of the following statements drawn from the passage is opinion rather than fact?

Ⓐ The main crop was corn.
Ⓑ The Iroquois used wampum (hollow beads) for money.
Ⓒ These factors made the Iroquois a dominant power.
Ⓓ Records were woven into wampum belts.
Ⓔ The Iroquois nation consisted of five main tribes.

30. Which of the following best describes the geographic location of the five Iroquoian tribes?

Ⓐ The northeastern United States as far west as the Mississippi River
Ⓑ Southern Canada
Ⓒ Cayuga
Ⓓ New York State
Ⓔ The League of Nations

31. Which of the following best describes why the area occupied by the Iroquois was called the long house of the Iroquois?

Ⓐ The tribes were arranged as though they occupied different sections of a long house.
Ⓑ The Iroquois lived in structures called long houses.
Ⓒ The close political ties among tribes made it seem that they were all living in one house.
Ⓓ The Iroquois had expanded their original tribal lands through conquest.
Ⓔ It took weeks to walk the trail connecting all the tribes.

32. According to the passage, which of the following best describes the economic basis for the Iroquoian economy?

   (A) Wampum
   (B) Corn
   (C) Agriculture
   (D) Conquest
   (E) Warfare

QUESTIONS 33–38 ARE BASED ON THIS PASSAGE.

Europeans had started to devote significant resources to medicine when Louis Pasteur was born December 7, 1822. By the time he died in the fall of 1895, he had made enormous contributions to science and founded microbiology. At 32, he was named professor and dean at a French university dedicated to supporting the production of alcoholic beverages. Pasteur immediately began work on yeast and fermentation. He found that he could kill harmful bacteria in the initial brewing process by subjecting the liquid to high temperatures. This finding was extended to milk in the process called pasteurization. This work led him to the conclusion that human disease could be caused by germs. In Pasteur's time, there was a widely held belief that germs were spontaneously generated. Pasteur conducted experiments that proved germs were always introduced and never appeared spontaneously. This result was questioned by other scientists for over a decade. He proved his theory of vaccination and his theory of disease during his work with anthrax, a fatal animal disease. He vaccinated some sheep with weakened anthrax germs and left other sheep unvaccinated. Then he injected all the sheep with a potentially fatal dose of anthrax bacteria. The unvaccinated sheep died while the vaccinated sheep lived. He developed vaccines for many diseases and is best known for his vaccine for rabies. According to some accounts, the rabies vaccine was first tried on a human when a young boy, badly bitten by a rabid dog, arrived at Pasteur's laboratory. The treatment of the boy was successful.

33. What is topic of this passage?

   (A) Microbiology
   (B) Pasteur's scientific discoveries
   (C) Germs and disease
   (D) Science in France
   (E) Louis Pasteur

34. What does the process of pasteurization involve?

   (A) Inoculating
   (B) Experimenting
   (C) Hydrating
   (D) Heating
   (E) Fermenting

35. Which of the following statements could most reasonably be inferred from this passage?

    Ⓐ The myth of spontaneous generation was dispelled immediately following Pasteur's experiments on the subject.

    Ⓑ The pasteurization of milk can aid in the treatment of anthrax.

    Ⓒ Pasteur's discoveries were mainly luck.

    Ⓓ Even scientists don't think scientifically all the time.

    Ⓔ Injecting sheep with fatal doses of anthrax is one way of vaccinating them.

36. Which of the following statements can be implied from this passage?

    Ⓐ That germs do not develop spontaneously was already a widely accepted premise when Pasteur began his scientific work.

    Ⓑ Scientists in European countries had made significant progress on the link between germs and disease when Pasteur was born.

    Ⓒ Europe was ready for scientific research on germs when Pasteur conducted his experiments.

    Ⓓ Most of Pasteur's work was the replication of other work done by French scientists.

    Ⓔ The theory that germs could cause human disease was not yet accepted at the time of Pasteur's death.

37. Which of the following choices best characterizes the reason for Pasteur's early work?

    Ⓐ To cure humans

    Ⓑ To cure animals

    Ⓒ To help the French economy

    Ⓓ To study germs

    Ⓔ To be a professor

38. According to this passage, the rabies vaccine

    Ⓐ was developed after Pasteur had watched a young boy bitten by a rabid dog.

    Ⓑ was developed from the blood of a rabid dog, which had bitten a young boy.

    Ⓒ was developed from the blood of a young boy bitten by a rabid dog.

    Ⓓ was developed in addition to the vaccines for other diseases.

    Ⓔ was developed in his laboratory where a young boy had died of the disease.

QUESTIONS 39–40 ARE BASED ON THIS PASSAGE.

I believe that there is extraterrestrial life—probably in some other galaxy. It is particularly human to believe that our solar system is the only one that can support intelligent life. But our solar system is only an infinitesimal dot in the infinity of the cosmos and it is just not believable that there is not life out there—somewhere.

39. What is the author of this passage proposing?

  Ⓐ That there is other life in the universe
  Ⓑ That there is no life on earth
  Ⓒ That humans live on other planets
  Ⓓ That the sun is a very small star
  Ⓔ That we should explore other galaxies

40. The words *infinitesimal* and *infinite* are best characterized by which pair of words below?

  Ⓐ Small and large
  Ⓑ Very small and very large
  Ⓒ Very small and limitless
  Ⓓ Large and limitless
  Ⓔ Small and very large

QUESTIONS 41–44 ARE BASED ON THIS PASSAGE.

"It is just possible that some of our readers may not know who Flipper is. For their benefit we make haste to explain that Flipper is the solitary colored cadet now at West Point. Flipper's friends declare that he is getting along finely in his studies, and
Line that he is quite up to the standard of the average West Point student. Nevertheless
(5) they intimate that he will never graduate. Flipper, they say, may get as far as first class when he will be 'slaughtered.'

"A correspondent of the *New York Times* takes issue with this. He says there are many 'old heads' who believe Flipper will graduate with honor, and he thinks so too.

"The *Chicago Tribune* finds it difficult to come to any conclusion concerning Flip-
(10) per's chances for graduating. It says: 'It is freely asserted that Flipper will never be allowed to graduate; that the prejudice of the regular army instructors against the colored race is insurmountable, and that they will drive away from the Academy by persecution of some petty sort any colored boy who may obtain admittance there. The story does not seem to have any substantial basis; still, it possesses considerable vitality.'"

41. The main focus of this passage is

  Ⓐ race relations at West Point.
  Ⓑ Flipper's future at West Point.
  Ⓒ the hypocrisy of race prejudice.
  Ⓓ disagreements between rival papers.
  Ⓔ unfairness in the military.

42. Which of the statements below is the author most likely to agree with?

  Ⓐ Flipper's friends do not think he deserves to graduate.
  Ⓑ The *Chicago Times* story is false.
  Ⓒ Flippers biggest problem is the high-ranking officers at West Point.
  Ⓓ Flipper deserves a fair chance to graduate.
  Ⓔ Flipper will be killed before he is allowed to graduate.

43. In line 5 the author uses the word "intimate" to mean

    Ⓐ to show a relationship.
    Ⓑ imply.
    Ⓒ declare.
    Ⓓ forswear.
    Ⓔ emotional awareness.

44. Based on the passage, which of the following questions have regular army instructors asked themselves about Flipper's graduation?

    Ⓐ Why should we pass someone who is obviously inferior?
    Ⓑ Why not let him pass, and the whole world would see what a poor officer he is?
    Ⓒ Why should we be worried about what the newspapers write?
    Ⓓ What is the point in failing him—it will just draw more attention to his cause?
    Ⓔ Where does it say that we have to pass anybody?

QUESTION 45 IS BASED ON THIS PASSAGE.

Albert Payson Terhune (1872–1942) was a famous author about dogs. He lived on an estate called "The Place" in suburban New Jersey. The Place was filled with collies. Terhune wrote over thirty books about dogs that were popular mainly with younger audiences. Terhune never became the great writer that he wanted to become. Many of his plots were called stilted and overly optimistic. But his unique ability to write about the relationship between dogs and human beings has never been matched in American literature.

45. The author of this passage suggests that despite the criticism and the lack of an adult audience for his books, Terhune's books are timeless because they

    Ⓐ focus on dogs.
    Ⓑ are set in a suburban setting.
    Ⓒ appeal to a largely young audience.
    Ⓓ show kinship.
    Ⓔ show optimism.

QUESTION 46 IS BASED ON THIS PASSAGE.

Security among aircraft has become a central aspect of American life. Passengers are regularly screened before they enter an aircraft. But much of the cargo that is transported by air goes uninspected. Most of the explosive materials found in air shipments have been uncovered from tips from foreign governments. All of this leads me to the inescapable conclusion that we should divert a lot of our efforts screening airline passengers to screening airline cargo.

46. Which of the following statements, if true, is MOST likely to weaken the author's position about screening airline passengers?

   Ⓐ Airline passengers can hide explosives in body cavities, which makes it much harder to detect them.

   Ⓑ There are many more pieces of air cargo than there are air passengers, making it more difficult to screen packages than passengers.

   Ⓒ Increased screening of packages does not mean that there has to be decreased screening of air passengers.

   Ⓓ Tips from foreign governments may not always be available and not always accurate and we cannot rely on those tips to find troublesome packages.

   Ⓔ The chances of being killed on a plane that blows up because of a bomb are a lot less than the chances of being killed on the highways of America.

QUESTIONS 47–52 ARE BASED ON THE FOLLOWING PASSAGES.

I

   Abraham Lincoln is usually rated among the top three presidents of the United States. Some point to his role as president during the Civil War, while others remark on his famous, brief Gettysburg Address.

Line
(5)
   Lincoln is often cast as antislavery, but the record paints a different picture. He wanted to win the Civil War and preserve the Union, but ending slavery was not his main objective. His much praised Emancipation Proclamation freed only the slaves in rebellious states. While he felt that slavery was morally wrong, he admitted that he was not quite sure how to solve the problem. He was opposed to giving blacks the right to vote and stated in the famous Lincoln-Douglas debates that, "I will say then

(10)
that I am not, nor ever have been, in favor of bringing about in any way the social and political equality of the white and black races."

II

   Abraham Lincoln was a brilliant president, and he is ranked first in more polls and expert surveys. Lincoln is most associated with the end of slavery in the United States. He often expressed the view that slavery was morally wrong but often noted that he

(15)
was at a loss to find a way to end it under the current Constitution.

   He was a politician running for office, and he frequently found himself in elections in which being antislavery would have cost him the election. In those circumstances, probably most famously in the Lincoln-Douglas debates, he made statements to counter the charge that he was in favor of negro equality, knowing that to say

(20)
otherwise would have cost him the election. Lincoln's statements were a means to an end, but they must be judged by the Thirteenth Amendment abolishing slavery in the United States, which was passed before his assassination.

47. The authors of these passages agree that

   Ⓐ Lincoln was a brilliant president.
   Ⓑ Lincoln was the best president of the United States.
   Ⓒ Lincoln is most associated with ending slavery in the United States.
   Ⓓ Lincoln was a politician.
   Ⓔ The Thirteenth Amendment, known as the Emancipation Proclamation, was associated with Lincoln.

48. Reviewing the passages, we can see that the author of passage II mentions which of the following not mentioned in passage I?

    Ⓐ Lincoln-Douglas debates
    Ⓑ Lincoln was a politician
    Ⓒ Lincoln felt slavery was morally wrong
    Ⓓ The Emancipation Proclamation
    Ⓔ Lincoln's roots in Illinois

49. Which of the following statements best describes the relationship among the passages?

    Ⓐ The passages each mention the Lincoln-Douglas debates.
    Ⓑ Each passage consistently emphasizes Lincoln's antislavery stance.
    Ⓒ The first passage gives Lincoln more credit for ending the Civil War than the second passage.
    Ⓓ Each passage points out that Lincoln did not think slavery was morally wrong.
    Ⓔ The first passage is less forgiving of Lincoln's views of slavery than the second passage.

50. Which of the following extends an action mentioned in the first passage?

    Ⓐ The Thirteenth Amendment
    Ⓑ The Lincoln-Douglas debates
    Ⓒ Freeing slaves in confederate states
    Ⓓ Lincoln's statements as a means to an end
    Ⓔ The Union is preserved

51. Which of the following, if added as the last sentence in the first passage, would weaken the author's stance in that paragraph?

    Ⓐ This just reinforced his pro-slavery views.
    Ⓑ Most observers saw this as a purely political statement.
    Ⓒ Observers were not surprised by this comment.
    Ⓓ He inadvertently omitted "economic."
    Ⓔ This statement just agreed with previous comments.

52. In line 4 of the first passage, the word *cast* most nearly means

    Ⓐ embedded.
    Ⓑ portrayed.
    Ⓒ shadowed.
    Ⓓ molded.
    Ⓔ thrown.

Sun	Mon	Tue	Wed	Thu	Fri	Sat
	1 8:00 A.M. Aerobics A 10:00 A.M. Pilates A 2:00 P.M. Bicycle A	2 8:00 A.M. Aerobics B 10:00 A.M. Pilates B 2:00 P.M. Bicycle B	3 8:00 A.M. Aerobics A 10:00 A.M. Pilates B 2:00 P.M. Bicycle A	4 8:00 A.M. Aerobics C 10:00 A.M. Pilates A 2:00 P.M. Bicycle C	5 8:00 A.M. Aerobics B 10:00 A.M. Pilates C 2:00 P.M. Bicycle A	6 2:00 Swimming 1
7 OFF	8 8:00 A.M. Aerobics D 10:00 A.M. Pilates D 2:00 P.M. Bicycle D	9 10:00 A.M. Aerobics A 1:00 P.M. Pilates A 4:00 P.M. Bicycle A	10 OFF	11 8:00 A.M. Aerobics E 10:00 A.M. Pilates D 2:00 P.M. Bicycle E	12 6:00 P.M. Swimming 1	13 10:00 A.M. Swimming 3
14 OFF	15 8:00 A.M. Aerobics D 10:00 A.M. Pilates E 2:00 P.M. Bicycle D	16 OFF	17 8:00 A.M. Aerobics G 10:00 A.M. Pilates G 2:00 P.M. Bicycle G	18 6:00 P.M. Swimming 3	19 8:00 A.M. Aerobics A 10:00 A.M. Pilates B 2:00 P.M. Bicycle C	20 OFF
21 10:00 A.M. Swimming 2	22 OFF	23 8:00 A.M. Aerobics D 10:00 A.M. Pilates E 2:00 P.M. Bicycle F	24 8:00 A.M. Aerobics G 10:00 A.M. Pilates G 2:00 P.M. Bicycle G	25 OFF	26 8:00 A.M. Aerobics E 10:00 A.M. Pilates E 2:00 P.M. Bicycle E	27 2:00 P.M. Swimming 4

53. Quinn's college training program requires him to participate in a certain number of activities. He must participate once in each of the lettered and numbered activities for aerobics, pilates, bicycling, and swimming. Because of his schedule, he cannot participate in activities on Mondays and Thursdays.

Which of the following is the best strategy for Quinn to follow to complete the Pilates E activity as early in the month as possible?

Ⓐ Quinn should complete the Pilates E activity on the third day of the month.
Ⓑ Quinn should complete the Pilates E activity on the ninth day of the month.
Ⓒ Quinn should complete the Pilates E activity on the fifteenth day of the month.
Ⓓ Quinn should complete the Pilates E activity on the twenty-third day of the month.
Ⓔ Quinn should complete the Pilates E activity on the twenty-sixth day of the month.

54. Which of the following is the best explanation of why Quinn would take Aerobics A on the ninth of the month?

Ⓐ Aerobics A was offered later that day than on any other day.
Ⓑ There were three hours to rest between aerobics and pilates, not the two hours on other days.
Ⓒ This was the first time Aerobics A was not offered on a Monday or Thursday.
Ⓓ Bicycle A was offered on Friday the fifth and he wanted to avoid a conflict.
Ⓔ There were no activities scheduled for Wednesday the ninth of the month.

55. Based on the calendar, which of the following activities could Quinn have participated in *just one* single time?

Select all that apply.

A Swimming 3
B Aerobics A
C Aerobics D

_____

Even with the glacier covering Alaska, the Aleuts had established a culture on the Aleutian Islands off southern Alaska by 5000 B.C.E. Once glaciers melted in the area, the Eskimo and Intuit tribes established a culture in northern Alaska about 1800 B.C.E. This hunting fishing society has retained much of its ancient character. Navajo peoples lived in these same northern locales before migrating to the Southwest sometime between 1200 C.E. and 1500 C.E. Primitive woodland cultures developed in the northeastern United States about 3000 B.C.E. These cultures included Algonquin tribes such as the Shawnee and the Iroquois Federation. There is evidence that northern woodland tribes may have been exposed to outside contact five hundred years before the arrival of Europeans after Columbus. [Dates labeled B.C.E were previously labeled BC, and dates labeled C.E. were previously labeled A.D.]

56. What Native American group established a culture in about 5000 years ago?

Ⓐ Aleut
Ⓑ Algonquin
Ⓒ Eskimo
Ⓓ Intuit
Ⓔ Navajo

WRITING TEST

40 ITEMS 40 MINUTES

2 CONSTRUCTED RESPONSES   60 MINUTES

Usage

> **Directions:** You will read sentences with four parts underlined and lettered. Determine whether one of the underlined parts contains grammatical, word use, or punctuation errors. If so, mark that letter. If there are no errors, mark E.

1. A professional golfer told the new golfer that professional instruction or more
   (A)   (B)
   practice improve most golfers' scores. No error.
            (C)   (D)   (E)

2. It was difficult for the farmer to comprehend the unhappiness he
            (A)   (B)
   encountered among so many of the rich produce buyers in the city. No error.
            (C)   (D)   (E)

3. No goal is more noble—no feat more revealing—as the exploration of space.
                  (A)   (B)   (C)   (D)
   No error.
   (E)

4. The soccer player's slight strain from the shot on goal led to a pulled muscle,
                        (A)   (B)   (C)
   resulted in the player's removal from the game. No error.
   (D)   (E)

5. The young college graduate had no family to help her but she was fortunate
            (A)   (B)
   to get a job with a promising school district superintendent and
                        (C)
   eventually became a superintendent herself. No error.
   (D)   (E)

6. He was concerned about crossing the bridge, but the officer said that it was
         (A)   (B)   (C)
   all right to cross. No error.
   (D)   (E)

7. As the students prepared to take the test, they came to realize that it was not
                    (A)   (B)
   only what they knew and also how well they knew how to take tests. No error.
                        (C)   (D)   (E)

8. As <u>many</u> as a ton of bananas may have <u>spoiled</u> when the <u>ship</u> was <u>stuck</u> in the

   Ⓐ   Ⓑ   Ⓒ   Ⓓ

Panama Canal. <u>No error.</u>

          Ⓔ

9. Employment agencies <u>often place</u> newspaper advertisements <u>when no</u>

                    Ⓐ   Ⓑ

jobs <u>exist</u> to get the names of <u>potential</u> employees on file. <u>No error.</u>

   Ⓒ   Ⓓ   Ⓔ

10. Visitors <u>to New York can</u> expect to <u>encounter people</u>, noise, and

               Ⓐ   Ⓑ

<u>finding themselves in traffic</u> just <u>about any day of the</u> week. <u>No error.</u>

          Ⓒ   Ⓓ   Ⓔ

11. It <u>was obvious</u> to Kim that neither her family <u>or her friends</u> could

    Ⓐ   Ⓑ

<u>understand why</u> the study <u>of science was</u> so important to her. <u>No error.</u>

       Ⓒ   Ⓓ   Ⓔ

12. While <u>past safaris</u> had entered the jungle to hunt <u>elephants with rifles</u>, this safari

         Ⓐ   Ⓑ

had only a <u>single armed</u> guard to protect <u>the tourists as</u> they took photographs.

             Ⓒ   Ⓓ

<u>No errors.</u>

   Ⓔ

13. <u>Buddhism is an</u> interesting <u>religion</u> because Confucius <u>was born</u> in India,

     Ⓐ   Ⓑ   Ⓒ

but the religion never <u>gained lasting</u> popularity there. <u>No error.</u>

                   Ⓓ   Ⓔ

14. John Dewey's <u>progressive</u> philosophy <u>influenced</u> thousands of teachers;

              Ⓐ   Ⓑ

however, Dewey was often <u>displeased</u> with <u>there</u> teaching methods. <u>No error.</u>

                  Ⓒ   Ⓓ   Ⓔ

15. <u>While only</u> in the school for <u>a few weeks</u>, the gym teacher <u>was starting to</u>

     Ⓐ   Ⓑ   Ⓒ

<u>felt comfortable</u> with the principal. <u>No error.</u>

    Ⓓ   Ⓔ

16. The <u>carnival</u>, which <u>featured</u> a wild <u>animal act</u> was due to <u>arrive</u> in town

     Ⓐ   Ⓑ   Ⓒ   Ⓓ

next week. <u>No error.</u>

        Ⓔ

17. While the bus driver waited, the motor runs and uses expensive gasoline.
    Ⓐ   Ⓑ Ⓒ   Ⓓ
    No error.
       Ⓔ

18. Having needed to eat and earn money, the college graduate decided it was
         Ⓐ   Ⓑ   Ⓒ

    time to look for a job. No error.
       Ⓓ   Ⓔ

Sentence Correction

> **Directions:** You will read sentences with some or all of the sentence underlined, followed by five answer choices. The first answer choice repeats the underlined portion and the other four present possible replacements. Select the answer choice that best represents standard English without altering the meaning of the original sentence. Mark that letter on the test or the answer sheet.

19. The dean was famous for delivering grand sounding but otherwise unintelligible speeches.

    Ⓐ but otherwise unintelligible speeches.
    Ⓑ but in every other way speeches that could not be intelligible.
    Ⓒ but speeches which were not that intelligent.
    Ⓓ but otherwise speeches that could be understood.
    Ⓔ but speeches that could be unintelligible.

20. The hiker grew tired greater as the day wore on.

    Ⓐ The hiker grew tired greater
    Ⓑ The hiker grew tired more
    Ⓒ The hiker grew greater tired
    Ⓓ The hiker's tired grew greater
    Ⓔ The hiker grew more tired

21. The man knew that to solve the problem now can be easier than putting it off for another day.

    Ⓐ to solve the problem now can be easier
    Ⓑ to solve the problem now is easier
    Ⓒ to solve the problem now can be less difficult
    Ⓓ solving the problem now can be easier
    Ⓔ to try to solve the problem now

22. Lee's <u>mother and father insists that</u> he call if he is going to be out after 8:00 P.M.

   (A) mother and father insists that
   (B) mother and father insist that
   (C) mother and father insists
   (D) mother and father that insist
   (E) mother and father that insists

23. The weather forecaster said that people living near the shore should be prepared <u>in the event that</u> the storm headed for land.

   (A) in the event that
   (B) if the event happened and
   (C) the event
   (D) if
   (E) and

24. After years of observation, the soccer coach concluded that women soccer players were more aggressive than <u>men who played soccer.</u>

   (A) men who played soccer.
   (B) men soccer players.
   (C) soccer playing men.
   (D) those men who played soccer.
   (E) men.

25. The stockbroker advised her client to sell the stock before it <u>could no longer be popular</u>.

   (A) could no longer be popular.
   (B) could be popular no longer.
   (C) may be popular no longer.
   (D) could become unpopular.
   (E) was no longer popular.

26. Bringing in an outside consultant usually means that it will take too long for the consultant to understand what's going on, <u>the functioning of the office will be impaired</u>, and because a new person has been introduced into the company, it will create dissension.

   (A) the functioning of the office will be impaired
   (B) the impairment of office functioning will follow
   (C) caused impairment in office functioning
   (D) office functioning impairment will occur
   (E) it will impair the functioning of the office

27. The primary election was very important because winning could give the candidate a much more clearer mandate.

    Ⓐ important because winning could give the candidate a much more
    Ⓑ important because winning there could give the candidate a much more
    Ⓒ important because a win there could give the candidate a
    Ⓓ important because winning could give the candidate a
    Ⓔ important because a loss there would be devastating

28. She had become a doctor with the noble purpose of saving lives; however, the process of applying for medical benefits and the responsibilities for managing the office had become her primary and overriding concern.

    Ⓐ the process of applying for medical benefits and the responsibilities for managing the office had become her primary and overriding concern.
    Ⓑ applying for medical benefits and managing the office had become her main concerns.
    Ⓒ applying for medical benefits, and the responsibilities for managing the office had become her primary and overriding concern.
    Ⓓ applying for medical benefits and office work had become her main concern.
    Ⓔ she soon found out that being a doctor was not noble.

29. Among the most popular television programs are those that critics classify is soap operas.

    Ⓐ is soap operas.
    Ⓑ are soap operas.
    Ⓒ as soap operas.
    Ⓓ in soap operas.
    Ⓔ with soap operas.

30. If a person has the ability in music, then he should try to develop this ability by taking music lessons.

    Ⓐ has the ability in music
    Ⓑ has musical ability
    Ⓒ can play an instrument
    Ⓓ is a talented musician
    Ⓔ is interested in music

31. <u>The players on the national team were supposed by some of their countrymen to have almost superhuman ability</u>.

    Ⓐ The players on the national team were supposed by some of their countrymen to have almost superhuman ability.

    Ⓑ The players on the national team had superhuman ability, according to some of their countrymen.

    Ⓒ The players in the national team were better at the sport than most of their countryman.

    Ⓓ Suppose the players on the national team were not good enough, thought some of their countrymen.

    Ⓔ Some of their countrymen thought that the players on the national team had almost superhuman ability.

QUESTIONS 32–36 ARE BASED ON THE FOLLOWING PASSAGE.

Gettysburg Address

(1) At the end of the Battle of Gettysburg, more than 51,000 Confederate and Union soldiers were wounded, missing, or dead. (2) Pennsylvania governor Andrew Curtin commissioned David Wills, an attorney, to purchase land for a proper burial site for the deceased Union soldiers. (3) <u>Wills acquired 17 acres for the cemetery, which was planned and designed by landscape architect William Saunders.</u>

    (4) The cemetery was dedicated on November 19, 1863. (5) <u>The main speaker for the event Edward Everett, was one of the nation's foremost orators.</u> (6) President Lincoln was also invited to speak "as Chief Executive of the nation, formally to set apart these grounds to their sacred use by a few appropriate remarks." (7) At the ceremony, Everett spoke for more than two hours; Lincoln spoke for two minutes.

    (8) President Lincoln had given his brief speech a lot of thought. (9) <u>He saw meaning in the fact that the Union victory</u> at Gettysburg coincided with the nation's birthday; but rather than focus on the specific battle in his remarks, he wanted to present a broad statement about the larger significance of the war. (10) He invoked the Declaration of Independence and its principles of liberty and equality, and he spoke of "a new birth of freedom" for the nation. (11) In his brief address, he continued to reshape the aims of the war for the American people—transforming it from a war for Union to a war for Union and freedom. (12) Lincoln expressed disappointment in the speech initially.

32. Which of the following sentences, added after sentence 12, would provide the most fitting conclusion to this paragraph?

    Ⓐ But it has come to be regarded as one of the most elegant and eloquent speeches in U.S. history.

    Ⓑ He eventually realized he was no match for a great orator.

    Ⓒ The continuation of the Civil War made the initial reaction final.

    Ⓓ It became clear to him that he had been somewhat successful in rewriting history.

    Ⓔ But on the train trip back to Washington he completely dismissed the matter.

33. In the context of this passage, what is the best replacement for the underlined portion of sentence 3, shown below?

Wills acquired 17 acres for the cemetery, which was planned and designed by landscape architect William Saunders.

Ⓐ Leave as is.
Ⓑ Delete it.
Ⓒ The 17-acre cemetery was designed by William Saunders.
Ⓓ William Saunders designed the cemetery
Ⓔ Wills acquired the land for the cemetery, which was designed by William Saunders.

34. In the context of this passage, which of the following is the best addition to the end of sentence 4?

Ⓐ , after the battle.
Ⓑ , in Pennsylvania.
Ⓒ , with the battle still raging.
Ⓓ , near Gettysburg.
Ⓔ , before the war ended.

35. In the context of this passage, which of the choices below is the best suggestion to revise the underlined portion of sentence 9, shown below?

He saw meaning in the fact that the Union victory

Ⓐ He saw meaning in the fact that the North's victory
Ⓑ He saw special meaning in Union victory
Ⓒ He saw meaning in the very fact that the Union victory
Ⓓ He saw meaning because the Union victory
Ⓔ He saw meaning in the Union victory

36. In the context of this passage, which choice below is the best revision of Sentence 5 shown below?

The main speaker for the event Edward Everett, was one of the nation's foremost orators.

Ⓐ Leave as is.
Ⓑ The primary speaker for the event Edward Everett, one of the nation's foremost orators.
Ⓒ The main speaker for the event Edward Everett, as the nation's foremost orator.
Ⓓ The main speaker for the event, Edward Everett, was one of the nation's foremost orators.
Ⓔ The first speaker for the event Edward Everett, as one of the nation's outstanding orators.

37. Robert Dereko, "The Key to a Successful Relationship Is Often in the Differences," *New Square News* February 18, 2014, accessed March 23, 2014.

The citation above is from which of the following types of sources?

Ⓐ An online article
Ⓑ A newspaper article
Ⓒ A blog
Ⓓ A book
Ⓔ An interview

38. A friend is writing a paper about the Holocaust. Which of the following could be a primary source for this paper?

Ⓐ Notes from a guard about the Holocaust prison camp
Ⓑ A book about the Holocaust by the daughter of a Holocaust survivor
Ⓒ Handwritten notes from a Holocaust survivor about her life after the Holocaust
Ⓓ A list of names of those killed in concentration camps provided by a government
Ⓔ A visit to the site of the Auschwitz Concentration Camp

39. Which of the following would be correctly cited as a secondary source about the first moon landing?

Ⓐ A video of that moon landing
Ⓑ A book about the moon landing by an astronaut on that original lander
Ⓒ A book about space travel by an astronaut
Ⓓ A sample of rocks collected on the moon after the lunar lander touched down
Ⓔ A recording of an astronaut on that first lander as it touched down on the moon

40. In a paper about the origins of the term *Uncle Sam* to personify the U.S. government during the War of 1812, which of the following pieces of information is directly relevant to the paper?

Ⓐ It is believed that during the War of 1812, soldiers used the initials U.S. to arrive at "Uncle Sam."
Ⓑ During the War of 1812 British troops sacked the Capitol Building in Washington, DC.
Ⓒ During the War of 1812 Frances Scott Key is reputed to have written the "Star Spangled Banner" while a prisoner on a ship in Baltimore Harbor but did not include a reference to Uncle Sam.
Ⓓ The author of the paper has an uncle named Sam and so is familiar with Uncle Sam.
Ⓔ In 1989, the U.S. Congress officially recognized "Uncle Sam Day."

ARGUMENTATIVE CONSTRUCTED RESPONSE

30 MINUTES

Directions: You have 30 minutes to complete this constructed-response question. Use a word processor, but not the spell or grammar check, to type a brief response based on this topic.

A college student who received a poor grade in a class should be able to have any record of the class and the grade removed from his or her transcript.

Describe the extent to which you agree or disagree with this statement. Support your response with specific details, examples, and experiences.

Write a brief outline here.

INFORMATIVE/EXPLANATORY CONSTRUCTED RESPONSE

30 MINUTES

> **Directions:** You have 30 minutes to read two position papers on a topic and then type a constructed response based on the topic. Use a word processor, but not the spell or grammar check. The response should discuss the important points in the topic.
>
> Read the topic and sources below. It is good to spend time organizing your thoughts and planning your response before you start to write. You MUST write on the given topic, and you MUST include references to the sources.
>
> This response gives you a chance to demonstrate how well you can write and include sources in your writing. That means you should focus on writing well and using examples and references, all while being sure to cover the topic presented. While how much you write is not a specific scoring criteria, you will certainly want to write several meaningful paragraphs.

Topic

Pumping gas is one of the most common of daily experiences. You drive up to the pump, swipe your credit card, select the grade, put the nozzle in the gas filler tube, and depress the lever. You may even be able to set the pump to operate "automatically," and the pump stops when the pump's sensors indicate that the tank is full. There are signs that tell you to turn off your engine and not to introduce any flammable items into the situation but no one to check to see that you follow the rules. At this writing, that cannot happen in New Jersey, Oregon, and some localities. In those states and localities a station employee must operate the pump.

Read the two source passages below. Then type an essay that highlights the most important aspects of the positions and explain why they are important. Your essay should refer to EACH of the sources and must CITE the sources as you refer to them or provide direct quotations. You may also use your own experiences and readings.

Self-Service—Even if You Can—Service Yourself Is Dangerous and Costs Jobs (Andrews, web access 10/17/2014)

In all but two states a person can fill his or her own gas tank with fuel. Those states are New Jersey and Oregon. So a reasonable question is why these two states still have decades-old laws against fueling self-service. Before the discussion let me point out that the "traditional" gas stations in New Jersey and Oregon employ over 20,000 people. A little simple math indicates that we would add over 500,000 employees by eliminating self-service stations.

There are two clear reasons for a ban on self-service stations. The first is that these stations discriminate against the disabled. A disabled person is always discriminated against at self-service stations. The only issue is the extent of that discrimination, and since many self-service stations combine fuel dispensing with a convenience store, there is often only one employee present. That person cannot leave the store and the disabled person is just out of luck. The typical self-service station always violates federal law, and why that practice is allowed to continue is unclear to me.

Some think that the absence of employees at non-self-service stations would lower costs. But this is not true. Self-service stations pay much more for liability insurance, at least equal to the cost of actual employees, than non-self-service.

First, that makes the point that self-service stations are inherently less safe than non self-service stations. That is what all the statistics show as well, so the safety reason for banning self-service stations is hard to argue with. It also sharpens the issue of paying employees to pump gas. That seems a much better choice than paying an insurance company.

What may seem a "no-brainer" in favor of self-service stations turns out to be a no-brainer against them.

Self-Service—Can 48 States Really Be Wrong
(Callman, web access 9/28/2014)

You can make lots of arguments in favor of or against self-service filling stations. But I will start with the most obvious one. You can refuel your car, yourself, in all but 2 states, New Jersey and Oregon. In each one of those states the laws forbidding self-service gas stations are many decades old. It is simple: most people prefer to pump gas themselves and not hand over a credit card to a gas station employee.

So, yes, when you look at the big picture, you have to understand that 48 states really cannot be wrong. The citizens of these states have looked at all the issues, looked at all the pros and cons, and have reached a conclusion—self-serve stations are better than non-self-serve stations. There are undoubtedly many reasons, besides convenience, for their decisions. They have looked at them all.

The primary reason given for opposition to self-service stations is safety. But self-service opponents know that the safety requirements for self-service gas are more stringent than the requirements for employee-operated pumps. Besides that, it is just as easy for a poorly-paid gas station employee to cause an accident as it is for the self-service pump operator. There are some legitimate concerns about the very few disabled people who cannot get out of a car to fuel his or her vehicles. The truth is that very few of these people are driving and there is always a way to get help. The other day I was at a self-service station and a person who seemed to require a wheelchair just rolled down the window and asked another person to fuel the car. It worked great.

This is one of those times when the vast majority has it right. It is better to be able to fuel your vehicle yourself than to have to rely on an attendant, some of whom are not that attendant.

Write a brief outline here.

MATHEMATICS TEST

56 ITEMS   85 MINUTES

Directions: Choose the correct answer(s).

1. The triangle on the coordinate grid below was translated down 3 units and left 2 units. What is the coordinate of point C after these translations?

   Ⓐ (–1, 1)
   Ⓑ (0, –4)
   Ⓒ (0, 3)
   Ⓓ (5, –3)
   Ⓔ (5, 0)

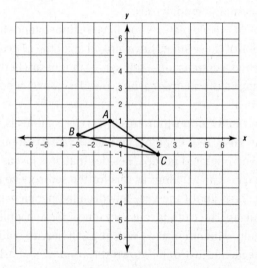

2. A machine used to flatten asphalt has two cylindrical rollers. The larger cylinder has a diameter of 5 feet. The smaller cylinder has a diameter of 3 feet. In one job, the machine travels once along a stretch of asphalt 320 feet long. What is the combined distance traveled by both cylindrical rollers during that job?

   Ⓐ 203π feet
   Ⓑ $32\pi/320$ feet
   Ⓒ 8π (320) feet
   Ⓓ 640π feet
   Ⓔ 640 feet

3. The heights of seven cell phone towers are 280 feet, 270 feet, 320 feet, 90 feet, 130 feet, and 105 feet, while the height of the seventh tower is unknown. However, the height of the seventh tower is different from any of the other heights, and is the median height of the seven towers. Which of the following could NOT be the height of the seventh tower?

   Ⓐ 91
   Ⓑ 135
   Ⓒ 167
   Ⓓ 200
   Ⓔ 269

4. The graph below shows part of a linear equation plotted on the coordinate plane. The graph actually extends infinitely in both directions. What would the *y* value be if the graph was extended to *x* value equals –190? Type your answer in the box below.

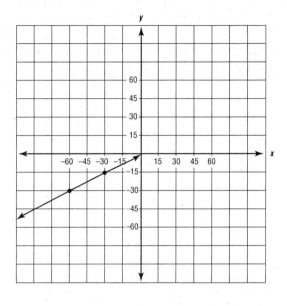

5. The figure below shows the lower portion of a right circular cone. If the height of the entire cone is 16, what is the volume of the missing top part of the cone?

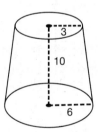

The volume of a right circular cone with the base radius *r* and height *h* is $\frac{1}{3}\pi r^2 h$.

- (A) 6π
- (B) 18π
- (C) 72π
- (D) 96π
- (E) 192π

6. Which of the following addition examples is equivalent to $\frac{3x+6y}{12}$?

    (A) $\frac{x}{4} + \frac{y}{2}$

    (B) $\frac{2x}{4} + \frac{2y}{2}$

    (C) $\frac{x}{2} + \frac{y}{4}$

    (D) $\frac{4}{x} + \frac{3}{y}$

    (E) $\frac{x}{4} + \frac{y}{2}$

7. Using 3.14 for ▯, what is the best estimate of the circumference of the circle on the coordinate below?

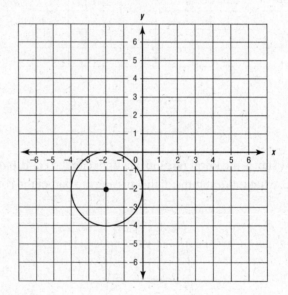

    (A) 6.28

    (B) 12.56

    (C) 24.02

    (D) 25.12

    (E) 50,24

8. A triangle has three sides of different lengths. The length of a < length of b < length of c. It also has three different angles. The measure of angle x is < the measure of angle y < the measure of angle z. Indicate all the angles that could not be opposite side c.

    [A] Angle x

    [B] Angle y

    [C] Angle z

    [D] One of the angles that measures 180°

    [E] None of the angles

9. At sea level, sound travels about 34,000 cm per second, while light travels almost instantaneously. You see a lightning bolt, and 5 seconds later you hear the thunderclap associated with that lightning bolt. Which of the following is the best estimate of how far away the lightning bolt was using scientific notation?

 Ⓐ 17.0×10^4
 Ⓑ 1.7×10^5
 Ⓒ 1.7×10^6
 Ⓓ 0.17×10^6
 Ⓔ $170,000 \times 10^0$

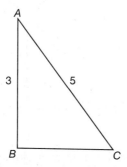

10. Which of the statements below is true about the triangle above?

The triangle is not drawn to scale.

 Ⓐ The measure of angles A and B total more than 90°.
 Ⓑ The area of the triangle is 6 square units.
 Ⓒ The perimeter of the triangle is 15 units.
 Ⓓ The area of the triangle is $7\frac{1}{2}$ square units.
 Ⓔ The perimeter of the triangle is 11 units.

x	y
0	−5
3	4
6	13
9	22
12	31

11. Which of the following equations creates the pattern in the table above?

 Ⓐ $y = 4x - 5$
 Ⓑ $y = 2x - 2$
 Ⓒ $y = 3y - 5$
 Ⓓ $y = 3x - 5$
 Ⓔ $y = 3x + 13$

12. A representative of the magazine advertising department is responsible for 9 to 10 full-page ads, 12 to 14 half-page ads, and 15 to 20 quarter-page ads per issue. The minimum and maximum numbers of ads that each representative is responsible for are

Ⓐ 9 and 20
Ⓑ 9 and 15
Ⓒ 15 and 20
Ⓓ 36 and 44
Ⓔ 10 and 20

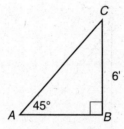

13. Construction workers laid out this triangular plot of land. What is the area of land inside the triangle?

Ⓐ $3\sqrt{3}$ square feet
Ⓑ $6\sqrt{3}$ square feet
Ⓒ 6 square feet
Ⓓ 18 square feet
Ⓔ 36 square feet

14. Which of the following expresses the relationship between x and y shown in the table?

x	y
0	1
3	7
6	13
7	15
9	19

Ⓐ $y = 3x - 2$
Ⓑ $y = 2x + 1$
Ⓒ $y = x + 3$
Ⓓ $y = 2x - 2$
Ⓔ $y = 2x + 3$

15. It took Liz 12 hours to travel by train from New York to North Carolina at an average speed of 55 miles per hour. On the return trip from North Carolina to New York, Liz traveled by bus and averaged 45 miles per hour. How much longer was her return trip?

Ⓐ $2\frac{2}{3}$ hours

Ⓑ $3\frac{2}{3}$ hours

Ⓒ $4\frac{2}{3}$ hours

Ⓓ 5 hours

Ⓔ $6\frac{2}{3}$ hours

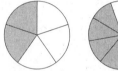

16. In the figure above, about what percent of the regions are shaded?

Ⓐ $66\frac{2}{3}$ %

Ⓑ 40%

Ⓒ 25%

Ⓓ 60%

Ⓔ $33\frac{1}{3}$ %

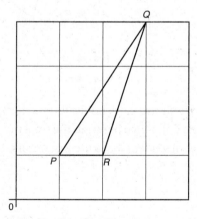

17. The graph is drawn on the coordinate plane, the vertex of angle R is at (6, 3). The vertex at angle Q is reflected across the y-axis. What are the new coordinates of the vertex of the reflected angle Q?

Ⓐ (12, –9)

Ⓑ (–9, +12)

Ⓒ (16, 3)

Ⓓ (6, –3)

Ⓔ (–6, –9)

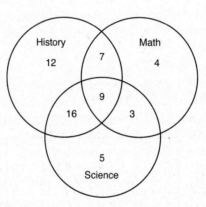

18. Three points *P*, *Q*, and *R*, are on this number line. The sum of the coordinates of points *P* and *Q* is 6. Point *R* is between points *P* and *Q*. Which of the following could be the coordinates for point *R*?

Ⓐ +1
Ⓑ −1
Ⓒ −5
Ⓓ −6
Ⓔ +6

19. *C* is 5 more than half of *B*. Which of the following expressions states this relationship?

Ⓐ $C + 5 = B/2$
Ⓑ $C = \frac{1}{2}B + 5$
Ⓒ $C + 5 = 2B$
Ⓓ $C + 5 > B/2$
Ⓔ $C + 5 < B/2$

20. The Venn diagram above shows the school subjects taken by members of the school's sport teams. What is the difference between the total number of students enrolled in history and the number of students who are just enrolled in history?

Ⓐ 56
Ⓑ 42
Ⓒ 32
Ⓓ 23
Ⓔ 9

21. $\sqrt{300 \times 3} =$

    Ⓐ $10\sqrt{3}$

    Ⓑ $3\sqrt{30}$

    Ⓒ 90

    Ⓓ $9\sqrt{10}$

    Ⓔ 30

Time	8 A.M.	9 A.M.	10 A.M.	11 A.M.	12 Noon
Temp	50°	55°	60°	60°	70°
Time	1 P.M.	2 P.M.	3 P.M.	4 P.M.	
Temp	75°	80°	70°	65°	
Time	5 P.M.	6 P.M.	7 P.M.	8 P.M.	
Temp	55°	50°	50°	45°	

22. The above table shows the temperature tracked for a 12-hour period of time. Which graph best illustrates this information?

Ⓐ
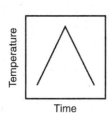

Ⓓ
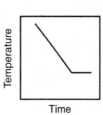

Ⓑ
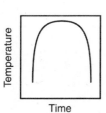

Ⓔ
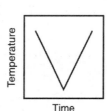

Ⓒ
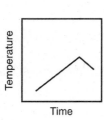

23. A rectangular garden measures 23 feet by 63 feet. What is the greatest number of nonoverlapping 5-foot square plots that can be ruled off in this garden?

    Ⓐ 48

    Ⓑ 57

    Ⓒ 58

    Ⓓ 289

    Ⓔ 290

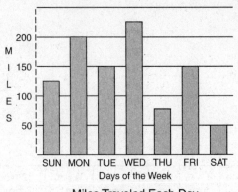

Miles Traveled Each Day
on a Family Camping Trip

24. The bar graph shows the number of miles a family traveled each day on a camping trip. Approximately how many miles did the family travel on average each day?

Ⓐ 125 miles

Ⓑ 200 miles

Ⓒ 175 miles

Ⓓ 140 miles

Ⓔ 100 miles

25. Which choice below is the same as $\dfrac{7}{xy} \div \dfrac{x}{14}$?

Ⓐ $98x^2y$

Ⓑ $\dfrac{7}{14xy}$

Ⓒ $\dfrac{x^2y}{98}$

Ⓓ $\dfrac{98}{x^2y}$

Ⓔ $\dfrac{1}{2}y$

26. A junior high school has a teacher-student ratio of 1 to 15. If there are 43 teachers, how many students are there?

Ⓐ 645

Ⓑ 430

Ⓒ 215

Ⓓ 630

Ⓔ 600

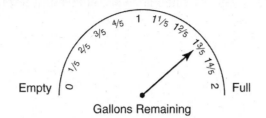

Empty · Full

Gallons Remaining

27. The gauge shows the amount of gas in the tank after mowing the lawn. If the tank was full at the start of mowing, which of the following is the best estimate of how many "mows" are left?

Ⓐ 2
Ⓑ 3
Ⓒ 4
Ⓓ 5
Ⓔ 6

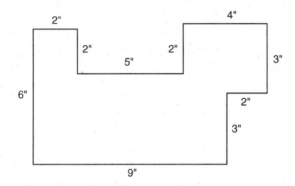

28. A floor plan is drawn with a scale of 5 feet per inch. If the diagram represents the floor plan, what is the actual perimeter of the house?

Ⓐ 38 inches
Ⓑ 38 feet
Ⓒ 200 feet
Ⓓ $7\frac{2}{5}$ feet
Ⓔ 190 feet

29. Mary must make tablecloths for 12 banquet tables. She needs a piece of cloth 5 ft. by 8 ft. for each tablecloth. Each cloth must be made from the same bolt and cannot be sewn. Of the five bolts listed here, which one must be eliminated due to insufficient material?

Ⓐ 25 yd. remaining on an 8-ft. wide bolt
Ⓑ 33 yd. remaining on a 6-ft. wide bolt
Ⓒ 25 yd. remaining on a 5-ft. wide bolt
Ⓓ 20 yd. remaining on an 8-ft. wide bolt
Ⓔ 36 yd. remaining on a 7-ft. wide bolt

30. Blaire bought a pair of shoes at 25 percent off the regular price of $40.00. She had a coupon, which saved her an additional 15 percent off the sale price. What price did she pay for the shoes?

Ⓐ $24.00
Ⓑ $15.00
Ⓒ $25.50
Ⓓ $11.25
Ⓔ $27.50

31. Points *L*, *M*, *N*, and *O* are on the same line. The ratio of *LM* to *NO* is 3:2. Which could NOT be values for *LM* and *NO*?

Ⓐ $LM = 15; NO = 10$
Ⓑ $LM = 12; NO = 9$
Ⓒ $LM = 3; NO = 2$
Ⓓ $LM = 0.75; NO = 0.5$
Ⓔ $LM = 1; NO = \dfrac{2}{3}$

32. Store A has DVDs in packs of 3 for $15.60. Store B sells DVDs for $6.00 each. How much is saved (if any) on each DVD if you buy six DVDs from Store A instead of 6 DVDs from Store B?

Ⓐ $3.40
Ⓑ $.80
Ⓒ $1.80
Ⓓ $2.40
Ⓔ There is no saving.

33. Two different whole numbers are multiplied. Which of the following could not result?

Ⓐ 0
Ⓑ 1
Ⓒ 7
Ⓓ 19
Ⓔ 319

34. Which of the following does not have the same value as the others?

Ⓐ $(0.9 + 0.2) \times 3.2$
Ⓑ $(0.9 \times 3.2) + (0.2 \times 3.2)$
Ⓒ $0.9 + (0.2 \times 3.2)$
Ⓓ $3.2 \times (0.2 + 0.9)$
Ⓔ $3.2 \times (1.1)$

35. Each of the following is $66\frac{2}{3}$ percent of 50 EXCEPT

 Ⓐ $0.66\overline{6} \times 50$

 Ⓑ 0.66×50

 Ⓒ $\frac{2}{3} \times 50$

 Ⓓ $.66\frac{2}{3} \times 50$

 Ⓔ $\frac{26}{39} \times 50$

36. A calculator displays a multiple-digit whole number ending in 0. All the following statements must be true about the number EXCEPT:

 Ⓐ it is an even number.

 Ⓑ it is a multiple of 5.

 Ⓒ it is a power of 10.

 Ⓓ it is a multiple of 10.

 Ⓔ it is the sum of 2 odd numbers.

37. Some values of Y are more than 50. Which of the following could not be true?

 Ⓐ 60 is not a value of Y.

 Ⓑ 45 is not a value of Y.

 Ⓒ There are Y values more than 50.

 Ⓓ All values of Y are 50 or less.

 Ⓔ Some values of Y are more than 50.

38. A pedometer shows distance in meters. A distance of 0.5 kilometers would have a numerical display that is

 Ⓐ 100 times as great.

 Ⓑ twice as great.

 Ⓒ half as great.

 Ⓓ 1000 times as great.

 Ⓔ $\frac{1}{10}$ times as great.

39. Which of the following shows the least to greatest ordering of the fractions?

 Ⓐ $\frac{12}{13}, \frac{99}{100}, \frac{25}{24}, \frac{17}{16}, \frac{5}{4}$

 Ⓑ $\frac{99}{100}, \frac{25}{24}, \frac{17}{16}, \frac{5}{4}, \frac{12}{13}$

 Ⓒ $\frac{25}{24}, \frac{12}{13}, \frac{99}{100}, \frac{5}{4}, \frac{17}{16}$

 Ⓓ $\frac{17}{16}, \frac{5}{4}, \frac{25}{24}, \frac{12}{13}, \frac{99}{100}$

 Ⓔ $\frac{5}{4}, \frac{12}{13}, \frac{17}{16}, \frac{99}{100}, \frac{25}{24}$

40. Two dice are rolled. What is the probability that the sum of the numbers is even?

    (A) $\dfrac{1}{2}$

    (B) $\dfrac{16}{36}$

    (C) $\dfrac{3}{4}$

    (D) $\dfrac{1}{12}$

    (E) $\dfrac{5}{6}$

41. If the product of P and 6 is R, then the product of P and 3 is

    (A) $2R$

    (B) $R/2$

    (C) $\dfrac{1}{2}P$

    (D) $2P$

    (E) $P/6$

42. The multiplication and division buttons on a calculator are reversed. A person presses $\boxed{\div}\ \boxed{5}\ \boxed{=}$ and the calculator displays 625. What answer should have been displayed?

    (A) 125

    (B) 625

    (C) 25

    (D) 50

    (E) 250

43. If V, l, w, and h are positive numbers and $V = l \times w \times h$, then $l =$

    (A) $\dfrac{1}{3}whv$

    (B) $\dfrac{v}{wh}$

    (C) $\dfrac{lw}{v}$

    (D) vlw

    (E) $w(v + h)$

44. If 0.00005 divided by $X = 0.005$, then $X =$

    (A) 0.1

    (B) 0.01

    (C) 0.001

    (D) 0.0001

    (E) 0.00001

45. The product of two numbers is 900. One number is tripled. In order for the product to remain the same, the other number must be

Ⓐ multiplied by 3.

Ⓑ divided by $\frac{1}{3}$.

Ⓒ multiplied by $\frac{1}{3}$.

Ⓓ subtracted from 900.

Ⓔ quadrupled.

46. Which of the following could be the face of the cross section of a cylinder?

Ⓐ

Ⓓ

Ⓑ

Ⓔ

Ⓒ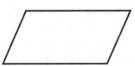

47. Quinn needs to buy enough fencing to enclose a 3 foot by 4 foot piece of land and to build a diagonal fence from one corner to the other. How much fencing is needed?

Ⓐ 12 feet

Ⓑ 14 feet

Ⓒ 17 feet

Ⓓ 19 feet

Ⓔ 20 feet

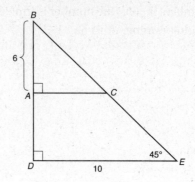

48. In triangle *BDE* what is the length of side *AD*?

Ⓐ 16
Ⓑ 10
Ⓒ 4
Ⓓ 2
Ⓔ 1

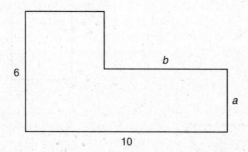

49. Which of the following dimensions would be needed to find the area of the figure?

Ⓐ *a* only
Ⓑ *b* only
Ⓒ neither *a* nor *b*
Ⓓ both *a* and *b*
Ⓔ either *a* or *b*

50. Deena finished the school run in 52.8 seconds. Lisa's time was 1.3 seconds faster. What was Lisa's time?

Ⓐ 51.5 seconds
Ⓑ 54.1 seconds
Ⓒ 53.11 seconds
Ⓓ 65.8 seconds
Ⓔ 52.93 seconds

51. Quinn had 5 weeks to practice the violin before the concert. He practiced an average of 7 hours a week. In one of the weeks he practiced 7 hours. He practiced 2 hours more than that during each of two other weeks. In one other week he practiced 10 hours. To the nearest whole number how many hours did he practice in the remaining week?

Ⓐ 0
Ⓑ 5
Ⓒ 7
Ⓓ 9
Ⓔ 35

52. Manuel and Ellen are conducting a probability experiment. The auditorium is emptying out of students after a play and more than a hundred students are walking single file down the hall. Starting at one, Manuel writes down the number of each third student (the first number he writes down is 3). Also starting at one, Ellen writes the number for each fourth student. Counting stops when they reach the hundredth student. When the experiment is over how many numbers are written twice?

Ⓐ 6
Ⓑ 8
Ⓒ 10
Ⓓ 12
Ⓔ 16

53. There are a total of 28 vehicles in the parking lot. Some are cars, while some are SUVs. Which of the following could be the ratio of cars to SUVs?

Ⓐ 2 to 3
Ⓑ 3 to 4
Ⓒ 4 to 7
Ⓓ 5 to 7
Ⓔ 6 to 10

54. A store offers merchandise for half off the listed price (L). Each of the following choices represents this result EXCEPT

Ⓐ $0.50 \times L$
Ⓑ $L - .50L$
Ⓒ $\dfrac{L}{2}$
Ⓓ $\dfrac{5L}{10}$
Ⓔ $\dfrac{L}{0.50}$

55. A car travels 40 kilometers an hour. Which of the following gives the approximate speed of the car in miles per hour?

Ⓐ $\dfrac{16}{100} \times 40$

Ⓑ 0.6×40

Ⓒ $32 \times \dfrac{40}{2} \times \dfrac{1}{10}$

Ⓓ $0.6 \times 10 \times 40 \times \dfrac{1}{10}$

Ⓔ $\dfrac{60}{10} \div (\dfrac{1}{40} \times 30 \times 2)$

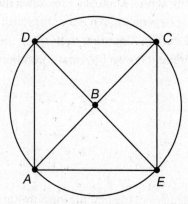

56. Point B is at the center of the circle shown above. Which of the following must be true?

Select all that apply.

Ⓐ $\overline{AC}$ is a chord.

Ⓑ $\overline{AE}$ is a radius.

Ⓒ $\overline{BE}$ is a radius.

Ⓓ $\overline{AB}$ is a diameter.

Ⓔ $\overline{BD}$ is a chord.

ANSWER KEY
Practice Core 2

READING TEST

1. C	11. C	21. C	31. A	41. B	51. B
2. D	12. E	22. A	32. C	42. D	52. B
3. A	13. C	23. E	33. B	43. B	53. D
4. E	14. B	24. B	34. D	44. A	54. C
5. D	15. B	25. D	35. D	45. D	55. A, D
6. B	16. C	26. D	36. C	46. C	56. B
7. B	17. E	27. B	37. C	47. D	
8. B	18. D	28. D	38. D	48. B	
9. A	19. B	29. C	39. A	49. E	
10. D	20. B	30. D	40. C	50. A	

WRITING TEST

Usage

1. C	4. D	7. C	10. C	13. E	16. C
2. E	5. C	8. A	11. B	14. D	17. C
3. C	6. E	9. E	12. B	15. D	18. A

Sentence Correction

19. A	23. D	27. D	31. E	35. D	39. B
20. E	24. B	28. B	32. A	36. D	40. A
21. D	25. E	29. C	33. B	37. B	
22. B	26. E	30. B	34. E	38. A	

MATHEMATICS TEST

1. B	11. C	21. E	31. B	41. B	51. A
2. E	12. D	22. A	32. B	42. C	52. B
3. A	13. D	23. A	33. B	43. B	53. B
4. −95	14. B	24. D	34. C	44. B	54. E
5. B	15. A	25. D	35. B	45. C	55. C
6. E	16. B	26. A	36. C	46. E	56. A, C
7. B	17. B	27. C	37. D	47. D	
8. A, B, D, E	18. A	28. E	38. D	48. C	
9. C	19. B	29. C	39. A	49. D	
10. B	20. C	30. C	40. A	50. A	

EXPLAINED ANSWERS

Reading

1. **(C)** This choice paraphrases the last sentence of the passage.

2. **(D)** The author includes details about the moon's cycle and the earth's revolution as factors contributing to the development of the current calendar.

3. **(A)** The author explains the difference with the description and an example.

4. **(E)** The passage constantly refers to what youth do not know about AIDS.

5. **(D)** This choice paraphrases the third sentence in the paragraph.

6. **(B)** The passage uses many synonyms of this word to describe young people's knowledge of AIDS.

7. **(B)** This choice paraphrases the first sentence in the passage.

8. **(B)** The author says, and then gives an example to show, that men are discriminated against just as much as women.

9. **(A)** Drafted, in the sense used here, means to be inducted into the armed forces against one's will.

10. **(D)** *Alice in Wonderland*, a fanciful story about a young girl's adventures underground, has underlying figurative meanings.

11. **(C)** The passage states that *Understanding Alice* contains original text with marginal notes, indicating that the marginal notes are written next to the main text.

12. **(E)** Music is more than notes and varies with the mood of the performer.

13. **(C)** The passage refers to rockets as ordnance or weapons used by the British.

14. **(B)** *Ravished* is the best choice and describes what happens when a town is sacked.

15. **(B)** The last sentence of the first paragraph says that most Americans remember Perry, but not where he served.

16. **(C)** Francis Scott Key must have been able to distribute his "Star Spangled Banner" in America, so he must have been released by or escaped from the British.

17. **(E)** The second sentence in the paragraph identifies the United States as the aggressor.

18. **(D)** The answer to this question is in the first sentence of the passage.

19. **(B)** The next to the last sentence in the first paragraph indicates that these programs do not teach about spelling or word meanings.

20. **(B)** The type of computer used and teaching methods are not mentioned in the passage.

21. **(C)** The fourth sentence in the first paragraph explains that the author likes having a program to perform the mechanical aspects.

22. **(A)** This question can be answered from information in the passage's last paragraph.

23. **(E)** This choice paraphrases the first sentence in the last paragraph.

24. **(B)** This information is found in the first sentence of the first paragraph.

25. **(D)** The author wants to share what he or she learned about the *Hardy Boys* books.

26. **(D)** The author is more disappointed than anything else upon learning that a favorite childhood author did not really exist.

27. **(B)** A ghost writer is someone who writes books but does not receive credit.

28. **(D)** Every other choice is an acceptable replacement for the word *awe*.

29. **(C)** The word "dominant" is subjective and open to interpretation, which makes this choice an opinion and not a fact. Recall that an opinion can be true.

30. **(D)** This information is contained in the first sentence of the first paragraph.

31. **(A)** This choice is supported by the last sentence in the first paragraph.

32. **(C)** The first sentence of the second paragraph provides this information.

33. **(B)** This paragraph is about Pasteur's scientific discoveries and not about Pasteur the person.

34. **(D)** This answer can be found in lines 5–6 of the passage.

35. **(D)** The passage contains examples of scientists who opposed Pasteur's theories even though Pasteur had proven his theories scientifically.

36. **(C)** The first sentence indicates that Europeans had already started to devote resources to medicine when Pasteur was born, and theories about germs existed when Pasteur began his work.

37. **(C)** The passage mentions that his early work was at a university dedicated to supporting an important product of the French economy.

38. **(D)** The third from last sentence in the passage mentions that Pasteur developed vaccines for many diseases.

39. **(A)** This choice paraphrases the first sentence in the paragraph.

40. **(C)** *Infinitesimal* means very small, and *infinite* means without limit.

41. **(B)** Each paragraph in the passage discusses the likelihood that Flipper will graduate from West Point. The main focus of the passage is on his future at West Point.

42. **(D)** The author wrote the article as an objective story, but includes information about support for Flipper and never indicates the author's personal view that Flipper does not deserve to graduate. One is left with the feeling that the absence of this negative view of Flipper indicates that the author believes Flipper deserves a fair chance.

43. **(B)** In this context, the word "intimate" means "to imply" or "to indicate indirectly."

44. **(A)** The passage states that "the prejudice of the regular army instructors against the colored race is insurmountable." It would follow that these instructors would question why they should pass an obviously inferior person.

45. **(D)** The final paragraph indicates that of all the qualities of Terhune's books it is the relationship, or kinship, between humans and dogs that has never been matched in American literature. This accounts for Terhune's books timelessness.

46. **(C)** The author's message about less need for screening passengers as opposed to screening cargo is weakened by a statement that more screening of cargo does not mean there has to be less screening of passengers.

47. **(D)** Both passages note that Lincoln was president of the United States, a political office. That means he was a politician. While only stated directly in the second passage it is a common thread in both passages. The other choices are found in only one of the two passages.

48. **(B)** Only the second passage mentions that Lincoln was a politician.

49. **(E)** The first passage points out more examples of Lincoln's pro-slavery views than the second passage. For Choice A, both passages mention the Lincoln-Douglas debates, but this fact does not describe the relationship between the passages.

50. **(A)** The Thirteenth Amendment abolishing slavery extended freedom to slaves in Confederate states not found in the Emancipation Proclamation.

51. **(B)** Passage I is most direct in pointing out Lincoln's pro-slavery statements. To say these statements were made for purely political reasons implies that the statements were not deeply held personal views and diminishes their impact.

52. **(B)** *Cast* is a word with many meanings. In this context, it means "portrayed." Lincoln is often portrayed as antislavery.

53. **(D)** The twenty-third day of the month is the first day that Pilates E is not scheduled on a Monday or a Thursday.

54. **(C)** The best explanation is that this was not the first time during the month that Quinn could take Aerobics A.

55. **(A, D)** Quinn cannot attend classes on Mondays and Thursdays, and Swimming 3 is on a Thursday. Aerobics A is available on a number of days when Quinn can attend. Note that there are many other activities listed that Quinn could chose to attend one single time.

56. **(B)** Civilization is about 200 years into the Common Era (c.e.), so a civilization 5,000 years old would have been established about 3,000 years Before the Common Era (b.c.e.). Scanning the passage you see that there is only one date 3,000 b.c.e., the date of the Algonquin culture in the northeastern United States. The most common error is selecting A because those settlements were established 5,000 b.c.e., or 7,000 years ago.

Writing

USAGE

1. **(C)** This singular verb should end in *s*.
2. **(E)** This sentence contains no errors.
3. **(C)** The phrase *as the* should be replaced by the word *than*.
4. **(D)** *Resulted* should be replaced by *resulting*.
5. **(C)** It is not possible to tell whether the school district or the superintendent is promising.

6. **(E)** This sentence contains no errors.

7. **(C)** Replace *and also* with *but also*.

8. **(A)** Replace *many* with *much*.

9. **(E)** This sentence contains no errors.

10. **(C)** Remove *finding themselves in* to maintain the parallel development of this sentence.

11. **(B)** Replace *or* with *nor*.

12. **(B)** This phrase makes it seem that elephants are armed with rifles.

13. **(E)** This sentence contains no errors.

14. **(D)** Replace *there* with *their*.

15. **(D)** Replace *felt* with *feel*.

16. **(C)** A comma is missing following the word *act*.

17. **(C)** Replace *waited* with *waits*.

18. **(A)** Replace *having needed* with *needing*.

SENTENCE CORRECTION

19. **(A)** The underlined portion is acceptable as written.

20. **(E)** Use this replacement for the awkward wording in the original sentence.

21. **(D)** Use this replacement for the awkward wording in the original sentence.

22. **(B)** The plural verb does not end in *s*.

23. **(D)** Use the word *if* in place of the wordy underlined phrase.

24. **(B)** This wording is clearer and more understandable than the original wording in the sentence.

25. **(E)** The correct verb is *was*, rather than *could . . . be*.

26. **(E)** Use this replacement to maintain the parallel structure of the sentence.

27. **(D)** The words *much more* in the original sentence are not needed. Choice C is not correct because it unnecessarily changes the sentence.

28. **(B)** Use this more direct wording to replace the underlined portion of the sentence.

29. **(C)** Replace *is* with *as*.

30. **(B)** Use this more direct wording to replace the underlined portion of the sentence.

31. **(E)** Use this more direct wording to replace the underlined portion of the sentence.

32. **(A)** This choice best reflects the tone of the passage and does provide the most fitting conclusion.

33. **(B)** This sentence adds nothing to the passage, which is about the Gettysburg Address. Deleting the sentence takes nothing away from the meaning of the passage.

34. **(E)** This choice, alone, would remind the reader that Lincoln's Gettysburg Address came before the war's end.

35. **(D)** You should always edit out "the fact that" from any written work. Choices B, D, and E accomplish that task. However, choices B and E do not make sense in context, leaving D as the only correct choice.

36. **(D)** The word *as* can be an adverb, a conjunction, a preposition, or even a noun. What it cannot be is a verb. This sentence does not have a verb, and D solves that problem by including the verb "was."

37. **(B)** It is an article from a newspaper. The article was accessed online, as is the case for many newspaper articles, but there is no evidence that it is an online article.

38. **(A)** A primary source is firsthand information. The only primary source on this list is the notes from a concentration camp guard.

39. **(B)** The book by a participating astronaut in that original lander is a secondary source because the events were recalled after the fact. Choices A, D, and E are primary sources. Choice C is a general reference and neither a primary nor a secondary source.

40. **(A)** This is the only choice, correct or not, that refers to the origins of the name "Uncle Sam." None of the other choices directly address the origin of the name "Uncle Sam."

Argumentative Essay

Compare your essay to the sample essay that follows. You may want to show your essay to an English expert for further evaluation.

This essay would likely receive 5 or 6 out of 6 points (510 words).

I think that the idea of removing any record of a poor grade in a class and any record of the class from a transcript is one of the worst ideas I've ever heard of. A transcript is a record of work in college and that record should not be tampered with. I am going to explain why and try to explain why people might think it is a good idea for them and why that does not make it right.

A class and a grade on a final transcript is a record of what has happened in a college classroom. It is a reflection of what happens between a professor and a student. If a students got a poor grade there is certainly a good reason for it. Not only would this practice strike at the very basis of academic it would encourage students to pay less attention to their studies, knoing that they could just have any grade they wanted to have removed. Besides that there are many ways besides their performance in class that a student can stop a grade from appearing on their final record. The first is to withdraw. Every college has withdrawal policies that allow a students to leave a class and have no grade recorded. Often students can withdraw very late from a class, even after they know what their grade will be. The second thins is grade appeal. Every college has a grade appeal process. In what I see at the college I attend if a student really did not deserve a grade the grade will be overturned on appeal. Most colleges also have hardship provisions. That means say you were in a hospital, or something else tragic happeed in your life, a college committee can decide not to record your grade on a transcript. But once the grade is there after all the things to protect students then it belongs there.

There will be some people who write in favor of this statement because they apply it to themselves. They say "wow" it would be great if I could just go through my transcript and remove every grade and course I did not like. Of course that is what they are going to write.

But it is so serving of themselves that we just can't pay attention to them. It would be giving the wrong people a say over what is happening in our college where there are already enough questions about the quality of what goes on there. Why not just take the tuition money and let the students write their own grades.

To summarize my position I disagree with the statement about a college student being able to have any grade and class removed from their transcript. There are already many, many safeguards for students to stop the grade from appearing or to challenge a grade if it is incorrect or was because of some hardship. Things are bad enough as they are without removing this one last tiny bit of honesty in colleges and universities throughout the country.

Informative/Explanatory Essay

Compare your essay with the sample essays that follow. You may want to show your essay to an English expert for further evaluation.

This essay would receive a 5, but probably not a 6.

I never thought of self-serve gas stations as an issue that could lead to a useful analysis, but I see that's not true. The issue raises a number of fundamental questions. Both authors seem to agree that safety and dealing with disabled drivers, while Andrews alone raises the issue of jobs and Callman alone raises the issue of popular support.

I want to say immediately that Andrews point that requiring attendants would create about 500,000 jobs carries the day for me. Entry level jobs are hard to come by, and I believe his point that the extra liability premiums are certainly no more than the cost of the new jobs.

Pumps operated by station employees eliminates the issue of servicing disabled people. I am suspicious of Callman's statement about a disabled person getting another driver to refuel the car. It just seems too convenient, and I would not want to give my credit card to someone I did not know. Besides, and if an employee was present this arrangement would not be necessary. Besides, from what I know, it's legal to only refuel your own car.

The safety issue seems to be a little less clear. Andrews makes the issue of higher liability costs, while Callman mentions increased safety requirements for self-service stations. It seems to make sense that stations with pumps operated by employees would be safer for patrons than self-pumped gas. But neither author gives us any information about comparative safety of either type of station.

Callman's populous argument about the majority being correct reads like an example of an faulty argument. That the practice is widespread is interesting, but it does not prove that self service stations are the best approach.

Andrew's argument for jobs, and Callman's silence on this issue, convinces me that requiring that attendants dispense all gasoline is a strong enough point on its own. It is clear to me that the extra cost of employees would be offset by the reduction in insurance costs.

Discussion

This essay clearly defines the main issues and points out which position papers refer to which issues. The essay quickly identifies the main issue and then fully reviews the other issues, bringing in the author's own perspective. The essay is long enough, well developed, and is free of meaningful errors in usage and grammar. The essay uses information from the two position papers but only by paraphrase and somewhat casually cites the appropriate position paper. It would be easy for a rater to place this essay in the upper third; however, the lack of any direct quotations and the somewhat casual citing would likely limit the highest possible score on this essay to a 5.

This essay would receive a 3, but probably not a 4.

It jumps right out on top of you. We need jobs, and having people working in gas stations would create jobs, so let us have a law that says only employees can pump gas. That is the point made by Anderson, "We would add over 500,000 employees by eliminating self-service stations." Half a million jobs. Do we really need more discussion. The discussion is over.

All the rest of the arguments don't amount to much compared to jobs. Anderson says you can tell self-service stations are more dangerous because the liability insurance is higher. Callman write "it's just as easy for poorly-paid gas station employee to cause an accident as it is for the self-service pump operator. Neither argument is a real winner.

Callman claims to have witnessed disabled drivers getting help from other drivers at self-service stations. Anderson says in a response that "The typical self-service station always violates federal law. They each make a point and it's hard to tell who is really correct. I guess there should be some way of a disabled driver to get help at a self-serve.

So this brings us back to the issue of jobs. The unemployment rate in the country is high, and it is very high for those without a college degree. A gas station job would provide an opportunity for unskilled workers. These workers would make money, be able to support themselves, and be able to contribute to society. When I first began to read these position papers it seemed it was about gas stations, but it's really about people and providing work for them. How can we turn our backs on a plan that will add so many jobs?

Discussion

This essay is fairly well developed, although there are errors, including sentence fragments. The writer refers to the position papers and associates the sources with information drawn from the papers. However, the essay is not developed enough to earn a score in the upper third, and this lack of development also means that the typical grader would not assign a score of 4.

This essay would likely earn a score of 2.

One of these essays mentions job growth from non-self-serve stations. The other person doesn't mention job growth at all. One essays says that self-service stations are more dangerous than regular stations, and the other person says they are really not more dangerous.

When it comes to disabled people, one essay says that self-service stations break the law because there is no one to pump gas for the disabled, but the other person says that other customers are there to help the disabled. Personally I think people probably are discriminated against.

The conclusion I reach from all this is that the jobs issue is the only issue the second essay dos not have a response to. To me, that means that the jobs issue is the main point and the one we should pay the most attention to.

Discussion

An essay this short with some citations could never earn a score above 3. The absence of any citations and poor development mean that the highest score possible is a 2. The score could not be higher unless both the development and the citations were significantly improved.

Mathematics

1. **(B)** Point C begins at coordinates $(2, -1)$.
   Shift down 3 units: $y = -1$. Subtract 3: $(-1) - 3 = -4$. The new y value is -4.
   Shift left 2 units: $x = 2$. Subtract 2: $(2) - 2 = 0$. The new x value is 0.
   After the shift, the coordinates of point C are $(0, -4)$.

2. **(E)** Each roller must travel 320 feet so the combined distance traveled by both rollers must be 640 feet, even though each roller will have a different number of rotations.

3. **(A)** The median will be some number between 130 and 270, although we will not know exactly what that is. Any number NOT between 130 and 270 could not be the median. Choice A, 91, is the only number that meets that criteria. All the other choices could be the median, even though you do not know if any of them is the actual median.

4. **(-95)** The y value changes -15 for every change of -30 on the x axis. So the y value changes at half the rate of the x axis. At that rate, a point with a value of $x = -190$ would have a y value of -95.

5. **(B)** The "trick" to solving the problem is to notice that the missing part is also a cone. You can see that the radius of this cone is 3 from the diagram. Subtract $16 - 10 = 6$ to find the height of the missing cone. You have the dimensions you need to solve the problem: $r = 3$, $h = 6$
   Substitute the values in the formula:
   $$\frac{1}{3}\pi r^2 h$$
   $$\frac{1}{3}\pi(3)^2\, 6 = \frac{1}{3}\pi\,(9)\,(6) = \pi\left(\frac{1}{3}\right)(9)(6) = \pi(3)(6) = 18\pi$$
   Leave the answer in π form.

6. **(E)** Rewrite the fraction as two fractions: $\dfrac{3x}{12} + \dfrac{6y}{12}$
   Write in simplest form: $\dfrac{x}{4} + \dfrac{y}{2}$

7. **(B)** You have to know the formula for the circumference of a circle is πd ($2\pi r$). Use 3.14 for π. The diameter of the circle is 4. It does not matter that the x and y coordinates are negative because that has nothing to do with the diameter of the circle.
   Let's calculate $\pi d = 3.14 \times d = 3.14 \times 4 = 12.56$

8. **(A, B, D, E)** In a triangle, the longest side is opposite the largest angle. C is the longest side, and z is the largest angle. This means that side and that angle must be opposite each other, and angles a and y cannot be opposite each other. Choice D is also correct because no angle in a triangle can measure 180°. E is correct because just two of the angles could not be opposite side c.

9. **(B)** Start by multiplying $5 \times 34{,}000$ cm $= 170{,}000$ cm.
   Write the answer using scientific notation, which has a digit in the one's place multiplied by a power of 10.
   That is 1.7×10^5.
   Note that choices A, D, and E are mathematically correct but do not correctly represent the number using scientific notation.

10. **(B)** The triangle is a right triangle, and the best approach to answering this question is to see that the sides of the triangle form the Pythagorean triple: 3, 4, 5. Now find the area of $A = \dfrac{(3 \times 4)}{2} = 6$.

11. **(D)** Keep in mind that each x pair in the table must work in the equation. Some answers just work for one pair. It is best to follow a step-by-step approach. The pair (0, 5) is a hint that subtraction by 5 may be involved. Only D works for every (x, y) pair.

12. **(D)** Add the three smaller numbers and then the three larger numbers to find this answer.

13. **(D)** Recognize this triangle as a 45°–45°–90° triangle. That means both legs have the same length of 6 feet. Use the formula for the area of a triangle

$A = \dfrac{1}{2} \, bh. \; A = \dfrac{1}{2} \, (6)(6) = \dfrac{1}{2} \times 36 = 18.$

The area is 18 square feet.

14. **(B)** Multiply x by 2 and then add 1 to find y.

15. **(A)** Multiply 12 times 55 = 660 to find the total length of the trip. Divide 660 by $45 = 14\dfrac{2}{3}, \ldots$ to find the number of hours for the return trip.

Subtract $14\dfrac{2}{3} \, \square \, 12 = 2\dfrac{2}{3}$.

16. **(B)** The shaded parts of 3 circles total $\dfrac{2}{5} + \dfrac{5}{9} + \dfrac{1}{4} = \dfrac{72}{180} + \dfrac{100}{180} + \dfrac{45}{180} = \dfrac{217}{180}$.

Because there are three circles divide by 3. That's like multiplying by $\dfrac{1}{3}$.

$\left(\dfrac{1}{3} \times \dfrac{217}{180} \right) = \dfrac{217}{540} =$ about 40 percent. The trick to finding the total shaded part is to consider the 3 circles as 1 circle.

17. **(B)** Each line on the grid represents 3 units. That means point Q is at (9, 12). As a point is reflected across the y axis, the new point has the same y coordinate but the opposite of the x coordinate. The coordinate of the new point Q is (–9, +12).

18. **(A)** Points P and Q could be +6 and 0, +5 and +1, +4 and +2, +2 and +4, +1 and +5, or 0 and +6. That means point R must be between +6 and 0. The only choice that meets this requirement is A. Choice E, +6, is incorrect because point R would have to be less than +6 to be between +6 and 0.

19. **(B)** This equation correctly expresses the relationship.

20. **(C)** There are 16 + 12 + 9 + 7 = 44 students enrolled in history. Twelve of these students are enrolled only in history. The difference between all the students enrolled in history and the number of students just enrolled in history is 44 – 12 = 32.

21. **(E)** $\sqrt{300 \times 3} = \sqrt{900} = 30$ or $\sqrt{300 \times 3} = \sqrt{3 \times 3 \times 100} =$ $\sqrt{3} \times \sqrt{3} \times \sqrt{100} = \sqrt{3} \times 10 = 3 \times 10 = 30$

22. **(A)** This graph best represents the steady movement up and then down of the temperatures.

23. **(A)** $5\overline{)23}$ $= 4$ R 3; $5\overline{)63}$ $= 12$ R 3; $4 \times 12 = 48$.

24. **(D)** $(125 + 200 + 150 + 225 + 75 + 150 + 50) \div 7 =$ the average (139.3) miles per day. 140 is closest.

25. **(D)** Invert the divisor and then multiply.

$$\frac{7}{xy} \div \frac{x}{14} = \frac{7}{xy} \times \frac{14}{x} = \frac{98}{x^2 y}$$

26. **(A)** Write the proportion $\frac{1}{15} = \frac{43}{x}$, cross multiply to get $x = 645$.

27. **(C)** The lawnmower tank total capacity equals 2g. The amount left in the tank is $1\frac{3}{5}$ g. $2 - 1\frac{3}{5} = \frac{2}{5}$ g. The amount used for 1 mowing: $1\frac{3}{5} \div \frac{2}{5} = 4$.

    This is the number of "mows" still possible.

28. **(E)** Add the perimeters to find the total of 38 inches; $5 \times 38 = 190$.

29. **(C)** Choice C yields a piece 75 feet by 5 feet. Mary needs a piece 96 feet by 5 feet.

30. **(C)** $0.25 \times \$40 = \$10$; $\$40 - \$10 = \$30$; $0.15 \times \$30 = \$4.50$; $\$30 - \$4.50 = \$25.50$.

31. **(B)** The ratio of *LM* to *NO* is 3:2. Choice B does not reflect this ratio.

32. **(B)** Three DVDs cost \$15.60 at Store A and \$18.00 at Store B. The saving for all three DVDs is \$2.40. The saving on one DVD is \$0.80.

33. **(B)** The product of two whole numbers is 1 only if both whole numbers are 1.

34. **(C)** The value of C is 1.54. The value of each of the other choices is 3.52.

35. **(B)** $66\frac{2}{3}$ percent is written as $\frac{2}{3}$ or in decimal form as $0.66\overline{6}$ where the line over the last 6 shows that the 6 repeats endlessly. $0.66\overline{6}$ is not equal to 0.66. Choice B is the only choice that does not represent $66\frac{2}{3}$ percent correctly.

36. **(C)** Powers of 10 are 1 (10^0), 10 (10^1), 100 (10^2), 1000 (10^3). The calculator could be displaying 20, which is not a power of 10.

37. **(D)** If some of the values of *Y* are more than 50, then all of the values of *Y* could NOT be less than 50.

38. **(D)** The display would show 500, which is 1000 times (0.5).

39. **(A)** Find the fractions greater than 1. That is $\frac{12}{13}$ and $\frac{99}{100}$. Cross multiply

    $\frac{12}{13} \diagdown \frac{99}{100} = \frac{1{,}283}{1{,}200}$. The bottom product is smaller, so the first fraction is smaller.

40. **(A)** There are 36 possible outcomes. Half of these outcomes are even and half are odd.

41. **(B)** $6 \cdot P = R$. Divide both sides by 2 to get $3 \cdot P = R/2$.

42. **(C)** When the $\div$ key was pressed, the calculator multiplied: $125 \times 5 = 625$. The correct answer is $125 \div 5 = 25$.

43. **(B)** $V = l \times w \times h$. Divide both sides by $w \times h$ to get $\dfrac{V}{wh} = l$.

44. **(B)** Dividing by 0.01 is the same as multiplying by 100.

45. **(C)** Divide by 3 to reverse tripling the other number. Multiplying by $\dfrac{1}{3}$ is the same as dividing by 3.

46. **(E)** Imagine a cylinder with a height equal to its diameter. The vertical cross section of this cylinder is a square.

47. **(D)** Use the Pythagorean formula to find the length of the diagonal.
$3^2 + 4^2 = x^2$ $25 = x^2$ $x = 5$ feet
Find the perimeter $3 + 3 + 4 + 4 = 14$ feet
Add the perimeter and the length of the diagonal $14 + 5 = 19$ feet

48. **(C)** Recognize this as a 45°–45°–90° triangle. This means that sides $\overline{BD}$ and $\overline{DE}$ are the same length. The length of $\overline{DE}$ is 10. The length of $\overline{AB}$ is 6. The length of $\overline{AD}$ is $10 - 6 = 4$.

49. **(D)** Neither a nor b can be determined from the information on the figure. Both dimensions are needed to find the area.

50. **(A)** Faster times are represented by smaller numbers. Subtract $52.8 - 1.3$ to find Lisa's time.

51. **(A)** Quinn practiced an average of 7 hours a week for 5 weeks. That is 35 hours in all. Use addition to solve this problem. He practiced 7 hours in one week, $7 + 2 = 9$ hours in each of two weeks, and 10 hours in the fourth week. Add to find the total number of hours: $7 + 9 + 9 + 10 = 35$. That equals the total number of hours he practiced. That means he did not practice at all in one of the weeks. That means the correct answer is 0. It is incorrect to divide 35 by 5 and get 7, and it is incorrect to divide 35 by 4, which is 8.75, or 9 to the nearest whole number.

52. **(B)** The first number written twice is 12. ($12 = 3 \times 4$.) The next number written twice is 24. The numbers increase by 12. So the question is how many multiples of 12 are there from 1 to 100. We can just write the numbers 12, 24, 26, 28, 60, 72, 84, 96. That is 8. Or we can divide 100 by 12 and ignore the remainder; 100 divided by $12 = 8$ without the remainder.

53. **(B)** Solving this problem involves a little trial and error. Start to eliminate answers. Multiply each term of the ratio by an estimated factor and add to see if you can get 28.
(A) Try 5 as the factor $(5 \times 2) + (5 \times 3) = 25$. No factor will get us to 28.
(B) Try 4 $(4 \times 3) + (4 \times 4) = 28$. This is the correct ratio.
(C) Try 3 $(3 \times 4) + (3 \times 7) = 33$. No factor will get us to 28.
(D) Try 2 $(2 \times 5) + (2 \times 7) = 24$. No factor will get us to 28.
(E) Try 2 $(2 \times 6) + (2 \times 10) = 32$. No factor will get us to 28.

54. **(E)** Half off the listed price means the same thing as 0.5 times the listed price or $\frac{1}{2}$ times the listed price.

Choice E is $\frac{L}{0.50} = \frac{L}{\frac{1}{2}} = 2L$. That is twice the listed price.

The other choices all show half the listed price.

(A) $0.50 \times L = 0.5 L$ – one half the listed price

(B) $L - .50L = 0.5L$

(C) $\frac{L}{2} = L \times \frac{1}{2} = 0.5 L$

(D) $\frac{5L}{10} = \frac{5}{10} L = 0.5L$

55. **(C)** One mile is about 1.6 kilometers so the correct answer will represent 1.6×40.

Answer C is correct. It is best to rearrange it as $32 \times \frac{1}{10} \div 2 \times 40 = \frac{3.2}{2} \times 40 = 1.6 \times 40$. The other answers are incorrect.

(A) $\frac{16}{100} \times 40 = 0.16 \times 40$ is incorrect

(B) 0.6×40 is incorrect.

(D) $0.6 \times 10 \times 40 \times \frac{1}{10} = 0.6 \times 40$.

(E) $\frac{60}{10} \div (\frac{1}{40} \times 30 \times 2) = \frac{3}{4} \times 2 = \frac{6}{4} = \frac{3}{2} = 6 \times \frac{2}{3}$.

56. **(A, C)** Choice A is correct because a chord is a line segment connecting two points on a circle. Choice C is correct because a radius is a line segment connecting the center of a circle to a point on the circle. Choice B is incorrect because $\overline{AE}$ does not connect the center of a circle to a point on the circle. Choice D is incorrect because $\overline{AC}$ does not connect two points on a circle and pass through the center. Choice E is incorrect because $\overline{BD}$ does not connect two points on a circle.

PART V
Principles of Learning and Teaching

Principles of Learning and Teaching Review

10

COMPUTER DELIVERED

70 Multiple-Choice Questions (75% of test)

Two Instructional Scenarios with two constructed response questions for each scenario (25% of test)

Two hours to complete all the questions

You can take the PLT in four areas:

Early Childhood (5621)	**Grades K–6 (5622)**
Grades 5–9 (5623)	**Grades 7–12 (5624)**

The PLT is based on Core Standards 2 through 10 of the Interstate New Teacher Assessment and Support Consortium (INTASC). You can review the INTASC Standards with explanations at *www.ccsso.org/content/pdfs/corestrd.pdf.*

PASSING THE PLT

There is more than enough review information, test strategies, and test items in this book to pass the PLT. Remember, you are not competing with others for the highest score; you just need the minimum passing score for your state certification.

Important Scoring Information

Each state's passing score for the PLT is in the lower 25 percent of all scores, and many passing scores are in the lower 10 percent. That means the vast majority of test-takers pass the test. The high likelihood that you will pass the test is an important part of your preparation.

The raw score is the number of items you answer correctly or the number of constructed response points you earn. The raw score determines your scale score, which is the basis for passing the test. Different versions of the test are at different difficulty levels, and the raw passing scores vary from version to version. There is specific information about the percentile ranks of the scale scores for each test. The 25th percentile means that 75 percent of test takers scored above that score.

HOW TO PREPARE FOR THE PLT

Follow these steps to prepare for the PLT.

QUICK REVIEW CHECKLIST

Chapter 10: Principles of Learning and Teaching Review

☐ Read the review material.

Chapter 11: PLT Constructed Response Strategy and Practice

☐ Review the PLT Test Strategies on pages 407–409.

☐ Read the Practice PLT Scenario on page 410.

☐ Answer the Practice PLT Constructed-Response Items on page 412.

☐ Review the Constructed-Response Answers beginning on page 414.

Chapter 12: Principles of Learning and Teaching Practice Test

☐ Complete the PLT Practice Test beginning on page 421.

☐ Review the PLT Practice Test Explained Responses and Answers beginning on page 452.

COMPLETE PRINCIPLES OF LEARNING AND TEACHING REVIEW

This PLT review is organized under the four main areas tested on the PLT.

1. Students as Learners
2. Instructional processes
3. Assessment
4. Professional Development, Leadership, and Community

1. STUDENTS AS LEARNERS

Human Development

PHYSICAL DEVELOPMENT

Adequate nutrition in mothers is essential for proper fetal development. Adequate nutrition and exercise are essential for a child's physical growth. Inadequate nutrition can hamper growth and lead to inattentiveness and other problems that interfere with learning.

Alcohol and drug abuse by mothers can cause irreparable brain damage to unborn children. Children of drug-and-alcohol-abusing mothers tend to have lower birth weights. Low birth weight is associated with health, emotional, and learning problems. Alcohol and drug addiction, smoking, stress, and adverse environmental factors are among the other causes of abnormal physical and emotional development.

During the first 12 months after birth, the body weight of infants triples and brain size doubles. Infants crawl by about 7 months, eat with their hands at about 8 months, sit up by about 9 months, stand up by about 11 months, and walk by about 1 year.

From 12–15 months to 2.5 years, children are called toddlers. During this period, children become expert walkers, feed themselves, evidence self control, and spend a great deal of their time playing. This period is characterized by the word *no* and is also when children begin bowel training.

The preschool years span the time from the end of toddlerhood to entry into kindergarten. Children start to look more like adults, with longer legs and a shorter torso. Play continues but becomes more sophisticated.

The elementary school years refer to ages 6–10 in girls but 6–12 years in boys. During this period children enter a period of steady growth. Most children double their body weight and increase their height by one-half. Play continues but involves more sophisticated games and physical activities, often involving groups or teams of other children.

Adolescence begins at about age 10 for girls but at about age 12 for boys. The growth rate spurt begins during this time. Because this period begins earlier for girls than for boys, girls are more mature than boys for a number of years. Sexual and secondary sex characteristics appear during this time. Most adolescents rely heavily on peer group approval and respond to peer pressure.

COGNITIVE DEVELOPMENT

Jean Piaget

Jean Piaget is the most prominent of cognitive psychologists who believe that students develop concepts through a series of stages. Stage theory is currently the most popular form of child development.

According to Piaget, children proceed through a fixed but uneven series of stages of cognitive development. His stages help us understand the general way in which students learn and develop concepts.

Action and logic versus perception are at the center of Piaget's theory. He believed that children learn through an active involvement with their environment. He also believed that students have developed a concept when their logical understanding overcomes their perceptual misunderstanding of the concept.

His conservation experiments explain this last point. In conservation of number, students are shown two matched rows of checkers. The child confirms that there are the same number of checkers in each row. Then one row of checkers is spread out and the child is asked if there are still the same number of checkers. Children who believe there are more checkers in one of the rows do not understand the concept of number because their perception holds sway over their logic.

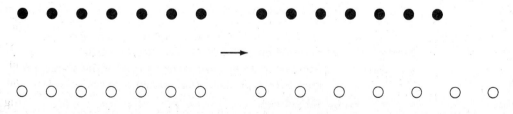

Piaget presents these four stages of cognitive development.

- Sensorimotor (birth to 18 months)—Children exhibit poor verbal and cognitive development. Children develop the idea of object permanence (out of sight not out of mind) during this stage.

- Preoperational (18 months to 7 years)—Children develop language and are able to solve some problems. Students' thinking is egocentric, and they have difficulty developing concepts. For example, students in this stage may not be able to complete the conservation of number task shown above.
- Concrete operational (7–12 years)—Students' thinking becomes operational. This means that concepts become organized and logical, as long as they are working with or around concrete materials or images. During this stage, students master the number conservation and other conservation tasks, but most students do not understand symbolic concepts.
- Formal operational (12+ years)—Children develop and demonstrate concepts without concrete materials or images. In this stage, students think fully in symbolic terms about concepts. Children become able to reason effectively, abstractly, and theoretically. Full development of this stage may depend on the extent to which children have had a full range of active manipulative experiences in the concrete operational stage.

PERSONALITY DEVELOPMENT

Freud's psychoanalytic theories have profoundly affected modern thought about psychological and personality development. He believed that humans pass through four stages of psychosexual development: oral, anal, phallic, and genital. The personality itself consists of the id, ego, and superego. According to Freud, an integrated personality develops from the gratification experienced at each of these stages.

PSYCHOSOCIAL DEVELOPMENT

Eriksen built on Freud's work and partitioned the life span into eight psychosocial stages. An emotional crisis at each stage can lead to a positive or negative result. The result achieved at each stage determines the development pattern for the next stage. Four of these stages fall within the school years.

Stage	Characteristic	Description
Kindergarten	Initiative vs. Guilt	Children accepted and treated warmly tend to feel more comfortable about trying out new ideas. Rejected children tend to become inhibited and guilty.
Elementary grades	Industry vs. Inferiority	Students who are accepted by their peer group and do well in school, and those who believe they are accepted and do well, are more successful than those who do not feel good about themselves.
Grades 6–9	Identity vs. Identity Confusion	Students who establish an identity and a sense of direction and who develop gender, social, and occupational roles experience an easier transition into adulthood than those students who do not establish these roles.
Grades 10–12	Intimacy vs. Isolation	Students who have passed successfully through the other stages will find it easier to establish a relationship with a member of the opposite sex. Those students who are unsuccessful at this stage may face an extremely difficult transition into adult life.

MORAL DEVELOPMENT

Kohlberg built on Piaget's original work to develop stages of moral development. Kohlberg proposed three levels of moral development with two stages at each level. His stages provide a reasonable approach to understanding moral development. Not everyone moves through all stages.

Preconventional Morality (preschool and primary grades)

STAGE 1 Children do not demonstrate a conscience but do react to fear of punishment. Children are very egocentric.

STAGE 2 Children still have no clear morality. Children concentrate on their own egocentric needs and let others do the same. Children may not be willing to help others meet their needs even though it would help other children meet their own needs.
[Some children and antisocial adults may not pass this stage.]

Conventional Morality (middle grades through high school)

STAGE 3 These children want to be good. They associate themselves with parents and other adult authority figures. They show concern for others and evidence a number of virtues and try to live up to expectations.

STAGE 4 These children shift from wanting to please authority figures to a more generalized sense of respect for rules and expectations. These children see their responsibility to maintain society through a strict enforcement of society's laws.
[Many adults do not progress beyond this stage of development.]

Postconventional Morality (high school and beyond)

STAGE 5 People at this stage differentiate between legality and morality. They have a more flexible view of right and wrong and realize that societal needs often take precedence over individual needs.

STAGE 6 Very few people reach this stage. Those at Stage 6 have pure, cosmic understanding of justice and dignity. These principles always take precedence when they conflict with what is considered legal or socially acceptable.

SOCIAL LEARNING THEORY

Social learning theory is a fairly new field. Social learning theorists seek to combine behavioral and cognitive learning theories along with other types of learning.

Albert Bandura is the leading social learning theorist. He believes that a great deal of learning can take place through modeling. That is, students often act the way they see others act, or they learn vicariously by observing others. Bandura believes that verbal explanations and reinforcement are also important and that students become socialized through systematic modeling of appropriate behavior. Students can also develop cognitive skills by observing a problem-solving process and learn procedures by observing these procedures in action.

NATURE VERSUS NURTURE

The relative effects of nature (heredity and genes) and nurture (environment and experience) on growth and development is still not resolved. Certain traits, sex, eye color, some forms of mental retardation, and susceptibility to some mental illnesses such as schizophrenia are linked to genes and heredity. However, other developmental questions are not clear, and even studies of twins separated at birth has not yielded the kind of conclusive results needed to draw conclusions.

ZONE OF PROXIMAL DEVELOPMENT

Lev Vygotsky developed the concept of the zone of proximal development (ZPD). The ZPD consists of those tasks the student cannot do without help but can do with help. Vygotsky held that teachers should present activities that are in a student's ZPD to encourage a realistic opportunity for advancement of student learning.

Scaffolding

Scaffolding applies Vygotsky's ZPD to the classroom, although scaffolding was not developed by Vygotsky. In scaffolding, a student receives help to learn something in his or her ZPD. The help is withdrawn in a measured way until the help becomes unnecessary. The term *scaffolding* was chosen because of its conceptual resemblance to the way a scaffold is removed, say, from a building as the scaffold is no longer needed for construction.

GARDNER'S MULTIPLE INTELLIGENCES

Howard Gardner presented a theory of multiple intelligences. He proposed the list of nine because he felt that the traditional view of intelligence did not reflect the wide range of ability demonstrated by students. His theory has received a cool reception from many psychologists because of a lack of empirical evidence. However, it has received a much better reception from those involved in education because of the theory's practical usefulness. Many educators believe that attention to the theory may encourage teachers to try alternate approaches when students are having difficulty learning. A list of Gardner's intelligences with brief explanations follows.

1. Spatial thinkers learn best by visualizing problems and solutions.
2. Linguistic thinkers may learn best through words and language.
3. Logical-mathematical thinkers may learn best through abstract and scientific thinking, and through solving numerical problems. It is said that this type of thinking is strongly related to traditional measures of intelligence.
4. Students with bodily-kinesthetic intelligence may learn best through physical activity, and are generally good at sports and dance.
5. Musical students may learn best by listening and these students tend to excel at singing and playing instruments.
6. Interpersonal thinkers may learn best by working with others and tend to be sensitive to the needs of others.
7. Intrapersonal thinkers may learn best by working alone and tend to be intuitive and introverted.
8. Naturalistic thinkers may learn best by relating subject matter to nature and to the world around them.
9. Existential thinkers suggest a person who can comprehend concepts beyond the actual information given.

MASLOW'S HIERARCHY OF NEEDS AND HUMAN MOTIVATION

Maslow's hierarchy of needs is a linear description of levels leading to the top level of self-transcendence. There are basic (deficiency) needs, which Maslow holds must be met for a person to be motivated to achieve the higher-level (being) needs. It is the achievement of one level of needs that "motivates" someone to pursue the next level of needs. Maslow holds that without motivation it is unlikely that the higher level of needs will be achieved.

Deficiency Needs

1. Biological and Physiological: hunger, thirst, bodily comforts
2. Safety: feel safe, personally secure, free from danger; and for adults, a secure employment
3. Belongingness and Love: be affiliated with others; and with a family, feel accepted and loved
4. Esteem: to gain approval, be seen as capable and have self-respect

Being Needs

5. Cognitive: to know, to understand, and explore
6. Aesthetic: the appreciation of and search for beauty, order, and form
7. Self-Actualization: to find self-fulfillment and realize one's potential
8. Self-Transcendence: to help others find self-fulfillment and self-realization

LEARNING STYLES IN THE CLASSROOM

There is an incredible variety of learning styles. A student's learning style may change as the student matures, and the style may be different for different types of learning and different subjects. There are some fundamental learning styles for a teacher to consider as he or she teaches. The three most frequently discussed styles are given below.

1. **AUDITORY** The student learns best through listening to spoken information.

   Try books on CD or books that can be "read" aloud by an e-reader. Encourage students to make oral reports, and try repeating difficult words or ideas. In general, allow for periods in which oral expression is as important as written expression.

2. **VISUAL-SPATIAL** The student learns best through reading and viewing tables, charts, and maps.

   Try writing words on the board as you speak, make provisions for a rich selection of books and other written learning materials, encouraging students to write reports or create PowerPoint presentations. Try handing out typed versions of complex instructions that you are giving orally.

3. **KINESTHETIC** The student learns best through physical activity and hands-on activities.

   The ideal is for a teacher to structure classroom learning to incorporate opportunities for all these learning styles. Naturally, there are physical and emotional needs to be met as well, and these needs may well be a determining factor in student success. Teaching is a complex business. Here is a brief summary of some ways that teachers can account for each of the listed learning styles.

Particularly in mathematics and science, give students opportunities to learn through hands-on experiences and experiments. Incorporate projects that students can work on in small groups at their own pace. Some educators recommend giving kinesthetic learners an opportunity to take breaks and to participate in field trips and role playing.

METACOGNITION

Metacognition is "knowing about knowing." In the classroom, metacognition includes what a student knows about him- or herself, what a student knows about strategies, or what a student knows about the topic to be learned or the problem to be solved. The term *metacognition* sounds exceptionally complex, but it can be as simple as noticing that one concept or skill is more difficult to learn than another.

Metacognition can help students perform cognitive tasks more effectively. Teachers can encourage metacognition in a number of ways. One metacognitive strategy is self-questioning (Have I solved a similar problem? What do I already know about this topic?). Other suggested strategies include using graphic representations such as flowcharts or concept maps. Still other educators recommend writing out thoughts or "thinking aloud" as effective metacognitive strategies.

VISUAL-PROCESSING PROBLEMS

Visual-processing problems arise when students have difficulty processing visual input. Visual-processing problems are particularly important in the elementary grades. Students can have perfect vision and still have visual-processing problems.

The most appropriate action for a teacher who suspects that a student may have difficulty processing visual information is to refer the child for a special test that can identify students with this problem. A regular vision test will not identify this problem and eyeglasses will not correct it.

Visual-processing problems usually create reading problems, but visual processing problems can create learning problems in other school subjects. Experts believe that as many as 80 percent of students may have visual-processing problems not severe enough to interfere with learning.

LEARNING DISABILITIES

The formal definition of learning disability comes from the Individuals with Disabilities Education Act (IDEA).

A learning disability is . . . a disorder in one or more of the basic psychological processes involved in understanding or in using language, spoken or written, that may manifest itself in an imperfect ability to listen, think, speak, read, write, spell, or do mathematical calculations, including conditions such as perceptual disabilities, brain injury, minimal brain dysfunction, dyslexia, and developmental aphasia.

Learning disabilities do not include, . . . learning problems that are primarily the result of visual, hearing, or motor disabilities, of mental retardation, of emotional disturbance, or of environmental, cultural, or economic disadvantage.

There are many different types of learning disabilities. A partial list is given below.

Dyslexia	Difficulty processing language	Problems reading, writing, spelling, speaking
Dyscalculia	Difficulty with math	Problems doing math problems, understanding time, using money
Dysgraphia	Difficulty with writing	Problems with handwriting, spelling, organizing ideas
Dyspraxia (Sensory Integration Disorder)	Difficulty with fine motor skills	Problems with hand-eye coordination, balance, manual dexterity
Auditory Processing Disorder	Difficulty hearing differences between sounds	Problems with reading, comprehension, language
Visual Processing Disorder	Difficulty interpreting visual information	Problems with reading, math, maps, charts, symbols, pictures

Attention-Deficit Disorder and Attention-Deficit Hyperactivity Disorder

The three main symptoms of a child with attention-deficit disorder (ADD) or attention-deficit hyperactivity disorder (ADHD) are inattention, hyperactivity, and impulsivity. Usually one of these symptoms is predominant. Not everything about students with ADD/ADHD has a negative impact on learning, and there are many successful people with ADD/ADHD. However, students who fit these classifications usually present a problem in a typical school setting.

INATTENTIVE: Inattentive students may be harder to identify because these students may not be disruptive. However, these students may not follow rules and directions, whether it is in interactions with teachers or with other students. These students may be unorganized.

HYPERACTIVE: Students are normally active, but students with hyperactive symptoms seem to be constantly on the move. They move suddenly from one activity to the next. Attempts to be still may be accompanied by what seems an involuntary movement such as tapping fingers or feet.

IMPULSIVE: Impulsive students lack self-control. They may make off-the-topic comments or ask irrelevant questions. They may break into other people's conversations or inappropriately move into another student's personal space.

There are many intervention programs for learning disabled students. However, the teacher should see the symptoms of these problems as behavior the student can likely not control. This step will help the teacher work with special educators and parents to develop effective classroom strategies.

Mental Retardation

A child under the age of 18 must meet two specific criteria to be classified as mentally retarded: (1) The child must have an IQ below 70; and (2) There must be meaningful limitations in at least two of three areas of adaptive behavior: social skills, daily living skills, and communication skills. Mental retardation is a disability and not a disease. There is no known cure for mental retardation. However, students with mental retardation can learn to function effectively within the limits of their disability.

An IQ score is determined by an IQ test. These tests have a mean score of 100 with a standard deviation of 15. That means a student classified as mentally retarded on the basis of these tests is at least two standard deviations below the mean. There are many causes of a low IQ score other than low intelligence, and it is very important to eliminate these causes before accepting the validity of the score.

> Here are the categories of mental retardation based solely on IQ scores.
>
> | Degree of Mental Retardation | IQ Score |
> | --- | --- |
> | Profound | less than 20 |
> | Severe | 20–34 |
> | Moderate | 35–49 |
> | Mild | 50–69 |

The other limitation required for a diagnosis of mental retardation is based on scores from an adaptive rating scale, which is based on the abilities a person is known to possess at a particular age. The evaluation and scale are administered and scored by a professional evaluator, and are typically beyond the responsibilities of a classroom teacher.

There are many such scales and each focuses on these three important areas of adaptive behavior.

> **Social skills** as demonstrated by interactions with family members, teachers, and peers.
>
> **Daily living skills** such as self-feeding, personal toilet habits, and dressing oneself.
>
> **Communication skills** such as understanding what someone is saying and the ability to respond orally to comments and questions.

Behavior Disorders in Children

Students classified with behavior disorders exhibit aberrant behavior that goes well beyond the problems normally demonstrated by children. These behavior disorders are particularly noticeable in the preschool years and in adolescence. The following biological and family factors make children most at risk for behavioral disorders: (1) low birth weight, (2) neurological damage, (3) early rejection, (4) separation from their parents, (5) physical and sexual abuse, or (6) being raised by mothers who have suffered physical or sexual abuse or who are living in poverty.

TYPES OF BEHAVIOR DISORDERS

Oppositional Defiant Disorder

Students exhibiting this disorder disobey rules formulated at home or in school. These students frequently argue and have temper tantrums, refuse to obey rules, defy authority, reject responsibility for their behavior, and show evidence of resentment and revenge seeking.

Conduct Disorder Behavior

Students exhibiting this disorder are usually older children or teens who disobey rules and laws formulated by the larger society, including laws that may lead to arrest and incarceration. These students may run away from home, not attend school, destroy property, or set fires. They may bully other students or steal, they may threaten to injure people or animals, and they may find themselves in youth detention facilities or in special programs.

DEVELOPMENTAL DELAYS

The IDEA is the source of the definition of developmental delay. These are students

> who [are] experiencing developmental delays as defined by the State and as measured by appropriate diagnostic instruments and procedures in one or more of the following areas: physical development, cognitive development, communication development, social or emotional development, or adaptive development; and who, by reason thereof, need special education and related services.

A teacher must be familiar with his or her state's definition of *developmental delay*, and, indeed, whether the state uses this term. A student may qualify for services as a developmentally delayed student in one state but not in another.

Developmental delays are determined by comparing what a child can do compared to the normal range of performance for children the same age. Developmental evaluations must be conducted by a trained professional. The evaluation typically focuses on five developmental areas.

Physical development
Cognitive development
Speech and language development
Social skills and emotional development
Child's ability to care for him- or herself

As long as a state defines the term and requires local school districts to use the term, a finding of developmental disabilities means special education services are available free of charge through the school system for children over the age of three.

AMERICANS WITH DISABILITIES ACT AND AMERICANS WITH DISABILITIES ACT AMENDED

The Americans with Disabilities Act (ADA) includes five main titles, but most important for education are the life activities defined more clearly in the Americans with Disabilities Act Amended (ADAA).

The ADA defines a covered disability as "a physical or mental impairment that substantially limits a major life activity."

Recently, the ADAA broadened the interpretations and added to the ADA examples of "major life activities" including, but not limited to, "caring for oneself, performing manual tasks, seeing, hearing, eating, sleeping, walking, standing, lifting, bending, speaking, breathing, learning, reading, concentrating, thinking, communicating, and working," as well as the operation of several specified "major bodily functions."

INCLUSION, MAINSTREAMING, AND LEAST RESTRICTIVE ENVIRONMENT

Inclusion, mainstreaming, and least restrictive environment (LRE) have different meanings.

LRE comes from the IDEA mandate that disabled students should be placed in learning settings whenever possible with students without disabilities. The term *LRE* does not refer to any particular setting, but emphasizes that the less a learning setting is like a traditional setting the more restrictive it is.

Inclusion has a more specific meaning. It means deliberately placing disabled students in regular classrooms with students who have no disabilities, when the disabled student can receive an appropriate education in the class. Inclusion reflects a more comprehensive plan than the less-used term *mainstreaming*, although the two terms still tend to be used interchangeably.

INDIVIDUALIZED EDUCATION PLAN

An individualized education plan (IEP) is required by the IDEA for a child who is classified as disabled by federal or state regulations. To qualify, the child's disability must have an adverse effect on the child's educational progress.

Once a child is found eligible for services, the school sets up an IEP team to develop the IEP. Specific IEP requirements may vary from state to state. An IEP team established by the school typically includes the student's teacher, the student's parents or guardian, a special education teacher, and someone to evaluate the child's evaluation reports, such as a school psychologist. The school may invite other experts to the meeting, and it is not unusual for the parents or guardian to arrange for an advocate or an attorney to join the team. It is also not unheard of for students beyond the primary grades to participate in the meeting.

The whole purpose of this effort is to bring everyone together to consider a child's strengths and deficits and to develop a plan that will best meet the child's educational needs. The IEP may include a wide variety of educational adaptations as well as work in a regular class.

The initial IEP must be accepted by the parents or guardian, or appealed within a set time, typically 10 days. Any member of the team may call a meeting to request an alteration to the IEP. An extensive system of conflict resolution procedures are set out in the statutory provisions.

SECTION 504 OF THE REHABILITATION SERVICES ACT

The best way to understand Section 504 of the Rehabilitation Services Act is to understand how it differs from the IDEA.

Section 504 has more lax requirements than the IDEA. That is, students may receive less assistance from schools with less overview and regulations under Section 504 than under IDEA. Section 504 covers a person's entire life span and safeguards the rights of persons with disabilities beyond education.

Schools are not required to identify students who qualify for services under Section 504, and parental permission is not required for students receiving 504 services. However, parents may raise concerns about the services and petition for a 504 hearing. Section 504 students have a plan but not an IEP. A Section 504 student is typically not placed in a special education setting.

SECOND-LANGUAGE ACQUISITION AND STRATEGIES FOR LEARNING ENGLISH AS A SECOND LANGUAGE

Second-language acquisition refers to learning a second language once a first language has already been learned. This typically happens in the United States when a student has learned the second language before the child comes to school.

The field of second-language acquisition often includes a number of terms such as English language learners (ELLs), English as a second language (ESL), English for speakers of other languages (ESOL), and English as a foreign language (EFL).

The ability of a student to learn a second language depends in large part on whether the second language is spoken at home. That makes it important to involve parents and guardians in an effective second-language acquisition program.

SHELTERED INSTRUCTION

The term *sheltered instruction* describes one approach teachers use to help ELLs. Sheltered instruction provides meaningful instruction in the content areas while students move toward English proficiency. The approach is notable since it frequently integrates Vygotsky's ZPD and Gardner's multiple intelligences. The approach is contrasted with other approaches for ELLs that offer content instruction below grade level while focusing primarily on a student's development of English skills.

One approach to sheltered instruction is the sheltered instruction observation protocol (SIOP). The SIOP model includes activities associated with the following interrelated activities.

- Lesson Preparation
- Building Background
- Comprehensible Input
- Strategies
- Interaction
- Practice/Application
- Lesson Delivery
- Review/Assessment

Each of the strategies is accompanied by a series of specific activities.

STUDENT MOTIVATION

Motivation

Most good lessons begin with a motivation. The motivation interests learners and focuses their attention on the lesson. It is also important to maintain students' motivation for the duration of the lesson.

The motivation for a lesson may be intrinsic or extrinsic. Intrinsic motivation refers to topics that students like or enjoy. Effective intrinsic motivations are based on a knowledge of what is popular or interesting to students of a particular age.

For example, you might introduce a lesson about the French and Indian War to older students by discussing the book and movie *Last of the Mohicans*. You might introduce a lesson on patterns to young children by picking out patterns in children's clothes. You might introduce a lesson on fractions to middle school students with a discussion about the stock market.

Extrinsic motivation focuses on external rewards for good work or goal attainment. Extrinsic rewards are most successful when used in conjunction with more routine work. Extrinsic motivations may offer an appropriate reward for completing an assignment or for other acceptable performance. Establish rewards for activities that most students can achieve and take care to eliminate unnecessary competition.

For example, you might grant a period of free time to students who successfully complete a routine but necessary assignment. You might offer the whole class a trip or a party when a class project is successfully completed. Special education programs feature token reinforcement in which students receive or lose points or small plastic tokens for appropriate or inappropriate activity.

Motivation needs to be maintained during the lesson itself. Follow these guidelines for teaching lessons in which the students remain motivated. Lessons will be more motivating if you have clear and unambiguous objectives, give the students stimulating tasks at an appropriate level, get and hold the students' attention, and allow students some choices. Students will be most motivated if they like the topic or activities, believe that the lesson has to do with them, believe that they will succeed, and have a positive reaction to your efforts to motivate them.

Individual work gives a further opportunity to use intrinsic motivation. Use the interests and likes of individual students to spark and maintain their motivation.

The extrinsic motivation of praise can be used effectively during a lesson. For praise to be successful, it must be given for a specific accomplishment (including effort) and it must focus on the student's own behavior. It does not compare behavior with other students or establish competitive situations.

2. INSTRUCTIONAL PROCESSES

Successful Learning

Research indicates that the following factors are likely to lead to successful learning.

- Students who are engaged in the learning process tend to be more successful learners, particularly when they are engaged in activities at the appropriate level of difficulty.
- Students learn most successfully when they are being taught or supervised as opposed to working independently.
- Students who are exposed to more material at the appropriate level of difficulty are more successful learners.
- Students are successful learners when their teachers expect them to master the curriculum and use available instructional time for learning activities.
- Students who are in a positive, uncritical classroom environment are more successful learners than students who are in a negative, critical classroom environment. This does

not mean that students cannot be corrected or criticized, but that students learn best when the corrections are done positively and when the criticisms are constructive.

- Students generally develop positive attitudes to teachers who appear warm, have a student orientation, praise students, listen to students, accept student ideas, and interact with them.

CLASSROOM INTERACTION

Flander's Interaction Analysis gives a way to understand how teachers teach. His scheme focuses on the kind of teacher talk and student talk in a classroom. In Flander's work, one of the following codes was assigned to every three seconds of classroom instruction. This kind of frequent coding and the numbers or precise names of the categories are not important. However, the coding system can help you understand how to structure successful learning experiences.

Indirect Teacher Talk

1. **ACCEPTS FEELINGS**—Teacher acknowledges and accepts students' feelings.
2. **PRAISES AND ENCOURAGES**—Teacher praises students' contributions and encourages students to continue their contributions.
3. **ACCEPTS OR USES STUDENTS' IDEAS**—Teacher helps students develop their own ideas and uses students' own ideas in the lesson.
4. **ASKS QUESTIONS**—Teacher asks questions about lesson content or solicits students' opinions. Rhetorical questions and questions not related to the lesson content are not included in this category.

Direct Teacher Talk

5. **LECTURES, EXPLAINS, OR DEMONSTRATES**—Teacher presents facts, opinions, or demonstrations related to the lesson topic.
6. **GIVES DIRECTIONS**—Teacher gives directions to which students are expected to comply.
7. **CRITICIZES OR JUSTIFIES AUTHORITY**—Teacher responds negatively to students, criticizes, or justifies authority.

Student Talk

8. **STUDENT TALK (RESPONSE)**—Student responds to a teacher's question. The correct answer is predictable and anticipated by the teacher.
9. **STUDENT TALK (INITIATION)**—Student initiates response that is not predictable. The response may follow an open-ended or indirect question from the teacher.
10. **SILENCE OR CONFUSION**—The classroom is silent or you can't make out what is being said.

Classroom Approaches

Effective classrooms are characterized by a variety of teaching approaches. The approaches should be tailored to the ability of the learner and the lesson objectives.

TEACHER-CENTERED APPROACHES

Teacher-centered approaches are characterized by teacher presentation, a factual question, and a knowledge-based response from the student.

Lecture or Explanation

You can present material through a lecture or an explanation. A lecture is a fairly long verbal presentation of material. Explanation refers to a shorter presentation. Lecture and explanation are efficient ways to present information that must be arranged and structured in a particular way. However, lecture and explanation may place learners in too passive a role.

Lecture and explanation work best under the following circumstances: (1) the lesson begins with a motivation, (2) the teacher maintains eye contact, (3) the teacher supplies accentuating gestures but without extraneous movements, (4) the presentation is limited to about 5–40 minutes depending on the age of the student, and (5) the objective is clear and the presentation is easy to follow and at an appropriate level.

Demonstrations

Demonstrations are lectures or explanations in which you model what you want students to learn. That is, you exhibit a behavior, show a technique, or demonstrate a skill to help students reach the objective. Demonstrations should follow the same general rules as lectures and the actual demonstration should be clear and easy to follow.

Teacher Questions

Teachers frequently ask questions during class. The following guidelines describe successful questions.

- Formulate questions so that they are clear, purposeful, brief, and at an appropriate level for the class.
- Address the vast majority of questions to the entire class. Individually addressed questions are appropriate to prepare "shy" students to answer the question.
- Avoid rhetorical questions.
- Use both higher and lower level questions on Bloom's Revised Taxonomy. All types of questions have their place.
- Avoid question-and-answer drills. A consistent pattern of teacher questions that call for responses at the first level of Bloom's Taxonomy is too limiting for most classrooms.
- Pause before you call on a student to answer the question, giving students an opportunity to formulate their responses.
- Call on a wide range of students to answer. Do not pick students just because they are either likely or unlikely to respond correctly.
- Wait 4 or 5 seconds for an answer. Do not cut off students who are struggling with an answer.
- Rephrase a question if it seems unclear or vague.
- Set a target for about 70 percent or so of questions to be answered correctly.

STUDENT-CENTERED APPROACHES—ACTIVE LEARNING

In a student-centered or active learning environment, the teacher ceases to be the prime presenter of information. The teacher's questions are more open-ended and indirect. Students will be encouraged to be more active participants in the class. This type of instruction is characterized by student-initiated comments, praise from the teacher, and the teacher's use of students' ideas.

Just because there is student involvement does not mean that the teacher is using a student-centered or active approach. For example, the pattern of questions and answers referred to as drill is not a student-centered approach.

Cooperative Learning

Students involved in cooperative learning work together in groups to learn a concept or skill or to complete a project. Students, in groups of two to six, are assigned or choose a specific learning task or project presented by the teacher. The group consults with the teacher and devises a plan for working together.

Students use many resources, including the teacher, to help and teach one another and to accept responsibilities for tasks as they complete their work. The students summarize their efforts and, typically, make a presentation to the entire class or the teacher.

Cooperative learning is characterized by active learning, full participation, and democracy within a clearly established structure. Cooperative learning also engages students in learning how to establish personal relationships and a cooperative working style.

Inquiry Learning

Inquiry learning uses students' own thought processes to help them learn a concept, solve a problem, or discover a relationship. This kind of instruction has also been referred to as Socratic. Inquiry learning often requires the most structure and preparation by the teacher. The teacher must know that the situation under study will yield useful results.

The teacher begins by explaining inquiry procedures to students, usually through examples. Next the teacher presents the problem to be solved or the situation that will lead to the concept or relationship. Students gather information and ask questions of the teacher to gain additional information. The teacher supports students as they make predictions and provide tentative solutions or results. Once the process is complete, the teacher asks students to think over and describe the process they used to arrive at the solution. This last step is referred to as a metacognition.

Resources for Instruction

You may have to assemble a number of resources for instruction. It often helps to jot down the resources you will need to teach a lesson or a unit. The materials you select should help the students meet the lesson objectives and match the teaching-learning approach you will use. The resources may include textual, manipulative, technological, and human resources.

Be sure to assemble in advance the materials you need to teach a lesson. The materials may include texts, workbooks, teacher-made handouts, or other printed materials. Check the materials to ensure that they are intact and in appropriate condition.

You may use manipulative materials to teach a lesson. Be sure that the materials are assembled and complete. Any laboratory materials should be tested and safe. Be sure that the materials are at an appropriate level for the students.

You may use technological resources, such as a computer, during your lesson. Be sure that the computer will be available during your lesson. Try the computer out and be sure that it is working. Be sure that any software you will use is at an appropriate grade and interest level and matches the objectives of the lesson.

You will frequently use human resources in your lesson. You may decide to cooperatively teach a lesson or unit with another teacher. This approach requires advanced planning and regular communication. You may need to arrange for a guest speaker to speak to the class about a particular topic.

Special education teachers frequently teach in consultive or collaborative roles. That is, they work in classrooms with regular education teachers. In this arrangement, teachers must coordinate their activities and agree on how they will interact during the lesson.

ADAPTING INSTRUCTION

Adapt instruction for the following factors, types of learners, and students.

AGE—Primary students should have more structure, shorter lessons, less explanation, more public praise, more small group and individual instruction, and more experiences with manipulatives and pictures. Older students should have less structure, increasingly longer lessons, more explanation, less public praise, more whole-class instruction, more independent work, and less work with manipulatives.

ACADEMICALLY DIVERSE

APTITUDE—Students exhibit different abilities to learn. You can provide differentiated assignments to enable students at different aptitude levels to maximize their potential.

READING LEVEL—Ensure that a student is capable of understanding the reading material. Do not ask students to learn from material that is too difficult. Identify materials at an appropriate reading level or with an alternative learning mode (tapes, material read to student). Remember that a low reading level does not mean that a student cannot learn a difficult concept.

LEARNING DISABLED—Learning-disabled students evidence at least a 2-year discrepancy between measures of ability and performance. Learning-disabled students should be given structured, brief assignments, manipulative experiences, and many opportunities for auditory learning.

VISUALLY IMPAIRED—Place the visually impaired student where he or she can most easily see the instruction. Use large learning aids and large print books. Use a multisensory approach.

HEARING IMPAIRED—Ensure that students are wearing an appropriate hearing aid. Students with less than 50 percent hearing loss will probably be able to hear you if you stand about 3 to 5 feet away.

MILDLY HANDICAPPED—Focus on a few, highly relevant skills, more learning time, and lots of practice. Provide students with concrete experiences. Do not do for students what they can do for themselves, even if it takes these students an extended time.

GIFTED—Gifted students have above average ability, creativity, and a high degree of task commitment. Provide these students with enriched or differentiated units. Permit them to test out of required units. Do not isolate these students from the rest of the class.

Cultural and Linguistic Diversity

SES (socioeconomic status)—Socioeconomic status and school achievement are highly correlated. Overall, students with higher SES will have higher achievement scores. In America, SES differences are typically associated with differences in race and ethnicity. However, the achievement differences are not caused by and are not a function of these differences in race or ethnicity. Rather, achievement differences are typically caused by differences in home environment, opportunity for enriched experiences, and parental expectations.

Teachers frequently have a higher SES than their students. These students often behave differently than teachers expect. The crushing problems of poor and homeless children may produce an overlay of acting out and attention problems. All this frequently leads the teacher to erroneously conclude that these students are less capable of learning. In turn, the teacher may erroneously lower learning expectations. This leads to lower school performance and a compounding of students' difficulty.

A teacher must consciously and forcibly remind herself or himself that lower SES students are capable learners. These teachers must also actively guard against reducing learning expectations for lower SES students.

There are appropriate ways of adapting instruction for students with different SES levels. For high SES students, minimize competitiveness, provide less structure, and present more material. For low SES students, be more encouraging, guard against feelings of failure or low self-esteem, and provide more structure. Do not lower learning expectations, but do present less material and emphasize mastery of the material.

CULTURALLY DIVERSE—Almost every class will have students from diverse cultural backgrounds. Use the values embedded in these cultures to motivate individual learners.

LINGUISTICALLY DIVERSE—The first language for many students is not English. In addition, a number of American students speak local variants of the English language. Teachers frequently, and erroneously, lower their learning expectations for these students. There are a number of useful strategies for adapting instruction for these students.

A number of students are referred to as Limited English Proficiency (LEP) who need English as a second language (ESL) instruction. Teaching English as a second language can be accomplished in the classroom, but often requires a specialist who works with students in "pull-out programs." When teaching these students, use simpler words and expressions, use context clues to help students identify word meaning, clearly draw students' attention to your speech, and actively involve students in the learning process.

CRITICAL THINKING

Critical thinking involves logical thinking and reasoning, including skills such as comparison, classification, sequencing, cause/effect, patterning, webbing, analogies, deductive and inductive reasoning, forecasting, planning, hypothesizing, and critiquing.

CREATIVE THINKING

Creative thinking involves creating something new or original. It involves the skills of flexibility, originality, fluency, elaboration, brainstorming, modification, imagery, associative thinking, attribute listing, and metaphorical thinking. The aim of creative thinking is to stimulate curiosity.

HIGHER-ORDER THINKING

This type of thinking is based on the higher levels of Bloom's revised taxonomy of educational objectives: cognitive domain, discussed on page 387. For example, skills and concepts that involve analysis, evaluation, and the creation of new knowledge are classified as higher-level thinking. Encouraging higher-order thinking is worth the extra effort because this type of thinking is more likely to be applied to new or unique situations.

INDUCTIVE AND DEDUCTIVE REASONING

Inductive reasoning leads the learner from the specific to the general. Deductive reasoning takes the learner from the general to the specific. A student who bases a conclusion on an observation is thinking inductively. In general, a student drawing a conclusion based on an established scientific fact is thinking deductively. Discovery and inquiry learning in science and mathematics are examples of inductive thinking.

PROBLEM SOLVING

In this approach students apply critical and creative thinking with established steps to solve a problem. This term is used most frequently in mathematics education in which students may use specific strategies such as clue words, working backward, and interpreting the remainder to solve a problem.

INVENTION

This approach asks students to create something new or better. As simple examples, a student might be challenged to invent a better approach to checking out at a food store or a better way to store books in a classroom.

MEMORIZATION AND RECALL

Memorizing and recalling information is at the lowest rungs on Bloom's taxonomy. Still, it is often important to remember and recall details and there are mnemonic devices available to improve recall. Examples of these devices are "Roy G. Biv" to remember the colors of the rainbow or "Please Excuse My Dear Aunt Sally" to recall the order in which arithmetic operations should be performed.

CONCEPT MAP

A concept map is a graphical tool for representing and organizing concepts. These concepts are usually shown as squares or circles and are connected with labeled arrows to show the downward flow of concept development. This technique is often referred to as concept mapping.

PROJECT APPROACH

This approach builds learning around the study of a particular topic rather than a particular skill or concept. In this way students learn a wide range of subject skills and concepts in the context of the topic.

LOCAL EXPERTS

This approach uses local experts from the community to help students learn. The experts may be parents or guardians of students in the class.

PRIMARY DOCUMENTS

This approach relies on original documents rather than a description of the document. For example, students would learn about the Revolutionary War by studying the Declaration of Independence rather than reading about the Declaration.

SERVICE LEARNING

This integrates service to the community and learning. This experiential approach to instruction seeks to teach students about civic responsibility while encouraging a lifetime of engagement with the community.

COMPUTERS AND THE INTERNET IN EDUCATION INCLUDING E-MAIL, WEB PAGES, CDS, DVDS, AND SMART BOARDS

Computers and computer-related technology are widely used in schools for tasks ranging from word processing to the presentation of graphics and sound. There are many computer-based effective instructional programs available. The Internet and SMART Boards are among the many technological applications being fully integrated into the schools. The Internet makes a wide array of information and media available to teachers and students. Hyperlinks to Internet websites can be integrated with text as students prepare papers and reports. Electronic e-mail gives those in the schools the ability to communicate electronically throughout the world. Services such as Skype permit students to videoconference using only a computer, a portable camera, and a microphone.

Teachers should be aware that the Internet also presents a number of dangers, from inappropriate content to an adult's ability to make inappropriate contact with students. Social networking sites are also very popular among students. These sites carry their own problems, as it is possible for someone to misrepresent someone else's picture and personal information, and because a person may be able to learn his or her personal information. Schools and teachers typically take steps to reduce the likelihood that these dangers will be present on a school's computers, but these efforts may not be universally successful.

Students may create copies of documents, images, and video on CDs and DVDs. Most modern computers are equipped with players for recording or playing these flat round disks. School are increasingly using e-book readers.

Interactive white boards, typically the trademarked SMART Boards, give teachers an interactive "chalk board" that can integrate text, images, and sound. Teachers frequently use SMART Boards to display PowerPoint presentations. The Board enables the teacher to write directly on the presentation images and to save the presentation along with the handwritten text. The graphic capabilities of the SMART Board increase each month and the use of these boards is becoming widespread.

In addition to the technology available for use in any learning setting, there is a wide array of adaptive devices to support learning and living for students who are disabled.

PLANNING INSTRUCTION

Common Core State Standards Initiative

The Common Core State Standards Initiative is a state-led effort coordinated by the National Governors Association Center for Best Practices (NGA Center) and the Council of Chief State School Officers (CCSSO). These standards define the knowledge and skills students should have within their K–12 education careers so that they will graduate high school able to succeed in entry-level, credit-bearing academic college courses and in workforce training programs. The standards:

- are aligned with college and work expectations;
- are clear, understandable, and consistent;
- include rigorous content and application of knowledge through high-order skills;
- build upon strengths and lessons of current state standards;
- are informed by other top performing countries, so that all students are prepared to succeed in our global economy and society; and
- are evidence based.

OBJECTIVES

All useful instruction has some purpose. Planning for instruction begins with choosing an objective that expresses this purpose. Objectives usually refer to outcomes, while goals usually refer to more general purposes of instruction. The terms *aim, competency, outcome,* and *behavioral objective* are also used to refer to an objective.

Objectives are often established by national or state organizations. The national or state English, mathematics, and science professional organizations may recommend objectives for their subject. The national or state organizations for speech, primary education, elementary education, preschool education, and special education may recommend objectives for specific grades or specialties.

Most school texts contain objectives, usually given for each text unit or lesson. These objectives are also reflected in national, state, and local achievement tests.

School districts usually have their own written objectives. There may be a scope and sequence chart that outlines the objectives for each subject and grade. The district may also have a comprehensive set of objectives for each subject and grade level.

TAXONOMY OF OBJECTS

Benjamin Bloom and others described three domains of learning: cognitive, affective, and psychomotor. The cognitive domain refers to knowledge, intellectual ability, and the other things we associate with school learning. The affective domain refers to values, interests, attitudes, and the other things we associate with feelings. The psychomotor domain refers to motor skills and other things we associate with movement.

Each domain describes various levels of objectives. The six levels on the revised cognitive domain, noted below, are most useful in classifying objectives. Students should be exposed to objectives at all levels of the taxonomy.

1. **REMEMBERING**—Remembering specifics, recalling terms and theories.
2. **UNDERSTANDING**—Understanding or using an idea but not relating it to other ideas.
3. **APPLYING**—Using concepts or abstractions in actual situations.
4. **ANALYZING**—Breaking down a statement to relate ideas in the statement.
5. **EVALUATING**—Judging a decision or critiquing according to a particular criteria.
6. **CREATING**—Creating new ideas or a new product or perspective.

CHOOSING AND MODIFYING OBJECTIVES

Initially, you will identify an objective from one of the sources noted previously. Consider these criteria when choosing and sequencing objectives.

- The objective should meet the overall goals of the school district.
- The objective should be appropriate for the achievement and maturation level of students in the class.
- The objective should be generally accepted by appropriate national, regional, or state professional organizations.

The objective you select may not exactly describe the lesson or unit you are going to teach. Modify the objective to meet your needs. You also may need to select or modify objectives and other plans to meet the needs of diverse student populations.

Your class may be academically diverse. You may teach special-needs students or you may have special-needs students in your class under the inclusion model. When you select and modify objectives for academically diverse students, consider the different achievement levels or learning styles of these students.

Your class may be culturally diverse. When you select and modify objectives for a culturally diverse class, consider the range of experiences and backgrounds found among the class. Do not reduce the difficulty of the objective.

Your class may be linguistically diverse. You may have limited English proficiency (LEP) students in your class. For a linguistically diverse class, take into account the limits that language places on learning. You may have to select or modify objectives to help these students learn English.

WRITING OBJECTIVES

An objective should answer the question: "What are students expected to do once instruction is complete?" Objectives should not describe what the teacher does during the lesson. Objectives should not be overly specific, involved, or complicated.

Whenever possible, objectives should begin with a verb. Here are some examples.

Not an objective:	I will teach students how to pronounce words with a silent *e*. [This is a statement of what the teacher will do.]
Not an objective:	While in the reading group, looking at the reading book, students will pronounce words with a silent *e*. [This statement is overly specific.]
Objective:	Sounds out words with a silent *e*. [This is an objective. It tells what the student is expected to do.]
Objective:	States what he or she liked about the trip to the zoo.
Objective:	Reads a book from the story shelf.
Objective:	Serves a tennis ball successfully twice in a row.

Do not limit objectives to skills or tiny bits of strictly observable behavior. Specific objectives are not limited objectives. Objectives can include statements that students will appreciate or participate in some activity. Objectives should include integrating subject matter, applying concepts, problem solving, decision making, writing essays, researching projects, preparing reports, exploring, observing, appreciating, experimenting, and constructing and making art work and other projects.

PLANNING TO TEACH THE LESSON

Once you have decided what to teach, you must plan how to teach it. Consider these factors as you plan the lesson or unit.

- Determine the prerequisite competencies. This is the knowledge and skills students must possess before they can learn the objective. Draw up a plan that ensures students will demonstrate prerequisite competencies before you teach the lesson.
- Determine the resources you need to help students reach the objective. The resources could include books, manipulatives, overhead transparencies, and other materials for you or the students to use. The resources could also include technological resources including computers or computer software and human resources including teacher aides, students, or outside presenters.
- Devise a plan to help students reach the objective. In addition to the factors discussed previously, the plan will usually include motivation and procedures.

Madeline Hunter posited the following important stages for effective lessons.

- Anticipatory set—Something that is said or done to prepare students and focus the students on the lesson.
- Objective and purpose—The teacher should state the objective of the lesson, and the students should be aware of the objective.
- Input—New information is presented during this stage.
- Modeling—The skills or procedures being taught or demonstrated.
- Checking for understanding—Following the instructional components in the previous two stages, the teacher should ensure that students understand the concept before moving to the next phases of the lesson.
- Guided practice—Students are given the opportunity to practice or use the concept or skill with the teacher's guidance.
- Independent practice—Students practice or use the concept on their own.

Classrooms are filled with the teacher's verbal and nonverbal communication. While most verbal communication is deliberate, much of nonverbal communication is expressed in ways that the teacher did not intend. A teacher can overtly develop a set of meanings for particular nonverbal communication that furthers the goal of a smoothly functioning classroom. These gestures should be carefully explained to students so that the students know the appropriate response. There are gestures that communicate approval, whereas others signal it is time to get back to work. Teachers can use gestures to tell students to take their seats, to get out their books, and for a whole host of routine classroom activities. Teachers should be sensitive to the cultural norms among their students. Moving into a student's personal space can be seen as approval by some students whereas others will see it as an unwanted intrusion. Even simple gestures like a "thumbs-up," universally seen as a sign of approval in this country, may be offensive to some learners.

A main focus of a teacher's communication is always to foster interactions and to stimulate discussions. The teacher pursues a wide range of strategies that embrace the full range of Bloom's Taxonomy and an energized approach to teaching.

The teacher will be there to help students formulate and flush out their ideas while continuing to probe learners for a deeper understanding of the subject matter. The teacher will create a safe environment where students feel comfortable taking risks and he or she will help students question facts and opinions to stimulate their curiosity in a way that furthers learning. The teacher will help students recall factual information needed for learning and then build on the recall to help students explore concepts. The teacher will help students learn how to engage in both convergent and divergent thinking.

Teaching for Student Learning

Planning instruction and implementing instruction are intertwined. Many of the points discussed here will have been considered during the planning process.

Classrooms are dynamic places. Students and teachers interact to further a student's learning and development. Follow these guidelines to establish a successful classroom and teach successful lessons.

Managing the Instructional Environment

Classroom management is a more encompassing idea than discipline or classroom control. Classroom management deals with all the things a classroom teacher can do to help students become productive learners. The best management system for any classroom will establish an effective learning environment with the least restrictions.

Teachers who are proactive and take charge stand the best chance of establishing an effective learning environment. Classroom management is designed to prevent problems, not react to them.

Classroom management begins with understanding the characteristics of students in your class.

CHARACTERISTICS OF STUDENTS

Some general statements about the students in a class can be made. For example, 3–7 percent of girls and 12–18 percent of boys will have some substantial adjustment problems. Prepare yourself for these predictable sex differences.

Boys are more physically active and younger children have shorter attention spans. Respond to this situation by scheduling activities when students are most likely to be able to complete them.

A teacher's management role is different at different grade levels. Prepare for these predictable differences in student reaction to teacher authority.

In the primary grades, students see teachers as authority figures and respond well to instruction and directions about how they should act in school. In the middle grades, students have learned how to act in school and still react well to the teacher's instruction.

In seventh through tenth grade, students turn to their peer group for leadership and resist the teacher's authority. The teacher must spend more time fostering appropriate behavior among students. By the last two years of high school, students are somewhat less resistant and the teacher's role is more academic.

Adolescents resent being touched and that teachers may anger adolescents by taking something from them. Avoid this problem by not confronting adolescent students.

There will be cultural differences among students. Many minority students, and other students, may be accustomed to harsh, authoritarian treatment. Respond to these students with warmth and acceptance. Many minority students will feel completely out of place in school. These students also need to be treated warmly and with the positive expectation that they will succeed in school.

Many other students may be too distracted to study effectively in school. These students may need quiet places to work and the opportunity to schedule some of their own work time.

Other factors, such as low self-esteem, anxiety, and tension, can also cause students to have difficulty in school.

CLASSROOM MANAGEMENT TECHNIQUES

The following guidelines for effective classroom management include techniques for dealing with student misbehavior.

Teacher's Role

Teachers who are good classroom managers understand their dual role as an authority figure and as someone who helps children adapt to school and to life. Teachers are authority figures. Students expect the teacher to be an authority figure and expect teachers to establish a clear and consistent classroom structure.

Teachers must also help students learn how to fit into the classroom and how to get along with others. Teachers fare better in their role as authority figures than they do in this latter role. But teachers who have realistic expectations and know how to respond to problems can have some success.

ESTABLISHING AN EFFECTIVE CLIMATE FOR MANAGEMENT

Classroom Physical Layout

There are several general rules to follow for a successful classroom layout. Set up the initial layout of the room so that you can see the faces of all the students. Rearrange the desks for individual and group work. Ensure that heavily used areas are free of all obstacles. Arrange the room so students do not have to stand in line, by having books and supplies available at several locations.

Classroom Leadership

Research indicates that the following factors are most important in establishing effective classroom leadership. Develop a cohesive class by promoting cooperative experiences and minimizing competition among class members. Identify and gain the confidence of peer leaders, particularly in Grades 7–10. Establish an authoritative, but not authoritarian, leadership style.

Depending on the grade level, set three to six reasonable, adaptable rules that describe the overall nature of acceptable and unacceptable behavior. The expectations that accompany these rules should be stated clearly. The rules should be posted for students to see.

Much of the first two weeks of school should be spent establishing these rules, which may be stated by the teacher and/or developed through class discussion. Once the rules are established and the expectations are understood, the teacher should follow through. Student misbehavior should be handled immediately and appropriately but without causing a confrontation or alienating the student from the class.

Effective classroom managers take steps to ensure that the majority of class time is spent on instruction. They also take steps to ensure that students use their seat work and other inclass study time to complete assignments.

Specific Management Techniques

There are some specific management techniques that a teacher can apply to all classes. These techniques are summarized here.

KOUNIN

Kounin is a well-known expert on classroom management. Research results show that a number of Kounin's management techniques are effective. The following techniques have the most research support.

Kounin noted that teacher with-it-ness is an important aspect of classroom management. In other words, teachers who are constantly monitoring and are aware of what is happening in the classroom are better managers.

Kounin also showed that effective managers' lessons have smoothness and momentum. By this he meant that these lessons are free of teacher behavior that interrupts the flow of activities or slows down lesson pacing.

Finally, Kounin showed that group alerting was an effective technique. In group alerting, the teacher keeps bringing uninvolved students back into the lesson by calling their attention to what is happening and forewarning them of future events.

CANTER AND CANTER

Canter and Canter developed an approach called assertive discipline. Their approach is popular but lacks the research support of the approach recommended by Kounin.

The Canters recommend a direct and assertive approach to problem children. They point out that passive and hostile reactions to student misbehavior are not effective. Among other approaches, they recommend that the teacher and students establish rules and post those rules in the classroom. During each class session, the teacher writes and then marks the names of students who have violated rules. One rule violation in a session requires no action. Two rule violations, and the student meets with the teacher after school. Three violations require a parental visit to the school.

CUEING

Cues are words, gestures, or other signals that alert students to a coming transition or that gain their attention. A cue may be spoken, such as "We'll be leaving for art in about 5 minutes. Take this time to get ready." Another cue might be, "Your group has about 15 minutes to complete your project."

Other cues are nonverbal. You may glance at a student or make eye contact to re-engage the student in the lesson. You may raise your arm or hold your hand in a particular way to gain attention. You may flick the classroom lights quickly to indicate that groups should stop working and return to whole-class instruction.

OTHER EFFECTIVE TECHNIQUES FOR MAINTAINING ATTENTION DURING A LESSON

The techniques listed below have proven effective in classrooms.

- Stand where you can scan and see the entire class.
- Ask questions of the whole class and then call on individuals for a response.
- Involve all students in the question-and-answer sessions and do not call on students just to catch them in a wrong answer or because they will give the correct answer.
- Gain attention through eye contact or a gesture.
- If a comment is required, make it very brief.
- Ensure that the material being taught is at an appropriate level.
- Base seat work or group work on an established system that is monitored closely and positively.

Changing Behavior

Students may act so unacceptably that their behavior must be changed. Here are some suggestions for changing behavior.

REINFORCEMENT

All teachers use positive reinforcement, whether through grades, praise, tokens, or other means. Teachers also use negative reinforcement by showing students how to avoid an undesirable consequence (poor grade) by doing acceptable work. Negative reinforcement is not punishment.

In the classroom you should increase the duration or quality of the desired behavior before reinforcing. Reach explicit agreements with students about the level of performance that will yield rewards (positive reinforcement). Praise is often an ineffective reinforcer.

CONTRACTS AND LOGS

You may be able to help children change behavior by using contracts or by asking students to maintain logs. These approaches cause students to think about their behavior and both have been proven effective.

When writing a contract, work with a student to establish desired learning goals or classroom behavior. The contract, signed by the teacher and the student, sets short-term goals for classroom conduct and academic achievement. A teacher may also ask students to maintain a log of their classroom behavior. A brief daily review of the log may improve behavior.

PUNISHMENT

Punishment is a temporary measure. It should be administered to improve student performance, not to make the teacher feel better. Limited punishment given for a specific reason when students are emotionally stable can be effective. Other punishments, such as extra work, punishment of the entire class, and corporal punishment, are usually not effective.

Effective punishment should be reasonable, deliberate, and unemotional. The punishment should also be short and somewhat unpleasant. The reason for the punishment should be clear, and the punishment should be accompanied by examples of appropriate behavior.

Teaching Reading and Language Arts

There are two competing models for reading and language arts instruction—phonics and whole language. The phonics approach is usually associated with drills, a teacher-centered classroom, and direct instruction. The whole language approach is usually associated with holistic teaching, a child-centered classroom, and cooperative learning groups.

PHONICS

In the phonics approach, children learn how to associate letters and groups of letters with sounds. A national reading study found this approach most effective for teaching reading. Once students learn to decode the language they learn what the words mean. This phonics approach is usually associated with basal readers. These readers contain basic passages and stories with a carefully controlled vocabulary. Stories in basal readers taken from literature sources are often changed to conform to the vocabulary reading level desired by those preparing the basal readers. Exercises accompanying basal readers frequently have one narrow correct answer.

Writing instruction in a phonics-based classroom emphasizes correct spelling. Students in these classrooms are expected to master the rules for spelling and grammar before they commit their thoughts to writing.

WHOLE LANGUAGE

Children using the whole language approach are often encouraged to decode words from their context. Proponents of the whole language approach point out that children entering school already have a spoken vocabulary of about 10,000 words. The whole language approach is usually associated with books students read outside of school with a more robust and varied vocabulary. Activities in whole language classrooms often include reading real literature and typically have a broader range of responses.

Writing instruction in a whole language-based classroom tolerates incorrect spelling and inappropriate grammatical usage. Students in these classrooms are expected to write thoughtfully and meaningfully with less emphasis on the rules of grammar and spelling. But recent research indicates that whole language does not effectively teach students to learn how to read.

MIDDLE GROUND

We do not want children to pronounce words correctly without knowing their meaning, and we do not want students who cannot decode a written word. We do need an approach that fosters both decoding and understanding to help students learn about language.

This seems to be the best advice for the classroom teacher. Use phonics to teach reading but also expose students to real stories. Incorporate a combination of narrow questions and questions that call for a broad understanding of the reading material. Ask students to master the rules of grammar and spelling, but encourage early drafts with less emphasis on these rules and more emphasis on meaning.

3. ASSESSMENT

Assessment Program

Every teacher evaluates instruction. The assessment program and the assessment instruments should measure mastery and understanding of important topics. The assessment program should also be used as a teaching tool. That is, the program should be used to help students learn and to improve instruction. The program should include authentic assessment of students' work as well as teacher-made and standardized tests.

Formative assessment information is usually gathered before or during teaching. Formative information is used to help you prepare appropriate lessons and assist students. Formative evaluations help teachers decide which objectives to teach, which instructional techniques to use, and which special help or services to provide to individual students.

Summative assessment information is usually gathered once instruction is complete. Summative evaluation is used to make judgments about student achievement and the effectiveness of the instructional programs. Summative evaluations lead to grades, to reports about a student's relative level of accomplishment, and to alterations of instructional programs.

Assessment information may be used for both purposes. For example, you may give a test to determine grades for a marking period or unit. You may then use the information from this test to plan further instruction and arrange individual help for students.

You may informally gather formative and summative information. Just walking around the room observing students' work can yield a lot of useful information. You can frequently discern the additional work that students need and identify different levels of student achievement.

Assessment Instruments

Tests have long been used to determine what students have learned and to compare students. Every test is imperfect. Many tests are so imperfect that they are useless. It is important to realize how this imperfection affects test results.

Some students are poor test takers. Every test assumes that the test takers have the opportunity to demonstrate what they know. A student may know something but be unable to demonstrate it on a particular test. Teachers must also consider alternative assessment strategies for these students.

Familiarize yourself with these basic assessment concepts.

- **ERRORS OF MEASUREMENT**—Every test contains errors of measurement. In other words, no one test accurately measures a student's achievement or ability. Carefully designed standardized tests may have measurement errors of 5 percent or 10 percent. Teacher-designed tests typically have large errors of measurement.

  A test result shows that a student falls into a range of scores and not just the single reported score. Focusing on a single score and ignoring the score range is among the most serious of score-reporting errors.

- **RELIABILITY**—A reliable test is consistent. That is, a reliable test will give similar results when given to the same person in a short time span. You cannot count on unreliable tests to give you useful scores. Use only very reliable standardized tests and be very aware of how important reliability is when you make up your own tests.

- **VALIDITY**—Valid tests measure what they are supposed to measure. There are two important types of validity: content validity and criterion validity.

  A test with high content validity measures the material covered in the curriculum or unit being tested. Tests that lack high content validity are unfair. When you make up a test it should have complete content validity. This does not mean that the test has to be unchallenging. It does mean that the questions should refer to the subject matter covered.

  A test with high criterion validity successfully predicts the ability to do other work. For example a test to be an automobile mechanic with high criterion validity will successfully predict who will be a good mechanic.

Norm-Referenced and Criterion-Referenced Tests

Norm-referenced tests are designed to compare students. Intelligence tests are probably the best-known norm-referenced tests. These tests yield a number that purports to show how one person's intelligence compares to everyone else's. The average IQ score is 100.

Standardized achievement tests yield grade-level equivalent scores. These tests purport to show how student achievement compares to the achievement of all other students of the same grade level.

A fifth grader who earns a grade level equivalent of 5.5 might be thought of as average. A second-grade student with the same grade equivalent score would be thought of as above average. About half of all the students taking these tests will be below average.

Standardized tests also yield percentile scores. Percentile scores are reported as a number from 0 through 100. A percentile of 50 indicates that the student did as well as or better than 50 percent of the students at that grade level who took the test. The higher the percentile, the better the relative performance.

Criterion-referenced tests are designed to determine the degree to which an objective has been reached. Teacher-made tests and tests found in teachers' editions of texts are usually criterion-referenced tests. Criterion-referenced tests have very high content validity.

Authentic Assessment

Standardized and teacher-made tests have significant drawbacks. These types of tests do not evaluate a student's ability to perform a task or demonstrate a skill in a real-life situation. These tests do not evaluate a student's ability to work cooperatively or consistently.

In authentic assessment, students are asked to demonstrate the skill or knowledge in a real-life setting. The teacher and students collaborate in the learning assessment process and discuss how learning is progressing and how to facilitate that learning. The idea is to get an authentic picture of the student's work and progress.

Students have an opportunity to demonstrate what they know or can do in a variety of settings. Students can also demonstrate their ability to work independently or as part of a group.

Portfolio assessment is another name for authentic assessment. Students evaluated through a system of authentic assessment frequently keep a portfolio of their work.

Effective Bridges

Creating Bridges Among Curriculum Goals and Students' Prior Experiences

One effective approach to instruction is to connect the curriculum goals with a student's prior experiences and knowledge. Consider these four ways to build a bridge between the curriculum and a student's prior knowledge.

Modeling

The term *modeling* means demonstrating a desired behavior or presenting a representation of an important theory, idea, or object. Each of these meanings can link curriculum goals with students' prior knowledge and experience.

Activating Prior Knowledge

Activating prior knowledge helps students recall what they already know about the material being studied. The teacher may encourage students to discuss what they already know, or the teacher may take the lead and directly discuss their prior knowledge. In either case, the activated prior knowledge is incorporated in instruction.

Anticipating Preconceptions of Students

Activating prior knowledge may actually reveal incorrect information that a student possesses, information that the student may believe to be accurate. Teachers function most effectively when they can anticipate and dispel these preconceptions.

Distinguishing Among Guided Practice, Independent Practice, and Homework

GUIDED PRACTICE: Guided practice offers students an opportunity to complete learning activities independently, but with the teacher or a knowledgeable classmate available to offer help and assistance. Guided practice is particularly effective when students are learning a new skill or concept.

INDEPENDENT PRACTICE: Independent practice places more responsibility on the student than guided practice. Independent practice is most effective when students are familiar with the material and when less help is required from another person.

HOMEWORK: Homework, literally work assigned to be done outside school, is most effective when students practice material that has already been learned in school. Homework can also foster a bond among parents, their children, and the schools and help establish responsibility for completing work as a preparation for the world of work that students will enter as adults.

4. PROFESSIONAL DEVELOPMENT, LEADERSHIP, AND COMMUNITY

The Reflective Practitioner

A teacher who is a reflective practitioner continuously reviews his or her own teaching methods, determines what methods create the most effective learning environment, and then adapts the methods to maximize learning. While using this sequence of teach–reflect–adapt, the teacher realizes that there are many effective teaching practices and that the process of reflection will enable the teacher to find the best approaches for the wide range of teaching situations that the teacher will encounter. A reflective practitioner is first and foremost an advocate for learners.

Reflective practitioners use a wide range of resources as they hone their craft. They stay abreast of professional literature, they form productive relationships with colleagues and administrators to share ideas, and they participate in professional development activities and are active members of professional associations.

Teacher–Parent Communication

Communication between parents and teachers is an essential part of effective instruction. The approaches listed below are proven strategies for effectively involving parents in a child's education.

Parent Surveys	Parent Classroom Visit
Positive Phone Calls	Weekly Folders
Class Newsletters	Flexible Scheduling for Conferences
Class Website and E-mail Updates	

Ethnicity, Opportunity, and Poverty and a Child's Life Outside the School

According to the recent census there were about 310 million people living in the United States. This country has the world's third largest population, accounting for about 5 percent of all the people living on earth. About 65 percent of the population is White and about 12 percent is African American/Black. White Hispanics and Latinos account for about 10 percent of the population, while 5 percent are Asian.

Much of a child's opportunity can be correlated with poverty, which in turn can be correlated with ethnicity and family structure. Poverty can have a striking impact on a child's ability to function and achieve in a school setting. Many of the learning problems attributed to schools are actually a function of the high level of poverty in many areas. Poverty is the most significant problem outside the school that teachers most accommodate for in the school setting.

About 20 percent of the children in the United States live below the poverty level, while many others live on the edges of poverty. About 30 percent of African American/Black and Hispanic children are disproportionately represented in this group. By contrast, some 13 percent of Asian children and about 12 percent of White children live below the poverty level.

Family structure has a significant impact on whether a child will be living in poverty. In families headed by a single woman, 30 percent live below the poverty level, whereas in families headed by single men, 17 percent live under the same circumstances. By contrast, about 6 percent of two-parent families live below the poverty level.

The School and Society

THE SCHOOL IN SOCIETY

The school is a part of society. It reflects the society and socializes students. To that end, the schools prepare students to function in society. Students are taught, directly and indirectly, acceptable social values and behavior.

The academic curriculum reflects society's expectations. Students are taught a generally accepted body of knowledge. Students are also prepared for society by being exposed to potential careers as a part of the school curriculum.

Every society has a culture. The culture combines the history of the society and the society's current norms. The culture includes customs, values, ethical and moral structures, religions and beliefs, laws, and a hierarchy of most valued contributions by members of society.

THE SCHOOL AS A SOCIETY

The school is a society in itself. The school society consists of a complex interrelationship of teachers, students, administrators, parents, and others. Each school has its own character, practices, and informal hierarchy. Generally speaking, new teachers must find a niche in the school's society to be successful. The school has a formal decision-making hierarchy of teachers, supervisors, principals, superintendents, and school boards. The new teacher must usually gain acceptance at each level of this hierarchy to experience success.

Each state in the United States has its own system of education. States are legally responsible for education. Locally elected or appointed school boards usually have the most direct legal impact on the schools. Within state and federal laws, school boards pay for the schools from tax receipts and other funds, hire teachers and administrators, approve curricula, and set school policy.

Many of the decisions made by school boards are affected by the amount of money available to the schools. Generally speaking, wealthier districts have more money to spend on schools. The difference in the funds available may create a difference in the quality of schooling.

Legal, Legislative, and Political Influences

WHO'S IN CHARGE OF EDUCATION

The Constitution of the United States does not assign the responsibility for education to the federal government, leaving this responsibility to each state. The state government, including the governor, the legislature, and the courts have the ultimate responsibility for public education. A state board or commission is usually responsible for the operation of the schools. A state commissioner of education reports to the state board.

The commissioner, in turn, oversees a state education department. The state education department is responsible for the state's daily responsibility for the schools. Other organizations in a state, including regional and county authorities, may have education responsibilities.

Local or regional boards of education are directly responsible for operating schools in their district or town. In more than 80 percent of the cases, these boards are elected. A local or regional superintendent of schools reports to the board and, along with other administrators and support staff, has the daily responsibility for operating the schools.

Building principals report to the superintendent and are responsible for the daily operations of their school building. Teachers have the responsibility for teaching their students and carrying out district and state education policies.

IT'S THE LAW

A complex set of federal, state, and local laws govern education. Court cases are changing the interpretation of these laws each day. Here is a brief summary of legal rights as they may apply to schools, teachers, and students. This summary should not be used to make any decisions related to school laws. Any specific interest in legal issues should be referred to a competent attorney.

Schools

- Schools may not discriminate against students, teachers, or others because of their race, sex, ethnicity, or religion. "Reverse discrimination" *may* be legal when hiring teachers, but it is not legal when dismissing teachers.
- Schools must make children's school records available to parents and legal guardians.
- Schools may remove books from the school library. However, a book may not be removed from the library just because a school board member or other school official does not agree with its content.

Teachers

- Teachers do not have to provide information unrelated to employment on an employment form or to an interviewer. You do not have to give your age, your marital status, sexual orientation, or any other unrelated information.

- Nontenured teachers usually have very limited rights to reappointment. Generally speaking, schools may not rehire a nontenured teacher for any reason. For example, the schools may simply say that they want to find someone better, that the teacher doesn't fit in, or that they just do not want to renew the contract.

- Teachers cannot be fired for behavior that does not disrupt or interfere with their effectiveness as teachers. However, even personal behavior away from school, which significantly reduces teaching effectiveness, might be grounds for dismissal.

- Pregnant teachers may not be forced to take a maternity leave. Decades ago, pregnant teachers were often forced to resign.

- Teachers may be dismissed or suspended for not doing their job. Any such action must follow a due process procedure.

- Teachers may be sued and be liable for negligence. Successful suits and actions against teachers have occurred when the evidence showed that the teacher could have reasonably foreseen what was going to happen or that the teacher acted differently than a reasonable teacher would have acted in that same situation.

- Teachers have the right to associate freely during off-school hours with whomever they wish. They may belong to any political party, religious group, or other group even if the group is not supported in the community or is disapproved of by board members, administrators, or others.

- Teachers have freedom of speech. Teachers have the same free speech rights as other citizens. They may comment publicly on all issues, including decisions of the school administrators or the school board. However, a teacher may not disclose confidential information or be malicious, and the statements cannot interfere with teaching performance. Teachers do not have unlimited academic freedom or freedom of speech in the classroom or elsewhere in the school. Teachers are not permitted to disrupt the school or the school curriculum.

- Corporal punishment is not unconstitutional. However, corporal punishment may be illegal and may only be administered according to the laws of the state. Teachers should never strike children in anger and should administer corporal punishment only as part of a due process procedure.

Students

- Handicapped students from ages 3 to 21 are entitled to a free and appropriate public education as a matter of federal law. This education should take place in the least restrictive environment available.

- Students have limited freedom of the press. Student newspapers supported by school funds may be reviewed and edited by school officials. However, papers paid for and produced by students off school property may not be censored by school officials.

- Students are entitled to due process. In particular, students have a right to a hearing and an opportunity to present a defense before being suspended. Students who pose a threat to others in the school are not entitled to this due process.

- Students have freedom of speech unless it causes a significant disruption in the school. They may display messages or symbols on their persons, and refuse to participate in the pledge of allegiance. However, they may not use speech considered vulgar or offensive.

Diversity

SOCIETY AND CULTURE

America is a multiethnic and multicultural society. Consequently, the culture of the community and the culture of the school varies widely depending on the school's geographic location, socioeconomic setting, and local norms. To understand schools, we must understand society and culture.

Anthropology and sociology provide a scientific basis for studying society and culture. Anthropology is the formal study of culture and the development of society. Much of the early anthropological work dealt with primitive cultures. However, in recent years anthropologists have turned their attention to communities and schools. Sociology is the study of how people behave in a group. Sociology can help us understand how students behave in school, how teachers function on a faculty, and how citizens interact in the community.

Culture is directly affected by the ethnicity of the community. Each ethnic group brings its own culture, its own language, and its own customs to this country.

Until recently, most immigrant groups have been acculturated. That is, they have largely adopted the dominant language and culture of the United States. Lately there has been a shift toward cultural pluralism in which immigrants maintain their cultural, and occasionally linguistic, identity.

Under cultural pluralism, the challenge is to provide equal educational opportunity while also providing for these cultural differences among students. There is little prospect, however, that non-English speakers will realize their full potential in the United States.

Socioeconomic status has a direct effect on culture and on the schools. As noted earlier, there is a strong correlation between SES and academic achievement. In the United States, groups, communities, and schools are stratified by social class. Social stratification often occurs within schools. Unlike many other countries, individuals are able to move among social classes, usually in an upward direction.

THE FAMILY

The family remains the predominant influence in the early lives of children. However, the nature of the American family has changed, and for the worse.

Divorce rates are very high and some say that a majority of Americans under 40 will be divorced. American families are fragmented, with about 30 percent of children living with a step-parent. About one-third of children are raised in one-parent families, and about two-thirds of these children live below the poverty level.

An increasing number of children, called latchkey children, return from school with no parents at home. School programs developed for these students cannot replace effective parenting.

In many respects, the school, social or religious institutions, peer groups, and gangs have replaced parents. This means that parents and families have less influence on children's values and beliefs.

The pressures of economic needs have drastically changed the American family. Less than 10 percent of American families have children, a mother at home, and a father at work. Over

30 percent of married couples have no children, and over 70 percent of mothers with children are working mothers.

ETHNICITY

A recent report indicates the population of the United States was about 74 percent Caucasian, 12 percent African American, 10 percent Hispanic, 3 percent Asian, and 1 percent Native American or Eskimo. Hispanics are the fastest growing ethnic group.

About 13 percent of the families in the United States live below the poverty level. Some 30 percent of African American and Hispanic families do so, and an astonishing 65 percent of Native American families also live below the poverty level.

Hispanics

Hispanics come predominantly from Mexico and from other countries in Central and South America and the Caribbean. Many Mexican American families have been in this country for more than 100 years. Puerto Ricans form another large Hispanic group.

Language is the primary difficulty faced by this ethnic group. About half of the Hispanics in this country speak Spanish as their first language.

The nature of the Hispanic population varies by region. Most Hispanics in California or their forebears are from Mexico. Many Hispanics living in and around New York City are from Puerto Rico or the Dominican Republic, while many Hispanics in Florida trace their ancestry to Cuba.

Hispanic students have more school problems than white students. Hispanics are disproportionately poor and low achieving, although as able as other students.

African Americans

African Americans have been in this country for centuries, but they began their lives here as slaves. There is not a recent history of large-scale African immigration to the United States.

Their status as slaves and second-class citizens denied African Americans the education, experience, and self-sufficiency needed for upward social mobility. Even when African Americans developed these qualities, they were frequently discriminated against just because of their race. It took almost 200 years from the founding of this country for the Supreme Court to rule that overt school segregation was unconstitutional. Of course, de facto segregation continues to exist.

Many African Americans have achieved middle class status. However, the overwhelming proportion of poor in urban areas are African Americans. The unemployment rate of young African Americans can be near 50 percent in some areas.

Native Americans

Groups of Eskimos and other Native Americans have lived on the North American continent for over 25,000 years. Most Native Americans living today are ancestors of tribes conquered and put on reservations about 100 years ago.

During this time of conquest, treaties made with tribes were frequently broken. Native Americans lost their lands and their way of life. They were made dependent on the federal government for subsidies and were not able to develop the education, experience, or self-sufficiency needed for upward mobility.

Native Americans have the largest family size and fastest growth rate of any ethnic group. They also have among the highest suicide and alcoholism rates of any ethnic group.

Native Americans are disproportionally poor and disenfranchised. They live in poverty often on reservations, and are often alienated when they move off reservations to metropolitan areas.

Asian Americans

Asian Americans are predominately Chinese and Japanese together with recent immigrants from Korea and Southeast Asia. Asian Americans represent a countertrend among American minorities. Their achievement and success tend to be above the national average.

Many recent Asian immigrants do not have the educational background of other Asian Americans. They tend to be more ghettoized and to attain a lower SES than other Asian Americans.

However, overall, Asian students perform better on American standardized tests than non-Asian students. This finding holds also for those Asian Americans who immigrated to this country unable to speak, read, or understand English.

Some researchers have said that a particular work ethic currently found in Asian countries together with a strong family structure are responsible for these trends.

Societal Problems

This decade finds our society beset with unprecedented problems of crime and violence, alcohol and drug abuse, sex, AIDS, high dropout rates, and child abuse. Many of these problems can be traced directly to poverty. Schools are a part of society so that they too are affected by these problems.

Crime and Violence

The number of serious crimes in the United States is at the highest level in memory. Students bring guns to school, and large urban areas report dozens of deaths each year from violent acts in school. Murder is the leading cause of death among African American teens. More than 70 percent of those who commit serious crimes are never caught. We live in a society where crime is rampant and crime pays.

Crime in school presents a particular problem for teachers. Some estimate that 3 to 7 percent of all students bring a gun with them to school. Students attack teachers every day in America. While this behavior is not defensible, attention to the principles of classroom management mentioned earlier can help in averting some of these incidents.

Alcohol and Drug Abuse

Alcohol is the most used and abused drug. Even though it is legal, there are serious short- and long-term consequences of alcohol use. Alcoholism is the most widespread drug addiction and untreated alcoholism can lead to death.

Tobacco is the next most widely used and abused substance. Some efforts are being made to declare tobacco a drug. Irrefutable evidence shows that tobacco use is a causative factor in hundreds of thousands of deaths each year.

Other drugs including marijuana, cocaine, heroin, and various drugs in pill form carry with them serious health, addiction, and emotional problems. The widespread illicit availability of these drugs creates additional problems. Many students engage in crimes to get money to pay for drugs. Others may commit crimes while under the influence of drugs. Still others may commit crimes by selling drugs to make money.

More than 90 percent of students have used alcohol by the time they leave high school. About 70 percent of high school graduates have used other illegal drugs. Awareness programs that focus on drug use can have some positive effects. However, most drug and alcohol abuse and addiction has other underlying causes. These causes must be addressed for any program to be effective.

Sex

Many teens and preteens are sexually active. While many of these children profess to know about sex, they do not. It is in this environment that we find increases in teenage pregnancies, abortions, dropouts, and ruined lives. Sex spreads disease. So we also note increases in syphilis, gonorrhea, and other sexually transmitted diseases.

About 10 percent of teenage girls will become pregnant. Teenage pregnancy is the primary reason why girls drop out of high school. These girls seldom receive appropriate help from the child's father and are often destined for a life of poverty and dependence.

AIDS

AIDS stands for Acquired Immune Deficiency Syndrome. AIDS is a breakdown in the body's immune system caused by a virus called HIV. This virus can be detected with blood tests. People with the HIV virus may take 10 years or longer to develop AIDS. Those who develop AIDS die.

The HIV virus is transmitted by infected blood and other bodily fluids. Sexual relations and contact with infected blood, including blood injected with shared hypodermic needles, are all examples of ways that AIDS can be transmitted. Some 2 to 5 percent of the teens in some urban areas may be HIV positive.

Students can try to avoid becoming HIV positive by reducing their risk factors. Abstinence from sex and never injecting drugs will virtually eliminate the likelihood that a teenager will become HIV positive. Less effective measures can be taken to help sexually active students reduce the likelihood of becoming HIV positive. Girls run a higher risk than boys of becoming HIV positive through sexual activity.

Acquiring the HIV virus is associated with drug and alcohol use. Even when students know the risks, and how to avoid them, alcohol and drug use can lower inhibitions and lead to unsafe practices.

Dropouts

About 10 percent of white students, 15 percent of African American students, and 30 percent of Hispanic students drop out of school. Dropout rates are worst in urban areas, with over half the students dropping out of some schools. High school dropouts are usually headed for a life of lower wages and poorer living conditions.

Many of these students feel alienated from society or school and need support or alternative learning environments. Intervention, counseling, and alternative programs such as therapeutic high schools, vocational high schools, and other special learning arrangements can help prevent a student from dropping out.

Child Abuse

Child abuse is the secret destroyer of children's lives. Some estimate that between two and three million children are abused each year. Child abuse is a primary cause of violent youth, runaways, and drug abusers.

Physical and sexual abuse are the most destructive of the abuses heaped upon children. Contrary to popular belief, most child abuse is perpetrated by family members, relatives, and friends. Younger children are often incapable of talking about their abuse and may not reveal it even when asked.

In many states, teachers are required to report suspected child abuse. When child abuse is suspected, a teacher should follow the guidelines given by the school, the district, or the state.

Principles of Learning and Teaching Test: Constructed-Response Strategy and Practice

11

This chapter contains an overview of Principles of Learning and Teaching (PLT) Test Strategy and Practice for constructed-response items. These constructed-response items count for 25 percent of your test score. The chapter includes a practice PLT case with practice questions and explained answers. Follow these steps to use this chapter.

USING THIS CHAPTER

☐ Review the Test Strategies on pages 407–409.

☐ Read the Practice PLT Scenario on page 410.

☐ Answer the Practice PLT Constructed-Response Items beginning on page 412 and review the answers beginning on page 414.

Chapter 10 contains a PLT Review.
Chapter 12 contains a complete PLT Practice Test.

TEST STRATEGIES

Multiple-Choice Strategies

You have about 1 minute for each multiple-choice question. There are helpful strategies for responding to the multiple-choice items on page 23. Use these strategies to answer the multiple-choice questions on the test. The multiple-choice items on the PLT are similar to the questions on the Elementary Education: Curriculum, Instruction, and Assessment (5011), although the questions on the PLT you take may be at a different grade level.

Constructed-Response Strategies

You have about 25 minutes for each case. That is about 5 minutes to review the case and about 7 minutes to think about and write each constructed response. You will write each constructed-response answer on a special single-page lined sheet provided with the test. Most often you will write 100 to 150 words. Readers are realistic about the length of your response. Try to print your answer; it will be easier to read.

Show that you get the idea.

Answer the question completely and directly.

Do not provide extra or unrelated information.

Show that you know about the case and about pedagogy as they relate to the question.

Support your answer.

A typical PLT constructed-response question asks for TWO of something. It may be TWO strategies, or TWO strengths, or TWO adaptations, or TWO of something else. Be sure to write TWO of whatever the question asks for and then explain why each of the two makes sense.

HERE'S HOW THEY SCORE YOU

Two readers, trained to evaluate answers using holistic scoring, will score your response. Holistic scoring means the scorer rates the response based on his or her informed impression, not on a detailed analysis. Each reader rates the response 2, 1, or 0. You have to communicate clearly, but English grammar itself is not evaluated.

2 You will earn a 2 for two clear statements that respond directly to the two points in the question with evident support and an explanation for each statement.

1 You will earn a 1 for one statement that responds directly to one of the two points in the question with evident support and an explanation for the statement. You can also earn a 1 if you provide two statements but one of the statements is deemed unresponsive to the question or if the explanation leaves something to be desired. For example, the question may ask for strategies for teaching two different subjects, but the response gives two strategies for teaching one subject. Or the question may ask for two additional strategies, and the response lists a strategy already mentioned in the case.

0 You will earn a score of 0 if your response does not address the question or if your response is too general or vague. For example, a question may ask for two additional strategies for teaching a lesson, and the response indicates that no additional strategies are necessary.

Most responses rated 2 have about 100 to 150 words. That does not mean that a response this long will always receive a 2. However, it does give you some idea about how long your response should be. Most responses rated 1 or 0 are shorter than responses rated 2. But many responses rated 0 or 1 that are off the point may be as long as a response that could be rated a 2.

USE YOUR TIME WISELY

Here is a plan for using your time to respond to each case. The times are recommendations. Monitor your time as you work on this activity to find the appropriate amount of time that you should devote to each step.

Case

Read the questions and skim the case (5 minutes).

- Read the three questions at the end of the case and then read the case.
- Skim the case looking for answers to the questions.
- Make notes on the case.
- Return to the questions.

Questions

1. **OUTLINE A RESPONSE (2 MINUTES).** Use this time to think. Read the question carefully to be sure you understand what it asks for. Jot down the two strategies, adaptations, strengths, or ideas called for in the question. Sketch a supporting detail or two under each.

2. **WRITE YOUR RESPONSE TO EACH QUESTION (4 MINUTES).** Use this time to write. Write directly and clearly. Print your answer on the response sheet. Plan to write about 100 to 140 words. That is about 25 to 35 words a minute. You can do that. Do not restate the question. Write your response on the sheet provided in the test materials. Responses written in the test booklet or elsewhere outside the response sheet will not be read.

   Follow these steps.

   - **Rewrite the first point from your outline.**
   - **Write a sentence or two with details to support the first point.** The details should support the point. Details tell how or why the point is important. Details can be explanations or examples.
   - **Rewrite the second point from your outline.** Then write at least one other sentence with details.
   - **Write a sentence or two with details to support this point.**

3. **REVIEW (1 MINUTE).** Compare your response to the item to be sure you have responded completely. Delete, add, or change words to clarify your response. Leave time to read your response. Raters understand that your response is a first draft, and they expect to see corrections. Thus, do not spend your time correcting minor grammatical or punctuation errors.

Let's apply these steps to a practice case.

What follows is a complete case with three constructed-response questions. Review the questions and the case and then answer the three constructed-response questions. A step-by-step review of how to answer Question 1 and sample constructed-response answers for all three questions follow.

SITUATION

Ms. DelCorso teaches a heterogeneous, self-contained, sixth-grade class of twenty-five students. She is working on her Professional Improvement Plan (PIP), which every teacher in the district prepares each spring. Ms. DelCorso has chosen four students in this class as the basis for her PIP. The principal will review Ms. DelCorso's PIP, and Ms. DelCorso will reflect on the process and respond.

Ms. DelCorso's First Step Is to Review Her Interactions with the Four Students

Mora is a hearing-impaired student. Mora's IEP requires me to wear a microphone and requires Mora to wear a wireless receiver tuned to the same frequency as my microphone. However, Mora refuses to wear the wireless device during class, and Mora's parents support her decision. Mora can read lips and watches very carefully; however, she misses out on important information in every class because Mora cannot hear me when she is looking at other students in the class.

Peter is a very bright student who is uncomfortable in social situations and something of an outcast among his peers. His test grades and standardized test scores have always been well above average in this class. He is someone who was used to achieving without effort. But lately his test grades have started to fall, and he has not responded to my efforts to help him complete all his homework assignments.

Luke is classified as a Learning Disabled student. He is easily distracted, and he almost never does his homework. He is a poor reader. He is easily frustrated and often abandons a task without giving it his full effort or attention. Luke regains his focus when I intervene and give him specific steps to follow.

Cynthia comes from a family of high achievers. Both of her parents are physicians, and she is driven to achieve beyond what her ability seems to justify. She is a perfectionist who can be very tense and nervous in class, and she works with a professional tutor at home each week. Her focus on schoolwork and her serious demeanor push her to the outer edges of the social group in her class.

Ms. DelCorso's PIP

Mora: Mora needs to use the wireless device to learn effectively in this class. My first step will be to call her parents and tell them that Mora is missing out on too much work because she does not wear the wireless device. I will ask for their support to encourage Mora to use the wireless device, and I will try to make clear how much language she misses each day and that this language deficit will create even more problems in later years. I will also talk to Mora to help her accept the device and point out that it is completely invisible to other students in the class.

Peter: I will bend the rules some to account for Peter's particular personality and learning style. I will provide him with study guides to help structure his homework and other learning activities and to help him review for tests. At the same time, I will open a channel of communication with Peter's parents and enlist them as partners in this effort, particularly to get Peter to do his homework.

Luke: I will establish a learning plan for Luke that requires him to come in on a regular basis to receive help. I will also give him an assignment pad that his parents will have to sign four nights a week. I will also try to motivate him to complete his homework by giving him extra-credit tickets for completed assignments that he can exchange for additional points toward his test grade.

Cynthia: Cynthia concerns me the most because her high expectations and insistence on perfection leave little room for flexibility, which may lead to even more significant problems. I will ask Cynthia to help other students to widen her friendship circle and to remove some of the focus from herself. I will also try to take the pressure off by giving her additional time for tests and other in-class activities.

The Principal's Response

Ms. DelCorso is a truly outstanding teacher, and I am always impressed with her work, as I am with her plan to deal with these four students. However, I recommend that she give further consideration to the following points.

- Parents are very defensive when speaking about their children's deficiencies, and parents are a very powerful force in our school district. We should be very careful about how we approach them, and any suggestions should be carefully considered and presented only after thorough discussion here at the school.
- Luke may benefit from extra-credit points, but how will we deal with the reactions of students and the parents of students who do not receive these points?
- I wonder if it is appropriate for a teacher to engage Cynthia in academic activities that are actually designed to further her social standing.

Ms. DelCorso's Reflection and Reaction

Thank you for your confidence in me, which I certainly have in you as a school administrator. I have reflected on my comments and your response, leading to these reactions.

I appreciate the concern and the delicate nature of dealing with parents, and I will be pleased to discuss my ideas and receive feedback before I engage in parental contact. However, I am very concerned about Mora in particular, and some appropriate action must be taken.

I see that overtly giving Luke extra credit may create problems with other students, and I will explore other ways to reward him when he completes his assignments.

Social activities are an integral part of the classroom environment and, in my opinion, Cynthia badly needs these social contacts to relieve pressure and to enhance her academic performance.

Practice PLT Constructed-Response Items

1. Review Ms. DelCorso's PIP in which she describes her plans for responding to each of four students in her class.

   - Choose TWO students and recommend one additional strategy Ms. DelCorso could have included in her PIP for each of these students.
   - Describe each strategy and explain why that strategy would be effective. Base your response on the sound principles of instructional planning.

2. Suppose that Ms. DelCorso and the principal have further discussions about parental involvement.

   - Recommend TWO strategies that Ms. DelCorso could use to effectively involve parents in the school.
   - Explain how each of the strategies you recommend could improve student learning. Base your answer on sound principles of communication and instructional planning.

3. The Principal's Response and Ms. DelCorso's Reflection and Reaction indicate that Luke needs reinforcement, but it should be done in a way that is unlikely to create problems with other students.

   - Describe TWO additional ways in which Luke could be rewarded for completing his assignments.
   - Explain why your suggestions will be effective and why they are unlikely to cause problems with other students. Base your answer on sound principles of classroom management and human interaction.

1. _____

   _____

   _____

   _____

   _____

   _____

   _____

   _____

   _____

2. _____

_____

_____

_____

_____

_____

_____

_____

_____

_____

3. _____

_____

_____

_____

_____

_____

_____

_____

_____

_____

_____

RATED RESPONSES

This section shows you how to apply the steps and gives examples of rated responses for the Practice Case.

Question 1

Review Ms. DelCorso's PIP in which she describes her plans for responding to each of four students in her class.

- Choose TWO students and recommend one additional strategy Ms. DelCorso could have included in her PIP for each of these students.
- Describe each strategy and explain why that strategy would be effective. Base your answer on sound principles of instructional planning.

Follow these steps.

1. **THINK:** I have to choose TWO *different* students. I'll pick Luke and Mora, for example. (You can pick any two students.)

   Then I have to come up with *one* additional PIP strategy for *each* student.

   I have to explain *why*, not how, each strategy will be effective.

2. **SKETCH AN OUTLINE:**

   Luke should use a microcomputer.

   Good for LD students.

   Mora's parents should come in to see how much she misses.

   Seeing is believing.

3. **WRITE YOUR ANSWER:** Review the scored sample responses that follow. A great many other responses could have earned these scores, so concentrate on the general form of each response.

4. **REVIEW YOUR ANSWERS TO BE SURE THEY ANSWER THE QUESTION:** For this activity, rewrite any of your answers that did not earn a score of 2.

This response would receive a score of 2.

It gives one additional strategy for each of two students and explains why the strategies would be effective. This response contains 129 words.

> I can think of something that Ms. DelCorso could have added to her PIP for Luke who is a learning-disabled student. Ms. DelCorso could have added a recommendation that Luke use a microcomputer to research topics on the Internet. Learning-disabled students in particular benefit from using computers to learn because working with a computer helps reduce distractions.
>
> Ms. DelCorso should consider adding this to Mora's PIP. Ms. DelCorso should ask one or both of Mora's parents to come to school and to observe Mora in class without the wireless device. This would let Mora's parents see for themselves how much Mora misses in class, and her parents would be a lot more likely to support Ms. DelCorso as she tries to convince Mora to wear the device.

This response would receive a score of 1.

It suggests TWO things that Ms. DelCorso should add to her PIP. But both suggestions are for the same student, and the question asks for a response for TWO different students. This response contains 116 words.

> I can think of something that Ms. DelCorso could have added to her PIP for Luke who is a learning-disabled student. Ms. DelCorso could have added a recommendation that Luke use a microcomputer to research topics on the Internet. Learning-disabled students in particular benefit from using computers to learn because working with a computer helps reduce distractions.
>
> Ms. DelCorso should also consider asking one or both of Luke's parents to come to school and to observe him in class as he works. This would let Luke's parents see for themselves how he works in class and help them understand and support Ms. DelCorso as she tries to help Luke focus on the material at hand and to give it his full attention.

This response would receive a score of 0.

It describes a useful process for arriving at a final PIP for Ms. DelCorso's students. However, it does not provide specific recommendations for any of the students. This response contains 97 words.

There are a number of things Ms. DelCorso could have added to her PIP. The principal suggests some, and I think that it is the process between these two professionals that is important. They should have a meeting to fully discuss additional recommendations and emerge with a consensus that both can support.

Once that process is complete, they should meet with the parents of the students to present their recommendations and receive parental feedback. Following that step, Ms. DelCorso and the principal should develop a final set of recommendations and use these recommendations to help the students.

Question 2

Suppose that Ms. DelCorso and the principal have further discussions about parental involvement.

- Recommend TWO strategies that Ms. DelCorso could use to effectively involve parents in the school.
- Explain how each of the strategies you recommend could improve student learning. Base your answer on sound principles of communication and instructional planning.

This response would receive a score of 2.

It provides two useful strategies for involving parents in school, and it explains how each strategy could improve student learning. This response contains 145 words.

> It is important to involve parents in school. This may be difficult if both parents work.
>
> Ms. DelCorso could send home a monthly folder of student work. Parents could review the work and teacher's comments then sign the folder and return it to Ms. DelCorso. This strategy could improve student learning because parents will have a good idea of the work their children are doing and the teacher's comments on the work. This will guide them in helping their child with work at home.
>
> Ms. DelCorso could hand out report cards to parents and their children at an after school meeting. This could improve student learning because the teacher can explain the report card and it will be clear to both the parents and the child how things are going and what work needs to be done in the next marking period.

This response would receive a score of 1.

It provides two useful strategies that relate to parents. However, only one of the strategies includes an explanation of how to involve parents in the school. This response contains 124 words.

> Ms. DelCorso should have a weekly class phone chain. She calls a few parents on the list to update information about classroom activities. These parents then call this information down through the chain. This approach will improve student learning because parents will be up-to-date on the most recent activities and assignments, and they will be able to help their children stay involved in class activities.
>
> Sixth-grade students have lives outside school. They have responsibilities with their parents. Ms. DelCorso should respect a child's parent and family time by not giving assignments and work that unnecessarily interfere with that time. This will help student learning by strengthening the family and by making sure that students have time to complete their work.

This response would receive a score of 0.

It provides strong support for the importance of parental involvement and acknowledges that Ms. DelCorso plans to involve parents. However, it does not give any specific approaches for involving parents in the school. This response contains 104 words.

> Parental involvement is one of just a few things that can make a real difference in school learning for students. So it is clear that involving parents in the school is definitely something that Ms. DelCorso should do.
>
> I can see that she already plans to involve parents because she is going to call Mora's parents. That is a good strategy. Ms. DelCorso probably has other ways to involve parents. I can't tell what they are. That is the reason why it is just not possible to make any recommendations without more information. That would not be a responsible approach to a school situation.

Question 3

The Principal's Response and Ms. DelCorso's reflection indicate that Luke needs reinforcement, but it should be done in a way that is unlikely to create problems with other students.

- Describe TWO additional ways in which Luke could be rewarded for completing his assignments.
- Explain why your suggestions will be effective and why they are unlikely to cause problems with other students. Base your answer on sound principles of classroom management and human interaction.

This response would receive a score of 2.

It presents two *additional* ways to reinforce Luke, explains why the suggestions will be effective, and explains why the suggestions are unlikely to cause problems with other students in the class. This response contains 157 words.

The token reinforcement activity the teacher mentioned can be effective, but it is very visible and it might cause problems with other students who will not receive the tickets.

Ms. DelCorso could use social reinforcement. She could praise him for completing his assignments and show that she is very pleased with his work. She could stand near him and react positively while he is completing the assignment. Social reinforcers have been proven effective, and it is unlikely that students will have a problem because these comments and actions are directed just to Luke.

Ms. DelCorso could also schedule a preferred activity for all her students to engage in when their regular assignments are complete. Luke could use the computer following the completion of his assignments. This Premack approach has proven effective in schools, and students will not have a problem with Luke having to complete an undesirable activity before he can participate with them in a desired activity.

This response would receive a score of 1. It describes two useful strategies and explains why each strategy should not cause a problem. However, the first strategy is already mentioned and so it is not an additional strategy. This response contains 129 words.

> Giving extra-credit tickets to Luke is a good idea, and it should motivate him to complete his assignments. The teacher can avoid problems with other students by giving the tickets to Luke privately and giving him the reward he gets for accumulating tickets after school when the other students are not around.
>
> Ms. DelCorso could set up some positive consequences when Luke does good work. It could just be a few words or a note sent home to his parents saying that he is doing a good job. These types of positive consequences have been proven to be effective at helping students work better. These types of consequences for Luke should not cause a problem for other students because they will be receiving their own positive consequences as well.

This response would receive a score of 0. It makes some valid points about reinforcement and teaching. However, it does not include any specific recommendations about reinforcement strategies for Luke. This response contains 58 words.

> This teacher should not be so concerned with specific types of reinforcement. It is too technical and no one really knows what will work with any given student. Ms. DelCorso should make herself accessible to every one of the students for extra help.
>
> Those are the things to concentrate on if you want to run an effective classroom.

Principles of Learning and Teaching Practice Test

12

TEST INFO BOX

Computer Delivered

2 hours

70 Multiple-Choice Items

2 Scenarios, each with 2 constructed responses

This sample full-length PLT contains all the elements of the real test. The test is given in paper-delivered or computer-delivered format. The trend is toward the computer-delivered format, and this test simulates the computer-delivered format. That means you will type your responses to the constructed test items and mark your answers directly on the multiple-choice test.

The PLT is given at four different levels: PLT Early Childhood, PLT K–6, PLT 5–9, and PLT 7–12. There is really a lot of overlap among the tests.

Follow the 2-hour time limit as you complete this practice test. You may begin with the constructed-response items that follow, or with the multiple-choice test on page 435.

There are two scenarios suited for Early Childhood/K–6 PLTs and two scenarios suited for 5–9 /7–12 PLTs. You will type two constructed responses to two questions from each of the two scenarios, just like the real PLT. The 70 multiple-choice items, just like the real PLT, include a range of grade levels.

Complete the Early Childhood/Elementary Scenario on page 425.

or

Complete the Grades 5–9, 7–12 Scenario on page 431.

Then complete the multiple-choice questions on page 435.

Fully explained answers begin on page 452.

ANSWER SHEET
Practice PLT Test

1. Ⓐ Ⓑ Ⓒ Ⓓ
2. Ⓐ Ⓑ Ⓒ Ⓓ
3. Ⓐ Ⓑ Ⓒ Ⓓ
4. Ⓐ Ⓑ Ⓒ Ⓓ
5. Ⓐ Ⓑ Ⓒ Ⓓ
6. Ⓐ Ⓑ Ⓒ Ⓓ
7. Ⓐ Ⓑ Ⓒ Ⓓ
8. Ⓐ Ⓑ Ⓒ Ⓓ
9. Ⓐ Ⓑ Ⓒ Ⓓ
10. Ⓐ Ⓑ Ⓒ Ⓓ
11. Ⓐ Ⓑ Ⓒ Ⓓ
12. Ⓐ Ⓑ Ⓒ Ⓓ
13. Ⓐ Ⓑ Ⓒ Ⓓ
14. Ⓐ Ⓑ Ⓒ Ⓓ
15. Ⓐ Ⓑ Ⓒ Ⓓ
16. Ⓐ Ⓑ Ⓒ Ⓓ
17. Ⓐ Ⓑ Ⓒ Ⓓ
18. Ⓐ Ⓑ Ⓒ Ⓓ
19. Ⓐ Ⓑ Ⓒ Ⓓ
20. Ⓐ Ⓑ Ⓒ Ⓓ
21. Ⓐ Ⓑ Ⓒ Ⓓ
22. Ⓐ Ⓑ Ⓒ Ⓓ
23. Ⓐ Ⓑ Ⓒ Ⓓ
24. Ⓐ Ⓑ Ⓒ Ⓓ
25. Ⓐ Ⓑ Ⓒ Ⓓ

26. Ⓐ Ⓑ Ⓒ Ⓓ
27. Ⓐ Ⓑ Ⓒ Ⓓ
28. Ⓐ Ⓑ Ⓒ Ⓓ
29. Ⓐ Ⓑ Ⓒ Ⓓ
30. Ⓐ Ⓑ Ⓒ Ⓓ
31. Ⓐ Ⓑ Ⓒ Ⓓ
32. Ⓐ Ⓑ Ⓒ Ⓓ
33. Ⓐ Ⓑ Ⓒ Ⓓ
34. Ⓐ Ⓑ Ⓒ Ⓓ
35. Ⓐ Ⓑ Ⓒ Ⓓ
36. Ⓐ Ⓑ Ⓒ Ⓓ
37. Ⓐ Ⓑ Ⓒ Ⓓ
38. Ⓐ Ⓑ Ⓒ Ⓓ
39. Ⓐ Ⓑ Ⓒ Ⓓ
40. Ⓐ Ⓑ Ⓒ Ⓓ
41. Ⓐ Ⓑ Ⓒ Ⓓ
42. Ⓐ Ⓑ Ⓒ Ⓓ
43. Ⓐ Ⓑ Ⓒ Ⓓ
44. Ⓐ Ⓑ Ⓒ Ⓓ
45. Ⓐ Ⓑ Ⓒ Ⓓ
46. Ⓐ Ⓑ Ⓒ Ⓓ
47. Ⓐ Ⓑ Ⓒ Ⓓ
48. Ⓐ Ⓑ Ⓒ Ⓓ
49. Ⓐ Ⓑ Ⓒ Ⓓ
50. Ⓐ Ⓑ Ⓒ Ⓓ

51. Ⓐ Ⓑ Ⓒ Ⓓ
52. Ⓐ Ⓑ Ⓒ Ⓓ
53. Ⓐ Ⓑ Ⓒ Ⓓ
54. Ⓐ Ⓑ Ⓒ Ⓓ
55. Ⓐ Ⓑ Ⓒ Ⓓ
56. Ⓐ Ⓑ Ⓒ Ⓓ
57. Ⓐ Ⓑ Ⓒ Ⓓ
58. Ⓐ Ⓑ Ⓒ Ⓓ
59. Ⓐ Ⓑ Ⓒ Ⓓ
60. Ⓐ Ⓑ Ⓒ Ⓓ
61. Ⓐ Ⓑ Ⓒ Ⓓ
62. Ⓐ Ⓑ Ⓒ Ⓓ
63. Ⓐ Ⓑ Ⓒ Ⓓ
64. Ⓐ Ⓑ Ⓒ Ⓓ
65. Ⓐ Ⓑ Ⓒ Ⓓ
66. Ⓐ Ⓑ Ⓒ Ⓓ
67. Ⓐ Ⓑ Ⓒ Ⓓ
68. Ⓐ Ⓑ Ⓒ Ⓓ
69. Ⓐ Ⓑ Ⓒ Ⓓ
70. Ⓐ Ⓑ Ⓒ Ⓓ

EARLY CHILDHOOD/ELEMENTARY SCENARIOS

SCENARIO 1

Situation

Ms. Kelly teaches second grade in a K–5 school. This is her fourth year of teaching. "I'm going to get this teaching down—definitely in the next 20 years," is her favorite thing to say to more experienced teachers in the school. She knew it was going to take a long time to become a master teacher, but she had no idea it would take this long. Ms. Kelly emphasizes appropriate classroom behavior.

DOCUMENT 1: CLASSROOM BEHAVIOR SIGN

DO UNTO OTHERS AS

YOU

WOULD HAVE THEM DO UNTO

YOU

DOCUMENT 2: PARTIAL LIST OF READING MATERIALS AND BOOKS

Gladstone's Basal Readers

Gladstone's Reading Workbooks

Gladstone's Phonics Workbooks

26 Fairmount Avenue

Babe, the Gallant Pig

Book of Slime

Dinosaur Bones

The Dog That Stole Home

Encyclopedia Brown and the Case of the Slippery Salamander

Finding Providence

Goin' Someplace Special

How We Crossed the West: The Adventures of Lewis and Clark

I, Amber Brown

In the Time of the Drums

Just Like Mike

Kate Shelley, Bound for Legend

Lizzie Logan, Second Banana

Red-Eyed Tree Frog

So You Want to Be President?

The Truth About Great White Sharks

DOCUMENT 3: MS. KELLY'S OBSERVATIONS ABOUT STUDENTS' READING PERFORMANCES

Janice: Janice has trouble when she has to sound out new words from the reading book. However, Janice easily remembers new sight words when I present them before she reads the story.

James: James remembers the sound of every letter. He can even sound out blends. But he has difficulty pronouncing new sight words when I present them. James can add quickly and accurately. The unusual thing is that James does not do well when he has word problems to solve.

Elizabeth: Elizabeth has difficulty when she reads stories from the basal text. But give her a book with many pictures at the same reading level as the basal text and she is able to get as much information out of the book as anyone else in the class. I am concerned that Elizabeth is really not able to read many words. Sometimes I think that Elizabeth gets most of her information from pictures. But it does not show up on any tests.

DOCUMENT 4: PORTION OF THE PRINCIPAL'S NOTES ABOUT HER LAST OBSERVATION MEETING WITH MS. KELLY

I observed the class reading a science-fiction story. Ms. Kelly had a large print version of the book in front of the class. Each student has his or her own version of the book. Some students followed along in their own books, while others followed along on Ms. Kelly's large print book.

The story is about astronauts who land on a friendly planet where they find friendly but impish aliens. In the story, Nayr the alien tries to trick the astronauts away from their spaceship so that Nayr can look inside. As I left Ms. Kelly's classroom, the students were enjoying the story. They read aloud, asked and answered questions, and enjoyed the wonder of this trip to an imaginary planet.

During our meeting Ms. Kelly told me she enjoys hearing her students during choral reading. She said, "There is just something about hearing the sound of all their voices together. And they help one another as they read. I just love it."

Ms. Kelly also told me she is considering implementing a program on reading and mathematics to help her students become more mathematically literate. She also wondered aloud whether to use primarily a whole language approach or primarily a phonics approach in her classroom.

Scenario 1: Practice PLT Constructed-Response Items

1. Suppose that Ms. Kelly and the principal are discussing effective classroom management practices.

    ■ Describe TWO strategies that Ms. Kelly could use for her approach to classroom management described in Document 1.
    ■ Explain why each of the strategies you recommend would be effective. Base your answer on sound principles of classroom management.

2. Document 2 includes a list of the different types of reading materials used in Ms. Kelly's classroom.

    ■ Describe TWO approaches that describe how Ms. Kelly could use these resources to establish an effective reading program in her classroom.
    ■ Explain why each of the approaches you recommend would be effective. Base your answer on sound principles of instructional planning.

3. Document 4, a portion of the principal's observation notes, indicates that Ms. Kelly was considering implementing a plan to integrate reading and mathematics.

    ■ Recommend TWO ways that Ms. Kelly could implement that plan.
    ■ Explain why each of the ways you recommend would be effective. Base your answer on sound principles of instructional planning.

Situation

Derek is a student in a mathematics class. Ms. Stendel, Derek's teacher, notices that he has trouble with some relatively simple computation problems. She also notices that Derek is frequently distracted during class. Ms. Stendel is an experienced teacher, and she decides to establish a portfolio of documents about Derek that she can later share with the psychologist and others.

DOCUMENT 1: SUMMARY OF PRIOR CLASSROOM NOTES

Derek's ability test scores and his insights and comments during class reveal that he is unusually intelligent. When I ask him to do something he can complete quickly or to solve a problem mentally, he is amazing. But he gets completely bogged down when we work on projects over several days or when he has to complete a longer project on his own. He often seems distracted and tense in class.

DOCUMENT 2: MS. STENDEL'S CLASSROOM OBSERVATION OF DEREK

I have just given the class a project to work on for thirty minutes that involves solving two mathematics problems. The first problem requires logical thinking, whereas the second problem involves complicated addition, subtraction, multiplication, and division. The students do not have their calculators. Derek is working in a group with four other students. I will observe that group and Derek in particular and record my observations.

The five students are seated around a table, and each student has a copy of the problem to be solved. Derek seems disinterested. But then he starts talking about things unrelated to the problem. He asks other students what they are doing after school. He suggests that the group talk about other things besides the problem in front of them. He brings up a soccer game that will be played on Saturday.

Some of the students seem interested in his distraction, but the group decides to focus on the first problem. Derek is not happy, and he sulks and withdraws from the group and stares at his copy of the problem. The other students are talking about the first problem when Derek interrupts them saying, "I've got it."

He will not tell the other students what his answer is and just continually says "That's wrong" when other students suggest solutions. I cannot tell whether he actually has the answer, but based on my past experiences, I think he probably does. Derek is somewhat more involved in the group now, and the group keeps working, with no help from him, on the first problem. He pushes his chair onto the back two legs and just rocks back and forth saying things like "No—that's not it."

After fifteen minutes the group has not solved the first problem, and Derek will not share the solution he says he has. The group turns their attention to the second problem. Derek demonstrates a new level of confidence and a new level of participation even though he is still ignored by most of the group.

Students have sheets of plain paper, and Derek begins to work on his calculations for the second problem. Derek is right-handed, and I notice that he holds his pencil in an unusual way with his thumb pressing the pencil against his middle finger. There is just enough room for him to touch the pencil with his index finger. He moves the pencil using only his fingers to produce large and often hard-to-read numerals. I can see that the numerals are not aligned well.

I end my observation with everyone in the group doing calculations to solve the second problem. I pick up Derek's work from the table after the group breaks up and have included some of it below for this portfolio.

DOCUMENT 3: A SAMPLE OF DEREK'S CALCULATIONS

$$\begin{array}{r} 1 \\ 174 \\ +\ 286 \\ \hline 4510 \end{array}$$

$$\begin{array}{r} 31 \\ \times\ 42 \\ \hline 62 \\ 124 \\ \hline 186 \end{array}$$

$$\begin{array}{r} 121 \ R15 \\ 58 \overline{)7053} \\ 58 \\ \hline 125 \\ 116 \\ \hline 93 \\ 58 \\ \hline 15 \end{array}$$

DOCUMENT 4: MS. STENDEL'S CONVERSATION WITH DEREK AFTER SCHOOL ON THE DAY OF THE OBSERVATION

Ms. Stendel: Derek, can you stay just a minute?

Derek: OK.

Ms. Stendel: I was watching your group during math today.

Derek: I saw you sitting there.

Ms. Stendel: You seemed to know the answer to that first problem.

Derek: Yes—they're all stupid.

Ms. Stendel: But you would not tell them what your answer was.

Derek: Let them get it.

Ms. Stendel: But it could help them to know what your answer is.

Derek: I don't want to help them. They are very mean to me.

Ms. Stendel: But what if your answer was not correct?

Derek: It was.

Ms. Stendel: Will you tell me what it was.

Derek: I don't remember. Can I go now?

Ms. Stendel: OK, Derek I will see you tomorrow.

Scenario 2: Practice PLT Constructed-Response Items

4. Document 2, Ms. Stendel's Classroom Observation of Derek, indicates some of the problems that Derek has with group work.

    ■ Recommend TWO approaches that may enable Ms. Stendel to effectively involve Derek in cooperative group work.
    ■ Explain why each of the strategies you recommend would be effective. Base your answer on sound principles of instructional planning and classroom management.

5. Document 3 shows some of Derek's calculations in addition, subtraction, and multiplication, which include some computational errors.

    ■ Recommend TWO specific techniques Ms. Stendel could use to help Derek with his arithmetic computation.
    ■ Explain why each of the techniques you recommend would be effective. Base your answer on sound principles of instructional planning and informal assessment.

6. Assume that Ms. Stendel shares the conversation from document 4 with her supervisor.

    ■ Give TWO recommendations the supervisor might make for effectively dealing with Derek.
    ■ Explain why each of the approaches you recommend would be effective. Base your answer on sound principles of instructional planning and human development.

GRADES 5–9/7–12 SCENARIOS

SCENARIO 3

Situation

Ms. Brown has been teaching seventh grade for just one month. It is not unusual for her to work through the weekend preparing lessons. Ms. Brown is concerned about the time it takes for her to teach her lessons and about the interactions she has with certain students and parents. She is gathering information and seeking feedback to help her with these situations.

MS. BROWN'S CONVERSATION WITH A COLLEAGUE

Ms. Brown saw a colleague one day when she was shopping in the supermarket. Ms. Brown was pushing around a shopping cart, and in the child's seat Ms. Brown had her plan book.

"What are you doing?" asked the colleague.

"Shopping," said Ms. Brown, "and you never know when you're going to get an idea for a lesson."

"You've got to have some time for yourself," her colleague said.

"Not this year," sighed Ms. Brown.

SUPERVISOR'S SUMMARY REPORT ABOUT MS. BROWN

The lessons Ms. Brown prepares are wonderful. I always write complimentary remarks when I return her plans. As I often tell other teachers, Ms. Brown writes the best lesson plans I have ever seen.

Unfortunately, Ms. Brown is frequently unable to finish her lessons. Some beginning teachers prepare more information than they can present. That is not the case with Ms. Brown. It is just that she spends so much time trying to explain everything carefully and in great detail. The students are often not actively involved in the lesson.

When Ms. Brown checks homework assignments, the students act as though it is free time. They talk, take each other's personal property, exchange notes, and just generally make a nuisance of themselves. They should be reviewing their work and correcting mistakes.

Preparing good lessons that are unappreciated by students leaves her frustrated. Ms. Brown has begun to teach in a negative and critical fashion. She has had a few run-ins with parents. They complain that she does not treat their children fairly and that she is too demanding.

PRINCIPAL'S SUMMARY OF SOME PARENT COMMENTS ABOUT MS. BROWN

Ms. Sivar is one of the parents who think Ms. Brown is unfair. She told me, "My Tim doesn't finish his tests in Ms. Brown's class because the tests are too long." She added, "It is certainly not because he's fooling around."

Ms. Price, another parent, told me it is unfair for her daughter Estelle to get a B in Ms. Brown's class when all the test grades are A. "So what if she misses a few assignments," she snapped at me.

Mr. Allen told me it was unfair for his son Sam to have to take a test when Sam has been absent the previous day. He was very firm when he told me, "I don't care if Sam knew about the test at the beginning of the week. And I certainly don't care that Ms. Brown sent home a test guide. He wasn't in class the day before, and he shouldn't have to take the test."

MS. BROWN'S COMMENTS ABOUT FOUR STUDENTS IN HER CLASS

Tommy never brings his book to class, and this is not accidental. Other students come to class without necessary supplies, including a required notebook and something to write with.

Jill almost never pays attention in class, seldom follows directions, and almost never participates in learning activities. At the same time every day, Jill announces that she has to go to the girls' room. I know she does not.

Igor always walks in five minutes late. Always! Then he may wander in and out of the class. He deliberately does not copy down the homework assignment. With Igor, it's lots of hard work planning for few results.

Fadia never does any homework and annoys everyone around her. That is why I put her in the back of the class—by herself. Now all Fadia does is read library books or just falls asleep.

MS. BROWN'S DISCUSSION WITH THE GUIDANCE COUNSELOR

During a discussion with the guidance counselor, Ms. Brown learned that many of her colleagues had had similar problems with Fadia.

Ms. Brown told the guidance counselor, "I may not be able to get Fadia to do homework. But there is no way that I am going to tolerate her sleeping in my class."

The guidance counselor responded by saying, "I think you should call Fadia's parents to see if they can help with this problem."

Scenario 3: Practice PLT Constructed-Response Items

7. The Principal's summary of parental comments about Ms. Brown lists some of the issues parents have with Ms. Brown.

   - Describe TWO approaches that Ms. Brown could take to improve her relationships with parents.
   - Explain why each of the approaches you recommend would effectively improve that communication. Base your answer on sound principles of communication.

8. Ms. Brown's comments about several students and her discussion with the guidance counselor help describe some of the disciplinary issues Fadia has in school.

   - Recommend TWO approaches that Ms. Brown could use to reduce some of Fadia's disciplinary problems.
   - Explain why each of the strategies you recommend would be likely to reduce Fadia's disciplinary problems. Base your answer on sound principles of classroom management and human development.

9. Say that Ms. Brown and her supervisor are discussing the supervisor's summary report about Ms. Brown, with an emphasis on completing each lesson.

   - Describe TWO strategies the supervisor could recommend to Ms. Brown to enable her to complete most of the lessons she teaches.
   - Explain why each of the strategies you recommend would be effective. Base your answer on sound principles of instructional planning and classroom management.

Situation

Mr. Hayes worked in industry for years and has been teaching science about three years. He came to the school without formal certification under a plan for bringing experienced scientists into the teaching ranks. Mr. Shifts has been the principal of Everett High School as long as anyone can remember. As usual, this morning finds him out and about the school visiting classes. He is about to drop in on Mr. Hayes, a science teacher in the school. Mr. Shifts had praised Mr. Hayes to the school board as "the kind of person who can help our students learn about science in the world of work." But both he and Mr. Hayes have learned that schools and businesses are not the same. Lots of things that are effective in the workplace simply are not effective in a school.

PREOBSERVATION INTERACTION

The bell rang, and Mr. Shifts stood in the hall as the students streamed by. Things really had not changed since he was a student there. The students dressed differently, but they were really the same. From within the crowds of students he heard calls of "Hey Shifty." That had not changed since he was a student there either.

The last student entered the classroom, leaving the hall desolate again except for the hall monitors seated at each end. Mr. Shifts turned his attention to the classroom. He walked through the door to Mr. Hayes's room, went up to Mr. Hayes, and said, "Morning."

Mr. Hayes groaned. "It's June. I thought I was finished with observations this year."

"Just dropping by," said Mr. Shifts. "Nothing formal, but I'd like to see what's going on with some of the students. What are you teaching today?"

Mr. Hayes smiled a relieved sigh and said, "I'm teaching a lesson on photosynthesis. I am going to model this myself with an experiment in front of the class. I also considered setting up a series of activities and preparing a series of questions that will guide the students through the activities. But this way will be better."

"Great," said Mr. Shifts. "Mind if I stay a bit?"

"You know that you're welcome—always," said Mr. Hayes. Then he thought to himself, "I've got to become an administrator. And am I glad I didn't decide to use that touchy-feely student-based approach to teaching this lesson. These students will be itchy enough on a hot day like this."

MR. SHIFT'S OBSERVATION OF MR. HAYES

Mr. Hayes begins, "OK class, today we're going to learn about photosynthesis. Copy the homework questions from the board while I check the experiment." I think Mr. Hayes hopes the questions will motivate the students to learn about photosynthesis and motivate them to pay attention during the lesson.

Mr. Hayes also tells the students that the class will end with a short quiz on aspects of the subject that he is presenting, apparently to motivate them to pay attention during the lesson.

Mr. Hayes sets up the experiment, moving the apparatus around on his experiment table in front of the class. Some students are not copying the questions. Mr. Hayes notices and urges the students to "get busy." The apparatus consists of a beaker of water with a test tube turned upside down inside it; there is a green plant inside the test tube. A very bright light shines on the beaker and the test tube. The apparatus does seem to hold the attention of many students.

After the students have had enough time to copy the questions, Mr. Hayes begins the lesson and explains the results of the experiment. The test tube started out completely filled with water, but after a while the water was pushed down farther in the test tube, which Mr. Hayes explains shows that photosynthesis produces oxygen.

Mr. Hayes is very careful to highlight the key concepts as he conducts the experiment. I can see that the homework questions are all based on the key concepts in the lesson.

Mr. Hayes is demonstrating and explaining important concepts. Most of the students are paying attention, but only a few of them are taking notes.

In my opinion, Mr. Hayes is a good teacher, but he should try using the inquiry approach with these students. I think that many of them would have learned more from what was a very good lesson.

Scenario 4: Practice PLT Constructed-Response Items

10. Suppose that Mr. Shifts and Mr. Hayes are discussing Mr. Shift's observation with a focus on how to engage students in note taking during the experiment.

   - Recommend TWO strategies that Mr. Shifts could present to Mr. Hayes to ensure that most of the students take notes during the experiment.
   - Explain why each of the strategies you recommend would be effective. Base your answer on sound principles of instructional planning and classroom management.

11. In the Preobservation interaction, Mr. Hayes indicates he's glad he did not set up a series of student-based activities to complete the lesson.

   - Recommend TWO benefits the students might have derived from a student-based approach.
   - Explain why each of these benefits would come from a student-based approach. Base your answer on sound principles of instructional planning and learning theory.

12. The description of the principal includes his opinion that Mr. Hayes's work experience can relate science learning to the world of work.

   - Recommend TWO approaches that Mr. Hayes could use to relate his work experience to learning science in a way that would benefit students.
   - Explain why each of the approaches you recommend would be effective. Base your answer on sound principles of communication and instructional planning.

Directions: Use about 80 minutes for this section. These questions are not related to the scenarios. Use the answer sheet on page 423.

1. Teachers on the Carteret Elementary School technology committee are discussing computer use in classrooms. Lee Mombello raises the issue of equity. He says, "In a country where most homes have a computer and the Internet, many of our students have no access to computers outside the school. With this in mind, which of the following choices is the best policy for the committee to establish about the classroom use of computers?

   Ⓐ Special after-school computer clubs should be set up for students who do not have a computer at home.
   Ⓑ Teachers should integrate computers in their teaching whenever possible.
   Ⓒ Each student should be given their own computer to use at school and at home.
   Ⓓ The school should hire a technology specialist who will help teachers integrate computers in their classrooms.

2. Gerard Lancaster is a new teacher who wants to use cooperative learning groups to supplement a teacher-centered approach to social studies instruction. In order to accomplish that task, which of the following should Mr. Lancaster employ when compared to teacher-centered presentations?

   I. More student involvement
   II. More content coverage
   III. More varied outcomes
   IV. More brainstorming

   Ⓐ I and II
   Ⓑ I, III, and IV
   Ⓒ III and IV
   Ⓓ II, III, and IV

3. The Carson Hills school district is preparing a pamphlet about effective schools to distribute to teachers. Which of the following choices should be listed as characteristic of effective schools in the pamphlet?

   I. A climate of high expectations
   II. Accountability for student performance
   III. Eliminating standardized tests

   Ⓐ I only
   Ⓑ I and II
   Ⓒ III only
   Ⓓ II and III

4. Cindy Weiss is concerned about how she uses class time in her departmentalized fifth-grade English class. She realizes after a year of teaching that she must learn to be an effective classroom manager, which means that she will take steps to ensure that the majority of class time is devoted to

Ⓐ individual work.
Ⓑ on-task activities.
Ⓒ cooperative learning.
Ⓓ lecturing.

BASE YOUR ANSWERS TO QUESTIONS 5 AND 6 ON THIS SITUATION.

Frank Damico, a special education teacher, is working with Kathy McCoy in Kathy's fifth-grade class that includes mainstreamed students. Mr. Damico and Ms. McCoy have regular meetings with the parents of mainstreamed students in the class.

5. Which of the following best describes Frank Damico's role in the classroom?

Ⓐ Observe the mainstreamed students to identify the out-of-class support they need
Ⓑ Teach the entire class cooperatively with the teacher
Ⓒ Help the mainstreamed students during the teacher's lesson
Ⓓ Observe the nonmainstreamed students to get tips on their successful learning styles to pass on to the special education students

6. During one meeting a parent expresses extreme anxiety about how her child James is doing in school. The parent is concerned that continued academic problems will make it impossible for him to attend college or to be a success in life. Which of the following choices is the best response for these teachers to give?

Ⓐ "Don't be concerned; we are confident that James will do fine and be successful."
Ⓑ "We enjoy working with James, and we have the highest hopes for him."
Ⓒ "That James is still in a special education setting at this age indicates there are likely some real problems that may or may not be resolved over time."
Ⓓ "We are sorry you feel that way, but we just cannot discuss these things with parents."

7. Dr. Samson, the school principal, was explaining to a group of beginning teachers that children can learn vicariously, meaning that children can

Ⓐ learn by doing.
Ⓑ learn through a wide variety of activities.
Ⓒ learn if there is a clear structure.
Ⓓ learn from others' experiences.

8. Stan Powell makes extensive use of portfolio assessment in his anthropology class, and so he knows that the most significant difficulty with portfolio assessment reliability is that

 Ⓐ students put samples of widely different types of work in their portfolios.
 Ⓑ scoring machines don't work reliably with materials in portfolios.
 Ⓒ different teachers place different emphasis on the portfolios when giving grades.
 Ⓓ different teachers assign widely different grades to the same portfolio.

9. Repeated testing of a fourth-grade student in Ray Maw's class reveals an IQ in the 110–115 range, but the student's standardized test scores are two or more years below grade level. Which of the following is the most appropriate interpretation of these test scores?

 Ⓐ The student is a poor test taker.
 Ⓑ The student's achievement and potential match.
 Ⓒ The student is gifted.
 Ⓓ The student has a learning disability.

10. Ezequiel Sanchez administers an end-of-chapter test from the teacher's edition of a language arts text to students in his fourth-grade class. In all likelihood, this is a

 Ⓐ portfolio evaluation.
 Ⓑ standardized test.
 Ⓒ norm-referenced test.
 Ⓓ summative evaluation.

BASE YOUR ANSWERS TO QUESTIONS 11 AND 12 ON THESE PASSAGES.

The following excerpts present opinions about what is good and what is not good about direct instruction.

What's good about direct instruction? Direct Instruction (DI) is the most widely used instructional technique, and for good reason, it works. DI features a research-based curriculum and lessons that have been extensively field-tested and revised. The objective is to develop lessons that students understand the first time the lesson is taught. Each lesson builds on skills fully mastered in the previous lesson. Once a skill has been mastered, students are able to apply the skill to new situations. This emphasis on mastery and application enables the student to learn more complex and more difficult skills. The use of proven lessons lets DI move quickly and efficiently. Students are asked many questions in DI classes, giving them the opportunity for full skill mastery. DI uses achievement grouping for each curricular area to account for achievement differences among students. This grouping enables students to move at their own pace. Students are assessed frequently to facilitate additional help and reteaching. When DI is fully implemented, students in these classes regularly outperform students in other classes regardless of the teaching approach used in the other classes.

What's not good about direct instruction? Research shows that Direct Instruction (DI) is great for developing skills. But DI proponents use the research about DI's success in a skills environment to make arguments for its use in all school instruction. That kind of argument just can't be supported. There is no doubt that it is a fantastic approach for teaching early reading. Researchers agree that phonics is the best way to teach reading, and phonics instruction lends itself to a DI approach. But there is much more to a curriculum than skills, and there is much more to reading than phonics. Once students learn to read, they must explore language, read books on their own, and pursue their own interests. DI is probably the worst way to help students become independent and effective readers. DI might be fine for teaching mathematics skills, but the tightly controlled instruction found in DI is not the best way to help students become effective problem solvers. You get the idea—DI may be fine for narrow skills instruction, but it is not good for instruction that requires higher-order thinking and exploration.

11. The first passage supports which of the following types of student grouping?

Ⓐ Students should be grouped homogeneously in a way that ensures each student will work with every other student in the class in each curricular area.

Ⓑ Students should be grouped heterogeneously according to IQ score, and this grouping should be used for each curricular area.

Ⓒ Students should be grouped homogeneously for each individual curricular area.

Ⓓ Students should be grouped heterogeneously for each individual curricular area.

12. The second passage argues against using DI throughout the curriculum by making which of the following points?

Ⓐ DI has been tested only in an environment that supports skills development.

Ⓑ DI has proven very successful for teaching reading, and reading is an important part of every subject in the school curriculum.

Ⓒ DI places an emphasis on the mastery and application of school subjects, and these apply across the entire school curriculum.

Ⓓ DI is still an unproven approach to teaching, and so this approach should definitely not be used throughout the school curriculum.

---

13. Which of the actions by a teacher is LEAST likely to promote good communication with parents?

Ⓐ Make phone calls to parents.

Ⓑ Write personal notes on report cards.

Ⓒ Initiate a series of home/school letters.

Ⓓ Meet with groups of parents to discuss individual student achievement.

14. Responsibilities primarily attributed to local school boards include

    I. employing and supervising a superintendent.
    II. assigning teachers and staff to schools and designating their responsibilities.
    III. assigning individual pupils to schools.
    IV. evaluating district goals.

    Ⓐ I, II, and IV
    Ⓑ II and III
    Ⓒ I and IV
    Ⓓ I, III, and IV

15. Frank Carmody usually uses a lecture approach to present his history lessons. Which of the following approaches is most likely to help Mr. Carmody enhance instruction?

    Ⓐ Begin the lesson with a motivation.
    Ⓑ Focus his instruction on the entire class and avoid making eye contact with individual students.
    Ⓒ Walk around the room while he delivers his lecture.
    Ⓓ Choose a topic above the students' ability level.

16. Ms. Johanssen arranges her students in cooperative learning groups to work on photosynthesis, usually meaning that

    Ⓐ Ms. Johanssen cooperates fully with the students.
    Ⓑ Ms. Johanssen gives each group specific instructions on how to proceed.
    Ⓒ a person from each group reports the group's findings.
    Ⓓ each group of students gathers information about photosynthesis from the local Agriculture Department Cooperative Extension.

17. Mr. Rosspaph receives the results of a norm-referenced test indicating that a student has an IQ of 97, leading the teacher to the conclusion that

    Ⓐ the student has below-average intelligence.
    Ⓑ the student's intelligence is in the normal range.
    Ⓒ the student is mildly retarded.
    Ⓓ the standard deviation of the test is 3.

Faith Bisone is teaching a United States history class that is culturally and linguistically diverse. Many of the students in her class have a first language other than English, and many come from homes where English is not spoken. Ms. Bisone knows that the minority students in her class as a whole tend to have lower achievement scores than other students. She wants to familiarize herself with the difficulties these students have and with the teaching approaches that will be effective in her classroom.

18. The data about the achievement of minority students leads Ms. Bisone to the valid conclusion that

Ⓐ minority students are less capable learners than other students are.

Ⓑ the parents of minority students care less about their children's education.

Ⓒ learning expectations should be lowered for minority students.

Ⓓ minority students have fewer opportunities for enriched learning experiences at home.

19. Which of the following describes an acceptable approach to modifying the objectives or plans for this class?

Ⓐ Modify the plans to teach history topics about the parents' home countries.

Ⓑ Modify the objective to adjust its difficulty level.

Ⓒ Modify the plans to include direct instruction in English.

Ⓓ Modify the plans to account for the cultural heritage of those in the class.

20. Which of the following is consistent with Ms. Bisone using an ESL approach with a group of Limited English Proficiency students from the class?

Ⓐ Use context clues to help students identify English words.

Ⓑ Teach mathematics in the students' first languages.

Ⓒ Help students learn their native languages.

Ⓓ Encourage regional and local dialects.

21. When completing an assignment, most successful learning takes place when

Ⓐ students work independently in school.

Ⓑ students work supervised by a parent at home.

Ⓒ students work supervised by the teacher.

Ⓓ students work on a computer.

PRACTICE PLT

22. Ezequiel Sanchez uses a computer-based multimedia encyclopedia as part of his fourth-grade writing program. The multimedia encyclopedia includes hypertext links in most of its articles. To help understand how to use the hypertext links, Mr. Sanchez would best explain that

Ⓐ the links tie together very (hyper) important ideas in the passage.

Ⓑ clicking on a link gives additional information.

Ⓒ the links move or vibrate to draw attention to important ideas.

Ⓓ clicking on a link with a mouse cursor changes the link's color.

23. Felipe Victorino uses a token economy system to motivate students during a unit in his business class. Which of the following actions is most consistent with Mr. Victorino's approach?

Ⓐ Mr. Victorino provides token (symbolic) reinforcement for work completed by students as opposed to real or meaningful reinforcement.

Ⓑ Mr. Victorino distributes subway and bus tokens for reinforcement because this approach was pioneered in urban areas where many students took buses and subways to school.

Ⓒ Mr. Victorino posts a description of how students can earn points and then exchange a certain number of points for a more tangible reward.

Ⓓ Mr. Victorino posts a "token of my appreciation list" on the bulletin board and lists the names of students who perform outstanding work.

24. In her 10 years as a superintendent of schools, Dr. Kim Morgan has learned that, generally speaking, class discipline problems are most difficult during

Ⓐ Grades 2–3.

Ⓑ Grades 5–6.

Ⓒ Grades 8–9.

Ⓓ Grades 11–12.

25. A teacher working with ELL students is using a sheltered instructional approach. Which of the following is NOT a characteristic of a program using this approach?

Ⓐ The program integrates Vygotsky's zone of proximal development and Gardner's multiple intelligences.

Ⓑ The program features lessons taught below grade level.

Ⓒ The program moves students toward English proficiency.

Ⓓ The program places an emphasis on lesson preparation.

26. A teacher wants to encourage vicarious learning among students in the class, meaning that students sometimes learn

Ⓐ by doing.

Ⓑ through a wide variety of activities.

Ⓒ if there is a clear structure.

Ⓓ from others' experiences.

BASE YOUR ANSWER TO QUESTION 27 ON THIS CONVERSATION.

Here is a brief part of a conversation between Alex Whitby, a third-grade teacher, and Marciella Atkins, the school district reading specialist.

Alex: Thanks for coming by. I wanted to talk to you about one of my students.

Marciella: Which one.

Alex: Savaro—he's still having trouble with reading.

Marciella: I remember Savaro from last year in second grade.

Alex: I was thinking about more phonics—what do you think?

Marciella: That's OK—just remember that phonics does not help much . . .

27. Which of the following finishes the reading specialist's last sentence?

Ⓐ to associate sounds with printed letters
Ⓑ with reading comprehension
Ⓒ to attack new words independently
Ⓓ to develop a sight vocabulary

---

28. Tara Kirk is concerned about the way she responds to student's questions in science and wants to develop a more effective approach. The best advice for Ms. Kirk is to respond in which of the following ways?

   I. Encourage exploration of the answer with activities and materials that stimulate curiosity.
  II. Model good responding skills.
 III. Answer all items as quickly and concisely as possible.
 IV. Include children's questions in evaluation techniques.

Ⓐ I and II
Ⓑ III and IV
Ⓒ I, II, and III
Ⓓ I, II, and IV

29. Jovina Crockett is planning a lesson to integrate art with haiku, a Japanese poetic form.

Which of the following approaches is LEAST likely to meet Ms. Crockett's needs?

Ⓐ Use the computer as an artistic tool to illustrate the haiku.
Ⓑ Provide a display of classical Japanese paintings for children to color.
Ⓒ Provide clay as a means to illustrate their haiku.
Ⓓ Provide paints and brushes for illustrations of the haiku.

30. Sam Meletto, a second-grade teacher, and the principal are discussing Sam's reasons for instituting a whole-language program in his classroom. Which among the following is the best reason Sam could give?

Ⓐ Whole-language instruction is widely accepted.

Ⓑ It is not necessary to teach word recognition.

Ⓒ Children comprehend more after using a whole-language approach.

Ⓓ Children have a better attitude toward reading.

31. A student has auditory discrimination difficulties that have not led to a classification of learning disabled. The auditory discrimination difficulties are LEAST likely to result in

Ⓐ writing difficulties.

Ⓑ reading difficulties.

Ⓒ difficulty following verbal instructions.

Ⓓ sight vocabulary problems.

32. Damaris Jones and one of his students are discussing the student's most recent report card. Mr. Jones chooses his words carefully to have the most impact, and finally decides on these: "Your grades would have been better if all homework assignments were handed in." Which of the following approaches has the teacher decided to use?

Ⓐ Positive reinforcement

Ⓑ Reverse psychology

Ⓒ Threats

Ⓓ Negative reinforcement

33. Lisa is a student in DeShala Washington's third-grade class. At a parent-teacher conference, Lisa's mother says she has heard about the school using a basal reading program and asks what basal reading programs are NOT good for. Which of the following would be Ms. Washington's best response?

Ⓐ Skills are taught and developed in a systematic sequential manner.

Ⓑ They meet individual differences and needs of the child.

Ⓒ A basic vocabulary is established and reinforced.

Ⓓ Manuals provide a detailed outline for teaching.

34. Elizabeth Milano is an experienced fifth-grade teacher. Ms. Milano notices that one student in her class has particular difficulty when he is reading the problems in the mathematics textbook. In an effort to help this student, it would be most appropriate for Ms. Milano to recognize that this difficulty is most likely the result of

Ⓐ faulty word identification and recognition.

Ⓑ inability to locate and retain specific facts.

Ⓒ deficiencies in basic comprehension abilities.

Ⓓ inability to adapt to reading needs in this content field.

35. Tom Karel has a number of students in his class who are significantly below grade level in reading. Mr. Karel realizes that he needs to adapt social studies instruction for these students. Mr. Karel's choice among the following options would be appropriate EXCEPT to

Ⓐ use instructional materials that have a lower reading level.

Ⓑ use instructional materials with less difficult concepts.

Ⓒ read information about social studies to the students.

Ⓓ use recorded tapes that contain social studies information.

36. Frank Rios is a primary teacher who is incorporating authentic assessment in his evaluation techniques. That means that Mr. Rios will

Ⓐ collect and evaluate student work.

Ⓑ only use tests provided by the publisher of the books he uses.

Ⓒ only evaluate students in real situations outside of school.

Ⓓ collect evaluative information from other teachers.

37. Renita Lopez is teaching language arts in the upper elementary grades and wants to evaluate students' writing techniques and plan for further writing experiences.

Which of the following is the most appropriate choice?

Ⓐ Administer a standardized grammar test and use the scores as a planning device

Ⓑ Use a writing checklist to assess a variety of creative writing samples that include writing summaries and samples

Ⓒ Have students prepare a composition on a subject of their choice and holistically evaluate the composition

Ⓓ Have students answer a series of higher-level, short-answer questions about a specific writing sample

38. Sheneoi Goldman, a fifth-grade teacher, conducts science class using the inquiry approach.

Which of the following would a person be most likely to observe during Ms. Goldman's science class?

Ⓐ Ms. Goldman deliberately does not try out an experiment in advance of the class so everyone in the class sees the results together for the first time.

Ⓑ Ms. Goldman tells the students to avoid analyzing thought processes and rather to rely on what happens in the experiment.

Ⓒ Ms. Goldman presents a problem for the students to solve or a situation for them to explore.

Ⓓ Ms. Goldman asks students to present a problem for the class to solve or a situation for the class to explore.

QUESTIONS 39–42 ARE BASED ON THE FOLLOWING SITUATION.

Wayne Yarborough is in his fourth year as a social studies teacher at Roosevelt High School. He is giving some thought to the way he teaches. While teaching a social studies lesson, Mr. Yarborough can get the students' interest but he is not good at maintaining their interest. He uses a wide variety of questions as he teaches and is interested in changing and reinforcing appropriate student behavior.

39. Mr. Yarborough has the best chance of maintaining student interest in the lesson if

　Ⓐ　he is more animated.
　Ⓑ　the objectives are clear and unambiguous.
　Ⓒ　students understand what they are learning, which will help them learn other material later.
　Ⓓ　there are no choices available to students.

40. When questioning students, which of the following techniques should Mr. Yarborough generally follow?

　Ⓐ　Make sure students know who will answer a question before it is asked
　Ⓑ　Ask questions of the whole class
　Ⓒ　Ask questions of students who are not paying attention
　Ⓓ　Ask questions of students who usually have the correct answers

41. Mr. Yarborough knows that modeling is one appropriate way of modifying behavior.

Which of the following is an example of a good modeling technique?

　Ⓐ　Respond courteously to students' questions
　Ⓑ　Show students how to construct replicas of historic buildings
　Ⓒ　Demonstrate students' inappropriate behavior
　Ⓓ　Stress the importance of appearance and show students how to dress

42. Which of the following would be an appropriate way for Mr. Yarborough to reinforce student behavior?

　　I.　Grading on the basis of performance
　 II.　Praising appropriate behavior
　III.　Ignoring inappropriate behavior

　Ⓐ　I and II
　Ⓑ　I and III
　Ⓒ　II and III
　Ⓓ　II only

43. Chuck Galesky has been teaching for a few years but like most newer teachers, he still has some problems with discipline. He overhears the assistant principal say, "Chuck should try a more 'with-it' teaching approach to handle his discipline problems." This most probably means a

Ⓐ teacher is always aware of new disciplinary techniques.
Ⓑ teacher is always aware of current popular trends among students.
Ⓒ teacher is always aware of what is happening in the classroom.
Ⓓ teacher is well respected by other teachers.

44. Lisa Germanio has significant discipline problems with her ninth-grade students. However, if Ms. Germanio were teaching high school seniors, she would find that discipline is less difficult because

Ⓐ it is left to the administration.
Ⓑ it is the parents' concern.
Ⓒ students are less resistant.
Ⓓ teachers are less authoritative.

QUESTIONS 45 AND 46 ARE BASED ON THE FOLLOWING SITUATION.

Ingrid Johanssen is a science teacher who plans to begin the lesson by saying, "OK class, today we're going to learn about photosynthesis." The teacher wants to model photosynthesis for the students. She plans to write prerequisite competencies for the lesson on the board. Ms. Johanssen plans to use an inquiry approach and wants to motivate the students as much as possible.

45. Which of the following is the most powerful overall motivation Ms. Johanssen could use in the class?

Ⓐ Praise
Ⓑ Grades
Ⓒ Privileges
Ⓓ Learning

46. Which of the following best describes a prerequisite competency Ms. Johanssen plans to write on the board?

Ⓐ the knowledge and skills a teacher must possess to teach an objective
Ⓑ a subobjective to the main objective of the lesson
Ⓒ the basis for admitting students when they transfer from another school district
Ⓓ the knowledge and skills students must possess to learn an objective

47. Which of the following is an appropriate alteration to make to your curriculum to accommodate the needs of the recent immigrants in your class?

    Ⓐ lower the expectations for the group
    Ⓑ limit the amount of homework given
    Ⓒ teach in the native language
    Ⓓ require English proficiency to make progress in school

48. Stan Heligo is writing objectives based on the Taxonomy of Educational Objectives: Cognitive Domain, which means that he would teach which of these topics at the highest level of this taxonomy?

    Ⓐ evaluate a book
    Ⓑ understand a reading passage
    Ⓒ analyze a written paragraph
    Ⓓ apply a mathematics formula to a real situation

49. A teacher using Gardner's multiple intelligences as the basis for instruction is most likely to do which of the following?

    Ⓐ Implement interdisciplinary units
    Ⓑ Help students learn about each of the intelligences
    Ⓒ Eliminate assessments
    Ⓓ Allow students to determine criteria for quality

50. As part of an ongoing assessment program, a teacher uses criterion-referenced tests, meaning that these tests

    Ⓐ require students to reach certain criteria, which are usually minimum percentile scores.
    Ⓑ measure a student's ability as compared with specific criteria established by the testing company.
    Ⓒ measure a limited, specific body of knowledge.
    Ⓓ include only constructed-response answers.

51. Morina Meridcu is planning to teach a fourth-grade geography lesson. When it comes to ability level, Ms. Meridcu should present the lesson

    Ⓐ below students' ability level.
    Ⓑ above students' ability level.
    Ⓒ at students' ability level.
    Ⓓ in a way that does not take ability level into account.

52. A special education teacher joins a classroom teacher in class to help a mainstreamed student. The involvement of the special education teacher in the mainstreamed class is an example of

Ⓐ mainstreaming.

Ⓑ inclusion.

Ⓒ teacher-assisted intervention.

Ⓓ teacher-student conferencing.

53. The most appropriate reason a teacher in a school with a predominately minority population could have for a tracking system based on standardized tests is that

Ⓐ the standardized tests used to place students are deliberately designed to trick minority students.

Ⓑ tracking systems consistently discriminate against minority students.

Ⓒ the best teachers are always assigned to the highest- and lowest-achieving classes.

Ⓓ the school administration cannot be counted on to accurately report test scores.

54. A student is classified as learning disabled. The Child Study Team, which includes the student's teacher, is discussing the strategies to help the student learn to read and master language arts. Which of the following best describes an effective approach for the teacher to use with this student?

Ⓐ Use large-print books.

Ⓑ Use highly relevant reading materials.

Ⓒ Provide brief assignments and auditory learning.

Ⓓ Stress the importance of appearance and showing students how to dress.

55. Which of the following describes a classroom in which the teacher uses Glasser's reality therapy?

Ⓐ A student is on his or her own to discover the harsh reality of mistakes.

Ⓑ The teacher establishes clear rules and the rewards or punishment that accompany acceptable and unacceptable behavior.

Ⓒ The teacher explains all positive and negative outcomes in terms of the real world.

Ⓓ Students help develop rules and then accept the consequences of any rule breaking.

56. Ms. Cornell plans to incorporate metacognition in her lessons, meaning that she plans to

Ⓐ place an emphasis on subject matter objectives rather than process objectives.

Ⓑ engage students in examining their thought processes.

Ⓒ show students how to think about ideas in an abstract way.

Ⓓ show students how to tell the difference between what they actually know and what they think they know.

57. Which of the following is LEAST likely to promote good communication with parents?

Ⓐ Make a series of phone calls to parents at home.
Ⓑ Write personal notes on report cards for the parents to read.
Ⓒ Initiate a series of home/school letters mailed directly to parents.
Ⓓ Meet with groups of parents to discuss individual student achievement.

58. As an effective classroom manager, a teacher should be most careful to take steps that ensure the majority of class time is devoted to

Ⓐ individual work.
Ⓑ on-task activities.
Ⓒ lecturing.
Ⓓ group work.

59. Lucinda Crawford uses holistic scoring to evaluate her fifth-grade students' writing. She will make a brief presentation to the Board of Education about this method. This is best described as a scoring technique in which

Ⓐ essays are scored using advanced imaging technology.
Ⓑ essays are scored by several readers who do not discuss the essays.
Ⓒ readers rank essays relative to the "whole" of essays written for that testing cycle.
Ⓓ readers rank essays based on the overall impression, not on a detailed analysis of the essays.

60. The best approach for a teacher to follow after asking a question is to

Ⓐ call on a student immediately and ask for a quick answer.
Ⓑ wait until a student calls out the answer.
Ⓒ wait before calling on a student and then ask for a quick answer.
Ⓓ wait before calling on a student and allow four or five seconds for the student to answer.

61. Approximately what percentage of questions should the teacher expect to be answered correctly?

Ⓐ 90 percent
Ⓑ 75 percent
Ⓒ 40 percent
Ⓓ 20 percent

62. The LEAST effective setting for direct instruction is when students are

Ⓐ learning a skill.
Ⓑ having difficulty with a concept.
Ⓒ writing book reports.
Ⓓ learning to solve problems.

63. Research states characteristics of effective schools include all the following EXCEPT

   Ⓐ a climate of high expectations.
   Ⓑ a high proportion of instructional time spent on task.
   Ⓒ strong and effective leadership.
   Ⓓ eliminating standardized tests.

64. A teacher can help a student who is having difficulty in class by providing all of the following EXCEPT

   Ⓐ a quiet place to work.
   Ⓑ extensive homework to reinforce skills.
   Ⓒ a flexible schedule.
   Ⓓ a warm, supportive atmosphere.

65. Generally speaking, the factor that creates the most significant difference in the quality of individual schools is

   Ⓐ teacher knowledge.
   Ⓑ class size.
   Ⓒ parent/teacher communication.
   Ⓓ the student's SES.

66. Ellen Obutu keeps a portfolio of written work for students. In Ms. Obutu's opinion, Lionel's writing sample is well above average for ninth grade students at her school. A standardized language arts test administered last month shows Lionel has a writing grade equivalent of 7.9, which is above average for his class but below his grade level.

   Which of the following is the best description of Lionel's language arts achievement?

   Ⓐ Lionel's writing test scores are above grade level.
   Ⓑ Lionel is writing below average for his class.
   Ⓒ Lionel needs intensive help in writing.
   Ⓓ Lionel seems to do better when evaluated with an authentic assessment.

67. Which of the following is the most reasonable explanation of why Lionel's standardized test score is below grade level but above average for that class?

   Ⓐ The student answered fewer questions correctly for the ninth-grade level.
   Ⓑ The class did worse, on average, than the entire group that took the test.
   Ⓒ Half of those who take the test are below average.
   Ⓓ The averages are different because the number of students in each group is different.

68. Weekly planning differs from individual lesson plans in that

(A) weekly plans fit lessons and other activities into available time periods during the week, whereas lesson plans detail the lessons.

(B) weekly plans detail the lessons, whereas lesson plans fit into available time periods during the week.

(C) weekly plans should be prepared each week, whereas lesson plans should be prepared at the beginning of the year.

(D) weekly plans are usually kept by the teacher, whereas lesson plans are usually submitted written in a plan book.

69. A teacher wants to use Vygotsky's zone of proximal development as a main feature of classroom instruction. To effectively implement this strategy the teacher must

(A) be aware of what a student knows and what a student does not know.

(B) know a student's development stage according to Piaget's theory.

(C) be aware of how closely the teacher may approach a student during instruction.

(D) position the teacher's desk near the student's desk.

70. Piaget wrote that students learn through a process of equilibration. Which of the following classroom practices is most likely to promote this process?

(A) Teachers help students learn concepts using manipulative materials.

(B) Students learn concepts through the repeat practice method.

(C) Students learn concepts vicariously.

(D) Students actively learn concepts through their own experiences.

EXPLAINED RESPONSES AND ANSWERS

Constructed-Response Items

The essential elements of the responses to each constructed-response item are given below.

SCENARIO 1

1. You should give TWO strategies Ms. Kelly could use for her approach to classroom management. This item refers to Ms. Kelly's classroom sign, "DO UNTO OTHERS AS YOU WOULD HAVE THEM DO UNTO YOU." Your strategies should directly address that approach.

    Following each strategy, you should give a brief explanation of why the strategy would be successful. That is, you should highlight something about that strategy that will make it successful. That's different from describing how something will be successful, which means describing the impact of the approach in the classroom.

    For example, one strategy might be having students meet to agree on the consequences of not following the advice in the sign. You might say the strategy will be effective because it involves the active participation of all the students in the class.

    There are many other effective strategies.

2. You should give TWO ways Ms. Kelly should use the resources listed in the case to establish an effective reading program. These materials include both basal readers and children's literature. Your strategies should incorporate both types of reading materials.

    Following each of the ways of using the resources, you should explain why they would be effective. That means you should explain what there is about the approaches that would make them effective, and not about the effect they will have. There are many other effective strategies.

    For example, you could say that you will use the phonics workbook and the basal readers for a phonics-based program and then explain that phonics is the best way to teach students about reading. You could also say that you will use the children's books for a literature-based program.

3. You should give TWO ways that Ms. Kelly can implement a plan to integrate reading and mathematics in her classroom. The question does not specifically refer to the reading materials in Ms. Kelly's class.

    Following each of the ways for integrating reading and mathematics, you should explain why the approach you suggest will be effective. That means what there is about the approach that will make that approach effective.

    For example, you could say that you will teach reading through mathematics word problems and explain that the approach will be effective because improved reading ability will help students become better mathematics problem solvers.

    There are many other effective strategies.

SCENARIO 2

4. You should give TWO strategies to help ensure that most of Mr. Hayes's students are taking notes during the experiment. Mr. Shift's observation of Mr. Hayes gives most of the information you need to answer this question. Mr. Hayes spends a lot of time at

the beginning of the lesson getting the experiment ready and then demonstrating the experiment.

Following the description of each strategy, you should explain why the strategy would be effective—what there is about the strategy that would make it effective.

You might recommend that Mr. Hayes walk around the room and check on students to be sure they are taking notes and explain that this approach could be successful because students are more likely to take notes if someone is checking on their progress. A recommendation that Mr. Hayes give clear instructions to take notes would not be appropriate because Mr. Hayes gives clear instructions at the beginning of the class to copy questions from the board.

There are many other effective strategies.

5. You should give TWO examples of benefits that students could have derived from student-based activities in Mr. Hayes's class. Mr. Hayes's lesson was teacher-based and teacher-directed.

Following the description of each benefit, explain why the students would benefit from the activity.

You might recommend the inquiry approach that the principal describes at the end of his observation. In the inquiry approach students observe experiments and draw their own conclusions under the teacher's guidance. You could explain that students would benefit from this approach because they would be actively involved in the lesson.

There are many other effective strategies.

6. You should give TWO approaches that Mr. Hayes could use to relate his work experience and science in a way that will benefit students. The case history tells us that Mr. Hayes has worked in industry, but it does not tell us what type of industry he worked in. The principal did praise Mr. Hayes as someone who "can help our students learn about science in the world of work."

Following the description of each approach, explain why the approach would benefit students.

You might just say that Mr. Hayes could describe how the science that students were learning was important to the work he did in business and how the students' work in class would help prepare them for a science career. Explain that this approach would be effective because it would give students a real-world basis for studying science.

There are many other effective strategies.

SCENARIO 3

7. You should give TWO approaches Ms. Brown can take to improve her relationship with parents. All the complaints in the Principal's Summary are about testing and grades. Some of these complaints are bound to be self-serving, but they are still creating problems for Ms. Brown. Other parts of the scenario indicate that Ms. Brown may be trying to do too much, that she has difficulty with classroom discipline, and that she is frustrated and acts in a negative fashion. These problems with students cause them to complain to their parents. This does not seem to be an easy problem to solve.

Following each of the suggestions for improving relationships with parents, you should explain why it would be effective and what there is about the approach that will make it successful. For example, you could write that Ms. Brown could improve communication with parents through phone calls or through a regular newsletter. You could explain that this approach will be effective because parents respond positively to teachers who reach out to them.

There are many other effective strategies.

8. You should give TWO approaches that Ms. Brown could take to *reduce some* of Fadia's disciplinary problems. Fadia creates real problems for Ms. Brown, and it seems that Ms. Brown is overwhelmed by other aspects of the classroom. The guidance counselor gives some clear guidance to Ms. Brown when she recommends that Ms. Brown call Fadia's parents, although you do not know what approaches might emerge from that discussion. You know that Fadia's disciplinary problems occur in other classes, not just in this class.

Following each approach, you should tell why that approach is likely to reduce Fadia's disciplinary problems—what there is about the approach that will reduce some of the problems.

You might recommend that Ms. Brown structure high-interest activities for Fadia that will lead to her success and explain that this approach will be successful because Fadia will be less likely to bother others if she has work that holds her interest and offers the opportunity for success. A recommendation that Ms. Brown call the parents is not appropriate. This action might lead to an effective strategy for reducing Fadia's disciplinary problems, but it is not an effective strategy in itself. The answer should include only effective strategies.

There are many other effective strategies.

9. You should give TWO strategies the supervisor could recommend to Ms. Brown to enable her to finish her lessons. The Supervisor's Summary report reveals the supervisor thinks that one reason Ms. Brown's lessons are too long is because she spends too much time on details. The supervisor also mentions that students are not actively involved in the lessons.

Following each suggestion, you should explain why the strategy will be effective in reducing the length of her lessons—what there is about the strategy that will make it effective.

You might recommend that Ms. Brown actively involves the students in the lessons, using student feedback to move the lesson along, and explain that this approach is likely to be effective because it may help Ms. Brown stop providing too much detail. A recommendation that Ms. Brown prepare less material is not appropriate because the Supervisor's Summary indicates that Ms. Brown does not prepare more information than she can present.

SCENARIO 4

10. You should give TWO approaches that Ms. Stendel could use to effectively involve Derek in cooperative group work. Cooperative Learning is a group of students working as a team toward a goal that will be reported, with a focus on individual responsibility, decision making, reflection, and positive interaction. Ms. Stendel's observation of Derek indicates that he is highly intelligent but uncooperative, although he is more involved when he feels more comfortable and more in control.

Following the description of each approach, explain why this approach would effectively involve Derek in cooperative group work.

You might suggest that Ms. Stendel assign each student in the group a specific responsibility, such as leader, recorder, reporter, questioner, or assessor. Perhaps questioner would be the best role for Derek. Explain that this approach would help to effectively involve Derek in cooperative group work because it would give him a specific task and make him feel more in control of the situation.

There are many other effective strategies.

11. You should give TWO techniques to help Derek with computation, and the techniques should be specific. The first step is to analyze his errors. Derek has trouble renaming in addition, he adds 6 and 4 to get 10 and just writes the 10 in the sum instead of writing 0 in the ones place and renaming ten ones as one ten. He has trouble aligning the partial products in multiplication. In division he subtracts incorrectly at the last step of the computation.

Following the description of each technique, explain why this technique would effectively help Derek with his arithmetic computation.

You might recommend that Derek do his computation on graph paper, writing digits in each square on the paper. Explain that this approach will help him align digits and at least help him overcome the computational errors he makes by misaligning partial products in multiplication.

There are many other effective strategies.

12. You should give TWO recommendations that a supervisor might give for effectively dealing with Derek. Derek seems angry, rejected by, and alienated from the other students in the class. He is unwilling to interact with them, let alone cooperate.

Following the description of the recommendation, explain why the strategies you recommend would be effective.

The one thing missing in this report about Derek is any information about his parents or his home life. You might say that the supervisor would recommend that Ms. Stendel involve Derek's parents and explain that this would be effective because parental involvement is known to be effective and because the teachers could learn more about Derek and work with the parents to help him feel less alienated.

There are many other effective strategies.

Multiple-Choice Answers

1. **(B)** This policy statement gives the best guidance to ensure that students have the most opportunities to use computers. (A) and (C) The committee's work is focused on computer use in classrooms, and these policies do not address that area. (D) This policy is not within the committee's control, and it holds little promise of helping because it would require additional approval to implement.

2. **(B)** Consider each Roman numeral in turn.

   I. Correct—Group learning means more student involvement.
   II. Incorrect—Cooperative learning groups do not lead to more content coverage. In fact, teacher-directed lessons would most likely lead to more content coverage.
   III. Correct—The more people involved, the more varied the outcomes.
   IV. Correct—A cooperative learning group means more brainstorming.

   I, III, and IV are correct. That's choice (B).

3. **(B)** Consider each Roman numeral in turn.

   I. Correct—High expectations are a hallmark of effective schools.
   II. Correct—Students do better when teachers and administrators are held accountable for their performances.
   III. Incorrect—Standardized tests are used in effective schools.

   I and II are correct; that's choice (B).

4. **(B)** Spending more time on a task is among a relatively few classroom practices shown to enhance learning. It has a proven and more powerful impact than all the other choices listed. There is room in the classroom for all the other choices. However, if Ms. Weiss had to choose, as you do, she would choose choice (B).

5. **(C)** This choice accurately describes why the special education teacher is in the classroom, to help special education students while the teacher conducts the lesson. (A) Frank Damico's job is to be the support, not to arrange for support. (B) and (D) are incorrect because Mr. Damico's responsibility is not with nonmainstreamed students, although he may spend some time working with these students.

6. **(B)** This is the best response to give a parent. It is positive and truthful, and it neither holds out too much hope nor is too negative. (A) is too positive and unrealistically raises a parent's expectations. (C) is likely the most candidly honest of the four responses. But it is too stark, and it is not the kind of response that should be given at a parent-teacher conference. (D) unnecessarily puts the parent off.

7. **(D)** It is a definition; vicarious learning means that children can learn from others' experiences rather than from direct experience. None of the other choices reflect the definition of vicarious learning.

8. **(D)** Reliability means that the same work consistently receives the same evaluation. Many schools that implemented portfolio assessment had to alter their policies because different teachers assigned widely different grades to the same portfolio. Clear rubrics or standards have to be established for portfolio assessment to be effective. (A) It is not the diverse group of work students put in portfolios that causes the problem. Rather, it is the way teachers assess these samples. (B) Machines do not typically score the materials in a portfolio. (C) This may be an issue under some circumstances; however, it is not an issue of reliability.

9. **(D)** This is the classic test-based definition of a learning disability—at or above average ability but achievement two or more years below grade level. (A) is incorrect. There is nothing in this record to indicate that the student is a poor test taker, and the IQ score of 110–115 may indicate that the child is not a poor test taker. (B) is incorrect. The student's achievement is well below the student's potential. (C) is incorrect. These IQ test results are not high enough for a gifted classification.

10. **(D)** A summative evaluation assesses what a student has learned about a specific objective or objectives. (A) A portfolio evaluation relies on samples of students' actual work. (B) and (C) Standardized tests and norm-referenced tests are essentially the same type of test. These tests have been standardized on a large population of students. End-of-chapter tests are not standardized.

11. **(C)** The first passage supports ability grouping, which means students should be grouped homogeneously by achievement. The passage indicates that there should be a separate grouping for each curricular area. Choices (A) and (D) are incorrect because they call for heterogeneous grouping—grouping not based on achievement. Choice (B) is incorrect because it calls for a single grouping based on ability to be applied to each individual curricular area.

12. **(A)** The main argument against Direct Instruction (DI) in the second passage is that it has been proven effective only for skills instruction. (B) and (C) are incorrect because the answer choices support DI. The support found in choice (C) is from the first passage and not the second passage. (D) is incorrect because the second passage acknowledges that Direct Instruction is a proven form of instruction.

13. **(D)** This choice identifies the approach that Ms. Zimbui should not use. It is improper to discuss individual student achievement with groups of parents. Even if the parents seem to agree to share the results, the practice can only lead to problems. The remaining choices give examples of ways to promote effective communication with parents.

14. **(C)** In a sense, a school board is responsible for everything in a district, and very little can happen without some sort of approval by the board. In practice the board has a more limited number of primary responsibilities.
Consider each Roman numeral in turn.

   I. Correct—This is one of the board's most important responsibilities.
   II. Incorrect—This is primarily an administrative responsibility.
   III. Incorrect—The board may make policy about school assignments but very rarely actually assigns a student to a school.
   IV. Correct—This is another of the board's most important responsibilities. The board has a responsibility to ensure that the long-term and short-term goals are being met.

   I and IV are correct. That is choice (C).

15. **(A)** Research shows that starting a lecture with a motivation, compared to the other choices, is the most effective way to enhance instruction. (B) It is good to make eye contact with students during a lecture. (C) Walking around the room, alone, does not enhance instruction. (D) A topic above students' *ability* levels detracts from the effectiveness of a lecture.

16. **(C)** Students in cooperative learning groups devise their own plan and work actively together to gather information. Usually, one member of the group reports the group's findings. (A) This kind of cooperation does not describe cooperative learning groups. (B) The teacher gives cooperative learning groups the topic, but group members themselves devise a working plan. (D) A cooperative learning group may do this, but working with cooperative extensions does not describe cooperative learning groups.

17. **(B)** IQ tests have a mean of 100 and a standard deviation of 10, and IQ scores from 90 to 100 are in the normal range. That means that 97 is in the normal range and that the other choices are incorrect. There is no evidence from this score that this student is mentally retarded.

18. **(D)** Minority students as a whole are *not* less capable than other students, but as a whole they do have fewer opportunities for learning at home, which tends to lower achievement scores. (A) Minority students are not less capable. (B) Parents of minority students are as concerned about their student's education as much as other parents. (C) Ms. Bisone should not lower learning expectations for her students. High expectations lead to more learning.

19. **(D)** The acceptable approach is for Ms. Bisone to modify the plans to account for the cultural heritage of the students in her class. (A) The topics should be those regularly taught in the school's United States history courses. (B) The objective should be at the same difficulty level, although Ms. Bisone may adapt her teaching approach. (C) It is fine for Ms. Bisone to help her students understand English in the context of learning history, but she should not adapt her objectives to become English objectives.

20. **(A)** Every teacher is a reading teacher. ESL means English as a second language, and LEP means limited English proficiency. Teaching English as a second language includes using context clues to identify words. (B) Teaching mathematics in the first language is an example of bilingual education. (C) Teaching English as a second language does not include instruction in the foreign language. (D) Standard spoken English is the goal, and ESL instruction does not encourage regional or local dialects.

21. **(C)** Students typically learn most when they are supervised by a teacher. (A) Some students may learn most when they work independently, but that is not typical. (B) Some parents are capable of appropriate supervision, but that is not usually the case. (D) Some students may learn most while they complete an appropriate assignment on a computer, but that is not where most successful learning occurs.

22. **(B)** Clicking on a hypertext word reveals a definition or underlying meaning. Hypertext links to word definitions hold tremendous promise for reading instruction. (A) The links do not tie together "hyper" ideas. (C) Links do not usually move or vibrate to draw attention. (D) A link may change color when clicked, but that is to let you know that you have visited that link before.

23. **(C)** A definite reward schedule, some means of giving rewards (points, paper coupons, plastic tokens), and a means of redeeming tokens or points are the essential ingredients of a token economy. (A) The word *token* in this choice means figurative and does not mean a real token to be handed out to children.

24. **(C)** It is during these grades that students turn most to peer groups and are most resistant to authority. The activity that one sees in the early grades and the maturity later in high school typically present fewer discipline problems than choice (C).

25. **(B)** Note the word NOT in the item. Sheltered Instruction distinguishes itself from many other ELL approaches by offering content instruction at or above grade level. (A) is incorrect because sheltered instruction programs do integrate these two theories of instruction. (C) and (D) are incorrect because sheltered instruction does move students toward English proficiency, and this program does place an emphasis on lesson preparation.

26. **(D)** Vicarious learning means learning from the experiences of others. The remaining choices are incorrect because none of them reflects this approach.

27. **(B)** The reading specialist was most likely going to say phonics does not address word meaning or reading comprehension. Phonics primarily addresses word recognition and word pronunciation. Each of the remaining choices describes a benefit that can be derived directly from the phonics approach.

28. **(D)** Consider each Roman numeral in turn and then choose your answer.
    I. Correct. It is a good technique to handle a question with encouragement for more explanation.
    II. Correct. It is effective to demonstrate how to respond to questions.
    III. Incorrect. It is generally not a good idea to answer quickly. Ms. Kirk may be able to help the student find the answer for him- or herself.
    IV. Correct. Students' questions often reveal what is most difficult for them to understand and it is a good technique to include their questions in evaluations.
    I, II, and IV are correct; that is Choice (D).

29. **(B)** This is the least effective method because this choice, alone, does NOT integrate haiku with fine arts because only art is displayed. Each of the remaining choices describes an effective way of integrating haiku and art.

30. **(D)** Students develop a better attitude toward reading when they use the real literature found in a whole-language approach. (A) It may be reassuring that an approach is widely accepted, but that is never the best reason to use it. (B) Word recognition must always be taught. Students cannot read if they cannot recognize words. (C) Research does not uniformly support the conclusion that students comprehend better after using a whole-language approach. Rather, it seems a combination of approaches, including aspects of the whole-language approach, best develops reading comprehension.

31. **(D)** Notice the term LEAST LIKELY in the question. This choice is best because sight vocabulary does not rely on phonics, which requires students to establish a relationship between graphemes and phonemes. However, (A) writing difficulties and (B) reading difficulties can both be compromised by auditory discrimination difficulties. Obviously, (C) can be compromised by auditory discrimination difficulties.

32. **(D)** One example of negative reinforcement means explaining how to improve positive outcomes. (A) Positive reinforcement is praise or rewards for good work. (B) Reverse psychology is suggesting the opposite of what you want a student to do. (C) Threats, or bullying, are not appropriate classroom techniques.

33. **(B)** This choice is correct because a basal reading program is not designed to meet the individual needs of students. Note the word NOT in the item. A basal program is typically designed to be used with all students in a class. A basal program must be supplemented to meet the individual needs of students. The remaining choices describe some of the characteristics of a basal reading program.

34. **(D)** Ms. Milano notices the reading difficulty when the student is reading mathematics problems. This indicates that the difficulty is reading in the context of mathematics and there is no mention that the reading problem occurs elsewhere. The remaining choices are all potential causes of reading difficulties, but not this reading difficulty, even though they may contribute to the problem in some way.

35. **(B)** Just because a student is below grade level in reading does *not* mean he or she cannot understand social studies topics that are on or above grade level. Do not adapt instruction to less difficult topics on the basis of a low reading level. Each of the remaining choices represents an acceptable way to adapt social studies instruction for students who are reading significantly below grade level.

36. **(A)** Authentic assessment means Mr. Rios will observe students as they work or review students' actual work as described in this choice. (B) Mr. Rios would not uses tests as a part of authentic assessment, although he may use them for other purposes in his class. (C) Authentic assessment does not have to be conducted in real-life settings. (D) Mr. Rios would not rely on evaluative information from other teachers as a part of authentic assessment.

37. **(B)** This choice describes the best way to consistently determine a student's writing ability, and to prepare for the future. The teacher gathers specific information that can be used for future plans. (A) Standardized grammar tests do not reveal detailed information about a student's writing. (C) Holistic evaluations reflect the evaluator's view of the overall quality of the writing. A holistic evaluation does not yield a specific analysis that can lead to instructional plans. (D) is incorrect because it evaluates reading, not writing.

38. **(C)** This choice describes the essence of the inquiry approach—to solve problems as a way to understand scientific principles. (A) is incorrect because a teacher must have prior experience with an experiment so he or she can guide students. (B) is incorrect because students analyze their thought processes when using the inquiry approach. (D) is incorrect because the inquiry approach is student centered not teacher centered.

39. **(B)** Clear and unambiguous objectives are fundamental and crucial to maintaining interest. There is a difference between students being responsive and students being interested in a lesson. (A) An animated presentation may maintain students' interest in the teacher but not in the lesson at hand unless the teacher has clear objectives in mind. (C) Students are typically not interested in a lesson because it holds the promise of subsequent understanding. (D) Leaving students with no choice does not maintain their interest.

40. **(B)** Mr. Yarborough should address questions to the entire class. This increases the likelihood that students will pay attention and actively think about an answer. (A) This technique focuses on just one student, and only that student will be thinking about an answer to the question. (C) This is a poor questioning technique, although some teachers use it to bring students back into the discussion. (D) This is a poor questioning technique that keeps the majority of students from full participation.

41. **(A)** Modeling means Mr. Yarborough does things he wants his students to copy or emulate. This choice shows that he is engaging in exactly that kind of behavior. (B) This is a different kind of model than the one Mr. Yarborough has in mind. (C) Mr. Yarborough would not model inappropriate behavior to be copied. (D) Talking about the ways things should be or showing students how things should be is not modeling how things should be.

42. **(A)** Consider each Roman numeral in turn.

I. Correct. This is an example of reinforcing behavior.

II. Correct. This is also a way to reinforce student behavior.

III. Incorrect. This is not a way to reinforce behavior, but rather a negative reinforcement.

I and II are correct. That is Choice (A).

43. **(C)** The answer to this is common sense, but it also fits Kounin's definition of what "with-it" teaching means. (A) Just being aware of techniques does not mean you use them. (B) This choice means "with-it" in one sense, but it does not describe an approach to teaching. (D) The respect from peers described in this choice is not an approach to teaching.

44. **(C)** During the first two years of high school students tend to follow peer leaders. By the last two years of high school students are more responsive to adult authority. (A) and (B). Both apply equally to ninth graders as to seniors. (D) Teachers who are constructively authoritative are usually best at discipline.

45. **(B)** It might be nice to think otherwise, but more than any other factor, grades are by far the most powerful student motivation.

46. **(D)** A prerequisite competency refers to some skill or knowledge a student must possess to learn a competency. In the sense used here, competency does not refer to teachers. (A) A competency refers to what the student must learn or do. (B) A prerequisite competency comes before the main objective; it is not a part of the main objective. (C) The term *prerequisite competency* does not apply to admission or transfer requirements.

47. **(B)** Children from immigrant families will often not benefit from extensive homework because there may not be help available from parents. (A) Lowering expectations does not help these students. (C) Teaching in the native language will not help these students because they need to master English to enjoy viable careers. This is different from helping children make the transition from their native language to English, which could be helpful. (D) This requirement is not helpful since English proficiency is beyond the capability of most of these students. However, it may be useful to ask students to make progress toward English proficiency.

48. **(A)** Evaluation is at the sixth and highest level of Bloom's cognitive taxonomy. (B) Comprehension is at the second level on the hierarchy of learning objectives. (C) Analysis is the fourth level and (D) application is the third level.

49. **(A)** Gardner's theory supports the use of interdisciplinary units. Gardner's theory holds that students have many intelligences, not just a cognitive intelligence. Interdisciplinary units promote utilization of these multiple intelligences. (B) Students do not need to know about the intelligences. (C) and (D) There is nothing in Gardner's theory that supports the elimination of assessments nor having students establish the criteria for quality.

50. **(C)** A criterion-referenced test measures a specific and usually limited set of objectives. (A) is incorrect because the criterion referred to is unrelated to a percentile score. (B) is incorrect because a criterion-referenced test does not measure a student's ability. (D) is incorrect because this type of test is not limited to constructed-response answers.

51. **(C)** Students learn best when the lesson is at their level of ability. Students become too frustrated when asked to do something they cannot do. Naturally, there is a difference between ability level and achievement level. Students frequently learn successfully when reasonably challenged beyond their achievement level, but not beyond their ability level. Lessons at advanced achievement levels can be adapted to a student's ability level.

52. **(B)** Inclusion means that the student is encouraged to participate fully in his or her "regular" classroom, often with the assistance of an inclusion teacher. (A) is incorrect because, while mainstreaming means the education of special education students in "regular" classrooms, the question asks about the inclusion teacher, and this choice does not mention that teacher. (C) is incorrect because the instruction is not limited to integrating topics. (D) is incorrect because inclusion teaching focuses on the content taught in the lesson.

53. **(B)** Minority students' achievement test performances tend to fall below students' ability level. The result is that minority students are overrepresented in lower tracks. (A) is incorrect because the flaws in the standardized tests are not deliberately designed to ensure lower performance among minority students. (C) is incorrect because this statement is not always true and is not the most appropriate reason for opposing tracking. (D) is incorrect because an administrator would be most likely to inflate scores.

54. **(C)** Students who are learning disabled benefit most from brief, structured assignments and auditory opportunities for learning. (A) Large-print books are most appropriate for students who are visually impaired. (B) It is useful to provide highly relevant reading materials, but this is not the most effective approach for students who are learning disabled. (D) It is not appropriate to just let a student "test out" without appropriate achievement gains.

55. **(D)** Glasser's theory features consequences for inappropriate behavior developed cooperatively by the students and the teacher. (A) is incorrect because Glasser emphasizes a cooperative relationship between the teacher and the students. (B) is incorrect because the students also participate in establishing the rules and the consequences. (C) is incorrect because the reality therapy approach is designed for the classroom.

56. **(B)** Metacognition means a student thinking about learning and being aware of his or her thought processes. The remaining choices are completely unrelated to metacognition.

57. **(D)** This choice identifies the approach that should not be used. It is improper to discuss individual student achievement with groups of parents. Even if the parents consent to share the results, the practice can only lead to problems. The remaining choices give examples of ways to promote effective communication with parents.

58. **(B)** There is very little in education about which we are absolutely sure—but time on task is one of them. It is well established that students learn more when they spend more time on task. The main goal of a classroom manager is to promote learning, and this is clearly the best choice. (A), (C), and (D) can be effective forms of classroom management, but none of them can match the proven positive impact of time on task.

59. **(D)** Holistic scoring is based on the evaluators' informed impression of the writing sample, not on a detailed analysis. (A) This choice may remind you of a hologram, but it has nothing to do with holistic scoring. (B) Tests scored holistically are often evaluated by several readers, but this does not happen in Ms. Crawford's class. (C) Holistic scoring is not about this kind of whole.

60. **(D)** The teacher should use this approach because it gives students time to think about the answer and helps maintain students' attention to the question. (A) is incorrect because calling on students quickly does not give them adequate time to formulate a response. (B) is incorrect because calling out answers makes for a chaotic classroom. (C) is incorrect because nothing is gained by forcing students to answer quickly when a few more seconds would permit a full and complete answer.

61. **(B)** Among the choices given, it would be best for the teacher to ask questions that can be answered correctly about 70 percent of the time. This approach provides a mix of difficult and easier questions. (A) is incorrect because the questions would be too easy if the teacher expected 90 percent of them to be answered correctly. Answers (C) and (D) are incorrect because the questions are too difficult if the teacher expected as few as 40 or 20 percent to be answered correctly.

62. **(C)** Note the word LEAST in the question. (C) gives students many options for exploration. This activity is least like direct teaching than the other activities described in the other answer choices.

63. **(D)** Note the word EXCEPT in the question. Just eliminating standardized tests does not characterize effective schools. All of the other choices are characteristics of effective schools.

64. **(B)** Note the word EXCEPT in the question. This choice is the least effective way of helping a student who is having difficulty in class. Many children will not benefit from extensive homework because there may not be help available from parents. The remaining choices are all effective ways to help a student who is having difficulty.

65. **(D)** Research consistently shows that SES correlates most significantly with the quality of an individual school. A correlation does not establish a cause and effect; however, students from more affluent families tend to do better in schools.

66. **(D)** The only conclusive information in Lionel's profile is that he appears to do better on authentic assessments. Authentic assessments can give students an opportunity to demonstrate achievement that may not show up on standardized tests. Authentic assessments can also be statistically unreliable. (A) is incorrect because his score of 7.9 is below average for ninth grade. (B) is incorrect because the last sentence says his writing score is above grade level for his class. (C) is incorrect because a score one single year below grade level and an above-average writing sample does not support the need for intensive help in writing.

67. **(B)** The grade level is derived from the entire national group of students who took the test. It is quite common for test scores of a class, a school, or a school district to vary from these standardized scores. (C) This statement is generally true. Generally, half of the students nationally who take a standardized test are below grade level. However, this

statement does not explain Lionel's test scores. Choices (A) and (D) do not offer correct explanations for Lionel's test scores.

68. **(A)** A weekly plan allocates available time to lessons. (B) is incorrect because the plan descriptions are reversed in this choice. (C) is incorrect because the first part is correct, but the second part is not practical because not enough is known at the beginning of the year to prepare these plans. (D) is incorrect because it is usually just the opposite. Teachers usually hand in plan books containing weekly plans.

69. **(A)** The ZPD approach means a teacher gives a student help that the student is ready to receive. To accomplish this task, the teacher must understand what the student knows and does not know about the skill or topic to be learned. (B) is incorrect because the ZPD approach does not rely on a student's developmental stage but on what the student knows and does not know. (C) and (D) are incorrect because the ZPD approach is not related to the student's physical proximity to the teacher.

70. **(D)** Piaget embraced the notion that students should learn actively through their own experiences. (A) is incorrect because the process of equilibration focuses on the learner. (B) is incorrect because Piaget's process does not support drill and practice. (C) is incorrect because equilibration does not mean learning from others' experiences.

PART VI

Elementary Education

Including Full-Length Practice Tests with Explained Answers

Elementary Education: Curriculum, Instruction, and Assessment

13

PASSING THE ELEMENTARY EDUCATION: CURRICULUM, INSTRUCTION, AND ASSESSMENT TEST (0011, 5011)

There is more than enough review information, test strategies, and practice tests in this book to pass the Elementary Education (0011, 5011) test. Remember, you are not competing with others for the highest score, you just need the minimum passing score for your state certification.

The state passing scores for the Elementary Education (0011, 5011) are in the lower 25 percent of all scores, and many passing scores are in the lower 10 percent. That means the vast majority of test takers pass the test. The high likelihood that you will pass the test is an important part of your preparation.

The raw score is the number of items you answer correctly. The raw score determines your scale score, which is the basis for passing the test. Different versions of the test are at different difficulty levels and the raw passing scores vary from version to version. Visit the ETS PRAXIS website for the most recent information about state passing scores.

HOW TO PREPARE FOR THE CURRICULUM, INSTRUCTION, AND ASSESSMENT TEST (0011, 5011)

This chapter prepares you to take the Elementary Education: Curriculum, Instruction, and Assessment Test (0011, 5011). The chapter gives an overview of each test and full-length practice tests with explained answers.

The Curriculum, Instruction, and Assessment Practice Test begins on page 471.

Preparation Strategies

Other sections in this book will help you prepare for these tests. The PLT Review beginning on page 365 will help you prepare for this test. The Proven Test-Preparation Strategies on page 22 will help you prepare for all the tests. The Proven Test-Taking Strategies on page 23 will help you pass the Curriculum, Instruction, and Assessment test.

ELEMENTARY EDUCATION: CURRICULUM, INSTRUCTION, AND ASSESSMENT (0011, 5011)

Overview

This 2-hour test has 110 multiple-choice items. Most items relate directly to school settings, while some items are more general. According to ETS, the items are based on the material a new teacher should know. You will encounter items from many grade levels. The items are based on the overall areas of curriculum, instruction, and assessment. The test is also based on the content areas of Reading/Language Arts, Mathematics, Science, Social Studies, Arts (including music) and Physical Education, and General Knowledge items about teaching.

This section includes a full practice test with explained answers.

The test itself is structured in one of two ways: (1) content area organization, or (2) overall area organization.

OVERALL AREA ORGANIZATION

The items for each overall area are grouped together. The items for the content areas are randomly distributed under each overall area. For example, all the curriculum items are grouped together. The subject area items related to curriculum are arranged in no particular order in the curriculum items.

CONTENT AREA ORGANIZATION

The items for each content area are grouped together. The items for the overall areas are randomly distributed under each content area. For example, all the reading items are grouped together. The curriculum, instruction, and assessment items for reading are arranged in no particular order in the reading items.

Overall Areas

Each overall area below contains questions about each of the six content areas. The following include the topics on which you may be tested in each overall area.

CURRICULUM

Curriculum questions ask about how each instructional area is organized, as well as how to choose and use the instructional materials and other resources available for teaching the subject. That is, curriculum questions may ask you to communicate why a subject is important to learn, or how subject areas are related, or how to integrate within and across subject areas, or about the textbooks and other materials, including technological resources and software, available for instruction.

INSTRUCTION

Instruction questions ask you about specific teaching approaches for a subject area. That is, curriculum questions may ask you to describe how to find out what students know and build on this knowledge, or how to prepare instructional activities that integrate within and across subject areas, or to choose learning and teaching approaches which might include cooperative learning, or how to motivate students to learn.

ASSESSMENT

Assessment questions ask you how to devise and implement assessment strategies. That is, assessment questions might ask you about the appropriateness of text-based and other assessment strategies, or about how to use informal assessment techniques, about authentic or portfolio assessment, and appropriate interpretation and reporting of assessment results.

Content Areas

Each content area below contains questions about curriculum, instruction, and assessment. The following include the topics on which you may be tested in each content area.

READING/LANGUAGE ARTS (35 PERCENT OR 38 ITEMS)

- The general purpose of teaching reading and language arts, including literacy
- Methodology including readiness, comprehension, word recognition, and teaching techniques
- Strategies for integrating reading, writing, listening, and speaking, children's literature
- Learning theories applied to teaching reading and writing, including constructivism, behaviorism, multiple intelligences, Piaget's stages of cognitive development, and others
- Curriculum, including objectives, overall scope and sequence, and instructional materials
- Assessing and interpreting students' reading and writing development, including teacher-made tests, standardized tests, and authentic (portfolio) assessment

Some test items may ask you to analyze students' work.

MATHEMATICS (20 PERCENT OR 22 ITEMS)

- The general purpose of teaching mathematics
- Methodology including pre-number activities, problem solving, numeration, operations, algorithms, geometry, estimation, reasonableness of results, probability, elementary statistics, calculators, and computers
- Learning theories applied to teaching mathematics, including constructivism, behaviorism, multiple intelligences, Piaget's stages of cognitive development, and others
- Curriculum including objectives, overall scope and sequence, and instructional materials
- Assessing and interpreting students' mathematics development, including teacher-made tests, standardized tests, and authentic (portfolio) assessment

Some test items may ask you to analyze students' work.

SCIENCE (10 PERCENT OR 11 ITEMS)

- The general purpose of teaching science
- Teaching methodology; observing and describing, formulating and testing hypotheses, experiments, data and data presentation, health and safety
- Learning theories applied to teaching science, including constructivism, behaviorism, multiple intelligences, Piaget's stages of cognitive development, and others

- Curriculum including objectives, overall scope and sequence, and instructional materials
- Assessing and interpreting students' science development, including teacher-made tests, standardized tests, and authentic (portfolio) assessment

Some test items may ask you to analyze students' experiments or experimental results.

SOCIAL STUDIES (10 PERCENT OR 11 ITEMS)

- The general purpose of teaching social studies
- Teaching methodology; people, social organization, government, economics, communication, transportation, data and data representation, building models, impact of technology, planning and problem solving
- Learning theories applied to teaching, including constructivism, behaviorism, multiple intelligences, Piaget's stages of cognitive development, and others
- Curriculum including objectives, overall scope and sequence, and instructional materials
- Assessing and interpreting students' social studies development, including teacher-made tests, standardized tests, and authentic (portfolio) assessment

ARTS (INCLUDING MUSIC) AND PHYSICAL EDUCATION (10 PERCENT OR 11 ITEMS)

- The general purpose of teaching the arts, music, and physical education
- Methodology and activities, color, texture, design, rhythm, melody, harmony, timbre, cultural influences, art and music as therapy, creativity, indoor and outdoor safety, activities and games appropriate to developmental level and sports, movement, coordination
- Learning theories applied to teaching the arts, music, and physical education, including constructivism, behaviorism, multiple intelligences, Piaget's stages of cognitive development, and others
- Curriculum including objectives, overall scope and sequence, and instructional materials
- Assessing and interpreting students' art and physical education development, including teacher-made tests, standardized tests, and authentic (portfolio) assessment

GENERAL CURRICULUM, INSTRUCTION, AND ASSESSMENT (15 PERCENT OR 17 ITEMS)

- Psychological and social basis for instruction including child development, emotional development, social development, and language development
- Hierarchy of thinking skills and classroom questions
- Classroom organization, management, discipline, and motivation
- Learning theories applied to teaching, including constructivism, behaviorism, multiple intelligences, Piaget's stages of cognitive development, and others
- Curriculum including objectives, overall scope and sequence, and instructional materials
- Assessment and interpretation of students' development, including teacher-made tests, standardized tests, and authentic (portfolio) assessment
- Use and interpretation of assessment of results including fundamental test and measurement concepts
- Relationships with parents and other colleagues

Elementary Education: Curriculum, Instruction, and Assessment (0011, 5011) Practice Test

14

COMPUTER DELIVERED: 110 ITEMS, 2 HOURS

The items about Curriculum, Instruction, and Assessment are arranged under each content area. The test you take may have items organized by the overall areas of Curriculum, Instruction, and Assessment, with the content items arranged under each of these headings. There are many different versions of this test, and the version you take may have a different emphasis and focus than this practice test.

Take this test in a realistic, timed setting. The setting will be most realistic if another person times the test and ensures that the test rules are followed. If another person is acting as test supervisor, he or she should review these instructions with you and say "START" when you should begin a section and "STOP" when time is up.

You have 2 hours to complete the test. Keep the time limit in mind as you work. There is no penalty for guessing. You may write on the test and mark up the questions. Each item has four answer choices. Only one of these choices is correct.

Mark your choice on the test or the answer sheet on pages 473–474. Use a pencil to mark the answer. The actual test will be machine scored so completely darken in the answer space. Once the test is complete, correct the answer sheet and review the answer explanations.

When instructed, turn the page and begin.

ANSWER SHEET
Elementary Education
Practice Test

Reading/Language Arts

1. Ⓐ Ⓑ Ⓒ Ⓓ	11. Ⓐ Ⓑ Ⓒ Ⓓ	21. Ⓐ Ⓑ Ⓒ Ⓓ	31. Ⓐ Ⓑ Ⓒ Ⓓ
2. Ⓐ Ⓑ Ⓒ Ⓓ	12. Ⓐ Ⓑ Ⓒ Ⓓ	22. Ⓐ Ⓑ Ⓒ Ⓓ	32. Ⓐ Ⓑ Ⓒ Ⓓ
3. Ⓐ Ⓑ Ⓒ Ⓓ	13. Ⓐ Ⓑ Ⓒ Ⓓ	23. Ⓐ Ⓑ Ⓒ Ⓓ	33. Ⓐ Ⓑ Ⓒ Ⓓ
4. Ⓐ Ⓑ Ⓒ Ⓓ	14. Ⓐ Ⓑ Ⓒ Ⓓ	24. Ⓐ Ⓑ Ⓒ Ⓓ	34. Ⓐ Ⓑ Ⓒ Ⓓ
5. Ⓐ Ⓑ Ⓒ Ⓓ	15. Ⓐ Ⓑ Ⓒ Ⓓ	25. Ⓐ Ⓑ Ⓒ Ⓓ	35. Ⓐ Ⓑ Ⓒ Ⓓ
6. Ⓐ Ⓑ Ⓒ Ⓓ	16. Ⓐ Ⓑ Ⓒ Ⓓ	26. Ⓐ Ⓑ Ⓒ Ⓓ	36. Ⓐ Ⓑ Ⓒ Ⓓ
7. Ⓐ Ⓑ Ⓒ Ⓓ	17. Ⓐ Ⓑ Ⓒ Ⓓ	27. Ⓐ Ⓑ Ⓒ Ⓓ	37. Ⓐ Ⓑ Ⓒ Ⓓ
8. Ⓐ Ⓑ Ⓒ Ⓓ	18. Ⓐ Ⓑ Ⓒ Ⓓ	28. Ⓐ Ⓑ Ⓒ Ⓓ	38. Ⓐ Ⓑ Ⓒ Ⓓ
9. Ⓐ Ⓑ Ⓒ Ⓓ	19. Ⓐ Ⓑ Ⓒ Ⓓ	29. Ⓐ Ⓑ Ⓒ Ⓓ	
10. Ⓐ Ⓑ Ⓒ Ⓓ	20. Ⓐ Ⓑ Ⓒ Ⓓ	30. Ⓐ Ⓑ Ⓒ Ⓓ	

Mathematics

39. Ⓐ Ⓑ Ⓒ Ⓓ	45. Ⓐ Ⓑ Ⓒ Ⓓ	51. Ⓐ Ⓑ Ⓒ Ⓓ	57. Ⓐ Ⓑ Ⓒ Ⓓ
40. Ⓐ Ⓑ Ⓒ Ⓓ	46. Ⓐ Ⓑ Ⓒ Ⓓ	52. Ⓐ Ⓑ Ⓒ Ⓓ	58. Ⓐ Ⓑ Ⓒ Ⓓ
41. Ⓐ Ⓑ Ⓒ Ⓓ	47. Ⓐ Ⓑ Ⓒ Ⓓ	53. Ⓐ Ⓑ Ⓒ Ⓓ	59. Ⓐ Ⓑ Ⓒ Ⓓ
42. Ⓐ Ⓑ Ⓒ Ⓓ	48. Ⓐ Ⓑ Ⓒ Ⓓ	54. Ⓐ Ⓑ Ⓒ Ⓓ	60. Ⓐ Ⓑ Ⓒ Ⓓ
43. Ⓐ Ⓑ Ⓒ Ⓓ	49. Ⓐ Ⓑ Ⓒ Ⓓ	55. Ⓐ Ⓑ Ⓒ Ⓓ	
44. Ⓐ Ⓑ Ⓒ Ⓓ	50. Ⓐ Ⓑ Ⓒ Ⓓ	56. Ⓐ Ⓑ Ⓒ Ⓓ	

Science

61. Ⓐ Ⓑ Ⓒ Ⓓ	64. Ⓐ Ⓑ Ⓒ Ⓓ	67. Ⓐ Ⓑ Ⓒ Ⓓ	70. Ⓐ Ⓑ Ⓒ Ⓓ
62. Ⓐ Ⓑ Ⓒ Ⓓ	65. Ⓐ Ⓑ Ⓒ Ⓓ	68. Ⓐ Ⓑ Ⓒ Ⓓ	71. Ⓐ Ⓑ Ⓒ Ⓓ
63. Ⓐ Ⓑ Ⓒ Ⓓ	66. Ⓐ Ⓑ Ⓒ Ⓓ	69. Ⓐ Ⓑ Ⓒ Ⓓ	

Social Studies

72. Ⓐ Ⓑ Ⓒ Ⓓ	75. Ⓐ Ⓑ Ⓒ Ⓓ	78. Ⓐ Ⓑ Ⓒ Ⓓ	81. Ⓐ Ⓑ Ⓒ Ⓓ
73. Ⓐ Ⓑ Ⓒ Ⓓ	76. Ⓐ Ⓑ Ⓒ Ⓓ	79. Ⓐ Ⓑ Ⓒ Ⓓ	82. Ⓐ Ⓑ Ⓒ Ⓓ
74. Ⓐ Ⓑ Ⓒ Ⓓ	77. Ⓐ Ⓑ Ⓒ Ⓓ	80. Ⓐ Ⓑ Ⓒ Ⓓ	

ANSWER SHEET
Elementary Education
Practice Test

Arts and Physical Education

83. Ⓐ Ⓑ Ⓒ Ⓓ   86. Ⓐ Ⓑ Ⓒ Ⓓ   89. Ⓐ Ⓑ Ⓒ Ⓓ   92. Ⓐ Ⓑ Ⓒ Ⓓ
84. Ⓐ Ⓑ Ⓒ Ⓓ   87. Ⓐ Ⓑ Ⓒ Ⓓ   90. Ⓐ Ⓑ Ⓒ Ⓓ   93. Ⓐ Ⓑ Ⓒ Ⓓ
85. Ⓐ Ⓑ Ⓒ Ⓓ   88. Ⓐ Ⓑ Ⓒ Ⓓ   91. Ⓐ Ⓑ Ⓒ Ⓓ

General Knowledge

94. Ⓐ Ⓑ Ⓒ Ⓓ   99. Ⓐ Ⓑ Ⓒ Ⓓ   104. Ⓐ Ⓑ Ⓒ Ⓓ   109. Ⓐ Ⓑ Ⓒ Ⓓ
95. Ⓐ Ⓑ Ⓒ Ⓓ   100. Ⓐ Ⓑ Ⓒ Ⓓ   105. Ⓐ Ⓑ Ⓒ Ⓓ   110. Ⓐ Ⓑ Ⓒ Ⓓ
96. Ⓐ Ⓑ Ⓒ Ⓓ   101. Ⓐ Ⓑ Ⓒ Ⓓ   106. Ⓐ Ⓑ Ⓒ Ⓓ
97. Ⓐ Ⓑ Ⓒ Ⓓ   102. Ⓐ Ⓑ Ⓒ Ⓓ   107. Ⓐ Ⓑ Ⓒ Ⓓ
98. Ⓐ Ⓑ Ⓒ Ⓓ   103. Ⓐ Ⓑ Ⓒ Ⓓ   108. Ⓐ Ⓑ Ⓒ Ⓓ

READING/LANGUAGE ARTS

38 ITEMS

1. Fifth-grade students are starting to read a book about American colonists. Students are most likely to use context to learn the meaning of new social studies terms when the teacher

    Ⓐ shows students how to examine surrounding words and phrases.

    Ⓑ shows students how to use a dictionary and to distinguish among the various meanings of a word.

    Ⓒ asks students to try to activate their prior knowledge about the word's meaning.

    Ⓓ provides content material about American colonists and events occurring during Colonial times.

2. Which of the following would be most appropriate for an upper elementary teacher to use to evaluate students' writing techniques and plan for further writing experiences?

    Ⓐ Administer a standardized grammar test and use the scores as a planning device.

    Ⓑ Use a writing checklist to assess a variety of creative writing samples that include writing summaries and samples.

    Ⓒ Have the students prepare a composition on a subject of their choice and holistically evaluate the composition.

    Ⓓ Have the students answer a series of higher-level, short-answer questions about a specific writing sample.

3. Which of the following describes a prerequisite competency in language arts?

    Ⓐ The knowledge and skills a teacher must possess to teach about subject–verb agreement

    Ⓑ A sub-objective to the main objective about subject–verb agreement

    Ⓒ The test for admitting students to language arts classes when they come in from another school

    Ⓓ The knowledge and skills students must possess to learn about subject–verb agreement

4. Lisa writes well, understands verbal directions, but often has trouble understanding written directions. Her difficulty might be related to all of the following EXCEPT

    Ⓐ auditory discrimination.

    Ⓑ visual discrimination.

    Ⓒ sight vocabulary.

    Ⓓ context clues.

5. A lesson on reading comprehension strategies features semantic organizers, which means it could include all of the following EXCEPT

    Ⓐ to help students group words according to like characteristics.

    Ⓑ to ask students to find words ending in "e" in a group of words.

    Ⓒ to ask students to practice finding missing words in a group of sentences.

    Ⓓ to ask students to partition words into groups of nouns or verbs.

6. A student has trouble reading the problems in the mathematics textbook. This difficulty is most likely to be the result of

Ⓐ faulty word identification and recognition.

Ⓑ inability to locate and retain specific facts.

Ⓒ deficiencies in basic comprehension abilities.

Ⓓ inability to adapt to reading needs in this content field.

7. Which of the following goals would NOT be met through choral reading?

Ⓐ To help students to feel part of a group

Ⓑ To appreciate oral reading

Ⓒ To develop an interest in creative forms of language

Ⓓ To help students interpret meaning

8. A child has difficulty pronouncing a printed word. The problem may reflect all of the following EXCEPT

Ⓐ phonetic analysis.

Ⓑ sight vocabulary.

Ⓒ language comprehension.

Ⓓ context analysis.

9. Personal journals should NOT be used as a

Ⓐ record of feelings.

Ⓑ way to share thoughts with others.

Ⓒ means of expressing thought.

Ⓓ means for writing ideas.

10. Which of the following best describes a class activity that uses instructional scaffolding to help students learn the meaning of new words?

Ⓐ The teacher offers help to students as the students learn new words, and then slowly withdraws that help as students become proficient.

Ⓑ The teacher presents students with a clear structure so that students slowly "climb" to a final understanding of the meaning of new words.

Ⓒ The teacher shows students how to build a set of skills, such as meaning in context and dictionary usage, that enable students to use that "scaffold" of skills to build word meaning.

Ⓓ The teacher shows students how to build a "scaffold" of meanings and definitions and then how to associate words with the meaning they find in this existing structure.

11. The most important thing a student can do when writing is to

Ⓐ decide on the best order for presenting ideas.

Ⓑ have a clear beginning.

Ⓒ keep the audience and purpose in mind.

Ⓓ support the main idea.

12. Which of the following is NOT furthered by a phonics approach?

Ⓐ Associating sounds with printed letters
Ⓑ Reading comprehension
Ⓒ Attacking new words independently
Ⓓ Developing a sight vocabulary

13. At the beginning of a lesson the teacher says, "OK class, today we're going to learn about reading history." This type of statement is referred to as

Ⓐ an anticipatory set.
Ⓑ a motivation.
Ⓒ an objective.
Ⓓ an advanced organizer.

14. The second-grade teacher is considering a whole language approach. Which of the following is the best reason to institute the program?

Ⓐ Whole language instruction is widely accepted.
Ⓑ It is not necessary to teach word recognition.
Ⓒ Children comprehend more after using a whole language approach.
Ⓓ Children have a better attitude toward reading.

15. During a unit on animal stories, sixth-grade students read *Lad a Dog*, by Albert Payson Terhune. The teacher wants to use transactional strategy instruction to help students develop a deeper understanding of the cognitive process involved in understanding Lad's "motivations" as described in the book. Which of the following indicates the teacher is using this approach?

Ⓐ The teacher explicitly explains the processes involved in successful reading comprehension.
Ⓑ The teacher encourages students to explore the processes involved in successful reading comprehension.
Ⓒ The teacher and students cooperate to jointly explore the processes involved in successful reading instruction.
Ⓓ The teacher asks students to explore the processes involved in successful reading comprehension.

16. As a part of a writing program, a teacher uses a computer-based multimedia encyclopedia. The multimedia encyclopedia includes hypertext links in most of its articles. These hypertext links are highlighted words

Ⓐ that link together very (hyper) important ideas in the passage.
Ⓑ linked to underlying meanings.
Ⓒ that move or vibrate to draw attention to important ideas.
Ⓓ that can be clicked with a mouse cursor to change color.

17. A third-grade teacher who emphasizes the relationship between reading and mathematics posts this problem for his students to read critically and to solve.

Charles is traveling on a bus. Charles leaves work at 6:15 P.M. The bus travels 15 minutes on Forest Street, then 20 minutes on Quincy Avenue, then 25 minutes on Chestnut Street. What time does Charles get home?

The teacher most likely asked the students to read the problem critically in order to

Ⓐ experience a reading passage that included both words and numerals.
Ⓑ detect if there is too much or too little information in a passage.
Ⓒ notice that a story about a boy's life could include numerical information.
Ⓓ develop a visual image of the trip described in the passage.

18. A fourth-grade student hands in a writing assignment containing this sentence.

I are going swimming.

This assignment indicates that the student needs more help with which of the following?

Ⓐ Subject–verb agreement
Ⓑ Pronouns
Ⓒ Sentence fragments
Ⓓ Adjectives and adverbs

19. Your class reads a science fiction story about space travel. Which of the following actions on your part is most likely to help students differentiate between science fact and science fiction?

Ⓐ Guide students to understand that science fiction stories are creative writing and not based on science fact.
Ⓑ Guide students as they identify examples of science fact and science fiction based on the story they just completed.
Ⓒ Ask students to work independently to make their own list of science fact and science fiction.
Ⓓ Ask students to work independently as they identify examples of science fact and science fiction in the story they just completed.

20. Which of the following reading activities would engage a student at the highest level of the *Revised Taxonomy of Educational Objectives: Cognitive Domain*?

Ⓐ Evaluate a reading passage
Ⓑ Understand a reading passage
Ⓒ Analyze a reading passage
Ⓓ Apply the contents of a reading passage to a real-world situation

21. You have a number of long newspaper articles about whales. Which of the following approaches on your part is most likely to best inform students about the main idea(s) of each article?

Ⓐ Students work independently and summarize for themselves the main point(s) of each article.

Ⓑ Students work in cooperative learning groups to summarize and present the main point(s) of each article.

Ⓒ You present a brief summary of the main point(s) of each article.

Ⓓ You prepare a brief summary of the main point(s) of each article and distribute them to your students.

22. A young student writes about a sailor on a four-masted schooner. The student's writing contains this sentence.

He had enuf rope to tie up the boat.

Which of the actions on the part of the teacher listed below addresses the errors in the sentence?

Ⓐ Instruction on phonics-based word attack skills

Ⓑ Instruction on context-based word attack skills

Ⓒ Instruction on the use of homonyms

Ⓓ Instruction on variable spelling phonemes

23. A teacher wants to use a token economy system to motivate students during reading. Which of the following actions on the part of the teacher is most consistent with this approach?

Ⓐ The teacher provides token (symbolic) reinforcement for work completed by students as opposed to real or meaningful reinforcement.

Ⓑ The teacher distributes subway and bus tokens for reinforcement since this approach was pioneered in urban areas where many students took buses and subways to school.

Ⓒ The number of points that students can receive is posted and students may exchange a certain number of points for a more tangible reward.

Ⓓ The teacher posts a "token of my appreciation list" on the bulletin board and lists the names of students who perform outstanding work.

24. A teacher finished a three-day unit on nouns. He wants to be sure students learned the material in the unit. Which of the following assessment techniques would be best for the teacher to use?

Ⓐ Obtain and have the students complete a standardized assessment.

Ⓑ Prepare and have the students complete a teacher-made assessment.

Ⓒ Observe students' writing over the next week.

Ⓓ Review writing that students have previously completed.

25. A teacher wants to use the Orton-Gillingham approach with a student who is having difficulty reading. The following actions on the part of the teacher are consistent with that approach EXCEPT

Ⓐ teaching synthetic phonics.

Ⓑ generally discouraging independent reading.

Ⓒ emphasizing reading for meaning.

Ⓓ using a dictionary to learn word pronunciation.

26. A fourth-grade teacher wants to conduct an ongoing assessment of her language arts program. Which one of the following actions on the part of the teacher would NOT indicate that the assessment was underway?

Ⓐ The teacher walks around the room regularly observing students' writing.

Ⓑ The teacher asks students to hand in their written work at the end of the day.

Ⓒ The teacher gives students an in-class composition assignment about the environment.

Ⓓ The teacher regularly collects performance samples of students' work.

27. Which of the following would be the best opportunity for a formative evaluation of a student's writing?

Ⓐ A discussion with the student

Ⓑ A portfolio of the student's writing samples

Ⓒ Iowa Test of Basic Skills

Ⓓ End of unit test

28. You are meeting with the parents of a sixth-grade student to interpret their child's test scores. A standardized reading test shows the student at the 34th percentile in reading. Which of the following is the best explanation of this reading score?

Ⓐ "This means that your child did better on this test than all but 34 students."

Ⓑ "This means that your child did better than all but 34 percent of the students who took this test."

Ⓒ "This means that your child did better than 34 percent of the students who took this test."

Ⓓ "This means that your child has better reading ability than 34 percent of the students who took this test."

29. Parents of a fourth-grade child are meeting with the teacher to discuss the child's progress in language arts. A standardized English test shows a grade equivalent of 4.3. The average grade equivalent for the fourth grade in that school is 4.4. Which of the following is the best explanation of the child's language arts score?

Ⓐ "Your child is above average in language arts."

Ⓑ "Your child's language arts achievement is about average."

Ⓒ "Your child's language arts achievement is almost at the level of a 4-year-old."

Ⓓ "Your child's language arts achievement is below average."

30. A teacher is using an ESL approach to teach reading to a group of LEP students. Which of the following actions on the part of the teacher is most consistent with that approach?

Ⓐ Use context clues to help students identify English words.
Ⓑ Help students learn to read in the student's native language.
Ⓒ Translate English reading passages into the student's native language.
Ⓓ Ask students to bring in original literature in the student's native language.

31. A teacher administers an end of chapter test from the teacher's edition of a language arts text. In all likelihood, this is a

Ⓐ formative evaluation.
Ⓑ standardized test.
Ⓒ norm-referenced test.
Ⓓ summative evaluation.

32. A fourth-grade teacher keeps a portfolio of written work for a student. In her opinion, the writing samples are well above average for fourth-graders in that school. A standardized language arts test administered last month shows a writing grade equivalent of 3.2. Which of the following is the best description of the child's language arts achievement?

Ⓐ The child is above average in writing for his grade level.
Ⓑ The child is below average in writing for his grade level.
Ⓒ The child needs intensive help in writing at his grade level.
Ⓓ The child seems to do better when evaluated in real-world settings.

33. A fifth-grade student hands in this writing sample.

> I sat in the audience while my sister play
> the clarinet. I saw her play while sit there.
> I guess I will never be a profesional musician.

The teacher is most likely to help improve this student's writing by providing instruction in which of the following areas?

Ⓐ Nouns
Ⓑ Pronouns
Ⓒ Spelling
Ⓓ Verbs

34. A teacher wants to use cooperative learning groups for language arts instruction. Which of the following practices is LEAST consistent with this approach to classroom instruction?

Ⓐ Group members devise a working plan
Ⓑ Group members are actively involved in learning
Ⓒ Groups include 10 to 12 members
Ⓓ The teacher presents the project or topic to be worked on

35. A primary teacher wants to produce the most significant reading benefits for his students. Which of the following actions on the part of the teacher is most likely to create that benefit?

Ⓐ Providing a literature-rich environment
Ⓑ Providing effective phonics instruction
Ⓒ Providing opportunities for oral expression and listening
Ⓓ Using real literature sources instead of basal texts

36. A classroom teacher is using the whole language approach as a part of reading instruction. The whole language approach is based on the work of which of the following?

Ⓐ Marie Clay's Reading Recovery
Ⓑ James Pitman's Initial Teaching Alphabet
Ⓒ Jean Piaget's developmental levels of learning
Ⓓ John Dewey's Progressive Education movement

37. Which of the following is the most reasonable explanation of why a child's standardized reading test score is above grade level, but below average for that class?

Ⓐ The student correctly answered more questions on the first test.
Ⓑ The class did better on average than the entire group of students who took the test.
Ⓒ Half of those who take the test are below average.
Ⓓ The averages are different because the number of students in each group is different.

38. Which of the following is the most appropriate first step to modify plans to meet the needs of a student with a standardized reading score significantly below grade level?

Ⓐ Modify the plans to account for learning style.
Ⓑ Modify the plans to account for differences in achievement level.
Ⓒ Modify the plans to provide peer tutoring.
Ⓓ Modify the plans to incorporate alternative evaluation techniques.

MATHEMATICS

22 ITEMS

39. Here are some examples of a student's work.

$$
\begin{array}{r}
0.036 \\
\times\ \ 1.23 \\
\hline
0.4428
\end{array}
\qquad
\begin{array}{r}
1.24 \\
\times\ \ 1.04 \\
\hline
12.896
\end{array}
\qquad
\begin{array}{r}
5.79 \\
\times\ \ 2.4 \\
\hline
13.896
\end{array}
$$

The student continues to make the same type of error. Which of the following is the student's answer to 0.08×1.04?

- Ⓐ 0.0832
- Ⓑ 0.832
- Ⓒ 8.32
- Ⓓ 83.2

40. After examining the diagram of the polygon below the student states that the perimeter is 23 units. Which of the following statements by the teacher is most likely to help the student?

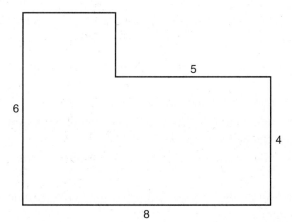

- Ⓐ Check your addition.
- Ⓑ Tracing each side of the shape with her finger, state the length of each side.
- Ⓒ Count the number of sides of the polygon.
- Ⓓ Use a rule for finding perimeter.

41. Which of the following is the best approach to teaching a first lesson on percent to a fourth-grade class?

    Ⓐ A written explanation of what a percent is
    Ⓑ A 100's chart
    Ⓒ Illustrations on the chalkboard
    Ⓓ Manipulative materials

42.

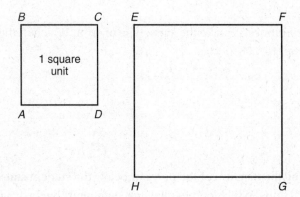

    After examining the illustration above, a student gave an answer of 2 for the area of the larger polygon. How can the teacher best help the student understand the error?

    Ⓐ Suggest the student trace the small square and compare that to the tracing of the larger square.
    Ⓑ Suggest the student get a ruler and measure.
    Ⓒ Suggest the student cut out the small square and find out how many small squares fit inside the large square.
    Ⓓ Suggest the student estimate the increase in distance between *BC* and *EF*.

43. Which of the following is the LEAST appropriate mathematics objective to teach using manipulative materials?

    Ⓐ Adding single-digit numbers
    Ⓑ Solving problems using the strategy "make an organized list"
    Ⓒ Adding double-digit numbers
    Ⓓ Dividing decimals

44. A teacher is planning a middle school mathematics unit. Which of the following would most likely lead to successful learning?

    Ⓐ Students are listening to a lesson at their ability level.
    Ⓑ Students are listening to a lesson and challenged beyond their ability level.
    Ⓒ Students are actively participating in a lesson at their ability level.
    Ⓓ Students are actively participating and challenged beyond their ability level.

45. A student consistently makes addition mistakes such as the one shown below.

$$13 + 9 = 112$$

Instruction in which of the following areas is most likely to help the student overcome this problem?

Ⓐ Lining up decimal points
Ⓑ Place value
Ⓒ Addition facts
Ⓓ Writing number sentences

46. A teacher wants to use one of Piaget's conservation tasks to check a student's number concept development. Which of the following actions on the part of the teacher represents a conservation task?

Ⓐ The teacher shows the student a group of attribute shapes. The child can match like shapes.
Ⓑ The teacher gives the student six-sided number cubes numbered 1–6. The child can place the cubes with the correct number on top when asked by the teacher.
Ⓒ The teacher shows the student a linear pattern of attribute blocks. The child can successfully duplicate the linear pattern formed by the teacher.
Ⓓ The teacher shows the student two matched rows of checkers. The child knows the number of checkers has not changed when one of the rows is spread out.

47. Given below is a list of mathematics concepts.

   I.   Multiplying 4×3
   II. Solving $3x = 12$
   III. Joining together 4 groups of 3 blocks
   IV. Drawing 3 lines vertically and 4 lines horizontally to create 12 crossing points

Which of the following best represents the order in which these concepts should be taught?

Ⓐ III, IV, I, II
Ⓑ III, I, IV, II
Ⓒ IV, III, II, I
Ⓓ IV, I, III, II

48. A teacher is considering reviewing arithmetic computation. For which of the following examples does a student need the most in-depth understanding of the relationship among arithmetic operations?

Ⓐ $7/9 \times 1/5 =$
Ⓑ $7/9 + 1/5 =$
Ⓒ $35 \div 7 =$
Ⓓ $392 + 26 =$

49. A primary goal of an upper-elementary grade school mathematics curriculum is that students should learn to use indirect measurement to find the height or length of objects. Which of the following student activities best helps meet that goal?

Ⓐ Students estimate the length of the hallway outside the classroom.

Ⓑ Students measure the length of the shadow cast by a pole.

Ⓒ Students use a tape measure to find the width of the classroom to find the width of another same-size classroom.

Ⓓ Students measure their own height, and then stand next to a pole to estimate the height of the pole.

50. A fifth-grade teacher wants to introduce students to the number pi (3.14159 . . .). The teacher plans to use the Internet to research the number. Which of the following actions on the part of the teacher will be LEAST helpful?

Ⓐ Use a search engine to look up pi.

Ⓑ Send e-mails to others to find out about pi.

Ⓒ Type in a web address that seems related to pi.

Ⓓ Use a chat program to discuss pi with others.

51. A teacher wants to give students experiences making triangles. Which of the following instructional aids will be most helpful?

Ⓐ String

Ⓑ Geoboard

Ⓒ Popsicle sticks

Ⓓ Ruler and pencil

52. A teacher is helping young students learn about counting. The teacher uses shapes as counters and makes sure students point to a shape each time they say the next numeral. Why is the teacher using this approach?

Ⓐ The teacher wants to be sure the students are paying attention to what they are doing.

Ⓑ The teacher wants to be sure students are developing eye-hand coordination.

Ⓒ The teacher is going to ask the students questions about the shapes once they have finished counting.

Ⓓ The teacher wants to be sure the students are not just saying counting words.

53. During a second-grade mathematics lesson, the teacher presents this problem.

There are 43 people on the camping trip.
If 5 people can fit in a tent, what is the least number of tents needed?

Which of the following is the best strategy for solving this problem?

Ⓐ Guess and check

Ⓑ Interpret the remainder

Ⓒ Make an organized list

Ⓓ Choose the operation

54. A student has difficulty aligning partial products in multiplication as shown below.

$$
\begin{array}{r}
119 \\
\times\ 258 \\
\hline
952 \\
515 \\
238 \\
\hline
\end{array}
$$

Which of the following actions is the most appropriate first step for the teacher to take?

Ⓐ Reteach the concept of place value.
Ⓑ Give the student graph paper to write the multiplication problems.
Ⓒ Reteach two-digit multiplication and then return to three-digit multiplication.
Ⓓ Show the child how to write placeholder zeroes in blank spaces of the partial products.

55. A primary teacher is about to engage the class in a lesson on adding the value of coins. Which of the following actions on the part of the teacher is most likely to motivate student interest in the lesson?

Ⓐ "Hi everyone—I have some make-believe coins. I'll hold them up and tell you what each coin is worth."
Ⓑ "Here are some make-believe coins. Pretend I am a bank. We'll add as you put the coins in."
Ⓒ "Does anyone know when coins were first used? It is interesting because coins were used a long time ago."
Ⓓ "Before we begin, let me review with you the value of each one of these coins. Knowing the value of the coins is the secret to our lesson today."

56. In a primary grade, each student is given a number line numbered 1 to 30, a group of 30 beans, paper, and pencil. The teacher then gives the students this problem.

There are 7 marbles in each bag, and there are 4 bags in all. Use any of the materials you have to find the total number of marbles in the four bags.

Which of the following learning approaches is most consistent with the teacher's actions?

Ⓐ Problem solving
Ⓑ Constructivist
Ⓒ Modeling
Ⓓ Manipulatives

57. A teacher discusses the results of a mathematics unit test with a student's parents. The student received 85 percent on the test. Which of the following is the best interpretation of this test score?

  Ⓐ This score shows that the child is above average in mathematics.
  Ⓑ This score puts the child at the 85th percentile.
  Ⓒ This score shows that the child did well on this test.
  Ⓓ This score shows that the child needs further review before moving on to the next chapter.

58. Each morning, a teacher presents a mathematics problem for students to solve during the day. Which of the following describes the most effective technique the teacher can use to assess students' solutions?

  Ⓐ Observation
  Ⓑ Standardized test
  Ⓒ Cooperative learning
  Ⓓ Portfolio assessment

59. A teacher establishes cooperative learning groups to work on mathematics projects, meaning that the teacher is most likely basing these efforts on the works of

  Ⓐ Howard Gardner.
  Ⓑ Johnson and Johnson.
  Ⓒ Madeline Hunter.
  Ⓓ Holdaway and Clark.

60. A school district committee wants to formulate a policy for calculator use. Which of the choices below represents the most appropriate policy?

  Ⓐ Calculators should be banned from classrooms until high school.
  Ⓑ Calculators should not be used when the reason for the lesson is to teach computation.
  Ⓒ Calculators should not be used to add, subtract, multiply, or divide. These operations should be completed only by hand.
  Ⓓ Calculators should be used only to check paper and pencil computations.

SCIENCE

11 ITEMS

61. A group of advanced fourth-graders had difficulty understanding the resistance (R)–fulcrum (F)–effort (E) characteristics of levers. Which of the following activities would best help students understand these concepts?

    Ⓐ Arrange a variety of levers RFE, FRE, and FER in order so that the students can demonstrate where to place a lever on a fulcrum to reduce or increase effort.

    Ⓑ Have students classify a group of pictorial representations of levers into RFE, FRE, and FER groups.

    Ⓒ Read a textbook description of each type of lever and list examples under each type.

    Ⓓ Chart the resistance and effort levels of different types of levers.

62. When responding to children's science questions, a teacher should do all the following EXCEPT

    Ⓐ encourage exploration of the answer with activities and materials that stimulate curiosity.

    Ⓑ model good responding skills.

    Ⓒ answer all items as quickly and concisely as possible.

    Ⓓ include children's questions in evaluation techniques.

63. All of the following describe how science educators apply Piaget's developmental theory in the science classroom EXCEPT

    Ⓐ using cooperative learning to teach science.

    Ⓑ having an age-appropriate textbook for the class.

    Ⓒ hands-on science experiments.

    Ⓓ organizing results through a systematic thinking process.

64. Young children have many experiences with capacity, including sand and water play. Why do so few children carry over these experiences to understanding volume?

    Ⓐ They have not progressed to that stage

    Ⓑ They usually overfill the containers

    Ⓒ They usually do not have enough variety of containers

    Ⓓ No one told them what they were doing

65. A teacher does an experiment in which a white light is refracted through a prism, which splits it into many colors, like the colors of a rainbow. This experiment is best used to demonstrate which of the following concepts?

Ⓐ The angle of incidence equals the angle of reflection.
Ⓑ Light rays travel in a straight line.
Ⓒ White light is formed by a combination of all these colors.
Ⓓ If all these colors were refracted through a prism, a white light would come out.

66. A fifth-grade teacher conducts a science class using the inquiry approach. Which of the following actions on the part of the teacher is most likely to occur?

Ⓐ The teacher deliberately does not try out an experiment in advance so the teacher and the children will discover the results together.
Ⓑ The teacher tells the students to avoid analyzing thought processes, but rather to rely on what happens in the experiment.
Ⓒ The teacher presents a problem for the students to solve or a situation for them to explore.
Ⓓ The teacher explains an experiment and the results and then asks students to try the experiment.

67. A teacher plans to give students some activities that will lead the students to discover a science concept. Which of the following best describes this approach to teaching?

Ⓐ Deductive
Ⓑ Skill
Ⓒ Concrete
Ⓓ Inductive

68. The following is a description of a science activity from a school district manual.

The teacher should have a piece of dense solid material such as lead that weighs about 500 grams and a less dense solid material such as ceramics or rubber that weighs the same. Let students handle the materials. Point out that the objects weigh the same, but are not the same size. Immerse the objects in water so that students can observe that the larger object displaces more water than the smaller object.

This activity is best used to teach which of the following?

Ⓐ Gravity and variable weights
Ⓑ Composition of materials
Ⓒ Density
Ⓓ Geological versus manufactured materials

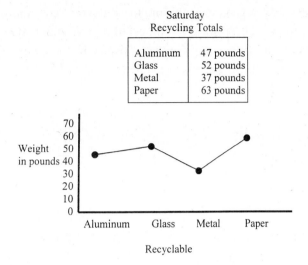

Saturday
Recycling Totals

Aluminum	47 pounds
Glass	52 pounds
Metal	37 pounds
Paper	63 pounds

Recyclable

69. Students visit the recycling center and gather information about the amount of different recyclables collected during one day. The students organize the information into a table and then sketch the graph, both of which are shown above.

Which of the following comments from the teacher to the students would most help students in future activities?

Ⓐ "You should use a straightedge to draw the lines in your graph."
Ⓑ "You should use a circle graph to show percents of the whole. This table and graph do not show percents of a whole."
Ⓒ "You should use a bar graph when quantities are not related."
Ⓓ "You should use kilograms instead of pounds for science results."

70. A teacher replicates a famous experiment. The teacher has a tennis ball and a plastic ball that weigh about the same, although the plastic ball is larger and has holes. The teacher drops the balls simultaneously from a second-story window to the ground below. After repeated experiments, a student standing on the ground always reports that the tennis ball hits first. The student writes this conclusion.

This experiment does not have the result I expected.
These two objects did not fall at the same rate.

Which of the following comments on the part of the teacher is most appropriate?

Ⓐ "Are you sure the balls were dropped at the same time?"
Ⓑ "Did you take into account all variables in the experiment?"
Ⓒ "Wasn't the Leaning Tower of Pisa experiment about falling objects found to be faulty?"
Ⓓ "Did you carefully weigh the two objects?"

71. Students drop a very large grapefruit from five different heights into a large container of sand. The grapefruit is dropped ten times from each height. After each drop the students measure the diameter of the crater formed by the grapefruit. The average, rounded diameter of the crater from each height is shown below.

Height of Drop	Average crater diameter
20 cm	1.6 cm
40 cm	3.2 cm
60 cm	4.8 cm
80 cm	6.4 cm
100 cm	8 cm

The results of this experiment would be a most useful activity for helping students integrate which of the following mathematics concepts with science?

Ⓐ Average
Ⓑ Addition of decimals
Ⓒ Multiplication by a decimal
Ⓓ Decimal representation

72. An advanced upper-elementary school social studies class learning about world geography looked at an outline map without place names. A teacher tells students they will use the Mediterranean Sea to locate a country. This activity would best evaluate a student's

    Ⓐ general knowledge of locations on a blank map.
    Ⓑ ability to distinguish between a sea and an ocean.
    Ⓒ ability to identify the African continent.
    Ⓓ knowledge of the location of the world's largest sea.

73. A multicultural approach to teaching social studies most appropriately includes

    Ⓐ a comparison of how different cultures respond to similar issues.
    Ⓑ how people from different cultures contribute to world events.
    Ⓒ how people around the world have common characteristics.
    Ⓓ how events in one part of the globe influence the rest of the world.

74. Which of the following is the most appropriate emphasis for an elementary school social studies program?

    Ⓐ Emphasize the learning of cultural facts in order to promote an overall cultural literacy.
    Ⓑ Focus on the role of the United States in the contemporary world.
    Ⓒ Prepare learners for competent participation in social, political, and economic life.
    Ⓓ Avoid students' discussion of divisive, value-laden issues.

75. Which of the following map and globe skills would be the most challenging to teach to a group of fifth-grade students?

    Ⓐ Locating on a map the state, county, and town of the school
    Ⓑ Coloring a map so that no two adjoining states, counties, or countries would have the same color
    Ⓒ Reading and using the key on the map
    Ⓓ Plotting factual information about a country on a specific map

76. A teacher wants to adapt social studies instruction for students who are significantly below grade reading level. The following actions on the part of the teacher are appropriate EXCEPT

    Ⓐ using instructional materials that have a lower reading level.
    Ⓑ using instructional materials with less difficult concepts.
    Ⓒ reading information about social studies to the student.
    Ⓓ using recorded tapes that contain social studies information.

> ### SCHOOL GRADING RULES
>
> A   91–100
> B   81–90
> C   71–80

77. A teacher constructs his own content-valid multiple-choice test to assess performance on a social studies unit. One student correctly answers 91 percent of the questions, while another student gets 89 percent correct. How confident should the teacher be about assigning grades according to the school grading rules?

   Ⓐ Very confident—the teacher should just follow the grading rules
   Ⓑ Very confident—the difference between the grades is clear
   Ⓒ Somewhat confident—the test is content-valid and probably measures important concepts
   Ⓓ Not confident—the errors of measurement in the test could eliminate the meaning of the difference between the scores

78. An upper-grade teacher shares five circle graphs with the class. The graphs show only the percent of publicly owned land in each of five cities that is devoted to parks, town buildings, and wildlife areas. The teacher asks students to compare the graphs, most likely to help students explore which of the following?

   Ⓐ Cost of town operations
   Ⓑ Concern for the environment
   Ⓒ Comparative town sizes
   Ⓓ Allocation of resources

79. A student gathers information about the amount of money in a state government's seven budget categories. In order to help others understand the relationship among the amounts spent in the budget categories, the student should represent the data graphically as a

   Ⓐ flowchart.
   Ⓑ circle graph.
   Ⓒ bar graph.
   Ⓓ line graph.

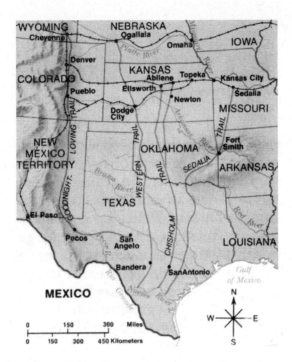

80. A sixth-grade teacher is going to teach a social studies lesson about cattle trails and railroads after the Civil War. The lesson is based on the map shown above. The teacher is most likely to explain that the Goodnight-Loving Trail turns north after Pecos because

    Ⓐ that is the way to Denver.
    Ⓑ the cattle drovers did not want to go into Mexico.
    Ⓒ of the mountains.
    Ⓓ of the Rio Grande River.

81. A teacher is going to conduct a social studies mediated reading thinking activity. Which of the following should the teacher do before reading begins?

    Ⓐ Give students a choice of the material to be read.
    Ⓑ Share responses to the reading with students.
    Ⓒ Predict what might be learned from the reading.
    Ⓓ Focus reading on identified purposes.

82. A teacher carefully planned a lesson on early American settlers and wrote an excellent lesson plan. Once the lesson is underway, the teacher's observation of the students indicates that the plan is clearly not working. The teacher should

    Ⓐ stay with the plan and analyze later why the plan was not successful.
    Ⓑ stay with the plan and discipline any students disrupting the lesson.
    Ⓒ stay with the plan and give other work to those students who can't keep up.
    Ⓓ abandon the plan and try another approach.

ARTS AND PHYSICAL EDUCATION

11 ITEMS

83. A middle-grade teacher developing a unit to integrate social studies and dance might include all of the following EXCEPT

Ⓐ dance styles from a variety of cultures.

Ⓑ cooperative learning groups to develop a project about dance during different time periods.

Ⓒ using the Internet to investigate ballet dance positions.

Ⓓ a video showing Native American dances.

84. Which of the following should be the main focus for an elementary school art program?

Ⓐ Help students acquire technical skills in drawing.

Ⓑ Make sure your students at least have experience coloring, painting, and using clay.

Ⓒ Help students gain appreciation of art, aesthetics, and human creativity.

Ⓓ Allow students to illustrate their written work in the way they feel most comfortable.

85. Rhythmic and movement activities are very often a part of today's elementary physical education programs. These activities lay the foundation for future folk and creative dance units. Which of the following is most important when planning for these activities?

Ⓐ Make sure the music is a lively and catchy tune.

Ⓑ Make sure you choose partners wisely.

Ⓒ Make sure you demonstrate each step so that each student can see you.

Ⓓ Make sure the basic approach is a gradual progression from individual to partner to group activities.

86. A fourth-grade teacher asks students to give their emotional response to a work of art. Which taxonomy of objectives is this lesson related to?

Ⓐ Psychomotor

Ⓑ Introspective

Ⓒ Cognitive

Ⓓ Affective

87. A teacher is conducting beanbag activities with very young students. These activities can integrate the movement of many body parts. Which of the following beanbag activities is the teacher most likely to do last?

Ⓐ Adding stunts in place with the beanbag
Ⓑ Performing locomotor movements with the beanbag
Ⓒ Tossing to self in place with the beanbag
Ⓓ Balancing the beanbag on various body parts

88. A teacher wants to assess a student's understanding of an instrumental music lesson while the lesson is underway. Which of the following most accurately characterizes how the assessment should be conducted?

Ⓐ The teacher should invite students to the teacher's desk to play the instrument.
Ⓑ The teacher should listen to students play during the lesson.
Ⓒ The teacher should invite students to the front of the class to play their instrument.
Ⓓ The teacher should record students' playing to evaluate later.

89. Which of the following is the best example of a teacher's instructional objective for a primary art lesson?

Ⓐ I will teach students how to create a finger painting.
Ⓑ I expect 60 percent of my students to complete a finger painting.
Ⓒ I will gather nontoxic finger paints, finger paint paper, a bowl of water, and a paper towel for each student.
Ⓓ Students will create a finger painting.

90. During a music lesson, the teacher notices that a child is very anxious about remembering musical notation. Which of the following is NOT an effective way for the teacher to respond to the needs of this child?

Ⓐ Don't draw attention to the student by providing emotional support.
Ⓑ Give extra time when practical for the student to learn the notation.
Ⓒ Reduce the tension with a little humor.
Ⓓ Don't criticize the student for his or her lack of progress.

91. A teacher wants to help a student understand the "meaning" of music. The plans call for a lesson on pitch. Which of the following does a student also need to learn to understand what the term "music" means?

Ⓐ Chord
Ⓑ Harmony
Ⓒ Duration
Ⓓ Timbre

92. Students are frequently active and noisy during physical education lessons, and it can be difficult to maintain discipline. At these times the teacher needs to recall that, above all, students usually expect the teacher to be

Ⓐ very assertive.
Ⓑ extremely understanding.
Ⓒ a tough taskmaster.
Ⓓ an authority figure.

93. A school's approach to education is built around the progressive schools movement founded by John Dewey. Which of the following is most likely to characterize the school's physical education program?

Ⓐ The physical education program is conducted in a teacher-centered very friendly classroom.
Ⓑ The physical education program is based on the future needs of society.
Ⓒ The physical education program is built around the needs of the child.
Ⓓ The physical education program is based on team sports and cooperation.

GENERAL KNOWLEDGE

17 ITEMS

94. Economically disadvantaged students, as a whole, tend to have lower achievement than other students, leading educators to the valid conclusion that

    Ⓐ economically disadvantaged students, as a whole, are usually less capable learners than other students.

    Ⓑ minority teachers are more effective with minority students.

    Ⓒ learning expectations should usually be lowered for minority students.

    Ⓓ economically disadvantaged students usually have fewer enriched learning opportunities at home.

95. A principal plans to distribute guidelines for classroom questioning techniques. Which of the following actions on the part of the teacher is generally most appropriate?

    Ⓐ Be sure students know who will answer a question before it is asked.

    Ⓑ Ask questions of the entire class, then call on a student.

    Ⓒ Ask questions of students who are not paying attention.

    Ⓓ Ask questions of students who usually have the correct answers.

96. A new sixth-grade teacher is trying to maintain attention during a lesson. Which of the following actions on the part of the teacher is most likely to be effective?

    Ⓐ The teacher stands where she can see the entire class.

    Ⓑ The teacher limits the number of students who participate in question-and-answer sessions.

    Ⓒ The teacher ensures that the material being taught is very difficult.

    Ⓓ The teacher does not proceed with the lesson if even a single student is not paying attention.

97. Research has shown that modeling can be an effective form of instruction. Which of the following actions on the part of the teacher is an example of appropriate modeling behavior?

    Ⓐ Show students how to construct replicas of historic buildings.

    Ⓑ Respond courteously to students' questions.

    Ⓒ Correct mispronounced words.

    Ⓓ Demonstrate students' inappropriate behavior.

98. A fifth-grade student has been classified as a special education student. The child study team determined that the student is learning disabled. Which of the following choices describes an appropriate placement for that student?

Ⓐ Place the child in a self-contained class with other learning disabled students and send the student out for music and art specials.

Ⓑ Place the student in a fifth-grade class with support from a special education teacher.

Ⓒ Place the student in a self-contained class with other learning disabled students, and send the student to a fifth-grade class for some subjects.

Ⓓ Place the student in a class that matches his or her reading level, and send the student out of class for other subject instruction as needed.

99. Four influential educators—Froebel, Herbart, Pestalozzi, and Rousseau—were born in the 1700s. Which of the following is an accurate statement about one of these educators?

Ⓐ Rousseau established the first kindergarten.

Ⓑ Froebel liberalized schools and called for understanding and patience.

Ⓒ Herbart formalized schools and called for structure and regularity.

Ⓓ Pestalozzi established the first Casa Bambini.

100. A teacher and student are discussing the student's most recent report card. The teacher explains that the student's grades would have been better if all homework assignments were handed in. This teacher is using

Ⓐ punishment.

Ⓑ reverse psychology.

Ⓒ threats.

Ⓓ negative reinforcement.

101. A teacher has a class that is culturally and linguistically diverse. Which of the following actions on the part of the teacher is an appropriate modification of the objectives or plans for this class?

Ⓐ Modify the objectives to focus more on basic skills.

Ⓑ Modify the objectives to reduce their difficulty level.

Ⓒ Modify the plans to teach the class in the foreign language.

Ⓓ Modify the plans to focus on the cultural heritage of those in the class.

102. A teacher puts only the teacher's name on the cover of a larger handout that includes two pages from a recent 100-page children's book. When it comes to copyright, in all likelihood the teacher has

    (A) not violated the copyright law because teachers are allowed to copy any books the teacher wishes to copy, as long as the books are for instructional purposes.

    (B) not violated copyright law because of the "fair-use" doctrine, which allows excerpts from books to be used for educational purposes.

    (C) violated the copyright law because the teacher did not give proper credit to the book's author and copyright holder of the book.

    (D) violated the copyright law because teachers actually have no right to copy copyrighted materials, even though teachers have been doing it for years.

103. A school district is preparing a pamphlet about effective schools. All of the following choices could be listed as characteristics of effective schools EXCEPT

    (A) a climate of high expectations.

    (B) a high proportion of instruction time spent on task.

    (C) accountability for student performance.

    (D) eliminating standardized tests.

104. Effective classroom managers take steps to ensure that the majority of class time is devoted to

    (A) individual work.

    (B) on-task activities.

    (C) cooperative learning.

    (D) lecturing.

105. Which of the following actions on the part of a teacher indicates that the teacher is using authentic assessment?

    (A) The teacher collects and evaluates student work.

    (B) The teacher uses standardized tests.

    (C) The teacher uses only tests that have been authenticated.

    (D) The teacher collects evaluative information from other teachers.

106. A fourth-grade teacher is using a cooperative learning approach. All of the following might occur EXCEPT

    (A) students get help from other students.

    (B) groups of two to six students work together.

    (C) group members consult with the teacher.

    (D) the teacher summarizes students' work.

107. A teacher seeks to use a constructivist approach to teaching. Which of the following actions on the part of the teacher is most consistent with that approach?

Ⓐ The teacher encourages students to respond quickly and alertly to questions.

Ⓑ The teacher encourages students to construct complex models of their thought processes.

Ⓒ The teacher encourages students to elaborate on their initial responses.

Ⓓ The teacher discourages students from creating metaphors.

108. A teacher using Gardner's multiple intelligences as the basis for instruction is most likely to use which of the following?

Ⓐ Implement interdisciplinary units.

Ⓑ Help students learn about each of the intelligences.

Ⓒ Eliminate assessments.

Ⓓ Allow students to determine criteria for quality.

109. Comprehensive testing of a fourth-grade student reveals an IQ in the 110–115 range, but standardized test scores are two or more years below grade level. Which of the following is the most appropriate interpretation of these test scores?

Ⓐ The student is a poor test taker.

Ⓑ The student's achievement and potential match.

Ⓒ The student is gifted.

Ⓓ The student has a learning disability.

110. The most significant difficulty with portfolio assessment is reliability in that

Ⓐ students put samples of widely different types of work in their portfolio.

Ⓑ scoring machines don't work reliably with materials in the portfolio.

Ⓒ different teachers place different emphasis on the portfolios when giving grades.

Ⓓ different teachers assign widely different grades to the same portfolio.

ANSWER KEY
Elementary Education Practice Test

READING/LANGUAGE ARTS

1. A	8. C	15. C	22. D	29. B	36. A
2. B	9. B	16. B	23. C	30. A	37. B
3. D	10. A	17. B	24. B	31. D	38. D
4. A	11. C	18. A	25. C	32. D	
5. C	12. B	19. B	26. C	33. D	
6. D	13. A	20. A	27. B	34. C	
7. D	14. D	21. B	28. C	35. B	

MATHEMATICS

39. C	43. D	47. A	51. B	55. B	59. B
40. B	44. C	48. B	52. D	56. B	60. B
41. D	45. B	49. B	53. B	57. C	
42. C	46. D	50. C	54. B	58. D	

SCIENCE

61. A	63. B	65. C	67. D	69. C	71. C
62. C	64. A	66. C	68. C	70. B	

SOCIAL STUDIES

72. C	74. C	76. B	78. D	80. C	82. D
73. A	75. D	77. D	79. B	81. D	

ARTS AND PHYSICAL EDUCATION

83. C	85. D	87. D	89. D	91. C	93. C
84. C	86. D	88. B	90. A	92. D	

GENERAL KNOWLEDGE

94. D	97. B	100. D	103. D	106. D	109. D
95. B	98. B	101. D	104. B	107. C	110. D
96. A	99. C	102. C	105. A	108. A	

Reading/Language Arts

1. **(A)** Choice (A) is correct. It describes how to use context clues to find the meaning of a word. Choice (B) is incorrect because using a dictionary is not using context to find meaning. Choice (C) is incorrect because prior knowledge is something students already know, not something students have to learn. Choice (D) is incorrect because content material will not help students understand word meaning.

2. **(B)** Choice (B) is correct. A writing checklist is an excellent way to determine a student's writing ability to prepare for further writing experiences. Choice (A) is incorrect. Standardized grammar tests do not reveal a student's writing ability. Choice (C) is incorrect. Holistic evaluations reflect the evaluator's overall view of the quality of the writing. A holistic evaluation does not yield a specific analysis that can lead to instructional plans. Choice (D) is incorrect. This assessment evaluates reading, not writing.

3. **(D)** Choice (D) is correct. A prerequisite competency refers to some skill or ability students must possess in order to learn an objective. That is, learning a prerequisite competency must come before learning the objective. Choice (A) is incorrect. The teacher certainly needs to have the knowledge and skills to teach about subject–verb agreement, but that is not what prerequisite competency means. Choice (B) is incorrect. A sub-objective is part of the objective. Learning a sub-objective does not come before learning the objective. Choice (C) is incorrect. A test is not a competency, even though it may assess prerequisite competencies for the listed objective.

4. **(A)** Choice (A) is correct. Note the word EXCEPT in the item. This choice has to do with listening and NOT reading. Difficulty with auditory discrimination does not itself interfere with reading. Early hearing problems can inhibit reading and writing development. However, Lisa writes well and understands verbal directions. Choices (B), (C), and (D) are incorrect. These choices could be the cause of Lisa's trouble understanding written directions. Of course, there are other factors that could cause her difficulty.

5. **(C)** Note the word EXCEPT in the question. This choice does not describe a semantic organizer because the missing words cannot be grouped according to a common characteristic or theme. Choices (A), (B), and (D) refer to semantic organizers because each involves grouping words according to common characteristics.

6. **(D)** Choice (D) is correct. The phrase "most likely" is key to answering this question. It is most likely that this student is having difficulty reading in the context of mathematics. We do not have any other information to base our decision on. Choices (A), (B), and (C) are incorrect. These choices may be a cause, just not the most likely cause.

7. **(D)** Choice (D) is correct. Note the word NOT in the item. Choral reading is a group of children reading aloud together. This setting does not help students interpret word meaning. Rather, the emphasis is on simultaneous, clear pronunciation. Choices (A), (B), and (C) are incorrect. These choices do describe some of the goals and benefits of choral reading.

8. **(C)** Choice (C) is correct. Note the word EXCEPT in the item. You do not have to understand the meaning of a word to pronounce it. This item points out the important distinction between recognizing a word and knowing what the word means. Word recognition and comprehension are both important parts of reading instruction. Choices (A), (B), and (D) are incorrect. Difficulty with any of these might make it harder for a child to pronounce a word. It is clear how difficulty with phonics, or difficulty with sight vocabulary might lead to the problem. Difficulty with content analysis could also lead to this problem. A young child reads the sentence, "Jamie went to the store." But the child does not remember if the "e" in "went" is pronounced "eh" or "ah." That is, the child is not sure if the word "went" is pronounced "went" or "want." But, the context of the word shows clearly the correct pronunciation is "went."

9. **(B)** Choice (B) is correct. Note the word NOT in the item. Personal journals are just that—personal. These journals are not a way to share thoughts with others. Students should use a different format, such as a response journal, to share their thoughts. Choices (A), (C), and (D) are incorrect. These choices describe appropriate ways of using personal journals.

10. **(A)** Choice (A) is correct. Scaffolding means to offer sufficient support for students to learn and then to slowly remove that support as students develop the desired understanding. Choices (B), (C), and (D) are incorrect because these choices offer incorrect definitions of instructional scaffolding.

11. **(C)** Choice (C) is correct. The phrase "most important" is key to answering this question. A student must have the audience and purpose in mind before he or she considers the order of presentation, writing a clear beginning, or the main idea. Choices (A), (B), and (D) are incorrect. These are important things for a student to do when writing, but not the most important of the four listed.

12. **(B)** Choice (B) is correct. Note the word NOT in the item. A phonics approach does not address word meaning or reading comprehension. Phonics addresses word recognition and word pronunciation. Educators frequently criticize overreliance on phonics for just this reason. Choices (A), (C), and (D) are incorrect. Each choice describes a benefit that can be derived from the phonics approach.

13. **(A)** Choice (A) is correct. An anticipatory set makes the student aware in advance of the lesson's content. Choice (B) is incorrect. A motivation interests the student in the lesson. Choice (C) is incorrect. An objective specifies what a student is expected to do once instruction is complete. Choice (D) is incorrect. An advanced organizer is an initial overview of the lesson's content.

14. **(D)** Choice (D) is correct. Students develop a better attitude toward reading when they use the real literature found in a whole language approach. Choice (A) is incorrect. It may be reassuring that an approach is widely accepted, but that is never the best reason to use the approach. Choice (B) is incorrect. Word recognition must always be taught. Students cannot read if they cannot recognize words. Choice (C) is incorrect. Research does not uniformly support the conclusion that students comprehend better after using a whole language approach. It seems that a combination of approaches, including aspects of the whole language approach, best develops reading comprehension.

15. **(C)** Choice (C) is correct. The word "transactional" in the term "transactional strategy instruction" means a give-and-take between students and teachers as they explore the processes involved in successful reading comprehension. Choice (A) is incorrect. This choice describes the direct explanation of cognitive processes. Both the direct explanation approach and the transactional strategy instruction approach hold tremendous promise for reading instruction. Choice (B) and choice (D) are incorrect. They explain neither of these approaches.

16. **(B)** Choice (B) is correct. Clicking on a hypertext word reveals a definition or underlying meaning. Hypertext links to word definitions hold tremendous promise for reading instruction. Choices (A), (C), and (D) are incorrect. The descriptions in these choices have nothing to do with hypertext terms.

17. **(B)** Choice (B) is correct. The problem does not provide enough information to determine what time Charles arrived home. The relationship between reading and mathematics is very important, and this is more a reading problem than a mathematics problem. A child might consider these points as the child tries to solve the problem. The problem never says that Charles arrived home. Charles left work at 6:15, but we don't know what time he got on the bus. We don't know that the bus is traveling toward his house.

18. **(A)** Choice (A) is correct. The singular subject "I" does not agree with the plural verb "are." Nonagreement of subject and verb should be addressed in the early grades. Choice (B) is incorrect. The use of the pronoun "I" is correct. Choice (C) is incorrect. This sentence contains a subject and a verb. Fragments are parts of sentences written as though they were sentences. Choice (D) is incorrect. There are no adjectives and no adverbs in this sentence, and none is called for.

19. **(B)** Choice (B) is correct. Guiding students as they work is a very effective strategy for teaching reading. Picking out science fact and science fiction in a space exploration science fiction story is certainly the best kind of guidance among the choices given. Choice (A) is incorrect. Many science fiction stories contain science fact. Choices (C) and (D) are incorrect. Working independently is one of the least effective ways to learn about reading because it lacks interaction with the teacher and with other students.

20. **(A)** Choice (A) is correct. Evaluation is the highest level in Bloom's Taxonomy. Choices (B), (C), and (D) are incorrect. They represent lower levels in the taxonomy.

21. **(B)** Choice (B) is correct. This is exactly the situation in which cooperative learning groups excel. Students learn from interaction in the group, from the presentation made by other groups, and from your reaction and others' reaction to the presentations. Choice (A) is incorrect. Working independently is one of the least effective ways to learn about reading because it lacks interaction with teachers and other students. Choices (C) and (D) are incorrect because the approaches involve direct instruction. A great many reading skills and objectives can best be taught through direct instruction. However, direct instruction is not the best approach for this situation.

22. **(D)** Choice (D) is correct. This student is a phonetic speller. "Enuf" is misspelled, but the student correctly followed phonics rules. This student needs instruction in the alternative spelling used for phonemes (sounds associated with letters and groups of

letters). For example, English spelling uses the letters "gh" to represent the "f" sound in "enough." Using many spellings for the same sound can make English a difficult language to learn. Choices (A) and (B) are incorrect. Word attack skills lead to the correct pronunciation of "enuf." Choice (C) is incorrect. "Enough" and "enuf" sound the same, so they are homonyms. However, confusing homonyms is not the problem here.

23. **(C)** Choice (C) is correct. A definite reward schedule, and some means of giving rewards (points, paper coupons, plastic tokens, etc.), and a means of redeeming tokens or points are the essential ingredients of a token economy. Choices (A), (B), and (D) are incorrect. None of these choices bears any resemblance to a token economy.

24. **(B)** Choice (B) is correct. For a brief unit such as this, a teacher-made assessment is almost always the best. There may also be an appropriate assessment available from a text publisher or other source, but this is clearly the best among the choices given. Choice (A) is incorrect. Standardized tests are used to establish an achievement level, or to compare results between students or groups of students. Standardized tests are not particularly useful for finding out whether or not a student has learned a particular skill or concept. Choice (C) is incorrect. The item states that the teacher wants to know whether the students have learned about nouns before going on. While observing students' written work over a week is an excellent assessment technique, it takes too long to meet the needs of this situation. Choice (D) is incorrect. Reviewing students' previous work, alone, will not help the teacher with this assessment.

25. **(C)** Choice (C) is correct. Note the word EXCEPT in the item. The Orton-Gillingham method does not emphasize reading for meaning. That is not to say that meaning is not important; it's just not an Orton-Gillingham emphasis. Choices (A), (B), and (D) are incorrect. The actions described in these choices are consistent with the Orton-Gillingham approach.

26. **(C)** Choice (C) is correct. Note the word NOT in the item. Note also the word "indicate," which means the incorrect choices do show an ongoing assessment is underway. This choice is correct because an in-class composition does not indicate that an ongoing assessment is underway. Choice (A) is incorrect. Observing students' work while they are writing indicates ongoing assessment is underway. Choice (B) is incorrect. The teacher's review of students' daily work indicates an ongoing assessment is underway. Choice (D) is incorrect. The regular collection of performance samples indicates an ongoing assessment is underway.

27. **(B)** Choice (B) is correct. A formative evaluation helps a teacher plan lessons. Samples of a student's writing best furthers that goal. Choice (A) is incorrect. A discussion with a student may help a teacher, particularly if the discussion follows a review of the student's writing, but a discussion is not the best opportunity for a formative evaluation. Choice (C) is incorrect. The Iowa Test of Basic Skills does not evaluate writing, and it is more useful as a summative evaluation than a formative evaluation. Choice (D) is incorrect. An end of unit test is also more useful as a summative evaluation.

28. **(C)** Choice (C) is correct. This answer correctly describes percentile rank. The 34th percentile means 34 percent of the scores are below that point. The 34th percentile also means that 66 percent of the scores are at or above that point. Choice (A) is incorrect. Percentile rank does not refer directly to the number of students. Choice (B) is incor-

rect. Another way to word this choice is ". . . did as well as or better than 66 percent of the students who took the test." That wording refers to the 66th percentile. Choice (D) is incorrect. Standardized reading tests measure performance on that test, not overall reading ability. Standardized scores may be a general guide to reading ability. However, an individual student may perform much better, or much worse, on a standardized test than his or her ability indicates.

29. **(B)** Choice (B) is correct. Standardized test scores indicate a range of grade levels, not one single grade level. The teacher's correct response is that the child is about average, meaning about average for that school. The word "about" in the teacher's explanation is important. It shows the teacher understands that reported grade levels are not precise. Choices (A) and (D) are incorrect. The reported grade equivalent is only slightly higher than the baseline 4.0, and in no significant way. If the test were given in the spring, as many are, the grade equivalent would be slightly below the average for all the students who took the test. But whether slightly above, or slightly below, the score indicates a range that is about average. Choice (C) is incorrect. The scores are reported in grade equivalents, not age equivalents.

30. **(A)** Choice (A) is correct. ESL means English as a Second Language. This approach encourages the teaching and use of English. Choices (B), (C), and (D) are incorrect. These choices are not consistent with an ESL approach.

31. **(D)** Choice (D) is correct. A summative evaluation assesses what a student learned about a specific objective or objectives. Choice (A) is incorrect. A formative evaluation helps a teacher plan lessons. Choices (C) and (D) are incorrect. A standardized test and norm-referenced test have been standardized or normed on a large population of students. End of chapter tests are not standardized.

32. **(D)** Choice (D) is correct. The only conclusive information is that the student appears to do better in real-world situations. This just underscores the importance of portfolio assessment. Even though portfolio assessment is often not a reliable indicator, portfolio assessment gives students the opportunity to demonstrate their "real-world" proficiency. Choices (A), (B), and (C) are incorrect. None of these explanations is supported by the reported results.

33. **(D)** Choice (D) is correct. The student's writing contains several verb tense shifts. In the first sentence, "sat" is past tense, while "play" is present tense. In the second sentence, "saw" is past tense, while "sit" is present tense. Choices (A) and (B) are incorrect. The nouns and pronouns are used correctly. Choice (C) is incorrect. The spelling error in the last sentence requires less of the teacher's attention than the tense shift errors.

34. **(C)** Choice (C) is correct. Note the word LEAST in the item. Groups with ten or twelve members are too large for effective interaction. Cooperative learning groups are typically limited to six members. Choices (A), (B), and (D) are incorrect. Each of these choices describes an essential element of cooperative learning groups.

35. **(B)** Choice (B) is correct. Reading is a unique skill, and different from language. Studies show that students benefit most from early, effective phonics instruction. This should not be taken to mean that every phonics program is effective. Choice (A) is incorrect. This is a good idea, of course, and it would likely improve language

development. But it is not a significant factor in reading development, particularly when compared to phonics instruction. Choice (C) is incorrect. Oral expression and effective listening are altogether different from reading. Choice (D) is incorrect. Replacing basal texts with real literature sources can help increase a student's interest in reading. However, this practice does not significantly contribute to reading development.

36. **(A)** Choice (A) is correct. Whole language is a direct descendent of Marie Clay's Reading Recovery programme. The programme was developed in New Zealand and became popular in the 1980s. Choice (B) is incorrect. Pitmans's Initial Teaching Alphabet (ITA) of 45 letters was first used in the early 1960s. Each ITA letter represents a phoneme (sound) in the English language. Choice (C) is incorrect. Piaget and his collaborator Barbel Inhelder posited several stages of child development. They argued that children should not be introduced to concepts until developmentally ready. Piaget made few recommendations about educational practice. Choice (D) is incorrect. Dewey's Progressive Education movement of the early 1900s featured practices similar to many of those found in the whole language approach. However, he did not emphasize using real literature sources and he is not credited with the founding of whole language.

37. **(B)** Choice (B) is correct. The reading grade level is based on the entire national group of students that took the test. In this case, the class as a whole performed better than the student, even though the student performed better than the national average. Choices (A) and (D) are incorrect. These are just meaningless statements about test scores. Choice (C) is incorrect. This statement is generally true. More or less half the students nationally who take a standardized test are below grade level. But this statement does not explain the student's test score situation.

38. **(D)** Choice (D) is correct. Students often perform better on alternative forms of assessment such as informal reading inventories than on standardized reading tests. The first step is to use alternative assessments to ensure that the reading level is actually low, and not just a function of the standardized test. Choice (A) is incorrect. Accounting for learning styles is not the first step, but it can be an effective approach to help students read better. There are many ways to categorize learning style, including multiple intelligences. Choice (B) is incorrect. It is obvious that this is a necessary step if the student is actually reading below grade level. Choice (C) is incorrect. Peer tutoring can be an effective technique, depending on the likelihood that the student will accept help from a classmate.

Mathematics

39. **(C)** Choice (C) is correct. It shows the student's incorrect answer. A rule for multiplying decimals is to multiply the numbers, to count the number of digits to the right of the decimal point in both factors, and to put that many decimal places in the answer. This student does not count "0" when it appears to the right of the decimal point. Choice (A) shows the right answer to the problem: $0.08 \times 1.04 = 0.0832$. There are a total of four digits to the right of the decimal point. The student should move the decimal point four places to the left to get 0.0832. Choices (B) and (D) do not show the student's incorrect answer.

40. **(B)** Choice (B) is correct. The student failed to include the side that has no indicated length. Tracing each side will eventually lead the student to realize the omission. The length of the missing side is $8 - 5 = 3$, and the correct perimeter is 26 units. Choice (A) is incorrect. The student added correctly, but omitted the length of a side. Choice (C) is incorrect. Counting the sides may help the student realize the length of a side is missing, but choice (B) is most likely to help. Choice (D) is incorrect. The student did use the rule "add the sides to find the perimeter," but omitted the length of a side.

41. **(D)** Choice (D) is correct. It is always best to teach a first lesson with manipulative materials. It is most important that elementary students handle materials during the first stage of the learning process. Choices (A), (B), and (C) are incorrect. In general, the concept should be taught in the following order:

    1. (D)
    2. (B)
    3. (C)
    4. (A)

42. **(C)** Choice (C) is correct. A student is most likely to be helped if he or she actually sees four small squares fit inside the large square. Choice (A) is incorrect. Tracing and comparing might help the student, but choice (C) is the best way. Choice (B) is incorrect. A ruler might help the student calculate the area, but the task here is to help the student see the relationship visually. Choice (D) is incorrect. Estimating the increase in distance might also help the student calculate the area, but choice (C) is best.

43. **(D)** Choice (D) is correct. Note the word LEAST in the item. Dividing decimals is too complex to represent with manipulatives. Choice (A) is incorrect. Counters can help students learn single digit addition. Choice (B) is incorrect. Students might use this strategy to find how many ways to arrange three different shapes in order. Shapes or other objects can be used to represent elements in the list. Choice (C) is incorrect. Tens blocks or bean sticks can help students learn addition of double-digit numbers.

44. **(C)** Choice (C) is correct. Students learn best when the lesson is at their level of *ability*. They become too frustrated when asked to do something they cannot do. While true as a general statement, it may be difficult to accurately determine a student's ability level. Naturally, there is a difference between ability level and achievement level. Students frequently learn successfully when reasonably challenged beyond their *achievement* level, but not beyond their ability level.

45. **(B)** Choice (B) is correct. This student has trouble with place value. Look below to see the example written vertically. The student adds 9 and 3, for a total of 12 (1 ten and 1 one). But the student writes 12 in the sum, rather than renaming 10 ones as 1 ten.

$$\begin{array}{r} 13 \\ +\,9 \\ \hline 112 \end{array} \qquad\qquad \begin{array}{r} 1 \\ 13 \\ +9 \\ \hline 22 \end{array}$$

Student's error.   **Correct.**

46. **(D)** Choice (D) is correct. This is the classic number conservation task. One matched row of checkers is spread out after a student realizes the original rows contain the same number of checkers. Students who realize the rows still contain the same number of checkers are said to conserve number.

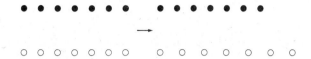

47. **(A)** Choice (A) is correct. Mathematics concepts, in this case multiplication, should be generally taught in this order:

1. Manipulatives
2. Visual representation
3. Symbolic representation

48. **(B)** Choice (B) is correct. These two fractions must share a common denominator before a student can find the sum with the addition algorithm. Finding a common denominator requires a student to think, and then to use multiplication before adding. Choice (A) is incorrect. Multiplying fractions is the only understanding required. The answer is already in the simplest form. Choice (C) is incorrect. A student must know to "invert the divisor" and then multiply. Students do not have to understand the relationship between multiplication and division to complete this task. Choice (D) is incorrect. An understanding of a relationship among arithmetic operations is not required to complete this problem.

49. **(B)** Choice (B) is correct. This activity best helps meet the goal of indirect measurement. Indirect measurement means to measure the length of one thing, and then use that measurement and mathematics to find the length or height of something else. If a student knows the length of the pole's shadow and the length of a ruler's shadow, the student can use mathematics to indirectly find the height of the pole. Choice (A) is incorrect because estimation is not the same as indirect measurement, even though estimation is an important measurement concept. Choice (C) is incorrect because the students do not use mathematics to find the width of the other classroom. Choice (D) is incorrect because this choice describes another type of estimation based on a person's height.

50. **(C)** Choice (C) is correct. Note the word LEAST in the item. The least helpful way to find information is to just type in a web address. Frequently, information about a subject is not found at a web address with that name. You also have to enter the correct suffix (.com, .edu, .gov, .net, and so on). Choice (A) is incorrect. Using a search engine is the best way to locate information on the Internet. Choices (B) and (D) are incorrect. These are not the best ways to find information on the Internet, but you may find someone to e-mail, to send messages to, or to chat with in real time.

51. **(B)** Choice (B) is correct. The geoboard is the instructional aid of choice for making triangles and other polygons. The geoboard consists of a board or piece of plastic with nails or pegs evenly spaced horizontally and vertically. Elastic bands are used to form shapes, and the elastic bands can be easily manipulated. Choice (A) is incorrect. You

can create triangles with string, but it is very cumbersome. Choice (C) is incorrect. You can create triangles with sticks, but you need glue and it is too time-consuming. The sticks are not easily manipulated. Choice (D) is incorrect. You can create triangles with a ruler and pencil, but the drawn lines cannot be manipulated.

52. **(D)** Choice (D) is correct. Just because a student can say counting words in order does not mean the student can count. You may have seen a child correctly count to five as the child counts seven objects. It is the correspondence between the counting words and the objects being counted that is important. Choices (A), (B), and (C) are incorrect. None of these is the reason the teacher is using this approach.

53. **(B)** Choice (B) is correct. In order to solve this problem, the student must interpret the remainder to mean that an extra tent is needed. That is, 9 tents are needed for the camping trip. Choices (A), (C), and (D) are incorrect. None of these strategies are correct.

$$\begin{array}{r} 8 \ \text{R}\,3 \\ 5\,\overline{\smash{)}43} \\ \underline{40} \\ 3 \end{array}$$

54. **(B)** Choice (B) is correct. This step is first because this student's difficulty is mechanical, not conceptual. The multiplication is completed correctly, and the student tries to put the digits in the correct places. Writing digits in boxes on the graph paper usually solves this problem. Choice (A) is incorrect. Teaching place value is not likely to resolve this difficulty. If the graph paper doesn't help, the next step might be to reteach place value. Choice (C) is incorrect. Reteaching multiplication with fewer digits will not help. This student does not appear to have difficulty with multiplication. Choice (D) is incorrect. Teaching to use zeros as placeholders may not solve the alignment problem. If the graph paper does not work, the next step might be to use zeros as placeholders.

55. **(B)** Choice (B) is correct. This choice draws attention to the coins and actively involves students in the lesson. Choice (A) is incorrect. It sounds interesting, but it does not involve students in the lesson. Choice (C) is incorrect. The question of where coins came from may be interesting to some, but usually not to a class of primary students. Choice (D) is incorrect. This choice is an anticipatory set designed to focus students on the lesson.

56. **(B)** Choice (B) is correct. This is a constructivist approach to teaching. Students are allowed to choose the resource or resources to "construct" their solution to this problem. Choices (A) and (D) are incorrect. True, there is a problem to be solved, and students can use manipulatives; however, problem solving and manipulatives are not general approaches to teaching, and not the most important aspect of this lesson. Choice (C) is incorrect. The teacher does not model a solution to the problem.

57. **(C)** Choice (C) is correct. The test is not standardized, and there is no information about how other students did on the test. The best interpretation among those given that is the student did well. Choice (A) is incorrect. The test is not standardized and there is no comparative information available about the meaning of the score. Choice (B) is incorrect. A score of 85 percent correct does not mean the score is at the 85th

percentile. Choice (D) is incorrect. There is nothing about the score to indicate that further review is necessary. A perfect score on an end of chapter test is not required to move on to the next chapter.

58. **(D)** Choice (D) is correct. Students may be working on the problem at different times of the day. The best approach is for students to submit written samples of their solutions for the teacher to review. Choice (A) is incorrect. It will be too difficult to observe all the students as they work on the solution. Choice (B) is incorrect. A standardized test is not appropriate to assess student's solutions to these problems. Choice (C) is incorrect. Cooperative learning is not itself an assessment tool.

59. **(B)** Choice (B) is correct. David and Roger Johnson are widely credited for their pioneering work on cooperative learning, and for their work *Learning Together and Alone. Cooperative, Competitive, and Individualistic Learning.* Choice (A) is incorrect. Howard Gardner is best known for his work on Multiple Intelligences. Choice (C) is incorrect. Madeline Hunter is best known for her direct instruction model and for the lesson plan format based on that model. Choice (D) is incorrect. Holdaway and Clark are best known for their work on literacy development.

60. **(B)** Choice (B) is correct. This is the most common way to limit the use of calculators. If students are learning a computation method, calculators should not be used. But when students need to compute, particularly to solve problems, the calculator can be used. Students use calculators on many tests, including the PSAT, the SAT, and the ACT. One challenge on these tests is to determine when a calculator will help, when a calculator may help, and when a calculator will not help, and may even hurt.

Science

61. **(A)** Choice (A) is correct. It is best to help students learn through actual experience. Choices (B), (C), and (D) are incorrect. Each of these choices has value; however, none of them are the best response to this item.

62. **(C)** Choice (C) is correct. Note the word EXCEPT in the item. A teacher should not be quick to answer a question; the teacher may be able to help the student find the answer himself or herself. Choices (A), (B), and (D) are incorrect. These are all appropriate ways of responding to student's science questions.

63. **(B)** Choice (B) is correct. Note the word EXCEPT in the item. This approach does not incorporate Piaget's developmental theory. Piaget emphasizes developmental appropriateness, not age appropriateness. Choices (A), (C), and (D) describe a way to apply Piaget's child development theory.

64. **(A)** Choice (A) is correct. Understanding capacity means understanding that the amount of liquid does not change just because its appearance changes. Volume is a specific measure of how much something holds (2 cubic feet). Students can understand capacity without being ready to understand volume.

65. **(C)** Choice (C) is correct. The prism separates out all the colors that white light consists of. Choices (A) and (B) are incorrect. These choices accurately represent science con-

cepts, but this experiment does not demonstrate either of these concepts. Choice (D) is incorrect because a prism separates colors; it does not combine them.

66. **(C)** Choice (C) is correct. This choice describes the essence of the inquiry approach. Choice (A) is incorrect. A teacher should try out experiments in advance. Choice (B) is incorrect. The inquiry approach encourages analysis of thought processes. Choice (D) is incorrect. The inquiry approach encourages students to conduct experiments and observe results without prior guidance.

67. **(D)** Choice (D) is correct. Inductive teaching helps a student to discover science concepts by leading the student from examples to a generalization. Choice (A) is incorrect. The deductive approach is the opposite of the inductive approach. Deductive teaching leads from rules to examples, and can be effective in many settings. Choices (B) and (C) are incorrect. Neither of these choices describes the inductive approach to teaching.

68. **(C)** Choice (C) is correct. Two objects can weigh the same, but have different densities. The rubber or ceramic solid object is not as dense as the lead solid object. If two solid objects weigh the same, the one that displaces the least water is most dense. Choice (A) is incorrect. The activity does not have to do with gravity. However, the weight of an object does depend on gravity. An object will weigh less on the surface of the moon than on the surface of the earth. However, the mass or amount of the object is the same on earth as it is on the moon. Choices (B) and (D) are incorrect. These answers are not related to the activity.

69. **(C)** Choice (C) is correct. Use a bar graph when quantities are unrelated to one another. A line graph is used when the quantities are related to one another. For example, use a line graph to show temperature change throughout a day, but these quantities in the item are unrelated, and a bar graph is appropriate. Choice (A) is incorrect. The table and graph were made "on site" and their informal appearance is acceptable under those circumstances. Choice (B) is incorrect. This choice correctly describes when to use a circle graph, but a circle graph is not appropriate here. Choice (D) is incorrect. It is fine to use kilograms, but pounds are just as good. The data at the recycling center was probably reported in pounds.

70. **(B)** Choice (B) is correct. The experiment is similar to the Leaning Tower of Pisa experiment that helped establish that all objects fall at the same rate. These objects likely did not land at the same time because air pressure and wind slowed the fall of the plastic ball. The students did not take these variables into account. By the way, the objects don't have to be the same weight to fall at the same rate. For better results, try this experiment with an orange and a grape.

71. **(C)** Choice (C) is correct. To integrate mathematics with science, multiply the height of the fall by 0.8 to find the diameter of the crater.

Social Studies

72. **(C)** Choice (C) is correct. A student who can identify the African continent can easily locate the Mediterranean to the north of that continent. Choice (A) is incorrect because a general knowledge of locations does not help with this specific location choice. Choice (B) is incorrect because knowing the difference between a sea and an ocean will

not help students to locate the Mediterranean Sea. Choice (D) is incorrect because the Mediterranean Sea is third on the list of the world's largest seas. The South China Sea is the largest.

73. **(A)** Choice (A) is correct. A multicultural approach emphasizes the varying experiences across cultures. The intent of a multicultural approach is to help students recognize differences and yet develop a unified bond among the students. Choices (B), (C), and (D) are incorrect. These choices do not characterize a multicultural approach.

74. **(C)** Choice (C) is correct. This choice represents a consistent emphasis of the National Council for the Social Studies Standards. Choices (A) and (B) are incorrect. These might be teaching goals in a social studies program, but never the overall emphasis of the program. Choice (D) is contrary to the standards.

75. **(D)** Choice (D) is correct. Plotting information on a map is the most complex skill. In fact, it involves many skills including map reading, understanding information to be plotted, devising a plotting key, and others. Choices (A), (B), and (C) are incorrect. These are all useful skills and activities, but none of them are the most challenging skill on the list.

76. **(B)** Choice (B) is correct. Note the word EXCEPT in the item. Just because a student is below grade level in reading does not mean the student cannot understand on-level or above-level social studies topics. Do not adapt instruction to less difficult topics on the basis of a low reading level. Choices (A), (C), and (D) are all incorrect. Each represents an acceptable way to adapt social studies instruction for students reading significantly below grade level.

77. **(D)** Choice (D) is correct. The teacher should not be confident. Errors of measurement that occur on all teacher-made tests quite likely eliminate any meaning in the difference between these scores. Choice (A) is incorrect. The teacher should not be very confident. Choice (B) is incorrect. The teacher should not be very confident, and the difference between the scores of two percent does not mean much. Choice (C) is incorrect. Content validity means the test actually measures the content in the social studies unit. Content validity does not mean the test is reliable. Reliability loosely means the test consistently yields the same results when given to the same types of students.

78. **(D)** Choice (D) is correct. The graphs clearly show how each town allocates the important resource of town-owned land. Choice (A) is incorrect because the graphs do not reveal any information about cost. Choice (B) is incorrect because the graphs, themselves, do not reveal information about concern for the environment. A town might have large natural areas, but still have plants with large smokestack emissions that pollute the air. Choice (C) is incorrect because the graphs show only percents.

79. **(B)** Choice (B) is correct. A circle graph best displays this type of comparative data. Choice (A) is incorrect. A flowchart shows the steps for completing a task. Choice (C) is incorrect. A bar graph represents information by the length of a bar. Choice (D) is incorrect. A line graph plots data against two axes.

80. **(C)** Choice (C) is correct. The map shows the mountains blocking the way west. Choice (A) is incorrect. That is the way to Denver, but the trail continues west after Denver and

the trail would not turn north except for the mountains. Choices (B) and (D) are incorrect. Mexico and the Rio Grande River are too far away to cause this turn.

81. **(D)** Choice (D) is correct. The teacher directs a mediated reading thinking activity. Students are asked to read a particular passage for a particular purpose. Choices (A), (B), and (C) are incorrect. These might be appropriate actions by the teacher in other circumstances. However, these choices do not characterize a mediated reading thinking activity.

82. **(D)** Choice (D) is correct. Plans often fail, and for many reasons; it is a reality of teaching, particularly for beginning teachers. The teacher should then try to find alternative ways to teach the lesson. Choices (A), (B), and (C) are incorrect. Do not stick with a failed plan. That is not to say a teacher should abandon a plan at the first sign of trouble. However, let the plan go if it is "clearly not working."

Arts and Physical Education

83. **(C)** Choice (C) is correct. Notice the word EXCEPT in the question. This is the only choice that does not integrate dance with social studies. It just directs students to an activity strictly about dance. Choices (A), (B), and (D) all integrate dance with a social studies topic.

84. **(C)** Choice (C) is correct. This is the most appropriate focus for an elementary school art program. This general focus might include the more specific activities found in the other choices. Choices (A), (B), and (D) are incorrect. While these may be appropriate art activities, none is as an appropriate main focus for an art program as choice (C).

85. **(D)** Choice (D) is correct. Contemporary elementary school physical education programs focus on movement activities. This choice describes one of the important aspects of these movement programs. Choices (A), (B), and (C) are incorrect. These approaches may be appropriate in certain circumstances, but none of these choices are the most important when planning this activity.

86. **(D)** Choice (D) is correct. The affective domain presents a taxonomy for feelings and emotions. Choice (A) is incorrect. The psychomotor domain presents a taxonomy for movement. Choice (B) is incorrect. There is no introspective domain. Choice (C) is incorrect. The cognitive domain presents a taxonomy for cognitive processes.

87. **(D)** Choice (D) is correct. Balancing is the most advanced individual activity given here.

The correct order of these activities is:

1. (C)
2. (A)
3. (B)
4. (D)

88. **(B)** Choice (B) is correct. Listening to students is the best way to find out how they are doing. Choices (A) and (C) are incorrect. These choices interrupt the flow of the lesson

and call too much attention to the student. Choice (D) is incorrect. This choice does not permit assessment during the lesson.

89. **(D)** Choice (D) is correct. An objective should describe clearly what the student is expected to do at the completion of instruction. Choices (A) and (B) are incorrect. These choices describe what the teacher will do, not what the student will do. Choice (C) is incorrect. This choice describes what the teacher will do to prepare for the lesson.

90. **(A)** Choice (A) is correct. Note the word NOT in the item. It is fine to provide emotional support even if other students notice. Choices (B), (C), and (D) are incorrect. These are all appropriate ways to respond to the child who is anxious about learning music notation.

91. **(C)** Choice (C) is correct. Music consists of pitch, the actual frequency or sound of a note, and duration. Choice (A) is incorrect. A chord is many different pitches occurring simultaneously. Choice (B) is incorrect. Harmony is a chord with duration. Choice (D) is incorrect. Timbre refers to the unique sound produced by musical instruments; for example, horns (trumpet, trombone) have a similar timbre.

92. **(D)** Choice (D) is correct. Students expect the teacher to be an authority figure. Students may complain, but an authority figure is what students expect and what it is usually best to give them. Choices (A), (B), and (C) are incorrect. Students do not have these general expectations of a teacher, and authority figures do not have to act in one of these ways.

93. **(C)** Choice (C) is correct. Dewey's approach put the child and the child's needs at the center of the curriculum and at the center of the school. Choice (A) is incorrect. Dewey's approach was child centered, not teacher centered. Choice (B) is incorrect. Dewey's approach did not reflect the future needs of society. Choice (D) is incorrect. Team sports do not necessarily reflect Dewey's philosophy.

General Knowledge

94. **(D)** Choice (D) is correct. Economically disadvantaged students are not less capable, but as a group, economically disadvantaged students do have fewer home learning opportunities, which leads to lower achievement scores. Choices (A), (B), and (C) are false.

95. **(B)** Choice (B) is correct. It is generally most appropriate to address questions to the entire class. This maximizes the number of students who are thinking about the answer. Choices (A), (C), and (D) are incorrect. These choices represent incorrect questioning techniques.

96. **(A)** Choice (A) is correct. The best advice among the four choices is to stand where you can see all the students. Choices (B), (C), and (D) are incorrect. These choices represent inappropriate management techniques.

97. **(B)** Choice (B) is correct. Modeling means demonstrating the behavior students should replicate. Choices (A), (C), and (D) are incorrect. None of these is an example of appropriate modeling behavior.

98. **(B)** Choice (B) is correct. This choice describes the least restrictive environment that meets the child's need for support. Choices (A) and (C) are incorrect. Primary placement in a self-contained special education class is too restrictive. Choice (D) is incorrect. Reading level alone should never be used to place a student.

99. **(C)** Choice (C) is correct. Herbart formalized schools, and much of the formal structure of American schools is due to his influence. Choice (A) is incorrect. Rousseau was a philosopher who advocated liberalizing education and wrote an influential book, *Emile*. Choice (B) is incorrect. Froebel founded the first kindergarten (child's garden). Choice (D) is incorrect. Pestalozzi popularized Rousseau's ideas and called for learning through activity. Maria Montessori established the first Casa Bambini.

100. **(D)** Choice (D) is correct. Negative reinforcement means explaining how to avoid negative consequences. Choice (A) is incorrect. Punishment is negative consequences brought on by inappropriate behavior. Choice (B) is incorrect. Reverse psychology is suggesting the opposite of what you want a student to do. Choice (C) is incorrect. Threats, or bullying, are not appropriate teacher behavior.

101. **(D)** Choice (D) is correct. It is appropriate to alter the objectives or plans to focus on the cultural heritage of those in the class. Choices (A), (B), and (C) are incorrect. It is not appropriate to adopt these practices in a culturally and linguistically diverse class.

102. **(C)** Choice (C) is correct. The teacher has violated the copyright law because the teacher did not give appropriate credit to the book's author and copyright holder. Choice (A) is incorrect, in part, because teachers may not use copyrighted material as a substitute for purchasing it. Choice (B) is incorrect. The fair-use doctrine has limitations, and one of those limitations includes crediting the source of the work. Moreover, in this case it might appear that the pages from the children's book were the teacher's own work. Choice (D) is incorrect. Teachers are allowed to make copies of copyrighted materials when the use of these materials falls within the fair-use doctrine.

103. **(D)** Choice (D) is correct. Note the word EXCEPT in the item. Standardized tests are used in effective schools. Choices (A), (B), and (C) are incorrect. These choices represent the characteristics of effective schools.

104. **(B)** Choice (B) is correct. More than any of the other factors, research shows that students learn more when they spend more time on task. Choices (A), (C), and (D) are incorrect. These choices can be effective techniques, but are not as important as time on task.

105. **(A)** Choice (A) is correct. Authentic assessment means a teacher observes students as they work or reviews their work product. Portfolio assessment is a form of authentic assessment. Choices (B), (C), and (D) are incorrect. These choices do not describe authentic assessment.

106. **(D)** Choice (D) is correct. Note the word EXCEPT in the item. In cooperative learning, students summarize the results of their cooperative work. Choices (A), (B), and (C) are incorrect. All of these choices are characteristics of cooperative learning groups.

107. **(C)** Choice (C) is correct. A constructivist approach encourages students to construct their own understanding of concepts. One way students do this is to build on their

initial responses. Choice (A) is not correct. A more reflective approach to questions is in keeping with the constructivist approach. Choice (B) is not correct. This is not the kind of construction that constructivists have in mind. Choice (D) is not correct. The constructivist approach encourages students to create metaphors.

108. **(A)** Choice (A) is correct. Gardner's theory supports the use of interdisciplinary units. Gardner's theory posits that students have many intelligences, not just a cognitive intelligence. Interdisciplinary units promote utilization of these multiple intelligences. Choices (B), (C), and (D) are incorrect. These choices do not reflect Gardner's theory.

109. **(D)** Choice (D) is correct. This is the classic test-based definition of a learning disability—ability at or above average but achievement two or more years below grade level. Choice (A) is incorrect. There is nothing in this record to indicate that the student is a poor test taker, and the IQ score of 110–115 may indicate that the child is not a poor test taker. Choice (B) is incorrect. The student's achievement is well below the student's potential. Choice (C) is incorrect. These IQ test results are not high enough for a gifted classification.

110. **(D)** Choice (D) is correct. Reliability refers to the same work consistently receiving the same evaluation. A school that implemented portfolio assessment had to reconsider its decision because different teachers assigned widely different grades to the same portfolio. Clear rubrics or standards have to be established in order to reliably evaluate portfolios. Choice (A) is not correct. It is not the diverse group of work students put in portfolios that causes the problem; rather, it is the way teachers assess these samples. Choice (B) is not correct. Machines do not typically score the materials in a portfolio. Choice (C) is not correct. The different emphases teachers give to the importance of a portfolio is not an issue of reliability.

Elementary Education: Multiple Subjects

15

An older test and a newer test are currently used by states to measure content knowledge. Each is still in use; however, the shorter older test, Elementary Education: Content Knowledge, is being phased out. The newer longer test, Elementary Education: Multiple Subjects, is replacing the older test. This chapter focuses on the newer test, but the tests are so similar that this chapter is equally useful to help you prepare for the older test.

Both Elementary Education: Multiple Subjects and Elementary Education: Content Knowledge focus on the four main areas of Reading/Language Arts, Mathematics, Social Studies, and Science.

NEWER TEST Elementary Education: Multiple Subjects (5031)

There are four separate timed subtests.

Reading and Language Arts (5032)	**65 multiple-choice items**	**60 minutes**
Mathematics (5033)	**40 multiple-choice items**	**50 minutes**
Social Studies (5034)	**55 multiple-choice items**	**50 minutes**
Science (5035)	**50 multiple-choice items**	**50 minutes**

This test is given in a computer-delivered format only.

Each item has four answer choices.

You may use a scientific or four-function calculator.

OLDER TEST Elementary Education: Content Knowledge (5014)

There are 120 multiple-choice questions, with 30 questions each in the same four areas covered on Elementary Education: Multiple Subjects. The test is given in a paper-delivered and computer-delivered format. You may use a calculator on this test.

PASSING THE ELEMENTARY EDUCATION: MULTIPLE SUBJECTS AND THE ELEMENTARY EDUCATION: CONTENT KNOWLEDGE TESTS

There is more than enough review information, test strategies, and practice tests in this book to help you prepare for these tests. For example, the Core reading and mathematics tests earlier in this book provide very useful preparation for the mathematics test and portions of the reading test. The Elementary Education: Curriculum, Instruction, and Assessment Test in Chapter 14 also includes questions on the four curricular areas covered by these tests. The PLT review in Chapter 10 and the PLT test itself in Chapter 12 offer additional guidance.

If you are preparing for the Content Knowledge test, the longer Multiple Subjects test provides you with more practice. Remember that you are not competing with others for the highest score; you just need the minimum passing score for your state certification.

The state passing scores for these tests are near the score of the lower 25 percent of all test takers, sometimes even near the score of the lower 10 percent. That means the vast majority of test takers pass the test. The high likelihood that you will pass the test is an important part of your preparation.

These tests draw on a vast bank of items, so tests vary in question type and difficulty. That may even mean finding very similar questions on the test you take. The raw score is the number of items you answer correctly. Your raw score determines your scale score, which is the basis for passing the test. Different versions of these tests can be vastly different and are at different difficulty levels. That means the raw passing score will vary, sometimes significantly, from version to version.

Visit the ETS Praxis website for the most recent information about state passing scores.

HOW TO PREPARE FOR THE MULTIPLE SUBJECTS AND THE CONTENT KNOWLEDGE TESTS

This chapter prepares you to take the longer Multiple Subjects test and the Content Knowledge test. The chapter gives an overview of these tests and Chapter 16 provides a full-length practice test with explained answers. Practice items on pages 475–496 are particularly helpful.

Preparation Strategies

Other sections in this book will help you prepare for these tests. The Proven Test Preparation Strategies on page 22 will help you prepare for both tests. The Proven Test-Taking Strategies on page 23 will help you pass both tests as well.

Learning to Read

Reading is the most important subject addressed in school. Students who cannot read effectively are denied access to most other learning. There are dire practical consequences for those who cannot read. Teaching reading is a sophisticated, technical process that requires careful study.

This section reviews five areas of reading instruction: phonemic awareness, phonics, fluency, vocabulary, and text comprehension. You will find a description of each topic, some specific examples, and a summary of the most current research about reading instruction.

PHONEMIC AWARENESS

Here are some essential definitions related to phonemic awareness.

Phoneme

A phoneme is the smallest part of *spoken* language that makes a difference in the meaning of words. Phonemes are represented by letters between slash marks. English has about forty-one phonemes. A few words have one phoneme, but most words have more than one phoneme: The word "at" has two phonemes, one for each letter; "check" has three phonemes (/ch/ /e/ /k/).

Grapheme

A grapheme is the smallest part of *written* language that represents a phoneme in the spelling of a word. A grapheme may be just one letter, such as "b" or "s" or several letters, such as "sh" or "ea."

Phonics

Phonics is the fairly predictable relationship between phonemes and graphemes.

Phonemic Awareness

Phonemic awareness is the ability to hear, identify, and manipulate the individual sounds—phonemes—in spoken words.

Phonological Awareness

Phonological awareness is a broad term that includes phonemic awareness. In addition to phonemes, phonological awareness activities can involve work with rhymes, words, syllables, and onsets and rimes.

Onset and Rime

Onsets and rimes are parts of spoken language that are smaller than syllables but larger than phonemes. An onset is the initial consonant(s) sound of a syllable (the onset of bag is b-; of swim, sw-). A rime is the part of a syllable that contains the vowel and all that follows it (the rime of bag is -ag; of swim, -im).

Children learn phonemes—the sounds of a language—before they learn to read. Phonemic awareness is the ability to notice, think about, and work with those individual sounds in spoken words. Children who have well-established phonemic awareness skills generally find it easier to read and spell than children who do not.

Phonemic awareness is not phonics, as we can see from the definitions above. Phonemic awareness is not the same as phonological awareness, although phonemic awareness is a subcategory of phonological awareness. The focus of phonemic awareness is narrow—identifying and manipulating the individual sounds in words. The focus of phonological awareness is much broader. It includes identifying and manipulating larger parts of spoken language, such as words, syllables, and onsets and rimes—as well as phonemes. It also encompasses awareness of other aspects of sound, such as rhyming, alliteration, and intonation.

Here are some activities to build phonemic awareness.

PHONEME ISOLATION—recognize individual sounds in a word.

PHONEME IDENTITY—recognize the same sounds in different words.

PHONEME CATEGORIZATION—recognize a word with a sound that does not match the sounds in other words.

PHONEME BLENDING—combine the phonemes to form a word. Then they write and read the word.

PHONEME SEGMENTATION—break a word into its separate sounds, saying each sound.

PHONEME DELETION—recognize the word that remains when a phoneme is removed from another word.

PHONEME ADDITION—make a new word by adding a phoneme to an existing word.

PHONEME SUBSTITUTION—substitute one phoneme for another to make a new word.

Phonemic Awareness Instruction Helps Children Learn to Read.

Phonemic awareness instruction aids reading comprehension primarily through its influence on word reading. For children to understand what they read, they must be able to read words rapidly and accurately. Rapid and accurate word reading frees children to focus their attention on the meaning of what they read. Of course, many other things, including the size of children's vocabulary and their world experiences, contribute to reading comprehension.

Phonemic Awareness Instruction Helps Children Learn to Spell.

Teaching phonemic awareness, particularly how to segment words into phonemes, helps children learn to spell. The explanation for this may be that children who have phonemic awareness understand that sounds and letters are related in a predictable way. Thus, they are able to relate the sounds to letters as they spell words.

Phonemic Awareness Instruction Is Most Effective When Children Are Taught to Manipulate Phonemes by Using the Letters of the Alphabet.

Phonemic awareness instruction makes a stronger contribution to the improvement of reading and spelling when children are taught to use letters as they manipulate phonemes than when instruction is limited to phonemes alone. Teaching sounds along with the letters of the alphabet is important because it helps children to see how phonemic awareness relates to their reading and writing.

If children do not know letter names and shapes, they need to be taught them along with phonemic awareness. Relating sounds to letters is, of course, the heart of phonics instruction, which is discussed later in this section.

Phonemic Awareness Instruction Is Most Effective When It Focuses on Only One or Two Types of Phoneme Manipulation.

Children who receive instruction that focuses on one or two types of phoneme manipulation make greater gains in reading and spelling than children who are taught three or more types of manipulation.

PHONICS

Phonics is the relationships between the letters (graphemes) of written language and the individual sounds (phonemes) of spoken language. It teaches children to use these relationships to read and write words. Phonics instruction teaches children a system for remembering how to read words. The alphabetic system is a mnemonic device that supports our memory for specific words.

Systematic Phonics Instruction Is More Effective than Non-Systematic or No Phonics Instruction.

Systematic phonics instruction is the direct teaching of a set of letter–sound relationships in a clearly defined sequence. The set includes the major sound/spelling relationships of both consonants and vowels.

Systematic and Explicit Phonics Instruction Significantly Improves Kindergarten and First-Grade Children's Word Recognition and Spelling.

Systematic phonics instruction produces the greatest impact on children's reading achievement when it begins in kindergarten or first grade.

Both kindergarten and first-grade children who receive systematic phonics instruction are better at reading and spelling words than kindergarten and first-grade children who do not receive systematic instruction.

Systematic and Explicit Phonics Instruction Significantly Improves Children's Reading Comprehension.

Systematic phonics instruction results in better growth in children's ability to comprehend what they read than non-systematic or no phonics instruction. This is not surprising because the ability to read the words in a text accurately and quickly is highly related to successful reading comprehension.

Systematic and Explicit Phonics Instruction Is Effective for Children from Various Social and Economic Levels.

Systematic phonics instruction is beneficial to children regardless of their socioeconomic status. It helps children from various backgrounds make greater gains in reading than non-systematic instruction or no phonics instruction.

Systematic and explicit phonics instruction is particularly beneficial for children who are having difficulty learning to read and who are at risk for developing future reading problems.

Systematic phonics instruction is significantly more effective than non-systematic or no phonics instruction in helping to prevent reading difficulties among at risk students and in helping children overcome reading difficulties.

Systematic and Explicit Phonics Instruction Is Most Effective When Introduced Early.

Phonics instruction is most effective when it begins in kindergarten or first grade. To be effective with young learners, systematic instruction must be designed appropriately and taught carefully. It should include teaching letter shapes and names, phonemic awareness, and all major letter–sound relationships. It should ensure that all children learn these skills. As instruction proceeds, children should be taught to use this knowledge to read and write words.

Phonics Instruction Is Not an Entire Reading Program for Beginning Readers.

Along with phonics instruction, young children should be solidifying their knowledge of the alphabet, engaging in phonemic awareness activities, and listening to stories and informational texts read aloud to them. They also should be reading texts (both out loud and silently) and writing letters, words, messages, and stories.

EXAMPLES OF NON-SYSTEMATIC PROGRAMS

Here are examples of non-systematic programs that may be important in other ways but that do not achieve the essential outcomes of systematic phonics instruction.

Literature-Based Programs That Emphasize Reading and Writing Activities.

Phonics instruction is embedded in these activities, but letter–sound relationships are taught incidentally, usually based on key letters that appear in student reading materials.

Basal Reading Programs That Focus on Whole-Word or Meaning-Based Activities.

These programs pay only limited attention to letter–sound relationships and provide little or no instruction in how to blend letters to pronounce words.

Sight-Word Programs That Begin by Teaching a Sight-Word Reading Vocabulary of from 50 to 100 Words.

Only after they learn to read these words do children receive instruction in the alphabetic principle.

Adding Phonics Workbooks or Phonics Activities.

Just adding phonics workbooks or phonics activities to these programs has not been effective. Such "add-ons" tend to confuse rather than help children to read.

FLUENCY

Fluency means to read a text accurately and quickly. Fluent readers recognize words automatically and they group words quickly to help them gain meaning. Fluent readers read aloud effortlessly and with expression. Readers who have not yet developed fluency read slowly, word by word. Their oral reading is choppy and plodding.

Fluency is the bridge between word recognition and comprehension. Fluent readers can concentrate on meaning because they do not have to concentrate on decoding words. Less fluent readers, however, must focus their attention on the words and not on meaning.

Fluency develops gradually through substantial practice. At the earliest stage of reading development, students' oral reading is slow and labored and even when students recognize many words automatically, their oral reading may still not be fluent. To read with expression, readers must be able to divide the text into meaningful chunks and know when to pause appropriately.

Fluency varies, depending on what readers are reading. Even very skilled readers may read in a slow, labored manner when reading texts with many unfamiliar words or topics. For example, readers who are usually fluent may not be able to fluently read unfamiliar technical material.

Repeated and Monitored Oral Reading Improves Reading Fluency and Overall Reading Achievement.

Students who read and reread passages orally as they receive guidance and/or feedback become better readers. Repeated oral reading substantially improves word recognition, speed, and accuracy as well as fluency. To a lesser but still considerable extent, repeated oral reading also improves reading comprehension. Repeated oral reading improves the reading ability of all students throughout the elementary school years. It also helps struggling readers at higher grade levels.

Round-robin reading means students take turns reading parts of a text aloud (though usually not repeatedly). But round-robin reading in itself does not increase fluency. This may be because students only read small amounts of text, and they usually read this small portion only once.

Students should read and reread a text a certain number of times or until a certain level of fluency is reached. Four rereadings are sufficient for most students. Oral reading practice is increased through the use of audiotapes, tutors, and peer guidance.

No Research Evidence Currently Confirms That Silent, Independent Reading with Minimal Guidance Improves Reading Fluency and Overall Reading Achievement.

One of the major differences between good and poor readers is the amount of time they spend reading. But research has not yet confirmed whether independent silent reading with minimal guidance or feedback improves reading achievement and fluency. Neither has it proven that more silent reading in the classroom cannot work. But the research does suggest that there are more beneficial ways to spend reading instructional time than to have students read independently in the classroom without reading instruction.

Students Should Hear Models of Fluent Reading.

Primary teachers should read aloud daily to their students. By reading effortlessly and with expression, the teacher is modeling how a fluent reader sounds during reading. After a teacher models how to read students should reread the selection.

A teacher should encourage parents or other family members to read aloud to their children at home. The more models of fluent reading the children hear, the better. Of course, hearing a model of fluent reading is not the only benefit of reading aloud to children. Reading to children also increases their knowledge of the world, their vocabulary, their familiarity with written language, and their interest in reading.

Students Should Read Orally from Text They Can Easily Master.

Fluency develops as a result of many opportunities to practice reading with a high degree of success. Therefore, students should practice orally rereading text that contains mostly words that they know or can decode easily. In other words, the texts should be at the students' independent reading level, which means the student can read it with about 95 percent accuracy. If the text is more difficult, students will focus so much on word recognition that they will not have an opportunity to develop fluency.

The text your students practice rereading orally should also be relatively short—probably 50–200 words, depending on the age of the students. You should also use a variety of reading materials, including stories, nonfiction, and poetry. Poetry is especially well suited to fluency practice because poems for children are often short and they contain rhythm, rhyme, and meaning, making practice easy, fun, and rewarding.

VOCABULARY

Vocabulary refers to the words people must know to communicate effectively. In general, vocabulary can be described as oral vocabulary or reading vocabulary. Oral vocabulary refers to words used in speaking or recognized in listening. Reading vocabulary refers to words we recognized or used in print.

Vocabulary plays an important part in learning to read. As beginning readers, children use the words they have heard to make sense of the words they see in print. Beginning readers have a much more difficult time reading words that are not already part of their oral vocabulary.

Vocabulary also is very important to reading comprehension. Readers cannot understand what they are reading without knowing what most of the words mean. As children learn to read more advanced texts, they must learn the meaning of new words that are not part of their oral vocabulary.

Children Learn the Meanings of Most Words Indirectly, Through Everyday Experiences with Oral and Written Language.

Children learn word meanings indirectly in three ways:

Children Engage in Oral Language Daily.

Young children learn word meanings through conversations with other people, especially adults. As they engage in these conversations, children often hear adults repeat words several times. They also may hear adults use new and interesting words. The more oral language experiences children have, the more word meanings they learn.

Children Listen to Adults Read to Them.

Children learn word meanings from listening to adults read to them. Reading aloud is particularly helpful when the reader pauses during reading to define an unfamiliar word and, after reading, engages the child in a conversation about the book. Conversations about books help children to learn new words and concepts and to relate them to their prior knowledge and experience.

Children Read Extensively on Their Own.

Children learn many new words by reading extensively on their own. The more children read on their own, the more words they encounter and the more word meanings they learn.

Teaching Specific Words Before Reading Helps Both Vocabulary and Reading Comprehension.

Before students read a text, it is helpful to teach them specific words they will see in the text. Teaching important vocabulary before reading can help students learn new words and comprehend the text.

Extended Instruction That Promotes Active Engagement with Vocabulary Improves Word Learning.

Children learn words best when they work actively with the words over an extended period of time. The more students use new words and the more they use them in different contexts, the more likely they are to learn the words.

Repeated Exposure to Vocabulary in Many Contexts Aids Word Learning.

Students learn new words better when they encounter them often and in various contexts. When the students read those same words in their texts, they increase their exposure to the new words.

WORD-LEARNING STRATEGIES

Of course, it is not possible for teachers to provide specific instruction for all the words their students do not know. Therefore, students also need to be able to determine the meaning of words that are new to them but not taught directly to them. They need to develop effective word-learning strategies. Word-learning strategies include:

1. how to use dictionaries and other reference aids to learn word meanings and to deepen knowledge of word meanings;
2. how to use information about word parts to figure out the meanings of words in text; and
3. how to use context clues to determine word meanings.

Using Dictionaries and Other Reference Aids.

Students must learn how to use dictionaries, glossaries, and thesauruses to help broaden and deepen their knowledge of words, even though these resources can be difficult to use. The most helpful dictionaries include sentences providing clear examples of word meanings in context.

PARTS OF WORDS

Word parts include *affixes* (prefixes and suffixes), *base words*, and *word roots*.

AFFIXES are word parts that are "fixed to" either the beginnings of words (prefixes) or the ending of words (suffixes). The word "unremarkable" has two affixes, a prefix "un" and a suffix "able."

BASE WORDS are words from which many other words are formed. For example, many words can be formed from the base word migrate: migration, migrant, immigration, immigrant, migrating, migratory.

WORD ROOTS are the words from other languages that are the origin of many English words. About 60 percent of all English words have Latin or Greek origins.

Using Context Clues

Context clues are hints about the meaning of an unknown word that are provided in the words, phrases, and sentences that surround the word. Context clues include definitions, restatements, examples, or descriptions. Because students learn most word meanings indirectly, or from context, it is important that they learn to use context clues effectively.

TEXT COMPREHENSION

Comprehension is the reason for reading. Without comprehension, reading is a largely meaningless activity. Good readers are both purposeful and active as they read.

Good Readers Are Purposeful.

Good readers have a purpose for reading. They may read to find out how to use a food processor, read a guidebook to gather information about national parks, read a textbook to satisfy the requirements of a course, read a magazine for entertainment, or read a classic novel to experience the pleasures of great literature.

Good Readers Are Active.

Good readers think actively as they read. To make sense of what they read, good readers engage in a complicated process. Using their experiences and knowledge of the world, their knowledge of vocabulary and language structure, and their knowledge of reading strategies (or plans), good readers make sense of the text and know how to get the most out of it. They know when they have problems with understanding and how to resolve these problems as they occur.

Over 30 years of research has shown that instruction in comprehension can help students understand what they read, remember what they read, and communicate with others about what they read.

Specific Comprehension Strategies Help Improve Text Comprehension.

Comprehension strategies are conscious sets of steps that good readers use to make sense of text. Comprehension strategy instruction helps students become purposeful, active readers who are in control of their own reading comprehension.

The following six strategies appear to have a firm scientific basis for improving text comprehension.

METACOGNITION. Metacognition can be defined as "thinking about thinking." Good readers use metacognitive strategies to think about and have control over their reading. Before reading, they might clarify their purpose for reading and preview the text. During reading, they might monitor their understanding, adjusting their reading speed to fit the difficulty of the text and "fixing up" any comprehension problems they have. After reading, they check their understanding of what they read.

COMPREHENSION MONITORING. Comprehension monitoring is a critical part of metacognition. Students who are good at monitoring their comprehension know when they understand what they read and when they do not. They have strategies to "fix up" problems in their understanding as the problems arise. Research shows that instruction, even in the early grades, can help students become better at monitoring their comprehension.

USING GRAPHIC AND SEMANTIC ORGANIZERS. Graphic organizers illustrate concepts and interrelationships among concepts in a text, using diagrams or other pictorial devices. Graphic organizers may be maps, webs, graphs, charts, frames, or clusters. Semantic organizers (also called semantic maps or semantic webs) are graphic organizers that look somewhat like a spider web. In a semantic organizer, lines connect a central concept to a variety of related ideas and events.

Regardless of the label, graphic organizers can help readers focus on concepts and how they are related to other concepts. Graphic organizers help students read to learn from informational text in the content areas, such as science and social studies textbooks and trade books. Used with informational text, graphic organizers can help students see how concepts fit common text structures. Graphic organizers are also used with narrative text, or stories, as story maps.

RECOGNIZING STORY STRUCTURE. Story structure refers to the way the content and events of a story are organized into a plot. Students who can recognize story structure have greater appreciation, understanding, and memory for stories. In story structure instruction, students learn to identify the categories of content (setting, initiating events, internal reactions, goals, attempts, and outcomes) and how this content is organized into a plot. Often, students learn to recognize story structure through the use of story maps. Story maps, a type of graphic organizer, show the sequence of events in simple stories. Instruction in the content and organization of stories improves students' comprehension and memory of stories.

SUMMARIZING. A summary is a synthesis of the important ideas in a text. Summarizing requires students to determine what is important in what they are reading, to condense this information, and to put it into their own words. Instruction in summarizing helps students identify or generate main ideas; connect the main or central ideas; eliminate redundant and unnecessary information; and remember what they read.

Students Can Be Taught to Use Comprehension Strategies.

In addition to identifying which comprehension strategies are effective, scientific research provides guidelines for how to teach comprehension strategies.

Effective Comprehension Strategy Instruction Is Explicit, or Direct.

Research shows that explicit teaching techniques are particularly effective for comprehension strategy instruction. In explicit instruction, teachers tell readers why and when they should use strategies, what strategies to use, and how to apply them. The steps of explicit instruction typically include direct explanation, teacher modeling ("thinking aloud"), guided practice, and application.

DIRECT EXPLANATION. The teacher explains to students why the strategy helps comprehension and when to apply the strategy.

MODELING. The teacher models, or demonstrates, how to apply the strategy, usually by "thinking aloud" while reading the text that the students are using.

GUIDED PRACTICE. The teacher guides and assists students as they learn how and when to apply the strategy.

APPLICATION. The teacher helps students practice the strategy until they can apply it independently.

Effective Comprehension Strategy Instruction Can Be Accomplished Through Cooperative Learning.

Cooperative learning (and the closely related concept, collaborative learning) involves students working together as partners or in small groups on clearly defined tasks. Cooperative learning instruction has been used successfully to teach comprehension strategies in content-area subjects. Students work together to understand content-area texts, helping each other learn and apply comprehension strategies. Teachers help students learn to work in groups, demonstrate comprehension strategies, and monitor student progress.

Effective Instruction Helps Readers Use Comprehension Strategies Flexibly and in Combination.

Good readers must be able to coordinate and adjust several strategies to assist comprehension. Multiple-strategy instruction teaches students how to use strategies flexibly as they are needed to assist their comprehension. In a well-known example of multiple-strategy instruction called "reciprocal teaching," the teacher and students work together so that the students learn these four comprehension strategies.

1. Ask questions about the text they are reading;
2. Summarize parts of the text;
3. Clarify words and sentences students don't understand;
4. Predict what might occur next in the text.

Teachers and students use these four strategies flexibly as they are needed in reading literature and informational texts.

LANGUAGE

Humans use language, including gestures and sounds, to communicate. Humans first used gestures, but it was spoken language that opened the vistas for human communication. Language consists of two things: the thoughts that language conveys and the physical sounds, writing, and structure of the language itself.

Human speech organs (mouth, tongue, lips, etc.) were not developed to make sounds but they uniquely determined the sounds and words humans could produce. Human speech gradually came to be loosely bound together by unique rules of grammar.

Many believe that humans developed their unique ability to speak with the development of a specialized area of the brain called Broca's area. If this is so, human speech and language probably developed in the past 100,000 years.

The appearance of written language about 3500 B.C. separates prehistoric from historic times. Written language often does not adequately represent the spoken language. For example, English uses the 26-letter Latin alphabet, which does not represent all the English sounds.

THE ENGLISH LANGUAGE

The English language emerged 1,500 years ago from Germanic languages on the European continent and developed primarily in England. American English is based on the English language and includes words from every major language including Latin, Greek, and French.

English is spoken throughout Australia, Canada, the United Kingdom, and the United States. It is the most universally accepted language in the world, and only Chinese is spoken by more people. In all likelihood, English will become even more prominent as the world's primary language.

Some experts estimate that there are over 1,000,000 English words, more than any other language in the world. Sounds and letters do not match in the English language. For example, the word spelled t-o-u-g-h is pronounced *tuf*. The rock group Phish also reminds us of this variation, which often makes English words difficult to pronounce and spell.

Language has a structure and a function. The structure of a language refers to the way words and sentences are combined to create effective communication. The function of a language is the ability to use language to think and communicate. Understanding language development means understanding how each of these aspects develops.

Much of the recent work on structural language development is related to Chomsky's work. Chomsky says that the "old" explanations of language development, modeling and reinforcement, were incorrect. This is not to say that language cannot be learned through these methods because this task is accomplished every day as people learn a foreign language. Rather, Chomsky says that this model-repeat-reinforce approach is not the way that children actually learn language.

Chomsky holds that children possess an innate ability to learn language, both words and structure, merely through exposure. To bolster his argument, Chomsky points out that most grammatical mistakes made by children actually follow the general grammatical rules of the language and that the children's errors often represent exceptions to these rules.

For example, a child may say "Lisa goed to the store" instead of "Lisa went to the store." Chomsky would say, *goed* is structurally sound and represents a good grasp of the English language. The child would certainly say *hopped* if Lisa had gotten to the store that way. The problem is created because the past tense for go is an exception to the past tense formation rule.

Vygotsky is a prominent psychologist who studied the relationship between thought and language. A contemporary of Piaget, he pointed out that thought and language are not coordinated during the sensorimotor and most of the preoperational stages. That is, from birth through about age 6 or 7, thought and language develop independently, with language being primarily functional.

As students move toward the concrete operational stage, their language also becomes operational. That is, thought and the structural and functional aspects of language become integrated, and students can use language to think and solve problems.

Teachers can foster language development most effectively by constantly encouraging and enabling students to express themselves by speaking and writing. Students should be encouraged to integrate writing and speaking with all subject matter, and writing and speaking should be the overarching classroom objectives to be developed in every lesson. In all cases, teachers should help children communicate in standard English while in school.

ASSESSMENT PROGRAM

Every teacher evaluates instruction. The assessment program and the assessment instruments should measure mastery and understanding of important topics. The assessment program should also be used as a teaching tool. That is, the program should be used to help students learn and to improve instruction. The program should include authentic assessment of students' work as well as teacher-made and standardized tests.

Formative assessment information is usually gathered before or during teaching. Formative information is used to help you prepare appropriate lessons and assist students. Formative evaluations help teachers decide which objectives to teach, which instructional techniques to use, and which special help or service to provide to individual students.

Summative assessment information is usually gathered once instruction is complete. Summative evaluation is used to make judgments about student achievement and the effectiveness of the instructional programs. Summative evaluations lead to grades, to reports about a student's relative level of accomplishment, and to alterations of instructional programs.

Assessment information may be used for both purposes. For example, you may give a test to determine grades for a marking period or unit. You may then use the information from this test to plan further instruction and arrange individual help for students.

You may informally gather formative and summative information. Just walking around the room observing students' work can yield a lot of useful information. You can frequently discern the additional work that students need and identify different levels of student achievement.

ASSESSMENT

Tests have long been used to determine what students have learned and to compare students. Every test is imperfect. Many tests are so imperfect that they are useless. It is important to realize how this imperfection affects test results.

Some students are poor test takers. Every test assumes that the test taker has the opportunity to demonstrate what he or she knows. A student may know something but be unable to demonstrate it on a particular test. You must also consider alternative assessment strategies for these students.

Familiarize yourself with these basic assessment concepts.

- Errors of Measurement—Every test contains errors of measurement. In other words, no one test accurately measures a student's achievement or ability. Carefully designed standardized tests may have measurement errors of 5 percent or 10 percent. Teacher-designed tests typically have large errors of measurement.

  A test result shows that a student falls into a range of scores and not just the single reported score. Focusing on a single score and ignoring the score range is among the most serious of score-reporting errors.

- Reliability—A reliable test is consistent. That is, a reliable test will give similar results when given to the same person in a short time span. You cannot count on unreliable tests to give you useful scores. Use only very reliable standardized tests and be very aware of how important reliability is when you make up your own tests.

- Validity—Valid tests measure what they are supposed to measure. There are two important types of validity: content validity and criterion validity.

  A test with high content validity measures the material covered in the curriculum or unit being tested. Tests that lack high content validity are unfair. When you make up a test it should have complete content validity. This does not mean that the test has to be unchallenging. It does mean that the questions should refer to the subject matter covered.

  A test with high criterion validity successfully predicts the ability to do other work. For example, a test to be an automobile mechanic with high criterion validity will successfully predict who will be a good mechanic.

HOW MUCH SHOULD I REVIEW

There is always a reasonable question about the amount you should review. The idea is to review neither too little nor too much.

Think about the scale score you need to pass and how that translates into the required number correct on the test. As tests go, the low required scale score makes these very reasonable tests to pass. We are always asked about the number correct needed to pass a test. It is unclear, and it varies from one test version to the other. However, our best GUESS is you need to get 65 to 75 percent correct to reach the 25th percentile.

Mathematics, English, vocabulary, and reading review are in this book as well as links to Web-based reviews for the rest of the test. We think you will like this approach because it will give you more flexibility.

To that end, we scoured the Internet to find the best review sites. Naturally we wanted sites that would provide a useful review, as well as remain active for a long time. Those were our two criteria. All the links we list were active at press time. Websites are constantly being added to the Internet, and you can always go online and do your own search, but we think the sites mentioned below will serve you well.

For overall subject review, we were frequently drawn to the Wikipedia sites. These sites are under constant review and scrutiny, and because they include many links, you can easily pursue further review, if you choose to. That helps you avoid being trapped in an overwhelmingly long review. This does not mean all Wikipedia articles are useful, but questionable articles are usually flagged.

You can just go directly to *en.wikipedia.org* and enter your own search terms in the box on the left.

Reading/Language Arts

READING

___ Chapter 7 contains an extensive vocabulary and reading review.

ENGLISH AND WRITING

___ Chapter 5 contains a thorough English and writing review.

READING/LANGUAGE INSTRUCTION

This paper from the National Reading Panel gives an excellent introduction to the fundamental concepts of reading along with a summary of effective reading practices.

____ *www.nichd.nih.gov/publications/nrp/findings.cfm*

"Teaching Reading is Rocket Science" is a practical overview of teaching reading.

____ *www.aft.org/pubs-reports/downloads/teachers/rocketsci.pdf*

LITERATURE

Children's Literature

Comprehensive summary from the University of Connecticut with useful additional links.

____ *www.southernct.edu/%7Ebrownm/300hlit.html*

This detailed Wikipedia article about children's literature includes a chronological list of well-known children's authors and an extensive list of other useful links for further study.

____ *en.wikipedia.org/wiki/Children's_literature*

English Literature

All literature written in English is referred to as English literature.

This Wikipedia article is the most useful concise review of English literature that we have found. It includes many additional links for further study.

_____ *en.wikipedia.org/wiki/English_literature*

American Literature

This Wikipedia article is the most useful brief review we found of American literature.

_____ *en.wikipedia.org/wiki/American_literature*

Mathematics

Chapter 6 on contains a thorough mathematics review with ample practice. You may use a four-function calculator or a scientific calculator during the test, so use the calculator you will bring to the test as you complete the activities in this chapter.

For additional practice, complete the Core Mathematics tests on page 266 and page 332.

History

UNITED STATES HISTORY

This link from Wikipedia gives an overview of United States history, with many links for further study.

_____ *en.wikipedia.org/wiki/History_of_the_United_States*

This time line of United States history from Wikipedia gives links to specific historical periods beginning in the 1400s.

_____ *en.wikipedia.org/wiki/Timeline_of_United_States_history*

This link-based United States history review gives a fairly thorough overview of United States history and allows you to select the historic periods or events you want to study.

_____ *countrystudies.us/united-states/*

UNITED STATES GEOGRAPHY

This overview of United States geography from Wikipedia provides many links to additional reviews and maps.

_____ *en.wikipedia.org/wiki/Geography_of_the_United_States*

UNITED STATES GOVERNMENT

This United States government overview from Wikipedia gives a thorough overview with links for any additional study you may choose to pursue.

_____ *en.wikipedia.org/wiki/United_States_Government*

WORLD HISTORY

Wikipedia world history overview provides a complete overview with additional links for further study.

_____ *en.wikipedia.org/wiki/History_of_the_world*

Science

We feature these Wikipedia links about life science (biology), earth science, physical science, the history of science, and even for inquiry-based science instruction. All these sites contain many links for further study. Most other online sites typically contain too much information and will not give you the opportunity to limit your study.

EARTH SCIENCE

_____ *en.wikipedia.org/wiki/Earth_science*

LIFE SCIENCE (BIOLOGY)

_____ *en.wikipedia.org/wiki/Biology*

PHYSICAL SCIENCE

_____ *en.wikipedia.org/wiki/Physical_science*

INQUIRY-BASED SCIENCE INSTRUCTION

_____ *en.wikipedia.org/wiki/Inquiry-based_science*

HISTORY OF SCIENCE

_____ *en.wikipedia.org/wiki/History_of_science*

Elementary Education Practice Test: Multiple Subjects

16

The items in this practice test are organized by content area: Reading/Language Arts, Mathematics, Social Studies, and Science. You may use a basic four-function calculator or a scientific calculator on this test. The calculator must be solar or battery powered. You cannot use a noisy calculator, a calculator with a paper tape, or a pocket organizer. There are many different versions of this test, and the version you take may have a different emphasis and focus than this practice test.

There are four separately timed subtests. Keep the time limit in mind as you work. There is no penalty for guessing. Each item has four answer choices. Exactly one of these choices is correct.

Mark your choice on the test to simulate the computer-delivered test. Use a pencil to mark the test. Once the test is complete, correct your answers and review the answer explanations.

When instructed, turn the page and begin.

ANSWER SHEET
Elementary Education Practice Test

Subtest 5032 Reading/Language Arts

1. Ⓐ Ⓑ Ⓒ Ⓓ	18. Ⓐ Ⓑ Ⓒ Ⓓ	35. Ⓐ Ⓑ Ⓒ Ⓓ	52. Ⓐ Ⓑ Ⓒ Ⓓ
2. Ⓐ Ⓑ Ⓒ Ⓓ	19. Ⓐ Ⓑ Ⓒ Ⓓ	36. Ⓐ Ⓑ Ⓒ Ⓓ	53. Ⓐ Ⓑ Ⓒ Ⓓ
3. Ⓐ Ⓑ Ⓒ Ⓓ	20. Ⓐ Ⓑ Ⓒ Ⓓ	37. Ⓐ Ⓑ Ⓒ Ⓓ	54. Ⓐ Ⓑ Ⓒ Ⓓ
4. Ⓐ Ⓑ Ⓒ Ⓓ	21. Ⓐ Ⓑ Ⓒ Ⓓ	38. Ⓐ Ⓑ Ⓒ Ⓓ	55. Ⓐ Ⓑ Ⓒ Ⓓ
5. Ⓐ Ⓑ Ⓒ Ⓓ	22. Ⓐ Ⓑ Ⓒ Ⓓ	39. Ⓐ Ⓑ Ⓒ Ⓓ	56. Ⓐ Ⓑ Ⓒ Ⓓ
6. Ⓐ Ⓑ Ⓒ Ⓓ	23. Ⓐ Ⓑ Ⓒ Ⓓ	40. Ⓐ Ⓑ Ⓒ Ⓓ	57. Ⓐ Ⓑ Ⓒ Ⓓ
7. Ⓐ Ⓑ Ⓒ Ⓓ	24. Ⓐ Ⓑ Ⓒ Ⓓ	41. Ⓐ Ⓑ Ⓒ Ⓓ	58. Ⓐ Ⓑ Ⓒ Ⓓ
8. Ⓐ Ⓑ Ⓒ Ⓓ	25. Ⓐ Ⓑ Ⓒ Ⓓ	42. Ⓐ Ⓑ Ⓒ Ⓓ	59. Ⓐ Ⓑ Ⓒ Ⓓ
9. Ⓐ Ⓑ Ⓒ Ⓓ	26. Ⓐ Ⓑ Ⓒ Ⓓ	43. Ⓐ Ⓑ Ⓒ Ⓓ	60. Ⓐ Ⓑ Ⓒ Ⓓ
10. Ⓐ Ⓑ Ⓒ Ⓓ	27. Ⓐ Ⓑ Ⓒ Ⓓ	44. Ⓐ Ⓑ Ⓒ Ⓓ	61. Ⓐ Ⓑ Ⓒ Ⓓ
11. Ⓐ Ⓑ Ⓒ Ⓓ	28. Ⓐ Ⓑ Ⓒ Ⓓ	45. Ⓐ Ⓑ Ⓒ Ⓓ	62. Ⓐ Ⓑ Ⓒ Ⓓ
12. Ⓐ Ⓑ Ⓒ Ⓓ	29. Ⓐ Ⓑ Ⓒ Ⓓ	46. Ⓐ Ⓑ Ⓒ Ⓓ	63. Ⓐ Ⓑ Ⓒ Ⓓ
13. Ⓐ Ⓑ Ⓒ Ⓓ	30. Ⓐ Ⓑ Ⓒ Ⓓ	47. Ⓐ Ⓑ Ⓒ Ⓓ	64. Ⓐ Ⓑ Ⓒ Ⓓ
14. Ⓐ Ⓑ Ⓒ Ⓓ	31. Ⓐ Ⓑ Ⓒ Ⓓ	48. Ⓐ Ⓑ Ⓒ Ⓓ	65. Ⓐ Ⓑ Ⓒ Ⓓ
15. Ⓐ Ⓑ Ⓒ Ⓓ	32. Ⓐ Ⓑ Ⓒ Ⓓ	49. Ⓐ Ⓑ Ⓒ Ⓓ	
16. Ⓐ Ⓑ Ⓒ Ⓓ	33. Ⓐ Ⓑ Ⓒ Ⓓ	50. Ⓐ Ⓑ Ⓒ Ⓓ	
17. Ⓐ Ⓑ Ⓒ Ⓓ	34. Ⓐ Ⓑ Ⓒ Ⓓ	51. Ⓐ Ⓑ Ⓒ Ⓓ	

Subtest 5033 Mathematics

1. Ⓐ Ⓑ Ⓒ Ⓓ	11. Ⓐ Ⓑ Ⓒ Ⓓ	21. Ⓐ Ⓑ Ⓒ Ⓓ	31. Ⓐ Ⓑ Ⓒ Ⓓ
2. Ⓐ Ⓑ Ⓒ Ⓓ	12. Ⓐ Ⓑ Ⓒ Ⓓ	22. Ⓐ Ⓑ Ⓒ Ⓓ	32. Ⓐ Ⓑ Ⓒ Ⓓ
3. Ⓐ Ⓑ Ⓒ Ⓓ	13. Ⓐ Ⓑ Ⓒ Ⓓ	23. Ⓐ Ⓑ Ⓒ Ⓓ	33. Ⓐ Ⓑ Ⓒ Ⓓ
4. Ⓐ Ⓑ Ⓒ Ⓓ	14. Ⓐ Ⓑ Ⓒ Ⓓ	24. Ⓐ Ⓑ Ⓒ Ⓓ	34. Ⓐ Ⓑ Ⓒ Ⓓ
5. Ⓐ Ⓑ Ⓒ Ⓓ	15. Ⓐ Ⓑ Ⓒ Ⓓ	25. Ⓐ Ⓑ Ⓒ Ⓓ	35. Ⓐ Ⓑ Ⓒ Ⓓ
6. Ⓐ Ⓑ Ⓒ Ⓓ	16. Ⓐ Ⓑ Ⓒ Ⓓ	26. Ⓐ Ⓑ Ⓒ Ⓓ	36. Ⓐ Ⓑ Ⓒ Ⓓ
7. Ⓐ Ⓑ Ⓒ Ⓓ	17. Ⓐ Ⓑ Ⓒ Ⓓ	27. Ⓐ Ⓑ Ⓒ Ⓓ	37. Ⓐ Ⓑ Ⓒ Ⓓ
8. Ⓐ Ⓑ Ⓒ Ⓓ	18. Ⓐ Ⓑ Ⓒ Ⓓ	28. Ⓐ Ⓑ Ⓒ Ⓓ	38. Ⓐ Ⓑ Ⓒ Ⓓ
9. Ⓐ Ⓑ Ⓒ Ⓓ	19. Ⓐ Ⓑ Ⓒ Ⓓ	29. Ⓐ Ⓑ Ⓒ Ⓓ	39. Ⓐ Ⓑ Ⓒ Ⓓ
10. Ⓐ Ⓑ Ⓒ Ⓓ	20. Ⓐ Ⓑ Ⓒ Ⓓ	30. Ⓐ Ⓑ Ⓒ Ⓓ	40. Ⓐ Ⓑ Ⓒ Ⓓ

ANSWER SHEET
Elementary Education
Practice Test

Subtest 5034 Social Studies

1. Ⓐ Ⓑ Ⓒ Ⓓ	16. Ⓐ Ⓑ Ⓒ Ⓓ	31. Ⓐ Ⓑ Ⓒ Ⓓ	46. Ⓐ Ⓑ Ⓒ Ⓓ
2. Ⓐ Ⓑ Ⓒ Ⓓ	17. Ⓐ Ⓑ Ⓒ Ⓓ	32. Ⓐ Ⓑ Ⓒ Ⓓ	47. Ⓐ Ⓑ Ⓒ Ⓓ
3. Ⓐ Ⓑ Ⓒ Ⓓ	18. Ⓐ Ⓑ Ⓒ Ⓓ	33. Ⓐ Ⓑ Ⓒ Ⓓ	48. Ⓐ Ⓑ Ⓒ Ⓓ
4. Ⓐ Ⓑ Ⓒ Ⓓ	19. Ⓐ Ⓑ Ⓒ Ⓓ	34. Ⓐ Ⓑ Ⓒ Ⓓ	49. Ⓐ Ⓑ Ⓒ Ⓓ
5. Ⓐ Ⓑ Ⓒ Ⓓ	20. Ⓐ Ⓑ Ⓒ Ⓓ	35. Ⓐ Ⓑ Ⓒ Ⓓ	50. Ⓐ Ⓑ Ⓒ Ⓓ
6. Ⓐ Ⓑ Ⓒ Ⓓ	21. Ⓐ Ⓑ Ⓒ Ⓓ	36. Ⓐ Ⓑ Ⓒ Ⓓ	51. Ⓐ Ⓑ Ⓒ Ⓓ
7. Ⓐ Ⓑ Ⓒ Ⓓ	22. Ⓐ Ⓑ Ⓒ Ⓓ	37. Ⓐ Ⓑ Ⓒ Ⓓ	52. Ⓐ Ⓑ Ⓒ Ⓓ
8. Ⓐ Ⓑ Ⓒ Ⓓ	23. Ⓐ Ⓑ Ⓒ Ⓓ	38. Ⓐ Ⓑ Ⓒ Ⓓ	53. Ⓐ Ⓑ Ⓒ Ⓓ
9. Ⓐ Ⓑ Ⓒ Ⓓ	24. Ⓐ Ⓑ Ⓒ Ⓓ	39. Ⓐ Ⓑ Ⓒ Ⓓ	54. Ⓐ Ⓑ Ⓒ Ⓓ
10. Ⓐ Ⓑ Ⓒ Ⓓ	25. Ⓐ Ⓑ Ⓒ Ⓓ	40. Ⓐ Ⓑ Ⓒ Ⓓ	55. Ⓐ Ⓑ Ⓒ Ⓓ
11. Ⓐ Ⓑ Ⓒ Ⓓ	26. Ⓐ Ⓑ Ⓒ Ⓓ	41. Ⓐ Ⓑ Ⓒ Ⓓ	
12. Ⓐ Ⓑ Ⓒ Ⓓ	27. Ⓐ Ⓑ Ⓒ Ⓓ	42. Ⓐ Ⓑ Ⓒ Ⓓ	
13. Ⓐ Ⓑ Ⓒ Ⓓ	28. Ⓐ Ⓑ Ⓒ Ⓓ	43. Ⓐ Ⓑ Ⓒ Ⓓ	
14. Ⓐ Ⓑ Ⓒ Ⓓ	29. Ⓐ Ⓑ Ⓒ Ⓓ	44. Ⓐ Ⓑ Ⓒ Ⓓ	
15. Ⓐ Ⓑ Ⓒ Ⓓ	30. Ⓐ Ⓑ Ⓒ Ⓓ	45. Ⓐ Ⓑ Ⓒ Ⓓ	

Subtest 5035 Science

1. Ⓐ Ⓑ Ⓒ Ⓓ	14. Ⓐ Ⓑ Ⓒ Ⓓ	27. Ⓐ Ⓑ Ⓒ Ⓓ	40. Ⓐ Ⓑ Ⓒ Ⓓ
2. Ⓐ Ⓑ Ⓒ Ⓓ	15. Ⓐ Ⓑ Ⓒ Ⓓ	28. Ⓐ Ⓑ Ⓒ Ⓓ	41. Ⓐ Ⓑ Ⓒ Ⓓ
3. Ⓐ Ⓑ Ⓒ Ⓓ	16. Ⓐ Ⓑ Ⓒ Ⓓ	29. Ⓐ Ⓑ Ⓒ Ⓓ	42. Ⓐ Ⓑ Ⓒ Ⓓ
4. Ⓐ Ⓑ Ⓒ Ⓓ	17. Ⓐ Ⓑ Ⓒ Ⓓ	30. Ⓐ Ⓑ Ⓒ Ⓓ	43. Ⓐ Ⓑ Ⓒ Ⓓ
5. Ⓐ Ⓑ Ⓒ Ⓓ	18. Ⓐ Ⓑ Ⓒ Ⓓ	31. Ⓐ Ⓑ Ⓒ Ⓓ	44. Ⓐ Ⓑ Ⓒ Ⓓ
6. Ⓐ Ⓑ Ⓒ Ⓓ	19. Ⓐ Ⓑ Ⓒ Ⓓ	32. Ⓐ Ⓑ Ⓒ Ⓓ	45. Ⓐ Ⓑ Ⓒ Ⓓ
7. Ⓐ Ⓑ Ⓒ Ⓓ	20. Ⓐ Ⓑ Ⓒ Ⓓ	33. Ⓐ Ⓑ Ⓒ Ⓓ	46. Ⓐ Ⓑ Ⓒ Ⓓ
8. Ⓐ Ⓑ Ⓒ Ⓓ	21. Ⓐ Ⓑ Ⓒ Ⓓ	34. Ⓐ Ⓑ Ⓒ Ⓓ	47. Ⓐ Ⓑ Ⓒ Ⓓ
9. Ⓐ Ⓑ Ⓒ Ⓓ	22. Ⓐ Ⓑ Ⓒ Ⓓ	35. Ⓐ Ⓑ Ⓒ Ⓓ	48. Ⓐ Ⓑ Ⓒ Ⓓ
10. Ⓐ Ⓑ Ⓒ Ⓓ	23. Ⓐ Ⓑ Ⓒ Ⓓ	36. Ⓐ Ⓑ Ⓒ Ⓓ	49. Ⓐ Ⓑ Ⓒ Ⓓ
11. Ⓐ Ⓑ Ⓒ Ⓓ	24. Ⓐ Ⓑ Ⓒ Ⓓ	37. Ⓐ Ⓑ Ⓒ Ⓓ	50. Ⓐ Ⓑ Ⓒ Ⓓ
12. Ⓐ Ⓑ Ⓒ Ⓓ	25. Ⓐ Ⓑ Ⓒ Ⓓ	38. Ⓐ Ⓑ Ⓒ Ⓓ	
13. Ⓐ Ⓑ Ⓒ Ⓓ	26. Ⓐ Ⓑ Ⓒ Ⓓ	39. Ⓐ Ⓑ Ⓒ Ⓓ	

65 ITEMS   60 MINUTES

1. A teacher would NOT do which of the following when using a basal reading approach?

    Ⓐ Teach skills in a systematic sequential manner
    Ⓑ Meet individual differences and the needs of a child
    Ⓒ Establish and reinforce a basic vocabulary
    Ⓓ Use manuals that provide a detailed outline for teaching

2. A student has difficulty pronouncing a printed word. This difficulty may reflect all of the following EXCEPT

    Ⓐ phonetic analysis.
    Ⓑ sight vocabulary.
    Ⓒ language comprehension.
    Ⓓ content analysis.

3. A teacher would ensure that personal journals are NOT used as a

    Ⓐ record of thoughts and feelings.
    Ⓑ way to share thoughts with others.
    Ⓒ means of expressing thoughts and insights.
    Ⓓ means for writing ideas.

4. A teacher would NOT use a phonics approach to further which of the following?

    Ⓐ Associating sounds with printed words
    Ⓑ Reading comprehension
    Ⓒ Attacking new words independently
    Ⓓ Developing a sight vocabulary

5. During a unit on animal stories, sixth-grade students read *Lad a Dog* by Albert Payson Terhune. The teacher wants to use transactional strategy instruction to help students develop a deeper understanding of the cognitive process involved in Lad's "motivations," as described in the book. That approach is in use when the teacher

    Ⓐ explicitly explains the process involved in successful reading comprehension.
    Ⓑ encourages students to explore the process involved in successful reading instruction.
    Ⓒ and students cooperate to explore the processes involved in successful reading instruction.
    Ⓓ asks students to explore the processes involved in successful reading instruction.

6. A fourth-grade student hands in a writitng assignment containing this sentence:

    I are going swimming

    This sentence indicates that the student needs help with

    Ⓐ subject-verb agreement.
    Ⓑ pronouns.
    Ⓒ sentence fragments.
    Ⓓ adjectives and adverbs.

7. Students read a science fiction story about space travel. The best choice among the following for a teacher to help students distinguish between science facts and science fiction is to

    Ⓐ guide students to understand that science fiction stories are creative writing and these stories are not based on science facts.
    Ⓑ guide students as they identify examples of science facts and science fiction.
    Ⓒ ask students to work independently to make their own lists of science facts and science fiction.
    Ⓓ ask students to work independently as they identify examples of science facts and science fiction in the story just read in class.

8. A teacher is using an ESL approach to teach reading to a group of LEP students. Which of the teacher's actions described below is most consistent with that approach?

    Ⓐ Use context clues to help students identify English words
    Ⓑ Help a student learn to read in the student's native language
    Ⓒ Translate English reading passages into the student's native language
    Ⓓ Ask students to bring in original literature in their native language

9. A primary-grade teacher wants to produce the most significant reading benefits for his students. Which of the following teacher's actions is most likely to create that benefit?

    Ⓐ Provide a literature-rich environment
    Ⓑ Provide effective phonics instruction
    Ⓒ Provide opportunities for oral expression and learning
    Ⓓ Use real literature sources instead of basal texts

10. Which of the following "spoken" examples does NOT point out the difficulty of using the twenty-six-letter alphabet to represent spoken English?

    Ⓐ "Live and on stage the rock group Phish"
    Ⓑ "The new tuf truck line from Tough Trucks"
    Ⓒ "*I* before *e*, except after *c* and when sounded like *a* as in 'neighbor' and 'weigh'"
    Ⓓ "It's a terrrr-iffffic day here at the car wash"

QUESTIONS 11 AND 12 REFER TO THE FOLLOWING POEM.

My life falls on silence nigh
I am alone in saying the good-bye
For while a love has lost its day
A love unknown is a sadder way

11. The word *nigh* in line 1 means

   Ⓐ clear.

   Ⓑ complete.

   Ⓒ near.

   Ⓓ not.

12. This poem describes

   Ⓐ loving someone and being rebuffed.

   Ⓑ being loved by someone you do not love.

   Ⓒ loving someone who loves another person.

   Ⓓ loving someone without acknowledgment.

-----

13. A teacher uses phonemic awareness instruction with students because

   Ⓐ it focuses on many types of phoneme manipulation.

   Ⓑ it is taught as phonological awareness.

   Ⓒ students learn the sounds along with the phonemes.

   Ⓓ students understand that phoneme awareness is the same as phonics.

14. Based on recent research, which of the following is the best approach to teach reading to young children?

   Ⓐ Sight-word programs

   Ⓑ Literature-based programs

   Ⓒ Phonics instruction integrated with literature-based approaches

   Ⓓ Phonics programs

15. Recent research demonstrates that silent independent reading

   Ⓐ has not been shown to improve reading achievement.

   Ⓑ has been shown to improve reading achievement but not fluency.

   Ⓒ has not been shown to improve reading achievement, but it has been proven to improve reading fluency.

   Ⓓ has been shown to improve both reading achievement and fluency.

16. Which of the following is the best example of the phonemic awareness skill of phonemic identity?

    Ⓐ A child recognizes the sound of *w* in the word *was.*

    Ⓑ A child recognizes the sound of the word *was.*

    Ⓒ A child recognizes the sound of *w* is the same as *was* and *want."*

    Ⓓ A child substitutes the sound of *w* in *was* with the sound of *h* to form the new word *has.*

17. Which of the following is NOT an effective text comprehension strategy?

    Ⓐ Using graphic organizers

    Ⓑ Careful detailed reading

    Ⓒ Employing metacognition

    Ⓓ Writing summaries

18. According to researchers, which of the following is the most effective way for children to develop phonemic awareness?

    Ⓐ Become familiar with an appropriate number of symbolic phonemic spellings such as /b/ /eI/

    Ⓑ Focus on the unique sounds of each phoneme

    Ⓒ Learn how the building blocks of individual phonemes combine to form sounds that are more complex

    Ⓓ Learn phonemic awareness along with the letters of the alphabet

19. The main reason that a teacher's presentation is ineffective when read directly from projected visuals is the

    Ⓐ information on the visuals is relatively unimportant.

    Ⓑ students can read the visuals.

    Ⓒ students often cannot see the visuals.

    Ⓓ teacher loses eye contact with the students.

20. A teacher introduces onsets and rimes as the

    Ⓐ beginning stages of reading through rhyming words.

    Ⓑ initial consonant in a syllable and the part of the syllable that contains the vowel.

    Ⓒ beginning of a line of poetry and the end of the line of poetry that actually contains a rhyme.

    Ⓓ beginning of a word that does not show the rhyme and the end of the word that does rhyme.

21. During reading activities, a teacher uses phoneme deletion activities to promote phonemic awareness by

    Ⓐ breaking a word into separate sounds and saying each sound aloud.

    Ⓑ recognizing the sounds in a word that do not match the sounds in another word.

    Ⓒ recognizing the word remaining when a phoneme is removed from a longer word.

    Ⓓ substituting one phoneme for another to make a new word.

22. When it comes to phonics and the predictable relationship between graphemes and phonemes, experts generally hold that

    Ⓐ systematic and explicit phonics instruction is the essential element of early grade reading programs.

    Ⓑ literature-based instruction that emphasizes reading and writing, not phonics, is the essential element of early grade reading programs.

    Ⓒ sight-word programs are more important than phonics and are the essential element in early grade reading programs.

    Ⓓ basal programs that focus on whole word or meaning-based activities, not phonics, are the essential element of early grade reading programs.

23. According to recent research, which of the following approaches is most likely to improve a student's reading fluency?

    Ⓐ Round robin reading in which students take turns reading a passage

    Ⓑ Monitored oral reading

    Ⓒ Silent independent reading

    Ⓓ Hearing models of fluent reading

24. A teacher most likely uses semantic organizers to help students

    Ⓐ understand the meaning of words, expressions, and sentences in relation to reference and truth.

    Ⓑ identify the underlying structure of a story.

    Ⓒ relate pictures and diagrams in the text to the text itself.

    Ⓓ identify related ideas and concepts in a text.

25. Which of the following would indicate to a teacher that a student is using a metacognitive approach to reading comprehension?

    Ⓐ A student grasps the overall structure of a story.

    Ⓑ A student summarizes the essence of a story.

    Ⓒ A student adjusts his or her reading speed.

    Ⓓ A student works cooperatively with others to comprehend a story.

26. It is most likely that a child has learned the meaning of a word

Ⓐ indirectly, through context clues.
Ⓑ directly, through phonics learning experiences.
Ⓒ indirectly, through everyday experiences.
Ⓓ directly, through phonemic learning experiences.

USE THIS PARAGRAPH TO ANSWER QUESTION 27.

The computers in the college dormitories are actually more sophisticated than the computers in the college computer labs, and they cost less. It seems that the person who bought the dormitory computers looked around until she found powerful computers at a low price. The person who runs the labs just got the computers offered by the regular supplier.

27. The best statement of the main idea of this paragraph is

Ⓐ it is better to use the computers in the dorms.
Ⓑ the computers in the dorms are always in use, so, for most purposes it is better to use the computers in the labs.
Ⓒ it is better to shop around before you buy.
Ⓓ wholesale prices are usually better than retail prices.

USE THIS PRESENTATION TO ANSWER QUESTION 28.

Using percentages to report growth patterns can be deceptive. If there are 100 new users for a cereal currently used by 100 other people, the growth rate is 100 percent. However, if there are 50,000 new users for a cereal currently used by 5 million people, the growth rate is 1 percent. The 1 percent growth is much larger than the 100 percent growth. It seems clear that this growth rate of 1 percent is preferable to the growth rate of 100 percent. While percentages provide a useful way to report growth patterns, we must know the initial number the growth percentage is based on.

28. Which of the following experts would most likely be concerned with a presentation such as the one described above?

Ⓐ A marketing specialist who conducts various types of market research
Ⓑ A sociologist who studies the actions and interactions of people
Ⓒ A nutritionist who helps people make decisions about which foods to eat
Ⓓ A supermarket manager who decides how much and what type of food to order each week

USE THIS PASSAGE TO ANSWER QUESTION 29.

Charles Dodgson, a non-American writing under the pen name Lewis Carroll, wrote *Alice's Adventures in Wonderland*. The book is so filled with symbolism that a book titled *Understanding Alice* contains the original text with marginal notes explaining the symbolism.

29. The passage refers to the symbolism found in *Alice in Wonderland*, meaning that the story

    Ⓐ was written in a foreign language.
    Ⓑ contained many mathematical symbols.
    Ⓒ contained no pictures.
    Ⓓ has a figurative meaning.

USE THE PARAGRAPH BELOW TO ANSWER QUESTIONS 30 AND 31.

(1) All of my visits to the park came well before a series of fires that burned the park. (2) I have some very happy memories about the time I spent in Yellowstone National Park. (3) The U.S. national park system is extensive and very large. (4) However, most of the land dedicated to the park system is in the western states.

30. Which of the following choices represents the most logical way to order the sentences from the paragraph above?

    Ⓐ 4, 3, 2, 1
    Ⓑ 4, 3, 1, 2
    Ⓒ 3, 4, 1, 2
    Ⓓ 3, 4, 2, 1

31. Which of the following revisions to a sentence in the paragraph above would improve the overall style of the reordered passage?

    Ⓐ Sentence 1—All of my visits to Yellowstone Park came well before a series of fires that burned the park.
    Ⓑ Sentence 2—I have some very happy memories about the time spent in Yellowstone National Park.
    Ⓒ Sentence 3—The U.S. national park system is extensive.
    Ⓓ Sentence 4—However, most of the land dedicated to the park system is in the western United States.

---

32. Literature written specifically for children did not appear until the

    Ⓐ 1500s.
    Ⓑ 1600s.
    Ⓒ 1700s.
    Ⓓ 1800s.

33. I grew up in Kearny, New Jersey, now known as Soccer Town, USA. I played football in high school and barely knew that the soccer team existed. However, a look back at my high school yearbook revealed that the soccer team won the state championship. We had a 0.500 season.

Which of these techniques is used by the author of this passage?

Ⓐ Exposition
Ⓑ Reflection
Ⓒ Argumentation
Ⓓ Narration

34. Which of the following words or word pairs would NOT be used to coordinate sentence elements?

Ⓐ And
Ⓑ Either or
Ⓒ But
Ⓓ When

35. Many English words follow common spelling patterns. Which of the following words has a pronunciation that does not follow the spelling pattern usually associated with that word?

Ⓐ Save
Ⓑ Axe
Ⓒ Sleigh
Ⓓ Neat

36. The root *frac* in the word *fraction* means

Ⓐ break.
Ⓑ eighths.
Ⓒ part.
Ⓓ piece.

37. The speaker described her teen years and spoke about the arguments she had with her brothers and sisters. Then the speaker told the audience that she and her siblings were now the best of friends.

This account of the speaker's presentation best characterizes

Ⓐ argumentation.
Ⓑ exposition.
Ⓒ narration.
Ⓓ propaganda.

QUESTION 38 REFERS TO THE FOLLOWING PASSAGE.

In response to my opponent's question about my record on environmental issues, I want to say that the real problem in this election is not my record. Rather the problem is the influence of my opponent's rich friends in the record industry. I hope you will turn your back on his rich supporters and vote for me.

38. What type of rhetorical argument does this passage reflect?

  Ⓐ Narration
  Ⓑ Reflection
  Ⓒ Argumentation
  Ⓓ Exposition

I love gingerbread cookies, which are flavored with ginger and molasses. I can remember cold winter days when my brother and I huddled around the fire eating gingerbread cookies and sipping warm apple cider. In those days, gingerbread cookies came in many shapes and sizes. When you eat a gingerbread cookie today, you have to bite a "person's" head off.

39. Why did the author of the passage above put quotes around the word "person"?

  Ⓐ To emphasize the difference between gingerbread cookies that appear as people rather than windmills
  Ⓑ Because gingerbread cookies often don't look like people
  Ⓒ To emphasize the most popular current shape of gingerbread cookies
  Ⓓ To emphasize that the word *person* is not to be taken literally.

40. A young student writes about a sailor on a four-masted schooner. The student's writing contains this sentence:

> He had enuf rope to tie up the boat

The most effective way for a teacher to address the errors in this sentence is to provide instruction on

  Ⓐ phonics-based word skills.
  Ⓑ context-based word skills.
  Ⓒ the use of homonyms.
  Ⓓ variable spelling phonemes.

41. Which of the following would be the best opportunity for a teacher to use formative evaluation of a student's writing?

  Ⓐ A discussion with the student
  Ⓑ A portfolio of the student's writing
  Ⓒ The Iowa Test of Basic Skills
  Ⓓ An end-of-unit test

42. A fifth-grade student hands in this writing sample:

> I sat in the audience while my sister play
> the clarinet. I saw her play while sit there.
> I guess U will never be a professional musician

The teacher is most likely to help improve this student's writing by providing instruction in

Ⓐ nouns.
Ⓑ pronouns.
Ⓒ spelling.
Ⓓ verbs.

43. The speaker, a class visitor, described her teen years and spoke about the arguments she had with her brothers and sisters. Then the speaker told the class that she and her siblings were now the best of friends.

The account of the speaker's presentation best characterizes

Ⓐ argumentation.
Ⓑ exposition.
Ⓒ narration.
Ⓓ propaganda.

44. A teacher writes "You ain't going to no party," and asks students to evaluate the sentence from the standpoint of structure and function. The most appropriate response from the students is that the quote

Ⓐ effectively communicates in function and structure.
Ⓑ effectively communicates in function but not in structure.
Ⓒ effectively communicates in structure but not in function.
Ⓓ effectively communicates in neither function nor structure.

45. "Peter Piper picked a peck of pickled peppers"

A teacher would use the sentence above as an example of

Ⓐ alliteration.
Ⓑ euphemism.
Ⓒ hyperbole.
Ⓓ metaphor.

46. Which of the following words or word pairs would NOT be used to coordinate sentence elements?

Ⓐ And
Ⓑ Either or
Ⓒ But
Ⓓ When

USE THE FOLLOWING FOR QUESTIONS 47 AND 48.

The teacher shows students two lines from a haiku poem.

Ah autumn coolness
hand in hand paring away

47. Which of the following *could* students correctly write as the third line in the poem?

Ⓐ In the wetness
Ⓑ Branches and leaves
Ⓒ Eggplants and cucumbers
Ⓓ Til the end of day

48. The word *paring* in the haiku above means

Ⓐ putting together.
Ⓑ doubling up.
Ⓒ cutting off.
Ⓓ planting fruit.

_____

49. The Hubble space telescope observes space from Earth's orbit. This expensive telescope completely revolutionized astronomy because it is free of distortions caused by the atmosphere. Hubble has helped to discover galaxies that are many billions of light years away from Earth, which actually lets scientists study events that happened billions of years ago. This telescope has helped demonstrate that the universe is expanding, and we now know more about the universe than ever before. However, with all these discoveries we do not seem to be closer to the answer to the ultimate question. "How did the universe originate?"

The author's primary purpose for writing this passage is most likely to

Ⓐ give description about how the Hubble telescope operates.
Ⓑ narrate the history of space exploration.
Ⓒ present a key unanswered question.
Ⓓ describe the power of modern telescopes.

50. In which sentence is the underlined word used correctly?

Ⓐ The rider grabbed the horse's <u>reigns</u>.
Ⓑ The teacher just began her <u>lessen</u>.
Ⓒ The dog's collar showed <u>its</u> address.
Ⓓ The road offered a steep <u>assent</u> to the plateau.

51. Which of the following sentences contains a subordinate clause?

Ⓐ When Dorothy takes a trip to the beach, she always feels happier.
Ⓑ Dorothy takes a trip to the beach, and she always feels happier.
Ⓒ A trip to the beach makes Dorothy feel happier.
Ⓓ I feel happier when I take a trip to the beach.

52. In which of these sentences is the underlined word used correctly?

Ⓐ The reduction from two lanes to one lane had no <u>affect</u> on traffic.

Ⓑ One positive <u>effect</u> of construction is decreased neighborhood traffic.

Ⓒ The bridge construction did not really <u>effect</u> our lives.

Ⓓ The engineer is reviewing how car traffic <u>effects</u> the bridge's strength

53. Some oral presentation experts suggest that a speaker should use rhetorical questions to capture the attention of an audience, meaning the speaker should ask questions

Ⓐ that engage audience members in a rhetorical response.

Ⓑ to determine audience members' knowledge of rhetorical techniques.

Ⓒ to which no response is expected.

Ⓓ to which audience members already know the answer.

54. Which word below would a teacher introduce in class to demonstrate a pronunciation that does not follow the spelling pattern for that word?

Ⓐ Dave

Ⓑ Axe

Ⓒ Sleigh

Ⓓ Neat

55. Which of the sentences below would a teacher introduce as grammatically incorrect, that would be grammatically correct, except for the irregular nature of English verb construction?

Ⓐ Blaire bringed the car to the mechanic.

Ⓑ Blaire hopped happily down the street.

Ⓒ Blaire were practicing a play.

Ⓓ Blaire speak to her friend yesterday.

56. Which of the following sentences contains a possessive pronoun?

Ⓐ They were happy to have the day off.

Ⓑ John likes to ride his bike.

Ⓒ We do not know what to do with them.

Ⓓ They do not know whom to ask first.

57. In which of the following sentences is the underlined word used correctly?

Ⓐ The ropes helped the mountain climber with her <u>ascent</u>.

Ⓑ The runner <u>assented</u> the winner's platform.

Ⓒ The diver <u>accented</u> to the lowest depths of the ocean.

Ⓓ The tree limb stood in the way of the cat's <u>assent</u> up the old oak tree.

USE THE PASSAGE BELOW TO ANSWER QUESTIONS 58 AND 59.

(1) Choosing educational practices sometimes seems like choosing fashions. (2) Fashion is driven by whims, tastes, and the zeitgeist of the current day. (3) The education system should not be driven by these same forces. (4) Three decades ago, teachers were told to use manipulative materials to teach mathematics. (5) But consider the way mathematics is taught. (6) In the intervening years, the emphasis was on drill and practice. (7) Now teachers are told again to use manipulative materials. (8) Even so, every teacher has the ultimate capacity to determine his or her teaching practices.

58. Which of the following revisions to a sentence in this passage would be most likely to improve the style of the passage?

Ⓐ Sentence 1—The choice of educational practices sometimes seems like choosing fashions.

Ⓑ Sentence 3—The education system should not have to react to these forces.

Ⓒ Sentence 5—But consider mathematics and the way it is taught.

Ⓓ Sentence 8—Even so, every teacher can determine his or her teaching practices.

59. Which of the following describes the best way to rearrange sentences to improve the organization of the passage?

Ⓐ Move sentence 2 before sentence 1.

Ⓑ Move sentence 4 before sentence 3.

Ⓒ Move sentence 5 before sentence 4.

Ⓓ Move sentence 6 before sentence 5.

_____

60. Most people feel at least some stage fright, particularly at the beginning of an oral presentation. The best strategy listed below for handling this stage fright is to

Ⓐ begin with a well-thought-through introduction.

Ⓑ explain your nervousness to the audience.

Ⓒ make extra use of hand and arm movements.

Ⓓ use the entire stage; move actively to maintain your focus.

BASE YOUR ANSWERS TO QUESTIONS 61 AND 62 ON THIS EXCERPT
FROM AN ORAL PRESENTATION.

Jean Piaget is world famous for his research on child development. According to Piaget's research, children are at the concrete operational stage of development for most of their elementary school years. However, in the early school years students are usually in the pre-operational stage. During the preoperational stage of development, students do not grasp many fundamental concepts. Helping children make the transition from preoperational to concrete operational stages means striking a balance between not teaching a concept and teaching the concept with concrete materials.

61. Which of the following best characterizes this presentation?

Ⓐ It is primarily a narration.
Ⓑ It is primarily opinion.
Ⓒ It is primarily an exposition.
Ⓓ It is primarily a reflection.

62. Which of the following sentences, when added to the presentation, would make it primarily a persuasive presentation?

Ⓐ Piaget conducted most of his developmental research on just a few children.
Ⓑ Children may be hurt if instruction is not based on Piaget's stages.
Ⓒ Primary teachers are most likely to encounter students who are at the preoperational stage.
Ⓓ Piaget frequently collaborated with Barbel Inhelder.

_____

63. Which of the following is usually the focus of an epic?
Ⓐ Profound feelings or ideas
Ⓑ Love and chivalry
Ⓒ Political ideas
Ⓓ A single mythological figure

BASE YOUR RESPONSES TO QUESTIONS 64 AND 65 ON THIS STORY
ABOUT THE FOX AND THE GRAPES.

A fox was strolling through a vineyard, and after a while he came upon a bunch of grapes. The grapes had just ripened, but they were hanging high up on the vine. It was a hot summer day and the fox wanted to get the grapes to drink a little grape juice.

The fox ran and jumped to reach the grapes but could not reach them. Then the fox went a great distance from the grapes and ran as fast as possible and jumped as high as he could. He still did not reach the grapes. For over an hour, the fox ran and jumped but—no luck. The fox was never able to reach the grapes and had to give up. The fox walked away, sullenly proclaiming, "Those grapes were probably sour."

64. The structure of this story indicates that it is a

Ⓐ legend.
Ⓑ fable.
Ⓒ lyric.
Ⓓ satire.

65. The point made by this story is that

Ⓐ height makes right.
Ⓑ the longer the run, the shorter the triumph.
Ⓒ it is easy to despise what you cannot get.
Ⓓ the fox would have done better by trying to solve the problem in a more clever way.

40 ITEMS   50 MINUTES

1. If the original price is $83.00, what would be the sale price if the sale took off 35 percent?

    Ⓐ $136.25
    Ⓑ $53.25
    Ⓒ $53.95
    Ⓓ $41.50

2. What percent of 125 is 105?

    Ⓐ 84%
    Ⓑ 0.84%
    Ⓒ 119%
    Ⓓ 1.19%

3. Ms. Stendel's class is forming groups. When they form groups of 2, 3, or 4 students, there is never anyone left over. How many are in the class?

    Ⓐ 24
    Ⓑ 25
    Ⓒ 21
    Ⓓ 30

4. A number divided by 0.01 equals 1,000. What is the number?

    Ⓐ 0.01
    Ⓑ 0.1
    Ⓒ 1.0
    Ⓓ 10

5. Which of the following fractions has the least value?

    Ⓐ $\dfrac{46}{30}$

    Ⓑ $\dfrac{241}{159}$

    Ⓒ $\dfrac{240}{97}$

    Ⓓ $\dfrac{195}{97}$

6. It took the oil truck 3 hours to fill the empty oil tank pumping at 100 gallons an hour. How long will it take another oil truck to fill the same empty tank pumping 80 gallons an hour?

    Ⓐ $2\frac{2}{5}$ hours

    Ⓑ $3\frac{2}{5}$ hours

    Ⓒ $3\frac{3}{8}$ hours

    Ⓓ $3\frac{3}{4}$ hours

7. On a map, 2 centimeters represents 300 kilometers. A road is 3,000 kilometers long.

    How long will it be on the map?

    Ⓐ 10 cm
    Ⓑ 20 cm
    Ⓒ 150 cm
    Ⓓ 300 cm

NAILS
$0.98 a one pound box
Three pound box for $2.55

---

8. The above sign shows the sale price of nails. You buy three pounds. How much is saved per pound by buying a three pound box?

    Ⓐ $3.53
    Ⓑ $1.57
    Ⓒ $0.39
    Ⓓ $0.13

9. Which of the following measures could NOT be the height of a real building?

    Ⓐ 0.3 kilometers
    Ⓑ 60,000 millimeters
    Ⓒ 23 centimeters
    Ⓓ 29 meters

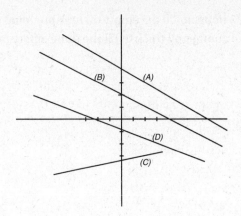

10. In the above graph, which line segment passes through the point (–2, 3)?

    Ⓐ Line Segment *A*

    Ⓑ Line Segment *B*

    Ⓒ Line Segment *C*

    Ⓓ Line Segment *D*

11. Which of these events has a probability of $\frac{1}{8}$?

    Ⓐ Flipping a head on a penny after flipping two tails

    Ⓑ Picking a red sock out of a drawer with four red socks and four black socks

    Ⓒ Picking two red socks out of a drawer with 16 red socks

    Ⓓ Flipping three pennies and getting all heads

12. Which of the following would be an estimate of the answer to 0.004913×0.04108?

    Ⓐ 0.02

    Ⓑ 0.002

    Ⓒ 0.0002

    Ⓓ 0.00002

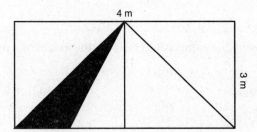

13. In the diagram above, what is the area of the shaded region?

    Ⓐ 1 m^2

    Ⓑ 1.5 m^2

    Ⓒ 2 m^2

    Ⓓ 2.5 m^2

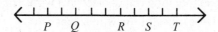

14. The number line above shows the relationship of points P, Q, R, S, and T. The product of Q and R is 1.00. What do we know about the points on the number line?

Ⓐ Points Q and R are less than 1.
Ⓑ Only Point Q is a negative number.
Ⓒ Point Q is more than 2.
Ⓓ The product of P and Q is less than 1.

MOST POPULAR BABY NAMES IN ONE TOWN			
Girls		Boys	
1990	2010	1990	2010
Michele	Lisa	Michael	William
Jennifer	Alexandra	Steven	Dylan
Lisa	Michelle	Joseph	Michael
Stephanie	Jillian	Peter	Gregory
Christine	Jennifer	Robert	
Alexandra			

15. Which of the following includes all the correct statements about the popular name table above?

  I 60 percent of the names popular in 1990 were also popular in 2010.
  II William was not popular in 1990.
  III 40 percent of the names popular in 2010 were not popular in 1990.
  IV Lisa and Michele accounted for 40 percent of all the popular names in 1990.

Ⓐ I and II
Ⓑ I only
Ⓒ II, III, and IV
Ⓓ II only

16. Some birds in the zoo weigh 10 pounds or less. Which of the following is consistent with this statement?

Ⓐ All birds weigh less than 10 pounds.
Ⓑ There are some 100-pound birds.
Ⓒ There is a 5-pound bird.
Ⓓ There may be some birds who weigh more than 10 pounds.

17. In which of the following choices is the answer closest to 30×0.02?

Ⓐ $0.1 + 0.2 \times 0.2$
Ⓑ $0.5 \times (0.4 + 0.8)$
Ⓒ $(0.9 - 0.3) \times 2.0 - 1.0$
Ⓓ $0.6 \times 1.0 - 1.0$

18. The electrician has a 50 foot long roll of electrical wire. The electrician uses 9 feet 8 inches of the wire. How much of the wire is left?

Ⓐ 41 ft 4 in
Ⓑ 41 ft 2 in
Ⓒ 40 ft 4 in
Ⓓ 40 ft 2 in

19. A rectangle has an area of 56.7 cm² and a width of 3 cm. What is the perimeter of the rectangle?

Ⓐ 170.1 cm
Ⓑ 113.4 cm
Ⓒ 43.8 cm
Ⓓ 18.9 cm

20. $0.1 + 0.001 =$

Ⓐ $\frac{11}{100}$

Ⓑ $\frac{1,001}{10,000}$

Ⓒ $\frac{101}{1,000}$

Ⓓ $\frac{11}{1,000}$

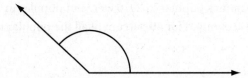

21. A protractor is used to measure the above angle. What is the approximate angle measure?

Ⓐ 60°
Ⓑ 130°
Ⓒ 45°
Ⓓ 240°

22. These shadows were cast at exactly the same time right next to one another.

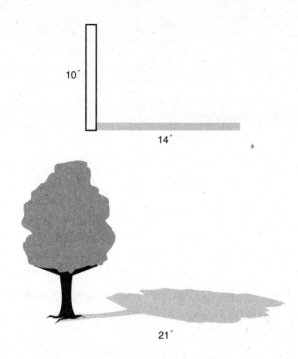

10´

14´

21´

About how tall is the above tree?

Ⓐ 25 ft

Ⓑ 15 ft

Ⓒ 17 ft

Ⓓ 29 ft

23. An even number has two different prime factors. Which of the following could be the product of those factors?

Ⓐ 6

Ⓑ 12

Ⓒ 36

Ⓓ 48

24. Use this diagram to answer this item.

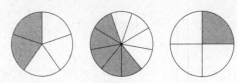

What is the sum of the shaded regions?

Ⓐ $1\frac{1}{5}$

Ⓑ $1\frac{1}{10}$

Ⓒ $1\frac{12}{90}$

Ⓓ $1\frac{37}{180}$

25. Two types of elevators travel up and down inside a very tall building. One elevator starts at the first floor and stops every x floors. Another elevator starts at the first floor and stops every y floors.

Which of the following is the best way to find at which floors both elevators stop?

Ⓐ Find the common multiples of x and the multiples of y.
Ⓑ Find the common factors of x and y.
Ⓒ Find the prime factors of x and y.
Ⓓ Find the divisors of x and y.

26. What is the value of the 7 in 1.37×10^{-2}?

Ⓐ $\frac{7}{10}$

Ⓑ $\frac{7}{100}$

Ⓒ $\frac{7}{1,000}$

Ⓓ $\frac{7}{10,000}$

27. Use this number line to answer the item that follows.

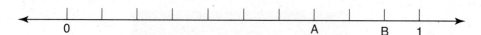

Which of the following could NOT be found on the number line between Point A and Point B?

Ⓐ $\frac{27}{34}$

Ⓑ $\frac{79}{86}$

Ⓒ $\frac{81}{91}$

Ⓓ $\frac{38}{54}$

28. The school received $5300 to use for eight different activities. A total of 91% of the money was allocated for seven of the activities, with the remainder used for the school trip. How much money was used for the school trip?

Ⓐ $477
Ⓑ $663
Ⓒ $757
Ⓓ $4,293

29. Use this list of numbers to answer the item that follows.

524

516

528

512

502

551

The teacher demonstrates how to use front-end estimation to estimate the sum of these numbers. He ignores the numerals in the ones place and just adds the numerals in the hundreds and tens places.

What is the difference between the teacher's estimate and the actual sum?

Ⓐ 6
Ⓑ 10
Ⓒ 18
Ⓓ 23

30. Use this chart to answer the item below.

Diameter	Circumference
2	6.28
3	9.42
4	12.56
5	15.70

The table above shows the diameter and circumference of several circles. Which of the graphs below best represents these data?

(A)

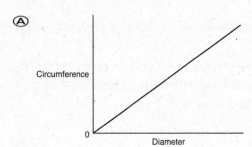

(B)

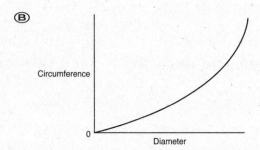

(C)

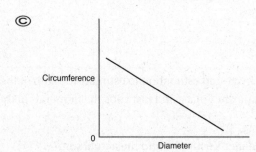

(D)

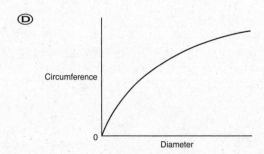

31. Use this coordinate grid to answer the question that follows.

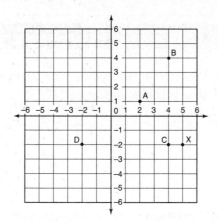

Point X is on a line with a slope of –1, meaning that which of the other points is also on that line?

Ⓐ A
Ⓑ B
Ⓒ C
Ⓓ D

32. Use this equation to answer the item below.

$3x - 1/5 \, (x + 5) = -x/5 + 33$

Which of the equations below could have been a step on the way to solving the equation above?

Ⓐ $3x = 33$
Ⓑ $3x = 34$
Ⓒ $13x = 156$
Ⓓ $15x = 170$

33. Use this diagram to answer the item below.

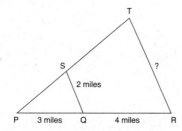

Engineers are building two bridges to span a deep canyon. They arranged the roads and bridges to form two similar triangles. △PQS is similar to △PRT. If the bridge from Q to S is two miles long, how long is the bridge from R to T?

Ⓐ 3.0 miles
Ⓑ 3.66 miles
Ⓒ 4.66 miles
Ⓓ 9.33 miles

34. Use this table to answer the item below.

January	February	March	April	May	June	July	August	September	October	November	December
3	7	6	4	8	7	8	6	4	3	2	2

The table above shows the amount of precipitation each month, to the nearest inch. What is the median of these precipitation amounts?

Ⓐ 3

Ⓑ 4

Ⓒ 5

Ⓓ 6

35. Which of the following graphs shows a line with both *x*-intercept and *y*-intercept equal to 1?

Ⓐ
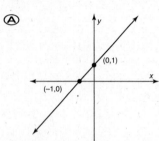

Ⓑ
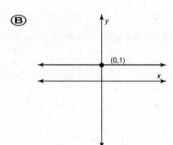

Ⓒ
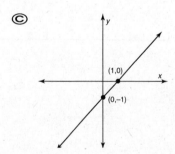

Ⓓ
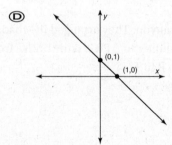

36. C is 5 more than half of B. Which of the following expressions states this relationship?

Ⓐ C + 5 = B/2
Ⓑ C = 1/2B + 5
Ⓒ C + 5 = 2/B
Ⓓ C + 5 > B/2

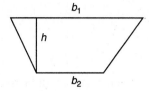

37. If the lengths of the bases in the trapezoid $A = \frac{h}{2}(b_1 + b_2)$ are doubled, what is the formula for the area of the new trapezoid, using the original height and base measurements?

Ⓐ $A = \frac{h}{2}(b_1 + b_2)$

Ⓑ $A = 2h(b_1 + b_2)$

Ⓒ $A = \frac{h}{4}(b_1 + b_2)$

Ⓓ $A = h(b_1 + b_2)$

38. The points (−4, +3) and (+4, −3) are plotted on the coordinate grid. At what point would a line connecting these two points cross the *y*-axis?

Ⓐ (+1, 0)
Ⓑ (0, 0)
Ⓒ (0, −1)
Ⓓ (−1, 0)

39. Beth's front walk is 58 feet long. If *y* stands for yards, which of the following number statements best represents the distance?

Ⓐ $19y + 0.1y$
Ⓑ $19y + 1/3y$
Ⓒ $19y$
Ⓓ $19.1y$

40. In a standard deck of 52 cards, what is the probability of being dealt a king, a queen, or a jack?

Ⓐ $\frac{1}{3}$

Ⓑ $\frac{2}{13}$

Ⓒ $\frac{3}{13}$

Ⓓ $\frac{4}{13}$

55 ITEMS   50 MINUTES

1. What is the connection among the following items?

   - FDIC
   - Tennessee Valley Authority
   - Civilian Conservation Corps
   - Agricultural Adjustment Act

   Ⓐ They are all programs enacted by President Herbert Hoover.

   Ⓑ They are all federal works programs.

   Ⓒ They all resulted from World War II.

   Ⓓ They are all programs enacted by President Franklin Roosevelt.

2. Which of the following shows the correct order of the listed events in United States history?

   I   Reconstruction

   II   Sherman's March to the Sea

   III   Surrender at Appomattox Courthouse

   IV   Approval of the XIII Amendment

   Ⓐ I, II, III, IV

   Ⓑ II, III, I, IV

   Ⓒ II, I, III, IV

   Ⓓ IV, II, III, I

3. All the following happened in full or in part as a result of World War I EXCEPT

   Ⓐ World War II.

   Ⓑ the Depression.

   Ⓒ the growth of the Nazi Party.

   Ⓓ the Yalta Agreement.

4. Go west young man.

   Which of the following items is best characterized by this statement?

   Ⓐ The age of exploration

   Ⓑ Manifest destiny

   Ⓒ Zionism

   Ⓓ The Peace Corps

5. The cause of liberty becomes a mockery if the price to be paid is the wholesale destruction of those who are to enjoy liberty.

The quote from Mohandas Gandhi is best reflected in which of the following statements about the American civil rights movement?

Ⓐ Bus boycotts are not effective because innocent boycotters are punished.
Ⓑ Nonviolence and civil disobedience are the best approaches to protest.
Ⓒ Desegregation laws were a direct result of freedom marches.
Ⓓ America will never be free as long as minorities are oppressed.

6. This poster depicts

Ⓐ the horrors of animal cruelty in early U.S. history.
Ⓑ the breakup of the United States leading to the Civil War.
Ⓒ the need for the colonies to ratify the Constitution.
Ⓓ the need for the colonies to unite against England.

7. The primary impact of early colonization on North America was that

Ⓐ more than half of the indigenous population died from disease.
Ⓑ trade goods were available for shipment back to Europe.
Ⓒ religiously oppressed minorities came in large numbers to North America.
Ⓓ England expanded the British Empire to include North America.

8. In which region of the United States did Algonquin-speaking people primarily live?

    Ⓐ A
    Ⓑ B
    Ⓒ C
    Ⓓ D

    _____

9. President Hoover's approach to the Depression can best be characterized as:

    Ⓐ the immediate establishment of work and relief programs.
    Ⓑ immediately making loan programs available to the unemployed.
    Ⓒ acting slowly while imposing strict rules that stabilized the stock market.
    Ⓓ acting slowly while establishing a program to loan money to employers.

10. What was the intent of Lincoln's Emancipation Proclamation?

    Ⓐ To free all slaves
    Ⓑ To free slaves not in Washington, D.C.
    Ⓒ To free slaves in the confederate states
    Ⓓ To free immediately all slaves who fought for the North and to free all other slaves at war's end

11. What happened to the English soldiers who fired on colonial protestors, killing five, including Crispus Attucks, during the Boston Massacre?

    Ⓐ They returned to England before they could be tried.
    Ⓑ They were defended by colonial patriots, including John Adams.
    Ⓒ They were found guilty but were freed by English soldiers dressed as colonials.
    Ⓓ They were acquitted primarily because Crispus Attucks was African-American.

12. In the debate during the late 1700s over a stronger versus a weaker federal government, which group took the position for a weaker federal government?

 Ⓐ The Federalists
 Ⓑ The Jeffersonians
 Ⓒ The Whigs
 Ⓓ The Hamiltonians

13. During which of the following conflicts involving England did the nursing efforts of Florence Nightingale become famous?

 Ⓐ American Revolutionary War
 Ⓑ Crimean War
 Ⓒ World War I
 Ⓓ World War II

14. How were the negotiations about the Common Market concluded?

 Ⓐ The United States was accepted as a provisional member of the Common Market.
 Ⓑ Britain and Western Europe agreed to form a Common Market.
 Ⓒ The Common Market, including England, Western Europe, China, and Russia, was established.
 Ⓓ The Common Market was denied most-favored-nation status by the United States.

15. In *Plessy v. Ferguson* the Supreme Court ruled that

 Ⓐ segregated schools were legal.
 Ⓑ segregation in rail travel was illegal.
 Ⓒ separate but equal accommodations were legal.
 Ⓓ the Black Codes were legal.

16. During the Spanish-American War in the late 1890s, the battleship *Maine* was sunk in the harbor at

 Ⓐ Boston.
 Ⓑ Havana.
 Ⓒ New York.
 Ⓓ Madrid.

17. What event is often identified as the cause of the American Revolution?

Ⓐ The death of Catherine the Great
Ⓑ The defeat of Napoleon at Waterloo
Ⓒ The French Revolution
Ⓓ The Townshend Acts

18. Which American military figure had a role in the Mexican-American War and John Brown's Raid at Harper's Ferry?

Ⓐ Philip Kearny
Ⓑ Robert E. Lee
Ⓒ Zachary Taylor
Ⓓ William Travis

19. When Christopher Columbus sailed he

Ⓐ never returned to Europe from his explorations.
Ⓑ first established a settlement in what is now the state of North Carolina.
Ⓒ never reached the mainland of North America.
Ⓓ first established a settlement in what is now the state of Virginia.

20. Which line in the table below correctly matches a description with the name of an event leading up to the Revolutionary War?

Line	Event	Description
1	Sugar Act	This act put a limit on the amount of sugar that the colonies could import.
2	Stamp Act	This act placed a tax on each legal document prepared in the colonies.
3	Boston Massacre	Several dozen colonial militia, including Crispus Attucks, were killed without provocation in the Boston Massacre.
4	Boston Tea Party	Hundreds of colonists dressed as Indians attacked the main tea warehouses around Boston Harbor and threw the cases of tea into the water.

Ⓐ Line 1
Ⓑ Line 2
Ⓒ Line 3
Ⓓ Line 4

21. During the state ratification process following the Constitutional Convention, the *Federalist Papers* were authored to support the ratification. In response, Anti-Federalists expressed their concerns, which were

Ⓐ there should be no federal or national government.
Ⓑ the Constitution replaced the Articles of Confederation, which formed a nation just from southern states.
Ⓒ the Constitution did not adequately protect individual rights.
Ⓓ the states could not properly ratify a document that established a federal government.

22. Use this excerpt from the U.S. Constitution to answer the item below.

Article II.

[Section 1] The executive Power shall be vested in a President of the United States of America. He shall hold his Office during the Term of four Years, and, together with the Vice President, chosen for the same Term, be elected, as follows:

Each State shall appoint, in such Manner as the Legislature thereof may direct, a Number of Electors, equal to the whole Number of Senators and Representatives to which the State may be entitled in the Congress: but no Senator or Representative or Person holding an Office of Trust or Profit under the United States, shall be appointed an Elector.

What is the impact of Article II, Section 1, on the election of the president of the United States of America?

Ⓐ The president of the United States is elected directly by the people of the United States.
Ⓑ The president of the United States is elected by a majority of the states.
Ⓒ The president of the United States can be elected by less than a majority of the voters.
Ⓓ The number of presidential electors is equal to the number of representatives.

23. The Declaration of Independence featured six self-evident truths including which of the following?

Ⓐ The right of the people to alter or abolish a destructive government
Ⓑ Governments derive their power from the law.
Ⓒ Freedom of religion, speech, press, assembly and petition
Ⓓ Right to bear arms

24. Which of the following is the most accurate account of the battle leading up to the surrender of the British general Cornwallis at Yorktown in Virginia on October 17, 1781?

Ⓐ American troops trapped Cornwallis in and around Yorktown and forced him to surrender.

Ⓑ American troops and the American Navy surrounded Cornwallis at Yorktown and forced him to surrender.

Ⓒ French troops and American troops surrounded Cornwallis at Yorktown and forced him to surrender.

Ⓓ The French Navy and American troops surrounded Cornwallis at Yorktown and forced him to surrender.

25. In understanding the impact of the Civil War on all Americans it is worth noting that

Ⓐ over six million prisoners were held in northern and southern camps.

Ⓑ the entire towns of Gettysburg and Atlanta were devastated and their entire populations were killed.

Ⓒ just as many men as women were killed during the war.

Ⓓ one in every thirty Americans was killed or wounded.

26. The Jim Crow south emerged following Reconstruction, in part because of

Ⓐ the Supreme Court's decision in the *Amistad* case that freed the slaves held on the ship.

Ⓑ the Supreme Court's decision in *Plessy v. Ferguson* that ruled separate but equal accommodations were legal.

Ⓒ the Supreme Court's decision in *Marbury v. Madison* that established the court's right to rule that federal actions were unconstitutional.

Ⓓ the Supreme Court's decision in *Brown v. Board of Education* that essentially overturned the *Plessy v. Ferguson* ruling.

27. Which line in the table below does NOT correctly match a person or people in the War of 1812 with a description of what they did?

Line	Person/people	Description
1	Francis Scott Key	Wrote the *Star Spangled Banner.*
2	British Troops	Sacked and burned Washington, D.C.
3	Andrew Jackson	Fought the Battle of New Orleans
4	Commodore Perry	Fought the British in Baltimore Harbor

Ⓐ Line 1
Ⓑ Line 2
Ⓒ Line 3
Ⓓ Line 4

28. After the slave ship *Amistad* was seized by the American Coast Guard in 1839

Ⓐ the Supreme Court ruled that the Africans aboard the ship were the property of their owners.
Ⓑ authorities learned that slaves aboard had revolted, killing several crew members.
Ⓒ the current president Van Buren and the past president Adams sided with the slave owners.
Ⓓ the Africans from the ship were given land to settle in upstate New York.

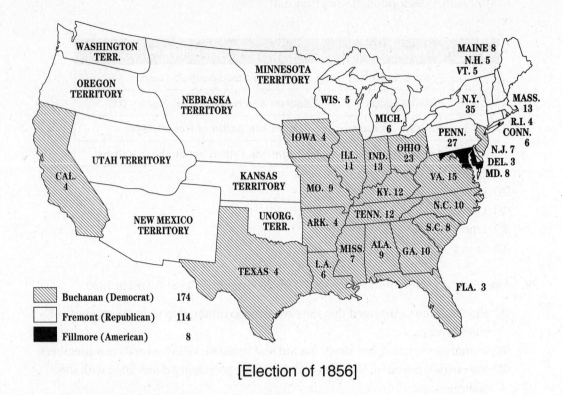

[Election of 1856]

29. The numbers in each state on this map show

Ⓐ the number of counties in each state.

Ⓑ the number of representatives from each state.

Ⓒ the electoral votes in each state.

Ⓓ the number of representatives won by the victorious party in each state.

30. What conclusion might you reasonably draw from this map?

Ⓐ Were it not for Texas and California, Fremont would have won the election.

Ⓑ Buchanan supported the rebel cause.

Ⓒ Fremont was favored by the northernmost states.

Ⓓ Fremont was favored by the states that fought on the Union side in the Civil War.

QUESTIONS 31–32 ARE BASED ON THIS MAP.

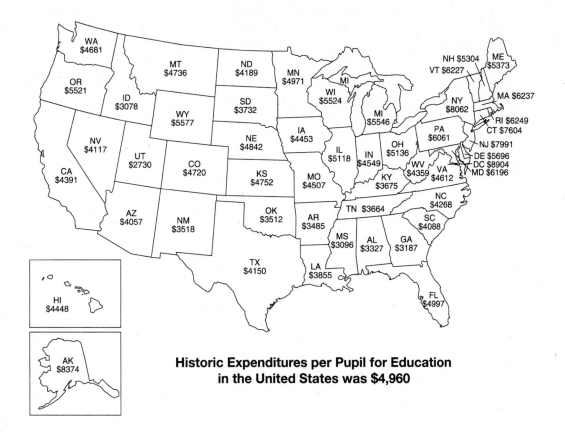

**Historic Expenditures per Pupil for Education
in the United States was $4,960**

31. You can deduce from the map that teachers' salaries were probably lowest in

 Ⓐ Georgia, Alabama, and Idaho.
 Ⓑ South Dakota, Tennessee, and Oklahoma.
 Ⓒ Kentucky, Louisiana, and New Mexico.
 Ⓓ Florida, Hawaii, and Iowa.

32. You can deduce from the map that school taxes are probably highest in

 Ⓐ the southeastern states.
 Ⓑ the northeastern states.
 Ⓒ the northwestern states.
 Ⓓ the southwestern states.

33. According to the law of supply and demand,

 Ⓐ decreased supply results in increased prices.
 Ⓑ increased prices result in increased demand.
 Ⓒ increased supply results in decreased demand.
 Ⓓ decreased demand results in increased prices.

USE THIS GRAPH TO ANSWER QUESTIONS 34 AND 35.

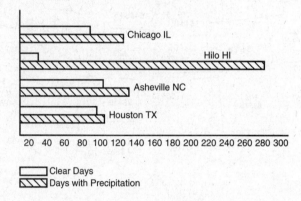

[Average Clear Day and Days with Precipitation]

34. A correct interpretation of this graph is, on average,

 Ⓐ most days in Houston have precipitation.
 Ⓑ less than 10 percent of the days in Hilo have no precipitation.
 Ⓒ most days in Asheville have no precipitation.
 Ⓓ most days in Chicago have precipitation.

35. A business may be moved to one of the four cities on the graph. What conclusion can be drawn from the graph to help make the final decision?

 Ⓐ On average, most precipitation in Hilo is from brief afternoon thundershowers.
 Ⓑ On average, Asheville gets only a few inches of snow.
 Ⓒ On average, Asheville and Chicago receive about the same amount of precipitation.
 Ⓓ On average, Houston has the most days without precipitation.

36. What action by the states is needed to amend the Constitution of the United States?

 Ⓐ None, the Constitution is a federal document.
 Ⓑ Congress must ratify amendments submitted by the states.
 Ⓒ Two-thirds of the states may agree to amend the Constitution.
 Ⓓ Three-quarters of the states must ratify amendments approved by Congress.

37. What impact did the Russian Revolution have on World War I?

  Ⓐ The Russian Revolution had no impact because it occurred much earlier than World War I.
  Ⓑ The Russian Revolution had no impact because the fighting was in Europe.
  Ⓒ The Russian Revolution had an impact because Russia left the war.
  Ⓓ The Russian Revolution had an impact because it was the cause of World War I.

38. Which of the following denotes the activity that separates prehistoric from historic times?

  Ⓐ Use of tools
  Ⓑ Use of fire
  Ⓒ Writing on clay tablets
  Ⓓ Use of the wheel

39. Robespierre's role during the French Revolution was

  Ⓐ as an adviser to Marie Antoinette and a defender of the throne who opposed the Reign of Terror.
  Ⓑ as the head of the Committee of Public Safety, which conducted the Reign of Terror.
  Ⓒ as an adviser to Napoleon and in this role reported to Napoleon about the Reign of Terror.
  Ⓓ heading the storming of the Bastille but later opposed the excesses of the Reign of Terror.

40. Which of the following fought a war with Britain in South Africa during 1879?

  Ⓐ The French
  Ⓑ The Dutch
  Ⓒ The Bantu
  Ⓓ The Zulu

41. Which Allied leaders met at Potsdam in 1945?

  Ⓐ Churchill, de Gaulle, Roosevelt, Stalin
  Ⓑ Churchill, de Gaulle, Truman, Stalin
  Ⓒ Stalin, Churchill, Truman
  Ⓓ Churchill, Roosevelt, Stalin

42. The main effect of the Treaty of Utrecht signed in 1713 was that

  Ⓐ France lost North American possessions to England.
  Ⓑ the Spanish Empire was partitioned.
  Ⓒ Britain recognized the United States after the Revolutionary War.
  Ⓓ Holland and Switzerland were officially formed.

43. Say that Company A and Company B try to raise money by selling bonds to the public. Which of the following would be the primary cause of the interest rate for Company A's bonds to be much higher than Company B's bonds?

Ⓐ Company A's bonds have a higher risk.
Ⓑ Company's B's bonds have a higher risk.
Ⓒ Company A's management wants to reward its investors.
Ⓓ Company B's management wants to reward its investors.

44. Use the map below to answer the question that follows.

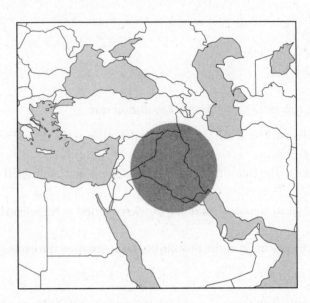

The shaded area on the map best represents the location of which of the following ancient civilizations?

Ⓐ Egypt New Kingdom
Ⓑ Hellenistic Greece
Ⓒ Kush Kingdom
Ⓓ Mesopotamia

45. Which of the following best describes the area in which the Kush Kingdom developed?

Ⓐ Jungle
Ⓑ Desert
Ⓒ Plain
Ⓓ Mountains

46. Use this list to answer the question below.

> Civilization began on an island
> Home to the Myceneans and the Minoans
> Invaded by the Dorians
> Location of Sparta

The description given above best describes which of the following ancient civilizations?

Ⓐ Assyria
Ⓑ Egypt
Ⓒ Greece
Ⓓ Phoenicia

47. Which of the following best describes the impact of the Crusades, which took place from about 1100 to 1300 C.E. (A.D.)?

Ⓐ Richard the Lionheart conquered the "holy land."
Ⓑ Muslims and Jews were massacred.
Ⓒ The crusaders established the country of Turkey.
Ⓓ The pope moved from Rome to Constantinople.

48. Which of the following began shortly after the Battle of Acton, about 38 B.C.E. (B.C.)?

Ⓐ Roman civil wars
Ⓑ the Pax Romana
Ⓒ Caesar was assassinated
Ⓓ The decline of the Roman Empire

49. Feudalism in Japan was most like feudalism in Europe in that

Ⓐ shoguns were like lords.
Ⓑ Christians were persecuted.
Ⓒ leaders were overthrown by the people.
Ⓓ shoguns were like popes.

50. The Reformation in Europe led to which of the following developments?

Ⓐ The establishment of protestant religions in Spain
Ⓑ The rediscovery of literature and art
Ⓒ The painting of the Sistine Chapel
Ⓓ The establishment of the Church of England

51. Which of the following is most closely associated with the early development of civilization?

Ⓐ The Upper Nile River and the Lower Nile River
Ⓑ The Tigris River and the Euphrates River
Ⓒ The Mediterranean Sea and the Red Sea
Ⓓ The Caspian Sea and the Black Sea

52. Which of the countries listed below fits the following description?

This land juts out into one sea and has another sea next to it. It includes a large island off its tip, and there are a great many other islands nearby.

Ⓐ Egypt
Ⓑ Greece
Ⓒ Switzerland
Ⓓ Austria

53. Which of the following describes a main impact of the end of Feudalism in Japan in the late 1800s?

Ⓐ Lords lost their lands
Ⓑ Samurai became more important
Ⓒ Industrialism declined
Ⓓ Shoguns gained power

54. Which cattle trail goes from San Antonio to Abilene?

   Ⓐ Chisholm
   Ⓑ Sedalia
   Ⓒ Goodnight-Loving
   Ⓓ Western Trail

55. Which cattle trail passes through the fewest states?

   Ⓐ Chisholm
   Ⓑ Sedalia
   Ⓒ Goodnight-Loving
   Ⓓ Western Trail

50 ITEMS, 50 MINUTES

1. The word *ecology* refers to what area of scientific study?

   Ⓐ The methods for keeping the environment clean
   Ⓑ The relationships between organisms and their habitats
   Ⓒ The effect of industrial and residential pollution on water resources
   Ⓓ The methods for determining the quality of water and the atmosphere

USE THIS INFORMATION TO ANSWER QUESTIONS 2 AND 3.

Average Ounces Gained per Animal		
Week #	HF1	HF2
1	4	9
2	3	4
3	2	3
4	1	2
5	1	2
6	1	1

2. An experiment is set up to determine the effects of a new hamster food HF2 as compared to the effects of a current hamster food HF1. Each group receives the same quantity of food and the same attention. From the above data choose the best conclusion for the experiment.

   Ⓐ HF2 group gained more weight.
   Ⓑ HF1 group lived longer.
   Ⓒ HF2 group got more protein.
   Ⓓ HF1 group got better nutrition.

3. What appropriate criticism might a scientist have of this experiment?

   Ⓐ Averages should not be used in this type of experiment.
   Ⓑ The null hypothesis is not stated in the appropriate form.
   Ⓒ Hamsters are not found as pets in enough homes for the experiment to be widely applicable.
   Ⓓ The experiment does not describe sufficient controls to be valid.

4. Which of the following paths best describes how blood circulates in the human body?

   Ⓐ Out from the heart along veins and arteries and back to the heart through the same veins and arteries

   Ⓑ Out from the heart through arteries and back to the heart through veins

   Ⓒ Out from the heart along veins and back to the heart through ducts

   Ⓓ Out from the heart through capillaries and back to the heart through arteries

5. Which of the following best illustrates heat transfer through conduction?

   Ⓐ A person feels heat when they stand near an electric stove.

   Ⓑ A person feels heat when they stand in the sunlight.

   Ⓒ A person feels heat when they stand in front of a hot air blower.

   Ⓓ A person feels heat when they touch a steam radiator.

6. Which of the following most correctly shows the makeup of Earth's atmosphere?

   Ⓐ Oxygen 78 percent, nitrogen 21 percent

   Ⓑ Oxygen 58 percent, nitrogen 41 percent

   Ⓒ Oxygen 41 percent, nitrogen 58 percent

   Ⓓ Oxygen 21 percent, nitrogen 78 percent

7. An aphid is a slow-moving insect that sucks juices from plants. Some ants feed on "honeydew," the excrement produced by the aphid. The ants protect the aphids and help the aphids get food. This relationship between these ants and aphids is best characterized by the term

   Ⓐ mutualism.

   Ⓑ competition.

   Ⓒ parasitism.

   Ⓓ predation.

8. What does heat measure?

   Ⓐ The amount of reflection of energy off a surface

   Ⓑ The ratio of friction to air temperature

   Ⓒ The speed of moving molecules

   Ⓓ The rate of convective energy

9. Written as a formula, Newton's Second Law of Motion is
(F)orce = (M)ass × (A)cceleration.

Which of the following is the best explanation of this law?

   Ⓐ Something heavier will move slower than something lighter.

   Ⓑ It is easier to move something if it has less mass.

   Ⓒ The more acceleration you apply the less mass there is.

   Ⓓ The more mass there is means there is more force applied to it.

10. Which of the following would NOT contribute to the process of photosynthesis?

   Ⓐ Water
   Ⓑ Sunlight
   Ⓒ Glucose
   Ⓓ Carbon dioxide

11. Which of the following is a true statement about DNA?

   Ⓐ All DNA determines human traits.
   Ⓑ Genes occupy specific locations on RNA.
   Ⓒ DNA carries genetic codes throughout the cell.
   Ⓓ DNA contains chromosomes.

12. Where did Earth's early oxygen supply come from?

   Ⓐ It came from anaerobic cells.
   Ⓑ Early molecules gave off energy.
   Ⓒ It came from photosynthesis.
   Ⓓ It came from aerobic cells.

13. Compared with cells, a virus is best characterized as

   Ⓐ advanced.
   Ⓑ parasitic.
   Ⓒ primitive.
   Ⓓ spirilla.

14. Use the diagram below to answer the question that follows.

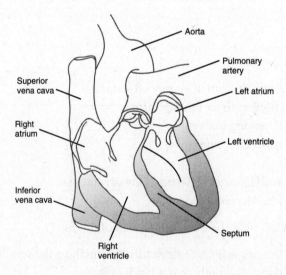

From which chamber does oxygen-poor blood leave the organ shown to go to the lungs?

   Ⓐ Left atrium
   Ⓑ Left ventricle
   Ⓒ Right atrium
   Ⓓ Right ventricle

15. Which one of the body systems listed below includes a mechanical process?

 Ⓐ Nervous system
 Ⓑ Digestive system
 Ⓒ Endocrine system
 Ⓓ Immune system

USE THE DIAGRAM BELOW TO ANSWER QUESTIONS 16 AND 17.

Shown below is a simplified diagram of the kelp forest food web with the sea otter. The sea otters' favorite food is the sea urchin. The sea urchins' favorite food shown in the diagram is kelp.

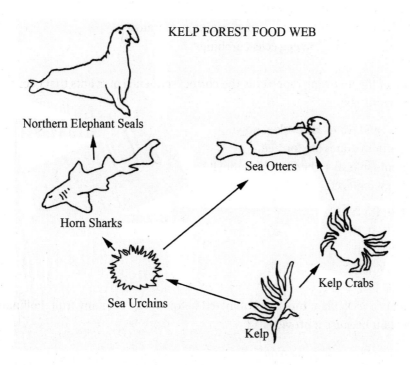

KELP FOREST FOOD WEB

16. It is most correct to say that energy in this food web

 Ⓐ flows in both directions.
 Ⓑ flows upward in this food web.
 Ⓒ does not flow in either direction.
 Ⓓ flows downward in this food web.

17. Which of the following is the most likely short-term outcome if sea otters were hunted to extinction?

 Ⓐ The number of sea urchins would be greatly reduced.
 Ⓑ The number of algae would be greatly increased.
 Ⓒ The number of kelp would be greatly reduced.
 Ⓓ The number of plankton would be greatly increased.

18. Some cells respire aerobically while others respire anaerobically. Fermentation is an example of anaerobic respiration in that the process

    Ⓐ occurs only during cell division.
    Ⓑ does not require oxygen.
    Ⓒ only occurs in aquatic animals.
    Ⓓ produces oxygen.

19. Which of the following examples of cell reproduction results in a doubling of the number of chromosomes?

    Ⓐ A human egg cell is formed.
    Ⓑ A human sperm cell is formed.
    Ⓒ A human cell enters the metaphase stage of mitosis.
    Ⓓ Human sperm and egg cells combine.

20. Which of the following represents the correct sequence of events that occurs during photosynthesis?

    I CO_2 and water are broken down.
    II Carbohydrates are formed.
    III Sunlight is absorbed by chlorophyll.
    IV Plant emits O_2.

    Ⓐ I, II, III, IV
    Ⓑ I, III, II, IV
    Ⓒ III, I, II, IV
    Ⓓ II, IV, I, III

21. In most cases, a plant must be pollinated before it can bear any fruit. Pollination is important because it provides

    Ⓐ sperm to fertilize the plant.
    Ⓑ a rich culture in which seeds and fruits can develop.
    Ⓒ the medium in which plant fertilization takes place.
    Ⓓ a way to attract bees.

22. Which of the following creates a chemical reaction?

    Ⓐ Mixing hot water from two glasses in a single glass
    Ⓑ Mixing raisins and cashews
    Ⓒ Mixing water and cement
    Ⓓ Mixing sand and seashells

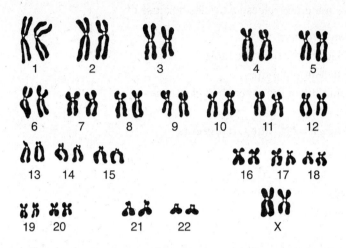

23. What conclusion could you reach about the person whose chromosomes are shown above?

   Ⓐ The person is a man.
   Ⓑ The person is a woman.
   Ⓒ The person has an abnormal gene.
   Ⓓ The person has more genes than usual.

24. Meiosis is an important cell reproduction process. This process always involves

   Ⓐ cells making carbon copies of themselves.
   Ⓑ the formation of zygotes.
   Ⓒ the creation of cells equal to all others in terms of DNA.
   Ⓓ the formation of gametes.

25. A ball is dropped and falls freely to Earth. Which of the following graphs best represents the relationship between the velocity of the ball and the time it has fallen?

Ⓐ
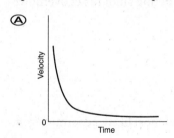

Ⓒ
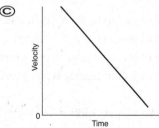

Ⓑ
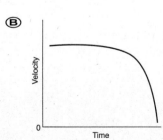

Ⓓ
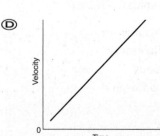

26. Radioactive materials release particles because of

Ⓐ their environment.

Ⓑ their place in the periodic table.

Ⓒ their nuclear make-up.

Ⓓ the instability of the outer shell electrons.

27. In the formula $E = MC^2$ the C represents

Ⓐ energy.

Ⓑ mass.

Ⓒ velocity.

Ⓓ the speed of light.

28. You are floating on a lake in a boat about 100 yards from the shore. You can hear someone talking at the shoreline. What is the best way to explain this phenomenon?

Ⓐ Sound travels faster through air.

Ⓑ Sound travels faster through water.

Ⓒ Sound traveled from the shore because of the materials the boat was constructed of.

Ⓓ An echo causes the sound to be heard.

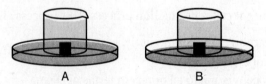

A   B

29. Identical beakers (above) were filled with water. The overflow was caused by the different solid objects placed in the beakers. The size of the objects cannot be determined. What is the most likely explanation of the differing amounts of overflow?

Ⓐ The object in beaker A is heavier.

Ⓑ The object in beaker B is heavier.

Ⓒ The object in beaker A has more mass.

Ⓓ The object in beaker B has more mass.

30. What type of rock, millions of years from now, would most likely be formed from current animal remains?

Ⓐ Conglomerate

Ⓑ Sedimentary

Ⓒ Igneous

Ⓓ Metamorphic

31. Through which of the media listed below will sound travel the fastest?

    Ⓐ Air
    Ⓑ Stone
    Ⓒ Water
    Ⓓ Vacuum

32. Which diagram shows object • to have the most potential energy?

Ⓐ

Ⓒ

Ⓑ

Ⓓ

33. There are 12 electrons in an element with a neutral charge. How many protons does it have?

    Ⓐ 3
    Ⓑ 4
    Ⓒ 6
    Ⓓ 12

34. The half-life of uranium is 82 years. Approximately how much of a mass of uranium would remain after 330 years?

    Ⓐ $\frac{1}{2}$

    Ⓑ $\frac{1}{4}$

    Ⓒ $\frac{1}{8}$

    Ⓓ $\frac{1}{16}$

35. Which of the following is most likely when you remove one light from a string of lights and all the lights go out?

Ⓐ A circuit breaker burned out.
Ⓑ All the other lights burned out when you removed the light.
Ⓒ The lights are wired in parallel.
Ⓓ The lights are wired in series.

36. When ironing clothes, the heat is transferred from the iron to the clothes by

Ⓐ convection.
Ⓑ acceleration.
Ⓒ radiation.
Ⓓ conduction.

37. You take a topography course at a college. Which of the following describes the possible subject matter of the course?

Ⓐ The moon's surface features
Ⓑ The solar system
Ⓒ The relationships between organisms and their habitat
Ⓓ Earth's atmosphere

38. Which diagram below shows earth's position at the beginning of summer in the southern hemisphere?

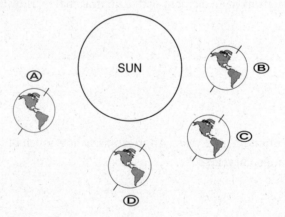

QUESTION 39 IS BASED ON THIS DIAGRAM.

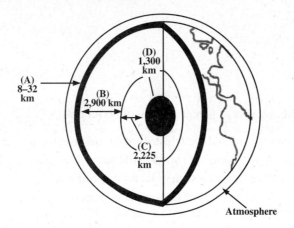

39. In the diagram above, what letter labels the mantle?

    Ⓐ A
    Ⓑ B
    Ⓒ C
    Ⓓ D

40. In electricity, what does the ohm measure?

    Ⓐ Resistance
    Ⓑ Current flow
    Ⓒ Current force
    Ⓓ Magnetic flux

41. What is the pattern of air circulation in the pressure system on the weather map
    shown above?

    Ⓐ Around to the right
    Ⓑ Around to the left
    Ⓒ Through it to the north
    Ⓓ Through it to the south

42. Which type of rock is usually found near the surface of the Earth?

    Ⓐ Sedimentary
    Ⓑ Metamorphic
    Ⓒ Igneous
    Ⓓ Cretaceous

43. Which of the following is a correct statement about matter?

    Ⓐ Matter cannot be created, nor destroyed, nor converted into energy.
    Ⓑ The mass of an object on the moon is the same as its mass on Earth.
    Ⓒ The weight of matter is the sum of its atomic numbers.
    Ⓓ Once established, the form of matter cannot change.

44. A person puts a black cloth over a pile of snow to make the snow melt faster. Why is that?

    Ⓐ The black cloth absorbs more sunlight and more heat.
    Ⓑ The black cloth holds the heat in close to the snow.
    Ⓒ The black cloth reflects more light and so it gets warmer
    Ⓓ The black cloth is the opposite color from the white snow.

45. Which of the following best describes plate tectonic theory?

    Ⓐ Molten material from within the Earth pushes up on portions of the Earth called plates causing volcanoes and earthquakes.
    Ⓑ Certain roughly circular portions of the Earth's surface called plates are subjected to pressure causing them to turn left or right causing earthquakes.
    Ⓒ The Earth's surface consists of a series of plates that float slowly on the material beneath the surface.
    Ⓓ Over time, portions of the Earth's surface crack or break in a fashion similar to the way plates break when dropped.

46. A solar eclipse occurs when the

    Ⓐ moon hides the sun from some or all of the Earth.
    Ⓑ moon casts a shadow on some of the Earth.
    Ⓒ Earth covers the moon with a shadow.
    Ⓓ Earth casts a shadow on the moon.

47. You weigh a lump of clay on Earth and then weigh the same lump of clay on the moon. Which of the following accurately summarizes the result?

Ⓐ The weight and the mass both remain the same on the moon as on Earth.

Ⓑ The mass is altered by its presence on the moon. Consequently, the clay will have a different weight on the moon than on the Earth.

Ⓒ The mass of the clay remains the same on the moon as on Earth, but the weight will be different on the moon than it is on Earth.

Ⓓ The clay's weight is different on a scale while on the moon than it was on Earth, but the mass is the same on the moon as on Earth, so the actual weight of the clay is the same on the moon as it is on Earth.

48. An object travels at a constant speed over 90 feet in four minutes. What is the velocity?

Ⓐ 360 feet

Ⓑ 360 feet per minute

Ⓒ 22.5 feet

Ⓓ 22.5 feet per minute

49. Which of the following involves the most work?

Ⓐ Using all your might to try to lift a 50 story building.

Ⓑ Holding 100 pounds of weight perfectly still over your head.

Ⓒ Lifting 10 pounds over your head.

Ⓓ Dropping 100 pounds of weight to the floor.

50. A scientist working in the Sierra Nevada Mountains comes across some hail that had just fallen. The scientist cuts a piece of hail in half and finds a series of rings, much like tree rings. What information could the scientist find from the approximate number of rings?

Ⓐ How long the hailstone had been in the atmosphere

Ⓑ How long the hailstone was in space before falling to Earth

Ⓒ How many miles above the surface of the Earth the hailstone was before it began to fall

Ⓓ How many times the hailstone was blown from lower to higher altitudes

SUBTEST 5032 READING/LANGUAGE ARTS

1. B	11. C	21. C	31. C	41. B	51. A	61. C
2. C	12. D	22. A	32. C	42. D	52. B	62. B
3. B	13. C	23. B	33. D	43. C	53. C	63. D
4. B	14. D	24. D	34. D	44. B	54. B	64. B
5. C	15. A	25. C	35. B	45. A	55. A	65. C
6. A	16. C	26. C	36. A	46. D	56. B	
7. B	17. B	27. C	37. C	47. C	57. A	
8. A	18. D	28. A	38. C	48. C	58. D	
9. B	19. B	29. D	39. D	49. C	59. C	
10. D	20. B	30. D	40. D	50. C	60. A	

SUBTEST 5033 MATHEMATICS

1. C	7. B	13. B	19. C	25. A	31. A	37. D
2. A	8. D	14. D	20. C	26. D	32. B	38. B
3. A	9. C	15. D	21. B	27. B	33. C	39. B
4. D	10. B	16. D	22. B	28. A	34. C	40. C
5. B	11. D	17. B	23. A	29. D	35. D	
6. D	12. C	18. C	24. D	30. A	36. B	

SUBTEST 5034 SOCIAL STUDIES

1. D	9. D	17. D	25. D	33. A	41. C	49. A
2. B	10. C	18. B	26. B	34. C	42. B	50. D
3. B	11. B	19. C	27. D	35. D	43. A	51. B
4. B	12. B	20. B	28. B	36. C	44. D	52. B
5. B	13. B	21. C	29. C	37. C	45. C	53. A
6. D	14. B	22. C	30. C	38. C	46. C	54. A
7. A	15. C	23. A	31. A	39. B	47. B	55. A
8. A	16. B	24. D	32. B	40. D	48. B	

SUBTEST 5035 SCIENCE

1. B	9. B	17. C	25. D	33. D	41. B	49. C
2. A	10. C	18. B	26. C	34. D	42. A	50. D
3. D	11. D	19. D	27. D	35. D	43. B	
4. B	12. C	20. B	28. D	36. D	44. A	
5. D	13. C	21. A	29. C	37. A	45. C	
6. D	14. D	22. C	30. B	38. B	46. A	
7. A	15. B	23. B	31. B	39. B	47. C	
8. C	16. B	24. D	32. C	40. A	48. D	

Subtest 5032 Reading/Language Arts

1. **(B)** Note the word NOT in the item. A basal reading program is not designed to meet the individual needs of students. A basal program is designed for all students, typically for all students in the United States. A basal program must be supplemented to meet the individual needs of students.

2. **(C)** Note the word EXCEPT in the item. You do not have to understand the meaning of a word to pronounce it. This item points out the important distinction between recognizing a word and knowing what the word means. Word recognition and comprehension are both important parts of reading instruction.

3. **(B)** Note the word NOT in the item. Personal journals are just that—personal. These journals are not a way to share thoughts with others. Students should use a different format, such as a response journal, to share their thoughts.

4. **(B)** Note the word NOT in the item. A phonics approach does not address word meaning or reading comprehension. Phonics addresses word recognition and word pronunciation. Educators frequently criticize overreliance on phonics for just this reason.

5. **(C)** The word *transactional* in the term *transactional strategy instruction* means a give-and-take between students and teachers as they explore the processes involved in successful reading comprehension.

6. **(A)** The singular subject "I" does not agree with the plural verb "are." Nonagreement of subject and verb should be addressed in the early grades.

7. **(B)** Guiding students as they work is a very effective strategy for teaching reading. Picking out science facts and science fiction in a space exploration science fiction story is certainly the best kind of guidance among the choices given.

8. **(A)** ESL means English as a second language. This approach encourages the teaching and use of English.

9. **(B)** Reading is a unique skill and different from language. Studies show that students benefit most from early, effective phonics instruction. This should not be taken to mean that every phonics program is effective.

10. **(D)** Choices (A), (B), and (C) point out the kind of spelling difficulties regularly encountered in the English language. (D) does not have such a problem but emphasizes the *r* sound by repeating the letters a number of times.

11. **(C)** The word *nigh* means "near" in space or time.

12. **(D)** The passage tells us that love falls on silence and that love unknown is sad, leading to the conclusion that the passage is about loving without acknowledgment.

13. **(C)** Phonemic awareness is the ability to hear, identify, and manipulate phonemes in spoken words. (A) is incorrect because phonemic manipulation is just one part of phonemic awareness. (B) is incorrect because phonological awareness includes phonemic

awareness but also includes words and syllables. It is not effective to include words and syllables with phonemic awareness. (D) is incorrect because phonemic awareness is not the same as phonics.

14. **(D)** According to experts, the research overwhelmingly supports the phonics program, alone, as the best approach to teach reading to young children. (A), (B), and (C) are all incorrect because research of the programs listed, including the blended phonics approaches, shows that they are not as effective as phonics alone.

15. **(A)** Studies have consistently failed to confirm that silent reading helps students become better readers. (B), (C), and (D) are all incorrect because research does not show that silent reading improves either reading achievement or reading fluency.

16. **(C)** Phonemic identity means to recognize the same sound in different words. (A) is incorrect because it is an example of phoneme isolation. (B) is incorrect because it is an example of phoneme blending. (D) is incorrect because it is an example of phoneme substitution.

17. **(B)** Careful detailed reading is not an effective text comprehension strategy. Good readers use strategies that are more flexible. (A), (C), and (D) are all incorrect because each of these choices presents an effective text comprehension strategy.

18. **(D)** This approach is most effective because it helps children see how phonemes relate directly to their reading and writing. (A) is incorrect because there is never a reason to introduce children to phonemic symbols. (B) and (C) are incorrect because, while they can be effective phonemic awareness approaches, they are not the most effective approaches.

19. **(B)** It can be an insult to read a visual aloud when audience members can read it for themselves. That does not mean you cannot summarize or call attention to visuals. (A), (C), and (D) are all incorrect because these choices are not the primary reason why you should not read directly from visuals.

20. **(B)** The linguistic definition of onset and rhyme is exactly as presented in this answer choice. Choices (A), (C), and (D) are all incorrect because they have nothing to do with the linguistic definition of onset and rhyme.

21. **(C)** Phonemic deletion means to remove the phonemes from one word and to leave another word for students to identify. In an easy example, remove the /s/ from *stack* to form *tack*. (A) is incorrect because phoneme segmentation involves saying each phoneme in a word. (B) is incorrect because the technique of phoneme categorization involves recognizing a sound not found in another word. (D) Phonemic substitution is the term for the technique of substituting one phoneme for another to make a new word.

22. **(A)** Early grade students need systematic and explicit phonics instruction to become good readers. This approach is not the only approach that could be included; however, it is the only approach that must be included. (B), (C), and (D) are all incorrect because they are examples of nonsystematic phonics approaches. The evidence is clear that these nonsystematic approaches are not as effective in early grades as systematic phonics approaches.

23. **(B)** Fluency is the ability to read accurately and quickly. Monitored oral reading that includes feedback from the teacher is the most effective way to help a student achieve fluency. (A) is incorrect because round robin reading does not increase fluency, probably because each student reads a relatively small part of the passage. (C) is incorrect because there is no current evidence that silent independent reading improves fluency or reading comprehension, although there is no final proof that it does not help. (D) is incorrect because, while students need to hear models of fluent reading, this approach is less likely to improve fluency than choice (B).

24. **(D)** Semantic organizers are a special type of graphic organizer that may look like a spider web and help students identify related events and concepts in a text. (A) is incorrect because semantic organizers are not related to the linguistic study of semantics described in this choice. (B) and (C) are incorrect because they describe some types of graphic organizers but not semantic organizers.

25. **(C)** Metacognition means thinking about thinking, and in this case thinking about reading. A student who adjusts his or her reading speed is thinking about the reading process and reacting appropriately. (A) is incorrect because understanding story structure is an effective comprehension technique, but it is not metacognition. (B) is incorrect because summarizing a story is another effective comprehension strategy that is not metacognition. (D) is incorrect because cooperative learning can be an effective way to learn comprehension strategies, but cooperative learning is neither an approach to reading comprehension nor a metacognitive strategy.

26 **(C)** Children are surrounded by a world of words, and they learn most words by talking with others, overhearing conversations, and reading themselves. (A) is incorrect because context clues are an important way for children to learn word meanings, but context clues are just a part of the indirect experiences that lead to understanding a word's meaning. (B) and (D) are incorrect because explicit phonics instruction and phonemic awareness instruction are essential, but these are not the way children learn the *meaning* of most words.

27. **(C)** Most of this paragraph is devoted to a discussion of buying computers, not using computers. The person buying the dorm computers got a better deal because she shopped around. (A) is incorrect because the paragraph does not tell us the dorm computers are better to use, just that they are more sophisticated. (B) is incorrect because nothing in the paragraph indicates that the dorm computers are always in use. (D) is incorrect because there is no indication in the paragraph that either person bought the computers wholesale. Even though you might think this statement is generally true, it does not flow from the paragraph.

28. **(A)** A marketing specialist is most likely among those listed to be interested in the study described in the presentation. The question is about the study, which describes growth rates for certain kinds of cereal. The question does not ask about the conclusion based on the study. (B) is incorrect because there is nothing in the study that addresses how people act or interact. (C) is incorrect because there is nothing in the study that would help a nutritionist decide which foods to recommend. (D) is incorrect because a supermarket manager could be interested in which type of cereal is most popular but not in the study described in the presentation.

29. **(D)** Any reference to symbolism in *Alice in Wonderland* refers to the story's figurative meaning. (A) is incorrect because Charles Dodgson was English, and he wrote in English. (B) is incorrect because, while *Alice in Wonderland* includes mathematical ideas, it does not contain many mathematical symbols. (C) is incorrect because although the original work actually contained some pictures, and even if it did not, the book's symbolism would not refer to the absence of this imagery.

30. **(D)** Sentence 4 only makes sense after reading sentence 3. Sentence 1 only makes sense after reading sentence 2. Choice (D), alone, shows this arrangement. (A), (B), and (C) are all incorrect because they do not show the correct sentence order.

31. **(C)** Replacing "extensive and very large" with "extensive" improves the style because the original phrase is too wordy. (A) is incorrect because there is no need to add Yellowstone to sentence 1 since this proper noun appears a number of times earlier in the reordered paragraph. (B) is incorrect because removing the pronoun "I" from sentence 2 does not improve the style. (D) is incorrect because replacing "states" with "United States" changes the meaning slightly and does not improve the style.

32. **(C)** The first books written for children appeared during the 1700s. Books such as *Gulliver's Travels* were adult books that appealed to some children.

33. **(D)** The author is narrating, or telling a story, about a part of his life.

34. **(D)** The word *when* is used to subordinate sentence elements. All of the other choices are used to coordinate sentence elements.

35. **(B)** Words with *a* pronounced as in *axe* usually do not end in "e." The word axe does not follow a regular spelling pattern. (A), (C), and (D) are all incorrect because each choice follows the regular spelling pattern for words pronunciation.

36. **(A)** The word *fraction* developed from the root *frac*, which means breaking something into pieces.

37. **(C)** The speaker is telling a story about her life.

38. **(C)** The speaker is clearly trying to convince the audience of his or her position and uses several rhetorical devices to that end.

39. **(D)** The quotes are the standard way to indicate the word "person" is not to be taken literally. The word "person" obviously refers to the gingerbread cookies. The other choices are incorrect because none of them describes a standard use of quotes around a word.

40. **(D)** This student is a phonetic speller. *Enuf* is misspelled, but the student correctly followed phonics rules. This student needs instruction in the alternative spelling used for phonemes (sounds associated with letters and groups of letters). For example, English spelling uses the letters *gh* to represent the *f* sound in *enough*. Using many spellings for the same sound can make English a difficult language to learn.

41. **(B)** A formative evaluation helps a teacher plan lessons, not determine student performance. Samples of a student's writing best furthers that goal.

42. **(D)** Choice (D) is correct. The student's writing contains several verb tense shifts. In the first sentence, "sat" is past tense, while "play" is present tense. In the second sentence, "saw" is past tense, while "sit" is present tense.

43. **(C)** The speaker is telling a story about her life.

44. **(B)** Language has two main aspects—function and structure. Language function refers to the ability to communicate. Language structure refers to the way words are used in a language. The structure of the quote is inappropriate; however, we know what it means.

45. **(A)** Alliteration refers to the repetition of an initial consonant in nearby words.

46. **(D)** The word *when* is used to subordinate sentence elements. All of the other choices are used to coordinate sentence elements.

47. **(C)** Haiku follows a 5-7-5 syllabic scheme with no rhyming. Choice (C) alone meets these criteria.

48. **(C)** The word *paring* means to "cut off." Do not confuse this word with its homonym *pairing*.

49. **(C)** The author's clear intent is to draw attention to the question about the origin of the universe. Choice A is incorrect because the author provides no information about how the telescope operates. Choice B is incorrect because there is no mention of space exploration. Choice D is incorrect because the author indicates the telescopes have not been able to answer the key question in the final sentence.

50. **(C)** This sentence correctly uses the possessive form of *its*. The other underlined words are homonyms (words that sound the same but are spelled differently) of the correct word.

51. **(A)** The subordinate or dependent clause is underlined below. This clause depends on the other clause in the sentence and it makes no sense on its own. <u>When Dorothy takes a trip to the beach</u>, she always feels happier.(B) is incorrect because each clause in this sentence makes sense on its own, so these are independent and not dependent clauses. (C) and (D) are incorrect because they have a single independent clause.

52. **(B)** *Effect* is usually a noun that typically means "consequence." *Affect* is a verb that typically means "act on." The word *effect* is used correctly as a noun in this choice to show that decreased traffic is a consequence of construction. (A) and (C) are incorrect because changing *affect* to *effect* or *effect* to *affect* would make these choices correct. (D) is incorrect because changing *effect* to *affect* would make this choice correct.

53. **(C)** This is the definition of a rhetorical question, a question to which no response is expected. (A) and (B) are incorrect because a rhetorical question has nothing to do with rhetoric or rhetorical techniques. (D) is incorrect because audience members may or may not know the answer to a rhetorical question.

54. **(B)** Words with *a* pronounced as in *axe* usually do not end in *e*. The word *axe* does not follow a regular spelling pattern. (A), (C), and (D) are all incorrect because each choice follows the regular spelling pattern for word pronunciation.

55. **(A)** Substitute *brought* for *bringed*. The word *bringed* would be appropriate, except for the irregular nature of English verb construction. (B) and (C) are incorrect because the verbs *hopped* and *practicing* are used correctly in the sentence. (D) is incorrect because, while a writer should substitute *spoke* for *speak*, the problem is not caused by the irregular nature of English verb construction.

56. **(B)** The pronoun *his* shows possession. The bike belongs to John. (A) is incorrect because the pronoun *they* does not show possession. (C) is incorrect because neither the pronoun *we* nor the pronoun *them* shows possession. (D) is incorrect because neither the pronoun *they* nor the pronoun *whom* shows possession.

57. **(A)** *Ascent* means the "process of going upward," which is what the mountain climber is doing. (B) is incorrect because *assented* means "agreed," and it does not make sense for the runner to agree the winner's platform. (C) is incorrect because *assented* means to "go up," but the diver is going down. (D) is incorrect because *assent* means "to agree," and it does not make sense for a cat to assent a tree.

58. **(D)** This sentence is too wordy. Replace the wordy "has the ultimate capacity to" with "can" to improve the style of the passage. (A) is incorrect because this change removes the parallel structure of the original sentence. (B) is incorrect because changing the words *driven by* to *react to* changes the meaning of the sentence and does not improve the style. (C) is incorrect because it alters the meaning from "consider the way mathematics is taught" to "consider mathematics," and it does not improve the style of the passage.

59. **(C)** The thought expressed in sentence 5 comes naturally before the thought expressed in sentence 4 and it makes sense to move it. (A), (B), and (D) are all incorrect because the sentences referred to in these choices are correct as placed in the passage.

60. **(A)** There is nothing like being prepared for the introductory part of your presentation. This approach is most likely among those listed to get a speaker through initial stage fright. (B) is incorrect because you should never share your stage fright or uncertainty with an audience. (C) and (D) are incorrect because, while these can be effective techniques, these techniques are not likely to help alleviate stage fright.

61. **(C)** The main purpose of an expository presentation is to explain, and this presentation explains about Piaget and his operational stages. (A) is incorrect because a narration tells a factual or fictional story. (B) is incorrect because the presentation conveys only facts. (D) is incorrect because a reflection describes a scene, a person, or an emotion.

62. **(B)** The intent of a persuasive presentation is to convince the audience of a particular point of view. This sentence seeks to convince the audience members to incorporate Piaget's ideas in their teaching. (A), (C), and (D) are all incorrect because they just continue the explanation, which is the hallmark of an expository presentation, not a persuasive presentation.

63. **(D)** An epic focuses on a single mythological figure. (A) is incorrect because a lyric is most closely associated with profound feelings or ideas. (B) is incorrect because this theme is most closely associated with a novel. (C) is incorrect because this theme is most closely associated with a romance.

64. **(B)** This is a version of one of Aesop's better-known fables. (A) is incorrect because a legend is partially fiction but presented as fact. (C) is incorrect because lyrics are poems. (D) is incorrect because a satire uses irony and sarcasm to comment on the human condition.

65. **(C)** This choice paraphrases the moral of this story, often summarized as "sour grapes." (A), (B), and (D) are all incorrect because the sentiments expressed in these choices do not match the facts of the story.

Subtest 5033 Mathematics

1. **(C)** Use formula $a\%$ of b is c.

   $35\% \times \$83.00 \qquad = ?$
   $.35 \times \$83 \qquad\qquad = \$29.05$
   $\$83 - \$29.05 \qquad = \$53.95$

2. **(A)** Write a number sentence and solve.

   $\square\% \times 125 = 105$
   $\square\% = 105 \div 125 = 0.84 = 84\%.$

3. **(A)** This is the only answer choice divisible by 2, 3, and 4.

4. **(D)** You can approach the problem this way. $0.01 = \dfrac{1}{100}$. Dividing by $\dfrac{1}{100}$ is the same as multiplying by 100. $100 \times 10 = 1{,}000$. That is the answer. You could set it up as an equation.

   $X \div 0.01 = 1{,}000 \quad X \div 0.01 = X \cdot 100 \quad$ so $\quad X \cdot 100 = 1{,}000$
   Divide both sides by 10. $X = 10$

5. **(B)** Begin by looking quickly at all the fractions. Choice (C) is too high, more than 2—so is choice (D). Eliminate these. The only ones left are (A) and (B). Cross multiply to see which is greater. The smaller cross product is over the smaller fraction.

   $$\begin{array}{cc} 7314 & 7230 \\ \dfrac{46}{30} & \dfrac{241}{159} \\ x & \end{array}$$

6. **(D)** There are two steps to this solution. First multiply 3 and 100 to find out that there are 300 gallons in the tank. Then divide 300 by 80 to get 3.75 or $3\dfrac{3}{4}$ hours.

7. **(B)** Think it through. $300 \text{ km} \times 10 = 3{,}000 \text{ km}$. $2 \text{ cm} = 300 \text{ km}$, so $20 \text{ cm} = 3{,}000$ miles. Or use a proportion: $2/300 = x/3000$, $300x = 6000$, $x = 20$.

8. **(D)** Three single pounds costs $2.94. A three-pound box costs $2.55. Subtract: $\$2.94 - \$2.55 = \$.39$. Divide by 3. That's $0.13 a pound.

9. **(C)** 23 centimeters should jump right out at you. All the others work out to a reasonable height for some real building.

10. **(B)** Only this line segment passes through point $(-2, 3)$.

11. **(D)** There are eight possible combinations of heads and tails when you flip three coins. All heads (H H H) is one of those eight ($\frac{1}{8}$) possibilities.

12. **(C)** Round the numbers to 0.04 and 0.005. Multiply to get 0.0002.

13. **(B)** The entire region has an area of 12 m^2. One-eighth of the region is shaded. $\frac{1}{8} \times 12 = 1.5$.

14. **(D)** This is the correct answer because if the product of two different numbers is 1, then one of the numbers must be greater than 1 and the other must be less than 1. So Q must be less than 1, as is P. That means the product of P and Q must also be less than 1.

15. **(D)** II is the only correct statement about all the names when you take into account both girls' and boys' names.

16. **(D)** Choice (C) is not correct because we cannot know that there is a bird of that specific weight.

17. **(B)** $30 \times 0.02 = 0.6$. Remember to use order of operations as you calculate the answers. Choice (B) says find 0.5 or half of 1.2. That's what you are looking for.

18. **(C)** Remember that there are 12 inches in a foot.

$$\begin{array}{r} 50 \text{ ft} = 49 \text{ ft } 12 \text{ in} \\ -\ 9 \text{ ft } \ 8 \text{ in} \\ \hline 40 \text{ ft } \ 4 \text{ in} \end{array}$$

19. **(C)** First divide the area by the width to find the length of the rectangle. $56.7 \div 3 = 18.9$. Then add the lengths and the widths to find the perimeter $3 + 3 + 18.9 + 18.9 = 43.8$ cm.

20. **(C)** $0.1 + 0.001 = \dfrac{1}{10} + \dfrac{1}{1{,}000} = \dfrac{100}{1{,}000} \div \dfrac{1}{1{,}000} = \dfrac{101}{1{,}000}$

21. **(B)** The angle measure is between 90° and 180°. The only answer in that range is 130°.

22. **(B)** The pole casts a 10 foot shadow, while the tree casts a 21 foot shadow.

Set up a proportion $\qquad\qquad \dfrac{10}{14} = \dfrac{x}{21}$

Cross multiply $\qquad\qquad 14x = 210$

The tree is about 15 ft tall $\qquad x = 15$

23. **(A)** The number 6 has two different prime factors, 2 and 3. The product of 2 and 3 is 6 $2 \times 3 = 6$. (B), (C), and (D) are incorrect.
(B) The number 12 has two prime factors, 2 and 3. The product of 2 and 3 is not 12.
(C) The number 36 has two prime factors, 2 and 3. The product of 2 and 3 is not 36.
(D) The number 48 has two prime factors, 2 and 3. The product of 2 and 3 is not 48.

24. **(D)** The first region has 2/5 shaded, the second region 5/9, the third region 1/4.
    2/5 + 5/9 + 1/4
The denominators do not share common factors. Multiply them all to find the common denominator: $5 \times 9 \times 4 = 180$.
    2/5 + 5/9 + 1/4 = 72/180 + 100/180 + 45/180 = 217/180 = 1 37/180.
(A), (B), and (C) are all incorrect because these choices do not show the correct answer.

25. **(A)** The multiples of x and y will reveal at which floors each elevator stops. Find the common multiples to find at which floors both elevators stop.

For example, the multiples of 2 are 2, 4, 6, 8, 10, . . .

The multiples of 3 are 3, 6, 9, . . .

Using common multiples we can see that both elevators stop at the sixth floor. (B), (C), and (D) are all incorrect because the factors of a number are the same as the divisors of that number. Prime factors are factors that are also prime numbers. Divisors do not show at which floors elevators stop. The largest divisor of a number is the number itself.

26. **(D)** Begin by rewriting this expression: 10^{-2} means move the decimal point two places to the left.

$1.37 \times 10^{-2} = 0.0137$

The 7 is in the ten-thousandths place. It has a value of 7/10000.

(A), (B), and (C) are all incorrect because these choices do not show this answer.

27. **(B)** The number line shows from 0 to 1 with a mark every 0.1 (1/10). The letter A is located at 7/10 (0.7) and B is located at 0.9.

Use your calculator to find the decimal value of each fraction.

(A) 27/34 = 0.79 YES

(B) 79/86 = 0.92   NO

(C) 81/91 = 0.89 YES

(D) 38/54 = 0.703 YES

Only choice B is not between Point A and Point B.

28. **(A)** 91 percent is spent on other things and 9 percent is left for the class trip.

Use your calculator to find 9 percent of $5,300.

9 percent of $5,300 = 0.09 × $5300 = $477

(B), (C), and (D) are all incorrect because these choices do not show the correct answer.

29. **(D)** Use your calculator.

Find the estimate: 52 + 51 + 52 + 51 + 50 + 55 = 311<u>0</u>

Now find the sum: 524 + 516 + 528 + 512 + 502 + 551 = 3133

Subtract: 3133 − 3110 = 23

The difference between the sum and the estimate is 23.

(A), (B), and (C) are all incorrect because these choices do not show the correct answer.

30. **(A)** As the diameter increases, the circumference increases, and at a steady rate. That's because the formula for the circumference of a circle is πd. (B) is incorrect because this graph shows that the circumference increases at a faster rate than the diameter. (C) is incorrect because this graph shows that the circumference decreases as the diameter increases. (D) is incorrect because this graph shows that the circumference increases at a slower rate than the diameter.

31. **(A)** The slope of −1 means the line goes generally from upper left to lower right on the grid.

That alone eliminates Points B, C, and D. A slope of −1 means move right one square for every square down. A line through Point A and Point X follows that pattern and shows the slope of that line is −1.

32. **(B)** Work out some steps for solving the equation.

$$3x - 1/5\,(x + 5) = -x/5 + 33$$
$$3x - x/5 - 1 = x/5 + 33$$
$$3x = 34$$

We can stop here. This step matches choice (B).

(A), (C), and (D) are all incorrect because these choices do not show this answer.

33. **(C)** Corresponding sides of similar triangles are proportional.

Write a proportion.

$$\frac{3}{7} \qquad \frac{2}{x}$$

Cross-multiply.

$$3x = 14 \qquad x = 14/3 \qquad x = 4.66$$

(A), (B), and (D) are all incorrect because these choices do not show this answer.

34. **(C)** Arrange the rainfall amounts in order from least to greatest.

There are an even number of scores, so find the middle two scores.

$$2 \quad 2 \quad 3 \quad 3 \quad 4 \quad \underline{4} \quad \underline{6} \quad 6 \quad 7 \quad 7 \quad 8 \quad 8$$

These scores are different;

find the average.

$$4 + 6 = 10 \div 2 = 5$$

The median is 5.

(A), (B), and (D) are all incorrect because these choices do not show this answer.

35. **(D)** Read the graph to find an ordered pair where the first element is 1 (x intercept of 1) and another ordered pair where the second element is 1 (y intercept of 1). Graph D shows the ordered pairs (1, 0) and (0, 1). (A), (B), and (C) are all incorrect because these graphs do not show both an x intercept of 1 and a y intercept of 1.

36. **(B)** You can substitute the numerals and symbols for words

$$\underline{C} \text{ is } \underline{5} \text{ more than } \underline{\text{half of}} \ \underline{B}.$$
$$\underline{C} = 5 \quad + \quad \tfrac{1}{2} \ \underline{B}$$

This is the same as the equation C = ½B + 5. (A), (C), and (D) are all incorrect because these choices do not show the correct equation.

37. **(D)** The formula for the area of a trapezoid is $A = \dfrac{h}{2}\,(b_1 + b_2)$.

The bases b_1 and b_2 are doubled in the new trapezoid. The formula for the area of the new trapezoid using the original values of b_1 and b_2 is

$$A = \frac{h}{2}\,(2b_1 + 2b_2) = \frac{h}{2} \cdot 2(b_1 + b_2) = h \cdot \frac{1}{2} \cdot 2(b_1 + b_2) = h(b_1 + b_2)$$

(A), (B), and (C) are all incorrect because these choices do not show the correct formula for the area of the new trapezoid.

38. **(B)** The points are symmetrical and so the line passes through the origin, where the x axis and y axis cross. The coordinates for the origin are (0, 0). (A), (C), and (D) are all incorrect because these choices do not show the correct coordinates.

39. **(B)** There are three feet in a yard. Beth's front walk is 58 divided by 3 = 19 yards and 1 foot. A foot is 1/3 of a yard. 19 yards 1 foot = $19y + 1/3y$. (A), (C), and (D) are all incorrect because these choices do not show the correct number of yards.

40. **(C)** In a standard deck of cards, there are 12 "face cards"—4 kings, 4 queens, and 4 jacks—out of 52 possible cards.

$$P \text{ (face card)} = 12/52 = 3/13.$$

(A), (B), and (D) are all incorrect because these choices do not show the correct probability.

Subtest 5034 Social Studies

1. **(D)** These are just a few of the measures FDR implemented during the Depression.

2. **(B)** Sherman's march to the sea occurred during the Civil War and was followed by Lee's surrender to Grant at Appomattox Courthouse, Virginia. Reconstruction and the XIII amendment followed the war.

3. **(B)** The Depression occurred some 15 to 20 years after World War I.

4. **(B)** The manifest destiny of the United States was to stretch from ocean to ocean.

5. **(B)** Gandhi believed in and "popularized" nonviolence.

6. **(D)** This famous poster reflects the sentiment "United we stand, divided we fall."

7. **(A)** The question asks about the primary impact of early colonization *on* North America. There is no doubt that the primary impact *on* North America was the mass death of indigenous Americans, which began as soon as the first colonists arrived. Choices (B), (C), and (D) are incorrect because these choices do not describe the primary impact of early colonization *on* North America.

8. **(A)** The Algonquin-speaking tribes lived in this area. These tribes included the Iroquois Federation and other Northeast Indians. None of the other lettered regions identifies a primary location for Algonquin-speaking tribes.

9. **(D)** Hoover adopted a hands-off policy and only attempted a "trickle-down" approach by making money available to employers. Choices (A), (B), and (C) are incorrect because these choices refer to actions that Hoover did not take.

10. **(C)** The Emancipation Proclamation applied only to slaves in confederate states. Choice (B) is incorrect. Choices (A) and (D) refer to popular misconceptions about the intent of the Emancipation Proclamation.

11. **(B)** The English soldiers were defended by patriots, including John Adams, and acquitted on the grounds that they acted in self-defense. Choices (A) and (C) are factually incorrect. Choice (D) is incorrect because while Crispus Attucks was African-American, that was not the reason for the acquittal.

12. **(B)** The Jeffersonians favored a weaker federal government. (A) and (D) are incorrect because the Federalists, also known as the Hamiltonians, favored a stronger federal government and opposed the Jeffersonians. (C) is incorrect because the Whigs did not emerge as a political party until the early 1800s.

13. **(B)** It was during the Crimean War, which pitted Great Britain, France, and Turkey as allies against Russia, that Florence Nightingale became famous. The remaining choices

are incorrect because Florence Nightingale died in 1910 at the age of 90. She was not alive during the wars listed in these other choices.

14. **(B)** The Common Market includes only England and European countries. Choices (A), (C), and (D) are all incorrect statements about the outcome of the negotiations.

15. **(C)** In 1896 the Court ruled that separate but equal accommodations for black Americans were legal. The case of *Plessy v. Ferguson* did not address the issues in Choices (A), (B), or (D).

16. **(B)** The Spanish American War was fought in Cuba and the Philippines. The battleship *Maine* was sunk in Havana harbor, and not the other places listed.

17. **(D)** These taxation acts moved many colonists to revolution. (A) is incorrect because Catherine the Great died in 1796, after the Revolutionary War. (B) is incorrect because Napoleon was defeated in 1815, well after the Revolutionary War. (C) The French Revolution began in 1789, after the Revolutionary War.

18. **(B)** Robert E. Lee is the only military figure listed who had a role in both events. The Mexican-American War spanned 1846 to 1848. John Brown's raid took place in October 1859. (A) and (C) are incorrect because Philip Kearny and Zachary Taylor participated in the Mexican-American War, but were not at Brown's raid. (D) is incorrect because William Travis had passed away in 1836 before either event.

19. **(C)** Columbus sailed the Caribbean and landed in what is now the Dominican Republic and the island of Hispaniola. He never reached the mainland. (A) is incorrect because Columbus did return to Europe during his explorations. (B) is incorrect because Sir Walter Raleigh established a settlement in North Carolina. (D) is incorrect because John Smith established the Jamestown Colony in Virginia.

20. **(B)** This line includes an accurate description of the Stamp Act, which required a tax stamp for each legal document. (A) is incorrect because the Sugar Act limited the export of other commodities. (C) is incorrect because, while Crispus Attucks was killed in the Boston Massacre, five colonists, not dozens, were killed and there was provocation. (D) is incorrect because there were less than a few hundred colonists who boarded ships and dumped tea into the harbor.

21. **(C)** The Anti-Federalists were not opposed to a federal government, but they were concerned that the Constitution did not protect individual rights. (A) is incorrect because the Anti-Federalists were not opposed to a federal government. (B) is incorrect because the Articles of Confederation was the first American constitution and had nothing to do with the confederacy or the Civil War. (D) is incorrect because many of those who preferred the Articles of Confederation did not feature a central government and were concerned whether individual states could act to form a central government. However, this was not a view held by the Anti-Federalists.

22. **(C)** This Article of the Constitution establishes the Electoral College. The popular vote chooses electors, not the president. The electors then vote for the president. In three recent presidential elections, a candidate received a majority of the electoral votes but did not receive a majority of the popular vote. (A) is incorrect because this article says that the people of the United States do not directly elect the president. (B) is incorrect

because a plurality in a majority of the states is not enough to elect a president, even though most elected presidents do win in a majority of states. (D) is incorrect because as the article says, the number of electors is equal to the number of senators and representatives combined.

23. **(A)** This basic right was essential to formulate a document that abolished the British government. Look at the underlined portion of this excerpt from the Declaration of Independence.

> We hold these truths to be self-evident, that all men are created equal, that they are endowed by their Creator with certain inalienable rights, that among these are Life, Liberty and the Pursuit of Happiness. That, to secure these rights, Governments are instituted among Men, deriving their just powers from the consent of the governed. <u>That, when any form of government becomes destructive of these ends, it is the Right of the People to alter or abolish it.</u>

(B) is incorrect because the Declaration of Independence says that all men are created equal, with no exception for slaves, although delegates removed from a draft a section condemning the slave trade. (C) is incorrect because the First Amendment outlines these rights. (D) is incorrect because the Second Amendment mentions the right to bear arms.

24. **(D)** American troops trapped Cornwallis and his forces against the coast in Yorktown, Virginia, but the French fleet made it impossible for British forces to escape. (A), (B), and (C) are all incorrect because it was the combination of American troops and French naval forces that forced the British to surrender.

25. **(D)** This very high rate of dead and wounded shows that the Civil War had an impact on all Americans. (A) is incorrect because this is about twice the number of soldiers who fought on both sides during the Civil War. (B) is incorrect because, while there was damage to these towns, it was nothing like total devastation. (C) is incorrect because the number of women killed in the war was a tiny fraction of the estimated 700,000 soldiers who died on both sides.

26. **(B)** Jim Crow laws imposed racial segregation. The Supreme Court ruled shortly after the Civil War in *Plessy v. Ferguson* that it was legal to have "separate but equal" accommodations, opening the door for segregationist legislation. (A) is incorrect because the Court's ruling in the *Amistad* case was about twenty-five years before the Civil War began. (C) is incorrect because the Court's ruling in *Marbury v. Madison* was about sixty years before the Civil War. (D) is incorrect because the Court's ruling in *Brown v. Board of Education* was in 1954.

27. **(D)** Note the word NOT in the question. Perry was in charge of a small American fleet on Lake Erie, not in Baltimore Harbor. (A), (B), and (C) are all incorrect because they are accurate matches of a person or people with events during the War of 1812.

28. **(B)** Slaves aboard the *Amistad* revolted during a voyage to the United States and killed several crew members. (A) is incorrect because the Supreme Court eventually ruled in favor of the Africans and freed them. (C) is incorrect because Martin Van Buren wanted the Africans deported, while John Quincy Adams represented them before the Supreme Court. (D) is incorrect because the Africans did not receive any land.

29. **(C)** The map's caption reveals this information.

30. **(C)** Refer to the map, which shows that Fremont won most northern states.

31. **(A)** These states have the lowest per pupil expenditures.

32. **(B)** These states, as a group, have the highest per pupil expenditures.

33. **(A)** The law of supply and demand describes the relationship between the availability and cost of goods.

34. **(C)** On average, Asheville has 235 days without precipitation. Note that the graph does not show days that are cloudy but have no precipitation.

35. **(D)** This conclusion is correct. On average, Houston has 259 days without precipitation. Choice (C) is incorrect because the number of days with precipitation does not reveal the amount of precipitation.

36. **(D)** Three-quarters of the states must ratify any amendment passed by Congress.

37. **(C)** The Russian Revolution had a significant impact because Russia left World War I. The Russian Revolution effectively brought Russia's conflict with Germany to an end. Germany was able to recommit troops and resources from the Eastern Front. The remaining answer choices are factually incorrect.

38. **(C)** Introduction of writing separates prehistoric from historic times, and the first symbols were cuneiform symbols written on clay tablets. The remaining answer choices are important developments, but the dividing line between prehistory and history is the invention of writing.

39. **(B)** Robespierre was executed for his role as head of the Committee on Public Safety, which arranged the deaths of over 20,000 people during the Reign of Terror in France. His execution in July 1794 was a reaction against the Committee of Public Safety and the excesses of the Reign of Terror. The other choices are incorrect because Robespierre did not oppose the Reign of Terror.

40. **(D)** The Anglo-Zulu War was fought in 1879 between the British Empire and the Zulu Kingdom. None of the other listed countries was at war with the British in South Africa during 1879.

41. **(C)** The three World War II powers were represented at Potsdam by Communist Party general secretary Joseph Stalin, Prime Minister Winston Churchill, and President Harry S. Truman. Answers (A) and (B) are incorrect because de Gaulle never participated in this conference. Choice (D) is incorrect because Roosevelt died just months before the conference began. Clement Attlee replaced Churchill after Atlee was elected prime minister, but his name is not listed in the answer choices.

42. **(B)** As a result of the Treaty of Utrecht the Spanish Empire was partitioned. Spain's European territories were apportioned. Portugal had its sovereignty recognized over the lands between the Amazon and Oyapock rivers in Brazil. In addition, Spain ceded Gibraltar and Minorca to Great Britain. (A) is incorrect because France lost most of its North American possessions to Britain when the Treaty of Paris was signed in 1763.

43. **(A)** Companies only pay higher rates to attract investors. Riskier bonds are the primary reason one company pays a higher rate than another company. (B) is incorrect because

Company B's bonds would have a higher rate if those bonds had a higher risk. (C) and (D) are incorrect because rewarding investors would not be the primary cause for either company to pay higher rates.

44. **(D)** The lined area east of the Mediterranean and east of the Red Sea corresponds to Mesopotamia. This region contains the Tigris and Euphrates rivers. Historians often identify Mesopotamia as the birthplace of civilization. (A) is incorrect because Egypt is located south of the Mediterranean and west of the Red Sea. (B) is incorrect because Greece is located on the northern shore of the Mediterranean. (C) is incorrect because the Kush Kingdom is located south of Egypt and west of the Red Sea.

45. **(C)** The Kush Kingdom developed in Africa on a plain along the Nile River. (A) is incorrect because the African jungles are found south of where the Kush Kingdom developed. (B) is incorrect because the Kush Kingdom developed in sub-Saharan Africa south of the Sahara desert. (D) is incorrect because there are no significant mountains in the area where the Kush civilization developed.

46. **(C)** Greek civilization began on the island of Crete, and it was home to both the Minoans about 3000–1400 B.C.E. (B.C.) and the Myceans in about 1600–1100 B.C.E. Greece was invaded by the Dorians about 1100–800 B.C.E. Sparta is located in Greece. None of the other choices can claim these elements. (A) is incorrect because Assyria was located in Mesopotamia, an essentially landlocked region. (B) is incorrect because Egyptian civilization developed along the northern Nile River. (D) is incorrect because the Phoenician civilization developed along the eastern coast of the Mediterranean.

47. **(B)** Both Muslims and Jews were massacred during the Crusades by the Christian invaders. (A) is incorrect because even though Richard the Lionheart spent most of his time in the Crusades while he was king, he never captured the Holy Land. (C) is incorrect because the country of Turkey was founded in the 1920s. (D) is incorrect because the "Great Schism" occurred in 1054, splitting the Catholic Church and establishing a second patriarch in Constantinople.

48. **(B)** The Pax Romana, 200 years of peace, began just after the Battle of Acton. (A) is incorrect because the Roman civil wars started before the Battle of Acton. (C) is incorrect because Caesar was assassinated before the Battle of Acton. (D) is incorrect because the Roman Empire's growth began after the Battle of Acton.

49. **(A)** Feudalism refers to a European system in which knights offered protection in return for their service. The role of lords in this system very closely resembles the role of shoguns in Japan. (B) is incorrect because persecution is not an element of Feudalism. (C) is incorrect because the overthrow of leaders by "the people" may have occurred during Feudalism, but it is not a part of Feudalism. (D) is incorrect because a pope is a religious leader, and shoguns did have a religious role in Japan.

50. **(D)** The reform movement in Europe created Protestant religions, protesting Catholicism. Protestant religions spread to England and led to the creation of the Protestant Church of England. (A) is incorrect because the Reformation did not have a significant impact on religion in Spain, which remained a largely Catholic nation. (B) is incorrect because the rediscovery of literature and art occurred in the Renaissance, not the Ref-

ormation. (C) is incorrect because the ceiling of the Sistine Chapel was painted at about the same time the Reformation started, and it did not result from the Reformation.

51. **(B)** Civilization is associated with a written language, which was most likely invented by the Sumerians about 5,000 years ago near the confluence of the Tigris and Euphrates rivers. (A) is incorrect because the Nile River is certainly the center of important civilizations, but it is not where written language first appeared. (C) and (D) are incorrect because civilization did develop around the seas mentioned in the choices, but they are not the birthplace of civilization.

52. **(B)** Greece alone meets this description. It juts out into the Mediterranean Sea, has a coastline along the Aegean Sea, has a large island off the southern tip of the mainland, and has scores of Greek Islands nearby. (A) is incorrect because the Nile Delta extends a little into the Mediterranean Sea, but it does not jut out. Egypt has a long coastline with the Red Sea, but there are not a great many other islands nearby. (C) and (D) are incorrect because Chad and Afghanistan are landlocked.

53. **(A)** As feudalism ended, the feudal lords lost power to the emperor. (B) is incorrect because Samurai were the lord's private soldiers, and as the lords lost their lands, the Samurai became less important. (C) is incorrect because as agrarian feudalism ended, industrialism increased. (D) is incorrect because the shoguns were the lords that lost power.

54. **(A)** Find San Antonio in southern Texas and trace the Chisholm Trail to Abilene, Kansas. Notice that the trail splits as it enters Kansas.

55. **(A)** The Chisholm Trail passes through just three states, while the other four trails pass through at least four states. Notice that the trails go generally south to north, while the railroads go generally east to west.

Subtest 5035 Science

1. **(B)** Choice (B) is the definition of ecology. Ecology is a more general study of the world than the choices offered in (A), (C), and (D).

2. **(A)** This is the only conclusion supported by the data.

3. **(D)** The experiment does not describe how experimenters ensured that the HF2 group received no special attention, nor does it describe any other controls.

4. **(B)** Arteries carry blood away from the heart, and veins bring the blood back to the heart.

5. **(D)** Conduction means heat transfer by direct contact, as described in this choice. (A) and (B) are incorrect because these choices give examples of heat transfer by radiation (no physical contact). (C) is incorrect because this choice gives an example of heat transfer by convection (moving air).

6. **(D)** Most of the Earth's atmosphere is nitrogen. Oxygen makes up about 21 percent of the atmosphere. The remaining 1 percent of Earth's atmosphere is partitioned among trace elements and gases. Choices (A), (B), and (C) are incorrect because each choice includes the incorrect percents of oxygen and nitrogen in the atmosphere.

7. **(A)** Both the aphids and the ants benefit from this relationship. That is the definition of mutualism. (B) is incorrect because ants and aphids do compete. (C) is incorrect because one organism does not benefit at the expense of the other. (D) is incorrect because one species does not eat the other.

8. **(C)** Heat measures the speed of moving molecules. (A) and (D) might play a role in the speed of molecules. However, only (C) directly answers the question.

9. **(B)** This formula means—the more mass there is the more force you need to accelerate it. Less mass means you need less force. (A) A common sense example of a heavy airplane moving faster than a lighter bicycle explains why this answer is incorrect. (C) is incorrect because making something go faster at this speed does not reduce its mass. (D) is incorrect because more mass does not mean more force will be applied to it.

10. **(C)** Note the word NOT in the question. Glucose is produced by photosynthesis, but it does not contribute to photosynthesis. Choices (A), (B), and (D) are required for photosynthesis.

11. **(D)** A chromosome is a single piece of coiled DNA. (A) is incorrect because some DNA duplicates other strands of DNA. (B) is incorrect because this is a statement about RNA. (C) is incorrect because DNA varies from one species to another.

12. **(C)** The Earth's early supply of oxygen came from photosynthesis and not from the other choices listed. Oxygen is generally released as a "waste" product of photosynthesis.

13. **(C)** A virus is primitive in that it is simpler and less developed than a cell. (B) is incorrect because cells can also be parasitic.

14. **(D)** Oxygen-poor blood enters the lungs from the right ventricle. (A) is incorrect because oxygen-rich blood enters the left atrium from the lungs. (B) is incorrect because blood goes from the left ventricle to the body. (C) is incorrect because blood enters the right atrium from the body.

15. **(B)** The teeth help digestion through a mechanical process. Stomach muscle contractions during digestion are also a mechanical process. (A), (C), and (D) are all incorrect because none of these systems include a mechanical process.

16. **(B)** A fundamental truth of a food web is that energy flows upward as larger organisms eat smaller organisms. (A), (C), and (D) are all incorrect because these choices represent incorrect descriptions of energy flow in this food web.

17. **(C)** In the short term, the number of sea urchins will increase because sea urchins are the sea otters' favorite food. In turn, the number of kelp will decrease because they are the sea urchins' favorite food. (A) is incorrect because the number of sea urchins will increase with no sea otters to hunt them. (B) and (D) are incorrect because algae and plankton will decrease because increased numbers of sea urchins and sea stars eat them.

18. **(B)** Anaerobic respiration means respiration without oxygen. (A) is incorrect because anaerobic respiration is not related to cell division. (C) is incorrect because fermentation is the most commonly discussed example of anaerobic respiration. (D) is incorrect because anaerobic respiration does not produce oxygen.

19. **(D)** A human sperm cell and egg cell each has half the number of chromosomes normally found in an individual. When they combine, they form a zygote that has double the number of cells found in the sperm cell or the egg cell. (A), (B), and (C) are all incorrect because cell reproduction through mitosis maintains the number of chromosomes found in the parent cell.

20. **(B)** This is the correct sequence for photosynthesis.

21. **(A)** Pollen contains the sperm that fertilizes the egg cells found in the plant. (B) and (C) are incorrect because pollen provides neither a rich culture nor a medium for plant development or fertilization. (D) is incorrect because pollination does not attract bees, although flowers on some plants attract bees to their pollen.

22. **(C)** A chemical reaction forms a new substance. That is what happens when water and cement are combined to create concrete. (A) is incorrect because mixing two glasses of hot water does not create a chemical reaction, although chemical reactions can be formed when elements are heated, cooled, or burned. (B) and (D) are incorrect because when these kinds of things are "mixed," no chemical change takes place, so no chemical reaction takes place.

23. **(B)** The twenty-third pair of a female's genes has XX chromosomes, as shown here. (A) is incorrect because the twenty-third pair of a male's genes have XY chromosomes. (C) is incorrect because this choice cannot be confirmed from the information available in this diagram. (D) is incorrect because a person has twenty-three pairs of genes, as shown here.

24. **(D)** Gamete formation is a fundamental step in meiosis. (A), (B), and (C) are all incorrect because these steps are all common to mitosis, but not meiosis.

25. **(D)** Velocity is the rate at which an object moves. A free-falling object accelerates and increases velocity at a constant rate. This graph best represents that the velocity of a falling body increases as time increases. (A) is incorrect because this graph shows that velocity decreases as time increases, with a time delay. (B) is incorrect because there is no time delay in the increase of velocity, as this graph shows. (C) is incorrect because this graph shows that velocity decreases as time increases.

26. **(C)** The instability of the nucleus causes radioactive particles to be released.

27. **(D)** The speed of light is represented by C in this formula, which is Einstein's relativity equation.

28. **(D)** Echos frequently appear to enhance sound production around bodies of water.

29. **(C)** More mass means that there is more of the object, so the object with the most mass creates the most overflow.

30. **(B)** Sedimentary rocks are generally nearest the surface and contain the remains of living things.

31. **(B)** Sound travels through stone a little less than 20 times faster than it travels through air (Choice A) and about 4 times faster than it travels through water (Choice E). Choice (D) is incorrect because sound does not travel through a vacuum.

32. **(C)** The ball at the top of the ramp has the most potential for creating energy.

33. **(D)** Elements with neutral charges have a balance of electrons (negative charge) and protons (positive charge).

34. **(D)** 330 years is about 4×82. Multiply $\frac{1}{2}$ four times: $\frac{1}{2} \times \frac{1}{2} \times \frac{1}{2} \times \frac{1}{2} = \frac{1}{16}$.

35. **(D)** The result described in this item is a string of lights wired in series. Choices (A) and (B) are incorrect because neither is a likely outcome of removing a single bulb. Choice (C) is incorrect because the lights would not go out if the lights were wired in parallel.

36. **(D)** Conduction means heat transfer by physical contact.

37. **(A)** Topography is the study of the surface features of Earth, other planets, *moons*, and asteroids.

38. **(B)** The sun is facing directly at the southern hemisphere at this position.

39. **(B)** The Earth's mantle is the part of the Earth beneath the crust. (A) is incorrect because that labels the Earth's crust. (C) is incorrect because that labels the outer core. (D) is incorrect because that labels the inner core.

40. **(A)** The ohm measures resistance. (B) is incorrect because amp measures the current flow. (C) is incorrect because volt measures the current force. (D) is incorrect because the unit of measurement called the Weber measures magnetic flux.

41. **(B)** In the Northern Hemisphere, and so the United States, air circulates counterclockwise, to the left, around a low, and (A) clockwise around a high. This pattern is reversed in the Southern Hemisphere. Choices (C) and (D) do not describe a pattern of air circulation in a low-pressure system.

42. **(A)** Sedimentary rocks are found near the surface. (B) and (C) are incorrect because metamorphic and igneous rocks are found beneath the surface. (D) is incorrect because the term *cretaceous* refers to a time period, not a rock type.

43. **(B)** Mass is the amount of an object, and it does not vary. Weight is the force of gravity on mass, and weight does vary with gravity.

44. **(A)** Dark-colored material absorbs more sunlight and more heat than light-colored material. Light-colored material reflects more sunlight than dark-colored material.

45. **(C)** Plate tectonic theory shows that parts of the Earth's surface are slowly moving. Earthquakes, volcanoes, and mountain growth can occur along plate boundaries.

46. **(A)** A solar eclipse occurs when the moon hides some or all of the sun from the Earth. (B) is incorrect because this describes a lunar eclipse. Choices (C) and (D) do not describe a solar or a lunar eclipse.

47. **(C)** Weight measures the force of gravity on an object. Since gravity is lower on the moon, the clay will weigh less on the moon than it does on Earth.

48. **(D)** The formula is $d = vt$.
Divide both sides by t to get $v = d/t$.
Then substitute 90 feet for d and
4 minutes for t.
$v = 90$ feet/4 minutes
$v = 22.5$ feet per minute

49. **(C)** In science, work means movement of a body by force. This choice is the only one that involves movement. (A) and (B) are incorrect because these choices involve no movement so there is no work. (D) is incorrect because no force is involved when an object is dropped, which means there is no work.

50. **(D)** A new layer of water is added at lower levels and frozen as the hailstone is blown to an upper level. This process creates the rings. (A), (B), and (C) are all incorrect because none of these factors creates the rings in a hailstone.

PART VII

ParaPro Assessment Overview with Sample Items

ParaPro Assessment (0755, 1755) Overview with Sample Items

17

Many teachers become paraprofessionals before they become teachers. We offer this overview of the ParaPro Assessment for those pursuing that path.

TEST INFO BOX

This test is for Paraprofessional certification.

Registration and Other Test Information—*www.ets.org/parapro*
  2½ hours (150 minutes)

Reading   30 Multiple-Choice Items

Mathematics   30 Multiple-Choice Items

Writing   30 Multiple-Choice Items

Two-thirds of the items in each area focus on basic skills and knowledge. The other third focus on teaching.

TEST ADMINISTRATION
The ParaPro Assessment is administered as both a paper-delivered and a computer-delivered test. The test has an identical format for each administration type.

  Paper-delivered test administrations are given at test centers. Computer-delivered test administrations are typically given through participating school districts.

TEST SCORING
The ParaPro Assessment consists of 90 multiple-choice items. Test scoring is based on 75 predetermined items, but you will not know in advance which items they are.

  ParaPro test scores are reported on a scale of 420 to 480. Each state or school has its own passing score, and most required passing scores are below the 25th percentile. That usually means that about 60 percent to 72 percent will earn a passing score.

HOW TO PREPARE FOR THE PARAPRO ASSESSMENT

Here is a complete preparation for the ParaPro Assessment, which is very similar to preparation for the Core, although the Core tests are more difficult.

Follow these steps.

QUICK REVIEW CHECKLIST

Strategies

☐ Review the proven Test-Preparation Strategies on page 22.

☐ Review the Proven Test-Taking Strategies on page 23.
Do not review the Essay Strategies.

Writing

☐ Complete the Targeted Writing Test on page 65.

☐ Complete the indicated part of the English Review beginning on page 34.

You will find two Core Writing tests on pages 255 and 321 with explained answers. You can use these tests for extra English practice items, although there are question types on the ParaPro Assessment that do not appear on these tests.

Mathematics

☐ Complete the indicated part of the Mathematics Review beginning on page 91.
You do not have to complete the Problem-Solving Review on pages 148–151.

☐ Complete the Targeted Mathematics Test beginning on page 163 and review the answers.

There are two Core Mathematics Tests on pages 266 and 332 with explained answers. You can use these tests for extra mathematics practice, although some of the questions are harder than the questions on the ParaPro Assessment.

Reading

☐ Complete the Reading Strategies on page 197.

☐ Take and correct the Targeted Reading Test on page 220 and review the answers.

There are two Core Reading Tests on pages 237 and 305 with explained answers. You can use these tests for extra reading practice, although some of the questions may be harder than the questions on the ParaPro Assessment.

☐ Sample Items.

Complete the 24 sample ParaPro items on the following pages.

ANSWER SHEET
ParaPro Assessment
Sample Items

1. Ⓐ Ⓑ Ⓒ Ⓓ
2. Ⓐ Ⓑ Ⓒ Ⓓ
3. Ⓐ Ⓑ Ⓒ Ⓓ
4. Ⓐ Ⓑ Ⓒ Ⓓ
5. Ⓐ Ⓑ Ⓒ Ⓓ
6. Ⓐ Ⓑ Ⓒ Ⓓ
7. Ⓐ Ⓑ Ⓒ Ⓓ
8. Ⓐ Ⓑ Ⓒ Ⓓ

9. Ⓐ Ⓑ Ⓒ Ⓓ
10. Ⓐ Ⓑ Ⓒ Ⓓ
11. Ⓐ Ⓑ Ⓒ Ⓓ
12. Ⓐ Ⓑ Ⓒ Ⓓ
13. Ⓐ Ⓑ Ⓒ Ⓓ
14. Ⓐ Ⓑ Ⓒ Ⓓ
15. Ⓐ Ⓑ Ⓒ Ⓓ
16. Ⓐ Ⓑ Ⓒ Ⓓ

17. Ⓐ Ⓑ Ⓒ Ⓓ
18. Ⓐ Ⓑ Ⓒ Ⓓ
19. Ⓐ Ⓑ Ⓒ Ⓓ
20. Ⓐ Ⓑ Ⓒ Ⓓ
21. Ⓐ Ⓑ Ⓒ Ⓓ
22. Ⓐ Ⓑ Ⓒ Ⓓ
23. Ⓐ Ⓑ Ⓒ Ⓓ
24. Ⓐ Ⓑ Ⓒ Ⓓ

1. Lyndon Johnson was born in a farmhouse in central Texas in 1908. He grew up in poverty and had to work his way through college. He was elected to the United States House of Representatives in 1937 and served in the United States Navy during World War II. Following 12 years in the House of Representatives, he was elected to the United States Senate, where he became the youngest person chosen by any party to be its Senate leader.

The main idea of this passage is that

Ⓐ Lyndon Johnson spent a number of years in government.
Ⓑ Lyndon Johnson was successful because of his years spent in Texas.
Ⓒ Lyndon Johnson rose from poverty to achieve the presidency.
Ⓓ Lyndon Johnson was the youngest person to be chosen Senate leader.

USE THIS TABLE OF CONTENTS TO ANSWER QUESTIONS 2 AND 3.

Earth and Space Science

Table of Contents

2. On which page would a person start to look for information about Mars?

   Ⓐ 1
   Ⓑ 3
   Ⓒ 12
   Ⓓ 34

3. On which page would a person be most likely to find a discussion of how water can erode the Earth?

   Ⓐ 54
   Ⓑ 55
   Ⓒ 56
   Ⓓ 58

---

4. A student wants to use a word in place of *right* in this sentence. "You are *right* to want to keep your place in the movie line." The student uses a thesaurus to find four possible replacements for the word. Which of the replacements is correct?

   Ⓐ Accurate
   Ⓑ Correct
   Ⓒ Honorable
   Ⓓ Real

USE THIS PASSAGE TO ANSWER QUESTION 5.

Music consists of pitch, the actual sound of a note, and duration, how long the note lasts. Three different tones occurring together are called chords. Harmony is chords with duration. Pitches separated by specific intervals are called a scale. Most music is based on the scale found on a piano's white keys.

5. A student reading this paragraph has trouble understanding the meaning of the word *scale*. Which of the following could a paraprofessional say to best help the student understand the meaning of the word?

   Ⓐ "Reread the earlier parts of the paragraph for clues about the meaning of pitch and harmony."
   Ⓑ "Read the rest of the passage to get more information about scales."
   Ⓒ "Think of some everyday examples of scales."
   Ⓓ "Take your time, relax, and sound the word out."

6. $40 = 50\%$ of $\square$

A student needs help answering the question shown above. Which of the following is the best help a paraprofessional could offer to help the student find the answer?

Ⓐ Fifty times one hundred equals what?
Ⓑ Fifty percent is what part of 100%?
Ⓒ Fifty percent of what number equals forty?
Ⓓ What number would make this equation correct?

7.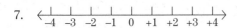

Where is $-\dfrac{9}{4}$ found on the number line above?

Ⓐ To the right of +1
Ⓑ Between 0 and 2
Ⓒ Between 0 and –2
Ⓓ To the left of –2

8. The circle graph below shows the percent distribution of eye colors among students in a class. If there are 30 students in the class, how many have blue eyes?

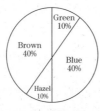

Ⓐ 8
Ⓑ 12
Ⓒ 18
Ⓓ 24

9. At the park, a train ride costs $1.25 and a horse ride costs $2.75. What is the cost of three train rides and four horse rides?

A paraprofessional is helping students write the correct expression to solve this word problem. Which of the following is the correct expression?

Ⓐ 3 + 4 ($1.25 + $2.75)
Ⓑ 3($1.25) + 4($2.75)
Ⓒ 3 + $1.25 + 4 + $2.75
Ⓓ 7($1.25 + $2.75)

10.

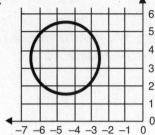

In the grid above, which point listed below is inside the circle?

(A) (–2, 3)

(B) (3, –2)

(C) (–4, 2)

(D) (2, –4)

11. At one school, $\frac{1}{3}$ of the students ride to school in a car, whereas $\frac{1}{2}$ of the students take the bus. What fraction of students at the school ride in a car or take the bus to school?

(A) $\frac{1}{6}$

(B) $\frac{1}{5}$

(C) $\frac{2}{5}$

(D) $\frac{5}{6}$

12. The list of numbers below shows a pattern. Each number is double the previous number. If things continue the same way, what will the sixth number be?

2   4   8   16   32

(A) 12

(B) 24

(C) 64

(D) 128

CHOOSE THE UNDERLINED PART THAT CONTAINS AN ERROR.

13. The tugboat <u>strains against</u> the <u>ship, revved</u> up its engines, <u>and was able to</u> <u>maneuver</u>
    Ⓐ   Ⓑ   Ⓒ   Ⓓ

    the ship into the middle of the channel.

14. A newspaper columnist <u>promised</u> <u>to print</u> the story about the <u>secret negotiations</u>
    Ⓐ   Ⓑ   Ⓒ

    concerning the sports stadium in <u>their</u> next column.
    Ⓓ

15. The <u>incredible</u> <u>intense</u> seminar held all <u>the participants</u> in a <u>hypnotic</u> trance.
    Ⓐ   Ⓑ   Ⓒ   Ⓓ

    _____

16. The developmental psychology of Jean Piaget still has an impact in schools,
    particularly on the education of young children.

    What is the subject of the sentence above?

    Ⓐ Developmental psychology
    Ⓑ Jean Piaget
    Ⓒ Developmental psychology of Jean Piaget
    Ⓓ Schools

17. It was not that long ago that glaciers covered much of the United States, leaving
    behind evidence of their visit as glacial moraines.

    What is the simple predicate in the sentence above?

    Ⓐ Covered
    Ⓑ Leaving
    Ⓒ Was
    Ⓓ Visit

USE THESE SENTENCES TO ANSWER QUESTION 18.

(1) I like to write about my favorite sports. (2) It is the most popular sport in the world. (3) That
means that I like to write about soccer. (4) Soccer is called football in most other countries.
(5) Football in this country is more rough than soccer. (6) That is another reason I like soccer.

18. As James looks over his essay, he realizes that sentences are out of order.
    What should he do to improve the sentence order?

    Ⓐ Move sentence (1) after sentence (2).
    Ⓑ Move sentence (2) after sentence (3).
    Ⓒ Move sentence (3) after sentence (4).
    Ⓓ Move sentence (4) after sentence (5).

The team captain was working on a letter to the team. The first draft of the outline for this letter is shown below.

A Letter to the Team

I. Team spirit
   A. Work together.
      1. Cooperate rather than compete.
      2. Put aside personal feelings.
   B. Support each other.
      1. Make positive comments.
      2. Don't be too critical.
      3. Make useful suggestions.

II. Team goals
   A. Have a successful season.
      1. Success is an attitude.
      2. Get our fans behind this.
   B. Win one game at a time.
      1. _____
      2. Forget any losses.

III. Team plays
   A. Play book.
      1. Don't lose it.
      2. Memorize the plays.
   B. _____
      1. Practice makes perfect.
      2. Review play execution.

19. Entry II.B.1. in the outline can't be read. Which of the following is the most likely entry for this line?

   Ⓐ Involve players' families.
   Ⓑ Get teachers involved.
   Ⓒ Focus on player commitment.
   Ⓓ Focus on today.

20. Which of the following is the best entry for III.B.?

   Ⓐ Play design
   Ⓑ Play evaluation
   Ⓒ Play practice
   Ⓓ Play distribution

21. Students have just learned that the letters *gh* can often sound like the letter *f*. They have seen some examples, such as *rough* and *tough*. Which of the following could a paraprofessional use to give students another example of a word that fits this pattern?

Ⓐ Enough
Ⓑ Ghost
Ⓒ Right
Ⓓ Ruff

USE THIS ASSIGNMENT TO ANSWER QUESTION 22.

Assignment: Collecting Data

Students are in groups of four with data collection sheets. The assignment is to find each person's height in inches, age in months, eye color, and hair color. Then after the data is collected, the students will take turns coming up to the front of the class, and each person will write one of the four results on the board.

22. According to the assignment, the students should come up to write results on the board

Ⓐ when they are called to the front of the class.
Ⓑ after the results from all the groups have been combined.
Ⓒ after the work for their group is complete.
Ⓓ if the results from their group matches the results from the entire class.

_____

23. A paraprofessional asks one group to go to the board according to the alphabetical order of their first names. It turns out that the four students in this group all have first names that begin with *B*. In which order should the paraprofessional call on students to go to the board?

Ⓐ Blakely, Bradley, Bryna, Bheardy
Ⓑ Bheardy, Blakely, Bradley, Bryna
Ⓒ Bradley, Blakely, Bheardy, Bryna
Ⓓ Bheardy, Bradley, Bryna, Blakely

24. $1000 \times 1 = 1000$
$1000 \times 0.1 = 100$
$1000 \times 0.01 = 10$
$1000 \times 0.001 = 1$

The pattern above would most likely be used to teach which of the following topics?

Ⓐ Addition
Ⓑ Subtraction
Ⓒ Place value
Ⓓ Division

EXPLAINED ANSWERS

1. **(C)** This paragraph describes how Lyndon Johnson rose from poverty to the presidency. Choice (A) is incorrect because, while the passage mentions his years in government, the main idea of the entire paragraph is choice (C) and is reflected in the topic sentence.

2. **(C)** The discussion of Planets and Asteroids begins on page 12. Mars is a planet, and page 12 is the page on which a person would start to look for information.

3. **(B)** Page 55 includes the discussion of external geological processes. Water erosion occurs on the surface of the earth, and so it is an external geological process.

4. **(B)** The context of the word *right* indicates that it means correct. A person is correct to want to keep his or her place in the movie line.

5. **(B)** If the student reads the rest of the passage, he or she will see a further explanation of a scale, which could help the student understand what a scale is.

6. **(C)** A student who thinks "fifty percent of what number is 40" can see that fifty percent of 80 is 40. The missing number is 80.

   The student could solve the equation:
   $40 = 50\%$ of ❏

   $40 = \dfrac{1}{2}x$

   $40 \times 2 = \dfrac{1}{2} \times 2x$

   $80 = x$

7. **(D)** $-\dfrac{9}{4} = -2\dfrac{1}{4}$, which is just to the left of –2.

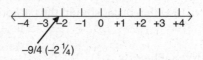

   $-9/4 \; (-2\,^{1}/_{4})$

8. **(B)** Follow these steps to find the answer.
   The graph shows that 40 percent of the students have blue eyes.
   $40\% = 0.4$
   $0.4 \times 30 = 12$

9. **(B)** The equation and an explanation are shown below.

3		($1.25)	+	4		($2.75)
Number of train rides	×	Cost of a train ride	+	Number of horse rides	×	Cost of a horse ride

10. **(C)** Point *B* and point *D* have a positive *x* value, and these points are to the right of 0 on the *x*-axis. These points are not on the grid. As shown below, point *A* and point *C* are on the grid, and only point *C* is inside the circle.

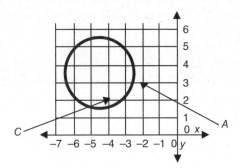

11. **(D)** This problem asks you to add $\frac{1}{3}$ and $\frac{1}{2}$.

That will show the fraction of students who either ride in a car or take the bus to school, combined.

$$\frac{1}{3} + \frac{1}{2} = \frac{2}{6} + \frac{3}{6} = \frac{5}{6}$$

12. **(C)** Continue the doubling pattern. The sixth number is 64.

$$2 \quad 4 \quad 8 \quad 16 \quad 32 \quad \underline{64}$$

13. **(A)** The verb tense of *strains* is incorrect. Replace the present tense *strains* with the past tense *strained* to agree with the other verbs *revved* and *was*.

14. **(D)** The pronoun *their* does not agree with antecedent *columnist*. Replace *their* with *his* or *her*.

15. **(A)** Replace *incredible* with the adverb *incredibly* to modify the adjective *intense*.

16. **(C)** The entire phrase "developmental psychology of Jean Piaget" is the subject. Choice (A) and Choice (B) do not fully communicate what the sentence is about.

17. **(A)** Notice first that *glaciers* is the subject of the sentence and that the verb *covered* describes what the glaciers did.

18. **(B)** The *It* in sentence 2 has nothing to refer to until you reverse the positions of sentence 1 and sentence 2.

19. **(D)** Of all the suggested entries, the advice to "Focus on today" fits best with the entry "Win one game at a time."

20. **(C)** The choice "Play practice" makes the most sense when compared to the entries that appear in III.B.1. and III.B.2.

21. **(A)** The word *enough* is pronounced *enuf*. In choices (B) and (C) the *gh* does not sound like *f*. Choice (D) does not contain the letters *gh*.

22. **(C)** The second sentence indicates that students should take turns coming up to the board after their group has completed its work.

23. **(B)** The first letter of each name is the same, so the second or third letter is used to determine alphabetical order: Bheardy, Blakely, Bradley, Bryna

24. **(C)** This is the best answer among the choices given. The pattern demonstrates the place values of tenths, hundredths, thousandths, and ten thousandths. The pattern does not show addition, subtraction, or division. "Multiplication," another possible correct answer, is not given as a choice.

Index

rounding of, 105
subtraction of, 115
whole numbers vs., 104–105
Decrease, percent of, 123
Deductive reasoning, 148, 384
Demonstrations, 380
Denominator, 107
Dependent events, 125
Developmental delays, 375
Diction
definition of, 49
homonyms, 50
idioms, 50
Dictionaries, 529
Direct instruction, 531
Direct teacher talk, 379
Distributive property of
multiplication over
addition, 115
Diversity, 401–403
Division, 111
of decimals, 116
equations solved by, 137
of fractions, 117
of integers, 131
of whole numbers, 114
Divorce, 401
Dropouts, 404
Drug abuse, 403–404
Dyscalculia, 373
Dysgraphia, 373
Dyslexia, 373
Dyspraxia, 373

E
Elementary Education:
Content Knowledge Test
passing of, 521–522
preparation for, 522–534
review, 534–537
test info box for, 521
Elementary Education:
Curriculum,
Instruction, and
Assessment Test
content areas, 468–471
overview of, 468–470
passing score for, 467
practice test, 471–519
preparation for, 467–468
Elementary Education:
Multiple Subjects Test
passing of, 521
practice test, 539–617
preparation for, 522–534

review, 534–537
test info box for, 521
E-mail, 385–386
English as a second language,
377, 383
English language, 532–533
English Review Quiz
description of, 28
essay, 31–32, 61–72
sentence correction, 28–29
study checklist for, 30–31
Equations, 136–137
Equilateral triangle, 141
Equivalent fractions, 107
Errors of measurement, 395,
534
Essays
argumentative. *See*
Argumentative essay
informative/explanatory.
See Informative/
explanatory essay
practice, 263–265, 290–293,
329–331, 349, 354–
356
rating scale for, 32–33
writing, 61–72
Estimation problems, 153–154
Ethnicity, 398, 402–403
Exclamation point, 55
Existential thinkers, 370
Explanation, 380
Explicit instruction, 525, 531
Exponents, 102–103
Extrinsic motivation, 378
Extrinsic rewards, 378

F
Family, 398, 401–402
Fluency, 526–527
Formal operational stage, 368
Formative assessment, 394,
533
Formulas, 133–134, 157
Fractions
addition of, 117
as percents, 120
comparing of, 108
definition of, 107
denominator of, 107
division of, 117
equivalent, 107
improper, 108
multiplication of, 108
numerator of, 107

percents as, 120–121
subtraction of, 117
Freedom of speech, 400–401
Frequency table problems,
155–156
Freud, Sigmund, 368
Fundamental counting
principle, 126
Future tense, 36

G
Gardner, Howard, 370
Geometric sequence, 152
Geometry, 139–141, 159–160
Gifted students, 383
Grapheme, 523
Graphic organizers, 530
Greatest common factor,
111–112
Guided practice, 397, 531

H
Handicapped students, 383, 400
Harmonic sequence, 152
Hearing impaired students, 382
Hexagon, 141
Hierarchy of needs, 371
High dropouts, 404
Higher-order thinking, 384
Hispanics, 402
Homework, 397
Homonyms, 50
Human development
cognitive, 367–368
moral, 369
nature versus nurture,
369–370
personality, 368
physical, 366–367
psychosocial, 368
social learning theory, 369
Human motivation, 371
Hunter, Madeline, 389

I
IDEA. *See* Individuals with
Disabilities Act
Identity properties, 115
Idioms, 50
IEP. *See* Individualized
education plan
Improper fractions, 108
Inclusion, 376
Increase, percent of, 121–123
Independent clause, 46